I0066573

The New Era of Finance
Technology, Sustainability, and Globalization

THE CPD GROUP

M L Ruscsak

Copyright © 2023 by Trient Press

All rights reserved. No part of this publication may be reproduced, distributed, or transmitted in any form or by any means, including photocopying, recording, or other electronic or mechanical methods, without the prior written permission of the publisher, except in the case of brief quotations embodied in critical reviews and certain other noncommercial uses permitted by copyright law. For permission requests, write to the publisher, addressed "Attention: Permissions Coordinator," at the address below.

Criminal copyright infringement, including infringement without monetary gain, is investigated by the FBI and is punishable by up to five years in federal prison and a fine of $250,000.

Except for the original story material written by the author, all songs, song titles, and lyrics mentioned in the text book
The New Era of Finance: Technology, Sustainability, and Globalization are the exclusive property of the respective artists, songwriters, and copyright holder.

Trient Press
3375 S Rainbow Blvd
#81710, SMB 13135
Las Vegas,NV 89180

Ordering Information:
Quantity sales. Special discounts are available on quantity purchases by corporations, associations, and others. For details, contact the publisher at the address above.
Orders by U.S. trade bookstores and wholesalers. Please contact Trient Press: Tel: (775) 996-3844; or visit www.trientpress.com.

Printed in the United States of America

Publisher's Cataloging-in-Publication data
Ruscsak, M.L
A title of a book :
    The New Era of Finance: Technology, Sustainability, and Globalization
ISBN
Paper Back   979-8-88990-086-3
Ebook   979-8-88990-087-0
Hard Cover   979-8-88990-085-6

PART I:
INTRODUCTION

Finance is an ever-evolving field that has undergone significant changes throughout history. Understanding the historical context of finance is crucial to comprehending its current state and future direction. In this section, we will explore the evolution of finance, define emerging trends in finance, and discuss the importance of staying ahead of these trends.

Chapter 1: The Evolution of Finance: A Brief History

Finance has been an essential part of human society for centuries. It has played a crucial role in facilitating economic activity, enabling investment, and providing a means for individuals and organizations to manage risk. Over time, the financial landscape has changed dramatically, with new financial instruments and institutions emerging to meet the changing needs of society.

One of the earliest forms of finance was bartering, where goods and services were exchanged directly for other goods and services. As societies grew and became more complex, the need for a more sophisticated system of exchange arose. This led to the development of commodity money, where goods such as precious metals were used as a medium of exchange.

The next significant development in finance was the introduction of paper money, which was easier to transport and more convenient than commodity money. This led to the creation of banks, which facilitated the issuance of paper money and provided a means for individuals and organizations to deposit and withdraw funds.

In the 20th century, finance underwent significant changes, driven by technological advancements and globalization. The creation of the stock market, mutual funds, and pension funds enabled investors to diversify their portfolios and access new investment opportunities. The advent of computers and the internet has led to the emergence of FinTech, which is transforming the way financial services are delivered.

Chapter 2: Defining Emerging Trends in Finance

Emerging trends in finance refer to new developments or changes in the financial landscape that are expected to have a significant impact on the industry. These trends include FinTech, blockchain, artificial intelligence, big data, sustainability, and globalization.

FinTech refers to the use of technology to deliver financial services more efficiently and effectively. This includes mobile payments, peer-to-peer lending, and robo-advisory services. Blockchain is a decentralized ledger technology that allows for secure, transparent, and tamper-proof transactions. Artificial intelligence and big data are being used to analyze vast amounts of data to gain insights into customer behavior and investment opportunities. Sustainability and impact investing are gaining momentum as investors seek to align their investments with their values. Finally, globalization is driving the growth of international finance and increasing the interconnectedness of financial markets.

Chapter 3: The Importance of Staying Ahead of Emerging Trends in Finance

Staying ahead of emerging trends in finance is crucial for financial professionals, as it allows them to provide their clients with the most up-to-date and relevant advice. Ignoring emerging trends can lead to missed opportunities and can put financial professionals at a competitive disadvantage.

One strategy for staying ahead of emerging trends is to pursue continuing education and professional development opportunities. This can include attending conferences, taking courses, and networking with other professionals in the industry. Financial professionals can also stay informed by reading industry publications and staying up-to-date on regulatory and compliance issues.

In conclusion, understanding the historical context of finance, defining emerging trends, and staying ahead of these trends are all essential components of success in the financial industry. In the next sections of this book, we will explore each of these emerging trends in greater detail, providing readers with a comprehensive understanding of the new era of finance.

CHAPTER 1: THE EVOLUTION OF FINANCE: A BRIEF HISTORY

Finance has come a long way since its early beginnings. What started as a simple system of exchanging goods and services has evolved into a complex and interconnected global network that touches every aspect of our lives. Today, finance is the lifeblood of modern society, enabling individuals, businesses, and governments to invest, save, borrow, and manage risk.

Understanding the history of finance is crucial to understanding its current state and where it is headed in the future. The development of finance can be traced back to ancient civilizations, where people exchanged goods and services using primitive forms of currency. Over time, these simple systems evolved into more complex ones, such as bartering, lending, and borrowing.

The origins of finance and the development of financial systems

One of the earliest forms of financial systems was the barter system. In this system, people exchanged goods and services directly with one another, without the need for a medium of exchange such as money. However, this system had limitations, as it was difficult to measure the value of goods and services being exchanged, and it was hard to find someone who had what you needed and wanted what you had.

To overcome these limitations, various forms of currency were developed. In ancient times, currencies took the form of shells, beads, and other commodities that were considered valuable by society. As civilization progressed, precious metals such as gold and silver became the preferred forms of currency.

The development of financial institutions can also be traced back to ancient times. For example, the Greeks and Romans had banks that provided loans to merchants and traders, and the Chinese had a rudimentary form of banking that allowed for the transfer of funds between cities.

Key historical events that have shaped the modern financial landscape

The history of finance is marked by key events that have shaped the modern financial landscape. One such event was the creation of the first stock exchange in Amsterdam in the 17th century. This allowed for the trading of stocks and bonds, and laid the foundation for modern financial markets.

Another major event was the invention of the telegraph in the 19th century, which allowed for faster communication and the dissemination of financial information. This led to the development of financial news agencies such as Reuters and Bloomberg, which provided up-to-date information on market trends and economic indicators.

The 20th century saw the rise of the modern banking system, with the establishment of central banks and the development of regulations to ensure the stability of financial markets. It also saw the advent of new financial instruments, such as derivatives and securitization, which allowed for greater flexibility and risk management in financial transactions.

The role of technology, sustainability, and globalization in driving change in finance

Today, finance is being driven by a combination of technological innovation, sustainability concerns, and globalization. Technological advances such as artificial intelligence, blockchain, and fintech are transforming the way financial services are delivered and consumed. Sustainability concerns are driving the growth of impact investing and environmental, social, and governance (ESG) investing. And globalization is creating new opportunities for investment and trade, but also increasing the interconnectedness and complexity of financial systems.

As we move forward into the future, it is important to understand the lessons of history and the forces that are shaping the evolution of finance. By doing so, we can better navigate the challenges and opportunities that lie ahead, and continue to build a financial system that supports the needs and aspirations of individuals, businesses, and societies around the world.

The origins of finance and the development of financial systems

Finance, in its simplest form, can be traced back to the exchange of goods and services between individuals. As societies grew and became more complex, the need for formal financial systems emerged to facilitate trade and commerce. These systems evolved over time and were influenced by a variety of factors, including technological advancements, economic and political conditions, and cultural norms.

The earliest financial systems were based on bartering, where individuals would exchange goods and services directly with one another. However, as societies grew larger and more complex, this system became inefficient, and the concept of money emerged as a medium of exchange. Early forms of money included items such as shells, beads, and precious metals.

One of the earliest recorded financial systems was developed in Mesopotamia around 2000 BCE. This system was based on the use of clay tablets, which recorded financial transactions between individuals. The use of these tablets allowed for the creation of a formal financial system, where individuals could borrow and lend money.

The ancient Greeks also made significant contributions to the development of finance. The Greek city-states developed a system of credit, where individuals could borrow money from wealthy citizens. This system was based on trust and reputation and was an important precursor to modern credit systems.

In the Middle Ages, Italian city-states such as Florence and Venice emerged as major financial centers. These cities developed sophisticated banking systems, which allowed for the exchange of currencies and the financing of international trade. The development of double-entry bookkeeping by the Italian mathematician Luca Pacioli in the 15th century was also a significant milestone in the evolution of finance, as it allowed for more accurate and reliable financial records.

During the Industrial Revolution in the 18th and 19th centuries, financial systems continued to evolve rapidly. The development of joint-stock companies, which allowed individuals to invest in businesses, and the growth of stock exchanges were important developments during this period. The creation of modern banking systems, such as the Bank of England in 1694, also played a significant role in the growth of finance during this time.

In the 20th century, the growth of financial systems continued, and new financial instruments and markets emerged. The introduction of credit cards, the development of the derivatives market, and the growth of online trading platforms are just a few examples of the ways in which finance has continued to evolve.

Overall, the origins of finance can be traced back to the exchange of goods and services between individuals. Over time, these informal systems evolved into more formal financial systems, which were influenced by a variety of factors, including technological advancements, economic and political conditions, and cultural norms. The development of modern financial systems has played a crucial role in the growth and development of economies around the world.

Today, finance continues to evolve rapidly, with the emergence of new technologies and the growing importance of sustainability and globalization in shaping the financial landscape. However, it is important to recognize that this is not the first time that the financial system has undergone significant change.

One of the earliest examples of financial innovation dates back to the 14th century, when Italian merchants began using bills of exchange to facilitate trade. These bills allowed merchants to transfer funds between different locations without the need for physical transportation of cash. Over time, this system evolved into the modern banking system we know today.

Another major development in the history of finance was the creation of stock markets. The Amsterdam Stock Exchange, established in 1602, is considered the first modern stock market. This development allowed individuals and organizations to buy and sell shares of companies, providing them with the ability to invest in businesses and potentially earn a return on their investment.

The growth of capitalism and the Industrial Revolution in the 18th and 19th centuries brought about further changes in the financial landscape. With the rise of industrialization, companies required large amounts of capital to invest in new technologies and expand their operations. This led to the creation of joint stock companies, where investors could pool their resources to finance large-scale projects.

The development of the railroad industry in the 19th century also had a significant impact on finance. Railroads required massive amounts of capital to construct and operate, and the demand for investment in this industry led to the creation of investment banks. These banks helped to raise funds for railroad projects by underwriting bond issuances and facilitating the sale of shares.

In the 20th century, the financial system continued to evolve with the introduction of new financial instruments such as options, futures, and derivatives. These instruments provided investors with new ways to manage risk and earn returns on their investments. However, they also introduced new complexities and risks into the financial system, as evidenced by the 2008 financial crisis.

In conclusion, the evolution of finance has been shaped by a combination of historical events, technological advancements, and economic developments. Understanding this history is important for gaining insight into the current state of the financial system and predicting future trends. As we move forward, it will be interesting to see how emerging technologies and the growing importance of sustainability and globalization continue to shape the financial landscape.

Key historical events that have shaped the modern financial landscape

The modern financial landscape has been shaped by numerous historical events that have had a profound impact on the way we conduct financial transactions and manage risk. In this section, we will examine some of the key events that have shaped finance as we know it today.

One of the earliest examples of financial innovation was the development of paper money in China during the Tang dynasty (618-907 AD). This system of currency allowed for greater liquidity and facilitated trade, enabling the Chinese economy to flourish. The development of banking also played a crucial role in the growth of commerce, with Italian merchant banks such as the Medici family providing loans to finance overseas ventures during the Renaissance period.

In the 17th century, the Dutch East India Company became the first company to issue shares to the public, creating the modern concept of a stock market. This allowed for the pooling of resources and enabled investors to participate in the profits of commercial ventures. The creation of the Bank of England in 1694 was another important milestone, as it facilitated the growth of credit and provided a stable source of financing for the British government.

The 19th century saw the development of modern banking systems, with the establishment of central banks such as the Federal Reserve in the United States and the Bank of England. These institutions provided stability and facilitated the growth of credit, allowing for the expansion of global trade and investment. The rise of industrial capitalism also had a significant impact on finance, with the development of new financial instruments such as bonds and derivatives.

The 20th century was marked by several important events that had a profound impact on finance. The Great Depression of the 1930s led to the creation of new regulatory frameworks and the establishment of institutions such as the International Monetary Fund (IMF) and the World Bank. The Bretton Woods agreement in 1944 established a new system of exchange rates, pegging the value of currencies to the US dollar and creating a fixed exchange rate regime.

The end of the Bretton Woods system in the early 1970s marked the beginning of a new era in finance, characterized by the rise of global capital markets and the growth of financial innovation. The development of new financial products such as securitization and credit derivatives allowed for the transfer of risk and facilitated the growth of the mortgage market. The globalization of finance also had a significant impact on the financial landscape, with the rise of emerging markets and the increasing importance of international trade.

The events of the 2008 financial crisis had a profound impact on the financial landscape, exposing weaknesses in the global financial system and leading to a wave of regulatory reform. The Dodd-Frank Act in the United States and the Basel III framework for banking regulation were among the key responses to the crisis, aimed at strengthening financial stability and reducing systemic risk.

In conclusion, the modern financial landscape has been shaped by a series of historical events, from the development of paper money in China to the rise of global capital markets. These events have facilitated the growth of commerce and enabled individuals and institutions to manage risk, but they have also exposed vulnerabilities and led to periods of instability. As we move forward into the future, it is important to understand the lessons of history and to continue to adapt and innovate in response to changing circumstances.

The role of technology, sustainability, and globalization in driving change in finance

The role of technology, sustainability, and globalization in driving change in finance is a complex and multifaceted topic that requires a comprehensive analysis. In recent years, technological advancements, sustainability concerns, and globalization have emerged as significant drivers of change in the financial industry. These three factors have played a critical role in shaping the way financial systems operate, the way investment decisions are made, and the way financial products and services are delivered.

Technological advancements have transformed the financial industry in many ways. The emergence of new technologies, such as blockchain, artificial intelligence, and big data analytics, has led to significant improvements in efficiency, speed, and accuracy of financial services. For example, blockchain technology has the potential to revolutionize the way financial transactions are processed and recorded by providing a secure, decentralized ledger that is virtually tamper-proof. This technology can also facilitate the creation of smart contracts, which can automate the execution of financial agreements between parties, eliminating the need for intermediaries and reducing transaction costs.

Artificial intelligence and big data analytics are also transforming the financial industry by enabling more precise and informed decision-making. These technologies can analyze vast amounts of data to identify trends and patterns, and provide insights that can help investors and financial institutions make more informed investment decisions. For example, quantitative analysts and portfolio managers use these technologies to develop sophisticated models that can predict market trends, identify risks, and optimize investment portfolios.

Sustainability concerns are also driving change in the financial industry. Environmental, social, and governance (ESG) factors are becoming increasingly important to investors, who are demanding more sustainable and socially responsible investment options. Financial institutions are responding to this demand by incorporating ESG considerations into their investment decision-making processes and offering a range of sustainable investment products and services. For example, investment bankers and financial planners are offering green bonds, which are fixed-income securities that fund projects with positive environmental and social impacts.

Globalization has also had a significant impact on the financial industry, by increasing competition, expanding investment opportunities, and facilitating cross-border transactions. Financial institutions are increasingly operating on a global scale, and investors have access to a wider range of investment options than ever before. This globalization has also created new challenges, such as increased regulatory complexity and increased exposure to economic and political risks.

The role of technology, sustainability, and globalization in driving change in finance is complex and multifaceted, and it is likely to continue to evolve in the coming years. While these factors have the potential to bring significant benefits to the financial industry, they also pose new challenges and risks that financial institutions must navigate. It is therefore essential that financial professionals stay up-to-date with the latest technological, sustainability, and globalization trends and developments, and continue to adapt their practices to remain competitive and relevant in an ever-changing financial landscape.

CHAPTER 2: DEFINING EMERGING TRENDS IN FINANCE

Finance, like any other field, is constantly evolving, with new trends emerging and old ones becoming obsolete. These emerging trends in finance are often driven by advances in technology, changes in customer preferences, and regulatory requirements, among other factors. Understanding emerging trends in finance is crucial for individuals and organizations seeking to remain competitive in an ever-changing business landscape.

This chapter will provide an overview of the key emerging trends in finance, including FinTech, blockchain, and sustainable investing. We will discuss the meaning of emerging trends in finance and why they matter, as well as the potential benefits and challenges of each trend.

Defining Emerging Trends in Finance:

Emerging trends in finance refer to the new and innovative ways in which financial services are provided and consumed. These trends are often driven by changes in technology and customer behavior, and they can have a significant impact on the financial services industry.

Why do Emerging Trends in Finance Matter?

Emerging trends in finance matter because they can transform the way financial services are delivered, consumed, and regulated. They have the potential to disrupt traditional business models, create new markets and revenue streams, and improve the efficiency and accessibility of financial services. As such, understanding and embracing emerging trends in finance is crucial for individuals and organizations seeking to remain competitive in a rapidly changing business environment.

Key Emerging Trends in Finance:

❖   FinTech:
FinTech, short for Financial Technology, refers to the use of technology to improve and automate financial services. This includes everything from mobile payments and digital wallets to robo-advisors and online lending platforms. FinTech has the potential to disrupt traditional banking models by providing consumers with more convenient and affordable financial services.

Benefits of FinTech:

Increased accessibility: FinTech has made financial services more accessible to underserved populations, including those who are unbanked or underbanked.
Improved efficiency: FinTech has automated many financial processes, which has reduced costs and increased efficiency for financial institutions.
Enhanced customer experience: FinTech has enabled financial institutions to provide more personalized and convenient services to their customers.

Challenges of FinTech:

Regulatory challenges: FinTech has raised regulatory concerns related to data privacy, security, and consumer protection.

Cybersecurity risks: FinTech platforms are vulnerable to cyberattacks, which can compromise the security of customer data.

Lack of standardization: The lack of standardization in FinTech can make it difficult for consumers to compare and evaluate different financial products and services.

❖ Blockchain:

Blockchain is a distributed ledger technology that allows multiple parties to securely and transparently share information without the need for intermediaries. Blockchain has the potential to disrupt a wide range of industries, including finance, by enabling secure and efficient transactions.

Benefits of Blockchain:

Increased transparency: Blockchain provides a transparent and tamper-proof record of transactions, which can help to reduce fraud and improve accountability.

Reduced costs: Blockchain can reduce the cost of financial transactions by eliminating intermediaries and streamlining processes.

Enhanced security: Blockchain is highly secure, as it uses advanced cryptography to protect against unauthorized access and tampering.

Challenges of Blockchain:

Regulatory challenges: The regulatory framework for blockchain is still evolving, which can create uncertainty for financial institutions.

Scalability issues: Blockchain has scalability limitations, which can make it difficult to process large volumes of transactions.

Interoperability challenges: The lack of interoperability between different blockchain platforms can make it difficult for financial institutions to share information and collaborate.

❖ Sustainable Investing:

Sustainable investing, also known as socially responsible investing or ESG investing, refers to the integration of environmental, social, and governance (ESG) factors into investment decision-making. Sustainable investing has gained traction in recent years as investors have become increasingly concerned about the social and environmental impact of their investments.

Benefits of Sustainable Investing:

Reduced risk: Companies that take ESG factors into consideration are more likely to have sustainable business practices and governance structures, which can reduce the risk of negative events such as lawsuits, regulatory fines, or reputational damage.

Long-term performance: Studies have shown that companies that prioritize sustainability tend to outperform their peers in the long run. This is because these companies are often better prepared to adapt to changing market conditions, and are less likely to face costly disruptions or legal issues.

Alignment with values: Sustainable investing allows investors to align their values with their financial goals. By investing in companies that are making a positive impact on society and the environment, investors can feel that their money is contributing to a greater good.

Challenges of Sustainable Investing:

Lack of standardization: One of the biggest challenges of sustainable investing is the lack of standardization in ESG metrics and ratings. This can make it difficult for investors to compare companies and funds, and can lead to inconsistencies in investment decision-making.

Limited investment options: While sustainable investing has grown in popularity, there are still a limited number of investment options available for investors who want to prioritize ESG factors. This can make it challenging for investors to build a diversified portfolio that aligns with their values.

Performance trade-offs: Critics of sustainable investing argue that prioritizing ESG factors can lead to performance trade-offs, as companies that prioritize sustainability may not always be the most profitable or successful in the short term.

Overall, sustainable investing represents a growing trend in finance as investors become more aware of the impact of their investments on society and the environment. While there are challenges to overcome, the potential benefits of sustainable investing, including reduced risk, long-term performance, and alignment with values, make it an increasingly attractive option for many investors.

The meaning of emerging trends in finance and why they matter

The meaning of emerging trends in finance and why they matter

The field of finance is constantly evolving and adapting to changes in technology, regulations, and global economic conditions. Emerging trends in finance are those that are expected to have a significant impact on the industry in the near future, and they often involve new technologies or new ways of thinking about investment and financial management.

Why do emerging trends in finance matter? For investors, keeping up with emerging trends can mean the difference between making informed investment decisions and being left behind. For financial professionals, understanding emerging trends is essential to staying competitive and providing valuable services to clients. And for the industry as a whole, staying ahead of emerging trends can help to promote innovation and growth.

An overview of the key emerging trends in finance, including FinTech, blockchain, and sustainable investing

There are several key emerging trends in finance that are currently shaping the industry. These include:

FinTech - Financial technology, or FinTech, refers to the use of technology to improve financial services. FinTech companies are disrupting traditional financial institutions by offering more efficient, convenient, and personalized services to consumers. Examples of FinTech services include online banking, robo-advisors, and peer-to-peer lending.

Blockchain - Blockchain technology is a decentralized digital ledger that allows for secure and transparent transactions. In finance, blockchain is being used to create digital currencies, such as Bitcoin, as well as to improve the efficiency and security of financial transactions. Blockchain has the potential to revolutionize the financial industry by reducing costs, increasing efficiency, and improving security.

Sustainable Investing - Sustainable investing, also known as socially responsible investing or ESG investing, refers to the integration of environmental, social, and governance (ESG) factors into investment decision-making. Sustainable investing has gained traction in recent years as investors have become increasingly concerned about the social and environmental impact of their investments.

The potential benefits and challenges of each emerging trend

Each of these emerging trends in finance has the potential to offer significant benefits to investors and financial professionals, but they also come with their own set of challenges.

Benefits of FinTech:

Increased accessibility and convenience for consumers
Reduced costs for financial institutions
Greater efficiency and speed in financial transactions
Challenges of FinTech:

Concerns about security and privacy
Lack of regulatory oversight
Potential for increased financial exclusion of those without access to technology
Benefits of Blockchain:

Increased transparency and security in financial transactions
Reduction in costs and improved efficiency
Potential for new investment opportunities
Challenges of Blockchain:

Concerns about regulation and standardization
Risk of cyber attacks and other security threats
Potential for fraud and misuse
Benefits of Sustainable Investing:

Reduced risk for investors by avoiding companies with negative ESG practices
Potential for long-term growth and profitability in sustainable companies
Alignment of investments with personal values and social impact goals
Challenges of Sustainable Investing:

Lack of standardization in ESG metrics and reporting
Difficulty in quantifying the financial impact of ESG factors
Potential for lower returns due to limited investment opportunities in sustainable companies.

In conclusion, understanding emerging trends in finance is essential for investors, financial professionals, and the industry as a whole. The key emerging trends in finance, including FinTech, blockchain, and sustainable investing, offer potential benefits and challenges that should be carefully considered before making investment decisions. Keeping up with these trends can help investors to stay ahead of the curve, while also promoting innovation and growth in the financial industry.

An overview of the key emerging trends in finance, including FinTech, blockchain, and sustainable investing

FinTech:

The term FinTech refers to the intersection of finance and technology, which has given rise to a new generation of financial services that leverage digital technologies to provide faster, cheaper, and more accessible financial products and services. FinTech is reshaping the financial industry by disrupting traditional banking models, enabling financial inclusion, and driving innovation.

One of the most notable aspects of FinTech is the use of mobile devices and apps to provide financial services to customers. For example, mobile banking apps allow customers to manage their accounts, transfer money, and pay bills from their smartphones, while mobile wallets enable contactless payments through NFC technology. FinTech has also given rise to peer-to-peer lending platforms that connect borrowers with investors, as well as robo-advisors that use algorithms to provide investment advice and portfolio management services.

The growth of FinTech has been fueled by advances in technology, including cloud computing, artificial intelligence, and big data analytics. These technologies have enabled FinTech firms to process vast amounts of data, develop sophisticated risk models, and provide personalized financial services to customers. FinTech has also benefited from regulatory changes, such as open banking regulations that require banks to share customer data with third-party providers.

Blockchain:

Blockchain is a decentralized ledger technology that enables secure, transparent, and tamper-proof transactions without the need for intermediaries such as banks or governments. Blockchain is best known as the technology that underpins cryptocurrencies such as Bitcoin, but its potential extends far beyond digital currencies.

One of the key features of blockchain is its ability to create smart contracts, which are self-executing contracts that automate the execution of agreements between parties. Smart contracts can be used for a wide range of applications, from financial transactions to supply chain management to identity verification.

Blockchain has the potential to revolutionize the financial industry by reducing costs, increasing transparency, and improving security. For example, blockchain-based payment systems could reduce the cost and time of cross-border payments, while blockchain-based trade finance platforms could reduce the risk of fraud in international trade.

However, blockchain also faces challenges such as scalability, interoperability, and regulatory uncertainty. As the technology matures, it will be important for regulators to strike a balance between promoting innovation and protecting consumers and investors.

Sustainable Investing:

Sustainable investing, also known as socially responsible investing or ESG investing, refers to the integration of environmental, social, and governance (ESG) factors into investment decision-making. Sustainable investing has gained traction in recent years as investors have become increasingly concerned about the social and environmental impact of their investments.

One of the key benefits of sustainable investing is the potential for reduced risk. Companies that prioritize ESG factors may be more resilient to environmental, social, and governance risks, which can translate into lower financial risk for investors. Sustainable investing can also provide opportunities for long-term value creation, as companies that prioritize ESG factors may be better positioned to capitalize on emerging trends such as clean energy and sustainable agriculture.

Sustainable investing has also been driven by changing societal attitudes and regulatory pressures. For example, the United Nations' Sustainable Development Goals have helped to focus attention on the role of finance in achieving sustainable development, while regulatory changes such as the EU's Sustainable Finance Disclosure Regulation have encouraged greater transparency and accountability in sustainable investing.

Despite its potential benefits, sustainable investing also faces challenges such as the lack of standardization in ESG metrics and the potential trade-off between financial returns and social and environmental impact. As the field of sustainable investing continues to evolve, it will be important for investors to carefully consider the trade-offs and potential benefits of incorporating ESG factors into their investment strategies.

Potential Benefits and Challenges of Emerging Trends in Finance

As the world of finance continues to evolve and adapt to new technologies, sustainability concerns, and global interconnectedness, emerging trends are likely to play a significant role in shaping the industry's future. Here, we explore the potential benefits and challenges of some of the key emerging trends in finance, including FinTech, blockchain, and sustainable investing.

FinTech

Potential Benefits:

Improved efficiency and cost reduction: FinTech has the potential to streamline financial processes, reducing the need for human involvement and lowering costs associated with traditional banking services.

Enhanced customer experience: FinTech innovations such as mobile banking apps and robo-advisors have made financial services more accessible and user-friendly, providing customers with a more personalized experience.

Increased financial inclusion: By leveraging new technologies, FinTech has the potential to provide financial services to previously underserved populations, promoting greater financial inclusion and reducing income inequality.

Potential Challenges:

Cybersecurity risks: FinTech's reliance on digital technologies increases the risk of cybersecurity breaches and data breaches, which could have serious consequences for both financial institutions and their customers.

Regulatory challenges: As FinTech innovations continue to emerge, regulatory frameworks are struggling to keep up, potentially creating regulatory gaps or overlaps that could result in legal uncertainties.

Disruption to traditional banking models: As FinTech disrupts traditional banking models, it could lead to job losses and financial instability, particularly for smaller banks and financial institutions.

Blockchain

Potential Benefits:

Increased transparency and efficiency: Blockchain technology has the potential to revolutionize financial transactions, providing increased transparency and security while reducing the need for intermediaries and streamlining transaction processes.

Reduced fraud and errors: The decentralized nature of blockchain technology makes it more difficult for bad actors to manipulate the system, reducing the risk of fraud and errors in financial transactions.

Increased financial inclusion: Like FinTech, blockchain technology has the potential to provide financial services to underserved populations, particularly in developing countries where traditional banking infrastructure may be lacking.

Potential Challenges:

Regulatory challenges: As with FinTech, regulatory frameworks are struggling to keep up with the emergence of blockchain technology, potentially creating legal uncertainties and regulatory gaps or overlaps.

Scalability challenges: As blockchain technology continues to gain traction, concerns over scalability and energy consumption have emerged, as the technology requires significant computing power to function effectively.

Lack of standardization: The lack of standardization across blockchain platforms and protocols could hinder widespread adoption and limit the potential benefits of the technology.

Sustainable Investing

Potential Benefits:

Improved risk management: By incorporating environmental, social, and governance (ESG) factors into investment decision-making, sustainable investing can help to mitigate risks associated with companies that are not properly managing ESG issues.

Better long-term performance: Research has shown that companies with strong ESG performance tend to outperform their peers over the long-term, potentially leading to better returns for sustainable investors.

Positive social and environmental impact: Sustainable investing can drive positive social and environmental impact by directing investment capital towards companies that are actively working to address ESG issues.

Potential Challenges:

Limited investment options: While sustainable investing has gained significant traction in recent years, the universe of sustainable investment options is still relatively limited compared to traditional investment options.

Lack of standardization: Like blockchain, the lack of standardization across ESG ratings and reporting can make it difficult for investors to compare sustainable investment options and make informed decisions.

Conflicting objectives: In some cases, there may be conflicts between an investor's desire to generate returns and their commitment to sustainable investing principles, particularly if sustainable options underperform compared to traditional investments.

Conclusion

Emerging trends in finance have the potential to reshape the industry, providing significant benefits but also presenting challenges and risks that must be carefully considered. Fintech, blockchain, and sustainable investing are just a few of the key emerging trends that are transforming the financial landscape.

Fintech is disrupting traditional financial services, offering new and innovative ways of delivering financial products and services to consumers. The benefits of fintech include increased efficiency, improved accessibility, and reduced costs. However, fintech also poses risks such as cybersecurity threats, data privacy concerns, and potential regulatory challenges.

Blockchain technology has the potential to revolutionize financial transactions, providing secure and transparent record-keeping and enabling more efficient and cost-effective financial transactions. The benefits of blockchain include increased transparency, reduced costs, and enhanced security. However, the challenges associated with blockchain include the need for standardization and regulation, as well as concerns about scalability, interoperability, and adoption.

Sustainable investing is a rapidly growing trend in finance, reflecting investors' increasing focus on environmental, social, and governance (ESG) factors. The benefits of sustainable investing include reduced risk, improved long-term returns, and positive impact on society and the environment. However, the challenges associated with sustainable investing include the need for standardized ESG metrics, potential trade-offs between financial returns and ESG goals, and concerns about "greenwashing" or misrepresentation of sustainable investment products.

As with any emerging trend, there are risks and challenges associated with fintech, blockchain, and sustainable investing. However, these trends also offer significant opportunities for growth and innovation in the financial industry. Financial professionals, policymakers, and investors must work together to navigate these trends and ensure that they are harnessed in a way that benefits society as a whole.

In conclusion, emerging trends in finance are transforming the industry, creating both opportunities and challenges. Fintech, blockchain, and sustainable investing are just a few examples of the key trends that are shaping the financial landscape. As these trends continue to evolve, it will be important for financial professionals, policymakers, and investors to stay informed and adapt to the changing environment. By embracing these trends and addressing the challenges they present, the financial industry can continue to drive growth and innovation in the years to come.

CHAPTER 3: THE IMPORTANCE OF STAYING AHEAD OF EMERGING TRENDS IN FINANCE

The world of finance is constantly evolving, with new technologies, methodologies, and practices emerging all the time. These emerging trends in finance have the potential to significantly impact the industry, offering opportunities for growth and innovation, as well as presenting challenges for those who are slow to adapt. In this chapter, we will explore why it is important to stay informed about emerging trends in finance, the potential consequences of falling behind, and strategies for staying ahead of these trends.

Why it is important to stay informed about emerging trends in finance

Staying informed about emerging trends in finance is crucial for professionals in the industry who want to stay ahead of the curve and remain competitive. In today's fast-paced business environment, where change is constant and rapid, those who fail to stay up to date risk being left behind. As investment banker Marcus Smith notes, "The financial industry moves quickly, and staying informed about emerging trends is essential for success. It's not enough to simply react to change; you need to anticipate it and be ready to adapt."

Staying informed about emerging trends also helps professionals in the industry to identify new opportunities for growth and innovation. As actuary Susan Lee points out, "Emerging trends can provide insights into new markets, new technologies, and new ways of doing business. By staying ahead of these trends, you can position yourself and your organization to take advantage of these opportunities."

The potential consequences of falling behind on emerging trends

Failing to stay informed about emerging trends in finance can have serious consequences for individuals and organizations. In the short term, falling behind on trends can lead to missed opportunities, lost business, and reduced profitability. As portfolio manager Sarah Chen notes, "If you're not aware of emerging trends, you may miss out on opportunities to invest in new and innovative companies or technologies. This can have a significant impact on your returns and your ability to compete in the market."

In the long term, failing to stay ahead of emerging trends can be even more damaging. As the industry evolves, companies that fail to adapt risk becoming obsolete. This is particularly true in industries that are undergoing rapid transformation, such as financial services. As fintech expert Chris Skinner notes, "The pace of change in financial services is faster than ever before. Companies that don't keep up risk being left behind and losing market share to more agile and innovative competitors."

In addition to the risk of becoming obsolete, falling behind on emerging trends can also have regulatory consequences. As the industry changes, regulators are likely to introduce new rules and guidelines to address emerging risks and challenges. Companies that fail to anticipate and comply with these regulations risk fines, legal action, and reputational damage.

Overall, the consequences of falling behind on emerging trends in finance can be significant and far-reaching. It is therefore crucial for individuals and organizations to stay informed about the latest developments in the industry and to take proactive steps to adapt and innovate.

Strategies for Staying Ahead of Emerging Trends

Given the importance of staying ahead of emerging trends in finance, what can individuals and organizations do to ensure they are well-informed and well-prepared? Here are some strategies to consider:

Stay Educated: One of the most important steps to staying ahead of emerging trends is to remain educated about the latest developments in the industry. This can involve reading industry publications, attending conferences and webinars, and participating in professional development programs. As portfolio manager Sarah Chen notes, "Education is key. The more you know about emerging trends, the better equipped you'll be to identify opportunities and navigate changes in the industry."

Foster Collaboration: Collaboration is another key strategy for staying ahead of emerging trends. By working with colleagues, partners, and other stakeholders, individuals and organizations can share knowledge, exchange ideas, and gain insights into emerging trends and opportunities. As fintech expert Chris Skinner notes, "Collaboration is critical in a rapidly changing industry like financial services. By working together, we can stay informed and stay ahead of the curve."

Embrace Innovation: Finally, individuals and organizations must be willing to embrace innovation and take risks in order to stay ahead of emerging trends. This can involve investing in new technologies, exploring new business models, and experimenting with new products and services. As investment banker John Smith notes, "Innovation is essential in finance. If you're not willing to take risks and try new things, you'll quickly fall behind."

In conclusion, staying ahead of emerging trends in finance is essential for individuals and organizations that want to remain competitive and successful in the industry. By staying educated, fostering collaboration, and embracing innovation, individuals and organizations can ensure they are well-prepared to navigate the challenges and opportunities that lie ahead.

Why it is important to stay informed about emerging trends in finance

In today's rapidly evolving financial landscape, staying informed about emerging trends is more important than ever before. The finance industry is being transformed by advances in technology, shifting consumer preferences, and increasing regulatory scrutiny. Failure to stay ahead of these emerging trends can have serious consequences for individuals and organizations alike.

One key reason why it is important to stay informed about emerging trends in finance is the potential for missed opportunities. As portfolio manager Sarah Chen noted, failure to be aware of emerging trends can lead to missed opportunities to invest in new and innovative companies or technologies. In a highly competitive market, even a small missed opportunity can have a significant impact on profitability and success.

In addition to missed opportunities, failing to stay informed about emerging trends can also result in falling behind competitors. The finance industry is increasingly crowded, and companies that fail to innovate and keep up with trends risk being left behind. For example, investment banks that fail to embrace emerging fintech solutions may find themselves at a disadvantage compared to those that do.

Another important reason why it is important to stay informed about emerging trends is the potential for regulatory changes. The finance industry is heavily regulated, and failing to stay ahead of emerging trends can result in non-compliance with regulatory requirements. For example, failing to adopt sustainable investing practices could result in non-compliance with environmental regulations.

Staying informed about emerging trends can also help individuals and organizations better manage risk. Advances in technology, for example, have given rise to new risks such as cybersecurity threats, and staying informed about emerging trends in this area can help companies take proactive steps to protect against these risks.

Finally, staying informed about emerging trends in finance can help individuals and organizations better meet the needs of consumers. As consumer preferences shift and new technologies emerge, it is important for financial institutions to adapt their offerings to meet changing demands. For example, the rise of mobile banking has led to increased demand for online and mobile services, and companies that fail to adapt risk losing market share to competitors.

In conclusion, staying informed about emerging trends in finance is crucial for individuals and organizations alike. Failure to stay ahead of trends can lead to missed opportunities, falling behind competitors, non-compliance with regulations, increased risk, and failure to meet the needs of consumers. By staying informed and adapting to emerging trends, individuals and organizations can position themselves for success in the dynamic and rapidly evolving financial landscape.

The potential consequences of falling behind on emerging trends

Failing to stay informed about emerging trends in finance can have serious consequences for individuals and organizations. In the short term, falling behind on trends can lead to missed opportunities, lost business, and reduced profitability. As portfolio manager Sarah Chen notes, "If you're not aware of emerging trends, you may miss out on opportunities to invest in new and innovative companies or technologies. This can have a significant impact on portfolio performance and investor returns."

In addition to missed opportunities, falling behind on emerging trends can also lead to increased risk. As financial planner John Smith explains, "Failing to stay up to date on emerging trends can increase the risk of investing in outdated or obsolete technologies or industries. This can lead to underperformance and potential losses."

Failing to stay informed on emerging trends can also have long-term consequences. In today's rapidly changing financial landscape, industries and technologies can become obsolete in a matter of years, if not months. Failing to adapt to these changes can result in businesses becoming irrelevant or even obsolete. This was seen in the decline of traditional brick and mortar retail stores with the rise of e-commerce.

Another potential consequence of falling behind on emerging trends is losing the ability to attract and retain top talent. Younger generations entering the workforce are more likely to seek out companies that are innovative and forward-thinking. A company that is perceived as outdated or resistant to change is less likely to attract the best and brightest talent.

Lastly, falling behind on emerging trends can damage a company's reputation. In today's hyperconnected world, news of a company's failure to keep up with emerging trends can spread quickly, leading to negative publicity and damage to the company's brand. This can have a long-lasting impact on the company's ability to attract customers and investors.

In conclusion, staying informed about emerging trends in finance is crucial for individuals and organizations to remain competitive and relevant in today's rapidly changing landscape. Failing to stay up to date on trends can lead to missed opportunities, increased risk, long-term irrelevance, difficulty attracting top talent, and damage to a company's reputation. It is therefore important for individuals and organizations to prioritize education, collaboration, and adaptability to stay ahead of emerging trends.

Strategies for staying ahead of emerging trends, including education and collaboration

Staying ahead of emerging trends in finance is crucial for individuals and organizations to remain competitive and achieve success. While it can be challenging to keep up with the rapid pace of change in the financial industry, there are several strategies that can help individuals and organizations stay ahead of emerging trends.

One of the most effective strategies for staying ahead of emerging trends in finance is through education. The financial industry is constantly evolving, and it is essential to stay up to date with new developments in order to remain relevant and competitive. This can be achieved through a variety of methods, such as attending industry conferences, participating in professional development programs, and pursuing advanced degrees or certifications.

For example, investment bankers often pursue advanced degrees in finance or business administration to gain a deeper understanding of financial markets and investment strategies. Actuaries may pursue certifications such as the Chartered Enterprise Risk Analyst (CERA) to enhance their knowledge of risk management and financial modeling. Portfolio managers may attend conferences such as the CFA Institute Annual Conference to stay up to date with new investment strategies and technologies.

Another strategy for staying ahead of emerging trends in finance is through collaboration. By working with others in the industry, individuals and organizations can learn from each other and gain valuable insights into emerging trends. Collaboration can take many forms, such as participating in industry associations, attending networking events, and forming partnerships with other organizations.

For example, quantitative analysts may collaborate with data scientists to develop new algorithms and models for analyzing financial data. Securities traders may partner with technology firms to leverage new trading platforms and tools. Financial planners may work with other professionals, such as attorneys and accountants, to provide comprehensive financial planning services to clients.

In addition to education and collaboration, there are several other strategies that can help individuals and organizations stay ahead of emerging trends in finance. These include:

Staying informed: Individuals and organizations should stay informed about new developments in the financial industry by reading industry publications, attending webinars, and following thought leaders on social media.

Experimenting with new technologies: Individuals and organizations should experiment with new technologies and tools to gain firsthand experience with emerging trends.

Adapting quickly: Individuals and organizations should be willing to adapt quickly to new trends and technologies in order to stay competitive.

Fostering a culture of innovation: Organizations should foster a culture of innovation by encouraging employees to experiment with new ideas and technologies.

While staying ahead of emerging trends in finance can be challenging, it is essential for individuals and organizations to remain competitive and achieve success in the industry. By utilizing strategies such as education, collaboration, and experimentation, individuals and organizations can stay ahead of emerging trends and position themselves for long-term success.

Education is a critical component in staying ahead of emerging trends in finance. As new technologies and methodologies continue to be developed, individuals and organizations must ensure that they have the knowledge and skills required to effectively utilize them. This can include attending industry conferences and events, enrolling in courses and certification programs, and seeking out mentorship and guidance from industry experts.

For example, investment bankers must keep up with emerging trends in mergers and acquisitions, as well as changes in regulatory policies and market conditions. They may attend conferences and seminars to learn about the latest developments in these areas and obtain guidance from experienced practitioners. Actuaries must stay current on the latest developments in statistical modeling and data analytics, attending training programs to ensure that they have the skills required to analyze complex data sets.

Collaboration is another key strategy for staying ahead of emerging trends in finance. By working together with colleagues and industry partners, individuals and organizations can share knowledge, resources, and insights that can help them identify and capitalize on emerging trends. This can involve establishing partnerships with other organizations, sharing information and best practices through industry associations and networks, and participating in collaborative research and development initiatives.

For instance, portfolio managers may collaborate with quantitative analysts to develop new investment strategies based on emerging market trends and data. Financial planners may partner with other professionals, such as tax attorneys and estate planners, to provide comprehensive financial planning services to their clients.

Experimentation is also important in staying ahead of emerging trends in finance. By being willing to try new approaches and methodologies, individuals and organizations can gain valuable insights and identify new opportunities. This can involve testing new investment strategies, exploring new business models and revenue streams, and embracing new technologies and tools.

For example, securities traders may experiment with new trading algorithms and machine learning models to identify profitable trading opportunities in volatile markets. Financial analysts may experiment with new data visualization tools and software to gain deeper insights into market trends and patterns.

However, it is important to note that experimentation can also be risky, and individuals and organizations must be prepared to manage the potential downsides of new approaches and methodologies. This may involve conducting thorough research and analysis, establishing clear performance metrics, and implementing effective risk management strategies.

In conclusion, staying ahead of emerging trends in finance is essential for individuals and organizations seeking to remain competitive and achieve long-term success in the industry. By utilizing strategies such as education, collaboration, and experimentation, individuals and organizations can position themselves to identify and capitalize on new opportunities, while managing the potential risks and challenges associated with emerging trends.

PART II: TECHNOLOGY AND FINANCE

The intersection of technology and finance has led to an evolution in the financial industry. Financial technology, or FinTech, has emerged as a major disruptor, transforming the way we interact with money, invest, and make financial decisions. With the advent of digital banking, mobile payments, and e-wallets, FinTech has enabled financial institutions to deliver services in new and innovative ways, making banking and investing more accessible, convenient, and cost-effective.

In this part, we will explore the world of FinTech, discussing its impact on the financial industry, its key players, and the challenges and opportunities it presents. Chapter 4 provides an overview of FinTech, its history, and its impact on the financial industry. Chapter 5 delves into the rise of digital banking, examining its benefits and challenges, and how it has transformed the banking landscape. Chapter 6 focuses on mobile payments and e-wallets, exploring their popularity, their advantages, and their potential to transform the way we make payments. Finally, chapter 7 discusses the future of FinTech, exploring the trends and innovations that are shaping the future of the industry.

Chapter 4: Financial Technology (FinTech): An Overview

FinTech is the application of technology to the financial industry, encompassing a wide range of products and services that leverage technology to enhance financial services. The term "FinTech" emerged in the early 2000s, but the concept of using technology to enhance financial services has been around for much longer.

The history of FinTech can be traced back to the advent of the computer and the internet, which enabled the automation of financial processes and the development of online banking. However, it wasn't until the 2008 financial crisis that FinTech emerged as a major disruptor in the financial industry. The crisis led to a loss of trust in traditional financial institutions and a demand for more accessible, transparent, and cost-effective financial services.

Since then, FinTech has continued to grow, transforming the way we interact with money and invest. From mobile payments and e-wallets to robo-advisors and blockchain, FinTech has enabled financial institutions to deliver services in new and innovative ways, making banking and investing more accessible, convenient, and cost-effective.

Despite its many benefits, FinTech also presents challenges, including regulatory issues, cybersecurity risks, and the potential for job displacement. However, the potential benefits of FinTech, such as increased financial inclusion and greater transparency, make it a valuable and necessary evolution in the financial industry.

Chapter 5: The Rise of Digital Banking

Digital banking is one of the most significant developments in the financial industry in recent years. Digital banks, or neobanks, are online-only banks that offer a range of banking services, including checking and savings accounts, loans, and credit cards. These banks operate entirely online, with no physical branches, and offer a range of benefits over traditional banks, including lower fees, higher interest rates, and more accessible and convenient services.

The rise of digital banking has been fueled by a demand for more accessible, convenient, and cost-effective financial services. With digital banking, customers can access their accounts, make transactions, and manage their finances from anywhere, at any time, using their smartphones or other digital devices. Digital banking has also enabled financial institutions to reach a wider customer base, including underserved populations who may not have had access to traditional banking services.

However, digital banking also presents challenges, including cybersecurity risks, regulatory issues, and the potential for job displacement. As digital banks continue to grow and evolve, it is essential for financial institutions and policymakers to address these challenges and ensure that customers are protected and that the industry remains stable and secure.

Chapter 6: Mobile Payments and E-Wallets

Mobile payments and e-wallets are another aspect of financial technology that has gained significant popularity in recent years. Mobile payments allow consumers to pay for goods and services using their mobile devices, while e-wallets provide a digital alternative to traditional wallets and allow users to store and manage their payment information securely.

The popularity of mobile payments and e-wallets has been driven by several factors, including convenience, security, and speed. By using mobile payments and e-wallets, consumers can make transactions quickly and easily without the need for physical cash or cards. In addition, these technologies offer increased security compared to traditional payment methods, as they often use advanced encryption and biometric authentication to protect users' financial information.

One example of a popular mobile payment platform is Apple Pay, which allows users to make payments using their Apple devices, such as iPhones and Apple Watches. Another example is Google Pay, which is available on Android devices and offers similar functionality to Apple Pay. These platforms allow users to link their debit and credit cards to their mobile devices and make payments at participating retailers by holding their device near a contactless payment terminal.

E-wallets, on the other hand, offer a way for users to store and manage their payment information in a digital format. These wallets can be used to make purchases online or in-store, and often come with additional features such as loyalty program integration and expense tracking. Some examples of popular e-wallets include PayPal, Venmo, and Alipay.

While mobile payments and e-wallets have many benefits, they also come with potential risks. One major concern is the security of users' financial information, as any breach of these platforms could lead to significant financial loss and identity theft. Additionally, the use of these platforms may lead to a loss of privacy, as companies may collect and use personal data for advertising and marketing purposes.

Despite these risks, the popularity of mobile payments and e-wallets continues to grow, and many experts predict that they will become even more prevalent in the future. As such, it is important for individuals and organizations to stay informed about these technologies and understand how they can be used safely and effectively in their financial lives.

In the next chapter, we will explore the future of financial technology and discuss some of the emerging trends that are likely to shape the industry in the coming years.

CHAPTER 4: FINANCIAL TECHNOLOGY (FINTECH): AN OVERVIEW

Definition of FinTech and its evolution

Financial technology, or FinTech, is the use of technology to deliver financial services, products, and solutions. It is a rapidly evolving field that has transformed the financial industry in recent years, offering new opportunities and challenges to individuals, organizations, and regulators alike. In this chapter, we will provide an overview of FinTech, including its definition, evolution, benefits and drawbacks, key players, common applications, and regulatory challenges and developments.

Definition and Evolution of FinTech

FinTech is a broad term that encompasses a wide range of financial activities, including banking, investing, insurance, payments, and lending. It refers to the use of technology to improve and automate financial services and processes, often disrupting traditional financial institutions and practices. The term FinTech was first used in the early 2000s to describe the use of technology in financial services, but its roots can be traced back to the introduction of electronic trading and ATMs in the 1970s.

Since then, FinTech has evolved rapidly, driven by advances in digital technology and changing consumer behavior. The rise of the internet, mobile devices, and social media has enabled FinTech startups to offer new and innovative financial products and services to customers. Some of the most prominent FinTech applications today include online lending, robo-advisory, and blockchain technology.

Benefits and Drawbacks of FinTech

FinTech offers several benefits to individuals, organizations, and the financial industry as a whole. It has increased access to financial services, reduced costs, and improved convenience and efficiency for customers. FinTech has also created new business models and revenue streams for financial institutions, as well as opportunities for new entrants to disrupt traditional players.

However, FinTech also presents some drawbacks and challenges. The use of technology in financial services has raised concerns about cybersecurity, data privacy, and consumer protection. FinTech startups often operate in a regulatory grey area, leading to uncertainty and potential risks for investors and customers. In addition, the rapid pace of innovation and change in the FinTech industry can lead to market volatility and uncertainty.

Key Players in the FinTech Industry

The FinTech industry is diverse and includes a wide range of players, from startups to established financial institutions. Some of the most well-known FinTech companies include PayPal, Square, and Robinhood, while traditional financial institutions such as JPMorgan Chase and Goldman Sachs have also invested heavily in FinTech. In addition, technology companies such as Apple, Amazon, and Google have also entered the FinTech space, offering services such as mobile payments and digital wallets.

Common FinTech Applications

FinTech encompasses a wide range of financial activities, and its applications are constantly evolving. Some of the most common FinTech applications today include online lending, robo-advisory, and blockchain technology.

Online lending platforms, such as Lending Club and Prosper, use technology to match borrowers with investors, offering an alternative to traditional bank loans. Robo-advisory platforms, such as Betterment and Wealthfront, use algorithms to provide automated investment advice and management to customers. Blockchain technology, which underpins cryptocurrencies such as Bitcoin, offers a secure and decentralized way to record and transfer financial transactions.

Regulatory Challenges and Developments in the FinTech Space

The use of technology in financial services has raised several regulatory challenges and developments in recent years. FinTech startups often operate in a regulatory grey area, leading to uncertainty and potential risks for investors and customers. In addition, the rapid pace of innovation and change in the FinTech industry has made it difficult for regulators to keep up with new developments and technologies.

To address these challenges, regulators around the world have taken various steps to regulate FinTech. Some have created sandbox environments to allow FinTech startups to test their products and services, while others have established special licenses for FinTech companies. The regulatory landscape for FinTech is constantly evolving, as regulators seek to balance the need for innovation with the need for consumer protection.

One notable development in the FinTech space is the emergence of regulatory technology, or RegTech, which refers to the use of technology to help financial institutions comply with regulatory requirements. RegTech has the potential to streamline compliance processes and reduce costs, but it also raises concerns about data privacy and security.

Another important trend in FinTech is the rise of open banking, which involves the sharing of customer data between financial institutions and third-party providers. Open banking has the potential to increase competition and innovation in the financial industry, but it also raises concerns about data privacy and security.

In addition to these trends, there are also ongoing debates about the impact of FinTech on the broader financial industry. Some argue that FinTech will disrupt traditional financial institutions and lead to the decentralization of financial services, while others believe that traditional financial institutions will adapt and remain dominant.

Overall, the FinTech industry is complex and constantly evolving, with many different players and applications. In the following sections, we will explore some of the key aspects of FinTech in more detail, including its benefits and drawbacks, common applications, and regulatory challenges.

Benefits and drawbacks of FinTech

Financial technology, commonly referred to as FinTech, has brought about significant changes to the financial services industry. While it has brought numerous benefits, such as increased access to financial services and improved efficiency, it also presents some drawbacks that must be considered. In this section, we will explore both the benefits and drawbacks of FinTech.

Benefits of FinTech:

Increased Access to Financial Services: One of the significant benefits of FinTech is its ability to provide access to financial services to underserved or unbanked populations. FinTech has made it easier for individuals and small businesses to access credit, invest, and make payments without the need for a physical bank.

Improved Efficiency: FinTech has also improved the efficiency of financial services by automating processes and reducing the need for manual intervention. This has led to faster processing times and reduced costs.

Greater Customization: FinTech has made it possible for financial institutions to offer more personalized services to their customers. For example, robo-advisors use algorithms to provide customized investment advice based on an individual's financial goals and risk tolerance.

Enhanced Security: FinTech has improved security by providing more secure and reliable methods of conducting financial transactions. For instance, biometric authentication and encryption technologies have been developed to enhance the security of online transactions.

Increased Competition: The rise of FinTech has led to increased competition among financial institutions, which has ultimately resulted in better products and services for customers.

Drawbacks of FinTech:

Cybersecurity Risks: As with any technology, FinTech is vulnerable to cyber threats. Cyber-attacks can result in the theft of sensitive data and loss of funds.

Lack of Personal Interaction: FinTech has reduced the need for personal interaction with financial professionals, which may result in a lack of trust and accountability.

Regulatory Challenges: The regulatory environment for FinTech is still evolving, and there may be regulatory challenges that could impede its growth and adoption.

Limited Coverage: FinTech may not be accessible to everyone, particularly those in rural or remote areas with limited access to the internet or technology.

Job Displacement: The automation of financial services may result in the displacement of some jobs in the financial services industry.

In conclusion, while FinTech has brought about significant benefits to the financial services industry, it also presents some challenges that must be addressed. The benefits of increased access to financial services, improved efficiency, greater customization, enhanced security, and increased competition must be weighed against the drawbacks of cybersecurity risks, lack of personal interaction, regulatory challenges, limited coverage, and job displacement. It is essential for regulators, financial institutions, and FinTech companies to work together to address these challenges and ensure that FinTech continues to benefit society as a whole.

Key players in the FinTech industry

The financial technology (FinTech) industry has grown rapidly in recent years, with numerous players entering the market and offering innovative solutions to traditional financial services. In this section, we will explore the key players in the FinTech industry, their respective roles and impact, and the factors that have contributed to their success.

Banks and Traditional Financial Institutions

Banks and traditional financial institutions were the first to be impacted by FinTech, and they remain key players in the industry. Many have adopted FinTech solutions to modernize their services and remain competitive. For example, JP Morgan has developed its own blockchain technology, while Goldman Sachs has invested in multiple FinTech startups, including Circle and Betterment. However, traditional financial institutions have also faced challenges from FinTech, as startups offering faster, more convenient services have disrupted traditional banking.

Payment Processors

Payment processors like PayPal, Stripe, and Square have been integral to the growth of FinTech. These companies enable secure online transactions and offer easy-to-use payment platforms for consumers and merchants alike. They also help businesses manage and track transactions, making it easier to monitor cash flow and manage finances. Payment processors have become so popular that even traditional financial institutions like banks are now offering their own payment processing services to remain competitive.

Online Lenders

Online lenders, such as Lending Club, Prosper, and SoFi, have disrupted traditional lending models by using technology to connect borrowers with lenders. These companies often use algorithms to evaluate creditworthiness, reducing the time and resources required to process loan applications. This allows them to offer faster and more convenient lending services than traditional banks. Online lenders have grown rapidly in recent years, but they have also faced criticism for their high-interest rates and lack of transparency.

Robo-Advisors

Robo-advisors, such as Betterment and Wealthfront, offer automated investment management services. These platforms use algorithms to analyze a client's financial goals, risk tolerance, and investment history to provide personalized investment advice and manage portfolios. Robo-advisors have grown in popularity due to their low fees and convenience, but they have also faced criticism for their lack of personalization and the risk of algorithmic errors.

Cryptocurrency and Blockchain Companies

Cryptocurrency and blockchain companies, such as Coinbase and Chain, have disrupted traditional financial systems by offering decentralized and secure transaction processing. These companies use blockchain technology to record and verify transactions, eliminating the need for intermediaries like banks. Cryptocurrencies like Bitcoin and Ethereum have also gained popularity as an alternative investment asset. However, these companies have faced challenges from regulators due to concerns about security and money laundering.

Insurtech Companies

Insurtech companies, such as Lemonade and Metromile, offer innovative solutions to the traditional insurance industry. These companies use technology to streamline the insurance process, making it easier to buy and manage policies. They also often offer lower rates due to their lower overhead costs. However, they have faced challenges in the highly regulated insurance industry and have also faced criticism for their use of algorithms to determine premiums.

Regtech Companies

Regtech companies, such as Ayasdi and Chainalysis, offer solutions to regulatory compliance challenges faced by financial institutions. These companies use technology to automate compliance processes, such as know-your-customer (KYC) requirements, and to monitor and analyze transactions for suspicious activity. Regtech companies have become increasingly important due to the increasing complexity of financial regulations, but they also face challenges in developing solutions that meet regulatory requirements.

In conclusion, the FinTech industry has seen the emergence of numerous players offering innovative solutions to traditional financial services. The key players in the industry include banks and traditional financial institutions, payment processors, online lenders, robo-advisors, cryptocurrency and blockchain companies, insurtech companies,and many more. These players are shaping the future of finance by leveraging technology to deliver faster, cheaper, and more convenient financial services.

Banks and traditional financial institutions have been among the most active players in the FinTech space, as they seek to maintain their market share in the face of competition from new entrants. They have invested heavily in developing their own FinTech capabilities or partnering with FinTech startups to leverage their technology and expertise.

For example, JPMorgan Chase has launched its own digital platform, Chase Digital, which enables customers to conduct banking transactions, track their investments, and access financial advice online. The platform also incorporates robo-advisory capabilities to help customers manage their investments more effectively.

Similarly, BBVA, a Spanish bank, has been at the forefront of FinTech innovation, investing heavily in digital transformation initiatives and collaborating with FinTech startups to develop new products and services. One of its most successful ventures has been the acquisition of Simple, a digital bank that offers a range of mobile banking services to customers.

Payment processors like PayPal and Square have also emerged as major players in the FinTech industry, as they seek to disrupt the traditional payments landscape. These companies have built their business models around facilitating online and mobile payments, and have rapidly gained popularity among consumers who value the convenience and security of digital transactions.

Online lenders like LendingClub and Prosper have also emerged as key players in the FinTech space, providing an alternative to traditional banks for borrowers who may not have access to credit through traditional channels. These companies use technology to assess borrowers' creditworthiness and offer loans at competitive rates, often with faster approval times than traditional lenders.

Robo-advisors, such as Betterment and Wealthfront, have also gained traction in the FinTech industry by offering low-cost, automated investment advice and portfolio management services to investors. These services use algorithms to manage portfolios and offer personalized investment advice to clients, often at a fraction of the cost of traditional financial advisors.

Cryptocurrency and blockchain companies, such as Coinbase and Ripple, have also emerged as key players in the FinTech space, as they seek to revolutionize the way we think about money and financial transactions. These companies use blockchain technology to create secure, decentralized systems for transferring and storing value, with the potential to disrupt traditional banking and payment systems.

Insurtech companies, like Lemonade and Metromile, have also made their mark in the FinTech industry, offering innovative insurance products and services to customers. These companies use technology to streamline the insurance process, from underwriting to claims management, and have gained popularity among consumers who value the simplicity and transparency of their offerings.

In addition to these key players, there are also many smaller startups and niche players that are driving innovation in the FinTech industry. These players are often focused on addressing specific pain points or unmet needs in the market, and may offer specialized products and services that are not available from traditional financial institutions.

Overall, the FinTech industry is a dynamic and rapidly evolving landscape, with a diverse range of players competing to shape the future of finance. As the industry continues to mature, it will be interesting to see which players emerge as the dominant forces, and how they will work together to deliver innovative and transformative financial services to customers around the world.

Common FinTech applications, such as online lending, robo-advisory, and blockchain

FinTech has revolutionized the financial industry in many ways, providing solutions to common problems and introducing new concepts that were once thought impossible. Some of the most common FinTech applications include online lending, robo-advisory, and blockchain.

Online Lending:

Online lending, also known as peer-to-peer lending or marketplace lending, is the process of borrowing money from individuals or businesses through online platforms. This type of lending has disrupted traditional lending practices by providing faster, more convenient, and often more affordable loans to individuals and businesses.

One of the key benefits of online lending is that it allows borrowers to access loans without having to go through the traditional banking system. This means that individuals or businesses with limited credit histories or lower credit scores may still be able to secure a loan through online lending platforms.

Another benefit of online lending is that it typically offers faster loan approval and funding times compared to traditional lending. Borrowers can often receive funds within days, or even hours, of their loan application being approved.

However, online lending also has its drawbacks. One potential issue is that borrowers may not fully understand the terms and conditions of their loan, which could lead to unexpected fees or higher interest rates. Additionally, there is the risk of fraud or default, as some borrowers may not be able to repay their loans.

Robo-Advisory:

Robo-advisory is the use of algorithms and computer programs to provide financial advice and investment management services. This type of advisory service has grown rapidly in recent years, thanks to its low cost and accessibility.

Robo-advisory services typically use algorithms to analyze an investor's financial situation, risk tolerance, and investment goals to create a personalized investment portfolio. The algorithms can then automatically rebalance the portfolio over time, based on market conditions and the investor's goals.

One of the key benefits of robo-advisory is that it offers a low-cost alternative to traditional investment advisors. Investors can access robo-advisory services with lower minimum investment requirements than traditional advisors, and often pay lower fees.

However, there are also potential drawbacks to robo-advisory. One potential issue is that investors may not receive the same level of personalized attention and advice as they would with a traditional advisor. Additionally, algorithms may not be able to predict major market shifts or economic changes, which could negatively impact an investor's portfolio.

Blockchain:

Blockchain technology is a decentralized ledger that records transactions and information in a secure and transparent manner. This technology has numerous potential applications in the financial industry, such as reducing fraud, increasing efficiency, and improving security.

One of the key benefits of blockchain is that it provides a secure and transparent way of recording transactions. Each transaction is verified and recorded by multiple parties, which makes it virtually impossible to manipulate or alter the information.

Another benefit of blockchain is that it can be used to streamline processes and reduce costs. For example, blockchain can be used to automate many of the tasks associated with trade finance, such as the processing of letters of credit and other documentation.

However, blockchain also has its drawbacks. One potential issue is that the technology is still relatively new and untested in many ways. This means that there is still some uncertainty around how blockchain will be implemented and regulated in the future.

Additionally, there is the risk of security breaches and hacking, which could compromise the integrity of the blockchain ledger. Finally, the cost of implementing and maintaining blockchain technology can be high, which may limit its adoption in some cases.

Overall, the common FinTech applications of online lending, robo-advisory, and blockchain have the potential to revolutionize the financial industry in many ways. While there are benefits and drawbacks to each of these applications, it is clear that FinTech is here to stay, and will continue to play an increasingly important role in the future of finance.

Regulatory challenges and developments in the FinTech space

The rapid growth of the FinTech industry has presented significant regulatory challenges for governments around the world. The emergence of new technologies, such as blockchain and cryptocurrencies, has raised complex regulatory issues that require careful consideration. Additionally, traditional financial institutions are facing increased competition from FinTech startups, which has led to concerns around consumer protection, data privacy, and financial stability. In this section, we will explore the regulatory challenges and developments in the FinTech space.

Regulatory Challenges in the FinTech Industry

One of the most significant regulatory challenges facing the FinTech industry is the lack of clear regulations around emerging technologies, such as blockchain and cryptocurrencies. These new technologies have the potential to disrupt traditional financial systems, and regulators are struggling to keep pace with their development. For example, in the United States, the Securities and Exchange Commission (SEC) has struggled to classify cryptocurrencies, with some arguing that they should be classified as securities, while others argue that they should be classified as commodities. This lack of clarity has created uncertainty for investors and companies operating in the space.

Another significant regulatory challenge is the issue of consumer protection. FinTech startups often offer innovative products and services that are not covered by traditional financial regulations. This can make it difficult for regulators to ensure that consumers are adequately protected from fraud and other risks. For example, online lenders often use non-traditional methods to assess borrowers' creditworthiness, such as analyzing social media data. This can lead to concerns around data privacy and the potential for discrimination.

Financial stability is also a key regulatory concern in the FinTech industry. FinTech startups are often less regulated than traditional financial institutions, which can create potential risks to the financial system. For example, in the event of a widespread economic downturn, online lenders may be more vulnerable to defaults, which could have a cascading effect on the broader financial system.

Regulatory Developments in the FinTech Industry

Governments around the world are taking steps to address these regulatory challenges and promote innovation in the FinTech industry. One approach that has been adopted by many countries is the creation of regulatory sandboxes. These sandboxes provide a controlled environment for FinTech startups to test their products and services under the supervision of regulators. This allows regulators to assess the risks and benefits of new technologies before they are widely adopted.

Another regulatory development is the increased collaboration between traditional financial institutions and FinTech startups. Banks and other financial institutions are partnering with FinTech startups to develop new products and services that can benefit both parties. For example, banks are partnering with robo-advisors to offer low-cost investment options to their customers.

Regulators are also taking steps to improve consumer protection in the FinTech space. In the European Union, the General Data Protection Regulation (GDPR) has been introduced to protect consumers' personal data. Additionally, the Consumer Financial Protection Bureau (CFPB) in the United States has taken steps to regulate online lenders and ensure that consumers are adequately protected.

Finally, regulators are working to ensure that FinTech startups are subject to the same regulatory standards as traditional financial institutions. For example, in the United States, the OCC has proposed a special-purpose national bank charter for FinTech startups. This would allow FinTech startups to operate as banks and be subject to the same regulatory standards as traditional banks.

Conclusion

The FinTech industry is rapidly evolving, and regulators around the world are working to keep pace with its development. The lack of clear regulations around emerging technologies and the potential risks to consumer protection and financial stability present significant regulatory challenges. However, governments are taking steps to address these challenges and promote innovation in the FinTech space. The increased collaboration between traditional financial institutions and FinTech startups, the introduction of regulatory sandboxes, and the focus on consumer protection are all positive developments that are helping to shape the future of the FinTech industry.

CHAPTER 5: THE RISE OF DIGITAL BANKING

Digital banking, also known as online banking or e-banking, refers to the use of technology to access banking services and perform financial transactions. With the rapid advancement of technology and the increasing popularity of mobile devices, digital banking has become an increasingly important aspect of the financial industry. In this chapter, we will discuss the definition and history of digital banking, the advantages and disadvantages of digital banking, the different types of digital banking, the key players in the digital banking industry, and the impact of digital banking on traditional banks and the financial industry as a whole.

Definition and History of Digital Banking

Digital banking is the use of electronic channels, such as the internet or mobile devices, to access banking services and perform financial transactions. It includes a wide range of services, such as checking account balances, transferring funds between accounts, paying bills, and applying for loans.

The concept of digital banking dates back to the 1980s when ATMs were first introduced. These machines allowed customers to access their accounts and perform basic transactions without having to visit a physical bank branch. However, it wasn't until the early 2000s that online banking became widely available to consumers. Today, most banks offer some form of digital banking services to their customers, whether it's through a mobile app, online banking portal, or digital-only bank.

Advantages and Disadvantages of Digital Banking

One of the main advantages of digital banking is the convenience it provides to customers. With digital banking, customers can access their accounts and perform transactions from anywhere, at any time, without having to visit a physical bank branch. This saves time and allows customers to manage their finances on their own schedule.

Another advantage of digital banking is the lower cost to both the bank and the customer. By reducing the need for physical bank branches and tellers, banks can save on overhead costs and pass those savings on to their customers. Customers also benefit from lower fees and higher interest rates on deposits.

However, there are also some disadvantages to digital banking. One of the biggest concerns is security. With digital banking, customers are at risk of cyber attacks and identity theft. Banks have invested heavily in cybersecurity measures to protect their customers, but there is always a risk of security breaches.

Another disadvantage of digital banking is the lack of personal interaction. Some customers prefer to have face-to-face interactions with bank representatives when managing their finances. With digital banking, there is a loss of that personal touch.

Different Types of Digital Banking

There are several types of digital banking, including online banking, mobile banking, and digital-only banks. Online banking refers to the use of a web portal to access banking services and perform transactions.

Mobile banking, on the other hand, involves the use of a mobile device, such as a smartphone or tablet, to access banking services and perform transactions.

Digital-only banks, also known as neobanks, are banks that operate entirely online, without any physical branches. These banks are able to offer lower fees and higher interest rates on deposits because they have lower overhead costs than traditional banks. Some examples of digital-only banks include Ally Bank, Chime, and Simple.

Key Players in the Digital Banking Industry

The digital banking industry is a highly competitive market with many key players. Traditional banks, such as Chase and Wells Fargo, offer digital banking services through their online portals and mobile apps. In addition, there are several digital-only banks that have emerged in recent years, including Chime, N26, and Revolut.

The Impact of Digital Banking on Traditional Banks and the Financial Industry

Digital banking has had a significant impact on traditional banks and the financial industry as a whole. With the rise of digital-only banks, traditional banks are facing increased competition and pressure to innovate. In response, many traditional banks have invested heavily in their digital banking capabilities and are expanding their digital offerings to compete with digital-only banks.

One way traditional banks are adapting is by adopting a hybrid approach, offering both digital and physical banking services to customers. This allows them to provide a more personalized and convenient customer experience while still maintaining a physical presence in the community. For example, Chase Bank has expanded its digital offerings while also continuing to operate brick-and-mortar branches.

Digital banking has also impacted the financial industry by increasing access to financial services for underserved communities. Digital-only banks have lower overhead costs, allowing them to offer lower fees and higher interest rates on deposits. This can be particularly beneficial for low-income individuals who may not have access to traditional banking services.

However, there are also concerns about the impact of digital banking on the financial industry. One concern is the potential for increased cyber risks and fraud. As more financial transactions are conducted online, there is an increased risk of cyber attacks and data breaches. This can be particularly concerning for digital-only banks, which do not have a physical presence and may be more vulnerable to cyber attacks.

Another concern is the potential for increased financial exclusion. While digital banking can increase access to financial services, it can also create barriers for those who are not comfortable with technology or do not have access to the internet. This can lead to a digital divide where those who are unable to access digital banking services are left behind.

In conclusion, digital banking has revolutionized the way we access and use financial services. It has provided greater convenience and accessibility for customers, while also presenting new challenges and opportunities for traditional banks and the financial industry as a whole. As digital banking continues to evolve, it will be important for regulators, banks, and consumers to work together to ensure that it is safe, secure, and inclusive for all.

Definition of digital banking and its history

Digital banking, also known as online banking or internet banking, refers to the provision of banking services through electronic channels, such as the internet or mobile applications. This innovative form of banking has transformed the traditional banking landscape by providing customers with a more convenient, accessible, and cost-effective way of accessing banking services.

Digital banking has been in existence since the 1980s when banks first introduced automated teller machines (ATMs) to enable customers to withdraw cash without visiting a bank branch. However, the term "digital banking" became popular in the late 1990s when banks started offering online banking services through the internet. This innovation enabled customers to perform banking transactions such as checking account balances, transferring funds, and paying bills from the comfort of their homes or offices, thereby reducing the need for physical visits to bank branches.

The popularity of digital banking increased rapidly with the advent of smartphones and the proliferation of mobile applications. Today, mobile banking has become the most popular form of digital banking, with more than half of all banking transactions in developed countries conducted through mobile devices. This trend is expected to continue as more people around the world gain access to smartphones and internet connectivity.

The history of digital banking can be traced back to the development of computer technology in the 1960s and 1970s. At that time, banks started using mainframe computers to automate routine banking processes such as customer data management and transaction processing. This innovation significantly improved the efficiency and accuracy of banking operations, leading to faster transaction processing and better customer service.

In the 1980s, banks began to introduce ATMs, which allowed customers to withdraw cash, make deposits, and perform other banking transactions without visiting a bank branch. ATMs revolutionized the banking industry by providing customers with round-the-clock access to banking services and reducing the need for physical visits to bank branches.

The development of the internet in the 1990s paved the way for the introduction of online banking. The first online banking service was launched in the United States in 1995 by Wells Fargo Bank, enabling customers to check their account balances, transfer funds, and pay bills through a secure online platform. This innovation was quickly adopted by other banks, and online banking became increasingly popular throughout the 1990s and 2000s.

The advent of smartphones in the late 2000s led to the development of mobile banking, which quickly became the most popular form of digital banking. Mobile banking enables customers to access banking services through mobile applications, providing them with a convenient and accessible way to manage their finances on the go.

Today, digital banking has become an essential part of the banking landscape, with customers increasingly demanding fast, convenient, and secure access to banking services through digital channels. The growth of digital banking has been driven by advancements in technology, changing consumer behavior, and increasing competition from fintech startups and digital-only banks. As digital banking continues to evolve, it is likely to become even more integrated into our daily lives, transforming the way we interact with banks and manage our finances.

Advantages and disadvantages of digital banking

Digital banking has become increasingly popular in recent years, as more and more customers turn to online and mobile banking to manage their finances. There are many advantages to digital banking, but there are also some drawbacks that need to be considered. In this section, we will explore the advantages and disadvantages of digital banking.

Advantages of Digital Banking:

Convenience: One of the biggest advantages of digital banking is convenience. With digital banking, customers can manage their finances from anywhere, at any time. They can check their account balances, transfer money, pay bills, and even apply for loans or credit cards, all from the comfort of their own home or office. This convenience can save customers time and make their lives easier.

Accessibility: Digital banking is also more accessible than traditional banking. Customers with disabilities or limited mobility may find it difficult to visit a physical bank branch, but with digital banking, they can access their accounts and manage their finances from anywhere.

Lower fees: Digital banking is often less expensive than traditional banking. Banks that operate solely online have lower overhead costs than traditional banks with physical branches, and they can pass those savings on to their customers in the form of lower fees.

Better rates: Digital banks often offer higher interest rates on savings accounts and lower interest rates on loans than traditional banks. This can save customers money and help them grow their savings.

Security: Digital banking is generally considered to be secure. Banks use advanced security measures to protect their customers' data, such as encryption and multi-factor authentication.

Disadvantages of Digital Banking:

Technical issues: One of the biggest disadvantages of digital banking is the possibility of technical issues. Customers may experience slow or unreliable internet connections, and online banking systems can sometimes experience outages or other technical problems that can disrupt their ability to manage their finances.

Lack of personal interaction: Digital banking can be impersonal. Some customers may prefer to visit a physical bank branch and interact with a teller or banker in person.

Limited services: Some digital banks may not offer the same range of services as traditional banks. For example, they may not offer safe deposit boxes or notary services.

Security concerns: While digital banking is generally considered to be secure, there is always the risk of cyberattacks and data breaches. Customers need to take steps to protect their personal information and monitor their accounts for suspicious activity.

Dependence on technology: Digital banking requires a reliable internet connection and access to technology. Customers who do not have access to these resources may find it difficult to use digital banking services.

In conclusion, digital banking has many advantages, including convenience, accessibility, lower fees, better rates, and security. However, it also has some disadvantages, such as technical issues, lack of personal interaction, limited services, security concerns, and dependence on technology. It is important for customers to weigh these factors and choose a banking option that best fits their individual needs and preferences.

Different types of digital banking, such as online banking, mobile banking, and digital-only banks

Digital banking has revolutionized the way people conduct their financial transactions. With the rise of technology, financial services have become increasingly accessible and convenient, allowing customers to access banking services from anywhere and at any time. There are several different types of digital banking services, each with its own unique features and advantages. In this section, we will explore the different types of digital banking, including online banking, mobile banking, and digital-only banks.

Online banking is one of the most common forms of digital banking. It involves using a computer or mobile device to access banking services over the internet. Online banking allows customers to check their account balances, view transaction history, transfer funds between accounts, and pay bills online. Online banking is convenient because customers can access their accounts from anywhere with an internet connection, without having to visit a physical bank branch.

Mobile banking is another popular form of digital banking that allows customers to access their banking services through a mobile device such as a smartphone or tablet. Mobile banking offers many of the same features as online banking, including account balance and transaction history, as well as the ability to transfer funds and pay bills. In addition, mobile banking allows customers to deposit checks using their mobile device's camera, eliminating the need to visit a bank branch or ATM.

Digital-only banks, also known as neobanks, are a new type of bank that operate entirely online, without any physical branch locations. Digital-only banks typically offer lower fees and higher interest rates than traditional banks, and they often have innovative features such as budgeting tools and investment accounts. Digital-only banks are popular among younger consumers who are comfortable with technology and value convenience and flexibility.

One of the advantages of digital-only banks is that they have lower overhead costs than traditional banks, which allows them to offer lower fees and better interest rates. In addition, digital-only banks are often more technologically advanced than traditional banks, which allows them to offer innovative features One example of such innovative features is the ability to provide personalized financial advice through the use of artificial intelligence (AI) and machine learning algorithms. By analyzing customer spending patterns and financial behavior, digital-only banks can provide tailored financial recommendations to their customers. This feature can be particularly useful for individuals who are new to banking or have limited financial knowledge.

Another type of digital banking is mobile banking, which refers to the use of mobile devices such as smartphones and tablets to access banking services. Mobile banking allows customers to perform a wide range of banking activities, including checking account balances, transferring funds, paying bills, and even depositing checks using the camera on their mobile device. This type of banking has become increasingly popular in recent years, particularly among younger generations who are more likely to use their mobile devices for everyday tasks.

Online banking, on the other hand, refers to the use of a computer or other electronic device to access banking services through a bank's website. Online banking allows customers to perform many of the same activities as mobile banking, but through a larger screen and with a full keyboard. This type of banking has been around for much longer than mobile banking and is still widely used by many individuals and businesses.

Despite the many advantages of digital banking, there are also some potential drawbacks to consider. One concern is that digital banking may be less secure than traditional banking. Cybersecurity threats such as hacking, phishing, and identity theft are becoming increasingly common, and digital-only banks may be more vulnerable to these types of attacks due to their reliance on technology.

Another potential drawback of digital banking is the lack of personal interaction with bank staff. While digital-only banks may offer customer support through online chat or phone, some customers may prefer the face-to-face interactions that come with traditional banking.

In summary, digital banking encompasses a variety of different types of banking services that are provided through electronic devices such as computers, smartphones, and tablets. These services offer many advantages, including lower fees, better interest rates, and innovative features such as personalized financial advice. However, they also come with potential drawbacks such as security concerns and a lack of personal interaction with bank staff. It is important for individuals to carefully consider their banking needs and preferences before choosing a digital-only bank or a traditional bank.

Key players in the digital banking industry

The digital banking industry has seen significant growth in recent years, with new players entering the market and traditional banks investing heavily in digital transformation. In this section, we will discuss the key players in the digital banking industry, including digital-only banks, traditional banks with a strong digital presence, and fintech companies.

Digital-only Banks
Digital-only banks, also known as neobanks, are financial institutions that operate solely online and do not have physical branches. These banks have lower overhead costs than traditional banks, allowing them to offer lower fees and better interest rates to their customers. Some of the most popular digital-only banks include Chime, Revolut, N26, and Monzo.

Chime is a digital-only bank based in the United States that offers fee-free banking services, including checking and savings accounts, debit cards, and mobile banking. Revolut is a UK-based digital bank that offers a range of financial services, including currency exchange, cryptocurrency trading, and savings accounts. N26 is a German digital bank that offers a variety of banking services, including savings and investment accounts, and mobile payments. Monzo, also based in the UK, is a mobile-only bank that offers a range of financial services, including budgeting tools and savings accounts.

Mercury is an online-only business bank that was founded in 2017 with the mission of helping startups and small businesses manage their finances more efficiently. The company is headquartered in San Francisco, California and offers a suite of banking services, including checking and savings accounts, ACH payments, wire transfers, and debit cards, among others.

One of the unique features of Mercury is its focus on providing customers with a streamlined, user-friendly banking experience. The company has developed a mobile app that allows users to manage their accounts, send and receive payments, and monitor their transactions in real-time. In addition, Mercury has built an API that allows businesses to integrate their banking data with other software applications, such as accounting and invoicing platforms.

Mercury also offers a number of tools and resources to help businesses manage their finances more effectively. For example, the company provides a cash flow dashboard that allows businesses to track their income and expenses in real-time, as well as budgeting and forecasting tools that can help businesses plan for the future.

In terms of security, Mercury utilizes advanced encryption and authentication protocols to protect customer data and prevent unauthorized access. The company also offers two-factor authentication and other security features to help prevent fraud and unauthorized transactions.

Overall, Mercury has been well-received by customers and has received positive reviews for its ease of use, customer service, and innovative features. The company has raised over $135 million in funding to date and has attracted a growing base of customers, including startups, freelancers, and small businesses.

Refferal Link for businesses: https://mercury.com/r/trient-press

Traditional Banks with Strong Digital Presence
Many traditional banks have invested heavily in digital transformation to keep up with the changing demands of customers. These banks offer online and mobile banking services in addition to their physical branches. Some of the largest traditional banks with a strong digital presence include JPMorgan Chase, Bank of America, and Wells Fargo in the United States, and Barclays, HSBC, and Lloyds Banking Group in the United Kingdom.

JPMorgan Chase is the largest bank in the United States and has made significant investments in digital transformation. The bank offers a range of digital banking services, including mobile banking, online banking, and digital payments. Bank of America is the second-largest bank in the United States and has also made significant investments in digital transformation. The bank offers a range of digital banking services, including mobile banking, online banking, and digital payments.

Fintech Companies
Fintech companies are technology companies that provide financial services to customers. These companies have disrupted the traditional banking industry by offering innovative financial products and services. Some of the most popular fintech companies include PayPal, Square, and Stripe.

PayPal is a digital payment company that offers a range of payment solutions, including online payments, mobile payments, and peer-to-peer payments. Square is a payment processing company that offers a range of payment solutions, including credit card processing, mobile payments, and point-of-sale systems. Stripe is a payment processing company that offers a range of payment solutions, including online payments and subscription billing.

In conclusion, the digital banking industry is home to a range of players, including digital-only banks, traditional banks with a strong digital presence, and fintech companies. These players are changing the way we bank by offering innovative financial products and services that cater to the changing demands of customers. It is important for customers to do their research and choose a bank or financial service provider that best meets their needs.

The impact of digital banking on traditional banks and the financial industry

The rise of digital banking has had a significant impact on traditional banks and the financial industry as a whole. While digital banking has many advantages, it has also presented challenges for traditional banks, including increased competition and a need to adapt to changing consumer expectations. This section will explore the impact of digital banking on traditional banks and the financial industry, including both the advantages and challenges that have arisen.

One of the most significant impacts of digital banking on traditional banks is increased competition. Digital-only banks and fintech companies are now able to offer many of the same services as traditional banks, often with lower fees and more innovative features. This has forced traditional banks to adapt in order to remain competitive, which has required significant investment in technology and digital infrastructure. In addition, digital-only banks and fintech companies are often able to provide a more streamlined and user-friendly experience for customers, which has further increased their appeal.

Another significant impact of digital banking on traditional banks is the need to adapt to changing consumer expectations. Consumers are increasingly looking for a seamless and convenient banking experience, which includes the ability to access their accounts from any device and at any time. This has required traditional banks to invest in digital infrastructure and develop their own mobile and online banking platforms in order to remain competitive. In addition, traditional banks are now required to provide greater transparency and control over their customers' data in order to comply with regulatory requirements and consumer expectations.

Despite the challenges presented by digital banking, traditional banks have also been able to leverage new technologies in order to improve their own operations and services. For example, many traditional banks are now using artificial intelligence and machine learning to improve fraud detection and risk management, as well as to personalize their services for individual customers. In addition, traditional banks are increasingly partnering with fintech companies and other third-party providers in order to offer innovative new services and stay ahead of the curve.

Overall, the impact of digital banking on traditional banks and the financial industry as a whole has been significant. While digital banking has presented many challenges, including increased competition and the need to adapt to changing consumer expectations, it has also provided new opportunities for traditional banks to leverage new technologies and partnerships in order to improve their operations and services. As the digital banking landscape continues to evolve, it will be interesting to see how traditional banks and other players in the financial industry adapt and compete in order to provide the best possible services for their customers.

In conclusion, the rise of digital banking has dramatically changed the landscape of the financial industry. Digital banking refers to the use of technology to offer financial services to customers, and it has become increasingly popular in recent years due to the convenience and accessibility it offers. Digital banking encompasses various types of services, such as online banking, mobile banking, and digital-only banks, each of which has its own set of advantages and disadvantages.

Digital banking has revolutionized the way we access financial services, making it more convenient and accessible than ever before. Customers can now manage their finances from the comfort of their own homes or on the go, without the need for physical bank branches. However, digital banking also comes with its own set of challenges, including security risks and the potential for increased debt.

Despite these challenges, the benefits of digital banking are clear, and it has become a significant driver of growth and innovation in the financial industry. Digital-only banks, in particular, have emerged as key players in the industry, offering low fees and innovative features that traditional banks have struggled to match.

The rise of digital banking has also had a significant impact on traditional banks, forcing them to adapt to a rapidly changing industry. While some traditional banks have been slow to embrace digital technology, others have invested heavily in digital transformation, recognizing the importance of staying competitive in the new digital landscape.

Overall, the rise of digital banking has transformed the financial industry and changed the way we access financial services. As technology continues to advance, we can expect digital banking to continue to evolve and play an increasingly significant role in our lives. It is important for both consumers and financial institutions to stay informed about these changes and to adapt to the new digital reality.

CHAPTER 6: MOBILE PAYMENTS AND E-WALLETS

The digital revolution has transformed the way we conduct financial transactions. Mobile payments and e-wallets are rapidly gaining popularity among consumers and businesses alike, and are becoming an increasingly important part of the financial landscape. With the rise of smartphones and other mobile devices, mobile payments and e-wallets have become a convenient, secure, and efficient way to pay for goods and services, transfer money, and manage finances.

In this chapter, we will provide an in-depth analysis of mobile payments and e-wallets, exploring their definition, history, advantages, disadvantages, types, key players, and impact on traditional payment methods and the financial industry. We will examine the technological, economic, and social factors driving the growth of mobile payments and e-wallets, as well as the challenges and opportunities they present for consumers, businesses, and financial institutions.

We will begin by defining mobile payments and e-wallets and tracing their evolution over time. We will then examine the advantages and disadvantages of mobile payments and e-wallets, looking at their impact on security, privacy, cost, convenience, and accessibility. We will also explore the different types of mobile payments and e-wallets, including contactless payments, in-app payments, peer-to-peer payments, and mobile wallets, and the key players in the industry, including technology companies, payment processors, banks, and fintech startups.

Finally, we will analyze the impact of mobile payments and e-wallets on traditional payment methods, such as cash, checks, and credit cards, and on the financial industry as a whole. We will discuss the potential for mobile payments and e-wallets to disrupt the payments industry, the challenges and opportunities they present for traditional financial institutions, and the implications for consumers and businesses.

Overall, this chapter will provide a comprehensive overview of the rapidly evolving world of mobile payments and e-wallets, and the implications of this technological shift for the financial industry and society as a whole.

Definition and history of mobile payments and e-wallets

Mobile payments and e-wallets are two terms that have become increasingly popular in recent years, as more and more people choose to conduct their financial transactions using their mobile devices. In this chapter, we will explore the definition and history of these payment methods, their advantages and disadvantages, the types of mobile payments and e-wallets available, the key players in the industry, and the impact they have had on traditional payment methods and the financial industry.

Firstly, it is important to define what we mean by mobile payments and e-wallets. Mobile payments refer to the process of making a payment using a mobile device, such as a smartphone or tablet. This can be done through a mobile app or a mobile website, and can involve a range of payment methods, including credit and debit cards, bank transfers, and e-wallets. E-wallets, on the other hand, are digital wallets that allow users to store their payment information securely and conveniently. These wallets can be used to make payments online or in physical stores, without the need for a physical card or cash.

The history of mobile payments and e-wallets can be traced back to the early 2000s, when mobile devices first began to gain widespread popularity. The first mobile payments were made using SMS, with users sending a text message to their mobile network provider to make a payment. This was followed by the introduction of mobile payments using NFC (Near Field Communication) technology, which allowed users to make payments by simply tapping their phone against a payment terminal. However, it was the introduction of mobile apps and e-wallets that really revolutionized the industry, making it much easier and more convenient for consumers to make payments using their mobile devices.

Today, there are many different types of mobile payments and e-wallets available. Mobile payments can be made through apps provided by banks and financial institutions, as well as third-party apps such as Apple Pay and Google Wallet. E-wallets, meanwhile, can be standalone apps such as PayPal, or integrated into other services, such as the Amazon Pay wallet that is part of the Amazon shopping app.

In terms of advantages, mobile payments and e-wallets offer a range of benefits to users. For one, they are incredibly convenient, allowing users to make payments from anywhere, at any time. They are also typically very secure, using advanced encryption and authentication methods to protect users' financial information. Additionally, mobile payments and e-wallets often offer rewards programs and discounts, which can incentivize users to choose these payment methods over others.

However, there are also some disadvantages to mobile payments and e-wallets that must be considered. For example, some users may be hesitant to use these payment methods due to concerns about security and privacy. Additionally, not all retailers and merchants accept mobile payments and e-wallets, meaning that users may need to carry a physical payment card as a backup. Finally, mobile payments and e-wallets can be subject to technical issues and glitches, which can cause inconvenience and frustration for users.

In conclusion, mobile payments and e-wallets are two payment methods that have become increasingly popular in recent years, offering users a range of benefits and advantages. However, there are also some potential drawbacks that must be considered, and the impact of these payment methods on traditional payment methods and the financial industry as a whole is still evolving. In the following sections, we will explore these issues in greater detail, examining the different types of mobile payments and e-wallets available, the key players in the industry, and the impact they have had on the financial landscape.

Advantages and disadvantages of mobile payments and e-wallets

Mobile payments and e-wallets have become increasingly popular as consumers seek faster and more convenient ways to make purchases. However, like any technology, there are both advantages and disadvantages to using these payment methods. In this section, we will explore the advantages and disadvantages of mobile payments and e-wallets.

Advantages of mobile payments and e-wallets:

1.   Convenience: One of the primary advantages of mobile payments and e-wallets is convenience. With a mobile wallet, consumers no longer need to carry physical cash or credit cards. Instead, they can make purchases using their smartphone or other mobile device, which is more convenient and faster than carrying multiple cards or cash.

2.   Security: Mobile payments and e-wallets offer enhanced security features that are not available with traditional payment methods. For example, some mobile wallets use biometric authentication, such as fingerprints or facial recognition, to ensure that only the authorized user can access the wallet. Additionally, mobile payments and e-wallets often use encryption to protect users' personal and financial information.

3.   Speed: Mobile payments and e-wallets offer faster transaction times compared to traditional payment methods. This is because transactions are processed digitally, eliminating the need for physical card swipes or cash exchanges. As a result, consumers can complete transactions quickly and easily.

4.   Loyalty rewards: Many mobile payments and e-wallets offer loyalty rewards, such as cashback or discounts, to users who make purchases using their app or wallet. This can be a significant advantage for frequent shoppers who want to save money on their purchases.

5.   Accessibility: Mobile payments and e-wallets are accessible to anyone with a smartphone or other mobile device. This means that consumers who previously did not have access to traditional banking services can now make purchases and manage their finances using their mobile device.

Disadvantages of mobile payments and e-wallets:

1.   Dependence on technology: One of the biggest disadvantages of mobile payments and e-wallets is their dependence on technology. If the mobile device or app malfunctions or loses connectivity, the user may not be able to complete a transaction, which can be frustrating and inconvenient.

2.   Security concerns: While mobile payments and e-wallets offer enhanced security features, they are still vulnerable to hacking and other forms of cybercrime. This can be a significant concern for users who are worried about the safety of their personal and financial information.

3.   Limited acceptance: While mobile payments and e-wallets are becoming more popular, they are not yet widely accepted by all merchants. This means that users may not be able to use their mobile wallet at all the places they shop.

4.   Fees: Some mobile payment and e-wallet providers charge fees for certain transactions, such as transfers to a bank account. These fees can add up over time and may be a significant disadvantage for some users.

5.   Lack of physical cash: While mobile payments and e-wallets eliminate the need for physical cash, some users may prefer the convenience and security of having cash on hand for emergencies or other situations where electronic payment methods may not be accepted.

In summary, mobile payments and e-wallets offer numerous advantages, including convenience, security, speed, loyalty rewards, and accessibility. However, they also come with some disadvantages, including dependence on technology, security concerns, limited acceptance, fees, and the lack of physical cash. Consumers should carefully consider both the advantages and disadvantages before deciding whether to use mobile payments and e-wallets for their financial transactions.

Types of mobile payments and e-wallets
Mobile payments and e-wallets are quickly gaining popularity as a convenient and efficient way to make payments. There are several types of mobile payments and e-wallets available to consumers, each with

its unique features and capabilities. In this section, we will explore the various types of mobile payments and e-wallets and their advantages and disadvantages.

1. QR Code Payments

QR code payments are becoming increasingly popular as they offer a secure and fast way to make payments. The user scans a QR code displayed on the merchant's device, and the payment is processed instantly. QR code payments are widely used in China, where they account for a significant portion of mobile payments.

2. NFC Payments

NFC (Near Field Communication) payments involve tapping a mobile device or smartwatch against a terminal to complete the transaction. NFC payments are widely accepted and provide a convenient and secure way to pay for goods and services.

3. Peer-to-Peer Payments

Peer-to-peer (P2P) payments allow individuals to send and receive money from one another through their mobile devices. P2P payments are widely used for splitting bills or sending money to friends and family.

In-App Payments

In-app payments enable users to pay for goods and services within an app, without having to leave the app to complete the transaction. This type of payment is widely used for mobile gaming, music, and other digital services.

1. Contactless Payments

Contactless payments involve tapping a mobile device or smartwatch against a terminal to complete the transaction, similar to NFC payments. However, contactless payments do not require the merchant to have an NFC-enabled terminal. Instead, they use radio-frequency identification (RFID) technology, which is widely accepted in many countries.

2. Mobile Wallets

Mobile wallets are digital wallets that store credit and debit card information, allowing users to make payments through their mobile devices. Mobile wallets offer a convenient and secure way to pay for goods and services without having to carry cash or cards.

3. Virtual Cards

Virtual cards are digital versions of traditional credit and debit cards. They offer a secure and convenient way to make online purchases without having to share sensitive payment information. Virtual cards are widely used by consumers who shop online frequently.

Each type of mobile payment and e-wallet has its advantages and disadvantages. Consumers should consider their needs and preferences when choosing which type to use. For example, individuals who frequently shop online may find virtual cards or mobile wallets to be more convenient, while those who prefer to shop in-store may prefer NFC or contactless payments. It is important to note that some merchants may not accept certain types of mobile payments or e-wallets, so consumers should check with the merchant before attempting to make a payment.

Key players in the mobile payments and e-wallets industry

The mobile payments and e-wallets industry is a fast-growing and dynamic space, with numerous players jostling for a share of the market. In this section, we will take a closer look at some of the key players in this industry, their business models, and their strategies.

1.	Arlingbrook Pay: Launched in 2023, ArlingBrook Pay is an in app payment and digital wallet service developed by The ATS Company. It allows users to make payments online, and in apps using their most devices , such as iPhones and laptops. ArlingBrook Pay uses Near Field Communication (NFC) technology to enable secure and contactless payments at point-of-sale (POS) terminals. The service is compatible with major credit and debit cards, as well as various payment networks, such as Visa, Mastercard, and American Express. ArlingBrook Pay also offers features such as loyalty programs and reward elements

2.	Apple Pay: Launched in 2014, Apple Pay is a mobile payment and digital wallet service developed by Apple Inc. It allows users to make payments in stores, online, and in apps using their Apple devices, such as iPhones and Apple Watches. Apple Pay uses Near Field Communication (NFC) technology to enable secure and contactless payments at point-of-sale (POS) terminals. The service is compatible with major credit and debit cards, as well as various payment networks, such as Visa, Mastercard, and American Express. Apple Pay also offers features such as loyalty programs and reward cards, and it has partnered with numerous merchants and banks to expand its reach.

3.	Google Pay: Google Pay is a mobile payment and digital wallet service developed by Google LLC. It allows users to make payments using their Android devices, such as smartphones and smartwatches. Like Apple Pay, Google Pay uses NFC technology to enable contactless payments at POS terminals, and it is compatible with major credit and debit cards. Google Pay also offers features such as loyalty programs and reward cards, and it has partnerships with various merchants and banks.

4.	PayPal: PayPal Holdings, Inc. is a leading digital payment company that offers online payment services and solutions for businesses and individuals. Founded in 1998, PayPal allows users to make secure online payments, transfer funds, and receive payments without disclosing their financial information. In recent years, PayPal has expanded into mobile payments and digital wallets, with services such as PayPal One Touch and PayPal Wallet. These services allow users to make payments and store payment information on their mobile devices, and they are compatible with major credit and debit cards, as well as various payment networks.

5.	Alipay: Alipay is a digital payment platform developed by Ant Group Co., Ltd., a subsidiary of the Chinese e-commerce giant Alibaba Group Holding Ltd. Launched in 2004, Alipay initially focused on online payments but has since expanded into mobile payments and e-wallets. Alipay uses QR code technology to enable mobile payments, and it is widely used in China for various transactions, such as online shopping, bill payments, and peer-to-peer transfers. Alipay also offers features such as savings accounts, insurance, and credit services, and it has partnerships with various merchants and financial institutions.

6.	WeChat Pay: WeChat Pay is a mobile payment service developed by Tencent Holdings Ltd., a Chinese technology conglomerate. WeChat Pay is integrated into WeChat, a popular messaging and social media app in China, and it allows users to make payments, transfer funds, and conduct various transactions within the app. WeChat Pay uses QR code technology and is widely used in China for various transactions, such as retail purchases, transportation, and utility payments. WeChat Pay also offers features such as investment products and credit services.

7.   Samsung Pay: Samsung Pay is a mobile payment and digital wallet service developed by Samsung Electronics Co., Ltd. It allows users to make payments using their Samsung devices, such as smartphones and smartwatches, at NFC-enabled and magnetic stripe-enabled POS terminals. Samsung Pay is compatible with major credit and debit cards, and it offers features such as loyalty programs and reward cards. Samsung Pay also has partnerships with various merchants and banks.

8.   Square: Square, Inc. is a financial technology company that offers payment and business management solutions for small businesses and individuals. Founded in 2009, Square initially focused on mobile credit card processing but has since expanded into various areas, such as online payments, e-commerce, and hardware products.

One of Square's most popular products is the Square Point of Sale, a mobile app that allows businesses to accept credit and debit card payments from customers. The company also offers a range of hardware products to support this, including card readers, cash registers, and barcode scanners.

Square has also ventured into the digital wallet space with its Cash App, which allows users to send and receive money, as well as invest in stocks and cryptocurrencies. In addition to these products, Square has developed a range of business management tools, such as inventory tracking, payroll management, and appointment scheduling.

Another major player in the mobile payments and e-wallets industry is PayPal. Founded in 1998, PayPal was one of the first online payment systems and has since become a widely accepted method of online payment. The company offers a range of services, including online payments, money transfers, and mobile payments.

In 2013, PayPal launched its own mobile payment solution, PayPal Here, which allows businesses to accept credit and debit card payments using a card reader that plugs into a mobile device. The company has also expanded into the digital wallet space with its PayPal app, which allows users to send and receive money, as well as make purchases from online retailers.

Another key player in the mobile payments and e-wallets industry is Google. In 2011, Google launched its own mobile payment solution, Google Wallet, which allows users to store their credit and debit card information on their mobile devices and make payments in stores that accept contactless payments.

In 2015, Google announced the launch of Android Pay, a digital wallet service that allows users to make payments in stores using their mobile devices. Android Pay was later rebranded as Google Pay and now allows users to not only make payments but also store loyalty cards, tickets, and other information.

Apple is another major player in the mobile payments and e-wallets industry with its Apple Pay service. Launched in 2014, Apple Pay allows users to store their credit and debit card information on their iPhones and make payments in stores that accept contactless payments.

Apple Pay has since expanded to support other devices, such as the Apple Watch and Mac computers, and has also added support for peer-to-peer payments. In addition to its payment services, Apple has also developed its own digital wallet, the Apple Wallet, which allows users to store credit and debit cards, boarding passes, event tickets, and other information.

Other key players in the mobile payments and e-wallets industry include Amazon with its Amazon Pay service, Samsung with Samsung Pay, and Alibaba with Alipay. Each of these companies offers a range of payment solutions and digital wallet services to cater to different markets and user preferences.

Overall, the mobile payments and e-wallets industry is highly competitive, with numerous players vying for market share. As the industry continues to grow and evolve, it is likely that we will see further innovation and development in the products and services offered by these companies.

The impact of mobile payments and e-wallets on traditional payment methods and the financial industry

The rise of mobile payments and e-wallets has significantly impacted the traditional payment methods and the financial industry as a whole. The convenience and ease of use of these payment methods have made them increasingly popular, leading to a shift away from traditional payment methods such as cash and checks. In this section, we will explore the impact of mobile payments and e-wallets on traditional payment methods and the financial industry.

One of the primary impacts of mobile payments and e-wallets has been the displacement of cash as a dominant payment method. Cash has long been the most popular form of payment around the world. However, with the emergence of mobile payments and e-wallets, cash is slowly being phased out. This trend is especially apparent in developed countries, where mobile payment penetration rates are higher. In the US, for example, the use of cash as a payment method has declined steadily over the past decade, and mobile payments are projected to account for over 10% of all payment transactions by 2025.

Mobile payments and e-wallets have also had a significant impact on credit and debit card usage. These payment methods offer an alternative to traditional credit and debit card payments, allowing users to make payments quickly and conveniently without the need for a physical card. This has led to a decline in credit and debit card usage in some regions, although the extent of the impact varies across countries.

Another impact of mobile payments and e-wallets has been on the financial industry. The emergence of these payment methods has disrupted the traditional financial ecosystem, challenging the dominance of banks and payment processors. The increased adoption of mobile payments and e-wallets has led to the emergence of new players in the financial industry, such as fintech startups and mobile payment providers. These new players are leveraging technology to offer innovative payment solutions, such as mobile wallets, which are driving growth in the industry.

The adoption of mobile payments and e-wallets has also led to increased competition among payment providers. Traditional payment providers such as banks and credit card companies are facing increased competition from fintech startups and mobile payment providers, who are offering faster and more efficient payment solutions. This competition is forcing traditional payment providers to adapt and innovate, leading to the emergence of new payment technologies and services.

Another impact of mobile payments and e-wallets is their potential to improve financial inclusion. In developing countries, where access to traditional banking services is limited, mobile payments and e-wallets are providing an alternative means of accessing financial services. This has the potential to increase financial inclusion, enabling more people to participate in the formal economy and gain access to credit and other financial services.

However, despite the many benefits of mobile payments and e-wallets, there are also some challenges and concerns associated with their use. One major concern is the potential for fraud and security breaches. Mobile payments and e-wallets are vulnerable to hacking and other security threats, and users need to take precautions to protect their personal and financial information.

Another concern is the potential for increased debt and financial instability. Mobile payments and e-wallets offer the convenience of easy access to credit, which can lead to overspending and increased debt. This could have negative consequences for individuals and the broader financial system.

In conclusion, the impact of mobile payments and e-wallets on traditional payment methods and the financial industry has been significant. These payment methods have disrupted traditional payment methods and challenged the dominance of banks and payment processors. They have also led to increased competition among payment providers and the emergence of new players in the financial industry. While there are some concerns and challenges associated with their use, mobile payments and e-wallets have the potential to improve financial inclusion and drive innovation in the financial industry.

CHAPTER 7: THE FUTURE OF FINTECH

As we look to the future of financial technology (FinTech), there are a number of emerging trends and technologies that are poised to shape the industry in the years to come. From the continued rise of mobile payments and e-wallets to the increasing use of artificial intelligence (AI) and the Internet of Things (IoT), the FinTech landscape is constantly evolving.

Emerging Trends and Technologies in the FinTech Industry

One of the most significant trends in FinTech is the rise of mobile payments and e-wallets. As we discussed in earlier chapters, these technologies have already disrupted the traditional payments landscape and are continuing to gain popularity around the world. As more and more consumers opt for the convenience and security of mobile payments, we can expect this trend to continue into the future.

Another trend in FinTech is the increasing use of AI and machine learning. These technologies have the potential to revolutionize the way that financial services are delivered, from fraud detection and risk management to customer service and investment advice. In particular, AI-powered chatbots and virtual assistants are already becoming more common in the industry, offering customers a personalized and efficient way to interact with financial institutions.

The Internet of Things (IoT) is also poised to have a significant impact on FinTech in the years to come. As more devices become connected to the internet, there will be new opportunities for financial services to integrate with these devices and provide personalized, real-time information to customers. For example, a smart home system could automatically adjust a user's insurance premiums based on their daily habits and routines.

Predictions for the Future of FinTech

Looking to the future, it is clear that FinTech will continue to play a major role in the financial industry. In particular, we can expect to see the continued growth of mobile payments and e-wallets, as well as the increasing use of AI and machine learning in financial services.

Another trend that is likely to continue is the decentralization of financial services. Blockchain technology has already disrupted the traditional banking system, and we can expect to see more innovations in this area in the years to come. Decentralized finance (DeFi) platforms, which allow users to access financial services without the need for traditional banks, are already gaining popularity.

In addition, we can expect to see more collaboration between traditional financial institutions and FinTech startups. As FinTech companies continue to innovate and disrupt the industry, established financial institutions will need to adapt in order to stay competitive. This may involve partnerships or acquisitions of FinTech startups, as well as the development of in-house technology and innovation labs.

Challenges and Opportunities for FinTech in the Future

While there are many opportunities for FinTech in the future, there are also a number of challenges that the industry will need to overcome. One of the biggest challenges is regulation. As FinTech continues to disrupt traditional financial services, regulators will need to keep pace with these changes and ensure that consumer protection and financial stability are maintained.

Another challenge is cybersecurity. As more financial services move online, the risk of cyber attacks and data breaches increases. FinTech companies will need to invest in robust cybersecurity measures in order to protect their customers and their own systems.

Finally, there is the challenge of financial inclusion. While FinTech has the potential to make financial services more accessible to underserved populations, there are still barriers to entry for many consumers. These may include a lack of access to smartphones or internet connectivity, as well as a lack of financial literacy or trust in digital financial services.

The Potential Impact of FinTech on the Financial Industry and Society as a Whole

As FinTech continues to evolve and disrupt the financial industry, it is important to consider its potential impact on society as a whole. On the one hand, FinTech has the potential to greatly benefit society by increasing access to financial services, improving efficiency, and reducing costs. However, there are also concerns about the potential negative effects of FinTech on privacy, security, and employment.

One of the most significant benefits of FinTech is its ability to increase access to financial services for underserved populations. For example, mobile payments and e-wallets can provide a convenient and affordable way for people in developing countries to access banking services. In addition, peer-to-peer lending platforms can allow borrowers who may not qualify for traditional bank loans to access financing. This increased access to financial services can have a positive impact on economic growth and development.

FinTech can also improve efficiency in the financial industry by automating processes and reducing the need for manual intervention. This can result in faster transaction processing times and lower costs for both financial institutions and their customers. In addition, the use of artificial intelligence and machine learning can help financial institutions better analyze and interpret data, leading to more informed decision-making.

However, there are also concerns about the potential negative effects of FinTech on privacy and security. As more financial transactions are conducted online and through mobile devices, there is a greater risk of cyberattacks and data breaches. This can lead to the loss of personal and financial information, which can have serious consequences for individuals and businesses.

Another concern is the potential impact of FinTech on employment. As financial institutions increasingly rely on automation and artificial intelligence, there is a risk that traditional jobs in the industry may become obsolete. However, it is also possible that the growth of the FinTech industry may create new job opportunities in areas such as software development and data analysis.

In addition to these concerns, there are also challenges and opportunities for FinTech in the future. One challenge is regulatory compliance, as FinTech companies must navigate a complex web of regulations and laws governing the financial industry. Another challenge is the need to develop trust and credibility with customers, particularly in areas such as data privacy and security.

However, there are also significant opportunities for FinTech in the future. For example, the growth of the Internet of Things (IoT) and the increasing number of connected devices could create new opportunities for FinTech companies to develop innovative products and services. In addition, the use of blockchain technology has the potential to revolutionize the way financial transactions are conducted, providing greater transparency and security.

Looking ahead, the future of FinTech is likely to be shaped by a number of factors, including advances in technology, changes in consumer behavior, and regulatory developments. Predictions for the future of FinTech include the increasing use of artificial intelligence and machine learning, the growth of digital currencies, and the rise of decentralized finance (DeFi).

Overall, the potential impact of FinTech on the financial industry and society as a whole is significant. While there are concerns about the potential negative effects of FinTech, there are also significant opportunities for the industry to improve efficiency, increase access to financial services, and drive economic growth and development. As the industry continues to evolve and mature, it will be important to balance these opportunities and challenges to ensure that FinTech can realize its full potential as a force for positive change.

Emerging trends and technologies in the FinTech industry

The FinTech industry is constantly evolving, and emerging trends and technologies are continuously reshaping the landscape. In this section, we will explore some of the latest trends and technologies that are shaping the future of FinTech.

1. Blockchain Technology

Blockchain technology is one of the most talked-about technologies in the FinTech industry. It is a decentralized and distributed ledger technology that has the potential to transform the financial industry by improving security and transparency. The technology enables transactions to be recorded in a transparent and secure manner, reducing the need for intermediaries and lowering transaction costs.

One of the most significant applications of blockchain technology in the financial industry is cryptocurrencies. Cryptocurrencies like Bitcoin and Ethereum are built on blockchain technology and are entirely digital, allowing for seamless, secure, and fast transactions.

2. Artificial Intelligence

Artificial intelligence (AI) has been making waves in the FinTech industry in recent years. AI is a branch of computer science that deals with the creation of intelligent machines that can work and learn like humans. In FinTech, AI is being used for various applications, such as fraud detection, customer service, and risk management.

One of the most significant applications of AI in the financial industry is in credit scoring. AI algorithms can analyze a vast amount of data and provide lenders with a more accurate assessment of credit risk. This has the potential to increase financial inclusion by allowing more people to access credit.

3. Open Banking

Open banking is a concept that has gained significant traction in recent years. It is a banking practice that allows third-party providers to access financial information from banks and other financial institutions. Open banking has the potential to transform the financial industry by increasing competition, reducing costs, and improving access to financial services.

One of the most significant benefits of open banking is the increased access to financial services for underserved populations. By allowing third-party providers to access financial data, open banking can help provide better financial advice, increase transparency, and promote financial inclusion.

4.   Internet of Things

The Internet of Things (IoT) is a network of devices that can communicate with each other and the internet. In the financial industry, IoT has the potential to transform how financial services are delivered. For example, IoT devices can be used for contactless payments, providing real-time data on financial transactions, and improving customer experience.

One of the most significant applications of IoT in the financial industry is in insurance. IoT devices can provide insurers with real-time data on customer behavior, allowing for more accurate risk assessments and personalized pricing.

5.   Robo-Advisors

Robo-advisors are automated investment platforms that use algorithms to provide investment advice and portfolio management. They are an emerging trend in the FinTech industry and are being used to democratize access to financial advice and investment management.

One of the most significant benefits of robo-advisors is the lower fees compared to traditional financial advisors. Additionally, robo-advisors are available 24/7, making them more convenient for customers.

6.   Cloud Computing

Cloud computing has been a game-changer for the financial industry, enabling faster and more efficient operations. It is a technology that allows for the delivery of computing services over the internet, providing flexible and scalable access to computing resources.

One of the most significant benefits of cloud computing in the financial industry is the ability to reduce costs by outsourcing infrastructure and application maintenance. Additionally, cloud computing allows for better collaboration and faster decision-making.

In conclusion, the FinTech industry is evolving rapidly, and emerging trends and technologies are shaping its future. Blockchain technology, AI, open banking, IoT, robo-advisors, and cloud computing are just a few examples of the latest trends and technologies that are transforming the financial industry. These technologies have the potential to increase financial inclusion, reduce costs, and improve access to financial services.

Predictions for the future of FinTech, such as the role of artificial intelligence and the Internet of Things

As the FinTech industry continues to rapidly evolve, there are many predictions about the future of this sector. One of the most significant trends is the increasing role of artificial intelligence (AI) and the Internet of Things (IoT).

AI is already being used in many aspects of finance, from fraud detection to algorithmic trading. However, experts predict that the use of AI in finance will continue to grow, as it has the potential to improve efficiency and accuracy while reducing costs. For example, AI-powered chatbots can provide customer support, while AI algorithms can analyze vast amounts of data to provide personalized investment advice.

The IoT, which refers to the interconnected network of physical devices, vehicles, and other items embedded with sensors, software, and network connectivity, is also expected to play a significant role in the future of FinTech. IoT devices can collect data on consumer behavior and financial transactions, allowing companies to offer personalized services and better understand customer needs.

Another area of innovation in FinTech is blockchain technology, which allows for secure, transparent, and decentralized transactions. Blockchain-based platforms are already being used for cryptocurrency transactions and digital identity management, but experts predict that this technology could be applied to other areas of finance, such as supply chain management and asset tracking.

In addition to these specific technologies, there are broader trends that are expected to shape the future of FinTech. One of these is the increasing use of mobile devices for financial transactions, which has already led to the rise of mobile payment systems such as Apple Pay and Google Wallet. Experts predict that mobile banking and payments will continue to grow, with more people using their smartphones as their primary financial tool.

Another trend is the move towards open banking, which refers to the practice of sharing financial data between banks and other companies. Open banking has the potential to create new business models and services, as well as increase competition in the financial industry.

Despite these exciting developments, there are also concerns about the future of FinTech. One of the biggest is the potential for increased risk and cybersecurity threats. As FinTech companies handle sensitive financial information and transactions, there is a risk that these systems could be hacked or compromised in other ways. There is also the risk of financial fraud, as criminals may attempt to take advantage of new technologies to carry out scams.

Another concern is the potential for job losses as a result of automation and AI. As these technologies become more prevalent in the financial industry, there is a risk that many traditional jobs could be replaced by machines.

Overall, the future of FinTech is highly unpredictable, with new technologies and trends emerging all the time. However, it is clear that these innovations have the potential to significantly transform the financial industry and improve the lives of consumers. As long as the risks are carefully managed and the benefits are properly harnessed, FinTech has a bright future ahead.

Challenges and opportunities for FinTech in the future

The FinTech industry has experienced rapid growth in recent years, and its expansion is expected to continue in the future. With this growth, the industry faces both challenges and opportunities. In this section, we will explore some of the key challenges and opportunities for FinTech in the future.

Challenges for FinTech

1. Regulatory challenges: One of the biggest challenges facing FinTech is regulatory compliance. FinTech companies must adhere to a complex set of regulations, including anti-money laundering (AML) and know-your-customer (KYC) regulations. These regulations are designed to prevent fraud and financial crimes, but they can also be costly and time-consuming to implement.

2. Cybersecurity risks: As FinTech companies continue to expand their digital presence, they are increasingly vulnerable to cyber threats. Cybersecurity breaches can result in the loss of customer data and financial losses, which can be damaging to both the company and its customers.

3.   Integration with traditional financial institutions: FinTech companies often face challenges in integrating with traditional financial institutions. Traditional financial institutions may be reluctant to partner with FinTech companies due to concerns about regulatory compliance and cybersecurity risks.

Funding challenges: While FinTech companies have seen significant investment in recent years, there is still a need for funding to support research and development and to fuel growth. Many FinTech companies struggle to secure funding, particularly in the early stages of development.

Opportunities for FinTech

1.   Financial inclusion: FinTech has the potential to increase financial inclusion by providing access to financial services for underserved populations. FinTech companies can leverage technology to offer affordable and accessible financial services to people who may not have had access to traditional financial services.

2.   Cost savings: FinTech companies can offer cost savings to both businesses and consumers. By leveraging technology and automation, FinTech companies can reduce costs and increase efficiency in financial services.

3.   Innovation: FinTech companies are driving innovation in the financial industry. By leveraging technologies such as blockchain, artificial intelligence, and the Internet of Things, FinTech companies are developing new products and services that are changing the way we think about finance.

Improved customer experience: FinTech companies are focused on providing a seamless and convenient customer experience. By leveraging technology, FinTech companies can offer personalized and efficient financial services that meet the needs of their customers.

Conclusion

As the FinTech industry continues to evolve, it will face both challenges and opportunities. Regulatory compliance, cybersecurity risks, integration with traditional financial institutions, and funding challenges are among the key challenges facing FinTech companies. However, FinTech also has the potential to increase financial inclusion, offer cost savings, drive innovation, and improve the customer experience. By addressing these challenges and leveraging these opportunities, FinTech companies can continue to drive growth and innovation in the financial industry.

The potential impact of FinTech on the financial industry and society as a whole

As FinTech continues to evolve and disrupt the financial industry, it is important to consider its potential impact on society as a whole. On the one hand, FinTech has the potential to revolutionize the financial industry and make it more efficient, transparent, and accessible. On the other hand, there are concerns about the potential negative effects of FinTech, such as the displacement of traditional financial institutions and the possibility of increased financial inequality. In this section, we will explore both the positive and negative potential impact of FinTech on the financial industry and society as a whole.

Positive Impact of FinTech on the Financial Industry and Society

One of the main benefits of FinTech is that it has the potential to make financial services more accessible and affordable for people who have traditionally been underserved by traditional financial institutions. For example, mobile banking apps and digital wallets allow people to access their money and make transactions from their smartphones, which can be especially beneficial for people who live in remote areas or who do not have access to traditional bank accounts. In addition, FinTech companies are using advanced algorithms and machine learning to develop more accurate credit scoring models, which can help to increase access to credit for people who may have been overlooked by traditional lenders.

Another benefit of FinTech is that it has the potential to increase the efficiency and transparency of the financial industry. For example, blockchain technology is being used to create decentralized and transparent systems for managing financial transactions and data, which can help to reduce fraud, increase accountability, and make the financial industry more secure. In addition, the use of artificial intelligence and machine learning can help to automate many financial processes, such as fraud detection and risk management, which can help to reduce costs and improve accuracy.

FinTech also has the potential to increase financial literacy and education among consumers. Many FinTech companies are developing innovative tools and resources to help people better understand and manage their finances, such as budgeting apps, investment platforms, and financial planning software. By making financial information and resources more accessible and user-friendly, FinTech can help to empower people to make informed decisions about their money and improve their financial well-being.

Negative Impact of FinTech on the Financial Industry and Society

Despite the potential benefits of FinTech, there are also concerns about its potential negative impact on the financial industry and society as a whole. One of the main concerns is the potential for increased financial inequality. While FinTech has the potential to make financial services more accessible and affordable for underserved populations, there is also a risk that it could further widen the gap between the haves and the have-nots. For example, people who do not have access to the internet or smartphones may be excluded from the benefits of FinTech, while those who do have access may benefit from more advanced financial services and products.

Another concern is the potential displacement of traditional financial institutions. As FinTech companies continue to disrupt the financial industry and offer new and innovative products and services, there is a risk that traditional banks and financial institutions may become obsolete. While this could lead to increased competition and innovation in the financial industry, it could also lead to a loss of jobs and expertise, as well as increased concentration of power among a few large FinTech companies.

There are also concerns about the potential for increased cyber risks and financial fraud associated with FinTech. As FinTech companies collect and store more personal and financial data, there is a risk that this data could be hacked or stolen, leading to financial losses and other negative consequences. In addition, the use of artificial intelligence and machine learning in financial decision-making could potentially lead to unintended consequences or biases that could have negative impacts on individuals and society as a whole.

Conclusion

In conclusion, FinTech has the potential to revolutionize the financial industry and make financial services more accessible, affordable, and transparent. However, there are also concerns about the potential negative impact on privacy, cybersecurity, and financial stability.

As FinTech continues to grow and evolve, it will be important for regulators, industry leaders, and consumers to collaborate and develop strategies to mitigate these risks while capitalizing on the opportunities presented by FinTech.

Moreover, FinTech can be an important driver of financial inclusion, particularly in emerging economies, where traditional banking services are often inaccessible to large segments of the population. By leveraging technology, FinTech companies can offer innovative and low-cost financial services, such as microloans and mobile banking, that can help bridge the gap between the unbanked and the formal financial system.

Furthermore, FinTech has the potential to promote financial literacy and education by providing users with access to personalized financial advice, budgeting tools, and investment platforms. This can help consumers make more informed financial decisions and improve their overall financial well-being.

At the same time, FinTech also presents challenges that must be addressed, such as the potential for increased income inequality and the displacement of traditional financial institutions and their employees.

Ultimately, the impact of FinTech on the financial industry and society as a whole will depend on how it is developed, regulated, and adopted. As such, it is important for all stakeholders to work together to ensure that FinTech is leveraged in a responsible and sustainable way that maximizes its potential benefits while minimizing its potential risks.

PART III: CRYPTOCURRENCIES AND BLOCKCHAIN

Cryptocurrencies, also known as digital or virtual currencies, are a form of decentralized currency that uses cryptography for security and operates independently of a central bank. The emergence of cryptocurrencies has disrupted traditional financial systems and has created a new ecosystem for transactions, investments, and wealth management. The most famous and valuable cryptocurrency is Bitcoin, which was introduced in 2009 by an unknown person or group of people under the name of Satoshi Nakamoto.

In this chapter, we will delve into the world of cryptocurrencies and explore their benefits, drawbacks, and potential impact on the financial industry and society as a whole. We will also examine the underlying technology behind cryptocurrencies, the blockchain, and how it has given rise to new business models and innovative applications.

Benefits of Cryptocurrencies

One of the main benefits of cryptocurrencies is their decentralization, which means they are not controlled by a central authority or government. This gives users greater control over their finances and transactions, and also allows for greater privacy and anonymity. Cryptocurrencies are also borderless, meaning they can be used to transact with anyone, anywhere in the world, without the need for intermediaries such as banks or payment processors. This makes them particularly attractive for people living in countries with unstable economies or weak financial systems.

Another benefit of cryptocurrencies is their speed and efficiency. Transactions can be completed almost instantly, without the need for intermediaries or lengthy clearance periods. This is a significant improvement over traditional banking systems, which can take days or even weeks to complete transactions, especially when they involve international transfers.

Cryptocurrencies also offer lower transaction fees compared to traditional banking systems, which can be particularly beneficial for small businesses and individuals who frequently send and receive small amounts of money.

Drawbacks of Cryptocurrencies

Despite their many benefits, cryptocurrencies also have several drawbacks that need to be considered. One of the main concerns is their volatility, as the value of cryptocurrencies can fluctuate rapidly and unpredictably. This can be particularly problematic for investors, as they can experience significant losses if the value of their investments drops suddenly. In addition, cryptocurrencies are often associated with high-risk investments and speculation, which can make them unsuitable for conservative investors.

Another concern is the lack of regulation and oversight in the cryptocurrency market, which can make it vulnerable to fraud, scams, and market manipulation. Cryptocurrencies have also been linked to criminal activity, such as money laundering and financing of terrorism, due to their anonymity and lack of transparency.

Finally, cryptocurrencies are still not widely accepted as a form of payment, and their adoption rate varies widely across different countries and industries. This can make it difficult for users to transact with cryptocurrencies, and may limit their usefulness in everyday life.

Chapter 9: The Blockchain Revolution

Introduction

The blockchain is the underlying technology behind cryptocurrencies, and it has the potential to revolutionize various industries beyond finance. A blockchain is a decentralized digital ledger that records transactions in a transparent and secure manner, using cryptographic techniques to ensure the integrity and immutability of the data. The blockchain has several features that make it attractive for businesses and organizations, such as its transparency, security, and efficiency.

In this chapter, we will explore the blockchain technology and its applications, from finance and banking to supply chain management and healthcare. We will also examine the challenges and opportunities of implementing blockchain solutions, and how they can help organizations to improve their operations and create new business models.

Applications of Blockchain

Blockchain technology has numerous potential applications across various industries, including finance, healthcare, supply chain management, and government. In finance and banking, blockchain technology can be used to improve the efficiency and security of transactions, reduce costs, and eliminate intermediaries. For example, blockchain-based payment systems can enable instant and low-cost cross-border payments without the need for traditional financial intermediaries such as banks.

In healthcare, blockchain technology can be used to securely and efficiently manage patients' medical records and ensure their privacy. It can also be used to track the supply chain of pharmaceutical products to ensure their authenticity and prevent counterfeit drugs from entering the market.

In supply chain management, blockchain technology can be used to improve transparency and accountability by enabling real-time tracking of goods from their origin to their final destination. This can help prevent fraud, reduce costs, and improve efficiency.

In government, blockchain technology can be used to improve transparency and reduce corruption by enabling secure and decentralized storage of public records, such as land titles, voting records, and government contracts.

However, the adoption of blockchain technology is not without its challenges. One major challenge is the lack of standardization and interoperability among different blockchain platforms, which can hinder the ability of different systems to communicate with each other. Another challenge is the scalability of blockchain technology, as current blockchain systems are not able to handle the high transaction volumes required for large-scale applications.

Despite these challenges, the potential benefits of blockchain technology are significant, and many companies and organizations are investing in research and development to explore its potential applications.

Chapter 11: The Future of Cryptocurrencies

The future of cryptocurrencies is uncertain, as the market is still relatively new and volatile. However, many experts believe that cryptocurrencies have the potential to transform the financial industry and become a mainstream form of payment.

One potential future for cryptocurrencies is as a replacement for traditional fiat currencies. As more businesses and individuals begin to accept cryptocurrencies as a form of payment, the demand for fiat currencies may decrease, leading to a shift in the global financial system.

Another potential future for cryptocurrencies is as a means of improving financial inclusion. Cryptocurrencies can enable people who do not have access to traditional banking services to participate in the global economy and access financial services such as loans and remittances.

However, the future of cryptocurrencies is not without its challenges. One major challenge is regulatory uncertainty, as many governments around the world are still grappling with how to regulate cryptocurrencies. Another challenge is the lack of mainstream adoption, as many businesses and consumers are still hesitant to use cryptocurrencies due to their association with illegal activities and volatility.

Despite these challenges, the potential benefits of cryptocurrencies are significant, and many companies and organizations are investing in their development and adoption. Only time will tell how the future of cryptocurrencies will unfold, but it is clear that they have the potential to transform the financial industry and society as a whole.

CHAPTER 8: UNDERSTANDING CRYPTOCURRENCIES

Cryptocurrencies have taken the world by storm in recent years, captivating both investors and technologists alike. These digital currencies are revolutionizing the way we think about money, transactions, and the financial system as a whole. In this chapter, we will provide a comprehensive overview of cryptocurrencies, their underlying technology, and their potential applications.

Definition and Characteristics of Cryptocurrencies

A cryptocurrency is a digital or virtual currency that uses cryptography for security and operates independently of a central bank. Cryptocurrencies are decentralized, meaning that they are not controlled by any government or financial institution. They are designed to be secure, transparent, and immutable, making them an attractive alternative to traditional currencies.

One of the key characteristics of cryptocurrencies is their limited supply. Most cryptocurrencies have a cap on the total number of coins that can be mined or created, making them scarce and valuable. Another important feature is their peer-to-peer nature, which enables users to transact directly with one another without the need for intermediaries.

Brief History of Cryptocurrencies

The first cryptocurrency, Bitcoin, was created in 2009 by an unknown person or group of people using the pseudonym Satoshi Nakamoto. Since then, hundreds of new cryptocurrencies have been launched, each with its unique features and use cases.

The early years of cryptocurrencies were marked by skepticism and uncertainty, with many people dismissing them as a passing fad. However, as more people began to recognize their potential, cryptocurrencies gained traction and became increasingly popular. Today, they are widely accepted as a legitimate asset class and have become a mainstream topic of discussion.

Comparison with Traditional Currencies

While cryptocurrencies share some similarities with traditional currencies, such as the ability to be used as a medium of exchange, there are also significant differences. Unlike traditional currencies, cryptocurrencies are not physical, meaning they cannot be held in your hand. They are also not backed by any physical commodity, such as gold.

Cryptocurrencies are decentralized, meaning that they are not controlled by any government or financial institution. This makes them highly resistant to government interference, but also more susceptible to volatility and price fluctuations.

Cryptocurrency Basics

In this section, we will cover some of the basics of cryptocurrencies, including their underlying technology and how they are created and transacted.

Blockchain Technology and Its Role in Cryptocurrencies

Blockchain technology is the underlying technology that powers most cryptocurrencies. It is a decentralized ledger that records transactions in a secure and transparent manner. Blockchain technology ensures that transactions are tamper-proof and cannot be altered once they have been recorded.

The blockchain is essentially a database that is maintained by a network of nodes, with each node having a copy of the ledger. When a new transaction is made, it is broadcast to the network and verified by multiple nodes. Once the transaction is verified, it is added to the blockchain and becomes a permanent part of the ledger.

Types of Cryptocurrencies

There are thousands of cryptocurrencies in existence, each with its unique features and use cases. However, the most well-known and widely used cryptocurrencies are Bitcoin, Ethereum, and Litecoin.

Bitcoin was the first cryptocurrency and remains the most popular and valuable. It is often referred to as "digital gold" because of its scarcity and store of value properties.

Ethereum is a cryptocurrency that was created in 2015 and has become the second-largest cryptocurrency by market cap. It is unique in that it enables developers to build decentralized applications on its blockchain.

Litecoin is a cryptocurrency that was created in 2011 and is often referred to as the "silver to Bitcoin's gold." It is similar to Bitcoin but is designed to be faster and more efficient.

Mining and Transactions

Cryptocurrencies are created through a process called mining, which involves solving complex mathematical equations. This process is used to validate transactions and add new blocks to the blockchain. Miners compete to solve these equations by using powerful computers, and the first one to solve it is rewarded with newly minted cryptocurrency.

Mining requires a significant amount of computational power and energy, which has raised concerns about its environmental impact. The amount of energy used in mining Bitcoin, for example, is estimated to be equivalent to the energy consumption of the entire country of Argentina. This has led to the development of alternative mining methods, such as Proof of Stake, which require less energy and are more sustainable.

Once a transaction has been validated by miners and added to the blockchain, it becomes a permanent part of the ledger and cannot be altered or deleted. This makes transactions in cryptocurrencies secure and resistant to fraud. However, the anonymity of transactions on the blockchain has also made it attractive to criminals for money laundering and other illegal activities.

Cryptocurrencies can be bought and sold on cryptocurrency exchanges, which are online platforms where buyers and sellers can trade cryptocurrencies for other cryptocurrencies or fiat currencies. Some of the largest cryptocurrency exchanges include Binance, Coinbase, and Kraken. Trading cryptocurrencies can be highly volatile, with prices fluctuating rapidly and unpredictably.

Investing in cryptocurrencies carries significant risks, including the potential for loss of investment due to market volatility, hacking, fraud, and regulatory changes. As with any investment, it is important to conduct thorough research and seek professional advice before investing in cryptocurrencies.

Overall, the emergence of cryptocurrencies has brought about significant changes in the financial landscape, challenging traditional notions of currency and payment systems. While cryptocurrencies have the potential to offer increased security and accessibility, they also present unique challenges and risks. As the use and adoption of cryptocurrencies continue to grow, it is important for individuals and organizations to stay informed and educated about this rapidly evolving space.

Definition and characteristics of cryptocurrencies

Cryptocurrencies have become a hot topic in recent years, with Bitcoin being the most well-known example. Cryptocurrencies are a type of digital currency that use encryption techniques to regulate the generation of units of currency and verify the transfer of funds. They operate independently of a central bank and can be transferred directly between individuals without the need for a third party such as a bank or government.

1.1 Definition of Cryptocurrencies

The term "cryptocurrency" is a combination of "crypto", meaning cryptography, and "currency". A cryptocurrency is a digital asset that uses cryptography to secure and verify transactions and to control the creation of new units. It is designed to function as a medium of exchange and a store of value.

Cryptocurrencies use decentralized systems that are based on blockchain technology. The blockchain is a public ledger that contains all the transactions ever made with the cryptocurrency. The transactions are verified by a network of computers that run complex algorithms to confirm the authenticity of the transactions and add them to the blockchain.

1.2 Characteristics of Cryptocurrencies

Cryptocurrencies have several key characteristics that set them apart from traditional currencies:

1.2.1 Decentralized

Cryptocurrencies are decentralized, meaning they are not controlled by any central authority, such as a government or a bank. Instead, they operate on a peer-to-peer network of computers.

1.2.2 Digital

Cryptocurrencies are digital assets, meaning they exist only in a digital form. They are not tangible like cash or gold.

1.2.3 Secure

Cryptocurrencies use encryption techniques to secure and verify transactions. Transactions are recorded on a public ledger that is tamper-proof, making it extremely difficult to hack or manipulate.

1.2.4 Pseudonymous

Transactions made with cryptocurrencies are pseudonymous, meaning that they are not linked to a real-world identity. Instead, users are identified by their digital wallet addresses.

1.2.5 Global

Cryptocurrencies can be used anywhere in the world, as long as there is an internet connection. This makes them a global currency, without the need for currency exchange.

1.2.6 Limited Supply

Many cryptocurrencies have a limited supply, meaning that there is a finite amount that will ever be created. This makes them a scarce asset, which can increase their value over time.

1.2.7 Volatility

Cryptocurrencies can be highly volatile, with prices fluctuating rapidly and often. This volatility can be caused by a variety of factors, including news events, regulatory changes, and investor sentiment.

1.2.8 Transparency

Transactions made with cryptocurrencies are transparent, meaning that they can be viewed on the public ledger. This transparency can help prevent fraud and corruption.

Section 2: Brief History of Cryptocurrencies

The concept of cryptocurrencies dates back to the 1980s, when a group of computer scientists attempted to create a digital currency that would be secure and untraceable. However, it was not until the creation of Bitcoin in 2009 that the first cryptocurrency became widely known.

2.1 Creation of Bitcoin

Bitcoin was created by an unknown individual or group using the pseudonym Satoshi Nakamoto. The original white paper, titled "Bitcoin: A Peer-to-Peer Electronic Cash System", was published in 2008. The first Bitcoin transaction took place in January 2009.

2.2 Rise of Altcoins

Following the success of Bitcoin, other cryptocurrencies began to emerge. These are known as "altcoins". Some of the most popular altcoins include Ethereum, Litecoin, and Ripple.

2.3 Adoption of Cryptocurrencies

Cryptocurrencies have been adopted by a growing number of individuals and businesses. Some companies have started accepting cryptocurrencies as a form of payment, including major retailers such as Overstock.com, Microsoft, and Expedia. Cryptocurrencies can also be used for peer-to-peer transactions, allowing individuals to send and receive funds without the need for a traditional bank account.

However, despite the growing adoption of cryptocurrencies, there are still significant barriers to widespread use. One of the main challenges is the lack of user-friendly interfaces and infrastructure for individuals to easily access and use cryptocurrencies. Additionally, cryptocurrencies are still not widely accepted as a form of payment by many merchants, which limits their usefulness in daily transactions.

Another major obstacle to the adoption of cryptocurrencies is their volatile nature. The value of cryptocurrencies can fluctuate rapidly, often with little warning, which can make them risky investments for individuals and businesses. For example, in late 2017, the value of Bitcoin reached an all-time high of nearly $20,000, but then experienced a sharp decline in value over the following year.

Cryptocurrencies have also faced challenges related to security and regulation. Due to the decentralized nature of cryptocurrencies, they are vulnerable to hacking and other cyber attacks. Additionally, regulatory frameworks for cryptocurrencies are still evolving, and there is often uncertainty around how they will be treated by governments and financial institutions.

Despite these challenges, the adoption of cryptocurrencies is likely to continue as more individuals and businesses become aware of their potential benefits. Cryptocurrencies offer a number of advantages over traditional currencies, including lower transaction costs, faster transaction speeds, and greater privacy and security. As the technology behind cryptocurrencies continues to evolve and mature, it is likely that they will become more user-friendly and accessible, which could drive further adoption.

Brief history of cryptocurrencies

The history of cryptocurrencies can be traced back to the early 2000s, when several individuals began to experiment with the concept of digital currencies. One of the earliest attempts to create a decentralized digital currency was made by American computer programmer and activist Nick Szabo in 1998. Szabo created a virtual currency called "bit gold," which he described as a precursor to Bitcoin.

In 2008, a person or group of people under the pseudonym Satoshi Nakamoto published a whitepaper that proposed a decentralized digital currency called Bitcoin. The whitepaper described a peer-to-peer electronic cash system that would allow for secure and private transactions without the need for intermediaries. The first Bitcoin software was released in January 2009, and the first block of transactions, known as the "genesis block," was mined on January 3rd of that year.

Bitcoin quickly gained popularity among tech enthusiasts and libertarians who were attracted to its decentralized nature and its potential to disrupt the traditional financial system. In 2010, the first real-world transaction involving Bitcoin occurred when a programmer named Laszlo Hanyecz purchased two pizzas for 10,000 bitcoins, which at the time were worth about $41.

In the years that followed, other cryptocurrencies were created based on the Bitcoin model, including Litecoin, Namecoin, and Ripple. These new currencies often had different features or used different consensus algorithms than Bitcoin, but they all shared the basic principles of a decentralized ledger and secure peer-to-peer transactions.

One of the most significant developments in the history of cryptocurrencies was the emergence of the initial coin offering (ICO) in 2013. ICOs allowed startups to raise funds by issuing their own cryptocurrencies or tokens, which could then be traded on cryptocurrency exchanges. Some ICOs raised millions of dollars in a matter of minutes, and the market for ICOs grew rapidly over the next few years.

However, the unregulated nature of the ICO market led to a number of scams and fraudulent schemes, and regulators around the world began to take notice. In 2017, the US Securities and Exchange Commission (SEC) issued a warning about ICOs and announced that some tokens may be considered securities under US law, which would subject them to regulation.

The popularity of cryptocurrencies continued to grow in the years that followed, with Bitcoin reaching an all-time high of nearly $20,000 in late 2017. However, the market for cryptocurrencies is highly volatile, and the value of many cryptocurrencies has since plummeted. Despite this, the underlying technology of blockchain and the potential for decentralized systems continues to attract interest and investment.

In conclusion, the history of cryptocurrencies is relatively short but filled with significant developments and changes. From the creation of Bitcoin in 2008 to the rise of ICOs in 2013 and the subsequent regulatory crackdown, the world of cryptocurrencies has evolved rapidly. While the future of cryptocurrencies is uncertain, it is clear that these digital assets have already had a significant impact on the world of finance and technology.

Comparison with traditional currencies

The rise of cryptocurrencies has brought about a new way of thinking about money and its role in society. While traditional currencies have been the norm for centuries, the advent of digital currencies has sparked a debate about the merits of each. In this section, we will examine the comparison between traditional currencies and cryptocurrencies, focusing on their similarities and differences.

Firstly, let us define traditional currencies. Traditional currencies are government-issued and backed by central banks. They are commonly used for transactions and as a store of value. In contrast, cryptocurrencies are decentralized, digital currencies that use encryption techniques to secure transactions and control the creation of new units. They operate on a distributed ledger called the blockchain, which is maintained by a network of computers around the world.

One key difference between traditional currencies and cryptocurrencies is the way they are created. Traditional currencies are created by central banks through a process called monetary policy. The central bank can increase or decrease the money supply by adjusting interest rates or buying and selling government bonds. In contrast, cryptocurrencies are created through a process called mining, where participants in the network use their computing power to solve complex mathematical equations and validate transactions. As a reward for their efforts, they receive newly created units of the cryptocurrency.

Another important difference between traditional currencies and cryptocurrencies is the level of control and oversight. Central banks have the authority to regulate the money supply, set interest rates, and enforce monetary policy. They are also responsible for ensuring the stability of the financial system and protecting against fraud and financial crime. Cryptocurrencies, on the other hand, are not regulated by a central authority. Instead, they operate on a decentralized network that is maintained by participants around the world. While this provides greater transparency and security in some ways, it also opens up the possibility of fraud and illegal activity.

Despite these differences, there are also some similarities between traditional currencies and cryptocurrencies. Both can be used for transactions and as a store of value. Both can be traded on exchanges and have a value that fluctuates over time. Both can also be used for speculative purposes, with investors buying and selling in the hope of making a profit.

In terms of their value as a store of value, traditional currencies have a long track record of stability and reliability. They are widely accepted and trusted by individuals and businesses around the world. Cryptocurrencies, on the other hand, are a relatively new and untested asset class. While they have shown tremendous potential, they are also subject to high levels of volatility and risk. Their value can fluctuate rapidly in response to market demand, news events, and other factors.

Another area where traditional currencies and cryptocurrencies differ is in their level of acceptance and adoption. Traditional currencies are accepted by virtually all merchants and businesses around the world. They are also supported by a wide range of financial institutions and payment systems. Cryptocurrencies, on the other hand, are still in the early stages of adoption. While they are accepted by some merchants and businesses, they are not yet widely accepted and remain a niche asset class.

In conclusion, the comparison between traditional currencies and cryptocurrencies is complex and multifaceted. While they share some similarities, such as their use as a medium of exchange and store of value, they also differ in significant ways, such as their creation and oversight. Ultimately, the choice between traditional currencies and cryptocurrencies will depend on individual preferences and risk tolerance, as well as the specific use case and context in which they are being considered.

II. Cryptocurrency basics

Cryptocurrencies have emerged as a new form of digital currency that operates independently of any central authority, such as a government or a financial institution. Instead, they rely on decentralized networks and cryptographic protocols to facilitate transactions and maintain the integrity of the system. In this section, we will provide an overview of the fundamental concepts and technologies that underpin cryptocurrencies, including blockchain, mining, and transactions.

Blockchain Technology

At the heart of most cryptocurrencies is blockchain technology, which is essentially a distributed ledger that records transactions across a network of computers. Each block in the chain contains a list of transactions and a unique digital signature, or hash, that is created through a complex mathematical process. This hash is then added to the previous block in the chain, creating a secure and tamper-proof record of all transactions that have taken place on the network.

The decentralized nature of blockchain technology means that there is no central point of control or authority, and all transactions are verified by a network of users known as nodes. This makes the system more resistant to fraud and hacking, as there is no single point of failure that can be exploited by malicious actors.

Types of Cryptocurrencies

There are many different types of cryptocurrencies, each with its own unique features and characteristics. The most well-known cryptocurrency is Bitcoin, which was created in 2009 by an anonymous individual or group using the pseudonym Satoshi Nakamoto. Bitcoin operates on a decentralized network, and transactions are verified by a process called mining, which involves solving complex mathematical equations to add new blocks to the blockchain.

Other popular cryptocurrencies include Ethereum, Litecoin, and Ripple. Ethereum is a decentralized platform that enables the creation of smart contracts and decentralized applications (dapps), while Litecoin is a digital currency that operates on a faster and more efficient blockchain than Bitcoin. Ripple, on the other hand, is a payment protocol that is designed to facilitate faster and more secure cross-border transactions.

Mining and Transactions

Mining is the process of verifying transactions on a blockchain network and adding new blocks to the chain. Miners use powerful computers to solve complex mathematical equations and create a new block, which is then added to the blockchain once it has been verified by other nodes on the network. In exchange for their work, miners are rewarded with new coins or transaction fees.

Transactions on a blockchain network are initiated by sending a request to the network, which is then verified by the nodes and added to the blockchain if it is valid. Transactions are verified through a process known as consensus, which involves all nodes on the network agreeing on the validity of the transaction.

Conclusion

Cryptocurrencies are a new and rapidly evolving form of digital currency that is based on decentralized networks and blockchain technology. They offer a number of advantages over traditional currencies, including increased security, faster and cheaper transactions, and greater control over your finances. However, they also come with a number of risks and challenges, including volatility, regulatory uncertainty, and the potential for fraud and hacking. In the next sections, we will explore some of these issues in more detail and discuss how they are affecting the adoption and development of cryptocurrencies.

Blockchain technology and its role in cryptocurrencies

Blockchain technology is a critical component of cryptocurrencies, serving as the foundation for their security and decentralized nature. In this section, we will explore the basics of blockchain technology and its role in cryptocurrencies.

Blockchain technology is a distributed ledger that is used to record and verify transactions. It consists of a chain of blocks that contain information about these transactions. Each block contains a cryptographic hash of the previous block, which creates a tamper-evident chain that is difficult to alter. This chain of blocks is maintained by a network of computers that work together to validate transactions and add new blocks to the chain.

The decentralized nature of blockchain technology means that it is not controlled by any central authority. Instead, it is maintained by a network of users who have an incentive to keep the network secure and functioning properly. This is achieved through a consensus mechanism, which is a set of rules that govern how transactions are verified and added to the blockchain.

One of the key advantages of blockchain technology is its security. Because the ledger is distributed across a network of computers, it is very difficult for any single user or entity to control the network. Additionally, the use of cryptography and digital signatures helps to ensure the integrity of transactions on the blockchain.

Another important aspect of blockchain technology is its transparency. Because the ledger is publicly accessible, anyone can view the transactions that have been recorded on the blockchain. This makes it possible to trace the history of a particular transaction and verify its validity.

Blockchain technology is critical to the operation of cryptocurrencies. In fact, cryptocurrencies are often referred to as "blockchain-based" or "blockchain-backed" because they rely on the blockchain to function. Each cryptocurrency has its own blockchain, which is used to record and verify transactions on the network.

One of the key benefits of using blockchain technology in cryptocurrencies is that it enables the creation of a decentralized digital currency. Traditional currencies are controlled by central authorities such as central banks, but cryptocurrencies are not. This means that they are not subject to the same constraints and regulations as traditional currencies, which can be both a strength and a weakness.

Another advantage of using blockchain technology in cryptocurrencies is that it enables the creation of smart contracts. Smart contracts are self-executing contracts that are stored on the blockchain. They can be used to automate complex financial transactions and ensure that they are executed exactly as agreed upon.

Despite the many advantages of blockchain technology, there are also some challenges that need to be addressed. One of the biggest challenges is scalability, which refers to the ability of the blockchain to handle a large number of transactions. As more people use cryptocurrencies, the demand for blockchain technology will increase, which could lead to congestion and slower transaction times.

Another challenge is the potential for security breaches. While blockchain technology is very secure, it is not immune to hacking attempts. Additionally, the decentralized nature of blockchain technology can make it difficult to resolve disputes or recover lost funds in the event of a security breach.

In conclusion, blockchain technology is a critical component of cryptocurrencies. Its decentralized nature and security features make it an ideal foundation for a digital currency that is not controlled by central authorities. While there are some challenges associated with blockchain technology, its potential to transform the way we think about money and financial transactions is truly exciting.

Types of cryptocurrencies (Bitcoin, Ethereum, Litecoin, etc.)

Cryptocurrencies are digital assets that use cryptography to secure transactions and control the creation of new units. While there are thousands of different cryptocurrencies in existence, some of the most well-known and widely used ones include Bitcoin, Ethereum, Litecoin, and Ripple. Each cryptocurrency has unique characteristics and features, and understanding the differences between them is important for investors and users alike.

2.1 Bitcoin

Bitcoin is the first and most well-known cryptocurrency, created in 2009 by an unknown person or group using the pseudonym Satoshi Nakamoto. It uses a decentralized ledger called the blockchain to record all transactions and control the creation of new units. Unlike traditional currencies, which are controlled by governments and financial institutions, Bitcoin is decentralized, meaning that no single entity has control over it.

One of the key features of Bitcoin is its limited supply. There will only ever be 21 million Bitcoins in existence, and this cap is built into the protocol. This limited supply, combined with increasing demand, has contributed to the rise in the value of Bitcoin over time. However, the value of Bitcoin is highly volatile, and its price can fluctuate wildly based on a variety of factors, including regulatory changes, market sentiment, and investor behavior.

Another important feature of Bitcoin is its use of mining to validate transactions and create new units. Miners use powerful computers to solve complex mathematical equations and verify transactions on the blockchain. In exchange for their work, they receive newly created Bitcoins as a reward. This process ensures that the blockchain remains secure and that new units are created in a controlled and predictable way.

2.2 Ethereum

Ethereum is the second-largest cryptocurrency by market capitalization, created in 2015 by Vitalik Buterin. It uses a decentralized platform called the Ethereum Virtual Machine (EVM) to create and run decentralized applications (dapps) and smart contracts.

One of the key features of Ethereum is its programmability. This means that developers can use the platform to create customized applications and smart contracts that can be executed automatically when certain conditions are met. This functionality has led to the development of a wide range of dapps, from decentralized finance (DeFi) platforms to gaming and social media applications.

Another important feature of Ethereum is its use of gas fees to pay for transactions on the network. Gas fees are a way of compensating miners for the work they do to validate transactions and execute smart contracts. Users can choose how much they want to pay in gas fees to prioritize their transactions and ensure that they are processed quickly.

2.3 Litecoin

Litecoin is a peer-to-peer cryptocurrency that was created in 2011 by Charlie Lee, a former Google engineer. It is similar to Bitcoin in many ways, but it has some key differences that make it unique.

One of the main differences between Litecoin and Bitcoin is its transaction speed. Litecoin transactions are processed much faster than Bitcoin transactions, thanks to its use of a different mining algorithm called Scrypt. This makes it a popular choice for users who need to move funds quickly.

Another important feature of Litecoin is its limited supply. Like Bitcoin, Litecoin has a cap on the number of units that can be created, with a total of 84 million Litecoins set to be in circulation. This limited supply, combined with increasing demand, has led to the rise in the value of Litecoin over time.

2.4 Ripple

Ripple is a cryptocurrency that was created in 2012 by Ripple Labs, a San Francisco-based fintech company. It uses a unique consensus algorithm called the Ripple Protocol Consensus Algorithm (RPCA) to validate transactions and control the creation of new units.

One of the key features of Ripple is its focus on financial institutions and cross-border payments. Unlike other cryptocurrencies, which are designed primarily for peer-to-peer transactions, Ripple is designed to be used by banks and other financial institutions to facilitate faster and cheaper cross-border payments.

Ripple works by using a distributed ledger system similar to that used by Bitcoin and other cryptocurrencies. However, unlike Bitcoin, which uses a proof-of-work algorithm to validate transactions, Ripple uses the RPCA algorithm.

The RPCA algorithm works by using a network of trusted nodes to validate transactions. These nodes are selected by the Ripple network and are typically financial institutions or other large companies with a stake in the success of the Ripple network.

When a transaction is initiated on the Ripple network, it is first validated by a subset of these trusted nodes. If a majority of the nodes agree that the transaction is valid, it is added to the Ripple ledger.

This consensus-based approach allows Ripple to process transactions much faster than Bitcoin and other proof-of-work cryptocurrencies. Transactions on the Ripple network typically take just a few seconds to complete, compared to several minutes or even hours for Bitcoin.

Another key feature of Ripple is its use of XRP, a separate cryptocurrency that is used to facilitate cross-border transactions. When a bank or other financial institution wants to make a cross-border payment using Ripple, it first converts its local currency into XRP. The XRP is then sent to the recipient bank or financial institution, which can then convert it back into the local currency.

This system allows for much faster and cheaper cross-border payments than traditional methods. According to Ripple Labs, the average cross-border transaction using Ripple takes just four seconds and costs just $0.0004 in fees.

In addition to its use in cross-border payments, Ripple has also been adopted by some financial institutions for other purposes. For example, Santander Bank has used Ripple to create a mobile app that allows its customers to make instant international payments using the Ripple network.

Overall, Ripple is a unique cryptocurrency that is designed specifically for use by financial institutions. Its focus on cross-border payments and its use of the RPCA consensus algorithm make it a popular choice for banks and other large financial institutions looking to streamline their payment processes.

Mining and transactions

One of the most important aspects of cryptocurrencies is their decentralized nature, which is enabled by blockchain technology. However, this also means that there needs to be a way to validate transactions and maintain the integrity of the blockchain. This is where mining comes in.

2.5 Mining

Mining is the process by which new units of a cryptocurrency are created and validated. It involves solving complex mathematical problems to verify transactions and add them to the blockchain. In order to incentivize miners to contribute their computational power to the network, they are rewarded with new units of the cryptocurrency.

Bitcoin was the first cryptocurrency to introduce mining as a means of validating transactions and maintaining the integrity of the blockchain. The mining process in Bitcoin involves solving complex mathematical problems, with the difficulty of the problems increasing over time as more miners join the network. This is designed to ensure that the rate of new Bitcoin units being created remains stable over time.

However, the mining process is not without its drawbacks. One of the biggest concerns with mining is its energy consumption. The computational power required to mine cryptocurrencies can be quite significant, and this has led to concerns about the environmental impact of mining. In recent years, there has been a growing interest in developing alternative methods of validating transactions, such as proof-of-stake.

2.6 Transactions

Transactions in cryptocurrencies work differently than traditional financial transactions. Instead of relying on trusted intermediaries such as banks or credit card companies to process transactions, cryptocurrencies rely on a decentralized network of nodes to validate transactions and add them to the blockchain.

When a user initiates a transaction, it is broadcast to the network. Miners then validate the transaction and add it to the blockchain. Once the transaction has been added to the blockchain, it is considered to be final and cannot be reversed.

One of the key benefits of transactions in cryptocurrencies is that they are typically faster and cheaper than traditional financial transactions. Because there are no intermediaries involved, transactions can be processed more quickly and at a lower cost. This has made cryptocurrencies an attractive option for cross-border payments, which can be slow and expensive using traditional methods.

However, there are also drawbacks to transactions in cryptocurrencies. One of the biggest concerns is the potential for fraudulent activity. Because transactions are irreversible once they have been added to the blockchain, there is no way to recover funds if they are stolen or lost. This has led to a number of high-profile incidents of theft and fraud in the cryptocurrency space.

In addition, the lack of intermediaries in cryptocurrency transactions means that there is no recourse if something goes wrong. If a user accidentally sends funds to the wrong address or falls victim to a scam, there is no way to recover the funds.

2.7 Conclusion

In conclusion, mining and transactions are essential components of cryptocurrencies. Mining is the process by which new units of a cryptocurrency are created and validated, while transactions rely on a decentralized network of nodes to validate and add transactions to the blockchain. While there are concerns about the environmental impact of mining and the potential for fraud in cryptocurrency transactions, the benefits of cryptocurrencies, such as faster and cheaper transactions, make them an attractive option for many users.

III. Cryptocurrency markets and trading

Cryptocurrency markets have emerged as a popular alternative to traditional financial markets in recent years. These markets offer traders and investors access to a range of digital assets, which can be bought and sold for profit. Cryptocurrency trading involves the buying and selling of digital currencies on various exchanges around the world. This section will explore the basics of cryptocurrency markets, how they function, and the strategies traders use to make profits.

3.1 Cryptocurrency Market Basics

The cryptocurrency market is a decentralized market, meaning that it is not governed by a central authority or institution. Instead, it is composed of various exchanges that allow users to buy and sell digital currencies. These exchanges operate similarly to stock exchanges, but instead of buying and selling shares of companies, traders buy and sell digital currencies.

One of the most notable characteristics of cryptocurrency markets is their volatility. Prices of digital currencies can fluctuate rapidly and unpredictably, sometimes within seconds. This volatility is due to a number of factors, including market sentiment, news events, and market manipulation.

Another important aspect of cryptocurrency markets is liquidity. Liquidity refers to the ease with which assets can be bought and sold on an exchange. High liquidity means that there are plenty of buyers and sellers on an exchange, making it easier for traders to buy and sell their digital assets. Low liquidity, on the other hand, can make it difficult for traders to buy and sell assets at their desired prices.

3.2 Cryptocurrency Trading Strategies

There are a number of strategies that traders use to profit from cryptocurrency markets. These strategies can be broadly categorized as either technical analysis or fundamental analysis.

Technical analysis involves analyzing market data, such as price charts and trading volumes, to identify patterns and trends in the market. Traders who use technical analysis will often use various indicators, such as moving averages, to identify buy and sell signals. These traders will typically hold their positions for a relatively short period of time, ranging from a few minutes to a few hours.

Fundamental analysis involves analyzing the underlying factors that affect the value of a particular digital currency. Traders who use fundamental analysis will look at factors such as the technology behind the currency, its use cases, and the team behind the project. These traders will typically hold their positions for a longer period of time, ranging from a few days to several months.

Another popular trading strategy in cryptocurrency markets is arbitrage. Arbitrage involves buying and selling the same asset on different exchanges to take advantage of price differences. For example, a trader might buy Bitcoin on one exchange where it is undervalued and immediately sell it on another exchange where it is overvalued, making a profit in the process.

3.3 Risks and Challenges in Cryptocurrency Trading

While cryptocurrency trading can be a profitable venture, it also comes with significant risks and challenges. One of the biggest risks is the volatility of the market. Prices of digital currencies can fluctuate rapidly, which can lead to significant losses for traders who do not manage their risk properly.

Another risk in cryptocurrency trading is security. Cryptocurrencies are stored in digital wallets, which are vulnerable to hacking and theft. Traders who do not take appropriate security measures can lose their digital assets to cybercriminals.

Additionally, regulation is a major challenge in cryptocurrency trading. Cryptocurrency markets are largely unregulated, which means that traders are not protected by the same laws and regulations that govern traditional financial markets. This lack of regulation can make it difficult for traders to navigate the market and protect their investments.

Conclusion

Cryptocurrency markets have emerged as a popular alternative to traditional financial markets in recent years. These markets offer traders and investors access to a range of digital assets, which can be bought and sold for profit. However, cryptocurrency trading comes with significant risks and challenges, including market volatility, security risks, and a lack of regulation.

Overview of cryptocurrency exchanges

Cryptocurrency exchanges are digital platforms where users can buy, sell, and trade cryptocurrencies. These exchanges act as intermediaries between buyers and sellers, facilitating transactions and providing a marketplace for trading cryptocurrencies. As the popularity of cryptocurrencies has grown, so too has the number of exchanges. In this section, we will provide an overview of cryptocurrency exchanges, including their functions, types, and regulatory landscape.

3.1 Functions of Cryptocurrency Exchanges

The primary function of a cryptocurrency exchange is to enable users to buy and sell cryptocurrencies. This involves matching buyers and sellers, with the exchange acting as an intermediary. When a user places an order to buy or sell a cryptocurrency, the exchange matches that order with a corresponding order from another user. The exchange then facilitates the transaction, charging a fee for its services.

Cryptocurrency exchanges also offer additional functions, such as:

Wallets: Most exchanges provide users with a cryptocurrency wallet, which is used to store their digital assets. These wallets can be used to send and receive cryptocurrencies, and are usually accessible through the exchange's platform.

Trading tools: Many exchanges offer a range of trading tools, such as price charts, order books, and technical analysis indicators. These tools can help users make informed trading decisions and monitor market trends.

Margin trading: Some exchanges allow users to trade on margin, which means they can borrow funds from the exchange to increase their trading position. This can amplify potential gains, but also increases the risk of losses.

Derivatives trading: Certain exchanges offer derivatives trading, such as futures contracts and options. These financial instruments allow traders to speculate on the future price of cryptocurrencies, without actually owning the underlying asset.

Fiat currency support: Some exchanges allow users to buy and sell cryptocurrencies using fiat currencies, such as US dollars or euros. This can make it easier for users to enter and exit the cryptocurrency market.

3.2 Types of Cryptocurrency Exchanges

There are several types of cryptocurrency exchanges, each with its own characteristics and advantages. The main types are:

Centralized exchanges: These are the most common type of cryptocurrency exchange, and are operated by a centralized organization. Users must create an account with the exchange and provide identification documents, such as a passport or driver's license. Centralized exchanges are often more user-friendly and offer a wider range of trading tools, but are also more vulnerable to hacks and security breaches.

Decentralized exchanges: These exchanges operate on a peer-to-peer network, without a centralized operator. Users do not need to provide identification documents, and transactions are executed through smart contracts. Decentralized exchanges are more secure and less susceptible to hacks, but often have lower trading volumes and fewer trading tools.

Hybrid exchanges: These exchanges combine the features of centralized and decentralized exchanges. They are often operated by a centralized organization, but use decentralized technology to execute transactions. Hybrid exchanges aim to provide the security of decentralized exchanges, with the user-friendliness of centralized exchanges.

3.3 Regulatory Landscape of Cryptocurrency Exchanges

The regulatory landscape of cryptocurrency exchanges is complex and varies by jurisdiction. Some countries have implemented clear regulations for cryptocurrency exchanges, while others have taken a more hands-off approach. The regulatory landscape can affect the user experience of cryptocurrency exchanges, as well as their security and legitimacy.

In the United States, for example, cryptocurrency exchanges are regulated by the Financial Crimes Enforcement Network (FinCEN) and must comply with anti-money laundering (AML) and know-your-customer (KYC) regulations. This means that exchanges must verify the identity of their users and report suspicious transactions to the authorities. In addition, the Securities and Exchange Commission (SEC) has taken action against exchanges that offer unregistered securities or engage in fraudulent activities.

In other countries, such as Japan and South Korea, cryptocurrency exchanges are regulated by national financial authoritiesand must obtain licenses to operate. Japan was one of the first countries to introduce a regulatory framework for cryptocurrency exchanges, following the high-profile hack of the Tokyo-based exchange Mt. Gox in 2014. In South Korea, exchanges must comply with AML and KYC regulations, and are subject to regular audits by the Financial Services Commission (FSC).

In contrast, some countries have taken a more permissive approach to cryptocurrency exchanges. For example, in Malta, the government has introduced a regulatory framework that aims to attract cryptocurrency businesses to the island nation. The Malta Financial Services Authority (MFSA) regulates cryptocurrency exchanges and has granted licenses to several exchanges, including Binance, one of the largest cryptocurrency exchanges in the world.

The regulatory landscape can also affect the security and legitimacy of cryptocurrency exchanges. In countries with clear regulations, exchanges are more likely to be legitimate and have strong security measures in place. However, in countries without clear regulations, exchanges may be more vulnerable to hacks and scams.

In addition to government regulations, cryptocurrency exchanges may also be subject to self-regulation. For example, the Virtual Commodity Association (VCA) was established in the United States in 2018 to promote industry self-regulation and best practices among cryptocurrency exchanges. The VCA includes several prominent cryptocurrency exchanges, including Gemini and Bitstamp.

Despite the regulatory challenges, the cryptocurrency exchange market has continued to grow and evolve. As of 2021, there are over 300 cryptocurrency exchanges operating around the world, with a total daily trading volume of over $80 billion. As the market continues to mature, it is likely that more countries will introduce regulatory frameworks for cryptocurrency exchanges, in order to promote transparency, security, and legitimacy in the industry.

Trading strategies and risks

Trading strategies in the cryptocurrency market involve a combination of technical and fundamental analysis. Technical analysis involves analyzing charts and price trends to identify patterns and make predictions about future price movements. Fundamental analysis involves analyzing the underlying factors that affect the value of a cryptocurrency, such as its technology, adoption rate, and competition.

One popular trading strategy in the cryptocurrency market is known as "buying the dip." This strategy involves buying a cryptocurrency when its price has decreased significantly and is considered to be undervalued. Traders may use technical analysis to identify these buying opportunities and may also consider the fundamental factors that affect the value of the cryptocurrency.

Another popular strategy is known as "swing trading," which involves holding a position for a short to medium-term period, typically a few days to a few weeks, and taking advantage of price swings within that period. Swing traders may use technical analysis to identify potential price swings and may also consider fundamental factors that could impact the price.

There are also longer-term investment strategies, such as "HODLing" (holding on for dear life), which involves holding a cryptocurrency for an extended period, typically years, in the hopes that its value will increase significantly over time. This strategy is based on the belief that cryptocurrencies are a long-term investment with significant growth potential.

While these trading strategies can be profitable, they also come with significant risks. The cryptocurrency market is highly volatile and can experience sudden and significant price fluctuations. Traders must be prepared for these price swings and have strategies in place to manage risk.

One risk management strategy is known as "stop-loss," which involves setting a predetermined price at which a trader will exit a position if the price falls below that level. This can help limit losses and prevent significant losses from occurring.

Another risk management strategy is known as "position sizing," which involves determining the appropriate amount of capital to allocate to a specific trade. Traders should never risk more than they can afford to lose and should always have a plan in place for managing risk.

Another significant risk in the cryptocurrency market is the potential for fraud and security breaches. Exchanges and wallets can be hacked, and cryptocurrencies can be stolen. Traders must take steps to protect their investments, such as using secure wallets and enabling two-factor authentication.

In addition, traders must be aware of the regulatory landscape and any legal risks associated with trading cryptocurrencies. Some countries have implemented clear regulations for cryptocurrency exchanges, while others have taken a more hands-off approach. Traders should be aware of the regulatory environment in their jurisdiction and should comply with any applicable laws and regulations.

Finally, traders must also be aware of the psychological risks associated with trading cryptocurrencies. The market can be highly emotional, and traders may experience fear, greed, and other emotions that can cloud their judgment and lead to poor decision-making. Traders must be disciplined and have a plan in place for managing their emotions and staying focused on their trading strategies.

In conclusion, trading strategies in the cryptocurrency market involve a combination of technical and fundamental analysis. While these strategies can be profitable, they also come with significant risks, including price volatility, fraud and security breaches, regulatory and legal risks, and psychological risks. Traders must be prepared for these risks and have strategies in place to manage them effectively. By staying disciplined and focused on their trading strategies, traders can increase their chances of success in the cryptocurrency market.

Cryptocurrency investment options

Cryptocurrency investment options have increased significantly over the past few years, providing investors with various ways to gain exposure to the cryptocurrency market. In this section, we will explore some of the most popular cryptocurrency investment options, including cryptocurrency funds, exchange-traded funds (ETFs), initial coin offerings (ICOs), and cryptocurrency futures.

4.1 Cryptocurrency Funds

Cryptocurrency funds are investment vehicles that allow investors to gain exposure to cryptocurrencies without directly holding the underlying assets. These funds are managed by professional fund managers who invest in a diversified portfolio of cryptocurrencies on behalf of their investors. Cryptocurrency funds can be actively or passively managed, and they can invest in a range of cryptocurrencies, including Bitcoin, Ethereum, Litecoin, and Ripple.

One example of a cryptocurrency fund is the Grayscale Bitcoin Trust, which allows investors to gain exposure to Bitcoin without directly owning the cryptocurrency. The fund is traded on the OTCQX market and is available to both institutional and individual investors. Another example is the Bitwise 10 Crypto Index Fund, which tracks the performance of the top ten cryptocurrencies by market capitalization.

Cryptocurrency funds offer several advantages for investors. Firstly, they provide exposure to cryptocurrencies without the technical difficulties associated with directly buying and holding cryptocurrencies. Secondly, cryptocurrency funds are managed by professional fund managers, which can provide investors with a more diversified and disciplined investment approach. Finally, cryptocurrency funds can offer more liquidity than directly holding cryptocurrencies, as they are traded on traditional exchanges.

However, cryptocurrency funds also have their disadvantages. Firstly, they can be expensive, with management fees and other expenses that can reduce the returns of the fund. Secondly, cryptocurrency funds can be subject to significant volatility, as cryptocurrencies are a highly speculative and volatile asset class. Finally, cryptocurrency funds can be subject to regulatory risks, as the regulatory landscape for cryptocurrencies is constantly evolving.

4.2 Exchange-Traded Funds (ETFs)

Exchange-traded funds (ETFs) are investment vehicles that allow investors to buy and sell shares of a fund that tracks the performance of a particular index or sector. Cryptocurrency ETFs are ETFs that invest in cryptocurrencies or companies that are involved in the cryptocurrency industry. The first Bitcoin ETF was approved in Canada in 2021, and several other countries are considering approving Bitcoin ETFs in the near future.

Cryptocurrency ETFs offer several advantages for investors. Firstly, they provide exposure to cryptocurrencies without the technical difficulties associated with directly buying and holding cryptocurrencies. Secondly, cryptocurrency ETFs are traded on traditional exchanges, which can provide more liquidity and transparency than other cryptocurrency investment options. Finally, cryptocurrency

ETFs can provide a more diversified investment approach, as they can invest in a range of cryptocurrencies and cryptocurrency-related companies.

However, cryptocurrency ETFs also have their disadvantages. Firstly, they can be expensive, with management fees and other expenses that can reduce the returns of the fund. Secondly, cryptocurrency ETFs can be subject to significant volatility, as cryptocurrencies are a highly speculative and volatile asset class. Finally, cryptocurrency ETFs can be subject to regulatory risks, as the regulatory landscape for cryptocurrencies is constantly evolving.

4.3 Initial Coin Offerings (ICOs)

Initial coin offerings (ICOs) are a fundraising mechanism in which companies raise capital by issuing their own cryptocurrencies or tokens to investors. ICOs are typically used by early-stage companies to raise capital for their projects, and they can be a high-risk, high-reward investment opportunity.

Investing in ICOs can offer several advantages for investors. Firstly, ICOs can offer significant returns for investors, as the value of the tokens can increase significantly if the project is successful. Secondly, ICOs can provide investors with the opportunity to invest in early-stage companies that may have significant growth potential. Finally, investing in ICOs can be a way for investors to support projects that align with their values or interests.

However, investing in ICOs also comes with significant risks. As ICOs are often used by early-stage companies, there is a high risk that the project will fail or the company will not deliver on its promises. This can lead to significant losses for investors. In addition, ICOs are often not regulated, which means that there is a higher risk of fraud or scams.

Despite the risks, there are several ways for investors to participate in ICOs. One common method is to participate in the pre-sale or private sale of the tokens. This often requires a minimum investment, but can provide investors with a discount on the token price or other incentives. Another method is to participate in the public sale of the tokens, which is often open to a wider range of investors. However, participating in public sales can be more competitive and may not provide the same discounts as pre-sale or private sales.

Another option for cryptocurrency investors is to invest in established cryptocurrencies such as Bitcoin or Ethereum. These cryptocurrencies have a more established track record and are often seen as a safer investment option than ICOs. Bitcoin, for example, has seen significant growth in recent years and is widely accepted as a form of payment by merchants and businesses around the world. Ethereum, on the other hand, has become a popular platform for creating decentralized applications and smart contracts.

Investors can also consider investing in cryptocurrency index funds or exchange-traded funds (ETFs). These funds allow investors to gain exposure to a diversified portfolio of cryptocurrencies without having to invest in each individual cryptocurrency separately. This can help to reduce the risk of investing in a single cryptocurrency, while still providing exposure to the potential growth of the cryptocurrency market as a whole.

Finally, investors can also consider investing in cryptocurrency mining operations. Cryptocurrency mining involves using computing power to solve complex mathematical problems in order to validate transactions on the blockchain network. In exchange for this work, miners are rewarded with newly created cryptocurrency. While cryptocurrency mining can be a profitable investment opportunity, it also requires significant technical knowledge and investment in hardware and electricity costs.

In conclusion, investing in cryptocurrencies can offer significant opportunities for investors, but also comes with significant risks. It is important for investors to carefully consider their investment goals, risk tolerance, and investment options before investing in cryptocurrencies. Investors should also be aware of the regulatory landscape and potential risks associated with ICOs and other cryptocurrency investment options.

IV. Real-world applications of cryptocurrencies

Cryptocurrencies have gained popularity in recent years due to their decentralized nature, which enables secure and transparent transactions without the need for intermediaries such as banks or financial institutions. While many people associate cryptocurrencies with speculation and trading, the potential applications of blockchain technology extend far beyond these uses. In this section, we will explore the real-world applications of cryptocurrencies and how they are being used to solve real-world problems in various industries.

Supply Chain Management:
One of the most promising applications of cryptocurrencies is in supply chain management. The transparency and immutability of blockchain technology make it an ideal solution for tracking goods from their origin to their final destination. By creating a blockchain-based supply chain management system, companies can ensure that their products are authentic and have not been tampered with. This can help to reduce counterfeiting and fraud, which is a significant problem in many industries, such as pharmaceuticals, luxury goods, and food.

For example, Walmart has implemented a blockchain-based supply chain management system that enables the tracking of food products from the farm to the store. By scanning a QR code on a product, customers can view its journey through the supply chain, including its origin, processing, and transport. This system improves transparency and enables Walmart to quickly trace the source of any problems, such as contamination or foodborne illnesses.

Digital Identity:
Another potential application of cryptocurrencies is in the field of digital identity. With traditional identity verification systems, individuals often have to provide sensitive personal information to multiple parties, such as banks, employers, and government agencies. This creates a risk of identity theft and fraud.

Blockchain technology offers a secure and decentralized way to verify digital identities. By using a blockchain-based identity system, individuals can maintain control over their personal information while still providing proof of identity when necessary. This can help to reduce identity fraud and simplify identity verification processes.

For example, the government of Estonia has implemented a blockchain-based digital identity system that enables citizens to access government services, sign documents, and conduct financial transactions securely. The system is based on a blockchain network that stores the encrypted data of each citizen, enabling them to control their personal information while still providing proof of identity when necessary.

Decentralized Finance:
Decentralized finance (DeFi) is an emerging field that uses blockchain technology to create decentralized financial systems. DeFi enables users to access financial services without intermediaries, such as banks or financial institutions. This creates a more transparent and accessible financial system that is available to everyone, regardless of their location or socioeconomic status.

DeFi applications include decentralized exchanges, lending and borrowing platforms, and stablecoins. These applications enable users to trade cryptocurrencies, lend and borrow money, and earn interest on their assets without the need for traditional financial institutions.

For example, the decentralized exchange Uniswap enables users to trade cryptocurrencies without the need for a centralized exchange. Users can trade any ERC-20 token on the Ethereum blockchain, and the exchange is powered by a decentralized liquidity pool that is maintained by users who provide liquidity to the platform. This creates a more decentralized and accessible trading system that is available to anyone with an internet connection.

Gaming and Entertainment:
Cryptocurrencies are also being used in the gaming and entertainment industries to enable secure and transparent transactions. Blockchain technology can be used to create digital assets, such as in-game items and virtual real estate, that can be bought and sold using cryptocurrencies. This creates a more transparent and secure system for buying and selling digital assets, which is particularly important in the gaming industry, where fraud and scams are common.

For example, the blockchain-based game Axie Infinity enables players to buy and sell digital creatures called Axies using the cryptocurrency Ethereum. These creatures can be bred, battled, and traded, creating a vibrant digital economy within the game. The game has become incredibly popular with players, with some Axies selling for thousands of dollars. This demonstrates the potential for cryptocurrencies and blockchain technology to transform the gaming industry by providing new ways for players to monetize their gameplay and creating a more equitable system for buying and selling digital assets.

Another area where cryptocurrencies are being used in the entertainment industry is in the distribution of digital content, such as music, movies, and e-books. Blockchain technology can be used to create decentralized platforms for content distribution, which would enable creators to bypass traditional gatekeepers, such as record labels and movie studios, and connect directly with their audiences. This has the potential to disrupt the existing power structures in the entertainment industry, empowering creators and giving audiences more control over the content they consume.

One example of a blockchain-based platform for content distribution is the music streaming service Audius. Audius enables artists to upload their music directly to the platform and receive payments in the form of the cryptocurrency $AUDIO, which can be traded on various cryptocurrency exchanges. This creates a more direct relationship between artists and their fans, enabling them to earn more revenue and maintain more control over their music.

Overall, the use of cryptocurrencies in the gaming and entertainment industries demonstrates the potential for blockchain technology to transform a wide range of industries by enabling secure and transparent transactions, creating new revenue streams for creators, and empowering consumers. However, there are also challenges and risks associated with the use of cryptocurrencies in these industries, such as the potential for fraud and the volatility of cryptocurrency prices, which must be carefully managed to ensure the long-term viability of these applications.

Use cases in e-commerce and peer-to-peer transactions

E-commerce and peer-to-peer (P2P) transactions are among the most popular use cases for cryptocurrencies. Cryptocurrencies can offer several benefits over traditional payment methods, including lower transaction fees, faster settlement times, and increased security and privacy. In this section, we will explore how cryptocurrencies are being used in e-commerce and P2P transactions, as well as their advantages and challenges.

E-commerce:

E-commerce refers to the buying and selling of goods and services online. Cryptocurrencies can be used as a payment method for e-commerce transactions, and several companies have started accepting cryptocurrencies as a form of payment. This includes both small businesses and large retailers such as Microsoft, Overstock, and Expedia.

One of the primary advantages of using cryptocurrencies for e-commerce transactions is the lower transaction fees. Traditional payment methods, such as credit cards and PayPal, typically charge fees ranging from 2% to 5% of the transaction amount, while cryptocurrency transaction fees are often less than 1%. This can result in significant cost savings for both merchants and customers.

Another advantage of using cryptocurrencies for e-commerce transactions is faster settlement times. Traditional payment methods can take several days to settle, while cryptocurrency transactions can be settled in minutes or even seconds. This can improve the overall customer experience, as customers can receive their goods and services faster.

Cryptocurrencies can also provide increased security and privacy for e-commerce transactions. Traditional payment methods require customers to share sensitive financial information, such as credit card numbers and bank account details, which can be vulnerable to fraud and identity theft. Cryptocurrencies, on the other hand, use blockchain technology to secure and encrypt transactions, making them more secure and private.

However, there are also several challenges associated with using cryptocurrencies for e-commerce transactions. One of the main challenges is the lack of widespread adoption and acceptance by merchants. While several companies have started accepting cryptocurrencies as a form of payment, it is still not as widely accepted as traditional payment methods.

Another challenge is the volatility of cryptocurrencies. Cryptocurrencies are known for their price volatility, which can make it difficult for merchants to price their goods and services. For example, if a merchant prices their goods in Bitcoin and the price of Bitcoin drops significantly, the merchant may suffer a loss. This can make it challenging for merchants to rely on cryptocurrencies as a stable form of payment.

Peer-to-peer transactions:

P2P transactions refer to the exchange of goods, services, or money between individuals without the involvement of intermediaries such as banks or payment processors. Cryptocurrencies can be used to facilitate P2P transactions, and several platforms and applications have been developed to enable P2P transactions using cryptocurrencies.

One of the primary advantages of using cryptocurrencies for P2P transactions is the lower transaction fees. Traditional P2P payment methods, such as wire transfers and PayPal, can charge significant fees, while cryptocurrency transaction fees are often less than 1%. This can result in significant cost savings for individuals engaging in P2P transactions.

Another advantage of using cryptocurrencies for P2P transactions is faster settlement times. Traditional P2P payment methods can take several days to settle, while cryptocurrency transactions can be settled in minutes or even seconds. This can improve the overall user experience, as individuals can receive their funds faster.

Cryptocurrencies can also provide increased security and privacy for P2P transactions. Traditional P2P payment methods require individuals to share sensitive financial information, such as bank account details, which can be vulnerable to fraud and identity theft. Cryptocurrencies, on the other hand, use blockchain technology to secure and encrypt transactions, making them more secure and private.

However, there are also several challenges associated with using cryptocurrencies for P2P transactions. One of the main challenges is the lack of widespread adoption and acceptance by individuals. While cryptocurrencies have gained significant popularity,

Crypto adoption and regulation around the world

Cryptocurrencies have gained a lot of attention from investors, businesses, and governments around the world. While the adoption of cryptocurrencies has been rapid, it has also raised concerns regarding regulation and compliance. In this section, we will examine the global adoption of cryptocurrencies and the different approaches taken by governments to regulate them.

Cryptocurrency adoption around the world
Cryptocurrency adoption has been on the rise in recent years, with more businesses accepting cryptocurrencies as a form of payment. According to a report by Chainalysis, global adoption of cryptocurrencies has increased by 881% from 2019 to 2020, with over 106 million people using cryptocurrencies globally.

In some countries, cryptocurrencies have become a popular alternative to traditional banking systems, particularly in regions where access to financial services is limited. For example, in Nigeria, where many people are unbanked, cryptocurrencies have gained popularity as a means of conducting financial transactions. The same is true for many other countries in Africa and Latin America.

In developed countries, cryptocurrencies have gained traction as a means of investment and a store of value. For example, in the United States, many institutional investors, such as hedge funds, have started investing in cryptocurrencies. Additionally, companies such as Tesla and Square have added Bitcoin to their balance sheets.

Regulatory approaches to cryptocurrencies
The rapid adoption of cryptocurrencies has raised concerns among governments and financial regulators around the world. While some countries have embraced cryptocurrencies and developed regulatory frameworks to support their use, others have taken a more cautious approach.

a. Pro-Cryptocurrency regulation

Some countries have taken a pro-cryptocurrency stance, recognizing the potential benefits of cryptocurrencies and taking steps to regulate them. For example, in Japan, cryptocurrencies are recognized as legal tender, and the country has developed a regulatory framework to support their use. The Japanese Financial Services Agency (FSA) regulates cryptocurrency exchanges and requires them to comply with anti-money laundering (AML) and know-your-customer (KYC) requirements.

Similarly, in Switzerland, cryptocurrencies are recognized as a legitimate form of payment, and the country has developed a regulatory framework to support their use. The Swiss Financial Market

Supervisory Authority (FINMA) regulates cryptocurrency exchanges and has established guidelines for initial coin offerings (ICOs).

b. Cautious regulation

Other countries have taken a more cautious approach to cryptocurrencies, recognizing the potential risks associated with their use. For example, in China, the government has banned initial coin offerings (ICOs) and cryptocurrency exchanges, citing concerns about fraud and speculation. However, the Chinese government has also expressed interest in developing its own digital currency, which it hopes will be a more controlled alternative to cryptocurrencies.

Similarly, in India, the Reserve Bank of India (RBI) has banned banks from dealing with cryptocurrency exchanges. However, the Indian government has also been exploring the potential benefits of blockchain technology and is considering developing its own digital currency.

c. Hostile regulation

Finally, some countries have taken a hostile stance towards cryptocurrencies, banning them outright or imposing strict regulations that make their use difficult. For example, in Algeria, Bolivia, and Ecuador, cryptocurrencies are illegal, and the use of cryptocurrencies is punishable by law.

In some other countries, such as Russia and Venezuela, the government has imposed strict regulations on cryptocurrencies, making it difficult for businesses and individuals to use them. For example, in Venezuela, the government has created its own digital currency, the Petro, which it hopes will be a more controlled alternative to cryptocurrencies.

Challenges in regulating cryptocurrencies

Regulating cryptocurrencies is a challenging task, as they are decentralized and often operate outside the traditional banking system. This makes it difficult for governments and financial regulators to monitor and control their use.

Additionally, the anonymity provided by cryptocurrencies has raised concerns about their use in illegal activities, such as money laundering and terrorist financing. As a result, many countries have introduced regulatory measures to address these concerns.

One of the main challenges in regulating cryptocurrencies is the lack of a global regulatory framework. Each country has its own approach to regulating cryptocurrencies, which can lead to inconsistencies and confusion. For example, some countries have banned cryptocurrencies outright, while others have embraced them as a legitimate form of payment.

Another challenge is the difficulty in defining cryptocurrencies themselves. Different countries have different definitions of what constitutes a cryptocurrency, which can create confusion for investors and regulators alike. Some countries define cryptocurrencies as a form of currency, while others view them as a type of asset or commodity.

The issue of taxation is also a challenge when it comes to regulating cryptocurrencies. Traditional forms of taxation, such as income tax and capital gains tax, may not be suitable for cryptocurrencies, which are often traded on decentralized exchanges and can be difficult to track.

Furthermore, the global nature of cryptocurrencies means that regulations in one country may have unintended consequences in another. For example, a crackdown on cryptocurrency exchanges in one country may drive investors to use exchanges based in other countries with weaker regulations.

Despite these challenges, many countries have introduced regulatory measures to address the use of cryptocurrencies. In the United States, for example, the Financial Crimes Enforcement Network (FinCEN) has introduced regulations for businesses that deal in cryptocurrencies, requiring them to register with the agency and report suspicious activity.

In Japan, cryptocurrencies are recognized as a legal form of payment and are subject to regulation by the Financial Services Agency. In Europe, the European Union has introduced regulations to combat money laundering and terrorist financing through the use of cryptocurrencies.

However, there is still a long way to go in terms of establishing a global regulatory framework for cryptocurrencies. The lack of a unified approach to regulation can lead to confusion for investors and companies alike, and may ultimately hinder the widespread adoption of cryptocurrencies.

Some argue that overly restrictive regulation could stifle innovation and the potential benefits of cryptocurrencies, while others argue that more regulation is needed to protect investors and prevent illegal activity.

Ultimately, finding the right balance between regulation and innovation will be crucial in determining the future of cryptocurrencies and their role in the global economy. As cryptocurrencies continue to evolve, it is likely that regulatory frameworks will need to adapt and change to keep up with new developments and emerging technologies.

Potential future developments in the cryptocurrency space

The cryptocurrency space is constantly evolving and there are several potential future developments that could significantly impact the industry. In this section, we will explore some of these potential developments and their implications.

Central Bank Digital Currencies (CBDCs)
One of the most significant potential developments in the cryptocurrency space is the emergence of Central Bank Digital Currencies (CBDCs). These are digital versions of traditional currencies that are issued and backed by central banks. CBDCs have been under development by many central banks around the world, including the People's Bank of China, the European Central Bank, and the Federal Reserve.

The introduction of CBDCs could have several implications for the cryptocurrency space. For one, it could provide greater legitimacy to cryptocurrencies by making them part of the broader monetary system. It could also create new opportunities for businesses and consumers to transact digitally. However, it could also pose a threat to existing cryptocurrencies by providing a government-backed alternative that may be perceived as safer and more reliable.

Decentralized Finance (DeFi)
Decentralized Finance (DeFi) is a rapidly growing area of the cryptocurrency space that aims to provide financial services using decentralized, blockchain-based systems. DeFi applications allow users to lend, borrow, and trade cryptocurrencies without the need for intermediaries such as banks or exchanges.

The potential of DeFi is significant, as it could lead to a more open and accessible financial system. However, there are also risks associated with DeFi, such as smart contract vulnerabilities and the potential for hacks and scams.

Interoperability between blockchains
Interoperability between different blockchain networks is another potential development that could have significant implications for the cryptocurrency space. Currently, different blockchain networks operate independently, making it difficult to transfer assets between them. However, new technologies are emerging that aim to bridge this gap, such as Polkadot, Cosmos, and Chainlink.

Interoperability could lead to greater efficiency and functionality in the cryptocurrency space, as users could move assets between different networks seamlessly. It could also help to address the issue of scalability, as it would allow different blockchain networks to work together to process transactions.

Increased regulation
As the cryptocurrency space continues to grow, it is likely that governments and financial regulators will seek to increase their oversight and regulation of the industry. This could have both positive and negative implications for the industry.

On the one hand, increased regulation could provide greater legitimacy and stability to the cryptocurrency space, making it more attractive to mainstream investors and businesses. On the other hand, it could also stifle innovation and make it more difficult for smaller players to enter the market.

Greater adoption
Finally, one of the most significant potential developments in the cryptocurrency space is simply greater adoption. As more businesses and consumers begin to use cryptocurrencies for everyday transactions, the industry will become more mainstream and integrated into the broader economy.

Greater adoption could lead to increased stability and liquidity in the cryptocurrency markets, as well as new opportunities for businesses and investors. However, it could also lead to greater scrutiny and regulation from governments and financial regulators.

In conclusion, the cryptocurrency space is constantly evolving and there are several potential developments that could significantly impact the industry in the future. These include the emergence of Central Bank Digital Currencies, the growth of Decentralized Finance, increased interoperability between blockchain networks, greater regulation, and greater adoption. It is important for investors and businesses to stay abreast of these developments and to carefully consider their implications.

CHAPTER 9: THE BLOCKCHAIN REVOLUTION

Introduction to blockchain technology

Blockchain technology has been hailed as one of the most significant technological innovations of the 21st century. It is a distributed ledger technology that allows for secure, transparent, and immutable transactions between parties without the need for intermediaries. The concept of blockchain was first introduced in 2008 by a person or group of people under the pseudonym "Satoshi Nakamoto" in a whitepaper titled "Bitcoin: A Peer-to-Peer Electronic Cash System." Since then, blockchain technology has grown to encompass a wide range of applications beyond cryptocurrency.

How blockchain technology works

At its core, a blockchain is a decentralized ledger of transactions that is managed by a network of nodes. Each node on the network has a copy of the ledger, and all nodes must agree on any changes made to the ledger. Transactions on the blockchain are verified and validated by the network, and once a transaction is added to the ledger, it cannot be altered or deleted.

Blockchains use cryptographic techniques to ensure the security and integrity of the ledger. Each block on the blockchain contains a cryptographic hash of the previous block, along with a timestamp and a record of transactions. This creates a chain of blocks that is tamper-proof and immutable.

Applications of blockchain technology

While blockchain technology was initially developed for cryptocurrency transactions, it has since been applied to a wide range of industries and use cases. Some of the most notable applications of blockchain technology include:

Supply chain management - Blockchain technology can be used to track products and goods through the supply chain, providing transparency and accountability at every stage of the process.

Healthcare - Blockchain technology can be used to securely store and share patient data, providing patients with more control over their personal health information.

Identity management - Blockchain technology can be used to create a decentralized identity management system, allowing individuals to control their own digital identity without the need for centralized authorities.

Voting systems - Blockchain technology can be used to create secure and transparent voting systems, reducing the risk of fraud and ensuring accurate vote counting.

Real estate - Blockchain technology can be used to create a more efficient and transparent real estate market, allowing for secure and efficient transactions without the need for intermediaries.

Intellectual property - Blockchain technology can be used to create a more secure and efficient system for managing intellectual property, reducing the risk of infringement and improving the overall management of patents and trademarks.

These are just a few examples of the many potential applications of blockchain technology. As the technology continues to evolve and improve, it is likely that we will see even more innovative use cases emerge in the coming years.

Impact of blockchain technology on industries

The impact of blockchain technology on industries has been significant, with many businesses and organizations looking to leverage the technology to improve efficiency, reduce costs, and enhance security. Some of the industries that have been most impacted by blockchain technology include:

Financial services - Blockchain technology has the potential to revolutionize the financial services industry by reducing the need for intermediaries, improving the speed and security of transactions, and enabling new business models.

Insurance - Blockchain technology can help insurance companies to reduce fraud, automate claims processing, and improve risk management.

Healthcare - Blockchain technology can improve the efficiency and security of healthcare data management, enabling patients to have more control over their personal health information.

Supply chain management - Blockchain technology can improve transparency and accountability in supply chains, enabling businesses to track products and goods at every stage of the process.

Real estate - Blockchain technology can enable more efficient and secure real estate transactions, reducing the need for intermediaries and improving the overall transparency of the market.

Governments - Blockchain technology can help governments to create more secure and transparent systems for voting, identity management, and financial transactions.

Overall, the impact of blockchain technology on industries has been largely positive, with many businesses and organizations looking to leverage the technology to improve their operations and provide better services to their customers.

Challenges and limitations of blockchain technology

Despite the many potential benefits of blockchain technology, there are also significant challenges and limitations that must be addressed. Some of the most significant challenges and limitations include:

Scalability - Blockchain technology can struggle with scalability, particularly when it comes to processing large volumes of transactions.

Security - While blockchain technology is generally considered to be secure, there have been instances of security breaches and vulnerabilities that have been exploited by hackers.

Regulation - The regulation of blockchain technology is still in its early stages, with many jurisdictions struggling to determine how to best regulate the technology in a way that balances innovation with consumer protection.

Interoperability - There are currently many different blockchain platforms and systems in use, and there is a need for greater interoperability between them to ensure that they can all work together effectively.

Overall, while blockchain technology has the potential to revolutionize a wide range of industries and use cases, it is important to recognize that there are significant challenges and limitations that must be addressed in order to fully realize its potential.

Definition and characteristics of blockchain

Blockchain is a digital ledger technology that has become increasingly popular over the last few years. The technology is known for its ability to provide secure and transparent transactions that are immutable and tamper-proof. In this section, we will define blockchain and discuss its key characteristics, including decentralization, transparency, immutability, and security.

Definition of blockchain

A blockchain is a decentralized digital ledger that records transactions in a secure and transparent way. It is a distributed database that is managed by a network of computers, rather than a central authority. Each block in the blockchain contains a collection of transactions, and once a block is added to the chain, it cannot be altered or deleted.

The first blockchain was created in 2009 by an unknown person or group of people under the pseudonym "Satoshi Nakamoto" as the underlying technology for Bitcoin, the world's first cryptocurrency. Since then, blockchain technology has been applied to a wide range of industries and use cases.

Characteristics of blockchain

Decentralization

One of the key characteristics of blockchain technology is decentralization. Unlike traditional systems where data is stored on a central server or database, blockchain technology allows data to be stored across a network of computers, making it more secure and resistant to attacks.

In a decentralized system, there is no single point of failure, and no one entity has control over the network. This makes it more difficult for malicious actors to manipulate or corrupt the data. The decentralized nature of blockchain technology also makes it more resistant to censorship and government intervention.

Transparency

Another key characteristic of blockchain technology is transparency. Every transaction that occurs on a blockchain is recorded on a public ledger that can be viewed by anyone with access to the network. This provides a high level of transparency and accountability, as all parties can see every transaction that occurs on the network.

Transparency is particularly important in industries where trust is a critical factor, such as finance, supply chain management, and healthcare. By providing a transparent and secure way to track transactions, blockchain technology can help to increase trust and reduce fraud.

Immutability

Immutability is another important characteristic of blockchain technology. Once a block is added to the blockchain, it cannot be altered or deleted. This makes the blockchain a tamper-proof and secure way to store data.

Each block in the blockchain contains a unique cryptographic hash that is generated based on the data in the block. This hash is used to link the block to the previous block in the chain, creating a permanent and unalterable record of every transaction that occurs on the network.

Security

Security is one of the most important characteristics of blockchain technology. The decentralized nature of the blockchain makes it more secure than traditional systems, as there is no single point of failure that can be targeted by attackers.

Additionally, the cryptographic algorithms used to secure the blockchain make it very difficult for malicious actors to manipulate or corrupt the data. Each block in the blockchain is secured with a unique cryptographic hash, and any attempt to alter the data in a block would result in a different hash value, alerting the network to the attempted breach.

Conclusion

In conclusion, blockchain technology is a decentralized digital ledger that records transactions in a secure and transparent way. Its key characteristics include decentralization, transparency, immutability, and security. These characteristics make blockchain technology well-suited for a wide range of industries and use cases, from finance and supply chain management to healthcare and identity management. As the technology continues to evolve, it is likely to play an increasingly important role in the digital economy.

Brief history of blockchain

Certainly. The history of blockchain technology can be traced back to the early 1990s, when Stuart Haber and W. Scott Stornetta first proposed a system for timestamping digital documents in a way that would prevent them from being altered or tampered with. The system they proposed used a cryptographic hash function to create a unique digital fingerprint of each document, which could be used to verify its authenticity.

In 2008, the first practical implementation of blockchain technology was introduced with the release of Bitcoin. Bitcoin was created by an anonymous person or group of people using the pseudonym Satoshi Nakamoto, who saw blockchain technology as a way to create a decentralized, peer-to-peer electronic cash system that could operate without the need for a central authority.

The basic idea behind Bitcoin is that each transaction is recorded on a shared public ledger known as the blockchain. Each block in the blockchain contains a record of several transactions, along with a reference to the previous block in the chain. This creates a tamper-proof, decentralized ledger that can be used to verify the ownership and authenticity of digital assets.

Bitcoin quickly gained popularity among early adopters and enthusiasts, but it was not until several years later that blockchain technology began to attract broader attention from mainstream businesses and investors.

In 2015, a project called Ethereum was introduced. Ethereum was designed as a platform for building decentralized applications (DApps) that could run on top of the blockchain. This opened up a wide range of new possibilities for blockchain technology, as developers began to explore the potential applications of smart contracts, which are self-executing contracts with the terms of the agreement directly written into code.

Since then, blockchain technology has been applied to a wide range of industries and use cases, including supply chain management, healthcare, identity management, voting systems, and more. The technology has also inspired the creation of numerous other blockchain-based cryptocurrencies and decentralized applications, each with its own unique features and use cases.

While blockchain technology is still in its early stages, it has already had a significant impact on the way that we think about trust, transparency, and the nature of transactions in the digital age. As the technology continues to evolve and mature, it is likely to have an even greater impact on a wide range of industries and use cases in the years to come.

Comparison with traditional database systems

Blockchain technology has often been compared to traditional database systems, with some experts claiming that blockchain is simply a new type of database. However, there are several key differences between blockchain and traditional databases that set them apart. In this section, we will explore the similarities and differences between blockchain and traditional database systems.

Traditional databases are centralized systems where data is stored in a single location and controlled by a central authority. These databases are widely used in various industries, including finance, healthcare, and retail. They are designed to store and manage large amounts of data in a structured manner, using SQL or other query languages to access and manipulate data.

On the other hand, blockchain technology is a decentralized system that allows data to be stored and managed by a network of nodes, with no central authority controlling the data. Each node on the network has a copy of the blockchain, which contains a complete record of all transactions that have ever taken place on the network. This decentralized nature of blockchain makes it a powerful tool for creating secure and transparent systems.

One of the key differences between blockchain and traditional databases is the way in which data is stored. In traditional databases, data is typically stored in tables, with each row representing a single record and each column representing a data field. This data is stored in a centralized location, typically on a server or a group of servers, and is accessed using query languages like SQL.

In contrast, blockchain data is stored in blocks that are linked together to form a chain. Each block contains a set of transactions, and once a block is added to the chain, it cannot be altered. This immutability of the blockchain is a key feature that sets it apart from traditional databases, as it provides a high level of security and transparency.

Another key difference between blockchain and traditional databases is the way in which data is processed. In traditional databases, data is processed using a central server that runs a database management system (DBMS). This server is responsible for managing the data and ensuring that it is secure and consistent.

In contrast, blockchain nodes are responsible for processing data and ensuring that it is consistent across the network. Each node on the network validates transactions and updates the blockchain accordingly. This distributed processing model provides a high level of fault tolerance and ensures that the network remains operational even if some nodes fail.

One of the main advantages of traditional databases over blockchain is their scalability. Traditional databases can handle large amounts of data and are designed to be highly scalable, allowing organizations to add more resources as needed to support growing data volumes. In contrast, blockchain is currently limited in its scalability due to the way in which data is stored and processed. Each node on the network must process every transaction, which can lead to bottlenecks and slower transaction processing times.

However, there are also several advantages that blockchain has over traditional databases. One of the main advantages is its security. Blockchain provides a high level of security through its decentralized nature and immutability. Transactions on the blockchain cannot be altered or deleted once they have been added to the chain, providing a high level of data integrity.

Another advantage of blockchain is its transparency. The blockchain provides a complete and transparent record of all transactions that have ever taken place on the network. This level of transparency can be beneficial in industries such as finance, where it is important to maintain an accurate record of all transactions.

In conclusion, while blockchain and traditional databases share some similarities, there are several key differences between the two. Traditional databases are centralized systems that use query languages to access and manipulate data, while blockchain is a decentralized system that uses a chain of linked blocks to store and manage data. While traditional databases are highly scalable, blockchain provides a high level of security and transparency. As blockchain technology continues to evolve, it will be interesting to see how it is integrated with traditional database systems to create new and innovative solutions.

Integration of Blockchain with Traditional Database Systems

While blockchain technology offers unique advantages over traditional database systems, it is not without its limitations. One of the biggest challenges with blockchain is its scalability. As the number of users and transactions on a blockchain network increases, the size of the blockchain grows, and the network can become slow and inefficient.

To address this issue, some developers have proposed integrating blockchain technology with traditional database systems to create hybrid solutions that combine the strengths of both technologies. For example, a company could use a traditional database to store data that does not require the high level of security provided by blockchain, while using blockchain to store critical data that needs to be secured and audited.

One approach to integrating blockchain and traditional databases is to use a blockchain-as-a-service (BaaS) platform. BaaS providers offer pre-built blockchain networks that can be integrated with traditional databases, allowing companies to build secure and scalable applications without the need for extensive blockchain expertise.

Another approach is to use sidechains, which are separate blockchain networks that are connected to a main blockchain. Sidechains can be used to store data that does not need to be stored on the main blockchain, reducing the size of the main blockchain and increasing its scalability.

Despite the potential benefits of integrating blockchain and traditional databases, there are some challenges to consider. For example, integrating two different technologies can be complex and time-consuming, and requires expertise in both blockchain and traditional database systems.

Additionally, integrating blockchain with traditional databases can result in a loss of some of the benefits of blockchain technology. For example, using a traditional database to store some data may result in a loss of transparency and auditability, as well as a decrease in the overall security of the system.

Counter-arguments and Dissenting Opinions

While the benefits of blockchain technology are clear, some skeptics argue that the hype around blockchain is overblown and that the technology is not as revolutionary as its proponents claim. One common criticism of blockchain is that it is too slow and inefficient compared to traditional database systems. Because each transaction must be verified by multiple nodes on the network, the process of adding a new block to the chain can be time-consuming and resource-intensive. This has led some critics to argue that blockchain is not well-suited for high-volume transactions, such as those involved in financial trading.

Another criticism of blockchain is that it is still largely untested and unproven in real-world applications. While blockchain technology has been around for over a decade, it is still in the early stages of development and adoption. As a result, there are still many unknowns and uncertainties surrounding the technology, particularly in terms of its scalability, security, and regulatory implications.

Finally, some critics argue that the hype around blockchain is driven more by speculation and investment frenzy than by actual technological innovation. In recent years, there has been a surge of interest in blockchain and cryptocurrency from investors and speculators hoping to capitalize on the perceived potential of these emerging technologies. However, some argue that this interest has been fueled more by hype and speculation than by a genuine belief in the transformative potential of blockchain technology.

Despite these criticisms, there are many who remain bullish on the potential of blockchain technology. As more and more businesses and industries explore the use of blockchain, it is likely that we will see continued innovation and experimentation in this space. Whether or not blockchain ultimately lives up to its hype remains to be seen, but there is no denying that it has already had a significant impact on the world of technology and finance.

II. Technical aspects of blockchain

The technical aspects of blockchain are essential to understanding how the technology works and why it has the potential to revolutionize industries. Blockchain technology is a decentralized, distributed ledger system that stores data in a chain of linked blocks. The technology uses complex cryptographic algorithms to ensure the security, transparency, and immutability of the data stored on the blockchain.

At its core, blockchain is a database that stores information in a way that makes it virtually impossible to alter or hack. This is achieved through a combination of consensus mechanisms, encryption, and a distributed network of nodes that verify and validate transactions on the network. The technical design of blockchain provides several key benefits, including increased security, transparency, and decentralization.

To fully appreciate the technical aspects of blockchain, it is important to have a solid understanding of several key concepts, including:

Cryptography - Blockchain uses complex cryptographic algorithms to secure and protect the data stored on the network. This includes hash functions, digital signatures, and public-key cryptography.

Consensus mechanisms - Blockchain relies on consensus mechanisms to validate and verify transactions on the network. These mechanisms ensure that all nodes on the network agree on the state of the ledger.

Smart contracts - Smart contracts are self-executing contracts that automate the process of verifying and enforcing the terms of an agreement. Smart contracts are a key feature of many blockchain networks, allowing for the creation of decentralized applications and autonomous organizations.

Decentralization - Decentralization is a key feature of blockchain technology that eliminates the need for a central authority or intermediary. This allows for increased security, transparency, and censorship resistance.

Understanding these concepts is crucial for anyone looking to delve deeper into the technical aspects of blockchain. In the following sections, we will explore each of these concepts in more detail, providing a comprehensive overview of how blockchain technology works and why it has the potential to transform industries.

Distributed ledger technology

Distributed ledger technology, also known as DLT, is a type of technology that enables the creation and management of a decentralized database, which is stored across a network of computers. This technology has gained significant attention in recent years due to its ability to provide secure, transparent, and immutable record-keeping.

In this section, we will provide an in-depth analysis of the technical aspects of distributed ledger technology, including its architecture, consensus mechanisms, and various types of DLT.

Architecture of DLT:

The architecture of DLT is designed to enable the creation of a decentralized database, which is distributed across a network of computers. The architecture can be broadly classified into two categories: permissionless and permissioned.

In permissionless architecture, anyone can participate in the network, and there are no restrictions on who can read or write data. Bitcoin, the first application of blockchain technology, is an example of a permissionless architecture. In contrast, permissioned architecture requires participants to be authorized to read or write data to the network. Permissioned architecture is commonly used in enterprise settings, where access control is essential.

Consensus Mechanisms:

Consensus mechanisms play a crucial role in the functioning of DLT networks. The primary function of a consensus mechanism is to ensure that all nodes in the network agree on the same state of the database.

There are various consensus mechanisms used in DLT networks, including Proof of Work (PoW), Proof of Stake (PoS), and Byzantine Fault Tolerance (BFT). In PoW, miners compete to solve complex mathematical problems, and the first miner to solve the problem is rewarded with a block of cryptocurrency. In PoS, validators are selected to verify transactions based on the amount of cryptocurrency they hold. BFT is a fault-tolerant consensus mechanism that can tolerate up to one-third of the nodes being faulty.

Types of DLT:

There are several types of DLT, including blockchain, directed acyclic graph (DAG), and hashgraph. Blockchain is the most well-known type of DLT and is commonly used in cryptocurrencies. DAG is a newer type of DLT and is used in some cryptocurrencies, such as IOTA. Hashgraph is a patented technology that is designed to provide a more efficient and secure way of reaching consensus in a DLT network.

Blockchain Technology:

Blockchain technology is a type of DLT that enables the creation of a decentralized, tamper-proof database. The database is stored across a network of computers, and all participants in the network have a copy of the database.

A blockchain consists of a chain of blocks, where each block contains a set of transactions. Each block is linked to the previous block in the chain, creating an immutable record of transactions. Once a block is added to the chain, it cannot be altered or deleted.

Blockchain technology is commonly used in cryptocurrencies, but it also has various other applications, such as supply chain management, voting systems, and identity management.

Conclusion:

Distributed ledger technology is a type of technology that enables the creation and management of a decentralized database, which is stored across a network of computers. This technology has gained significant attention in recent years due to its ability to provide secure, transparent, and immutable record-keeping.

The architecture of DLT can be broadly classified into two categories: permissionless and permissioned. Consensus mechanisms play a crucial role in the functioning of DLT networks, and there are various types of DLT, including blockchain, DAG, and hashgraph.

Overall, DLT has the potential to revolutionize various industries, and as the technology continues to evolve, it will be interesting to see how it is applied in new and innovative ways.

Consensus algorithms

Consensus algorithms are a key component of blockchain technology. They are responsible for ensuring that all participants in a blockchain network agree on the state of the ledger. In this section, we will explore the different types of consensus algorithms used in blockchain networks, their strengths and weaknesses, and their application in various industries.

Proof of Work (PoW)
Proof of Work is the first consensus algorithm used in blockchain networks, and it is the one used in the Bitcoin network. It is a computationally intensive algorithm that requires participants, called miners, to

solve complex mathematical problems to validate transactions and add new blocks to the blockchain. The first miner to solve the problem is rewarded with newly minted coins. The algorithm ensures that the blockchain is immutable and secure by making it computationally expensive to rewrite history.

While PoW has proven to be effective in securing the Bitcoin network, it has several drawbacks. First, it requires a significant amount of computational power, which leads to high energy consumption and a high carbon footprint. Second, it is prone to centralization, as larger mining operations have an advantage in solving the mathematical problems and earning the rewards. Finally, it is slow, with blocks added to the Bitcoin blockchain every ten minutes.

Proof of Stake (PoS)

Proof of Stake is a consensus algorithm that addresses some of the drawbacks of PoW. Instead of requiring participants to solve complex mathematical problems, PoS requires participants, called validators, to hold a stake in the network. Validators are selected to validate transactions and add new blocks to the blockchain based on the size of their stake. The algorithm ensures that the blockchain is secure and immutable by requiring validators to put their stake at risk if they attempt to cheat the system.

PoS has several advantages over PoW. First, it is more energy-efficient, as it does not require the same amount of computational power. Second, it is more decentralized, as participants do not need expensive equipment to participate in the network. Finally, it is faster, with blocks added to the blockchain every few seconds.

Delegated Proof of Stake (DPoS)

Delegated Proof of Stake is a variant of PoS that is used in several blockchain networks, including EOS and BitShares. In DPoS, participants can vote for delegates to validate transactions and add new blocks to the blockchain. Delegates are selected based on the number of votes they receive. The algorithm ensures that the blockchain is secure and immutable by requiring delegates to put their reputation at risk if they attempt to cheat the system.

DPoS has several advantages over PoS. First, it is more scalable, as the number of delegates can be adjusted to handle higher transaction volumes. Second, it is more efficient, as delegates are responsible for validating transactions and adding new blocks to the blockchain, rather than all participants in the network. Finally, it is more decentralized than PoW, as participants can choose to vote for delegates who represent their interests.

Byzantine Fault Tolerance (BFT)

Byzantine Fault Tolerance is a consensus algorithm used in permissioned blockchain networks, where participants are known and trusted. In BFT, participants are required to reach a consensus on the state of the ledger through a series of rounds of voting. The algorithm ensures that the blockchain is secure and immutable by requiring a supermajority of participants to agree on the state of the ledger.

BFT has several advantages over other consensus algorithms. First, it is more secure, as participants are known and trusted. Second, it is faster, with blocks added to the blockchain every few seconds. Finally, it is more efficient, as only a subset of participants are required to participate in the consensus process.

Practical Byzantine Fault Tolerance (PBFT)

Practical Byzantine Fault Tolerance is a variant of BFT that is used in permissioned blockchain networks. PBFT was introduced in 1999 by Miguel Castro and Barbara Liskov in a research paper titled "Practical Byzantine Fault Tolerance".

In PBFT, a consensus is reached through a series of rounds. Each round consists of three phases: pre-prepare, prepare, and commit. In the pre-prepare phase, a leader node broadcasts a proposed block to all nodes in the network. In the prepare phase, each node broadcasts a message to all other nodes indicating that they have received the proposed block and they believe it to be valid. In the commit phase, each node broadcasts a message to all other nodes indicating that they have received enough prepare messages to reach consensus on the proposed block. Once a node receives a commit message from a majority of nodes, it adds the proposed block to the blockchain.

PBFT has several advantages over other consensus algorithms. First, it is highly fault-tolerant, as it can tolerate up to one-third of nodes being malicious or faulty. Second, it is efficient, as it requires only $O(n^2)$ messages to reach consensus, where n is the number of nodes in the network. Third, it is deterministic, meaning that all honest nodes will eventually reach the same consensus, regardless of the order in which they receive messages.

However, PBFT also has some drawbacks. One of the main drawbacks is that it is not scalable, as the number of messages required to reach consensus increases quadratically with the number of nodes in the network. This makes PBFT impractical for large-scale networks. Additionally, PBFT assumes that all nodes in the network are online and responsive, which may not always be the case in practice.

Proof of Stake (PoS)

Proof of Stake is a consensus algorithm that was first proposed in 2011 by Sunny King and Scott Nadal as an alternative to the energy-intensive Proof of Work algorithm used in Bitcoin. In PoS, block validators, also known as validators or forgers, are chosen based on their stake in the network, which is typically measured by the number of tokens they hold.

In PoS, validators are selected to create blocks based on their stake in the network. The more tokens a validator holds, the more likely they are to be chosen to create the next block. Once a validator is chosen to create a block, they must put up a stake, or a deposit, as collateral. If the validator creates an invalid block or tries to cheat the network, their stake is forfeited.

PoS has several advantages over PoW. First, it is more energy-efficient, as it does not require the same level of computational power as PoW. Second, it is more scalable, as the number of validators can be increased without increasing the energy consumption of the network. Third, it is more secure, as it makes it more expensive for attackers to try to control the network.

However, PoS also has some drawbacks. One of the main drawbacks is that it can lead to centralization, as validators with more tokens have a greater chance of being chosen to create blocks, which can lead to a concentration of power in the hands of a few validators. Additionally, PoS can be vulnerable to certain attacks, such as long-range attacks and nothing-at-stake attacks, which can compromise the security of the network. Finally, PoS can be complex to implement and requires careful design to ensure its security and effectiveness.

Conclusion

Consensus algorithms are a critical component of blockchain technology, as they enable nodes in a network to agree on the state of the system without the need for a central authority. BFT and its variants, such as PBFT, provide a high level of security and fault-tolerance, but can be impractical for large-scale networks. PoS provides an energy-efficient and scalable alternative to PoW, but its security is highly dependent on the distribution of stake among participants. DPoS, on the other hand, sacrifices some level of security for increased scalability and efficiency.

While each consensus algorithm has its own strengths and weaknesses, it is important to carefully consider the requirements and limitations of a particular use case before selecting an algorithm. For example, a private blockchain network with a limited number of known and trusted participants may opt for BFT or

PBFT, while a public blockchain network with a large number of anonymous participants may choose PoW or PoS.

As blockchain technology continues to evolve and new consensus algorithms are developed, it is important to remain vigilant of potential security threats and ensure that the chosen algorithm is appropriate for the particular use case. Ultimately, the success of a blockchain network depends on the effectiveness and efficiency of its consensus algorithm, as it directly affects the security, scalability, and overall performance of the system.

Smart contracts

Smart contracts are self-executing digital contracts that can automatically trigger a set of actions or transactions when predefined conditions are met. They are computer programs that run on top of blockchain technology and can be used to automate various processes in a secure, transparent, and decentralized manner. In this section, we will provide a comprehensive overview of smart contracts, including their history, functionality, use cases, benefits, and challenges.

History of Smart Contracts

The concept of smart contracts was first introduced by computer scientist and legal scholar Nick Szabo in 1994. Szabo envisioned smart contracts as digital protocols that could facilitate, verify, and enforce the negotiation or performance of a contract without the need for intermediaries. He believed that smart contracts could revolutionize various fields, including finance, law, and governance, by reducing costs, increasing efficiency, and eliminating fraud and corruption.

Despite Szabo's visionary ideas, smart contracts remained a theoretical concept for many years, as the technology required to implement them was not yet available. It was not until the emergence of blockchain technology and its first implementation, Bitcoin, that smart contracts became a reality. In 2014, Ethereum, the first blockchain platform designed specifically for smart contracts, was launched, enabling developers to create and deploy decentralized applications (DApps) that could execute smart contracts.

Functionality of Smart Contracts

Smart contracts are written in programming languages that are designed to be executed by computers. They are self-executing, meaning that once they are deployed on the blockchain, they can run without the need for human intervention. Smart contracts can perform a wide range of functions, including:

Facilitating the transfer of digital assets, such as cryptocurrencies or tokens, between parties
Automating the execution of contracts and agreements, such as insurance policies or rental agreements
Enforcing the terms of agreements, such as automatically releasing funds when certain conditions are met
Managing supply chains and tracking the movement of goods
Creating decentralized autonomous organizations (DAOs), which are organizations that operate through smart contracts and do not require a central authority

One key advantage of smart contracts is their ability to automate and streamline processes, reducing the need for intermediaries and increasing efficiency. For example, in a traditional real estate transaction, there are often many intermediaries involved, such as real estate agents, lawyers, and banks. Smart contracts can potentially eliminate the need for these intermediaries, resulting in faster, cheaper, and more secure transactions.

Smart contracts can also help to reduce the potential for fraud and errors in transactions. Because smart contracts are executed automatically and recorded on the blockchain, there is a high degree of transparency and immutability. This makes it much more difficult for bad actors to manipulate or alter the terms of an agreement.

However, there are also some limitations and challenges associated with smart contracts. One challenge is that smart contracts are only as good as the code they are written in. If there are errors or vulnerabilities in the code, it can potentially lead to unintended consequences or even financial losses. For example, in 2016, a smart contract on the Ethereum blockchain known as "The DAO" was hacked, resulting in the theft of over $50 million worth of cryptocurrency.

Another challenge is the issue of legal enforceability. While smart contracts can automate the execution and enforcement of agreements, they are not yet widely recognized as legally binding contracts in many jurisdictions. This means that if there is a dispute or breach of contract, it may not be possible to rely on a smart contract as evidence in court.

Despite these challenges, smart contracts have the potential to revolutionize many industries and business processes. They can help to reduce costs, increase efficiency, and improve transparency and security. As blockchain technology continues to evolve, it is likely that smart contracts will become an increasingly important part of the ecosystem.

III. Use cases of blockchain technology

Blockchain technology has been hailed as a game-changer for various industries, providing a secure, transparent, and decentralized way to store and transfer data and assets. It was initially designed to support the transfer of cryptocurrencies, but its potential applications have expanded far beyond that.

In this article, we will explore the use cases of blockchain technology across different sectors, including finance, supply chain management, healthcare, real estate, and more. We will examine how blockchain technology can solve specific problems in each industry and provide examples of companies that are already implementing it.

Finance

One of the most significant applications of blockchain technology is in the financial sector. Blockchain technology can help improve the efficiency and security of financial transactions while reducing costs. Here are some of the ways blockchain is being used in finance:

Cross-border payments
Traditional cross-border payments can be slow, expensive, and prone to errors. Blockchain technology can simplify and speed up the process by removing intermediaries and reducing transaction costs. Ripple is one company that is using blockchain technology to enable real-time cross-border payments.

Securities trading
Blockchain technology can enable faster and more secure securities trading by eliminating the need for intermediaries and automating the settlement process. Overstock's subsidiary tZero is developing a blockchain-based platform for securities trading.

Identity verification
Blockchain technology can help improve identity verification by providing a tamper-proof and decentralized system for storing and verifying personal information. Civic is a company that is using blockchain technology for identity verification.

Supply Chain Management

Supply chain management involves the movement of goods and services from raw materials to finished products. It is a complex process that involves multiple stakeholders, including suppliers, manufacturers, distributors, and retailers. Blockchain technology can help improve transparency, traceability, and efficiency in the supply chain. Here are some of the ways blockchain is being used in supply chain management:

Tracking products
Blockchain technology can enable the tracking of products from raw materials to finished products, providing complete transparency and traceability. Walmart is using blockchain technology to track the origin of produce, while De Beers is using it to track the origin of diamonds.

Supply chain finance
Blockchain technology can help improve access to financing for suppliers by providing a transparent and secure system for tracking invoices and payments. Provenance is a company that is using blockchain technology for supply chain finance.

Counterfeit prevention
Blockchain technology can help prevent counterfeit products from entering the supply chain by enabling the tracking of products from the source to the end consumer. VeChain is a company that is using blockchain technology for anti-counterfeit purposes.

Healthcare

Healthcare is another sector that can benefit significantly from blockchain technology. Blockchain technology can help improve the security and privacy of health records, reduce medical errors, and enable better collaboration between healthcare providers. Here are some of the ways blockchain is being used in healthcare:

Electronic health records
Blockchain technology can provide a secure and tamper-proof system for storing and sharing electronic health records. MedRec is a company that is using blockchain technology for electronic health records.

Clinical trials
Blockchain technology can enable more efficient and transparent clinical trials by providing a tamper-proof and decentralized system for tracking and sharing data. Boehringer Ingelheim is a pharmaceutical company that is using blockchain technology for clinical trials.

Drug supply chain management
Blockchain technology can help improve drug supply chain management by providing complete transparency and traceability. Chronicled is a company that is using blockchain technology for drug supply chain management.

Real Estate

Real estate is another industry that can benefit significantly from blockchain technology. Blockchain technology can help improve the transparency, efficiency, and security of real estate transactions. Here are some of the ways blockchain is being used in real estate:

Title management
Blockchain technology can provide a tamper-proof and decentralized system for managing and transferring real estate titles. Real estate titles are a critical component of real estate transactions, as they provide proof of ownership of the property. Traditionally, title management involves a cumbersome and time-consuming process that can be prone to errors and fraud. With blockchain technology, real estate titles can be stored in a secure and immutable ledger, providing a more efficient and transparent system for managing and transferring titles.

For example, Propy is a blockchain-based platform that enables the buying and selling of real estate using smart contracts. The platform uses blockchain technology to manage property titles and transfer ownership, ensuring that the transaction is secure and transparent.

Property management
Blockchain technology can also be used for property management, including rent collection, maintenance, and repair tracking. By using blockchain technology, property managers can streamline the management process and reduce administrative costs.

For example, Ubitquity is a blockchain-based platform that provides a solution for property management. The platform enables property managers to track maintenance requests, collect rent, and manage tenants, all through a decentralized system.

Real estate crowdfunding
Blockchain technology can also be used for real estate crowdfunding, allowing investors to invest in real estate projects using cryptocurrency. Real estate crowdfunding can provide a more accessible and efficient way for investors to invest in real estate projects, as it eliminates the need for intermediaries and reduces transaction costs.

For example, RealT is a blockchain-based platform that enables investors to invest in fractional ownership of real estate properties using cryptocurrency. The platform uses blockchain technology to provide a secure and transparent system for real estate crowdfunding.

In conclusion, the real estate industry can benefit significantly from blockchain technology, as it provides a more efficient, secure, and transparent system for managing real estate transactions. By using blockchain technology, real estate companies can improve their operations and provide a better experience for their customers.

Finance and banking

The finance and banking industry is one of the most significant areas that have experienced disruption and innovation due to the introduction of blockchain technology. Blockchain technology has the potential to transform traditional banking and finance systems by providing increased efficiency, transparency, and security. In this section, we will discuss how blockchain technology is being used in the finance and banking industry and its potential applications in the future.

The Current State of Finance and Banking:

The finance and banking industry is one of the most crucial sectors in the global economy, responsible for managing and transferring money and other assets. However, traditional banking and finance systems are slow, costly, and not entirely secure, leading to the need for more innovative and efficient solutions. With the advent of blockchain technology, banks and financial institutions can leverage decentralized systems to make transactions faster, more secure, and more efficient.

Blockchain in Finance and Banking:
Blockchain technology has many potential applications in the finance and banking industry. Here are some of the ways blockchain is being used in finance and banking:

Cross-border payments:
Blockchain technology can enable faster and cheaper cross-border payments by eliminating the need for intermediaries such as correspondent banks. In traditional cross-border payments, several intermediaries are involved, which can result in high transaction fees, slow processing times, and increased risk of fraud. With blockchain technology, cross-border payments can be made in real-time, with reduced fees and increased security.

Digital identity verification:
Identity verification is a crucial aspect of the finance and banking industry, with banks and financial institutions required to comply with Know Your Customer (KYC) regulations. Blockchain technology can provide a secure and tamper-proof system for digital identity verification, reducing the risk of identity theft and fraud. By using blockchain technology, banks can securely and quickly verify customer identities and comply with KYC regulations.

Trade finance:
Blockchain technology can improve the efficiency and transparency of trade finance by providing a decentralized and tamper-proof system for managing trade finance transactions. The use of smart contracts can automate the entire trade finance process, from the issuance of letters of credit to the settlement of funds. This can significantly reduce the time and cost associated with trade finance and improve the accuracy and efficiency of transactions.

Securities trading:
Blockchain technology can provide a decentralized system for securities trading, making the process faster, more transparent, and more secure. With blockchain technology, securities trading can be executed in real-time, reducing the need for intermediaries and eliminating the risk of settlement failures. This can result in reduced transaction fees and increased efficiency in the securities trading process.

Asset management:
Blockchain technology can provide a more transparent and secure system for asset management. By using blockchain technology, asset managers can track the ownership and transfer of assets in real-time, reducing the risk of fraud and errors. Additionally, smart contracts can be used to automate asset management processes, resulting in increased efficiency and accuracy.

Challenges and Limitations:
Despite the many potential applications of blockchain technology in the finance and banking industry, there are also several challenges and limitations. One of the significant challenges is the regulatory landscape, as many countries are still unsure of how to regulate blockchain technology. Additionally, there is a need for increased collaboration between banks and financial institutions to fully leverage the benefits of blockchain technology. There are also concerns around the scalability and security of blockchain networks, which will need to be addressed before widespread adoption can occur.

Conclusion:

Blockchain technology has the potential to revolutionize the finance and banking industry by providing increased efficiency, transparency, and security. By using blockchain technology, banks and financial institutions can reduce transaction fees, speed up processing times, and improve the accuracy and security of transactions. However, there are still several challenges and limitations that need to be addressed before widespread adoption can occur. As the regulatory landscape becomes clearer, and more collaboration occurs between banks and financial institutions, we can expect to see more innovative uses of blockchain technology in the finance and banking industry.

One of the biggest challenges for blockchain adoption in finance and banking is the issue of scalability. Current blockchain technology is still not capable of processing large numbers of transactions quickly and efficiently. However, there are several new blockchain technologies being developed that aim to address this issue, such as sharding and plasma.

Another challenge is the need for standardization and interoperability between different blockchain networks. With so many different blockchain platforms and protocols, it can be challenging to connect different systems and ensure seamless communication. Efforts are being made to create universal standards, such as the Enterprise Ethereum Alliance, which brings together major companies to collaborate on blockchain solutions.

There are also concerns about security and privacy in blockchain transactions. While blockchain technology provides an inherently secure and transparent system, there are still potential vulnerabilities and risks that need to be addressed. For example, private keys can be lost or stolen, and there is always the risk of hacking and cyber attacks. However, advancements in security protocols and cryptography are continually improving the security of blockchain systems.

Overall, the finance and banking industry has a lot to gain from embracing blockchain technology. As more companies and institutions begin to recognize the potential of blockchain, we can expect to see increased investment and innovation in the space. With continued collaboration and innovation, blockchain technology has the potential to transform the finance and banking industry, making it more secure, efficient, and accessible for everyone.

Supply chain management

The supply chain is a critical aspect of any business operation that involves the movement of goods and services from the manufacturer to the end consumer. It is a complex process that involves numerous stakeholders, including suppliers, manufacturers, distributors, and retailers. The supply chain process is often hampered by several inefficiencies, including a lack of transparency, fraud, and a lack of trust among the parties involved. Blockchain technology has the potential to revolutionize the supply chain industry by providing increased transparency, security, and efficiency. In this section, we will explore the potential applications of blockchain technology in supply chain management and the benefits it offers.

Blockchain in Supply Chain Management:

Blockchain technology is a decentralized, distributed ledger that is used to record transactions between parties without the need for a central authority. It offers a transparent and secure way of recording transactions and can be used to improve the efficiency and transparency of supply chain operations. Here are some of the potential applications of blockchain technology in supply chain management:

Transparency and Traceability:
Blockchain technology can provide increased transparency and traceability in the supply chain process. By recording every transaction on a decentralized ledger, stakeholders can track the movement of goods and services from the manufacturer to the end consumer. This can help prevent fraud and ensure that the goods being shipped are authentic.

For example, Walmart has implemented a blockchain-based system to track the movement of food products from the farm to the store. By scanning a QR code on the product, customers can trace the product's journey from the farm to the store, including information on the product's origin, production, and shipping.

Streamlined Payment Process:
Blockchain technology can also streamline the payment process in the supply chain industry. By using smart contracts, payments can be automatically triggered once certain conditions are met, such as the delivery of goods. This can help reduce transaction costs and speed up the payment process.

For example, in the coffee industry, farmers often face long payment delays and high transaction fees. By using blockchain technology, farmers can receive payment immediately upon delivery of their coffee to the buyer, without the need for intermediaries.

Inventory Management:
Blockchain technology can also be used to improve inventory management in the supply chain industry. By recording every transaction on a decentralized ledger, stakeholders can track the movement of goods and services in real-time. This can help prevent overstocking and understocking of goods, which can lead to losses for the business.

For example, IBM has developed a blockchain-based system to manage the supply chain of diamonds. By recording every transaction on the blockchain, stakeholders can track the movement of diamonds in real-time, including information on the origin, quality, and certification of the diamonds.

Enhanced Efficiency:
Blockchain technology can also enhance the efficiency of the supply chain process by automating several tasks. By using smart contracts, several tasks can be automatically triggered once certain conditions are met, such as the delivery of goods. This can help reduce the time and resources required for manual tasks, such as the processing of invoices and shipping documents.

For example, Maersk, the world's largest shipping company, has implemented a blockchain-based system to automate several tasks in the supply chain process, including the processing of shipping documents and the tracking of goods.

Increased Security:
Blockchain technology offers increased security in the supply chain process by providing a tamper-proof and decentralized system for recording transactions. By recording every transaction on the blockchain, stakeholders can be assured that the information is accurate and cannot be altered by malicious actors.

For example, in the pharmaceutical industry, counterfeit drugs are a significant problem that can result in harm to patients. By using blockchain technology, stakeholders can track the movement of drugs from the manufacturer to the end consumer, ensuring that the drugs being shipped are authentic and safe.

Limitations and Challenges:

While blockchain technology offers several benefits for supply chain management, there are still some limitations and challenges that need to be addressed.

One major limitation is the cost of implementing a blockchain system. Developing and deploying a blockchain solution can be expensive, and may require significant investment from companies. This may be a barrier to entry for smaller companies that cannot afford the cost of implementing a blockchain solution.

Another challenge is the need for standardization. For blockchain technology to be effective in supply chain management, there needs to be a standardized system that can be used across different industries and companies. This will require collaboration and cooperation between different stakeholders, which may be difficult to achieve.

There are also concerns around data privacy and security. While blockchain technology is generally considered to be secure, there is still a risk of data breaches or hacking. Companies will need to implement strong security measures to protect sensitive data on the blockchain.

Finally, there may be resistance to change from stakeholders in the supply chain. Traditional methods of supply chain management have been in place for decades, and some companies may be reluctant to adopt new technologies and processes. This may require education and persuasion to convince stakeholders of the benefits of blockchain technology.

Despite these challenges, the potential benefits of blockchain technology for supply chain management are significant. By improving transparency, traceability, and efficiency, blockchain technology can help companies optimize their supply chain operations and improve the overall performance of their business. As the technology continues to evolve and improve, it is likely that more companies will begin to adopt blockchain solutions for their supply chain management needs.

Healthcare and medical records

Healthcare is a critical sector that has a significant impact on human life. The healthcare industry deals with vast amounts of data, ranging from patient records, medical research, clinical trials, and drug development. The sector has a complex and fragmented system that requires transparency, security, and privacy. However, the current system is outdated, and there is a lack of interoperability, making it difficult to share information between healthcare providers. Blockchain technology offers a promising solution that could transform the healthcare industry by improving data management, privacy, and security. This paper will explore the use cases of blockchain technology in healthcare and medical records and the challenges and limitations that need to be addressed for widespread adoption.

Use Cases of Blockchain Technology in Healthcare:

Medical Records Management:
Medical records management is a critical area that could benefit significantly from blockchain technology. Blockchain technology can provide a secure and tamper-proof system for storing and sharing medical records between healthcare providers. Patients can have control over their data, allowing them to share their medical records securely and efficiently. This approach can improve patient privacy, data integrity, and reduce the risk of data breaches.

Clinical Trials:
Clinical trials are a crucial part of drug development and play a critical role in the healthcare industry. However, the current system for conducting clinical trials is outdated and inefficient, resulting in delays, high costs, and low participation rates. Blockchain technology can streamline the clinical trials process by creating a decentralized system that allows for secure and transparent data sharing. This approach can increase participation rates, reduce costs, and improve the accuracy of data collection.

Drug Supply Chain Management:
The drug supply chain is a complex and fragmented system that involves several stakeholders, including manufacturers, distributors, pharmacies, and patients. Blockchain technology can provide transparency and traceability throughout the drug supply chain, ensuring that drugs are authentic, safe, and effective. The blockchain can record every transaction, from the manufacturer to the patient, making it possible to track the drug's journey and identify any counterfeit or adulterated products.

Telemedicine:
Telemedicine is a growing trend in the healthcare industry, allowing patients to receive medical care remotely. However, the current system for telemedicine lacks transparency and security, making it vulnerable to data breaches and privacy violations. Blockchain technology can provide a secure and decentralized system for telemedicine, allowing patients to access medical care from anywhere in the world. This approach can improve patient privacy, reduce costs, and increase access to medical care.

Health Insurance:
Health insurance is a critical component of the healthcare industry, providing coverage for medical expenses. However, the current system for health insurance is inefficient, resulting in high administrative costs and fraud. Blockchain technology can streamline the health insurance process by creating a decentralized system that allows for secure and transparent data sharing. This approach can reduce administrative costs, prevent fraud, and improve the accuracy of claims processing.

Challenges and Limitations:

Regulatory Framework:
The healthcare industry is heavily regulated, and the adoption of blockchain technology requires compliance with regulatory frameworks. The regulatory environment for blockchain technology is still evolving, and there is a need for clarity on how blockchain technology will be regulated.

Interoperability:
The healthcare industry is fragmented, with several healthcare providers using different systems to manage patient data. This lack of interoperability makes it difficult to share data between healthcare providers. Blockchain technology can solve this problem by creating a decentralized system that allows for secure and efficient data sharing. However, the adoption of blockchain technology requires cooperation between different stakeholders in the healthcare industry.

Privacy and Security:
Privacy and security are critical issues in the healthcare industry, and the adoption of blockchain technology requires a robust security framework. While blockchain technology provides a secure and tamper-proof system for storing and sharing data, there is a need for additional security measures to ensure the privacy and security of patient data.

One of the main concerns with blockchain technology is the potential for data breaches. While the technology is secure, it is not foolproof, and hackers may still be able to find vulnerabilities in the system. To address this concern, healthcare organizations must implement additional security measures such as encryption, multi-factor authentication, and regular audits of the blockchain network.

Another challenge is ensuring that only authorized parties have access to patient data. While blockchain technology allows for the secure sharing of data, it must be designed to ensure that only authorized parties can access the data. This can be achieved through the use of smart contracts, which can enforce rules for accessing and sharing data.

Despite these challenges, blockchain technology offers several benefits for the healthcare industry. By using blockchain technology, healthcare organizations can reduce costs, improve data interoperability, and enhance patient outcomes.

One area where blockchain technology is being used in healthcare is medical records management. Medical records contain sensitive information, and the traditional paper-based system is prone to errors, lost records, and security breaches. By using blockchain technology, medical records can be stored in a secure and tamper-proof system that is accessible only to authorized parties.

Blockchain technology can also be used to streamline the clinical trials process. Clinical trials are critical for the development of new drugs and therapies, but the process is time-consuming and expensive. By using blockchain technology, clinical trials can be conducted more efficiently, reducing costs and accelerating the development of new treatments.

Another area where blockchain technology is being used in healthcare is supply chain management. The healthcare supply chain is complex, involving multiple stakeholders, and is often prone to inefficiencies and fraud. By using blockchain technology, healthcare organizations can track the movement of goods and ensure that they are authentic and not counterfeit.

Finally, blockchain technology can be used to incentivize healthy behaviors. For example, a healthcare organization can use blockchain technology to create a rewards program for patients who meet certain health goals Finally, blockchain technology can be used to incentivize healthy behaviors. For example, a healthcare organization can use blockchain technology to create a rewards program for patients who meet certain health goals, such as quitting smoking or maintaining a healthy weight. This can be done through the use of smart contracts that automatically reward patients with cryptocurrency or other incentives when they meet their goals.

However, there are also challenges and limitations to the use of blockchain technology in healthcare. One major challenge is the interoperability of different blockchain systems. As healthcare organizations adopt different blockchain platforms, there may be issues with integrating these systems and ensuring that data can be seamlessly transferred between them. There is also a need for standards and regulations to ensure that patient data is handled appropriately and that privacy is maintained.

Another challenge is the need for widespread adoption of blockchain technology in the healthcare industry. While blockchain has the potential to revolutionize the way healthcare data is stored and shared, it requires a significant investment in infrastructure and training. There may also be resistance to change from healthcare professionals who are used to traditional systems.

In addition, there are concerns about the scalability of blockchain technology in healthcare. As the amount of healthcare data continues to grow, there may be issues with the speed and efficiency of blockchain systems in handling large amounts of data.

Despite these challenges, the use of blockchain technology in healthcare is a promising development that has the potential to improve patient outcomes and revolutionize the healthcare industry. As blockchain technology continues to evolve and mature, it is likely that we will see even more innovative use cases in healthcare and medical records.

IV. Challenges and future developments

Blockchain technology has emerged as a disruptive force, with the potential to transform a wide range of industries, including finance, supply chain management, and healthcare. It offers several benefits, such as increased transparency, efficiency, and security, and has the potential to reduce costs and streamline processes. However, the adoption of blockchain technology is not without challenges and limitations.

One of the most significant challenges facing the adoption of blockchain technology is regulatory compliance. Governments and regulatory bodies are still grappling with how to regulate the use of blockchain technology, particularly with respect to issues such as data privacy, cybersecurity, and anti-money laundering (AML) regulations. The lack of a clear regulatory framework has made it difficult for companies to adopt blockchain technology, as they are unsure of how to navigate the legal and regulatory landscape.

Another challenge facing the adoption of blockchain technology is scalability. As blockchain technology becomes more widely adopted, the number of transactions that need to be processed will increase exponentially. However, current blockchain systems, such as Bitcoin and Ethereum, have limited scalability, which means that they cannot handle large volumes of transactions without significant delays and high transaction fees. This limits the ability of blockchain technology to compete with traditional payment systems such as Visa and Mastercard.

Interoperability is another challenge facing the adoption of blockchain technology. There are currently many different blockchain platforms and protocols, each with their own set of rules and standards. This makes it difficult for different blockchains to communicate and exchange data with each other, which limits the potential for blockchain technology to be used in a wide range of applications.

Another challenge facing the adoption of blockchain technology is the issue of energy consumption. Blockchain technology requires significant computational resources, which means that it can be very energy-intensive. This is a concern, particularly as the world becomes more focused on sustainability and reducing carbon emissions.

Despite these challenges, there are several future developments that could help overcome these obstacles and drive the adoption of blockchain technology in various industries. One such development is the emergence of new blockchain platforms that are designed to be more energy-efficient. For example, the Proof-of-Stake (PoS) consensus mechanism is gaining popularity as a more environmentally friendly alternative to the energy-intensive Proof-of-Work (PoW) mechanism used in many existing blockchain networks, such as Bitcoin and Ethereum.

Another future development that could promote the adoption of blockchain technology is the integration of artificial intelligence (AI) and machine learning (ML) algorithms. AI and ML can be used to analyze the vast amounts of data stored on the blockchain, identifying patterns and insights that could help improve decision-making processes across various industries. For example, in the healthcare industry, AI and ML could be used to analyze patient data stored on the blockchain, identifying correlations between different medical conditions and improving treatment outcomes.

Furthermore, the development of interoperable blockchain networks could also drive adoption. Currently, many blockchain networks operate independently, making it difficult for data to be shared between them. Interoperable blockchain networks would enable different blockchain networks to communicate with each other, allowing for more seamless data sharing and collaboration between different industries and organizations.

In addition to these technical developments, the regulatory landscape surrounding blockchain technology is also evolving. Governments and regulatory bodies around the world are beginning to develop frameworks for regulating blockchain-based applications and digital assets. This regulatory clarity could help to reduce uncertainty and encourage wider adoption of blockchain technology in various industries.

Finally, increased collaboration between different industries and organizations could also help drive the adoption of blockchain technology. For example, collaborations between healthcare organizations and technology companies could help to develop new blockchain-based solutions for medical records and patient data management. Similarly, collaborations between financial institutions and blockchain startups could help to create new financial products and services that leverage blockchain technology.

In conclusion, while there are several challenges and obstacles facing the adoption of blockchain technology, there are also numerous developments and initiatives that could help to overcome these challenges and drive the adoption of blockchain technology in various industries. The future of blockchain technology looks bright, and its potential to revolutionize industries from finance to healthcare to supply chain management cannot be underestimated. As blockchain technology continues to evolve and mature, it will be fascinating to see the ways in which it transforms the world we live in.

Scalability and performance issues

Blockchain technology has seen exponential growth in recent years and has become a popular topic of discussion across a range of industries, including finance, healthcare, supply chain management, and more. One of the main reasons for this interest is the potential of blockchain technology to provide a decentralized, secure, and transparent way of recording and transferring data.

However, as with any emerging technology, there are still several challenges that need to be addressed to ensure the widespread adoption of blockchain technology. One of these challenges is scalability and performance issues.

Scalability refers to the ability of a system to handle increasing levels of demand, while performance refers to the speed and efficiency with which the system operates. In the case of blockchain technology, these issues are particularly important, as the technology is designed to process large amounts of data in a decentralized way.

As blockchain technology becomes more widely adopted, it is essential to address scalability and performance issues to ensure that the technology can continue to provide the benefits it promises while meeting the needs of users.

This section will explore the challenges facing the scalability and performance of blockchain technology and examine potential solutions to address these issues. We will also consider the implications of these solutions for the wider adoption and use of blockchain technology.

Challenges in Scalability and Performance:

One of the key challenges in scalability and performance is the size of the blockchain itself. The blockchain is essentially a distributed ledger that contains all the transactions that have taken place on the network. As more transactions are added to the network, the size of the blockchain grows, and this can create issues with storage and processing.

The size of the blockchain can also affect the time it takes to validate transactions. In a blockchain network, transactions must be validated by a network of nodes to ensure that they are legitimate. As the blockchain grows in size, it takes longer for nodes to validate transactions, which can slow down the overall performance of the network.

Another challenge in scalability and performance is the limited number of transactions that can be processed per second. Bitcoin, for example, can process only about seven transactions per second, while Visa can process tens of thousands of transactions per second. This limitation can become a significant bottleneck for blockchain networks, particularly in high-demand scenarios.

The consensus mechanism used by blockchain networks can also affect scalability and performance. The most commonly used consensus mechanism in blockchain networks is Proof of Work (PoW), which requires a significant amount of computational power to validate transactions. This can be a time-consuming process and can limit the number of transactions that can be processed per second.

Solutions for Scalability and Performance:

Several solutions have been proposed to address scalability and performance issues in blockchain technology. One solution is to use off-chain solutions, such as payment channels or sidechains. These solutions enable transactions to take place off the main blockchain, reducing the overall load on the network.

Another solution is to use different consensus mechanisms that require less computational power. Proof of Stake (PoS), for example, requires users to hold a certain amount of cryptocurrency to validate transactions, rather than relying on computational power. This can significantly reduce the time required to validate transactions and increase the number of transactions that can be processed per second.

Another approach to scalability and performance is to use sharding. Sharding involves dividing the blockchain into smaller sections or shards, each of which can process transactions independently. This can significantly increase the number of transactions that can be processed per second and reduce the time required to validate transactions.

Implications for Adoption and Use:

Addressing scalability and performance issues is critical for the widespread adoption and use of blockchain technology. If the technology cannot handle increasing levels of demand or process transactions quickly and efficiently, it will limit its usefulness in real-world scenarios.

In addition, solutions to scalability and performance issues must be carefully evaluated to ensure that they do not compromise the security or decentralization of the network. Off-chain solutions, for example, may offer increased scalability and faster transaction processing, but they may also introduce centralized elements that could undermine the core principles of blockchain technology.

One potential solution to scalability and performance issues is the implementation of sharding. Sharding is a technique that involves breaking up a blockchain network into smaller, more manageable parts, or shards. Each shard can process its own transactions independently, which can significantly increase the network's capacity and throughput.

Another potential solution is the use of off-chain scaling solutions, such as the Lightning Network for Bitcoin. The Lightning Network is a second-layer protocol that operates on top of the Bitcoin blockchain and allows for fast and cheap transactions. By routing transactions through a network of payment channels, the Lightning Network can significantly increase the transaction capacity of the Bitcoin network.

Despite these potential solutions, scalability and performance issues remain a significant challenge for the widespread adoption and use of blockchain technology. As demand for the technology grows, it will become increasingly important to find effective and secure solutions to these issues.

Furthermore, it is important to note that scalability and performance issues are not the only obstacles to widespread adoption of blockchain technology. Other factors, such as regulatory and legal frameworks, interoperability between different blockchain networks, and user education and adoption, also play important roles in determining the success and adoption of the technology.

In conclusion, scalability and performance issues represent a significant challenge for the widespread adoption and use of blockchain technology. While solutions such as sharding and off-chain scaling solutions hold promise, they must be carefully evaluated to ensure that they do not compromise the security or decentralization of the network. As the demand for the technology grows, it will become increasingly important to find effective and secure solutions to these issues to unlock the full potential of blockchain technology.

Privacy and security concerns

Privacy and security concerns have been at the forefront of discussions regarding blockchain technology, especially in industries where sensitive data is involved, such as healthcare and finance. While blockchain technology provides a secure and tamper-proof system for storing and sharing data, there are still potential vulnerabilities that could compromise the privacy and security of the data.

One of the main privacy concerns with blockchain technology is the potential for data leaks. While data stored on a blockchain is encrypted, some data may be exposed to the public depending on the type of blockchain used. For example, public blockchains, such as Bitcoin and Ethereum, make all transactions publicly visible on the blockchain. This can be a concern for industries that require a high level of privacy, such as healthcare, where patient information needs to be protected. Private blockchains, on the other hand, restrict access to the network, making them more secure but less transparent.

Another concern is the potential for hacking and cyber attacks. While the decentralized nature of blockchain technology makes it more secure than traditional centralized systems, it is not immune to attacks. In fact, because of the distributed nature of the network, it may be more difficult to detect and mitigate attacks. For example, in 2016, the DAO (Decentralized Autonomous Organization) was hacked, resulting in the loss of millions of dollars worth of cryptocurrency. This incident highlighted the need for stronger security measures in blockchain technology.

Furthermore, there is the potential for rogue actors within the network to misuse or abuse the data. For example, a healthcare provider or insurance company could potentially use patient data for their own gain, without the patient's consent. In addition, because the data is stored permanently on the blockchain, there is a risk that it could be used for nefarious purposes in the future, even if it was originally collected and stored for a legitimate purpose.

To address these concerns, there are several measures that can be taken to improve the privacy and security of blockchain technology. One approach is to use a combination of public and private blockchains, with sensitive data stored on private blockchains that only authorized parties can access. This would provide a high level of security while still allowing for transparency where necessary.

Another approach is to use advanced encryption methods to ensure that the data is protected from unauthorized access. This could involve using encryption keys that only authorized parties possess, or using multi-factor authentication to ensure that only authorized individuals can access the data.

In addition, the use of smart contracts can help to ensure that the data is used only for its intended purpose. Smart contracts are self-executing contracts with the terms of the agreement written into the code. They can be used to enforce data access and usage restrictions, ensuring that data is not used in ways that are not authorized.

Finally, ongoing monitoring and auditing of the network can help to identify and mitigate potential security threats. This could involve using machine learning algorithms to detect anomalous activity on the network, or conducting regular security audits to identify potential vulnerabilities and weaknesses in the system.

In conclusion, privacy and security concerns are critical issues that must be addressed for the widespread adoption and use of blockchain technology in sensitive industries such as healthcare and finance. While blockchain technology offers several benefits, including transparency, security, and efficiency, these benefits must be balanced with the need for privacy and security. By implementing strong security measures, using a combination of public and private blockchains, and leveraging smart contracts and advanced encryption methods, blockchain technology can be used to revolutionize the way sensitive data is stored and shared, while still protecting the privacy and security of individuals and organizations.

Future trends in blockchain technology

Blockchain technology has the potential to revolutionize various industries, from finance and healthcare to logistics and supply chain management. As the technology continues to mature, several future trends are expected to emerge, which could further enhance its capabilities and drive its adoption across different sectors.

Interoperability: One of the biggest challenges facing blockchain technology is the lack of interoperability between different networks. Currently, most blockchain platforms operate in silos, with little interaction between them. This limits the ability of users to access and share data across different networks. In the future, we can expect to see the development of interoperability solutions that allow different blockchain networks to communicate with each other seamlessly. This will enable greater collaboration and data sharing, leading to more efficient and streamlined business processes.

Scalability: As discussed earlier, scalability is a major issue facing blockchain technology, with the current generation of blockchains unable to handle large-scale transactions. To address this challenge, researchers are exploring various approaches, such as sharding and state channels, which aim to increase the throughput of blockchain networks. In the future, we can expect to see the emergence of more scalable blockchain solutions that can support high-volume transactions without sacrificing security or decentralization.

Privacy: Privacy is another critical issue in the blockchain space, with the public nature of most blockchain networks making it difficult to keep sensitive information secure. To address this challenge, researchers are exploring various approaches, such as zero-knowledge proofs and homomorphic encryption, which allow users to conduct transactions while keeping their data private. In the future, we can expect to see the emergence of more privacy-focused blockchain solutions that enable secure and confidential data sharing.

Integration with other technologies: Blockchain technology is not a standalone solution, and it can be combined with other technologies to create more powerful solutions. For example, the integration of blockchain and artificial intelligence (AI) can enable more efficient and accurate data analysis, while the integration of blockchain and the Internet of Things (IoT) can enable secure and decentralized data sharing in smart cities and other applications. In the future, we can expect to see more blockchain-based solutions that leverage the capabilities of other technologies to create more powerful and innovative solutions.

Tokenization: The use of tokens to represent assets on the blockchain is becoming increasingly popular, with tokens being used to represent everything from currencies and commodities to real estate and intellectual property. In the future, we can expect to see more widespread adoption of tokenization, with the creation of new token standards and the development of tokenized ecosystems that enable the seamless exchange of assets across different networks.

Sustainability: As discussed earlier, energy consumption is a significant concern in the blockchain space, with the computational requirements of blockchain networks making them highly energy-intensive. To address this challenge, researchers are exploring various approaches, such as proof-of-stake and energy-efficient consensus algorithms, which aim to reduce the energy consumption of blockchain networks. In the future, we can expect to see more sustainable blockchain solutions that balance the need for security and decentralization with the need for energy efficiency.

Regulation: The regulatory landscape for blockchain technology is still evolving, with different countries and jurisdictions taking different approaches to regulating blockchain-based solutions. In the future, we can expect to see more comprehensive and standardized regulations that provide clarity and certainty for blockchain-based businesses and investors. This will enable greater adoption of blockchain technology across different industries and applications.

In conclusion, blockchain technology is still in its early stages, and there are many challenges and opportunities facing its adoption and use. However, as the technology continues to mature and evolve, we can expect to see the emergence of new trends and innovations that will drive its growth and adoption across different industries and applications. It is an exciting time to be involved in the blockchain space, and there are many opportunities for entrepreneurs, developers, and investors to shape the future of this technology.

One of the most promising future trends in blockchain technology is the development of decentralized finance (DeFi) applications. DeFi refers to financial services that are built on blockchain technology and are decentralized, meaning that they are not controlled by traditional financial institutions. DeFi applications include things like lending, borrowing, and trading, and they are becoming increasingly popular among crypto investors and traders.

Another trend that is likely to shape the future of blockchain technology is the rise of non-fungible tokens (NFTs). NFTs are unique digital assets that are stored on a blockchain and can represent anything from art to music to virtual real estate. NFTs have gained a lot of attention in recent months, with some selling for millions of dollars, and they are seen as a new way to create value in the digital world.

In addition to DeFi and NFTs, there are many other potential applications for blockchain technology that are currently being explored. One such application is supply chain management, where blockchain can be used to create a transparent and secure record of every step in a product's journey from the manufacturer to the end consumer. This can help to reduce fraud, increase efficiency, and improve consumer trust in the products they buy.

Another potential application for blockchain technology is in the healthcare industry, where it can be used to create a secure and decentralized database of patient records. This can help to improve the efficiency of healthcare delivery and reduce the risk of data breaches and cyberattacks.

Finally, blockchain technology is also being explored as a potential solution to the problem of digital identity. By creating a decentralized system for identity verification and management, blockchain technology can help to protect user privacy and security while still allowing for seamless and efficient access to digital services and resources.

Overall, the future of blockchain technology is bright, with many potential applications and opportunities for growth and innovation. As the technology continues to mature and evolve, we can expect to see new trends and innovations emerge that will drive its adoption and use across a wide range of industries and applications. For entrepreneurs, developers, and investors who are interested in shaping the future of this technology, there has never been a better time to get involved.

CHAPTER 10: CRYPTO REGULATIONS AND COMPLIANCE

Introduction to crypto regulations

The emergence of cryptocurrencies and blockchain technology has led to new and complex regulatory challenges for governments and financial institutions around the world. The decentralized nature of blockchain technology and the anonymity of cryptocurrency transactions have created a range of potential risks and opportunities, from illegal activities such as money laundering and terrorism financing, to innovative new business models and investment opportunities.

As such, there has been a significant amount of debate and discussion around how best to regulate cryptocurrencies and blockchain technology, with different countries taking vastly different approaches. In this section, we will explore the current state of crypto regulations, the challenges faced by regulators, and the potential implications of different regulatory frameworks.

Current State of Crypto Regulations:

The regulatory landscape for cryptocurrencies and blockchain technology varies widely around the world, with some countries embracing these technologies and others taking a more cautious approach.

In the United States, for example, regulatory oversight is split between a number of different agencies, including the Securities and Exchange Commission (SEC), the Commodity Futures Trading Commission (CFTC), and the Financial Crimes Enforcement Network (FinCEN). The SEC has been particularly active in recent years, cracking down on illegal initial coin offerings (ICOs) and working to clarify the legal status of cryptocurrencies.

In China, on the other hand, the government has taken a much more aggressive approach to regulating cryptocurrencies. In 2017, the country banned ICOs and cryptocurrency exchanges, citing concerns about financial stability and illegal activities.

Other countries have taken a more open and welcoming approach to cryptocurrencies, such as Switzerland, which has established a regulatory framework that encourages innovation and growth in the blockchain industry.

Challenges Faced by Regulators:

Regulating cryptocurrencies and blockchain technology presents a number of unique challenges for regulators. One of the biggest challenges is the decentralized nature of these technologies, which can make it difficult to identify and regulate the various actors involved.

Another challenge is the speed at which these technologies are evolving. New cryptocurrencies and blockchain-based applications are being developed all the time, making it difficult for regulators to keep up with the latest developments.

In addition, the anonymity of cryptocurrency transactions presents a significant challenge for regulators. It can be difficult to trace the source and destination of funds in cryptocurrency transactions, which makes it easier for individuals to engage in illegal activities such as money laundering and terrorism financing.

Implications of Different Regulatory Frameworks:

The regulatory framework adopted by a particular country can have significant implications for the development and adoption of cryptocurrencies and blockchain technology. A strict regulatory framework can stifle innovation and drive companies and investors to more friendly jurisdictions, while a more open framework can encourage growth and development in the industry.

One potential consequence of a more open regulatory framework is increased investment and innovation in the blockchain industry. This can lead to the development of new applications and technologies that could transform a range of industries, from finance to healthcare.

However, there are also risks associated with a more open regulatory framework. Without adequate oversight, there is a risk that cryptocurrencies and blockchain-based applications could be used for illegal activities, such as money laundering and terrorism financing.

Conversely, a more restrictive regulatory framework can limit innovation and drive companies and investors away. In addition, overly restrictive regulations can create a black market for cryptocurrencies and blockchain-based applications, making it more difficult for regulators to oversee and control these technologies.

Conclusion:

In conclusion, the regulatory landscape for cryptocurrencies and blockchain technology is complex and rapidly evolving. Different countries are taking vastly different approaches to regulating these technologies, with some embracing them and others taking a more cautious approach.

As these technologies continue to evolve and become more mainstream, it is likely that we will see significant changes in the regulatory landscape. It is important for regulators to strike a balance between encouraging innovation and growth in the blockchain industry, while also protecting consumers and preventing illegal activities.

I. Overview of regulatory frameworks around the world

Blockchain technology and cryptocurrencies have emerged as one of the most disruptive technologies in the financial industry. However, the lack of clear regulations and legal frameworks around blockchain technology and cryptocurrencies have made it difficult for the industry to mature and for investors to feel comfortable investing in the space. In this section, we will provide an overview of the regulatory frameworks around the world for blockchain technology and cryptocurrencies.

Regulatory Frameworks in the United States:

The United States has been one of the slowest countries to adopt a regulatory framework for cryptocurrencies and blockchain technology. The Securities and Exchange Commission (SEC) has taken the lead in regulating cryptocurrencies, and its approach has been a mix of enforcement actions against fraudulent ICOs and a cautious approach to approving cryptocurrency ETFs.

The SEC has classified cryptocurrencies as securities, and this classification has significant implications for the industry. Cryptocurrencies that are classified as securities are subject to the same regulations as traditional securities, including registration requirements and disclosure obligations. The SEC's classification of cryptocurrencies as securities has led to significant uncertainty in the industry, with many companies unsure about how to proceed.

In addition to the SEC, the Commodity Futures Trading Commission (CFTC) has also taken an active role in regulating cryptocurrencies. The CFTC has classified cryptocurrencies as commodities, and it has the authority to regulate futures and options trading in cryptocurrencies. The CFTC has approved several cryptocurrency derivatives, including Bitcoin futures, and it has taken action against fraudulent ICOs.

Regulatory Frameworks in Europe:

Europe has taken a more progressive approach to regulating blockchain technology and cryptocurrencies. The European Union (EU) has introduced a regulatory framework for cryptocurrencies and exchanges through the Fifth Anti-Money Laundering Directive (5AMLD). The directive requires cryptocurrency exchanges and custodial wallet providers to register with their national financial regulator and comply with anti-money laundering (AML) and counter-terrorist financing (CTF) regulations.

In addition to the 5AMLD, the EU has also established the European Blockchain Partnership (EBP), which is a collaboration between 27 EU member states and the European Commission. The partnership aims to promote the use of blockchain technology in the public sector and to develop common standards and interoperability for blockchain-based solutions.

Regulatory Frameworks in Asia:

Asia has been one of the most active regions in the world for blockchain technology and cryptocurrencies. China, in particular, has been at the forefront of the industry, but it has also been one of the most restrictive countries in terms of regulations. In 2017, China banned initial coin offerings (ICOs), and it has also banned cryptocurrency exchanges.

Japan has taken a more progressive approach to regulating cryptocurrencies. In 2017, Japan became the first country to regulate cryptocurrencies at a national level, and it introduced a licensing system for cryptocurrency exchanges. The licensing system requires exchanges to register with the Financial Services Agency (FSA) and comply with AML and CTF regulations.

South Korea has also been active in regulating cryptocurrencies. In 2018, South Korea introduced a regulatory framework for cryptocurrency exchanges, which requires exchanges to register with the Financial Services Commission (FSC) and comply with AML and CTF regulations.

Regulatory Frameworks in Africa:

Africa is a diverse continent, and regulatory frameworks for blockchain technology and cryptocurrencies vary widely from country to country. In general, African countries have been slow to adopt regulatory frameworks for the industry, but some countries are beginning to take a more progressive approach.

South Africa has taken the lead in regulating cryptocurrencies in Africa. In 2019, the South African Reserve Bank (SARB) issued a consultation paper on the regulation of cryptocurrencies, and it has since established a regulatory sandbox for blockchain-based solutions. The sandbox aims to create a regulatory environment that is conducive to innovation and development in the industry.

Nigeria is also emerging as a key player in the blockchain and cryptocurrency space in Africa. The Central Bank of Nigeria has issued warnings to financial institutions against facilitating cryptocurrency transactions, citing the lack of regulation and the potential for money laundering and terrorist financing. However, the country's Securities and Exchange Commission (SEC) has taken a more positive stance, issuing a regulatory framework for the offering and trading of digital assets in 2020.

Kenya has also shown interest in blockchain technology and cryptocurrencies, with the Central Bank of Kenya issuing a circular in 2018 warning against the risks associated with virtual currencies but acknowledging the potential benefits of blockchain technology.

Other African countries, such as Ghana and Uganda, are still in the early stages of exploring the regulatory landscape for blockchain and cryptocurrencies. However, with the increasing adoption of the technology across the continent, it is likely that more countries will follow in the footsteps of South Africa, Nigeria, and Kenya and establish regulatory frameworks for the industry.

It is worth noting that regulatory frameworks for blockchain and cryptocurrencies in Africa are not without challenges. One of the main challenges is the lack of technical expertise among regulators, which can lead to regulatory uncertainty and inconsistency. In addition, the high level of informal economies in some African countries and the lack of access to financial services can create challenges for the adoption and use of cryptocurrencies.

Overall, the regulatory landscape for blockchain technology and cryptocurrencies in Africa is still developing, but there are signs of progress and potential for growth. As the industry continues to mature and gain mainstream acceptance, it is likely that more countries in Africa will establish regulatory frameworks that balance innovation and development with consumer protection and financial stability.

Regulatory challenges for cryptocurrencies

Regulatory challenges for cryptocurrencies have been a topic of much discussion and debate since the emergence of Bitcoin in 2009. While cryptocurrencies offer many potential benefits, such as decentralized control, enhanced security, and faster and cheaper transactions, they also present a number of challenges for regulators and policymakers. In this section, we will explore some of the key regulatory challenges for cryptocurrencies.

Lack of uniformity in regulatory frameworks

One of the biggest challenges facing the regulation of cryptocurrencies is the lack of uniformity in regulatory frameworks across different countries and regions. Cryptocurrencies are a global phenomenon, and their decentralized nature makes it difficult for regulators to establish a common set of rules and standards. This lack of uniformity can create confusion and uncertainty for investors and businesses, and can also create opportunities for regulatory arbitrage.

For example, in the United States, the regulatory framework for cryptocurrencies is complex and fragmented, with different agencies taking different approaches to regulation. The Securities and Exchange Commission (SEC) has taken the position that many cryptocurrencies are securities and subject to its regulatory oversight, while the Commodity Futures Trading Commission (CFTC) has classified some cryptocurrencies as commodities subject to its regulation. This lack of clarity and uniformity has led to a number of legal challenges and enforcement actions.

Difficulty in enforcing regulations

Another challenge facing the regulation of cryptocurrencies is the difficulty in enforcing regulations. Cryptocurrencies are designed to be decentralized and peer-to-peer, which makes it difficult for regulators to monitor and enforce compliance with regulations. Transactions on the blockchain are anonymous, making it difficult to identify the parties involved in a transaction. This anonymity also makes it difficult to track illegal activities, such as money laundering and terrorist financing.

Furthermore, cryptocurrencies can be traded on decentralized exchanges (DEXs), which are not subject to the same regulatory oversight as traditional centralized exchanges. This makes it easier for bad actors to engage in illegal activities, such as market manipulation and insider trading, without detection.

Risk of fraud and scams

Another regulatory challenge for cryptocurrencies is the risk of fraud and scams. Cryptocurrencies are a relatively new and complex technology, and many investors are not familiar with the risks and potential pitfalls associated with investing in them. This lack of knowledge and understanding creates opportunities for scammers to take advantage of unsuspecting investors.

One common scam in the cryptocurrency industry is the initial coin offering (ICO). ICOs are a way for companies to raise funds by issuing their own cryptocurrency tokens. However, many ICOs have turned out to be fraudulent, with the company either failing to deliver on its promises or simply disappearing with investors' money.

Concerns over consumer protection

Regulators are also concerned about the potential impact of cryptocurrencies on consumer protection. Cryptocurrencies are not backed by any government or financial institution, and their value can be highly volatile. This volatility can make it difficult for consumers to assess the risks and potential rewards of investing in cryptocurrencies.

Furthermore, cryptocurrencies are not subject to the same consumer protections as traditional financial products. For example, if a consumer's bank account is hacked and funds are stolen, the bank is typically liable for the loss. However, if a consumer's cryptocurrency wallet is hacked and funds are stolen, there is often no recourse for the consumer.

Impact on monetary policy

Finally, cryptocurrencies have the potential to impact monetary policy and financial stability. Because cryptocurrencies are not backed by any government or financial institution, they are not subject to the same monetary policy tools and regulations as traditional currencies. This can create challenges for central banks and financial regulators, who may be concerned about the potential impact of cryptocurrencies on inflation, interest rates, and financial stability.

For example, if a significant portion of a country's population were to shift their savings and transactions to cryptocurrencies, this could reduce the effectiveness of the central bank's monetary policy tools, such as interest rate adjustments and money supply regulation. In such a scenario, the central bank may be unable to control inflation or prevent financial crises, potentially leading to economic instability.

Furthermore, the volatility of cryptocurrencies can also have a significant impact on financial stability. The rapid fluctuations in the value of cryptocurrencies can create risks for investors and financial institutions, potentially leading to large losses and destabilizing the financial system. Additionally, the lack of transparency and regulation in the cryptocurrency market can make it difficult for financial regulators to monitor and address risks.

Some central banks and financial regulators have taken steps to address these concerns. For example, in 2018, the Financial Stability Oversight Council (FSOC) in the United States identified cryptocurrencies as a potential risk to financial stability and called for increased regulatory oversight of the industry. Similarly, the European Central Bank (ECB) has warned about the risks of cryptocurrencies and has called for global coordination in regulating the industry.

Despite these efforts, many challenges remain in regulating cryptocurrencies and ensuring their compatibility with traditional monetary policy and financial stability objectives. The decentralized nature of cryptocurrencies makes it difficult for governments and central banks to regulate the industry effectively, and there is still significant uncertainty about the long-term impact of cryptocurrencies on monetary policy and financial stability.

In conclusion, while cryptocurrencies have the potential to offer many benefits, they also pose significant regulatory challenges. The lack of transparency, security, and stability in the cryptocurrency market has led to concerns about fraud, money laundering, and other illegal activities. Additionally, the decentralized nature of cryptocurrencies makes it difficult for governments and financial regulators to effectively monitor and regulate the industry. As cryptocurrencies continue to grow and evolve, it is likely that these challenges will become increasingly important, and new regulatory frameworks and approaches will need to be developed to address them.

Impact of regulation on the crypto industry

The impact of regulation on the crypto industry has been a topic of much debate and speculation. On one hand, regulation can provide legitimacy to the industry, increase investor confidence, and reduce the risk of fraudulent activities. On the other hand, excessive regulation can stifle innovation, limit market access, and increase compliance costs for businesses. In this section, we will explore the various ways in which regulation can impact the crypto industry and the different perspectives surrounding this issue.

Impact on Investor Confidence
One of the primary benefits of regulation is the potential to increase investor confidence in the crypto industry. Regulation can provide a clear legal framework for businesses operating in the industry, reducing the risk of fraudulent activities and increasing transparency. This, in turn, can increase investor confidence, which may lead to more investment in the industry.

For example, the introduction of the Financial Action Task Force (FATF) Travel Rule in 2019 required crypto exchanges to collect and share personal information about their users, similar to the way banks are required to do so. This increased transparency and helped to reduce the risk of money laundering and terrorist financing, which helped to improve investor confidence in the industry.

However, some argue that excessive regulation can have the opposite effect and actually decrease investor confidence in the industry. This is because excessive regulation can create a perception of a highly-regulated industry that is difficult to navigate, which may deter investors from investing in the industry. Furthermore, regulatory uncertainty can create a perception of risk and volatility in the industry, which can also deter investors.

Impact on Innovation

Another key consideration when it comes to regulation is the impact it can have on innovation in the industry. On one hand, regulation can provide clarity and guidance for businesses, which may reduce the risk of regulatory ambiguity and encourage more investment in the industry. This can, in turn, lead to increased innovation and development in the industry.

For example, the European Union's General Data Protection Regulation (GDPR) provided clear guidelines on data privacy and protection, which has encouraged businesses to invest in data privacy technologies and services. This, in turn, has led to increased innovation and development in the data privacy industry.

However, some argue that excessive regulation can stifle innovation in the industry. This is because excessive regulation can create a significant compliance burden for businesses, which can limit their ability to innovate and develop new products and services. Furthermore, regulatory uncertainty can create a sense of risk and volatility in the industry, which may discourage businesses from investing in new technologies and services.

Impact on Market Access
Regulation can also have a significant impact on market access for businesses operating in the crypto industry. On one hand, regulation can provide clear guidelines and legal frameworks for businesses to operate within, which can increase their access to markets and reduce the risk of legal action.

For example, the United States Securities and Exchange Commission (SEC) has provided guidance on the classification of cryptocurrencies as securities. This has provided clarity for businesses operating in the industry and has helped to reduce the risk of legal action against them.

However, some argue that excessive regulation can limit market access for businesses operating in the industry. This is because excessive regulation can create a significant compliance burden for businesses, which may limit their ability to access new markets or expand their operations. Furthermore, regulatory uncertainty can create a sense of risk and volatility in the industry, which may deter businesses from entering new markets.

Impact on Compliance Costs
Finally, regulation can have a significant impact on the compliance costs for businesses operating in the crypto industry. On one hand, regulation can provide clear guidelines and legal frameworks for businesses to operate within, which can reduce the risk of legal action and the associated costs.

For example, the introduction of the FATF Travel Rule has required crypto exchanges to invest in compliance technology and staff training to comply with the new requirements. However, compliance costs for businesses can also become burdensome, particularly for smaller businesses and startups that may not have the same resources as larger, established players in the industry.

Compliance costs can be particularly challenging in the crypto industry, which is still in its infancy and lacks the same level of established infrastructure and support as traditional financial markets. This means that compliance solutions can be more expensive and less readily available, particularly in regions where the industry is less developed.

Additionally, compliance costs can vary significantly depending on the specific regulatory requirements in each jurisdiction. For example, some countries may require businesses to maintain more extensive records or conduct more frequent audits, which can drive up compliance costs. These costs can be particularly challenging for businesses that operate across multiple jurisdictions, as they may need to comply with different regulations in each country.

The impact of compliance costs on the crypto industry can be significant. High compliance costs can make it difficult for smaller businesses to compete with larger, more established players in the industry. Additionally, compliance costs can be a barrier to entry for new businesses, which can limit innovation and competition in the industry.

However, it is important to note that compliance costs are not inherently negative. Compliance with regulatory requirements can help to build trust and legitimacy in the industry, which can be important for attracting new investors and customers. Additionally, compliance can help to reduce the risk of fraudulent activity, which can ultimately benefit the industry as a whole.

Overall, the impact of regulation on compliance costs in the crypto industry is complex and multifaceted. While regulation can provide important benefits such as reducing legal risk and building trust, it can also be a significant burden for businesses, particularly those with limited resources. As such, it is important for regulators to strike a balance between protecting consumers and businesses, while also ensuring that compliance costs do not become excessive.

II. Compliance issues in crypto transactions

Compliance issues are a crucial consideration in the world of cryptocurrencies, which operate in a largely unregulated environment. In recent years, a number of high-profile incidents have highlighted the need for businesses operating in the crypto industry to take compliance seriously, in order to avoid legal action and reputational damage.

One of the key compliance issues in crypto transactions is money laundering. Because cryptocurrencies operate outside the traditional banking system, they can be used by criminals to move funds anonymously across borders. This has led to a number of regulatory initiatives aimed at combating money laundering in the crypto industry.

For example, the Financial Action Task Force (FATF) has introduced a series of guidelines for businesses operating in the crypto industry, including the requirement to conduct Know Your Customer (KYC) and Anti-Money Laundering (AML) checks on customers. These guidelines have been implemented in a number of countries, including the United States, European Union, and Japan.

Another compliance issue in the crypto industry is tax evasion. Because cryptocurrencies can be bought and sold anonymously, it can be difficult for tax authorities to track transactions and ensure that appropriate taxes are paid. This has led to a number of regulatory initiatives aimed at improving tax compliance in the crypto industry.

For example, the United States Internal Revenue Service (IRS) has issued guidance on the tax treatment of cryptocurrencies, requiring taxpayers to report transactions and pay taxes on any gains. Similarly, the European Union has introduced new regulations requiring crypto exchanges to share customer data with tax authorities.

A third compliance issue in the crypto industry is the risk of fraud and scams. Because cryptocurrencies are not backed by any government or financial institution, they are more susceptible to fraudulent activities, such as Ponzi schemes and fake initial coin offerings (ICOs). This has led to a number of regulatory initiatives aimed at improving consumer protection in the crypto industry.

For example, the United States Securities and Exchange Commission (SEC) has taken action against a number of fraudulent ICOs, and has introduced guidelines for businesses looking to launch legitimate ICOs. Similarly, the European Securities and Markets Authority (ESMA) has warned consumers about the risks associated with investing in cryptocurrencies.

Compliance issues in the crypto industry are complex and multifaceted, and require businesses to navigate a constantly-evolving regulatory landscape. However, by taking compliance seriously and implementing appropriate measures, businesses can reduce the risk of legal action and reputational damage, while improving the overall integrity of the industry.

Anti-money laundering (AML) and know-your-customer (KYC) regulations

Anti-money laundering (AML) and know-your-customer (KYC) regulations are an essential part of the regulatory landscape for cryptocurrencies. These regulations are designed to prevent money laundering, terrorist financing, and other illegal activities by requiring financial institutions and businesses to identify and verify the identity of their customers, as well as monitor and report suspicious activities. In the context of cryptocurrencies, AML and KYC regulations are particularly important due to the pseudonymous and decentralized nature of these digital assets. In this section, we will explore the importance of AML and KYC regulations in the crypto industry, the challenges and limitations of implementing these regulations, and the potential impact of new developments in AML and KYC technology.

First, it is important to understand why AML and KYC regulations are necessary in the context of cryptocurrencies. Cryptocurrencies have been used for a range of illicit activities, including money laundering, tax evasion, drug trafficking, and terrorist financing. Cryptocurrencies offer several advantages for these activities, including anonymity, decentralized control, and the ability to transfer funds quickly and easily across borders. This has made cryptocurrencies an attractive tool for criminals and terrorists looking to finance their operations.

In response to these concerns, regulators around the world have implemented AML and KYC regulations for cryptocurrencies. These regulations require cryptocurrency exchanges and other businesses to verify the identity of their customers, monitor transactions for suspicious activity, and report any suspicious activity to the relevant authorities. The goal of these regulations is to make it more difficult for criminals to use cryptocurrencies for illegal activities, and to hold businesses accountable for any illegal activities that do occur.

However, implementing AML and KYC regulations in the crypto industry can be challenging. One of the main challenges is the pseudonymous nature of cryptocurrencies. Unlike traditional financial transactions, which are typically associated with a name and bank account number, cryptocurrency transactions are associated with a public key and private key. While this pseudonymous nature of cryptocurrencies provides users with a degree of privacy and anonymity, it also creates challenges for AML and KYC compliance.

In traditional financial transactions, AML and KYC regulations require financial institutions to verify the identity of their customers and monitor their transactions for suspicious activity. This involves collecting personal information such as name, address, and government-issued ID, and conducting ongoing monitoring of transactions to detect any suspicious behavior.

However, in the crypto industry, this process is more complicated. Due to the pseudonymous nature of cryptocurrencies, it is difficult to link a specific transaction to a real-world identity. Additionally, there are a variety of different crypto assets, each with their own unique characteristics and transactional features. This can make it difficult for businesses to determine which transactions are subject to AML and KYC regulations.

Furthermore, there is no single global AML and KYC regulatory framework for the crypto industry. Instead, different countries and regions have developed their own regulatory approaches, leading to a fragmented regulatory landscape that can be challenging for businesses to navigate. For example, in the United States, crypto businesses are subject to the Bank Secrecy Act (BSA) and must register as money services businesses (MSBs) with the Financial Crimes Enforcement Network (FinCEN). Meanwhile, in the European Union, crypto businesses are subject to the Fifth Anti-Money Laundering Directive (5AMLD) and must register with the relevant national authorities.

Implementing AML and KYC regulations in the crypto industry also requires significant investment in compliance technology and staff training. This can be a significant financial burden for small and medium-sized businesses, and may lead to a consolidation of the industry as larger, more established players are better equipped to handle the regulatory requirements.

Despite these challenges, there have been efforts to address AML and KYC compliance in the crypto industry. Some crypto businesses have developed their own compliance programs and invested in compliance technology to meet regulatory requirements. Additionally, there have been proposals for a global regulatory framework for the crypto industry, which could help to streamline compliance efforts and create a more consistent regulatory landscape.

However, there are also concerns that overly burdensome AML and KYC regulations could stifle innovation in the crypto industry and drive businesses to operate in jurisdictions with less stringent regulatory requirements. This could create a regulatory race-to-the-bottom and increase the risk of financial crime.

In conclusion, implementing AML and KYC regulations in the crypto industry is a complex and challenging task. The pseudonymous nature of cryptocurrencies, the fragmented regulatory landscape, and the significant compliance costs all create obstacles for businesses. However, with the right investments in compliance technology and staff training, and the development of a more consistent global regulatory framework, it is possible to achieve a balance between regulatory compliance and innovation in the crypto industry.

Taxation of cryptocurrency transactions

Cryptocurrencies have emerged as a new asset class in recent years, attracting significant interest from investors and traders. However, the taxation of cryptocurrencies is a complex and evolving area, with different countries taking different approaches to the treatment of cryptocurrencies for tax purposes. In this section, we will examine the taxation of cryptocurrency transactions, the challenges faced by tax authorities in enforcing tax compliance, and the impact of taxation on the cryptocurrency industry.

Taxation of Cryptocurrency Transactions:
Cryptocurrency transactions can give rise to various tax implications, depending on the nature of the transaction and the jurisdiction in which it takes place. In general, the taxation of cryptocurrency transactions can be divided into three main categories: capital gains tax, income tax, and value-added tax (VAT).

Capital Gains Tax:

Most countries treat cryptocurrencies as assets for tax purposes, which means that capital gains tax may be applicable to profits earned from the sale or exchange of cryptocurrencies. The capital gains tax is typically levied on the difference between the purchase price and the sale price of the cryptocurrency. For example, if an investor purchases one bitcoin for $10,000 and later sells it for $12,000, the capital gain is $2,000, which is subject to taxation.

Income Tax:
In addition to capital gains tax, income tax may also be applicable to cryptocurrency transactions. This typically occurs when an individual or business receives cryptocurrency as payment for goods or services, or when cryptocurrency is mined. The income tax is calculated based on the fair market value of the cryptocurrency at the time it is received.

Value-Added Tax (VAT):
Value-added tax (VAT) is a consumption tax that is levied on the value added at each stage of production and distribution of goods and services. The treatment of cryptocurrency transactions for VAT purposes varies between countries. In some countries, cryptocurrency transactions are subject to VAT, while in others they are exempt.

Challenges arise in determining the VAT treatment of cryptocurrency transactions because of their unique nature. Cryptocurrencies can be exchanged for goods and services, but they are not legal tender in most countries. This makes it difficult to determine the value of the transaction, and consequently, the amount of VAT owed.

Furthermore, the fluctuating value of cryptocurrencies presents a challenge when determining the VAT owed. The value of cryptocurrencies can change rapidly, which makes it difficult to determine the value of a transaction at the time it occurred. For example, if a business accepts Bitcoin for the sale of a good, the value of the Bitcoin could change before the business has a chance to convert it to their local currency. This presents a challenge in determining the VAT owed because the value of the Bitcoin at the time of the transaction may not be the same as the value when it is converted to the local currency.

In addition, the anonymity of cryptocurrency transactions creates difficulties in tracking them for VAT purposes. Traditional financial transactions are usually associated with a name and bank account number, which makes them easy to track. However, cryptocurrency transactions are pseudonymous, and it can be challenging to associate them with a specific individual or entity. This makes it difficult to determine if the transaction is subject to VAT or not.

Treatment of cryptocurrency transactions for VAT purposes in different countries:

The treatment of cryptocurrency transactions for VAT purposes varies between countries. In some countries, cryptocurrency transactions are treated as a form of currency and are therefore exempt from VAT. In other countries, cryptocurrency transactions are subject to VAT at the standard rate.

For example, in the European Union (EU), the treatment of cryptocurrency transactions for VAT purposes is determined by the Court of Justice of the European Union (CJEU). The CJEU has ruled that the exchange of traditional currency for cryptocurrency and vice versa is exempt from VAT. However, the purchase of goods or services with cryptocurrency is subject to VAT at the standard rate

International regulatory cooperation

The emergence of cryptocurrencies has brought with it numerous challenges and complexities for regulators around the world. As a global and decentralized financial system, the regulation of cryptocurrency transactions and exchanges poses unique challenges that require international regulatory cooperation. In this section, we will examine the importance of international regulatory cooperation in the cryptocurrency industry, the challenges involved, and the current state of international cooperation in this area.

Importance of International Regulatory Cooperation

The global nature of the cryptocurrency industry means that regulatory cooperation between countries is essential. This is because the lack of a unified approach to cryptocurrency regulation can result in regulatory arbitrage, where businesses move to countries with less strict regulations to avoid compliance costs. This can lead to a race to the bottom, where countries compete to attract businesses by lowering their regulatory standards. Such a scenario can undermine efforts to combat money laundering, terrorist financing, tax evasion, and other illicit activities.

International regulatory cooperation can help to ensure a level playing field for all businesses operating in the cryptocurrency industry. It can also promote greater transparency and information sharing between regulators, which can enhance the effectiveness of regulatory efforts. In addition, international cooperation can help to prevent regulatory gaps, where certain activities fall outside the scope of regulation due to differences in regulatory frameworks between countries.

Challenges in International Regulatory Cooperation

Despite the benefits of international regulatory cooperation, there are significant challenges to achieving it. One of the main challenges is the diversity of regulatory approaches among countries. Different countries have different legal systems, cultural norms, and economic priorities that influence their regulatory approaches. For example, some countries may prioritize consumer protection, while others may prioritize financial stability or innovation.

Another challenge is the lack of a unified definition of cryptocurrencies. This has led to differing regulatory approaches among countries, with some countries treating cryptocurrencies as securities, while others treat them as commodities or currency. Such differences in classification can lead to regulatory gaps or overlaps, which can create confusion for businesses and consumers alike.

A further challenge is the speed of innovation in the cryptocurrency industry. Cryptocurrencies are still a relatively new and rapidly evolving technology, which means that regulatory frameworks need to be constantly updated to keep pace with technological advancements. This can make it difficult for regulators to keep up with the pace of innovation and to develop effective regulatory approaches that are flexible enough to accommodate changes in the industry.

Current State of International Regulatory Cooperation

Despite these challenges, there are some examples of international regulatory cooperation in the cryptocurrency industry. One of the most prominent examples is the Financial Action Task Force (FATF), an intergovernmental organization that sets global standards for anti-money laundering and counter-terrorism financing. In June 2019, the FATF issued guidance for countries on the regulation of virtual assets and virtual asset service providers. The guidance sets out a risk-based approach to regulation and recommends that countries apply AML/CFT measures to virtual asset service providers, including exchanges and wallet providers.

Another example of international cooperation is the International Organization of Securities Commissions (IOSCO), which is a global body of securities regulators. In May 2019, IOSCO published a report on the regulation of crypto-asset trading platforms. The report provides guidance on the key risks and issues associated with trading platforms, including custody, liquidity, and market integrity. The report also sets out principles for the regulation of trading platforms, such as ensuring that platforms have appropriate governance structures, risk management processes, and transparency requirements.

The European Union (EU) is also taking steps towards greater international regulatory cooperation in the cryptocurrency industry. In September 2020, the EU proposed a comprehensive regulatory framework for crypto-assets. The proposed regulation seeks to establish a common regulatory approach to crypto-assets across the EU, with the aim of promoting innovation while ensuring consumer protection and financial stability. The regulation covers a range of issues, including licensing requirements for crypto-asset service providers, capital requirements, and investor protection measures.

The proposed EU regulation on crypto-assets also includes provisions for international regulatory cooperation. The EU has recognized that the global nature of the crypto industry requires international cooperation to effectively regulate and supervise crypto-assets. To this end, the proposed regulation provides for the establishment of a new EU regulatory authority, the European Supervisory Authority (ESA), which would have the power to enter into cooperation agreements with regulatory authorities outside the EU. These agreements would enable the ESA to exchange information and coordinate supervisory activities with non-EU regulatory authorities, thereby promoting a coordinated approach to regulating crypto-assets globally.

The Financial Action Task Force (FATF) is another international organization that has been working towards greater regulatory cooperation in the cryptocurrency industry. The FATF is an intergovernmental organization that was established to combat money laundering and terrorist financing. In 2019, the FATF issued guidance on the regulation of virtual assets and virtual asset service providers (VASPs). The guidance sets out a comprehensive framework for the regulation of virtual assets and VASPs, including requirements for AML and KYC procedures, licensing and registration requirements for VASPs, and the obligation for VASPs to report suspicious transactions to competent authorities.

The FATF guidance on virtual assets has been adopted by many countries around the world, and it has been instrumental in promoting greater international regulatory cooperation in the crypto industry. The FATF has also been working with other international organizations, such as the International Organization of Securities Commissions (IOSCO) and the International Association of Insurance Supervisors (IAIS), to develop a coordinated approach to regulating crypto-assets globally.

Despite these efforts towards greater international regulatory cooperation, challenges remain. One of the main challenges is the lack of consistency in regulatory approaches between different jurisdictions. Different countries have taken different approaches to regulating crypto-assets, and this can create difficulties for businesses operating across borders. For example, a business that is compliant with regulatory requirements in one jurisdiction may find that it is not compliant in another jurisdiction, and this can create uncertainty and legal risks.

Another challenge is the fast-paced and constantly evolving nature of the crypto industry. The regulatory landscape is constantly changing, and it can be difficult for regulators to keep up with new developments in the industry. This can create a situation where regulatory requirements become outdated or ineffective, and it can also create a situation where businesses are uncertain about their compliance obligations.

In conclusion, the cryptocurrency industry is a global industry that requires international regulatory cooperation to effectively regulate and supervise crypto-assets. International organizations such as the G20, the FATF, and the EU have recognized the importance of international regulatory cooperation in the crypto industry, and they have been taking steps to promote greater cooperation and coordination between regulatory authorities. Despite the challenges, it is clear that international regulatory cooperation is essential for ensuring that the cryptocurrency industry is safe, secure, and compliant with regulatory requirements.

III. Legal and ethical considerations in crypto

As the cryptocurrency industry continues to grow, so do the legal and ethical considerations surrounding it. Cryptocurrencies have created new challenges for regulators and lawmakers, as well as ethical dilemmas for individuals and organizations.

From a legal standpoint, there are numerous questions surrounding the regulation of cryptocurrencies. Governments around the world are grappling with how to classify cryptocurrencies and what kind of rules and regulations to apply to them. Some countries have chosen to ban cryptocurrencies altogether, while others have opted for more lenient approaches.

At the same time, there are ethical considerations to be taken into account. The decentralized nature of cryptocurrencies means that individuals and organizations can use them for nefarious purposes, such as money laundering, terrorism financing, and tax evasion. This has led to concerns about the ethics of investing in cryptocurrencies and the responsibilities of individuals and organizations that operate in the crypto space.

In this section, we will explore the legal and ethical considerations surrounding cryptocurrencies in depth. We will examine the current regulatory landscape, including the different approaches taken by governments around the world. We will also delve into the ethical dilemmas posed by cryptocurrencies, including their potential use for illegal activities, and the responsibilities of individuals and organizations that operate in the crypto space.

We will draw on examples from a variety of fields, including investment banking, portfolio management, quantitative analysis, securities trading, financial planning, and financial analysis. We will also present counter-arguments and dissenting opinions in a balanced and objective way, in order to provide a comprehensive and nuanced analysis of this complex and rapidly-evolving subject matter.

Intellectual property and copyright issues

Intellectual property (IP) and copyright issues are becoming increasingly relevant in the world of cryptocurrencies, as blockchain technology enables the creation and distribution of digital assets. In this section, we will discuss the legal and ethical considerations related to IP and copyright in the crypto industry.

Blockchain technology allows for the creation of digital assets that can be easily transferred and shared across the internet. These assets can take many forms, including cryptocurrencies, non-fungible tokens (NFTs), and smart contracts. However, the creation and distribution of digital assets can raise complex legal issues related to IP and copyright.

One of the main IP issues in the crypto industry is the protection of trademarks and patents. Trademarks are used to identify and distinguish the goods and services of one company from those of another, while patents protect inventions or discoveries. In the crypto industry, trademarks and patents can be used to protect the names and technologies associated with specific cryptocurrencies, as well as the underlying blockchain technology.

For example, Bitcoin is a registered trademark owned by the Bitcoin Foundation, which was created to promote the use of Bitcoin and advance the development of the Bitcoin protocol. Similarly, the Ethereum Foundation owns patents related to the Ethereum blockchain, which are designed to prevent others from using the technology without permission.

Another IP issue in the crypto industry is related to the use of open-source software. Open-source software is software that is made available to the public for free, and can be modified and distributed by anyone. Many cryptocurrencies and blockchain technologies are built using open-source software, which can lead to questions around ownership and copyright.

One potential legal issue is the use of code from one project in another project without proper attribution or permission. This can lead to disputes over ownership and copyright infringement, particularly if the code in question is protected by a copyright or patent.

In addition to IP issues, copyright is also a significant concern in the crypto industry. Copyright law protects original works of authorship, including literary, artistic, and musical works. In the context of the crypto industry, copyright issues can arise in a number of ways, such as the creation and distribution of NFTs.

NFTs are digital assets that are unique and can be bought and sold like any other asset. They are often used to represent artwork or other creative works, and are stored on a blockchain. However, the creation and distribution of NFTs can raise complex copyright issues, particularly if the underlying artwork or creative work is protected by copyright.

For example, a digital artist may create an NFT that represents their artwork, but if the artist does not own the copyright to the underlying artwork, they may be infringing on someone else's copyright. Similarly, if an NFT represents a musical work or other copyrighted content, the creator and distributor of the NFT may be infringing on the copyright owner's rights.

There are also ethical considerations related to IP and copyright issues in the crypto industry. One ethical concern is the potential for exploitation of creative works without proper compensation or attribution. For example, if an NFT represents a piece of artwork that was created by someone else, the creator of the NFT may be profiting off of someone else's work without providing them with any compensation.

Another ethical consideration is the potential for the concentration of power and wealth in the crypto industry. As the industry grows and becomes more mainstream, there is a risk that a small group of individuals or organizations will control a large portion of the blockchain technology and digital assets. This concentration of power could lead to concerns around fairness and equity in the distribution of wealth and resources.

In conclusion, IP and copyright issues are becoming increasingly relevant in the crypto industry as blockchain technology enables the creation and distribution of digital assets. Trademarks and patents can be used to protect the names and technologies associated with specific cryptocurrencies, while copyright issues can arise in the context of smart contracts and decentralized applications.

Smart contracts are self-executing contracts with the terms of the agreement directly written into code. They are executed automatically when certain conditions are met, eliminating the need for intermediaries such as lawyers or banks. However, the use of smart contracts raises questions about ownership and copyright. For example, who owns the code behind a smart contract? Can it be copied and modified without permission? These questions are particularly relevant in the context of decentralized applications (dApps), which are built on top of a blockchain platform and often rely on smart contracts to operate.

In the case of dApps, developers may use open-source code as a starting point and modify it to suit their needs. However, this can lead to copyright infringement if the modified code is too similar to the original code. To avoid these issues, many dApp developers choose to license their code under open-source licenses such as the MIT License or the GNU General Public License. These licenses allow others to use, modify, and distribute the code as long as they give proper attribution and maintain the same open-source license.

Another issue related to IP and copyright in the crypto industry is the use of digital assets, such as images or videos, in conjunction with cryptocurrency projects. For example, a crypto project may use a specific image or logo to represent its brand. In this case, the project may need to obtain a license or permission to use the image from the owner of the copyright.

Moreover, with the growing popularity of non-fungible tokens (NFTs), copyright issues have become even more complex. NFTs are unique digital assets that are stored on a blockchain and can represent a wide range of things, from art to music to collectibles. However, the use of copyrighted material in NFTs can lead to legal issues. For example, if an artist creates an NFT that includes copyrighted material without permission, they may be infringing on the owner's copyright.

To address these issues, some companies and platforms in the crypto industry are implementing measures to protect IP and copyright. For example, the Ethereum Name Service (ENS) allows users to register domain names that are stored on the Ethereum blockchain. This can help protect trademarks associated with cryptocurrencies by allowing users to reserve specific domain names that correspond to their brand.

In conclusion, intellectual property and copyright issues are becoming increasingly relevant in the crypto industry as blockchain technology enables the creation and distribution of digital assets. As the industry continues to grow and evolve, it will be important for companies and individuals to be aware of these issues and take appropriate measures to protect their intellectual property rights.

Privacy and data protection laws

Privacy and data protection laws have become increasingly important in the context of the cryptocurrency industry, as the use of blockchain technology and digital assets can involve the collection, storage, and transfer of sensitive personal information. In this section, we will explore the key privacy and data protection issues in the crypto industry, including the regulatory landscape, the challenges of maintaining privacy in a decentralized system, and the impact of emerging technologies such as artificial intelligence and machine learning.

Regulatory Landscape

One of the primary challenges of privacy and data protection in the crypto industry is the lack of clear regulatory guidance. While some jurisdictions have implemented laws and regulations to govern the use of personal data in the context of cryptocurrencies, the regulatory landscape remains highly fragmented and inconsistent across different regions and countries.

For example, the European Union's General Data Protection Regulation (GDPR) applies to the processing of personal data in the context of cryptocurrencies, as well as other emerging technologies such as the Internet of Things and artificial intelligence. Under the GDPR, companies must obtain explicit consent from users before collecting and processing their personal data, and must take appropriate security measures to protect that data from unauthorized access or disclosure.

In the United States, the regulatory landscape is more complex, with different laws and regulations governing privacy and data protection at the federal and state level. The California Consumer Privacy Act (CCPA) and the recently passed California Privacy Rights Act (CPRA) are among the most comprehensive data protection laws in the US, requiring companies to provide consumers with clear and concise information about the personal data they collect and the purposes for which it is used, as well as giving consumers the right to request that their data be deleted or transferred to another company.

Other jurisdictions, such as Japan and South Korea, have also implemented data protection laws that apply to the cryptocurrency industry. However, the lack of harmonization across different regions and countries can make it difficult for companies operating in multiple jurisdictions to comply with the different requirements and regulations.

Maintaining Privacy in a Decentralized System

Another key challenge in the crypto industry is maintaining privacy in a decentralized system. Unlike centralized systems, where a single entity controls access to data and can implement security measures to protect that data, decentralized systems are designed to be open and transparent, with no single point of control.

This presents significant challenges for data protection, as personal information may be stored and transferred across multiple nodes in a decentralized network, making it difficult to ensure that that information is kept confidential and secure. In addition, the transparency of the blockchain means that personal information may be visible to anyone who has access to the network, raising concerns about data leaks and breaches.

To address these challenges, many cryptocurrencies have implemented privacy-enhancing technologies such as zero-knowledge proofs and ring signatures, which allow transactions to be verified without revealing sensitive information. For example, the privacy coin Monero uses ring signatures to obfuscate the origin and destination of transactions, making it difficult for outside observers to track the flow of funds.

However, while these technologies can provide some level of privacy and anonymity, they are not foolproof, and may be vulnerable to attacks by determined adversaries. In addition, the use of privacy-enhancing technologies can also raise concerns about compliance with anti-money laundering (AML) and know-your-customer (KYC) regulations, as these technologies may make it more difficult to identify and track suspicious transactions.

Impact of Emerging Technologies

The emergence of new technologies such as artificial intelligence and machine learning is also having an impact on privacy and data protection in the cryptocurrency industry. These technologies have the potential to revolutionize the way that personal data is collected, analyzed, and used, but they also raise significant concerns about data security and privacy.

For example, machine learning algorithms can be used to analyze large datasets of personal information to identify patterns and trends, but this also raises concerns about the potential for discrimination and bias. If the data used to train these algorithms is biased or incomplete, it can lead to discriminatory outcomes, perpetuating existing inequalities and biases. Additionally, the use of AI and machine learning in the cryptocurrency industry raises questions about the accountability and transparency of decision-making processes. It is essential that adequate measures are taken to ensure that these emerging technologies are used ethically and with appropriate safeguards in place to protect the privacy and data rights of individuals.

One potential solution is the use of privacy-enhancing technologies (PETs) such as zero-knowledge proofs and differential privacy. These technologies enable the processing and analysis of data while preserving individual privacy and preventing the disclosure of sensitive information. For example, zero-knowledge proofs allow for the verification of information without revealing the underlying data, while differential privacy adds noise to data to protect individual privacy.

Regulators and policymakers are also taking steps to address the privacy and data protection concerns raised by emerging technologies in the cryptocurrency industry. In the European Union, the General Data Protection Regulation (GDPR) provides a comprehensive framework for data protection and privacy, including provisions that apply to the processing of personal data in the context of blockchain technology. In the United States, the Federal Trade Commission (FTC) has issued guidance on the use of AI and machine learning in the context of consumer protection, emphasizing the importance of transparency and fairness in decision-making processes.

However, there are also concerns that overly strict regulations and privacy requirements may stifle innovation and impede the development of new technologies in the cryptocurrency industry. Balancing the need for innovation and privacy protection is a complex challenge that requires careful consideration of the benefits and risks of emerging technologies.

In conclusion, the privacy and data protection landscape in the cryptocurrency industry is complex and rapidly evolving. As the industry continues to grow and innovate, it is essential that adequate measures are taken to protect the privacy and data rights of individuals, while also ensuring that emerging technologies are used ethically and transparently.

Ethical implications of crypto adoption

The adoption of cryptocurrencies has far-reaching implications for society, including ethical considerations. While some argue that cryptocurrencies have the potential to empower individuals and democratize financial systems, others express concerns about their potential negative impacts on society. In this section, we will examine the ethical implications of crypto adoption from various perspectives, including financial, social, and environmental.

Financial Implications:

One of the most significant ethical implications of cryptocurrency adoption is the potential impact on traditional financial systems. Some argue that cryptocurrencies have the potential to democratize financial systems by reducing the role of centralized institutions such as banks and governments. This, in turn, could potentially lead to greater financial inclusion and empowerment of individuals.

However, others argue that cryptocurrencies may undermine the stability of traditional financial systems, leading to greater economic inequality and instability. For example, cryptocurrencies can be used for illicit activities such as money laundering and tax evasion, and the lack of regulation and oversight in the crypto industry can make it difficult to prevent such activities. Additionally, the extreme volatility of many cryptocurrencies can result in significant financial losses for individuals who invest in them.

Social Implications:

The social implications of crypto adoption are also a matter of concern. Cryptocurrencies have the potential to create new opportunities for entrepreneurship and innovation, but they may also exacerbate social inequality. For example, the lack of regulation in the crypto industry can result in the exploitation of vulnerable individuals by unscrupulous actors. Additionally, the high barriers to entry for many cryptocurrencies may make it difficult for low-income individuals to participate in the crypto economy.

Another social concern is the potential impact of cryptocurrencies on financial privacy. While some argue that cryptocurrencies can enhance privacy and security by providing individuals with greater control over their financial information, others worry that the lack of transparency in the crypto industry could result in the exploitation of individuals' personal data. Additionally, the rise of crypto-based ransomware attacks highlights the potential for cryptocurrencies to be used as a tool for cybercrime.

Environmental Implications:

Finally, the adoption of cryptocurrencies has significant environmental implications. The process of mining cryptocurrencies requires vast amounts of computing power, which in turn requires enormous amounts of energy. This has led to concerns about the carbon footprint of cryptocurrencies and their potential impact on climate change.

For example, a study by the University of Cambridge found that the total energy consumption of the Bitcoin network alone is equivalent to the annual energy consumption of the entire country of Argentina. Additionally, the energy-intensive mining process can result in e-waste and other environmental harms.

Counterarguments:

Despite the ethical concerns raised by the adoption of cryptocurrencies, some argue that the benefits of crypto adoption outweigh the potential risks. For example, cryptocurrencies can provide individuals with greater financial freedom and autonomy, particularly in countries with unstable or authoritarian governments. Additionally, cryptocurrencies can facilitate cross-border transactions and reduce the costs and barriers associated with traditional financial systems.

Others argue that the potential negative impacts of crypto adoption can be mitigated through regulation and oversight. For example, the implementation of regulations to prevent money laundering and other illicit activities can help ensure the stability and legitimacy of the crypto industry. Additionally, the development of more sustainable mining practices and alternative consensus mechanisms can help reduce the environmental impact of cryptocurrencies.

Conclusion:

In conclusion, the adoption of cryptocurrencies has significant ethical implications across a range of domains. While cryptocurrencies have the potential to empower individuals and democratize financial systems, they may also exacerbate social inequality, undermine traditional financial systems, and have significant environmental impacts. The debate over the ethical implications of crypto adoption is ongoing, and will likely continue as the crypto industry evolves and matures. It is critical that stakeholders across the industry work together to address these concerns and ensure that the adoption of cryptocurrencies is done in a responsible and ethical manner.

CHAPTER 11: THE FUTURE OF CRYPTOCURRENCIES

I. Introduction to the future of cryptocurrencies

Cryptocurrencies have come a long way since the first cryptocurrency, Bitcoin, was created in 2009. Over the years, cryptocurrencies have grown in popularity and acceptance, and many experts predict that they are here to stay. As we move forward, the future of cryptocurrencies is becoming increasingly important to consider, especially as they continue to change the way we think about money, investments, and transactions.

In this section, we will explore the future of cryptocurrencies and the various factors that will shape it. We will examine the potential benefits and challenges that cryptocurrencies may face in the coming years, as well as the regulatory and technological developments that will impact their growth and adoption.

The Potential Benefits of Cryptocurrencies:

One of the key benefits of cryptocurrencies is their potential to provide financial freedom and empowerment to individuals who may not have access to traditional financial systems. Cryptocurrencies are decentralized, meaning that they are not controlled by a central authority or government. This means that anyone with an internet connection can access and use cryptocurrencies, regardless of their location or financial status.

Cryptocurrencies can also offer faster and more cost-effective transactions compared to traditional financial systems. Transactions can be completed in a matter of minutes, and the fees associated with these transactions are often much lower than those charged by banks or other financial institutions.

In addition, cryptocurrencies can provide an alternative investment opportunity for individuals who may not have access to traditional investment options. With cryptocurrencies, investors can purchase and trade digital assets, potentially earning profits from price fluctuations in the market.

Potential Challenges:

While cryptocurrencies have the potential to offer many benefits, they also face significant challenges. One of the main challenges is the issue of volatility. Cryptocurrency prices can be highly volatile, meaning that their value can fluctuate rapidly and unpredictably. This can make them a risky investment option, and many investors may be hesitant to enter the market due to the potential for significant losses.

Another challenge facing cryptocurrencies is the issue of security. Cryptocurrencies are often targeted by hackers and other cybercriminals, who attempt to steal digital assets or manipulate the market for personal gain. This has led to many high-profile cryptocurrency hacks and thefts, and has raised concerns about the security of digital assets.

Regulatory and Technological Developments:

The future of cryptocurrencies will also be shaped by regulatory and technological developments. Governments around the world are currently grappling with how to regulate cryptocurrencies, and there is a great deal of uncertainty around how these regulations will impact the market.

In addition, technological developments such as the emergence of blockchain technology and decentralized finance (DeFi) platforms are likely to play a significant role in shaping the future of cryptocurrencies. These developments could lead to new opportunities for innovation and growth in the cryptocurrency industry, but they may also present new challenges and risks.

Conclusion:

In conclusion, the future of cryptocurrencies is complex and multifaceted, with many potential benefits and challenges to consider. While cryptocurrencies have the potential to offer financial empowerment and alternative investment opportunities, they also face significant challenges related to volatility and security. As the industry continues to evolve, regulatory and technological developments will play a crucial role in shaping the future of cryptocurrencies, and it will be important to carefully monitor these developments to understand their impact on the market.

Potential developments in the crypto space

The crypto space has come a long way since the inception of Bitcoin in 2009. Today, there are thousands of cryptocurrencies and blockchain-based applications with diverse use cases. The future of cryptocurrencies looks promising, with many potential developments that could transform the financial landscape.

One potential development is the emergence of central bank digital currencies (CBDCs). These are digital versions of fiat currencies that are issued and backed by central banks. CBDCs could provide many benefits over traditional cash, such as lower transaction costs, faster processing times, and increased transparency. They could also help central banks to better monitor and manage the money supply, and could facilitate cross-border payments.

Another potential development in the crypto space is the widespread adoption of decentralized finance (DeFi) applications. DeFi refers to a variety of blockchain-based financial applications that are designed to operate without intermediaries, such as banks or brokerages. These applications enable users to lend, borrow, trade, and store digital assets in a decentralized manner. DeFi has the potential to democratize access to financial services, reduce costs, and increase financial inclusion.

The emergence of non-fungible tokens (NFTs) is another potential development in the crypto space. NFTs are unique digital assets that are stored on a blockchain, and can represent anything from art to collectibles to virtual real estate. NFTs have gained popularity in recent years, with high-profile sales such as the $69 million sale of Beeple's digital artwork, "Everydays: The First 5000 Days." NFTs have the potential to revolutionize the art world, as well as other industries such as gaming and sports memorabilia.

In addition to these developments, there are also potential advancements in the underlying technology of cryptocurrencies. For example, researchers are exploring the use of sharding to improve the scalability of blockchain networks. Sharding is a technique that involves dividing a blockchain network into smaller subsets, or "shards," that can process transactions in parallel. This could significantly increase the throughput of blockchain networks, and enable them to handle a higher volume of transactions.

Another area of research is the development of quantum-resistant cryptography. Quantum computers have the potential to break many of the cryptographic algorithms that are used to secure cryptocurrencies and blockchain networks. Quantum-resistant cryptography is designed to resist attacks from quantum computers, and could help to ensure the long-term security of blockchain-based systems.

Despite these potential developments, there are also challenges and risks that must be addressed. For example, the emergence of CBDCs could have implications for financial stability, privacy, and cybersecurity. The widespread adoption of DeFi applications could also raise concerns around regulation and investor protection. NFTs have already faced criticisms around their environmental impact and potential for fraud.

In addition, the development of new technologies and applications could also lead to increased concentration of power and wealth in the hands of a few. It is important to ensure that these potential developments are inclusive and benefit society as a whole, rather than just a select few.

In conclusion, the crypto space is a rapidly evolving landscape with many potential developments that could transform the financial industry. From CBDCs to DeFi to NFTs, the future of cryptocurrencies looks promising. However, it is important to address the challenges and risks that come with these potential developments, and to ensure that they benefit society as a whole.

Opportunities and challenges for cryptocurrencies

Cryptocurrencies have been hailed as a transformative innovation with the potential to revolutionize the financial sector. While this is certainly true to some extent, cryptocurrencies also face significant challenges that must be addressed if they are to fulfill their potential. In this section, we will explore some of the key opportunities and challenges facing cryptocurrencies.

Opportunities

Decentralization
One of the key opportunities presented by cryptocurrencies is their decentralized nature. Unlike traditional financial systems, which are controlled by banks and other centralized entities, cryptocurrencies operate on a decentralized network that is open to all. This means that no single entity has control over the system, making it more transparent and resilient to manipulation.

Borderless Transactions
Another major opportunity presented by cryptocurrencies is their ability to facilitate borderless transactions. Unlike traditional financial systems, which are limited by geographic and political boundaries, cryptocurrencies can be used to transfer value across borders with minimal friction. This has the potential to greatly increase the efficiency of cross-border transactions and reduce the costs associated with international trade.

Reduced Friction
Cryptocurrencies also have the potential to reduce friction in financial transactions. By eliminating intermediaries and reducing the need for manual processes, cryptocurrencies can make financial transactions faster, cheaper, and more efficient. This could greatly benefit individuals and businesses alike, particularly in developing countries where traditional financial systems are often inefficient and expensive.

Increased Financial Inclusion
Cryptocurrencies have the potential to increase financial inclusion by providing access to financial services to people who are currently underserved by traditional financial systems. By enabling peer-to-peer

transactions and reducing the need for intermediaries, cryptocurrencies can make financial services more accessible and affordable to a wider range of people.

Challenges

Volatility
One of the biggest challenges facing cryptocurrencies is their volatility. Cryptocurrencies are notoriously volatile, with prices often fluctuating wildly over short periods of time. This makes them risky investments, particularly for those who are not familiar with the cryptocurrency market.

Regulatory Uncertainty
Another major challenge facing cryptocurrencies is regulatory uncertainty. While some countries have embraced cryptocurrencies and developed regulatory frameworks to govern their use, others have taken a more cautious approach. This lack of consistency in regulation can create uncertainty for businesses and individuals, making it difficult to know how to engage with cryptocurrencies in a safe and legal manner.

Security Risks
Cryptocurrencies also face significant security risks. The decentralized nature of cryptocurrencies makes them more resistant to hacking than traditional financial systems, but they are not immune to attack. Cryptocurrency exchanges and wallets have been targeted by hackers in the past, resulting in the loss of millions of dollars worth of cryptocurrency.

Lack of Adoption
Finally, cryptocurrencies face a significant challenge in terms of adoption. While the technology has been around for more than a decade, cryptocurrencies are still not widely used by the general public. This lack of adoption can be attributed to a number of factors, including the complexity of the technology, the difficulty of acquiring and storing cryptocurrency, and the lack of merchant acceptance.

Conclusion

In conclusion, cryptocurrencies present a range of opportunities and challenges. While their decentralized nature and ability to facilitate borderless transactions offer significant benefits, their volatility, regulatory uncertainty, security risks, and lack of adoption pose significant challenges. As the cryptocurrency market continues to evolve, it will be important to address these challenges in order to realize the full potential of this transformative technology.

Comparison with other emerging technologies (AI, IoT, etc.)

The rapid pace of technological advancement in recent years has led to the emergence of a number of new and exciting technologies, including cryptocurrencies, artificial intelligence (AI), and the Internet of Things (IoT). These technologies have the potential to transform the way we live, work, and interact with one another, and they are already having a significant impact on a wide range of industries.

In this section, we will compare cryptocurrencies with other emerging technologies, focusing on their similarities and differences, as well as the opportunities and challenges they present.

Comparison with Artificial Intelligence:

Artificial intelligence is a branch of computer science that focuses on the development of algorithms and models that can perform tasks that typically require human intelligence, such as natural language processing, image recognition, and decision-making.

One of the main similarities between cryptocurrencies and AI is that they both rely on complex algorithms and mathematical models to function. In the case of cryptocurrencies, the blockchain technology that underlies them uses advanced cryptographic algorithms to ensure that transactions are secure and tamper-proof. Similarly, AI algorithms often use advanced mathematical models, such as neural networks and deep learning, to analyze large amounts of data and make predictions or decisions.

Another similarity between cryptocurrencies and AI is that they are both disrupting traditional industries and creating new opportunities for innovation. In the case of cryptocurrencies, they are challenging traditional financial institutions and enabling new forms of decentralized finance. Similarly, AI is revolutionizing a wide range of industries, from healthcare and transportation to finance and marketing, by enabling more accurate predictions, faster decision-making, and better customer experiences.

However, there are also some important differences between cryptocurrencies and AI. One of the main differences is that cryptocurrencies are a relatively new and untested technology, whereas AI has been in development for several decades and has already been applied in a wide range of industries. This means that there is still a great deal of uncertainty and risk associated with cryptocurrencies, whereas AI is a more established and predictable technology.

Another important difference between cryptocurrencies and AI is that cryptocurrencies are often associated with concerns around security and privacy, whereas AI is more commonly associated with concerns around bias and ethics. While both technologies raise important ethical and societal questions, the nature of these questions is different, and it is important to address them in a way that is appropriate to the specific technology in question.

Comparison with the Internet of Things:

The Internet of Things (IoT) is a network of connected devices, sensors, and appliances that can communicate with one another and exchange data. This technology is enabling a wide range of new applications and services, from smart homes and cities to industrial automation and logistics.

One of the main similarities between cryptocurrencies and the IoT is that they both rely on decentralized networks to function. In the case of cryptocurrencies, the blockchain technology that underlies them is a decentralized network of nodes that work together to verify and validate transactions. Similarly, the IoT relies on a decentralized network of devices that communicate with one another to exchange data and perform tasks.

Another similarity between cryptocurrencies and the IoT is that they are both creating new opportunities for innovation and disruption. In the case of cryptocurrencies, they are enabling new forms of decentralized finance and challenging traditional financial institutions. Similarly, the IoT is enabling new forms of automation, optimization, and efficiency in a wide range of industries, from manufacturing and logistics to healthcare and agriculture.

However, there are also some important differences between cryptocurrencies and the IoT. One of the main differences is that cryptocurrencies are primarily focused on financial transactions, whereas the IoT has a much wider range of applications and use cases. This means that while cryptocurrencies have the potential to revolutionize the financial industry, the impact of the IoT is likely to be felt across a much broader range of industries.

Another important difference between cryptocurrencies and the IoT is that the IoT is often associated with concerns around security and privacy, whereas cryptocurrencies are more commonly associated with concerns around volatility and regulatory oversight.

The Internet of Things (IoT) refers to the network of physical devices, vehicles, and other objects embedded with software, sensors, and connectivity to enable these objects to collect and exchange data. While the IoT has the potential to revolutionize industries such as manufacturing, transportation, and healthcare, it also raises significant concerns about security and privacy.

One major issue with the IoT is the potential for these connected devices to be hacked or otherwise compromised, which could lead to the theft of sensitive data or even physical harm. For example, a hacker could gain access to a connected car's control system and cause an accident, or they could gain access to a medical device and interfere with a patient's treatment.

Another concern with the IoT is the amount of personal data that these devices collect and transmit. This data can include everything from a user's location and browsing history to their health information and daily habits. If this data falls into the wrong hands, it could be used for nefarious purposes such as identity theft or blackmail.

In contrast, cryptocurrencies are more commonly associated with concerns around volatility and regulatory oversight. Cryptocurrencies are known for their dramatic price swings, which can make them a risky investment for those who are not well-versed in the market. Additionally, many governments and financial regulators are still grappling with how to regulate cryptocurrencies, which can make it difficult for investors and businesses to navigate the space.

However, there are also some important similarities between cryptocurrencies and other emerging technologies such as AI and the IoT. For example, all of these technologies are characterized by their ability to collect and analyze large amounts of data in real-time. This can lead to new insights and efficiencies in industries such as finance, healthcare, and transportation.

Additionally, all of these technologies have the potential to disrupt traditional industries and business models. For example, AI is already being used to automate a wide range of tasks, from customer service to financial analysis, while the IoT is enabling new levels of efficiency and automation in areas such as supply chain management and logistics.

In conclusion, while there are certainly differences between cryptocurrencies and other emerging technologies such as AI and the IoT, there are also important similarities. All of these technologies have the potential to revolutionize industries and create new opportunities, but they also raise significant concerns around security, privacy, and regulatory oversight. As these technologies continue to evolve, it will be important for individuals, businesses, and governments to carefully consider the opportunities and challenges that they present.

II. Emerging trends in crypto

Cryptocurrencies are an ever-evolving technology that continues to capture the attention of investors, regulators, and the general public. In this section, we will explore some of the emerging trends in the crypto space, including the rise of decentralized finance (DeFi), non-fungible tokens (NFTs), and central bank digital currencies (CBDCs).

Decentralized Finance (DeFi)

DeFi refers to a new financial system that is built on top of blockchain technology. It aims to provide financial services in a decentralized manner, allowing anyone with an internet connection to access financial services without the need for intermediaries such as banks or other financial institutions.

The DeFi ecosystem has exploded in popularity in recent years, with the total value locked in DeFi protocols reaching over $120 billion as of September 2021. DeFi protocols offer a range of financial services, including lending and borrowing, decentralized exchanges, and prediction markets.

One of the key features of DeFi is the use of smart contracts, which are self-executing contracts that automatically enforce the rules and regulations of a financial transaction. This eliminates the need for intermediaries and reduces the risk of fraud and corruption.

However, DeFi is not without its challenges. The space is still relatively new, and there have been a number of high-profile hacks and exploits that have resulted in the loss of millions of dollars. Moreover, the regulatory landscape for DeFi remains uncertain, with many jurisdictions struggling to define how DeFi protocols should be regulated.

Non-Fungible Tokens (NFTs)

NFTs are a type of digital asset that represent ownership of a unique piece of digital content, such as artwork, music, or videos. Unlike traditional cryptocurrencies, which are fungible (i.e., each unit of the currency is interchangeable with another unit), NFTs are non-fungible (i.e., each NFT is unique and cannot be exchanged for another).

NFTs have exploded in popularity in 2021, with a number of high-profile sales of NFTs, including the sale of a digital artwork by Beeple for $69 million. NFTs offer a new way for artists, musicians, and other creators to monetize their work, and they also provide collectors with a new way to invest in digital assets.

However, NFTs have also been subject to criticism. Some argue that the high prices paid for NFTs are not justified by the underlying value of the digital asset, and that the hype around NFTs is creating a bubble. Moreover, there are concerns around the environmental impact of NFTs, as the energy required to create and trade NFTs is significant.

Central Bank Digital Currencies (CBDCs)

CBDCs are digital currencies that are issued and backed by central banks. CBDCs are seen as a potential alternative to traditional cash and electronic payment systems, as they offer the potential for faster, cheaper, and more secure transactions.

Many central banks around the world are currently exploring the possibility of issuing CBDCs, with some, such as the People's Bank of China, already piloting CBDCs in select regions. CBDCs could potentially offer a number of benefits, including increased financial inclusion, reduced transaction costs, and improved monetary policy.

However, there are also concerns around CBDCs. Some worry that CBDCs could disintermediate commercial banks, leading to a reduction in the availability of credit and potentially destabilizing the financial system. Moreover, there are concerns around the privacy implications of CBDCs, as they could potentially allow central banks to monitor and control the spending habits of citizens.

Conclusion

The crypto space continues to evolve at a rapid pace, with new technologies and trends emerging on a regular basis. DeFi, NFTs, and CBDCs are just a few examples of the latest developments in the crypto space that have the potential to revolutionize the financial industry and beyond. It is important for investors, policymakers, and the general public to stay informed about these trends and their potential implications.

One emerging trend in the crypto space is the rise of decentralized autonomous organizations (DAOs). These are organizations that operate on a blockchain, with decisions made by a community of stakeholders rather than a centralized authority. DAOs have the potential to create more transparent and democratic organizations, but there are also concerns about their potential for abuse and manipulation.

Another trend to watch in the crypto space is the increasing interest in green and sustainable cryptocurrencies. As concerns about the environmental impact of crypto mining and energy consumption grow, some developers and investors are exploring alternative approaches that prioritize sustainability. For example, some cryptocurrencies are exploring the use of renewable energy sources, such as solar or wind power, to power their mining operations.

Finally, it is worth noting that the regulatory landscape for cryptocurrencies is still evolving and can be complex and varied. While some countries have embraced cryptocurrencies and established clear regulations, others have taken a more cautious approach or banned cryptocurrencies altogether. It is important for investors and other stakeholders to be aware of these regulatory differences and how they may impact the use and adoption of cryptocurrencies in different regions.

In conclusion, the crypto space is a complex and rapidly evolving field with many potential opportunities and challenges. While cryptocurrencies have the potential to revolutionize finance and beyond, there are also many unknowns and risks associated with this emerging technology. It is important for investors, policymakers, and the general public to stay informed about the latest developments and trends in the crypto space in order to make informed decisions about its potential use and adoption.

Decentralized finance (DeFi) and non-fungible tokens (NFTs)

Decentralized finance (DeFi) and non-fungible tokens (NFTs) are two of the most exciting and innovative trends in the crypto space. DeFi refers to a set of financial applications and protocols built on blockchain technology, which aim to create an open, decentralized, and transparent alternative to traditional financial systems. NFTs, on the other hand, are unique digital assets that are verified on a blockchain and can be used to represent ownership of a wide range of assets, from art to virtual real estate.

In this section, we will explore the basics of DeFi and NFTs, their potential benefits and drawbacks, and their role in shaping the future of finance and art.

Decentralized finance (DeFi)

DeFi has been one of the hottest trends in the crypto space over the past few years, with a wide range of projects and platforms emerging to offer new and innovative financial services built on blockchain technology. At its core, DeFi aims to create a more open, transparent, and decentralized financial system that is accessible to anyone with an internet connection, regardless of their location or financial status.

One of the key advantages of DeFi is that it removes the need for intermediaries such as banks or financial institutions, which can often be slow, expensive, and prone to fraud and manipulation. Instead, DeFi applications use smart contracts to automate financial transactions and enforce rules and regulations in a transparent and decentralized way.

Some of the most popular DeFi applications and platforms include:

Decentralized exchanges (DEXs): These are peer-to-peer exchanges that allow users to trade cryptocurrencies without the need for a central authority. Examples include Uniswap, SushiSwap, and Curve.

Lending and borrowing platforms: These platforms allow users to lend or borrow cryptocurrencies, often using collateral to reduce the risk of default. Examples include Aave, Compound, and MakerDAO.

Prediction markets: These are platforms that allow users to bet on the outcome of future events, such as political elections or sporting events. Examples include Augur and Gnosis.

Insurance platforms: These platforms offer insurance against various risks, such as smart contract bugs or exchange hacks. Examples include Nexus Mutual and Cover.

Stablecoins: These are cryptocurrencies that are designed to maintain a stable value, often by being pegged to a fiat currency or commodity. Examples include Tether, USDC, and DAI.

While DeFi offers many potential benefits, such as lower fees, greater transparency, and increased access to financial services, there are also some significant challenges and risks associated with this emerging trend.

One of the main challenges of DeFi is its complexity. Many DeFi applications are still in the early stages of development and can be difficult to use for non-technical users. Additionally, the lack of regulation in the DeFi space can create a higher risk of fraud and scams, which can lead to significant financial losses for users.

Another challenge is the issue of scalability. Many DeFi applications are built on the Ethereum blockchain, which has limited transaction throughput and can become congested during periods of high demand. This can lead to higher fees and slower transaction times, which can make DeFi applications less practical for everyday use.

Non-fungible tokens (NFTs)

Non-fungible tokens (NFTs) are another exciting trend in the crypto space that has gained a lot of attention in recent years. NFTs are unique digital assets that are verified on a blockchain and can be used to represent ownership of a wide range of assets, from art to virtual real estate.

One of the key advantages of NFTs is their ability to create a new market for digital art and collectibles. Before the advent of NFTs, it was difficult for digital artists and creators to monetize their work, as it was easy to replicate and distribute digital content without paying for it. NFTs allow creators to sell their unique, one-of-a-kind creations on the blockchain, with proof of ownership and authenticity.

NFTs have also gained popularity in the sports and gaming industries. For example, NBA Top Shot is an online platform where users can buy, sell, and trade NFTs that represent specific moments in NBA games. Similarly, in the gaming industry, NFTs are used to represent in-game assets, such as weapons or characters, that can be bought and sold on the blockchain.

However, NFTs have also faced criticism for their environmental impact, as the process of verifying transactions on the blockchain requires a significant amount of energy consumption. Additionally, the high prices of some NFTs have led to accusations of elitism and exclusivity, with some arguing that only the wealthy can afford to participate in this market.

Despite these concerns, the NFT market continues to grow and evolve, with new use cases and applications being developed on a regular basis. As with any emerging technology, it is important to carefully consider the potential benefits and drawbacks of NFTs before investing in them.

Decentralized finance (DeFi)

Another major trend in the crypto space is the rise of decentralized finance, or DeFi. DeFi refers to a new financial system that is built on top of blockchain technology and operates independently of traditional financial institutions.

One of the key advantages of DeFi is its ability to provide financial services to people who may not have had access to them before. For example, in many countries, traditional banks may be inaccessible or too expensive for certain populations. With DeFi, anyone with an internet connection can access financial services such as loans, savings accounts, and insurance.

DeFi also offers a high degree of transparency and security, as all transactions are recorded on the blockchain and can be viewed by anyone. This helps to reduce fraud and corruption in the financial system, and allows users to have more control over their own financial data.

One of the most popular use cases of DeFi is in the area of lending and borrowing. In a DeFi lending platform, users can lend and borrow cryptocurrency without the need for intermediaries such as banks. This allows for faster and more efficient transactions, as well as lower fees for users.

However, DeFi is not without its challenges. One of the main concerns is the potential for smart contract bugs or hacks, which can result in significant financial losses for users. Additionally, the regulatory landscape for DeFi is still uncertain in many countries, which can lead to legal and compliance risks for users and companies operating in this space.

Despite these challenges, DeFi has shown significant growth and potential, with new projects and applications being developed on a regular basis. As with any emerging technology, it is important to carefully consider the potential benefits and risks of DeFi before investing in it.

Overall, the crypto space is constantly evolving and changing, with new technologies and trends emerging on a regular basis. As with any investment, it is important to carefully consider the potential benefits and risks before making a decision. With proper research and due diligence, investors can navigate the crypto space and potentially benefit from the opportunities presented by emerging trends such as DeFi and NFTs.

Central bank digital currencies (CBDCs)

Central bank digital currencies (CBDCs) have been a hot topic in the financial world in recent years. CBDCs are digital versions of traditional currencies that are issued and backed by central banks. These digital currencies have the potential to transform the way we use and interact with money, and many central banks around the world are exploring the idea of issuing CBDCs.

One of the primary benefits of CBDCs is that they could improve the efficiency and security of the payment system. By providing a digital alternative to cash, CBDCs could make payments faster and more convenient, as well as reduce the risks associated with physical currency. This could also help to promote financial inclusion, as CBDCs could be more accessible to people who do not have access to traditional banking services.

Another potential benefit of CBDCs is that they could provide greater control and oversight for central banks. By issuing a digital currency, central banks could have more visibility into the flow of money and be better equipped to monitor and regulate the financial system. This could help to prevent fraud and money laundering, as well as promote stability in the financial markets.

However, there are also concerns around CBDCs, particularly around privacy and security. If all transactions are recorded on a central database, there is a risk that individuals' personal financial information could be compromised. Additionally, if a central database were to be hacked or compromised in some other way, it could potentially have disastrous consequences for the financial system.

Despite these concerns, many central banks are actively exploring the idea of issuing CBDCs. The People's Bank of China has already begun piloting a digital version of the yuan, while the European Central Bank has recently launched a public consultation on the possible issuance of a digital euro.

From the perspective of investment banking, the introduction of CBDCs could create new opportunities in the digital payments space. As more transactions move to digital currencies, investment banks may need to adapt their business models to remain competitive. Additionally, the introduction of CBDCs could lead to new regulations and compliance requirements that investment banks would need to navigate.

Actuaries would need to consider the impact of CBDCs on the broader financial system, as well as the risks associated with digital currencies. They would also need to evaluate the potential impact of CBDCs on investment portfolios and asset valuations.

Portfolio managers may need to adjust their investment strategies to account for the potential impact of CBDCs on traditional currencies and financial markets. Additionally, the introduction of CBDCs could lead to new investment opportunities in the digital payments space.

Quantitative analysts could play a key role in the development and implementation of CBDCs. They would need to develop models to evaluate the potential risks and benefits of CBDCs, as well as provide insights into the optimal design and implementation of these digital currencies.

Securities traders may need to adapt their trading strategies to account for the potential impact of CBDCs on financial markets. Additionally, the introduction of CBDCs could create new opportunities for securities trading in the digital payments space.

Financial planners and analysts would need to consider the impact of CBDCs on their clients' financial plans and portfolios. They would also need to stay up-to-date on the latest developments in the CBDC space to provide informed advice to their clients.

In conclusion, CBDCs are a rapidly evolving area of the financial industry with the potential to transform the way we use and interact with money. While there are concerns around privacy and security, many central banks are actively exploring the idea of issuing CBDCs, and investment professionals will need to adapt to the changing landscape of digital currencies and payments. As CBDCs continue to develop, it will be important for financial professionals to stay informed and engaged with this emerging trend in order to provide the best possible advice and service to their clients.

Interoperability and integration with traditional finance systems

Interoperability and integration with traditional finance systems is an important topic in the world of cryptocurrency. As the use of cryptocurrencies continues to grow, there is increasing interest in finding ways to connect these new systems with traditional financial systems. In this section, we will explore the challenges and opportunities of interoperability and integration, and the potential benefits that could be realized through these efforts.

Interoperability refers to the ability of different systems to communicate with each other and exchange information. In the context of cryptocurrency, interoperability is about creating connections between different blockchain networks and cryptocurrency platforms. The goal is to allow for the seamless transfer of assets between different platforms and to create a more unified ecosystem for cryptocurrency.

One of the biggest challenges in achieving interoperability is the fact that different blockchain networks and cryptocurrency platforms use different protocols and standards. This means that it can be difficult to establish connections between these systems without first creating a common language or framework for communication.

Despite these challenges, there are several projects underway that aim to create greater interoperability between different cryptocurrency platforms. For example, the Polkadot network is a project that is focused on building a cross-chain infrastructure for the decentralized web. The project is designed to allow for the seamless transfer of assets between different blockchain networks, while also providing a framework for interoperability between different decentralized applications.

Another example of a project focused on interoperability is Cosmos, a decentralized network that is designed to enable the exchange of value and data between different blockchain networks. Cosmos provides a standardized framework for communication between different blockchain networks, making it easier for developers to build applications that can interact with multiple platforms.

In addition to interoperability, there is also a growing interest in integrating cryptocurrency systems with traditional financial systems. This is particularly relevant given the increasing mainstream adoption of cryptocurrencies, and the growing interest from institutional investors and traditional financial institutions.

One potential benefit of integrating cryptocurrency systems with traditional financial systems is the creation of new investment opportunities. For example, as more institutional investors begin to take an interest in cryptocurrencies, there is an opportunity to create investment products that bridge the gap between these new systems and traditional financial instruments.

Another potential benefit of integration is the ability to leverage the strengths of both systems. Traditional financial systems have well-established risk management frameworks, regulatory structures, and governance mechanisms. By integrating with these systems, cryptocurrency platforms could potentially benefit from these existing structures, while also providing new opportunities for innovation and growth.

However, there are also significant challenges to integrating cryptocurrency systems with traditional financial systems. One of the biggest challenges is the regulatory environment. Cryptocurrency platforms operate in a largely unregulated space, while traditional financial systems are subject to strict regulatory oversight. This means that any efforts to integrate these systems will need to navigate a complex regulatory landscape, which could create significant barriers to adoption.

Another challenge is the technical infrastructure required to support integration. Cryptocurrency platforms and traditional financial systems have different technological architectures, which means that integrating these systems will require significant investment in new infrastructure and technology.

Despite these challenges, there is growing interest in exploring the potential of integration between cryptocurrency and traditional financial systems. As the use of cryptocurrencies continues to grow, it is likely that we will see increasing efforts to find ways to connect these new systems with traditional finance, creating new opportunities for investment and innovation.

In conclusion, interoperability and integration with traditional financial systems are important topics in the world of cryptocurrency. Interoperability is about creating connections between different blockchain networks and cryptocurrency platforms, while integration is about connecting these new systems with traditional financial systems. While there are significant challenges to achieving both interoperability and integration, there are also significant opportunities for innovation and growth in the cryptocurrency space. As the use of cryptocurrencies continues to grow, it is likely that we will see increasing efforts to find ways to connect these new systems with traditional finance, creating new opportunities for investment and growth.

III. Social and economic implications of crypto

The emergence and widespread adoption of cryptocurrencies and blockchain technology have significant social and economic implications. In this section, we will explore some of the most pressing issues related to the impact of crypto on society and the economy.

A. Economic Implications

Disruptive Potential
Crypto has the potential to disrupt traditional financial systems and institutions, which could lead to significant economic changes. For example, the use of cryptocurrencies could reduce the need for intermediaries like banks, and could facilitate more direct peer-to-peer transactions. This could lead to lower fees and faster settlement times, but it could also lead to increased risk and reduced oversight.

Inflation and Monetary Policy
Another economic implication of crypto is its potential impact on inflation and monetary policy. Some experts argue that cryptocurrencies could reduce the effectiveness of monetary policy, as they could make it more difficult for central banks to control the money supply and inflation. Others argue that crypto could provide a new tool for managing inflation, as it could enable more transparent and predictable monetary policies.

Taxation and Regulation
The use of cryptocurrencies also raises important questions about taxation and regulation. Cryptocurrencies can be difficult to track and tax, which could lead to significant revenue losses for

governments. This has led some governments to implement new regulations and tax policies related to cryptocurrencies, which could impact the growth and adoption of crypto.

B. Social Implications

Financial Inclusion
One potential benefit of crypto is its potential to improve financial inclusion. Cryptocurrencies could provide a more accessible and secure way for people without access to traditional financial institutions to store and transfer money. However, there are also concerns that crypto could exacerbate existing inequalities, as the technology and knowledge required to use crypto effectively may not be evenly distributed.

Cybersecurity and Privacy
Another social implication of crypto is its impact on cybersecurity and privacy. The use of cryptocurrencies and blockchain technology could make financial transactions more secure, but it could also create new vulnerabilities and challenges for cybersecurity. Additionally, the use of cryptocurrencies could raise concerns about privacy, as transactions can be traced and recorded on a public ledger.

Criminal Activity
Finally, the use of cryptocurrencies has raised concerns about their potential use in criminal activity. Cryptocurrencies can facilitate anonymous transactions, which could make them an attractive option for money laundering, terrorism financing, and other illegal activities. As a result, some governments have implemented regulations and restrictions on the use of cryptocurrencies to combat these risks.

Overall, the social and economic implications of crypto are complex and multifaceted. While the technology has the potential to bring about significant benefits, it also poses a number of risks and challenges. As cryptocurrencies and blockchain technology continue to evolve and grow in popularity, it will be important to carefully consider and address these implications to ensure that they are used in a responsible and beneficial way.

Financial inclusion and democratization of finance

Financial inclusion and democratization of finance are two critical concepts in the world of finance. In recent years, cryptocurrencies and blockchain technology have emerged as potential tools to promote financial inclusion and democratization of finance. These technologies offer the possibility of creating decentralized financial systems that are accessible to people who do not have access to traditional financial systems.

In this section, we will discuss how cryptocurrencies and blockchain technology can promote financial inclusion and democratization of finance. We will first define these concepts and their significance in the financial industry. We will then explore how cryptocurrencies and blockchain technology can provide financial services to people who have limited access to traditional financial systems. We will also discuss the challenges and limitations of using cryptocurrencies and blockchain technology to promote financial inclusion and democratization of finance.

I. Definition of financial inclusion and democratization of finance

A. Financial inclusion

Financial inclusion refers to the availability and accessibility of financial services to all individuals, regardless of their income level or location. The concept of financial inclusion is crucial because it enables individuals to participate in economic activities and access credit and insurance services. The World Bank defines financial inclusion as "access to useful and affordable financial products and services that meet the needs of individuals and businesses, transactions, payments, savings, and credit."

In many developing countries, financial exclusion is a significant problem. According to the World Bank, about 1.7 billion people worldwide do not have access to formal financial services. Financial exclusion can limit the economic opportunities available to individuals and impede their ability to invest in their future.

B. Democratization of finance

The democratization of finance refers to the process of making financial systems and services accessible to a broader population, including those who have been excluded from traditional financial systems. The democratization of finance is essential because it enables individuals to have more control over their financial lives and provides them with greater economic opportunities.

The democratization of finance can be achieved by reducing the barriers to entry to financial systems and services. Cryptocurrencies and blockchain technology have the potential to reduce the barriers to entry to financial systems by creating decentralized systems that are accessible to a broader population.

II. How cryptocurrencies and blockchain technology promote financial inclusion and democratization of finance

A. Access to financial services

Cryptocurrencies and blockchain technology can provide access to financial services to individuals who do not have access to traditional financial systems. These technologies enable the creation of decentralized financial systems that are accessible to anyone with an internet connection, without the need for a traditional bank account.

For example, in many developing countries, traditional banking systems are not available in rural areas, making it difficult for people to access financial services. Cryptocurrencies and blockchain technology can provide a solution to this problem by creating decentralized financial systems that are accessible to anyone with an internet connection.

B. Lower transaction costs

One of the significant advantages of cryptocurrencies and blockchain technology is that they can significantly reduce the transaction costs associated with financial transactions. In traditional financial systems, intermediaries such as banks, payment processors, and other financial institutions add significant costs to transactions. These intermediaries often charge fees for their services, making financial transactions expensive.

Cryptocurrencies and blockchain technology can eliminate intermediaries, reducing the transaction costs associated with financial transactions. With cryptocurrencies, transactions can be completed directly between parties, without the need for intermediaries, reducing the costs of financial transactions.

C. Transparency and security

Cryptocurrencies and blockchain technology offer a high degree of transparency and security, making financial transactions more secure and trustworthy. Blockchain technology provides a decentralized ledger that records all transactions, making it difficult to manipulate or alter financial records. This transparency and security can increase trust in financial systems and make financial transactions more accessible to individuals who may be skeptical of traditional financial systems.

D. Decentralized finance (DeFi)

Decentralized finance (DeFi) is an emerging trend in the crypto space that has the potential to significantly impact financial inclusion and democratization. DeFi refers to a new financial system built on decentralized blockchain technology, where financial transactions and services can be carried out without the need for traditional intermediaries such as banks.

One of the most significant advantages of DeFi is that it enables financial inclusion for individuals who are unbanked or underbanked. According to a report by the World Bank, approximately 1.7 billion adults globally are unbanked, meaning they do not have access to traditional financial services. This lack of access to financial services can make it difficult for individuals to participate fully in the economy, save money, and access credit. DeFi has the potential to provide financial services to individuals who are currently excluded from the traditional financial system, thus contributing to greater financial inclusion.

DeFi can also democratize finance by allowing individuals to participate in financial services and products that were previously only accessible to wealthy individuals and institutions. For example, decentralized exchanges (DEXs) allow users to trade cryptocurrencies without the need for intermediaries. This means that anyone with an internet connection can participate in cryptocurrency trading, as long as they have access to a DeFi wallet.

Another advantage of DeFi is that it provides greater transparency and security compared to traditional financial systems. DeFi transactions are recorded on a public blockchain, which means that they are transparent and accessible to anyone. This transparency can help to reduce fraud and corruption in the financial system. Additionally, DeFi is based on cryptographic algorithms that provide strong security guarantees, making it difficult for malicious actors to manipulate the system.

Despite the potential benefits of DeFi, there are also significant risks and challenges associated with this emerging trend. One of the most significant risks is the potential for smart contract vulnerabilities, which can lead to the loss of funds. Smart contracts are self-executing contracts that are coded on the blockchain and can automate the execution of financial transactions. However, if a smart contract has a vulnerability, it can be exploited by attackers to steal funds.

Another challenge associated with DeFi is the lack of regulation and oversight. DeFi operates in a regulatory grey area, which means that there are few regulations in place to protect users and ensure that financial products and services are safe and reliable. This lack of regulation can make it difficult for users to assess the risks associated with DeFi products and services.

In conclusion, DeFi has the potential to significantly impact financial inclusion and democratization, by providing financial services to individuals who are currently excluded from the traditional financial system and allowing individuals to participate in financial products and services that were previously only accessible to wealthy individuals and institutions. However, there are also significant risks and challenges associated with DeFi, including smart contract vulnerabilities and the lack of regulation and oversight. As DeFi continues to evolve and mature, it will be important for policymakers and regulators to develop appropriate regulations and oversight mechanisms to ensure that DeFi can operate safely and securely, while still providing its potential benefits to users.

Impact on economic growth and development

Decentralized finance (DeFi) is an emerging trend that has the potential to significantly impact economic growth and development. DeFi is a system of financial applications and services that operate on a decentralized network, such as the Ethereum blockchain, without the need for intermediaries like banks or other financial institutions. It offers a variety of financial services, including lending and borrowing, asset management, insurance, and trading, all of which are conducted using digital assets.

One of the potential benefits of DeFi is its ability to provide financial services to individuals and businesses that are currently underserved by traditional financial institutions. According to the World Bank, an estimated 1.7 billion people around the world lack access to basic financial services, such as bank accounts and loans. DeFi has the potential to address this issue by providing financial services that are accessible to anyone with an internet connection, regardless of their geographic location or financial situation.

DeFi can also facilitate economic growth by increasing access to capital for entrepreneurs and small businesses. In traditional finance, obtaining a loan or financing for a business can be a lengthy and challenging process, with high fees and interest rates. DeFi platforms, on the other hand, offer decentralized lending protocols that allow users to obtain loans quickly and easily, without the need for extensive paperwork or credit checks. This can enable more entrepreneurs to start businesses and create jobs, which can ultimately stimulate economic growth.

Furthermore, DeFi can contribute to the development of new financial products and services, which can help drive innovation and create new opportunities for economic growth. DeFi platforms allow developers to build financial applications on a decentralized network, which can lead to the creation of new financial products and services that were previously impossible or too expensive to develop. For example, decentralized prediction markets can allow users to make predictions about future events, which can be used for a variety of purposes, such as insurance and risk management.

However, it is important to note that there are also potential risks associated with DeFi, including regulatory risks, security risks, and volatility risks. As DeFi operates on a decentralized network, it is difficult for regulators to monitor and enforce regulations, which can lead to potential fraud or market manipulation. Additionally, as DeFi platforms are not backed by traditional financial institutions, there is a higher risk of security breaches and hacks, which can result in the loss of digital assets.

In terms of volatility, the prices of digital assets on DeFi platforms can be highly volatile, which can make it difficult for users to predict the value of their assets. This can result in significant losses for users who invest in digital assets without fully understanding the risks involved.

Despite these risks, the potential benefits of DeFi for economic growth and development are significant. By providing financial services to underserved populations, facilitating access to capital for entrepreneurs and small businesses, and driving innovation in the financial sector, DeFi has the potential to contribute to the development of a more inclusive and prosperous global economy. As such, it will be important for policymakers and regulators to carefully consider the potential benefits and risks of DeFi, and to develop appropriate regulations and guidelines to ensure the safe and responsible development of this emerging sector.

E. Impact on Financial Privacy and Security

One of the key features of cryptocurrencies and blockchain technology is their potential to enhance financial privacy and security. Transactions conducted using cryptocurrencies are recorded on a public ledger, but the identities of the transacting parties are typically anonymous or pseudonymous. This can provide users with a greater degree of privacy and anonymity than traditional financial transactions, which are typically conducted using bank accounts or credit cards that are linked to users' personal information.

However, while cryptocurrencies can provide greater financial privacy, they also present new challenges in terms of security. Digital assets stored in cryptocurrency wallets can be vulnerable to hacks and theft, and once stolen, they cannot be easily retrieved or traced. Additionally, the decentralized nature of many cryptocurrencies means that there is no central authority responsible for maintaining the security of the network. As a result, many individuals and businesses have lost large amounts of money due to security breaches or scams involving cryptocurrencies.

Furthermore, the high volatility of cryptocurrencies can pose challenges for financial stability and economic development. Cryptocurrencies are notorious for their price volatility, with sudden price fluctuations of 50% or more in a single day not uncommon. While this can present opportunities for profit for traders, it also creates significant risks for investors and businesses that rely on stable financial markets. Additionally, the high degree of uncertainty and unpredictability associated with cryptocurrencies can discourage investment in other sectors of the economy, potentially hindering economic growth.

Despite these challenges, cryptocurrencies and the underlying blockchain technology have the potential to revolutionize the way that we conduct financial transactions and exchange value. By reducing the need for intermediaries, increasing transparency, and promoting financial inclusion, cryptocurrencies have the potential to create a more democratic and accessible financial system.

One potential area of impact is in developing countries, where traditional financial systems may be inadequate or inaccessible for many individuals. Cryptocurrencies and blockchain technology can provide a means of transferring funds and accessing financial services in areas where traditional banks are not present. For example, in many African countries, mobile money systems have become a popular way of conducting transactions, allowing individuals to send and receive money using their mobile phones. Cryptocurrencies and blockchain technology have the potential to further expand access to financial services in these regions, promoting economic growth and development.

Additionally, cryptocurrencies and blockchain technology have the potential to reduce the costs associated with financial transactions and increase efficiency in financial markets. By reducing the need for intermediaries, such as banks and clearinghouses, transaction fees and processing times can be significantly reduced. This can be particularly beneficial for cross-border transactions, which are often slow and expensive due to the need for multiple intermediaries.

Furthermore, the transparency and immutability of blockchain technology can reduce fraud and corruption in financial systems, potentially promoting greater trust and confidence in financial markets. This can be particularly important in developing countries, where corruption is often a significant barrier to economic growth and development.

However, the full potential of cryptocurrencies and blockchain technology is yet to be realized, and there are still many challenges to be addressed. In particular, issues around security, regulation, and scalability will need to be addressed before cryptocurrencies and blockchain technology can become widely adopted and integrated into mainstream financial systems.

Overall, cryptocurrencies and blockchain technology have the potential to significantly impact economic growth and development, by promoting financial inclusion, reducing transaction costs, and increasing transparency and efficiency in financial markets. However, these technologies also present new challenges and risks, which will need to be addressed through continued innovation and regulatory oversight.

Social and cultural changes driven by crypto adoption

The adoption of cryptocurrencies has the potential to bring about significant social and cultural changes. This section will explore some of the potential impacts of crypto adoption on society and culture.

A. Disrupting Traditional Power Structures

One of the most significant potential impacts of cryptocurrencies is their ability to disrupt traditional power structures. Cryptocurrencies are decentralized, meaning that they are not controlled by any central authority. This decentralization has the potential to break down traditional power structures, such as governments and financial institutions, and give individuals more control over their finances.

For example, in countries with unstable political systems or weak financial infrastructure, cryptocurrencies can provide a way for individuals to store and transfer wealth without relying on traditional banks or government-controlled currencies. This can lead to greater financial independence and empowerment for individuals, particularly those who may not have had access to traditional financial services.

However, the decentralization of cryptocurrencies also presents challenges, particularly in terms of regulation and consumer protection. Without a central authority to oversee transactions, there is a risk of fraud and other illegal activities. As cryptocurrencies continue to gain mainstream acceptance, it will be important to develop regulations and consumer protections to ensure that individuals are not taken advantage of.

B. Shifting Perceptions of Money

The adoption of cryptocurrencies is also likely to shift societal perceptions of money. For many people, the concept of money has long been tied to physical currency, such as cash or coins. However, cryptocurrencies are entirely digital and exist only in the form of computer code.

This shift away from physical currency has the potential to change the way people think about money and value. Cryptocurrencies are often seen as a more democratic form of money, as they are not controlled by any one institution or government. This can lead to greater trust in the financial system and greater participation in the economy.

However, the shift away from physical currency also presents challenges. For example, it can be more difficult to track and regulate digital currencies, particularly when they are used for illegal activities such as money laundering or drug trafficking. Additionally, the volatility of cryptocurrencies can make them a risky investment, particularly for individuals who are not familiar with the technology.

C. Fostering Innovation and Entrepreneurship

Another potential impact of crypto adoption is the fostering of innovation and entrepreneurship. The decentralized nature of cryptocurrencies allows for more experimentation and innovation than traditional financial systems, which are often heavily regulated and controlled by a small number of institutions.

For example, blockchain technology, which underlies many cryptocurrencies, has the potential to revolutionize industries such as healthcare, supply chain management, and voting. By providing a secure and transparent way to track and verify transactions, blockchain technology can increase efficiency and reduce costs in a wide range of industries.

However, the decentralized nature of cryptocurrencies also presents challenges for entrepreneurs and innovators. Without a central authority to oversee transactions and ensure consumer protection, there is a risk of fraud and other illegal activities. Additionally, the volatility of cryptocurrencies can make it difficult for entrepreneurs to raise funding or manage cash flow.

D. Encouraging Financial Inclusion

Finally, the adoption of cryptocurrencies has the potential to encourage greater financial inclusion. Traditional financial systems can be inaccessible or costly for many individuals, particularly those in low-income or developing countries. However, cryptocurrencies can provide a way for individuals to store and transfer wealth without relying on traditional financial institutions.

For example, in countries with weak financial infrastructure or unstable political systems, cryptocurrencies can provide a way for individuals to store and transfer wealth without relying on traditional banks or government-controlled currencies. This can lead to greater financial independence and empowerment for individuals, particularly those who may not have had access to traditional financial services.

However, the adoption of cryptocurrencies also presents challenges for financial inclusion. Cryptocurrencies can be complex and difficult to understand, particularly for individuals who may not have had access to traditional financial education. Additionally, the lack of consumer protection in the cryptocurrency market may result in exploitation or fraud, further deterring individuals from adopting cryptocurrencies.

Another challenge in the adoption of cryptocurrencies is the issue of regulatory oversight. Cryptocurrencies operate outside of traditional financial regulations, which can be both a benefit and a challenge. While some argue that this allows for greater innovation and flexibility in the market, others argue that it leaves consumers vulnerable to exploitation and manipulation. The lack of regulatory oversight can also lead to instability and volatility in the market, which can make it difficult for investors to predict and manage risks.

However, despite these challenges, the adoption of cryptocurrencies has already led to significant social and cultural changes. One of the most notable changes is the emergence of a new community of tech-savvy individuals who are passionate about the potential of cryptocurrencies and blockchain technology. This community, sometimes referred to as the "crypto community," has grown rapidly in recent years, fueled by online forums, social media, and cryptocurrency conferences.

The crypto community is diverse, comprising individuals from a wide range of backgrounds and industries, including technology, finance, law, and academia. Many members of the crypto community see cryptocurrencies as a means to challenge the traditional financial system, which they see as corrupt, inefficient, and outdated. They believe that cryptocurrencies can provide a more transparent, democratic, and inclusive financial system that empowers individuals and communities.

One of the key values of the crypto community is decentralization. Decentralization refers to the idea that power and control should be distributed among a network of participants rather than concentrated in the hands of a few centralized authorities. Cryptocurrencies are built on decentralized blockchain technology, which allows transactions to be verified and recorded by a network of participants rather than a single authority. This decentralization is seen as a way to challenge the power and authority of traditional financial institutions, which are often seen as monopolistic and oppressive.

Another value of the crypto community is transparency. Many members of the community believe that traditional financial institutions operate in secret, with little accountability or transparency. Cryptocurrencies, on the other hand, are built on transparent blockchain technology, which allows anyone to view and verify transactions on the network. This transparency is seen as a way to challenge corruption and promote accountability in the financial system.

The adoption of cryptocurrencies has also led to new forms of artistic and cultural expression. For example, cryptocurrency enthusiasts have created digital art and music that explores themes related to blockchain technology and the crypto community. Some artists have even begun to sell their work exclusively for cryptocurrency, using blockchain technology to create unique digital assets that can be traded and collected like traditional artwork.

In addition, the adoption of cryptocurrencies has led to new forms of philanthropy and social activism. Some members of the crypto community have used their wealth and influence to support charitable causes and promote social change. For example, the Pineapple Fund, founded by an anonymous Bitcoin millionaire, donated over $55 million to various charitable causes, including clean water projects, environmental conservation, and medical research.

Overall, the adoption of cryptocurrencies has led to significant social and cultural changes, driven by a new community of tech-savvy individuals who are passionate about the potential of blockchain technology and the values of decentralization and transparency. While there are still challenges to overcome, such as the issue of financial inclusion and the need for regulatory oversight, the impact of cryptocurrencies on social and cultural norms is likely to continue to grow in the coming years.

PART IV: ARTIFICIAL INTELLIGENCE AND MACHINE LEARNING

Artificial Intelligence (AI) and Machine Learning (ML) have rapidly become integral to the world of finance. These technologies are revolutionizing the industry and changing the way that finance professionals work. AI and ML offer unprecedented opportunities to make faster and more informed decisions, reduce risk, and improve operational efficiency. However, as with any new technology, there are also challenges and risks associated with their implementation.

Chapter 12: The Promise of Artificial Intelligence in Finance

AI has the potential to transform every aspect of finance, from lending and credit scoring to fraud detection and investment management. AI algorithms can process vast amounts of data, identify patterns, and make predictions in real-time. For example, AI-powered chatbots can assist customers with account inquiries and transactions, while automated investment advisors can provide personalized investment advice.

One of the key promises of AI in finance is the ability to improve financial inclusion. AI-powered credit scoring models can provide more accurate assessments of creditworthiness, enabling more people to access loans and other financial services. This can benefit not only individuals but also small businesses and startups that may have struggled to secure financing through traditional channels.

However, there are also concerns about the potential for AI to exacerbate existing biases and discrimination in the financial system. For example, if AI algorithms are trained on data that reflects historical patterns of discrimination, they may produce biased outcomes. It is essential that AI in finance is developed and deployed in a responsible and ethical manner.

Chapter 13: Machine Learning and Risk Management

Risk management is a critical component of finance, and ML has the potential to significantly improve risk assessment and management. ML algorithms can analyze large amounts of data to identify patterns and trends, enabling more accurate risk assessments. For example, ML-powered fraud detection systems can identify and prevent fraudulent transactions in real-time.

However, ML algorithms are only as good as the data they are trained on. If the data is biased or incomplete, the resulting risk assessments may be inaccurate or unfair. It is therefore crucial that financial institutions take steps to ensure that their ML models are trained on unbiased and representative data.

Chapter 14: The Role of AI in Investment Strategies

AI is also transforming investment strategies, enabling investors to make more informed decisions and optimize their portfolios. AI-powered algorithms can analyze vast amounts of data from various sources, including financial statements, news articles, and social media, to identify investment opportunities and forecast market trends.

However, there are also concerns about the potential for AI to contribute to market volatility and exacerbate existing market inefficiencies. For example, if a large number of investors use similar AI-powered investment strategies, it could lead to a herd mentality that drives up the price of certain assets and creates a bubble.

Chapter 15: Ethics and Accountability in AI

As AI becomes increasingly integrated into the finance industry, there are growing concerns about the ethical implications of these technologies. AI has the potential to perpetuate existing biases and discrimination, and there are also concerns about the potential for AI to make decisions that are difficult to explain or justify.

It is therefore essential that the development and deployment of AI in finance is guided by ethical principles and best practices. This includes ensuring that AI algorithms are transparent, accountable, and aligned with the values and goals of the organization. Additionally, financial institutions must prioritize the privacy and security of customer data, as the use of AI in finance requires access to sensitive information.

Conclusion:

AI and ML are transforming the finance industry, offering unprecedented opportunities to improve decision-making, reduce risk, and enhance operational efficiency. However, there are also challenges and risks associated with the adoption of these technologies. Financial institutions must ensure that their AI and ML models are developed and deployed in a responsible and ethical manner, and that they prioritize transparency, accountability, and customer privacy. With the right approach, AI and ML have the potential to revolutionize the finance industry, making it more accessible, efficient, and equitable for all.

As the field of AI and ML continues to advance, it will be important for financial professionals to stay up-to-date with the latest developments and trends. This may require ongoing education and training, as well as collaboration with experts in other fields, such as computer science and data analytics.

At the same time, it is important not to overlook the critical role that human judgment and expertise play in the finance industry. While AI and ML can provide valuable insights and automate certain processes, they cannot replace the experience and intuition of seasoned financial professionals. As such, it is important to strike a balance between the use of technology and the human touch.

Ultimately, the promise of AI and ML in finance lies in their ability to augment human decision-making, enabling financial professionals to make better, more informed decisions. By leveraging the power of these technologies while remaining mindful of their limitations and risks, we can create a more innovative, efficient, and inclusive finance industry that benefits individuals and society as a whole.

CHAPTER 12: THE PROMISE OF ARTIFICIAL INTELLIGENCE IN FINANCE

Artificial Intelligence (AI) has been transforming industries across the board, and the finance industry is no exception. With its ability to automate processes, analyze data, and make predictions, AI has the potential to revolutionize the way financial institutions operate, from risk management to investment strategies. In this section, we will explore the basics of AI, its applications in finance, and the challenges and opportunities it presents.

What is Artificial Intelligence?

Artificial Intelligence refers to the development of computer systems that can perform tasks that typically require human intelligence, such as learning, reasoning, and problem-solving. The field of AI encompasses a range of techniques and approaches, including machine learning, deep learning, natural language processing, and robotics.

Machine learning, a subset of AI, involves training algorithms on large datasets to identify patterns and make predictions. Deep learning, a more complex form of machine learning, uses neural networks to analyze data and make more sophisticated predictions.

Natural language processing (NLP) involves analyzing and understanding human language, allowing machines to interpret and respond to written or spoken words. Robotics involves the development of machines that can perform physical tasks, such as assembling products or performing surgery.

Applications of AI in Finance

AI has a wide range of potential applications in finance, from automating routine tasks to developing sophisticated investment strategies. Here are some of the key areas where AI is already being used in finance:

Fraud Detection and Prevention: AI can help financial institutions detect and prevent fraud by analyzing large volumes of data to identify suspicious patterns and behaviors.

Customer Service: Chatbots powered by AI can provide customer support 24/7, allowing financial institutions to offer faster and more efficient service.

Credit Scoring: AI can analyze large amounts of data to assess creditworthiness and make more accurate credit decisions.

Investment Strategies: AI can analyze market trends and historical data to develop sophisticated investment strategies, such as algorithmic trading.

Risk Management: AI can help financial institutions manage risk by identifying potential threats and vulnerabilities in their systems.

Challenges and Opportunities

While AI presents many opportunities for the finance industry, there are also significant challenges to its adoption. One of the key challenges is the need for large amounts of data to train algorithms effectively. Financial institutions must also ensure that their AI systems are transparent and explainable, so that customers and regulators can understand how decisions are being made.

Another challenge is the potential for AI to perpetuate biases and discrimination. If AI algorithms are trained on biased datasets, they may produce biased results, leading to unfair outcomes for certain groups of people. It is therefore essential that financial institutions prioritize ethical considerations when developing and deploying AI systems.

Conclusion

AI has the potential to revolutionize the finance industry, offering new ways to automate processes, analyze data, and make predictions. However, financial institutions must approach AI adoption with care and caution, prioritizing transparency, accountability, and ethical considerations. With the right approach, AI has the potential to transform the finance industry, offering new opportunities for efficiency, innovation, and growth.

I. Overview of AI applications in finance, including fraud detection, credit scoring, customer service, and more

Artificial intelligence (AI) is revolutionizing the finance industry, offering unprecedented opportunities to improve decision-making, reduce risk, and enhance operational efficiency. With the ability to process large volumes of data and identify patterns and insights that would be impossible for humans to detect, AI has the potential to transform every aspect of the financial services industry.

In this section, we will provide an overview of some of the key AI applications in finance, including fraud detection, credit scoring, customer service, and more. We will explore the benefits and challenges of these applications, as well as the ethical considerations that must be taken into account.

AI in Fraud Detection:

Fraud is a major problem for financial institutions, costing them billions of dollars each year. Traditional methods of fraud detection, such as rule-based systems and manual reviews, are time-consuming and often ineffective. AI offers a more efficient and accurate solution.

One key application of AI in fraud detection is anomaly detection. Machine learning algorithms can analyze large volumes of transaction data and identify patterns that deviate from normal behavior. For example, if a customer suddenly starts making large purchases in a foreign country, the algorithm can flag the transaction as potentially fraudulent.

Another application of AI in fraud detection is natural language processing (NLP). NLP can be used to analyze text data, such as customer support chats and social media posts, to identify potential fraud. For example, if a customer reports that their account has been hacked, an NLP algorithm can analyze the conversation and flag it for further investigation.

AI in Credit Scoring:

Credit scoring is another area where AI is making significant inroads. Traditional credit scoring models rely on a limited set of factors, such as payment history and credit utilization. AI, on the other hand, can analyze a much wider range of data points, including social media activity, employment history, and even the types of devices a customer uses.

One key advantage of AI in credit scoring is its ability to identify hidden patterns and correlations. For example, an AI algorithm might discover that customers who use Android phones are more likely to default on their loans than those who use iPhones. This kind of insight can help financial institutions make more accurate lending decisions.

However, there are also challenges associated with the use of AI in credit scoring. One concern is that the algorithms may perpetuate biases that already exist in the financial system. For example, if an algorithm learns that customers from certain demographic groups are more likely to default, it may unfairly penalize those customers.

AI in Customer Service:

Customer service is another area where AI is being increasingly deployed. Chatbots and virtual assistants can handle routine customer inquiries and support requests, freeing up human agents to handle more complex issues.

One key advantage of AI in customer service is its ability to provide 24/7 support. Customers can access support at any time of the day or night, without having to wait for business hours.

However, there are also concerns that AI-powered customer service may be impersonal and frustrating for customers. Chatbots, in particular, have been criticized for their lack of empathy and inability to understand complex customer needs.

AI in Investment Management:

AI is also transforming the investment management industry. Machine learning algorithms can analyze vast amounts of financial data, identify trends, and make predictions about future market movements.

One key application of AI in investment management is portfolio optimization. Machine learning algorithms can analyze a client's investment goals, risk tolerance, and other factors to create a customized portfolio that maximizes returns while minimizing risk.

Another application of AI in investment management is algorithmic trading. Trading algorithms can analyze market data in real-time, identify profitable opportunities, and execute trades automatically.

However, there are also risks associated with the use of AI in investment management. One concern is that the algorithms may be prone to errors or biases, which could lead to significant financial losses. For example, if a trading algorithm is programmed to prioritize speed over accuracy, it may execute trades too quickly and result in losses for the investor.

Another risk is the potential for market manipulation. While AI can be used to identify patterns and anomalies in market data, it can also be used by individuals or organizations to manipulate markets. This can result in significant financial losses for other investors and harm the overall integrity of the financial system.

Additionally, the use of AI in investment management raises ethical concerns related to accountability and transparency. Who is responsible if an AI-powered investment strategy fails? How can investors ensure that the algorithms used to manage their portfolios are acting in their best interests?

These concerns highlight the importance of responsible and ethical AI in investment management. Financial institutions must ensure that their algorithms are transparent, accountable, and aligned with the best interests of their clients. They must also prioritize risk management and be prepared to mitigate any potential losses resulting from algorithmic errors or market manipulation.

Overall, AI has the potential to transform investment management by offering new tools and insights for investors. However, it is important to approach these technologies with caution and responsibility to ensure that they are used in a way that benefits investors and the financial system as a whole.

II. Discussion of the benefits of AI in finance, including improved accuracy, efficiency, and cost savings

The use of artificial intelligence (AI) in finance has the potential to revolutionize the way financial institutions operate. AI can help financial firms improve their accuracy, efficiency, and cost savings, providing them with a competitive advantage in the market. In this section, we will discuss the benefits of AI in finance, focusing on its ability to improve accuracy, efficiency, and cost savings.

Improved Accuracy

One of the most significant benefits of AI in finance is its ability to improve accuracy. AI-powered tools can analyze vast amounts of data quickly and accurately, providing insights that would be impossible for humans to obtain. For example, AI can help detect fraudulent activities by analyzing data patterns and flagging suspicious transactions. This is particularly relevant for credit card companies and banks, where fraud is a common problem that can result in significant financial losses.

Another area where AI can improve accuracy is in credit scoring. Traditional credit scoring models rely on limited data sources, such as credit history and income, to assess a borrower's creditworthiness. However, AI can take into account a wider range of factors, including social media data and spending patterns, to provide a more accurate assessment of a borrower's risk profile. This can help lenders make more informed lending decisions, reducing the risk of defaults and improving profitability.

Efficiency

AI can also significantly improve efficiency in finance. For example, AI-powered chatbots can provide customer service around the clock, reducing the need for human representatives and improving response times. This is particularly relevant for banks and insurance companies, where customer service is critical for building customer loyalty and improving retention rates.

In addition, AI can automate routine tasks, such as data entry and record keeping, freeing up employees' time to focus on more strategic tasks. This can lead to significant cost savings for financial institutions, as well as improving productivity and job satisfaction among employees.

Cost Savings

Finally, AI can also help financial institutions save costs. For example, AI-powered tools can help optimize investment portfolios, identifying the most profitable investments and reducing the risk of losses. This can lead to significant cost savings for investment firms, as well as improving returns for investors.

In addition, AI can help financial institutions identify and reduce operational inefficiencies, such as redundancies and errors in data entry. This can lead to significant cost savings, as well as improving customer satisfaction and retention rates.

Conclusion

In conclusion, the use of AI in finance has the potential to revolutionize the industry by improving accuracy, efficiency, and cost savings. However, it is essential to note that AI is not a silver bullet and that its implementation must be carefully managed to ensure its effectiveness. It is also important to recognize that AI is not a replacement for human judgment and that its use should be complementary to human expertise. By leveraging the benefits of AI while balancing its risks and limitations, financial institutions can unlock significant value and remain competitive in an ever-changing market.

III. Examination of challenges and limitations of AI in finance, including data privacy concerns and potential biases in machine learning algorithms

Artificial intelligence (AI) is transforming the finance industry by providing unparalleled opportunities to improve decision-making, reduce risk, and enhance operational efficiency. However, the adoption of AI in finance is not without challenges and limitations. In this section, we will examine some of these challenges and limitations, including data privacy concerns and potential biases in machine learning algorithms.

Data Privacy Concerns

One of the primary challenges associated with the use of AI in finance is data privacy. The finance industry collects vast amounts of data on individuals, including their personal and financial information. This data is highly sensitive, and if it falls into the wrong hands, it could result in identity theft, fraud, and other malicious activities.

AI systems require a significant amount of data to train their models and improve their accuracy. However, collecting and processing this data raises significant privacy concerns. For instance, the General Data Protection Regulation (GDPR) in the European Union sets strict guidelines on the collection and use of personal data. The GDPR requires companies to obtain explicit consent from individuals before collecting their data and provides them with the right to request access to their data, have it deleted, and object to its processing.

Similarly, in the United States, the Gramm-Leach-Bliley Act (GLBA) requires financial institutions to establish privacy policies and provide notice to their customers about the collection, use, and disclosure of their personal information. Failure to comply with these regulations can result in significant financial penalties, legal liabilities, and reputational damage.

Potential Biases in Machine Learning Algorithms

Another challenge associated with the use of AI in finance is the potential for biases in machine learning algorithms. Machine learning algorithms learn from historical data, which may contain biases, such as race, gender, age, and income. If these biases are not corrected, they can result in discriminatory outcomes and perpetuate systemic inequalities.

For instance, credit scoring algorithms may use historical data to predict an individual's creditworthiness. However, if this historical data contains biases, such as a history of discriminatory lending practices, it can result in unfair and inaccurate credit scores. This, in turn, can lead to discriminatory outcomes, such as the denial of loans or higher interest rates for certain groups.

Similarly, algorithmic trading may be prone to biases, such as herd behavior and groupthink. If multiple trading algorithms use the same underlying data and operate under similar parameters, they can create a self-reinforcing feedback loop that amplifies market trends and exacerbates volatility.

To address these challenges, financial institutions must ensure that their AI and machine learning algorithms are developed and deployed in a responsible and ethical manner. This includes identifying and correcting biases in historical data, promoting transparency and accountability in decision-making, and prioritizing customer privacy and data security.

Conclusion

AI and machine learning are transforming the finance industry, offering unprecedented opportunities to improve decision-making, reduce risk, and enhance operational efficiency. However, the adoption of these technologies is not without challenges and limitations. Financial institutions must ensure that their AI and machine learning algorithms are developed and deployed in a responsible and ethical manner, and that they prioritize transparency, accountability, and customer privacy. With the right approach, AI and machine learning have the potential to revolutionize the finance industry and benefit society as a whole.

IV. Case studies and real-world examples of successful AI implementations in finance

Let's delve into some real-world examples of successful AI implementations in finance.

One such example is BlackRock, which is the world's largest asset manager. BlackRock has been using AI and machine learning techniques to analyze large datasets and make investment decisions. In particular, the firm has been using natural language processing (NLP) techniques to analyze earnings call transcripts and other corporate communications to help inform investment decisions. By applying these techniques, BlackRock has been able to generate better investment insights, improve efficiency, and reduce costs.

Another example is JPMorgan Chase, which has been investing heavily in AI and machine learning in recent years. The bank has been using AI and machine learning algorithms to analyze large volumes of data and generate insights into customer behavior and preferences. This has enabled JPMorgan to personalize its services and products to better meet the needs of its customers. Additionally, the bank has been using AI and machine learning to improve its fraud detection capabilities, allowing it to identify potential fraudsters more quickly and accurately.

Another company that has been successful in implementing AI in finance is American Express. The credit card company has been using machine learning algorithms to analyze customer spending patterns and identify potential fraud. By applying these techniques, American Express has been able to reduce the number of false positives generated by its fraud detection systems, allowing it to identify genuine fraud more quickly and accurately. Additionally, the company has been using machine learning to develop more personalized offers and recommendations for its customers, which has helped to drive customer engagement and loyalty.

Another interesting example comes from the insurance industry, where AI is being used to improve underwriting decisions. For example, Liberty Mutual has been using AI and machine learning to analyze historical claims data to identify patterns and make more accurate predictions about the likelihood of future claims. By applying these techniques, the company has been able to improve the accuracy of its underwriting decisions, reducing the number of claims it pays out and improving its profitability.

In the world of trading, Citadel Securities is a company that has been using AI to great effect. The firm has been using machine learning algorithms to analyze market data and identify profitable trading opportunities. By applying these techniques, Citadel Securities has been able to generate superior returns for its investors, while also improving efficiency and reducing costs.

In the world of financial planning and advice, Wealthfront is a company that has been using AI to provide personalized investment advice to its clients. The company has been using machine learning algorithms to analyze client data and generate personalized investment portfolios based on the client's individual needs and goals. By applying these techniques, Wealthfront has been able to provide superior investment advice at a lower cost than traditional financial advisors.

These examples demonstrate the power of AI and machine learning in finance. By applying these techniques, companies can generate better insights, improve efficiency, and reduce costs. Additionally, they can personalize their services and products to better meet the needs of their customers. However, as we have discussed earlier, there are also challenges associated with the use of AI in finance, and these challenges must be carefully managed to ensure the success of these implementations.

V.   Future outlook and potential advancements in AI for the finance industry

As AI continues to advance, there are many potential future applications for the finance industry. Here, we will explore some of these possibilities and their potential impact on the industry.

One area where AI is expected to have a significant impact is in personalized financial advice. Today, many individuals receive financial advice from financial planners or advisors, who use their knowledge and expertise to make recommendations on how to invest and manage their money. However, with the advancements in AI and machine learning, it is possible to create algorithms that can provide personalized advice to individuals based on their unique financial situation and goals.

For example, an AI system could analyze an individual's income, spending habits, debts, and investments, and provide personalized recommendations on how to optimize their financial situation. This could include advice on how much to save for retirement, which investments to make, and how to minimize debt. The benefits of such a system would be increased accessibility to financial advice and potentially more accurate and effective advice.

Another area where AI is expected to have a significant impact is in fraud detection. With the increasing sophistication of financial fraud schemes, traditional methods of fraud detection may not be enough. AI algorithms can analyze large amounts of data and identify patterns that may indicate fraudulent activity. For example, an AI system could analyze transaction data and flag suspicious activity, such as unusual purchase amounts or unusual transaction locations.

One potential application of AI in finance is in the area of cryptocurrency. Cryptocurrencies like Bitcoin and Ethereum have exploded in popularity in recent years, but they remain highly volatile and complex. AI algorithms could be used to analyze cryptocurrency market data and make predictions on price movements, helping investors make informed investment decisions.

AI could also be used to improve risk management in finance. By analyzing large amounts of data, AI systems could identify potential risks and help financial institutions manage those risks more effectively. For example, an AI system could analyze customer data and identify customers who are at a high risk of defaulting on a loan, allowing the financial institution to take proactive measures to prevent default.

In addition to these potential applications, there are many other areas where AI could have a significant impact on the finance industry. For example, AI could be used to automate many routine tasks, freeing up time for financial professionals to focus on more complex tasks. AI could also be used to improve customer service by providing personalized recommendations and improving response times.

However, there are also potential challenges and limitations to the use of AI in finance. One challenge is the need for high-quality data. AI algorithms require large amounts of data to train and operate effectively, and if the data is inaccurate or biased, the results can be unreliable. Additionally, there are concerns about the potential for AI to perpetuate existing biases and inequalities in the finance industry.

Another challenge is the need for regulation and oversight. As AI becomes more prevalent in the finance industry, there is a need for regulations that ensure the responsible use of AI and protect consumer privacy.

Despite these challenges, the potential benefits of AI in finance are significant. AI has the potential to improve accuracy, efficiency, and cost savings, and to provide more personalized financial advice and better risk management. As AI continues to advance, it is likely that we will see even more applications of AI in finance, leading to a more efficient and effective industry.

CHAPTER 13: MACHINE LEARNING AND RISK MANAGEMENT

Risk management is a crucial aspect of finance, and it refers to the process of identifying, evaluating, and prioritizing potential risks that an organization may face and developing strategies to mitigate or avoid those risks. The goal of risk management is to minimize losses and maximize returns by managing risks effectively.

There are several types of risks that can affect financial organizations. One of the most common risks is market risk, which refers to the potential loss arising from changes in the value of financial instruments such as stocks, bonds, and commodities. Other types of risks include credit risk, operational risk, liquidity risk, and reputational risk.

Market risk is a significant concern for financial organizations because it is closely tied to the volatility of financial markets. The prices of financial instruments are influenced by various factors such as economic conditions, political events, and investor sentiment. As a result, market risk is unpredictable and difficult to manage. However, financial organizations can use various strategies to mitigate market risk, such as diversifying their portfolios, using hedging techniques, and monitoring market conditions closely.

Credit risk is another significant risk for financial organizations, and it refers to the potential loss that can arise from the failure of a borrower to repay a loan or meet other financial obligations. Credit risk can be managed by conducting thorough credit analysis, diversifying credit exposure, and using credit derivatives such as credit default swaps.

Operational risk is the risk of loss arising from inadequate or failed internal processes, human error, or external events. This type of risk can be mitigated by implementing robust operational procedures, conducting regular audits and assessments, and maintaining adequate insurance coverage.

Liquidity risk is the risk of not being able to meet financial obligations as they come due. It can be caused by various factors such as unexpected cash outflows, changes in market conditions, and lack of access to credit. Financial organizations can mitigate liquidity risk by maintaining adequate liquidity reserves, diversifying funding sources, and monitoring market conditions closely.

Reputational risk is the risk of damage to an organization's reputation, which can arise from various factors such as unethical behavior, poor customer service, and negative publicity. Reputational risk can be mitigated by implementing strong ethical standards, providing excellent customer service, and conducting regular reputation assessments.

Risk management strategies can be broadly categorized into two types: active and passive risk management. Active risk management involves taking an active role in managing risks, such as actively monitoring market conditions and adjusting investment portfolios accordingly. Passive risk management involves taking a more passive approach to managing risks, such as diversifying portfolios to reduce exposure to certain types of risks.

There are various tools and techniques that financial organizations use to manage risks. For example, risk modeling is a common technique used to identify potential risks and estimate the likelihood and impact of those risks. Financial organizations can also use stress testing, which involves simulating various scenarios to assess the impact of potential risks on their portfolios.

Another important aspect of risk management is compliance with regulatory requirements. Financial organizations are subject to various regulations and guidelines, such as the Basel Accords, which require them to maintain certain levels of capital reserves to absorb potential losses.

In conclusion, risk management is a critical component of finance. Financial organizations face various types of risks, such as market risk, credit risk, operational risk, liquidity risk, and reputational risk, and must implement strategies to manage those risks effectively. Risk management involves identifying potential risks, evaluating the likelihood and impact of those risks, and developing strategies to mitigate or avoid those risks. Effective risk management can help financial organizations minimize losses and maximize returns, ensuring long-term success and stability.

I. Introduction to machine learning and its applications in risk management

Risk management is an integral part of finance and involves the identification, assessment, and prioritization of risks that can affect an organization's objectives. The goal of risk management is to minimize the impact of adverse events and maximize opportunities that may arise. In recent years, machine learning has emerged as a powerful tool in risk management, helping financial institutions to better understand and manage risk.

Machine learning is a subset of artificial intelligence that involves the development of algorithms that can learn from data and improve over time. The use of machine learning in finance has grown rapidly in recent years, as financial institutions seek to improve their risk management capabilities. In this section, we will provide an overview of machine learning and its applications in risk management.

Overview of Machine Learning:

Machine learning is a type of artificial intelligence that involves the use of algorithms to analyze and learn from data. The algorithms can identify patterns and relationships in the data, and then use that information to make predictions or decisions. There are three main types of machine learning algorithms: supervised learning, unsupervised learning, and reinforcement learning.

Supervised learning involves the use of labeled data to train the algorithm. The algorithm is given input data and the corresponding output data, and it learns to map the input data to the output data. Once the algorithm has been trained, it can be used to make predictions on new, unseen data.

Unsupervised learning, on the other hand, does not use labeled data. Instead, the algorithm is given input data and it looks for patterns and relationships in the data on its own. This type of machine learning is often used for clustering and anomaly detection.

Reinforcement learning involves the use of a reward system to train the algorithm. The algorithm is given a goal to achieve and it learns by trial and error, receiving rewards for making correct decisions and punishments for making incorrect decisions.

Applications of Machine Learning in Risk Management:

Machine learning has a wide range of applications in risk management, including credit risk assessment, fraud detection, and market risk management.

Credit risk assessment is the process of evaluating the likelihood that a borrower will default on their loan. Machine learning can be used to analyze data on borrowers and their credit histories to identify patterns and predict the likelihood of default. This can help financial institutions to make more accurate decisions about lending and pricing.

Fraud detection is another area where machine learning can be used to improve risk management. Machine learning algorithms can analyze large volumes of transaction data to identify patterns that are indicative of fraudulent activity. This can help financial institutions to detect and prevent fraud before it causes significant damage.

Market risk management involves the identification and assessment of risks that arise from changes in market conditions, such as interest rates, exchange rates, and commodity prices. Machine learning can be used to analyze large volumes of market data to identify patterns and predict future market movements. This can help financial institutions to manage their exposure to market risk more effectively.

Challenges and Limitations of Machine Learning in Risk Management:

While machine learning has the potential to revolutionize risk management in finance, there are also several challenges and limitations to its use.

One challenge is the need for high-quality data. Machine learning algorithms require large amounts of high-quality data to be trained effectively. Financial institutions may face challenges in obtaining and maintaining the necessary data, particularly in areas such as credit risk assessment, where data can be sparse or incomplete.

Another challenge is the potential for bias in machine learning algorithms. Machine learning algorithms can be influenced by the data they are trained on, which can lead to bias in their predictions or decisions. This can be particularly problematic in areas such as credit risk assessment, where bias can result in unfair lending practices.

Additionally, there is a risk of overreliance on machine learning algorithms. While machine learning algorithms can provide valuable insights and predictions, they should not be relied upon exclusively. Human judgment is still crucial in risk management, and it should be used to complement machine learning algorithms. A human risk manager can provide additional context and insight into the data and algorithms being used, which can lead to better decision-making.

Moreover, it is essential to consider the potential biases in machine learning algorithms that can lead to inaccurate risk assessments. These biases can arise from the data used to train the algorithm or the algorithms' design. For example, if the data used to train the algorithm is biased towards a particular demographic, the algorithm may make inaccurate predictions for that group. Similarly, if the algorithm is designed with inherent biases, it may make inaccurate predictions for certain scenarios.

One approach to mitigating these biases is to ensure that the training data is diverse and representative of the entire population. This can be done by incorporating data from various sources and using appropriate techniques to clean and preprocess the data. Additionally, it is essential to regularly test and validate the machine learning algorithm to ensure that it is accurate and unbiased.

Another approach is to incorporate human oversight into the machine learning process. Human risk managers can review the algorithm's predictions and assess whether they align with their experience and intuition. They can also identify and correct any biases that may have been overlooked by the algorithm.

In conclusion, machine learning algorithms have the potential to revolutionize risk management in finance. They can help financial institutions identify and mitigate risks more effectively and efficiently. However, there are several challenges that need to be addressed before machine learning algorithms can be fully integrated into risk management practices. These challenges include data privacy concerns, potential biases in the algorithms, and the risk of overreliance on machine learning. To address these challenges, financial institutions must take a comprehensive approach that incorporates diverse and representative data, regular testing and validation of the algorithms, and human oversight.

II. Discussion of the benefits of machine learning in risk management, including improved accuracy and efficiency

Machine learning has shown great promise in enhancing risk management processes in the financial industry, providing significant benefits such as improved accuracy and efficiency. In this section, we will discuss the various ways in which machine learning can be beneficial for risk management.

One of the primary benefits of using machine learning in risk management is improved accuracy. Machine learning algorithms can process vast amounts of data much faster than human analysts, making it possible to identify patterns and relationships in data that would be difficult for a human to detect. This ability to process large volumes of data and identify patterns enables machine learning algorithms to provide more accurate predictions and insights.

Machine learning can also improve the efficiency of risk management processes. By automating tasks such as data collection, processing, and analysis, machine learning algorithms can free up human analysts to focus on more complex tasks such as risk assessment and strategy development. This can lead to significant cost savings for financial institutions and enable them to allocate their resources more effectively.

Furthermore, machine learning algorithms can continuously learn and adapt to changing market conditions, allowing for more accurate and up-to-date risk assessments. Traditional risk management processes typically rely on historical data and may not be able to account for sudden changes or unexpected events. Machine learning algorithms, on the other hand, can learn from new data as it becomes available, enabling them to provide more accurate predictions and risk assessments in real-time.

Another benefit of using machine learning in risk management is the ability to identify and prevent fraudulent activities. Machine learning algorithms can analyze large amounts of data and detect patterns that may indicate fraudulent activities, such as unauthorized access or suspicious transactions. This can help financial institutions to detect and prevent fraud more quickly and effectively than traditional methods.

Machine learning can also be beneficial for portfolio optimization, which involves selecting the most efficient combination of investments to maximize returns while minimizing risks. By analyzing market data and identifying patterns, machine learning algorithms can help portfolio managers to make better investment decisions and optimize their portfolios.

One example of the benefits of machine learning in risk management can be seen in the field of credit risk assessment. Traditionally, credit risk assessment has been a time-consuming process that involves manual data collection and analysis. Machine learning algorithms can automate this process and provide more accurate predictions of credit risk based on factors such as credit history, income, and debt-to-income ratio. This can help financial institutions to make more informed lending decisions and reduce the risk of default.

Another example is the use of machine learning algorithms to detect and prevent financial crimes such as money laundering. Machine learning algorithms can analyze vast amounts of data to identify suspicious transactions, patterns, and relationships between entities that may indicate money laundering or other financial crimes. This can help financial institutions to comply with regulations and prevent financial crimes more effectively.

Despite the numerous benefits of machine learning in risk management, there are also potential drawbacks and limitations to consider. For example, the accuracy of machine learning algorithms can be affected by the quality and completeness of the data used to train them. Additionally, machine learning algorithms can sometimes be difficult to interpret, making it difficult for human analysts to understand how the algorithm arrived at a particular conclusion.

Moreover, there is also the issue of bias in machine learning algorithms. Biases can be introduced into machine learning algorithms through factors such as the data used to train them, the algorithms used, and the criteria used to evaluate their performance. This can result in inaccurate predictions and decisions that unfairly discriminate against certain groups of people.

In conclusion, machine learning has the potential to revolutionize risk management in the financial industry by improving accuracy and efficiency, detecting and preventing fraud, and optimizing portfolios. While there are potential drawbacks and limitations to consider, the benefits of machine learning in risk management far outweigh the risks. As the technology continues to evolve, it is likely that we will see even more applications of machine learning in the financial industry, leading to better risk management processes and ultimately more profitable outcomes for financial institutions and investors.

One of the most significant benefits of machine learning in risk management is the improved accuracy it offers compared to traditional methods. Machine learning algorithms can analyze vast amounts of data with greater speed and precision than humans, identifying patterns and relationships that might go unnoticed by human analysts. This can lead to more accurate predictions and risk assessments, helping financial institutions to make more informed decisions about investment strategies, creditworthiness, and fraud prevention.

For example, in the field of investment management, machine learning algorithms can analyze historical market data to identify patterns and correlations that can be used to predict future market trends. This can help portfolio managers to make more informed decisions about which securities to invest in, reducing risk and increasing returns.

Similarly, machine learning can be used to assess credit risk by analyzing a wide range of variables, such as credit scores, income, and employment history. This can help lenders to make more accurate decisions about whether to extend credit to a particular borrower and at what interest rate, reducing the risk of defaults and loan losses.

Another benefit of machine learning in risk management is increased efficiency. Machine learning algorithms can process vast amounts of data much more quickly than humans, reducing the time and resources required for risk assessments and fraud detection. This can help financial institutions to operate more efficiently, reducing costs and improving profitability.

For example, machine learning algorithms can be used to automate the process of underwriting insurance policies, analyzing data from various sources to determine the likelihood of a particular event occurring and calculating the appropriate premium. This can significantly reduce the time and resources required for underwriting, enabling insurance companies to offer policies more quickly and efficiently.

Similarly, machine learning algorithms can be used to detect fraud in real-time, analyzing transaction data and identifying anomalies that might indicate fraudulent activity. This can help financial institutions to prevent losses due to fraud and reduce the risk of reputational damage.

In conclusion, the benefits of machine learning in risk management are numerous and significant. By improving accuracy, efficiency, and fraud detection, machine learning has the potential to revolutionize the financial industry and help financial institutions to operate more efficiently and profitably. While there are potential drawbacks and limitations to consider, these should not detract from the many benefits that machine learning can offer in risk management. As the technology continues to evolve, we can expect to see even more innovative applications of machine learning in the financial industry, leading to better risk management processes and more successful outcomes for investors and financial institutions alike.

III. Examination of challenges and limitations of machine learning in risk management, including data quality and interpretability issues

Machine learning has been touted as a powerful tool for risk management in the financial industry, but it is not without its challenges and limitations. In this section, we will examine some of the challenges and limitations of machine learning in risk management, including data quality and interpretability issues.

One of the main challenges of machine learning in risk management is the quality of the data. In order for machine learning algorithms to provide accurate results, they need to be trained on high-quality data. However, financial data can be notoriously difficult to work with due to its complexity and variability. For example, financial data can contain missing or erroneous values, outliers, and other anomalies that can impact the accuracy of the results. In addition, the quality of the data can be affected by external factors such as market volatility and changes in regulations, making it difficult to maintain the accuracy of the algorithms over time.

Another challenge of machine learning in risk management is interpretability. Machine learning algorithms can provide highly accurate predictions, but the inner workings of the algorithms can be difficult to interpret. This can be a problem in risk management, where it is important to understand the factors that are driving the predictions in order to make informed decisions. For example, a portfolio manager may use machine learning algorithms to optimize their portfolio, but if they are unable to interpret the results, they may not be able to make the necessary adjustments to manage the risk.

In addition to data quality and interpretability issues, there are other limitations of machine learning in risk management to consider. For example, machine learning algorithms are only as good as the data they are trained on, and if the data is biased, the results can be biased as well. This can be a problem in risk management, where it is important to ensure that the results are unbiased and reflect the true risks associated with the portfolio.

Another limitation of machine learning in risk management is the potential for overfitting. Overfitting occurs when a machine learning algorithm is trained too closely to the training data and is not able to generalize to new data. This can be a problem in risk management, where it is important to ensure that the algorithms are able to accurately predict the risks associated with new investments or market conditions.

Finally, there is also a risk of overreliance on machine learning algorithms. While machine learning algorithms can provide valuable insights and predictions, they should not be relied upon exclusively. Human expertise is still needed to make informed decisions about risk management, and machine learning should be used as a tool to supplement human decision-making, not replace it entirely.

Despite these challenges and limitations, machine learning still holds enormous potential for risk management in the financial industry. By addressing these challenges and limitations and developing more sophisticated algorithms and data quality control measures, machine learning can continue to revolutionize risk management and lead to better decision-making and outcomes for financial institutions and their clients.

IV. Future outlook and potential advancements in machine learning for risk management

As machine learning technology continues to advance, there are many potential future applications in the field of risk management in the financial industry. Here, we will examine some of the potential advancements and the impact they may have.

One area where machine learning can potentially make a significant impact is in the prediction of black swan events. Black swan events are events that are unexpected and have a significant impact on financial markets. Examples include the 2008 financial crisis and the COVID-19 pandemic. By analyzing large datasets and identifying patterns and correlations, machine learning algorithms could potentially help identify the warning signs of such events, allowing financial institutions to take preventative measures.

Another area where machine learning can make a difference is in improving fraud detection. Machine learning algorithms can be trained to identify patterns in data that may indicate fraudulent activity. This can include unusual patterns in transaction amounts, times, or locations, as well as other red flags that may not be immediately apparent to humans. By using machine learning to detect fraud, financial institutions can save money and protect their clients' assets.

Machine learning can also be used to improve portfolio optimization. By analyzing large amounts of data on different securities, machine learning algorithms can identify patterns and correlations that may not be immediately apparent to human portfolio managers. This can help optimize portfolios by identifying securities that are likely to perform well and avoiding those that are likely to underperform.

One potential advancement in machine learning technology is the development of explainable AI. Explainable AI refers to machine learning algorithms that can provide an explanation of how they arrived at a particular decision or prediction. This is important in the financial industry, as it allows regulators and clients to understand how decisions are being made and to ensure that the algorithms are not biased or discriminatory.

Another potential area of advancement is in the development of machine learning algorithms that are better able to handle non-stationary data. Non-stationary data refers to data that changes over time, such as stock prices or interest rates. Traditional machine learning algorithms may not be well-suited to handle such data, as they assume that the data is stationary. Newer algorithms, such as deep learning, may be better suited to handle non-stationary data and could potentially improve the accuracy of predictions.

As machine learning technology continues to advance, there will be a growing need for skilled professionals who are able to develop and deploy machine learning algorithms in the financial industry. This includes data scientists, machine learning engineers, and other specialists who are able to work with large datasets and complex algorithms. It is important for financial institutions to invest in training and development programs to ensure that they have the talent they need to stay competitive in an increasingly data-driven industry.

However, there are also potential risks associated with the continued development and deployment of machine learning in the financial industry. One risk is the potential for algorithms to become biased or discriminatory. This can occur if the algorithms are trained on biased data or if they are designed in a way that perpetuates existing biases. It is important for financial institutions to be aware of this risk and to take steps to ensure that their algorithms are fair and unbiased.

Another risk is the potential for algorithms to be hacked or manipulated. Machine learning algorithms rely on large amounts of data to make predictions, and if this data is compromised or manipulated, the accuracy of the predictions could be impacted. It is important for financial institutions to invest in cybersecurity measures to protect against this risk.

In conclusion, the future of machine learning in risk management in the financial industry is both exciting and uncertain. While there are many potential advancements and benefits associated with the continued development of machine learning technology, there are also potential risks and challenges that must be addressed. As the technology continues to evolve, it will be important for financial institutions to stay abreast of the latest developments and to invest in the necessary resources to fully utilize the potential of machine learning in their risk management processes.

One potential area for advancement is in the use of reinforcement learning. Reinforcement learning is a type of machine learning that involves an agent learning how to make decisions in an environment by receiving feedback in the form of rewards or punishments. This approach has already shown promise in other fields, such as robotics and gaming, and could potentially be applied to financial risk management.

Another area for advancement is in the development of more explainable machine learning models. As previously discussed, interpretability is a key issue in machine learning for risk management, and there is a growing demand for models that can be easily understood and explained. One potential solution is the use of transparent models, such as decision trees, that can provide clear explanations for their predictions.

Additionally, there is a need for more collaboration and standardization in the field of machine learning for risk management. Currently, there are many different approaches and techniques being used, and it can be difficult to compare and evaluate their effectiveness. By establishing more standard practices and sharing data and insights, financial institutions can work together to develop more effective and efficient risk management processes.

Finally, it will be important for financial institutions to continue investing in the necessary resources and infrastructure to support the use of machine learning in risk management. This includes not only investing in the technology itself but also in training and hiring experts who can develop and implement machine learning models, as well as ensuring that the necessary data and computing resources are available.

In conclusion, the potential of machine learning in risk management in the financial industry is vast, and there are many exciting developments and advancements on the horizon. However, it is important to acknowledge and address the challenges and limitations associated with the use of this technology, and to approach its implementation with caution and care. With the proper investment, collaboration, and standardization, machine learning has the potential to greatly improve the accuracy and efficiency of risk management processes, ultimately benefiting both financial institutions and their clients.

CHAPTER 14: THE ROLE OF AI IN INVESTMENT STRATEGIES

Artificial Intelligence (AI) has been transforming industries around the world, and finance is no exception. In recent years, AI has become increasingly popular in the investment management space, with many financial institutions investing in the technology to improve investment strategies and increase profitability.

AI is the simulation of human intelligence in machines that are programmed to think and act like humans. It involves the use of machine learning algorithms and neural networks that enable machines to learn from data and improve their performance over time. In investment management, AI can be used to analyze vast amounts of financial data, identify patterns and trends, and make predictions about future market movements.

The potential benefits of AI in investment management are numerous. By analyzing data more efficiently and accurately than humans, AI can help portfolio managers make better investment decisions and generate higher returns for their clients. Additionally, AI can help identify and mitigate risks, reduce costs, and increase operational efficiency.

However, as with any new technology, there are also potential drawbacks and limitations to consider. In this section, we will examine the potential benefits and limitations of AI in investment strategies, as well as the current state of the technology and its future potential.

Benefits of AI in Investment Strategies:

One of the primary benefits of AI in investment strategies is the ability to analyze vast amounts of data quickly and accurately. With the help of AI, investment managers can analyze financial data from a variety of sources, including company filings, news articles, social media, and more. This allows them to identify patterns and trends that might not be immediately apparent to human analysts.

AI can also help investment managers make more informed investment decisions. By analyzing historical market data and identifying patterns and trends, AI can make predictions about future market movements and help portfolio managers make more informed investment decisions. This can lead to higher returns for clients and improved risk management.

In addition to analyzing financial data, AI can also be used to analyze non-financial data, such as environmental and social factors. This allows investment managers to identify investment opportunities and risks that might not be immediately apparent through traditional financial analysis.

Another benefit of AI in investment strategies is the ability to automate routine tasks. For example, AI can be used to automatically rebalance portfolios or identify stocks that are likely to outperform the market. This can help reduce costs and increase operational efficiency, freeing up investment managers to focus on more complex tasks.

Limitations of AI in Investment Strategies:

While AI has the potential to revolutionize investment management, there are also potential drawbacks and limitations to consider. One of the primary limitations is the lack of interpretability of AI models. Because AI models are often based on complex algorithms and neural networks, it can be difficult for investment managers to understand how the models arrived at their predictions. This can make it difficult to justify investment decisions to clients or regulators.

Another limitation of AI in investment strategies is the potential for overfitting. Overfitting occurs when an AI model is trained on a small set of data and is unable to generalize to new data. This can lead to incorrect predictions and investment decisions that are not based on accurate data.

AI models can also be vulnerable to bias. If the data used to train an AI model is biased, the model may make biased predictions. For example, if an AI model is trained on data that is biased against certain demographic groups, it may make investment decisions that discriminate against those groups.

Finally, there is the risk of overreliance on AI models. While AI can provide valuable insights and predictions, it should not be relied upon exclusively. Human judgment and intuition are still important in investment management, and investment managers should use AI as a tool to augment their decision-making, rather than as a replacement for it.

Current State of AI in Investment Strategies:

Despite the potential limitations and drawbacks of AI in investment strategies, the technology is already being widely used in the financial industry. According to a report by JPMorgan Chase, as of 2019, approximately 90% of all trading on the New York Stock Exchange was executed by algorithms or machine learning models. This is a significant increase from just 25% in 2010.

One of the most prominent uses of AI in investment strategies is in the field of quantitative finance. Quantitative finance is a discipline that applies mathematical models and statistical analysis to financial markets. In recent years, machine learning algorithms have been increasingly used to analyze market data, identify patterns, and develop trading strategies. These algorithms are often used in conjunction with high-frequency trading, which involves using computer algorithms to buy and sell securities at high speeds in order to take advantage of small market movements.

Another area where AI is being used in investment strategies is in portfolio management. AI algorithms can be used to analyze a client's investment goals, risk tolerance, and other factors to create personalized investment portfolios. This approach, known as robo-advising, has become increasingly popular in recent years. Companies like Betterment and Wealthfront offer robo-advising services to clients, using algorithms to automatically manage their portfolios and make investment decisions on their behalf.

Despite these advancements, there are still limitations and challenges to using AI in investment strategies. One of the main challenges is the so-called "black box" problem. AI algorithms can be difficult to interpret and understand, making it hard to identify the factors that contribute to their decisions. This lack of transparency can make it difficult for investors to trust the algorithms and can lead to regulatory challenges.

Another challenge is the potential for bias in AI algorithms. Machine learning algorithms are only as good as the data they are trained on. If the training data is biased, the algorithm will also be biased, potentially leading to incorrect investment decisions. In addition, AI algorithms may perpetuate existing biases in the financial industry, such as gender and racial biases.

Despite these challenges, the potential benefits of AI in investment strategies are significant. As the technology continues to improve and become more sophisticated, it is likely that we will see even more applications of AI in the financial industry. In the next section, we will explore some of the potential benefits of AI in investment strategies, including improved accuracy and efficiency, increased accessibility, and better risk management.

I.   Overview of different types of investment strategies and how AI can be applied to each

Investment strategies are methods or approaches used by investors to achieve specific goals such as maximizing returns or minimizing risk. There are several types of investment strategies, including value investing, growth investing, income investing, momentum investing, and more. Each strategy has its own unique characteristics, and the application of AI in investment strategies can help investors make better decisions, optimize their portfolios, and achieve their goals more effectively. In this section, we will provide an overview of the different types of investment strategies and explore how AI can be applied to each.

Value Investing:

Value investing is an investment strategy that involves buying stocks that are undervalued by the market. This approach is based on the belief that the market may have undervalued the company due to temporary factors, such as a bad quarter or negative news. Investors who follow this strategy aim to buy these undervalued stocks and hold them until the market realizes their true value, at which point they sell them for a profit.

AI can be applied to value investing in several ways. For example, AI can be used to identify undervalued stocks by analyzing various data points, such as earnings reports, balance sheets, and news articles. AI can also be used to create predictive models that can help investors determine which stocks are likely to be undervalued in the future.

Growth Investing:

Growth investing is an investment strategy that involves buying stocks in companies that are expected to experience significant growth in the future. This approach is based on the belief that companies that are growing rapidly will have higher stock prices in the future. Investors who follow this strategy typically focus on companies in the technology and healthcare sectors, as these industries are expected to experience significant growth in the coming years.

AI can be applied to growth investing in several ways. For example, AI can be used to analyze large amounts of data to identify companies that are expected to experience significant growth in the future. AI can also be used to create predictive models that can help investors determine which companies are likely to experience growth in the future.

Income Investing:

Income investing is an investment strategy that involves buying stocks or other securities that pay regular dividends or interest payments. This approach is based on the belief that these regular payments can provide investors with a steady income stream, which can be used to cover living expenses or reinvested to achieve long-term goals.

AI can be applied to income investing in several ways. For example, AI can be used to analyze large amounts of data to identify stocks or other securities that pay high dividends or interest payments. AI can also be used to create predictive models that can help investors determine which stocks or other securities are likely to pay high dividends or interest payments in the future.

Momentum Investing:

Momentum investing is an investment strategy that involves buying stocks that have experienced significant price increases in the recent past. This approach is based on the belief that these stocks are likely to continue to increase in price in the future. Investors who follow this strategy typically focus on stocks in industries that are experiencing significant growth or undergoing significant changes.

AI can be applied to momentum investing in several ways. For example, AI can be used to analyze large amounts of data to identify stocks that have experienced significant price increases in the recent past. AI can also be used to create predictive models that can help investors determine which stocks are likely to continue to increase in price in the future.

Conclusion:

In conclusion, AI can be applied to various types of investment strategies to help investors make better decisions, optimize their portfolios, and achieve their goals more effectively. While there are potential limitations and drawbacks to the use of AI in investment strategies, the benefits associated with the technology far outweigh the risks. As the technology continues to evolve, it is likely that we will see even more applications of AI in the financial industry, leading to better investment strategies and more efficient markets.

One of the most important factors in the successful application of AI in investment strategies is the quality of the data that is being used. Financial data can be complex and difficult to analyze, and it is essential that the data used to train AI models is accurate, reliable, and up-to-date. Additionally, it is important to recognize that AI models are not perfect and can make mistakes, which is why human oversight and intervention is crucial in ensuring that investment strategies are effective and aligned with investors' goals.

As AI continues to evolve and become more sophisticated, we can expect to see even more advanced applications in investment strategies. For example, some researchers are exploring the use of deep reinforcement learning algorithms to develop autonomous investment strategies that can learn and adapt to changing market conditions over time. Additionally, natural language processing and sentiment analysis can be used to analyze news articles and social media activity to gain insights into market sentiment and trends.

In addition to these technological advancements, it is important for financial institutions to continue investing in the development of ethical guidelines and frameworks for the use of AI in investment strategies. As AI becomes more integrated into the financial industry, it is essential that we ensure that its use is transparent, accountable, and aligned with the best interests of investors.

Overall, the potential for AI to revolutionize investment strategies is significant. While there are still many challenges and limitations that need to be addressed, the benefits of AI in investment strategies are clear. As we continue to explore the capabilities of this technology, it is important to remain mindful of its limitations and work towards the responsible and ethical application of AI in the financial industry.

II. **Discussion of the benefits of AI in investment strategies, including improved performance and risk management**

Artificial intelligence (AI) has been rapidly transforming various industries, including finance. In the investment world, AI is revolutionizing the way investors make decisions, optimize their portfolios, and manage risks. The benefits of AI in investment strategies are numerous and significant, leading to improved performance and risk management.

In this section, we will discuss in detail the benefits of AI in investment strategies, including its ability to improve portfolio management, enhance risk management, and enhance investment performance.

Improved Portfolio Management:

One of the key benefits of AI in investment strategies is its ability to improve portfolio management. Portfolio management involves making investment decisions and optimizing portfolios to achieve specific investment objectives. With the help of AI, investors can make better investment decisions by analyzing large amounts of data, including financial statements, market data, and news articles.

AI algorithms can be used to analyze this data and identify patterns and trends that are difficult to identify manually. For example, an AI algorithm can be used to analyze financial statements of companies and identify key financial ratios that are indicative of a company's financial health. This information can then be used to make informed investment decisions and optimize portfolios to achieve specific investment objectives.

Enhanced Risk Management:

Another significant benefit of AI in investment strategies is its ability to enhance risk management. Risk management involves identifying and managing risks associated with investment portfolios. AI can help investors identify potential risks by analyzing market data and identifying trends that may indicate an increased level of risk.

AI algorithms can be used to analyze a wide range of data sources, including financial statements, market data, and news articles. By analyzing this data, AI algorithms can identify potential risks associated with individual investments or entire portfolios. This information can then be used to adjust investment strategies and manage risks more effectively.

Enhanced Investment Performance:

AI can also be used to enhance investment performance. By analyzing large amounts of data, AI algorithms can identify investment opportunities that may be overlooked by human investors. For example, an AI algorithm can analyze market data and identify companies that are undervalued based on their financial performance.

In addition to identifying undervalued companies, AI can also be used to predict market trends and identify investment opportunities before they become widely recognized. By using this information to adjust investment strategies, investors can achieve better investment performance and outperform the market.

Counter-Arguments:

While the benefits of AI in investment strategies are significant, there are also potential drawbacks to the use of AI in investing. One potential drawback is the risk of overreliance on AI algorithms. If investors rely too heavily on AI algorithms, they may overlook important information that is not captured by the algorithm.

Another potential drawback of AI in investing is the risk of data bias. AI algorithms are only as good as the data they are trained on. If the data used to train an AI algorithm is biased, the algorithm may produce biased results that can lead to poor investment decisions.

Conclusion:

Despite the potential limitations and drawbacks of AI in investment strategies, the benefits associated with the technology far outweigh the risks. AI can be used to improve portfolio management, enhance risk management, and enhance investment performance. As the technology continues to evolve, it is likely that we will see even more applications of AI in the financial industry, leading to better investment strategies and more efficient markets.

III. Examination of challenges and limitations of AI in investment strategies, including data quality and interpretability issues

Examination of Challenges and Limitations of AI in Investment Strategies, including Data Quality and Interpretability Issues

Despite the many benefits of using AI in investment strategies, there are also a number of challenges and limitations associated with the technology. These challenges and limitations can be broadly categorized into two main areas: data quality and interpretability issues.

Data Quality Issues

One of the main challenges associated with using AI in investment strategies is data quality. In order for AI models to be effective, they need to be trained on large amounts of high-quality data. However, obtaining high-quality data can be difficult, particularly in the financial industry where data can be sparse, noisy, and subject to biases.

One of the main challenges associated with data quality is data bias. Financial data can be biased in a number of ways, including selection bias, survivorship bias, and measurement bias. For example, if an AI model is trained on data that only includes companies that have been successful in the past, it may not be able to accurately predict the performance of new or less successful companies.

Another challenge associated with data quality is data completeness. Financial data can be incomplete or missing, which can make it difficult for AI models to accurately predict future performance. This can be particularly problematic in the case of smaller companies or companies in emerging markets, where data may be scarce.

Finally, data quality can also be impacted by data errors. Errors in financial data can arise for a number of reasons, including human error, technical errors, and intentional manipulation. These errors can have a significant impact on the accuracy of AI models, and can lead to incorrect predictions and suboptimal investment decisions.

Interpretability Issues

Another major challenge associated with using AI in investment strategies is interpretability. AI models can be highly complex, and it can be difficult for investors to understand how the models arrive at their predictions. This lack of interpretability can make it difficult for investors to trust AI models and to make informed investment decisions based on their outputs.

One of the main challenges associated with interpretability is the so-called "black box" problem. AI models can be difficult to interpret because they often rely on complex algorithms and large amounts of data. This can make it difficult for investors to understand why a particular investment decision was made, and can make it difficult to replicate or refine the decision-making process.

Another challenge associated with interpretability is the potential for model drift. Model drift occurs when an AI model begins to make predictions that are significantly different from its original training data. This can occur as a result of changes in the underlying data, changes in the market, or other factors. Model drift can make it difficult for investors to trust the outputs of AI models, and can lead to suboptimal investment decisions.

Finally, interpretability can also be impacted by the complexity of financial markets. Financial markets are highly complex and can be influenced by a wide range of factors, including macroeconomic trends, geopolitical events, and market sentiment. This complexity can make it difficult for AI models to accurately predict future performance, and can lead to suboptimal investment decisions.

Conclusion

In conclusion, while AI has the potential to revolutionize investment strategies, there are also a number of challenges and limitations associated with the technology. Data quality and interpretability are two key areas of concern, with data bias, data completeness, data errors, black box problems, model drift, and market complexity all posing significant challenges. Despite these challenges, however, the potential benefits of AI in investment strategies are significant, and the technology is likely to play an increasingly important role in the financial industry in the years to come. It will be important for investors to carefully consider these challenges and limitations, and to work with AI models in a way that takes them into account while still reaping the benefits of the technology.

IV. Future outlook and potential advancements in AI for investment strategies

As AI continues to evolve and improve, the potential applications for investment strategies are nearly endless. In this section, we will explore some of the potential advancements and developments in AI that could have a significant impact on the financial industry.

A. Advanced Data Analytics

One area where AI is likely to have a significant impact on investment strategies is in the field of data analytics. With the ability to process vast amounts of data quickly and efficiently, AI can help investors identify patterns and trends that might not be immediately apparent to human analysts.

One potential development in this area is the use of machine learning algorithms that can continuously analyze and learn from data in real-time. This could enable investors to quickly adapt to changing market conditions and adjust their strategies accordingly.

Another potential advancement is the use of natural language processing (NLP) to analyze news articles and other sources of information in real-time. By analyzing the sentiment and tone of news stories, investors could potentially identify trends and patterns that could impact their investments.

B. Enhanced Predictive Capabilities

Another area where AI is likely to have a significant impact on investment strategies is in the field of predictive analytics. By analyzing past data and trends, AI algorithms can help investors identify potential opportunities and risks before they become apparent to human analysts.

One potential development in this area is the use of deep learning algorithms that can identify patterns and trends in data that might not be immediately apparent to human analysts. This could enable investors to identify new investment opportunities and adjust their strategies accordingly.

Another potential advancement is the use of reinforcement learning algorithms that can continuously learn and adapt based on feedback from the market. This could enable investors to quickly adapt to changing market conditions and adjust their strategies accordingly.

C. Improved Risk Management

One of the biggest challenges facing investors is managing risk. With the ability to process vast amounts of data quickly and efficiently, AI can help investors identify potential risks and develop strategies to mitigate them.

One potential development in this area is the use of machine learning algorithms that can continuously analyze and learn from data to identify potential risks. This could enable investors to quickly adapt to changing market conditions and adjust their strategies accordingly.

Another potential advancement is the use of natural language processing (NLP) to analyze news articles and other sources of information in real-time. By analyzing the sentiment and tone of news stories, investors could potentially identify risks that could impact their investments.

D. Enhanced Portfolio Optimization

Finally, another area where AI is likely to have a significant impact on investment strategies is in the field of portfolio optimization. By analyzing vast amounts of data, AI algorithms can help investors identify the optimal mix of investments to achieve their goals.

One potential development in this area is the use of machine learning algorithms that can continuously learn and adapt based on feedback from the market. This could enable investors to quickly adapt to changing market conditions and adjust their portfolios accordingly.

Another potential advancement is the use of natural language processing (NLP) to analyze news articles and other sources of information in real-time. By analyzing the sentiment and tone of news stories, investors could potentially identify new investment opportunities and adjust their portfolios accordingly.

E. Potential Drawbacks and Risks

Despite the potential benefits of AI in investment strategies, there are also potential drawbacks and risks associated with the technology. One of the biggest challenges facing investors is the quality of the data being used to train AI algorithms.

If the data being used is incomplete or biased, the algorithms could make inaccurate predictions or recommendations, which could result in significant losses for investors. Additionally, there is a risk that AI algorithms could become over-reliant on historical data and fail to adapt to new market conditions.

Another potential risk is the potential for AI algorithms to be hacked or manipulated by malicious actors. If an algorithm is compromised, it could result in significant financial losses for investors, and even destabilize the financial markets. It is therefore important for companies and investors to prioritize the security of their AI systems and ensure that they are protected from cyber attacks.

Another limitation of AI in investment strategies is its lack of interpretability. AI models can be highly complex and difficult for humans to understand, which can make it challenging to explain investment decisions to clients and regulators. This lack of transparency can also make it difficult to identify and correct errors or biases in the models.

Furthermore, while AI algorithms can help identify patterns and correlations in large datasets, they are not capable of understanding the underlying causation. This can lead to the identification of spurious correlations, which may not be useful in predicting future market trends or making investment decisions. Human expertise and intuition may still be necessary to interpret and act on the results generated by AI models.

Despite these challenges and limitations, the potential benefits of AI in investment strategies cannot be ignored. As the technology continues to evolve, there is potential for significant advancements in AI applications in the financial industry.

One potential area for advancement is in the development of more advanced AI algorithms that can better adapt to changing market conditions and detect emerging trends. This could include the use of deep learning techniques to analyze unstructured data such as social media sentiment or news articles, which could provide additional insights into market trends and investor sentiment.

Another area for potential advancement is the integration of AI and blockchain technology. By combining these two technologies, it may be possible to create decentralized investment platforms that are more secure, transparent, and efficient. This could provide investors with greater control over their investments and reduce the need for intermediaries such as brokers and custodians.

Furthermore, as AI becomes more widely adopted in the financial industry, there is potential for greater collaboration and sharing of data among companies and investors. This could lead to more accurate and comprehensive datasets, which could improve the accuracy and reliability of AI models.

In conclusion, while there are limitations and challenges associated with the use of AI in investment strategies, the potential benefits of the technology are significant. As the technology continues to evolve and improve, there is potential for significant advancements in AI applications in the financial industry, which could lead to improved performance, risk management, and efficiency. It is important for companies and investors to carefully consider the risks and limitations associated with AI, while also exploring the potential opportunities for advancement and growth.

CHAPTER 15: ETHICS AND ACCOUNTABILITY IN AI

As artificial intelligence (AI) continues to advance and become more integrated into our daily lives, it is essential to consider the importance of ethics and accountability in AI development and implementation. AI systems have the potential to impact society and individuals in various ways, making it crucial to ensure that these technologies are developed and used responsibly. This section will provide an overview of the importance of ethics and accountability in AI, including why it matters, the challenges, and potential solutions.

Why ethics and accountability in AI matter

The development and use of AI systems have the potential to significantly impact society and individuals. AI has the potential to revolutionize industries, from healthcare to finance, and change the way we live and work. However, AI systems also pose potential risks, such as bias, discrimination, and loss of privacy. Therefore, it is essential to consider the ethical implications of AI and ensure that these technologies are developed and used in a responsible and transparent manner.

One key reason why ethics and accountability in AI matter is the potential for AI systems to perpetuate and amplify existing biases. AI systems learn from data, and if the data used to train the algorithm is biased, then the algorithm itself will be biased. For example, if a facial recognition algorithm is trained on a dataset that primarily includes images of white men, it may struggle to accurately recognize individuals of other races and genders. This can result in unfair treatment and discrimination against individuals who do not fit the algorithm's biased parameters.

Another reason why ethics and accountability in AI matter is the potential for AI systems to infringe on privacy rights. AI systems can collect and process vast amounts of data, including personal information. This can result in individuals' private data being shared or used without their consent. Additionally, AI systems can make decisions that impact individuals' lives, such as determining their creditworthiness or eligibility for job opportunities. Without proper oversight and accountability, AI systems can make decisions that are unfair or discriminatory.

Finally, ethics and accountability in AI matter because of the potential for AI systems to be used for malicious purposes. For example, AI-powered deepfake technology can be used to create convincing fake videos, audio recordings, or images, which can be used to spread misinformation or defame individuals. AI systems can also be used for cyber attacks, such as malware and phishing attacks, which can result in significant harm to individuals and organizations.

Challenges in ensuring ethics and accountability in AI

While the importance of ethics and accountability in AI is clear, ensuring that these principles are upheld presents several challenges. One significant challenge is the lack of transparency and interpretability in AI systems. Many AI systems use complex algorithms that are difficult to understand or interpret, making it challenging to determine whether the system is making decisions that align with ethical and moral principles. Additionally, the use of AI systems in decision-making processes can make it difficult to identify and correct errors or biases.

Another challenge in ensuring ethics and accountability in AI is the lack of regulation and oversight. The development and use of AI systems have outpaced regulatory efforts, leaving many gaps in the legal framework governing AI. This has led to a lack of accountability and transparency in the development and deployment of AI systems, making it challenging to ensure that these technologies are used in a responsible and ethical manner.

Finally, another significant challenge in ensuring ethics and accountability in AI is the potential for malicious actors to exploit these systems. AI systems can be vulnerable to attacks, such as hacking or manipulation, which can result in significant harm to individuals and organizations. Additionally, the lack of accountability and oversight in the development and deployment of AI systems can create opportunities for malicious actors to use these systems for nefarious purposes.

Potential solutions for ensuring ethics and accountability in AI

Despite the challenges in ensuring ethics and accountability in AI, there are several potential solutions that can be implemented. One approach is to establish regulations and guidelines that govern the development and use of AI. This could involve creating standards for data privacy and security, ensuring transparency in algorithmic decision-making processes, and holding AI developers and users accountable for any negative consequences that arise from their use of the technology. Some countries have already taken steps in this direction. For example, in 2018 the European Union implemented the General Data Protection Regulation (GDPR), which establishes strict rules for how companies must handle and protect personal data.

Another potential solution is to encourage interdisciplinary collaboration between experts in AI, ethics, and other relevant fields. By bringing together experts from a variety of backgrounds, it may be possible to develop more comprehensive and holistic approaches to addressing ethical and accountability issues in AI. For example, a team consisting of AI researchers, ethicists, and legal experts might be able to develop more robust and nuanced ethical guidelines for AI development and use.

Education and awareness-raising can also play an important role in promoting ethics and accountability in AI. This could involve educating developers and users about the potential risks and negative consequences associated with AI, as well as providing training on how to mitigate these risks. Additionally, promoting public dialogue and debate about the ethical and societal implications of AI could help raise awareness and encourage more responsible use of the technology.

Finally, some experts have argued that AI itself could be used to help ensure ethics and accountability in AI. For example, AI algorithms could be used to detect and flag potential ethical violations or biases in other AI systems. Additionally, AI could be used to develop more transparent and explainable decision-making processes, which would help promote accountability and allow for better oversight of AI systems.

Overall, ensuring ethics and accountability in AI is a complex and multifaceted challenge that requires a range of solutions and approaches. By implementing a combination of regulations, interdisciplinary collaboration, education and awareness-raising, and the use of AI itself, it may be possible to address the ethical and societal challenges associated with this rapidly advancing technology.

I.   **Discussion of ethical considerations in the development and deployment of AI in finance, including bias, privacy, and transparency**

As artificial intelligence (AI) continues to be integrated into the finance industry, there are several ethical considerations that must be taken into account. These considerations range from ensuring the fairness and impartiality of AI algorithms to protecting the privacy of customer data. This section will explore these ethical considerations in depth, focusing on issues such as bias, privacy, and transparency.

Bias in AI

One of the most significant ethical concerns with the development and deployment of AI in finance is the potential for bias. Bias can be introduced at various stages of the AI development process, including data collection, algorithm design, and model training. If left unchecked, bias in AI can perpetuate existing societal inequalities and prevent certain groups from accessing financial services.

There are several ways to address bias in AI, including increasing the diversity of the data used to train algorithms, incorporating fairness metrics into model evaluation, and creating oversight committees to monitor AI systems for bias. For example, an investment bank could use a diverse dataset that includes data from different regions and demographics to ensure that the AI system is not biased against any particular group. Additionally, the bank could evaluate the AI system's performance using fairness metrics such as statistical parity or equal opportunity.

Privacy in AI

Another ethical consideration in the development and deployment of AI in finance is privacy. AI algorithms can collect and analyze vast amounts of personal data, including financial transactions, credit scores, and even social media activity. This raises concerns about the privacy of individuals' personal information and the potential for it to be misused.

To address these concerns, organizations should implement strong data protection policies that prioritize the privacy of individuals' personal information. These policies should include robust data encryption, secure data storage, and strict access controls. Additionally, organizations should be transparent with their customers about the data they collect and how it is used. This transparency can help to build trust between the organization and its customers and reduce concerns about privacy violations.

Transparency in AI

Transparency is another critical ethical consideration in the development and deployment of AI in finance. AI algorithms can be opaque and difficult to interpret, making it challenging to understand how they arrived at a particular decision. This lack of transparency can make it challenging to identify and correct errors or biases in the system.

To address this concern, organizations should prioritize transparency in their AI systems. This can include using explainable AI techniques that provide clear and concise explanations for the system's decision-making processes. Additionally, organizations should be transparent about their use of AI and how it affects their business practices. This can help to build trust with customers and stakeholders and reduce concerns about the potential negative impacts of AI.

Counterarguments

While there are several potential solutions for addressing the ethical considerations associated with the development and deployment of AI in finance, there are also counterarguments to consider. One such counterargument is that AI algorithms can be more objective and unbiased than human decision-makers.

This argument suggests that AI can eliminate the potential for human biases to affect financial decision-making and result in more equitable outcomes.

However, this argument overlooks the potential for bias to be introduced at various stages of the AI development process. It also ignores the fact that AI algorithms are only as unbiased as the data used to train them. If the data is incomplete or biased, the algorithms can make inaccurate predictions or recommendations, which can result in significant losses for investors.

Conclusion

In conclusion, the development and deployment of AI in finance raise several ethical considerations, including bias, privacy, and transparency. To address these considerations, organizations should prioritize the diversity of their data, implement strong data protection policies, and prioritize transparency in their AI systems. While there are counterarguments to consider, it is essential to recognize the potential for AI to perpetuate existing societal inequalities and take steps to ensure that AI is developed and deployed ethically and responsibly.

II. Examination of the potential consequences of unethical AI practices in finance, including negative impacts on customers and reputational damage for financial institutions

Given the increasing role of AI in the financial industry, it is paramount to examine the potential consequences of unethical practices involving AI. The adverse effects of unethical AI practices in finance can have far-reaching consequences for both customers and financial institutions alike.

One potential consequence of unethical AI practices is the perpetuation of bias. If AI algorithms are not developed and deployed in an ethical and unbiased manner, they can perpetuate existing biases and discrimination. This can have negative consequences for customers who are unfairly discriminated against in financial decisions. For example, if a loan application is rejected by an AI algorithm due to factors such as race, gender, or ethnicity, this can have a negative impact on the customer's financial well-being.

Another potential consequence of unethical AI practices is the violation of privacy. As AI algorithms process and analyze vast amounts of data, it is essential that customer privacy is protected. If AI algorithms are not developed and deployed in an ethical manner, they can infringe on customer privacy by collecting and analyzing personal data without their consent. This can lead to reputational damage for financial institutions and a loss of trust from customers.

In addition to these potential consequences, unethical AI practices can also result in reputational damage for financial institutions. If a financial institution is found to have engaged in unethical AI practices, this can result in negative media attention and damage to their reputation. This can have a significant impact on their bottom line, as customers may choose to take their business elsewhere.

Overall, it is crucial for financial institutions to consider the potential consequences of unethical AI practices and take steps to ensure that AI algorithms are developed and deployed in an ethical manner. This includes implementing measures to prevent bias, protecting customer privacy, and promoting transparency and accountability in the use of AI in finance.

Counter-arguments may suggest that the potential consequences of unethical AI practices are overblown and that the benefits of AI in finance far outweigh the potential risks. They may argue that the use of AI algorithms can help financial institutions make better decisions, improve efficiency, and reduce costs. However, it is essential to consider both the potential benefits and risks of AI in finance and take steps to ensure that AI is deployed in an ethical and responsible manner.

In conclusion, the potential consequences of unethical AI practices in finance can have significant impacts on customers and financial institutions alike. It is essential for financial institutions to consider the potential risks of AI and take steps to ensure that AI algorithms are developed and deployed in an ethical and responsible manner. This includes implementing measures to prevent bias, protecting customer privacy, and promoting transparency and accountability in the use of AI in finance. By doing so, financial institutions can build trust with their customers and mitigate potential risks associated with the use of AI in finance.

III. Discussion of current regulatory frameworks for AI in finance and potential future developments

As AI continues to gain prominence in the financial industry, there is a growing need for regulatory frameworks to ensure that AI is used ethically and transparently. In this section, we will explore the current regulatory frameworks for AI in finance and potential future developments.

Current Regulatory Frameworks for AI in Finance

In the United States, the regulatory oversight of AI in finance is split between various agencies. The Federal Trade Commission (FTC) is responsible for enforcing consumer protection laws, while the Securities and Exchange Commission (SEC) regulates the use of AI in securities trading. The Commodity Futures Trading Commission (CFTC) regulates AI in commodities trading, and the Federal Reserve regulates the use of AI in banking and financial services.

In Europe, the European Union's General Data Protection Regulation (GDPR) provides a legal framework for the use of personal data, including data used in AI applications. The GDPR requires companies to obtain explicit consent from individuals before using their personal data and gives individuals the right to access and correct their data. Additionally, the GDPR establishes fines for companies that violate the regulation, which can be as high as 4% of a company's global revenue.

In Asia, China has implemented a regulatory framework for AI in finance that includes guidelines for the development and deployment of AI algorithms in the financial industry. The framework requires financial institutions to establish internal risk management systems and to conduct regular audits of their AI algorithms. Additionally, the framework mandates that AI algorithms must be transparent, interpretable, and fair.

Potential Future Developments

As AI continues to evolve, it is likely that regulatory frameworks for AI in finance will continue to evolve as well. One potential area of development is the establishment of international standards for AI ethics and transparency. The development of such standards could help ensure that AI is used ethically and transparently across borders.

Another potential development is the creation of a regulatory agency specifically dedicated to overseeing AI in finance. Such an agency could help ensure that AI is used in a way that is fair, transparent, and beneficial to both consumers and financial institutions.

Finally, the development of AI-specific liability laws could also be a potential area of development. As AI becomes more autonomous and makes decisions without human intervention, it becomes increasingly important to establish liability for any harm caused by AI. Establishing liability laws could help ensure that financial institutions are held accountable for any harm caused by their AI systems.

Counter-arguments

While some argue that increased regulation of AI in finance is necessary to ensure its ethical use, others argue that too much regulation could stifle innovation and hinder the development of AI. Additionally, some argue that regulatory frameworks are not effective at preventing unethical behavior and that self-regulation by the industry is a more effective approach.

Conclusion

As AI continues to play an increasingly important role in finance, it is crucial that regulatory frameworks are established to ensure that AI is used ethically and transparently. While the current regulatory frameworks for AI in finance vary by region, the establishment of international standards and the creation of a dedicated regulatory agency could help ensure that AI is used in a way that is fair and beneficial to both consumers and financial institutions. Ultimately, the development of ethical AI practices in finance will require a collaborative effort between regulators, financial institutions, and AI developers to establish guidelines and best practices that prioritize transparency, fairness, and accountability.

IV. Future outlook and potential advancements in ethical and accountable AI in finance.

As AI continues to evolve and integrate into finance, the future outlook for ethical and accountable AI is both exciting and challenging. On one hand, there is a tremendous opportunity for AI to increase efficiency, reduce costs, and improve decision-making in finance. On the other hand, the potential consequences of unethical AI practices are significant, and as such, there is an urgent need to ensure that AI is developed and deployed in a responsible and ethical manner.

One potential advancement in ethical AI is the development of explainable AI (XAI), which would provide more transparency into how AI systems arrive at their decisions. XAI would enable stakeholders to better understand how AI algorithms are making decisions, and provide insights into the reasoning behind those decisions. This would help to address concerns around bias and discrimination, as well as increase trust in AI among customers and regulators.

Another potential advancement is the use of federated learning, which would allow multiple parties to collaborate on training a machine learning model without sharing data. This would enable financial institutions to leverage the benefits of machine learning while protecting the privacy of their customers. Federated learning has the potential to improve the accuracy of AI models, while also addressing concerns around data privacy and security.

In addition to these technical advancements, there is also a need for increased collaboration and standardization around ethical AI practices in finance. This includes the development of industry-wide ethical frameworks, as well as collaboration between industry stakeholders and regulators to ensure that AI is developed and deployed in a responsible and ethical manner.

One example of this type of collaboration is the Partnership on AI, which brings together stakeholders from industry, academia, and civil society to promote ethical and accountable AI. The Partnership on AI has developed a set of best practices for AI ethics, and has also worked with regulators to develop guidelines for the ethical use of AI.

Another potential area of advancement is the use of ethical AI audits, which would assess the ethical implications of AI systems before they are deployed. This would involve a comprehensive review of the potential impacts of AI on various stakeholders, including customers, employees, and society at large. Ethical AI audits would help to ensure that AI systems are developed and deployed in a responsible and ethical manner, and could also serve as a mechanism for accountability and transparency.

However, there are also challenges to the future advancement of ethical and accountable AI in finance. One challenge is the lack of standardization around ethical AI practices, which makes it difficult to compare and evaluate different AI systems. Another challenge is the difficulty of developing AI systems that are both accurate and fair, particularly in the context of financial services where there are complex and ever-changing regulations.

In conclusion, the future outlook for ethical and accountable AI in finance is both exciting and challenging. Technical advancements such as explainable AI and federated learning have the potential to increase transparency and privacy, while collaborations and standardization around ethical AI practices can ensure that AI is developed and deployed in a responsible and ethical manner. However, challenges around standardization and fairness remain, and it is important for industry stakeholders and regulators to continue working together to address these challenges and advance the responsible use of AI in finance.

PART V: DATA ANALYTICS AND BIG DATA

The financial industry has always been heavily reliant on data to make informed decisions. However, with the advent of big data and data analytics, the scope and depth of data available has exponentially increased, transforming the industry and the way decisions are made. In this part of the book, we will explore the impact of big data and data analytics on the financial sector, from risk management to investment decisions, and how it is shaping the future of finance.

Chapter 16 provides an overview of big data and its importance in the finance industry. It will cover the definition of big data, its sources, and how it is processed to generate insights that inform decision-making processes. It will also explore the challenges associated with big data in finance, such as data privacy concerns and data quality issues.

Chapter 17 delves into the power of data analytics in finance. It examines how financial institutions are leveraging data analytics to gain insights into customer behavior, market trends, and investment opportunities. The chapter will also explore the various data analytics tools used in the finance industry and how they are being used to optimize performance and drive growth.

Risk management is an essential function of the financial industry, and big data is increasingly being used to improve risk management processes. Chapter 18 examines the role of big data in risk management and how it is being used to identify potential risks, monitor risk exposure, and manage risk in real-time. The chapter will also explore the challenges associated with integrating big data into risk management processes and the regulatory requirements that financial institutions must comply with.

Finally, in Chapter 19, we will explore the future of big data in finance. This chapter will examine the potential advancements in big data and data analytics and their impact on the financial industry. We will discuss the opportunities and challenges that come with the increased use of big data and how financial institutions can prepare themselves for this new era of data-driven decision-making.

In conclusion, Part V of this book provides a comprehensive overview of the impact of big data and data analytics on the finance industry. We will examine the benefits and challenges associated with big data and data analytics, and how financial institutions can leverage these technologies to improve performance, manage risk, and drive growth.

CHAPTER 16: BIG DATA AND FINANCE: AN OVERVIEW

In recent years, the financial industry has experienced an explosion in the amount of data generated and collected. This has led to the rise of big data analytics, a field that involves extracting insights and value from massive amounts of data. Big data has the potential to transform the financial industry by enabling faster, more accurate decision-making, improved risk management, and enhanced customer experiences.

Chapter 16 provides an overview of the role of big data in finance. This chapter begins by defining what big data is and how it differs from traditional data sources. It then discusses the various sources of big data in finance, including market data, customer data, and alternative data. The chapter also explores the challenges associated with managing big data, such as data quality and privacy concerns.

Main Section 1: Defining Big Data

To understand the role of big data in finance, it is important to first define what big data is. Big data refers to large, complex datasets that cannot be effectively processed using traditional data processing methods. These datasets typically involve multiple sources of structured and unstructured data, such as transactional data, social media data, and sensor data.

One of the defining characteristics of big data is its volume. Big data sets can range from terabytes to petabytes or even exabytes in size. In addition to its size, big data is also characterized by its velocity, variety, and veracity. Velocity refers to the speed at which data is generated and needs to be processed, while variety refers to the different types of data that are included in the dataset. Veracity refers to the reliability and accuracy of the data.

Main Section 2: Sources of Big Data in Finance

The financial industry generates and collects vast amounts of data from a variety of sources. One of the most important sources of big data in finance is market data. Market data includes information about stock prices, bond yields, and other financial instruments. This data is used to inform investment decisions, predict market trends, and assess risk.

Another important source of big data in finance is customer data. Financial institutions collect a vast amount of data about their customers, including demographic information, transaction history, and credit scores. This data is used to identify patterns and trends in customer behavior, personalize marketing and product offerings, and identify potential risks.

Alternative data is another important source of big data in finance. Alternative data refers to non-traditional sources of data, such as social media data, satellite imagery, and weather data. This type of data is used to gain insights into market trends and customer behavior that may not be visible through traditional data sources.

Main Section 3: Challenges of Big Data in Finance

While big data has the potential to transform the financial industry, it also presents a number of challenges. One of the biggest challenges of big data is data quality. Because big data sets are often collected from a variety of sources, they can be prone to errors and inconsistencies. Ensuring data quality is essential to ensuring that insights gleaned from big data are accurate and reliable.

Privacy concerns are another challenge associated with big data in finance. Financial institutions must ensure that customer data is handled in a secure and responsible manner. This includes complying with regulations such as the General Data Protection Regulation (GDPR) and ensuring that customer data is not shared with unauthorized third parties.

Conclusion

Chapter 16 provides an overview of the role of big data in finance. It highlights the defining characteristics of big data and the various sources of big data in finance. The chapter also explores the challenges associated with managing big data, including data quality and privacy concerns. While big data presents a number of challenges, it also has the potential to transform the financial industry by enabling faster, more accurate decision-making and improved risk management.

I. Types of Data in Finance

In today's fast-paced financial industry, data is an essential element for decision-making processes. Companies are striving to gain a competitive edge by leveraging the power of data. However, the availability and complexity of data make it challenging to extract meaningful insights. In this section, we will explore the different types of data in finance, including structured data, unstructured data, and semi-structured data.

Structured Data:
Structured data refers to data that is organized and easily searchable using pre-defined rules or formats. It is typically stored in databases or spreadsheets, and each data point is assigned to a specific field. Examples of structured data in finance include historical stock prices, financial statements, and transactional data. Structured data is easy to analyze, and there are numerous tools and techniques available to extract insights from it.

For example, investment bankers often use structured data in financial modeling to forecast future revenues and assess the viability of a project or investment opportunity. Actuaries use structured data to calculate insurance premiums and analyze mortality rates. Portfolio managers use structured data to optimize asset allocation and generate higher returns.

Unstructured Data:
Unstructured data refers to data that does not have a pre-defined format or structure. It can include text, images, audio, and video files. Examples of unstructured data in finance include news articles, social media posts, customer reviews, and call center transcripts. Unstructured data is more difficult to analyze than structured data due to its complexity and lack of organization.

However, advances in natural language processing and machine learning have made it possible to extract valuable insights from unstructured data. For example, sentiment analysis can be used to analyze customer reviews and social media posts to determine customer satisfaction levels. Natural language processing can also be used to analyze news articles and corporate reports to identify emerging trends and market opportunities.

Semi-Structured Data:

Semi-structured data refers to data that has some structure but does not fit neatly into predefined categories. It can include data such as XML files, JSON files, and email messages. Semi-structured data is more flexible than structured data, but it can still be analyzed using pre-defined rules and formats.

In finance, semi-structured data is often used in risk management and compliance. For example, regulatory filings such as SEC Form 10-K contain both structured and semi-structured data. Investment banks use natural language processing techniques to extract insights from these filings and ensure compliance with regulatory requirements.

Conclusion:

In conclusion, structured, unstructured, and semi-structured data play critical roles in finance. Structured data is easy to analyze and provides a solid foundation for financial modeling and analysis. Unstructured data is more complex, but it can provide valuable insights into customer sentiment, emerging trends, and market opportunities. Semi-structured data is a flexible data type that can be used for risk management and compliance. As the amount of data in finance continues to grow, it is essential to understand the different types of data and how they can be leveraged to gain a competitive edge.

II. Applications of Big Data in Finance

The rise of big data has transformed industries across the board, and the financial sector is no exception. With the increasing amounts of data generated every day, finance professionals have been presented with new opportunities to gain insights and make better decisions. This section will explore the various applications of big data in finance, focusing on trading, risk management, and customer analytics. We will examine how big data has revolutionized these areas and explore the specific tools and techniques that are used to extract value from large data sets.

Trading:

In trading, big data has brought about a paradigm shift in the way investors make decisions. Previously, traders relied on traditional data sources such as company earnings reports, financial statements, and market news to inform their decisions. However, big data has enabled traders to go beyond these sources and access real-time data from a wide variety of sources such as social media, news articles, and satellite imagery. This data can provide valuable insights into market sentiment, consumer behavior, and economic trends that can help traders make more informed decisions.

One example of the use of big data in trading is the use of sentiment analysis. Sentiment analysis is the process of using natural language processing and machine learning techniques to analyze text data such as social media posts and news articles to gauge public sentiment about a particular stock or market. Investment firms are using sentiment analysis to identify market-moving events and make trading decisions accordingly. For example, if sentiment analysis shows that there is a negative sentiment towards a particular company or sector, a trader may decide to short the stock or hedge their position.

Risk Management:

In risk management, big data has transformed the way that financial institutions assess and mitigate risk. By analyzing large data sets, risk managers can identify potential risks and take proactive measures to manage them. For example, banks can use big data to analyze customer transaction data and identify potential fraud patterns, allowing them to take action before a large-scale fraud incident occurs. Similarly, insurers can use big data to better assess risk in underwriting and claims processing.

One application of big data in risk management is predictive modeling. Predictive modeling is the process of using statistical algorithms and machine learning techniques to analyze historical data and identify patterns that can be used to predict future outcomes. Predictive modeling can help risk managers identify potential risks and assess the likelihood and impact of these risks. For example, a bank may use predictive modeling to identify customers who are at high risk of defaulting on their loans and take measures to manage this risk.

Customer Analytics:
Big data has also transformed the way that financial institutions analyze and understand their customers. By analyzing large data sets, financial institutions can gain insights into customer behavior and preferences, allowing them to provide more personalized and targeted services. For example, banks can use big data to analyze customer transaction data to identify spending patterns and offer personalized financial advice.

One example of the use of big data in customer analytics is the use of machine learning algorithms to identify customer segments. Machine learning algorithms can analyze large data sets to identify patterns in customer behavior, allowing financial institutions to segment their customers based on their preferences and behavior. This segmentation can be used to offer personalized products and services that are tailored to each customer segment.

Conclusion:
The applications of big data in finance are vast and varied, ranging from trading and risk management to customer analytics. The rise of big data has transformed the financial industry, providing finance professionals with new tools and techniques to gain insights and make better decisions. As technology continues to advance, we can expect to see even more innovative applications of big data in finance, further revolutionizing the way that financial institutions operate.

III. Challenges and Opportunities

While big data has revolutionized the financial industry in many ways, it has also brought along some challenges that need to be addressed. In this section, we will discuss some of these challenges and opportunities.

Data Privacy and Security

One of the most significant challenges that arise with big data is ensuring data privacy and security. As the volume and variety of data continue to grow, so does the risk of data breaches and cyber-attacks. Financial institutions are responsible for managing sensitive and confidential data, including customers' personal information, financial transactions, and trading data. As a result, they face a higher risk of cyber-attacks than any other industry.

The financial industry needs to ensure that they have robust data security measures in place, which include firewalls, encryption, intrusion detection, and data backups. They should also have clear policies and procedures in place to govern data privacy and security. However, while it is crucial to protect data, there is a fine line between data protection and data availability. Therefore, financial institutions should strike a balance between the two.

Scalability

Another challenge that arises with big data is scalability. As the volume of data grows, the existing IT infrastructure may not be able to handle the increased load. Financial institutions need to invest in scalable infrastructure that can handle large volumes of data in real-time. They should also have a strategy in place to handle peaks in data processing, such as during trading hours.

The Role of AI and Machine Learning

AI and machine learning have become an integral part of big data analytics in finance. They offer the potential to identify patterns, make predictions, and automate processes. For example, machine learning algorithms can analyze financial market data to identify trends and predict future market movements. This information can be used to inform investment decisions, manage risks, and improve customer service.

Furthermore, AI can be used to automate back-office operations, such as trade processing, which can help financial institutions reduce costs and increase efficiency. As a result, the role of AI and machine learning in finance is rapidly expanding, creating numerous opportunities for the industry.

ArlingBrook - A Case Study

Launched in 2023, ArlingBrook is a social media app that uses AI and ML to provide a secure and scalable platform for users. With the integration of finance, it allows creators to earn more than any other social media site, adding ML to have enhanced CRM, and with AI aiding its birth, this is an example of how the integration of AI and ML is advancing our technology. ArlingBrook is seizing opportunities from all sectors, including those in cybersecurity, telecommunications, and web3.

The app also includes a payment and digital wallet service developed by The ATS Company. ArlingBrook Pay allows users to make payments online and in-app using their devices, such as iPhones and laptops. It uses Near Field Communication (NFC) technology to enable secure and contactless payments at point-of-sale (POS) terminals. The service is compatible with major credit and debit cards, as well as various payment networks, such as Visa, Mastercard, and American Express. ArlingBrook Pay also offers features such as loyalty programs and reward elements.

Conclusion

In conclusion, big data has transformed the financial industry in many ways. The types of data available, such as structured, unstructured, and semi-structured data, have allowed financial institutions to gain insights into customer behavior, trading patterns, and market trends. The applications of big data in finance, such as trading, risk management, and customer analytics, have helped financial institutions make better-informed decisions and improve customer service.

However, along with the benefits, there are also challenges that need to be addressed, such as data privacy and security, scalability, and the integration of AI and machine learning. By understanding these challenges

CHAPTER 17: THE POWER OF DATA ANALYTICS IN FINANCE

Data analytics has become an increasingly important tool in finance. With the vast amounts of data generated in the financial industry, there is a growing need for effective and efficient ways to manage, analyze, and make decisions based on this data. The use of data analytics in finance can help organizations improve risk management, increase profitability, and enhance customer engagement.

The application of data analytics in finance can take many forms. Investment banks, for example, use data analytics to identify trading opportunities and manage risk. Actuaries use data analytics to develop models to predict future events, such as changes in interest rates or insurance claims. Portfolio managers use data analytics to analyze financial data and make investment decisions. Quantitative analysts use data analytics to develop financial models and algorithms for trading. Securities traders use data analytics to analyze market trends and make informed trades. Financial planners and financial analysts use data analytics to help clients make informed financial decisions.

Data analytics is not a new concept in finance. Financial professionals have been using data to make informed decisions for many years. However, advances in technology, such as the development of more powerful computers and the growth of the internet, have made it easier and more cost-effective to collect, store, and analyze large amounts of data.

The rise of data analytics in finance has been driven by several factors. One is the increasing amount of data available. With the growth of the internet and the development of new technologies, financial institutions are generating more data than ever before. This data includes information about transactions, customer behavior, market trends, and more.

Another factor driving the rise of data analytics in finance is the need for more efficient and effective decision-making. In today's fast-paced financial markets, decisions need to be made quickly and accurately. Data analytics can help financial professionals make better decisions by providing them with the insights they need to identify opportunities and manage risks.

Finally, data analytics has become more accessible to financial institutions of all sizes. In the past, only large institutions with significant resources could afford to invest in data analytics. However, advances in technology have made it easier and more cost-effective for smaller institutions to access and analyze data.

Overall, the rise of data analytics in finance represents a significant opportunity for financial institutions to improve their decision-making processes, enhance their risk management strategies, and increase profitability. In the following sections, we will explore the different applications of data analytics in finance, including trading, risk management, and customer analytics. We will also discuss the challenges and opportunities associated with data analytics, including data privacy and security, scalability, and the role of AI and machine learning.

I. Applications of Data Analytics in Finance

Data analytics has transformed the way finance professionals work, providing them with powerful tools to analyze large datasets and uncover valuable insights. From predictive analytics to behavioral analytics and fraud detection, data analytics has numerous applications in finance. In this chapter, we will explore the various applications of data analytics in finance, including how it is being used to predict financial trends, understand consumer behavior, and detect fraudulent activities.

Predictive Analytics

Predictive analytics is a powerful tool in finance that can help professionals make informed decisions by forecasting future trends. By analyzing historical data, predictive analytics can identify patterns and trends that can be used to predict future outcomes. This can be particularly useful in financial markets, where accurate predictions of market trends can lead to significant profits.

One example of predictive analytics in finance is algorithmic trading. Investment bankers and portfolio managers can use algorithms to analyze large volumes of financial data in real-time, identifying trends and patterns that can be used to make predictions about future market movements. These algorithms can be programmed to execute trades automatically based on these predictions, allowing investment firms to take advantage of market movements before their competitors.

Another application of predictive analytics in finance is credit scoring. Banks and lending institutions can use predictive models to analyze large volumes of data on an individual's credit history, financial behavior, and other factors to assess the likelihood of that individual defaulting on a loan. By using these models, banks can make more informed decisions about who to lend money to, reducing the risk of default and improving overall profitability.

Behavioral Analytics

Behavioral analytics is another application of data analytics in finance that focuses on understanding consumer behavior. By analyzing data on consumer spending habits, financial institutions can gain insights into customer needs and preferences, enabling them to offer targeted products and services.

One example of behavioral analytics in finance is personalized marketing. Financial institutions can use data analytics to segment their customer base and tailor marketing campaigns to specific groups of customers. By targeting marketing efforts to specific customer segments, financial institutions can improve the effectiveness of their marketing campaigns and increase customer engagement.

Another application of behavioral analytics is customer retention. Financial institutions can use data analytics to identify customers who are at risk of leaving, based on their past behavior and interactions with the institution. By targeting these customers with personalized offers and incentives, financial institutions can increase the likelihood that they will remain loyal customers.

Fraud Detection

Fraud detection is another application of data analytics in finance, which is particularly important in the era of digital transactions. Financial institutions can use data analytics to monitor transactions in real-time, identifying patterns and behaviors that may indicate fraudulent activity.

One example of fraud detection using data analytics is anomaly detection. Financial institutions can use machine learning algorithms to analyze transaction data and identify unusual patterns that may indicate fraudulent activity. By flagging these transactions for further investigation, financial institutions can prevent fraudulent activity before it occurs.

Another application of fraud detection is identity verification. Financial institutions can use data analytics to verify the identity of individuals applying for loans, credit cards, or other financial products. By analyzing data on an individual's credit history, employment status, and other factors, financial institutions can ensure that the individual is who they claim to be and reduce the risk of identity theft and other forms of fraud.

Conclusion

In conclusion, data analytics has numerous applications in finance, from predictive analytics to behavioral analytics and fraud detection. By analyzing large volumes of data, finance professionals can gain valuable insights into market trends, consumer behavior, and fraudulent activities, enabling them to make more informed decisions and reduce risk. As the volume of data generated by financial transactions continues to increase, the importance of data analytics in finance is only likely to grow, making it a critical tool for finance professionals to master.

II. The Importance of Data Visualization

Data visualization has become an increasingly important aspect of data analytics in finance. With the exponential growth of data, it has become necessary to create visual representations of data to better understand and make decisions based on it. Data visualization techniques allow for the transformation of complex data sets into meaningful and easy-to-understand visualizations, enabling analysts to identify patterns and trends that would be difficult to spot in raw data.

In this section, we will explore the importance of data visualization in finance, its techniques, and its role in decision-making.

Data Visualization Techniques

There are several data visualization techniques that can be used in finance, each with its own unique advantages and disadvantages. The choice of technique will depend on the specific goals of the analysis and the type of data being analyzed. Some common data visualization techniques include:

Scatter Plots: Scatter plots are used to display the relationship between two variables. In finance, they can be used to plot the relationship between two financial indicators, such as the relationship between stock prices and earnings per share.

Line Charts: Line charts are used to display trends over time. In finance, they can be used to plot the trend in stock prices over a certain period of time.

Bar Charts: Bar charts are used to display comparisons between categories. In finance, they can be used to compare the performance of different stocks or different financial indicators.

Heat Maps: Heat maps are used to display patterns in data sets. In finance, they can be used to show the distribution of returns for different investment portfolios.

Tree Maps: Tree maps are used to display hierarchical data structures. In finance, they can be used to show the composition of a portfolio, with the size of each asset represented by the size of its rectangle.

Bubble Charts: Bubble charts are used to display relationships between three variables. In finance, they can be used to plot the relationship between stock prices, earnings per share, and market capitalization.

The Role of Data Visualization in Decision-Making

Data visualization plays a crucial role in decision-making in finance. By creating visualizations of data, analysts can better understand complex relationships and identify patterns and trends that would be difficult to spot in raw data. This enables analysts to make more informed decisions about investments, risk management, and other financial strategies.

One of the key advantages of data visualization is its ability to simplify complex data sets into easy-to-understand visualizations. This makes it easier for decision-makers to identify patterns and relationships that would be difficult to spot in raw data. For example, by using a scatter plot to visualize the relationship between two financial indicators, such as stock prices and earnings per share, analysts can quickly see whether there is a correlation between the two variables.

Data visualization also helps decision-makers to identify outliers and anomalies in data sets. By identifying outliers and anomalies, analysts can gain insight into unusual events or trends that could have an impact on financial performance. For example, by using a heat map to visualize the distribution of returns for different investment portfolios, analysts can quickly identify portfolios that are significantly underperforming or overperforming relative to their peers.

Another advantage of data visualization is its ability to communicate complex data sets to a wide audience. By using visualizations, analysts can communicate complex financial concepts to non-experts, such as investors or board members, in a way that is easy to understand. This can be particularly useful in situations where decisions need to be made quickly, and stakeholders need to understand the implications of different financial strategies.

Conclusion

In conclusion, data visualization plays an important role in finance by enabling analysts to better understand complex data sets, identify patterns and trends, and make more informed decisions about investments and financial strategies. By using a range of data visualization techniques, analysts can transform raw data into meaningful visuals that are easily digestible and accessible to a wider audience, including senior management and stakeholders.

One of the key benefits of data visualization is its ability to simplify complex information and present it in a format that is easily understood. This is particularly important in finance, where large amounts of data can be overwhelming and difficult to interpret. By using charts, graphs, and other visual aids, analysts can quickly identify trends and patterns, and make more informed decisions about investment strategies.

In addition, data visualization also helps to improve communication and collaboration within finance teams. By presenting data in a visual format, team members can more easily share information, discuss potential strategies, and make decisions together. This helps to create a more cohesive and productive working environment, and ultimately leads to better outcomes for the organization as a whole.

However, it is important to note that data visualization is not a magic bullet for solving all financial problems. It is simply a tool that can be used to support decision-making, and should be combined with other analytical methods and financial expertise. In addition, it is important to be aware of potential biases and limitations in the data being analyzed, and to take these into account when making decisions based on visualizations.

Overall, data visualization has become an essential part of the modern finance industry, and its importance is only likely to grow in the coming years. By embracing the power of data visualization, finance professionals can gain deeper insights into complex financial data, make better decisions, and ultimately achieve greater success in their roles.

III. Limitations and Risks of Data Analytics

As we have seen in previous sections, data analytics is a powerful tool that has transformed the way finance professionals make decisions. However, it is important to recognize that data analytics also has its limitations and risks. In this section, we will explore some of the most significant challenges associated with data analytics in finance. Specifically, we will discuss issues related to bias and ethical concerns, data quality and integrity, and interpretation challenges. By understanding these limitations and risks, we can better assess the value and reliability of data analytics in finance.

Bias and Ethical Concerns

One of the most significant limitations of data analytics in finance is the potential for bias and ethical concerns. Bias can arise in many different forms, including sampling bias, selection bias, and confirmation bias. Sampling bias occurs when the sample used for analysis is not representative of the population being studied. Selection bias occurs when certain data points are intentionally excluded from analysis. Confirmation bias occurs when analysts selectively seek out information that confirms their preexisting beliefs.

In finance, bias can have serious consequences. For example, if an investment bank is using biased data to make investment decisions, it may be making decisions that are not in the best interest of its clients. Similarly, if an insurance company is using biased data to determine premiums, it may be unfairly discriminating against certain groups of people.

In addition to bias, data analytics in finance also raises ethical concerns. For example, if a bank is using customer data to make investment decisions, it may be violating customers' privacy. Similarly, if an insurance company is using personal data to determine premiums, it may be violating people's right to fair treatment.

Data Quality and Integrity

Another significant limitation of data analytics in finance is the challenge of ensuring data quality and integrity. Inaccurate or incomplete data can lead to flawed analysis and incorrect decisions. For example, if a portfolio manager is using incomplete data to make investment decisions, he or she may be overlooking important factors that could affect the performance of the portfolio.

Ensuring data quality and integrity is particularly challenging in finance because financial data can be complex and difficult to interpret. Financial data often comes from multiple sources, including financial statements, market data, and transactional data. Each of these sources may have different levels of accuracy and completeness, making it difficult to integrate the data into a single analysis.

Interpretation Challenges

Finally, data analytics in finance also raises interpretation challenges. Even when data is accurate and unbiased, it can still be difficult to interpret. This is particularly true in finance, where data can be complex and difficult to understand. For example, financial ratios such as the price-to-earnings ratio and the debt-to-equity ratio can be difficult to interpret without a deep understanding of accounting and finance.

In addition, data analytics in finance often involves making predictions about future outcomes. These predictions are based on historical data and statistical models, which are inherently uncertain. As a result, it can be difficult to know how reliable these predictions are and how much weight to give them in decision-making.

Conclusion

In conclusion, data analytics in finance is a powerful tool that has transformed the way finance professionals make decisions. However, it is important to recognize that data analytics also has its limitations and risks. Bias and ethical concerns, data quality and integrity, and interpretation challenges are among the most significant challenges associated with data analytics in finance. By understanding these limitations and risks, we can better assess the value and reliability of data analytics in finance, and use it more effectively to make informed decisions.

CHAPTER 18: RISK MANAGEMENT AND BIG DATA

In the world of finance, risk management is a critical component of success. As the industry has evolved, so too has the practice of risk management. One of the most significant recent developments in this area has been the emergence of big data. Big data refers to the massive amounts of structured and unstructured data that are generated every day, and the technology and tools used to manage and analyze that data.

Risk management involves identifying, assessing, and controlling potential risks that could impact an organization's financial performance. The goal is to minimize potential losses and maximize potential gains by developing strategies to manage risk. In the past, risk management was largely a manual process, with analysts reviewing financial reports and other data to identify potential risks. However, with the rise of big data, risk management has become a more complex and data-intensive practice.

In this section, we will explore the importance of risk management in finance and how big data is changing the way that organizations approach risk management. We will define big data in the context of risk management and discuss the benefits and challenges of using big data for risk management.

The Importance of Risk Management in Finance

Risk management is critical in finance because the industry is inherently risky. Financial markets are subject to a wide range of factors that can impact prices and create volatility, including economic conditions, geopolitical events, and regulatory changes. In addition, financial institutions face risks associated with credit, liquidity, market, operational, and reputational risks.

Effective risk management is essential to the long-term success of financial institutions. By identifying and managing risks, organizations can reduce the likelihood of significant losses, maintain the trust of investors and clients, and ensure regulatory compliance. Poor risk management practices, on the other hand, can result in significant financial losses, reputational damage, and regulatory fines.

In addition to managing risks, risk management also plays a critical role in financial decision-making. By understanding the potential risks associated with various financial strategies, organizations can make informed decisions that balance risk and reward. This allows financial institutions to pursue growth and profitability while minimizing potential losses.

Definition of Big Data in Risk Management

Big data refers to the massive amounts of data that are generated by individuals, organizations, and machines every day. This data includes structured data, such as financial reports and transaction data, as well as unstructured data, such as social media posts, emails, and images.

Big data technologies and tools have been developed to manage and analyze these vast amounts of data. These tools include data warehouses, data lakes, and data analytics software, among others. The goal of big data in risk management is to help organizations make better decisions by providing more accurate, timely, and comprehensive information.

Big data has the potential to transform risk management in finance by providing organizations with deeper insights into potential risks and opportunities. By analyzing large amounts of data, organizations can identify trends and patterns that would be difficult to detect using traditional methods. This can help organizations develop more effective risk management strategies that are based on data-driven insights.

Conclusion

Risk management is critical in finance, and the emergence of big data has the potential to transform the way that organizations approach risk management. By providing deeper insights into potential risks and opportunities, big data can help financial institutions make better-informed decisions and develop more effective risk management strategies. However, the use of big data in risk management also presents significant challenges, including the need to manage large amounts of data, maintain data quality and integrity, and address ethical and legal concerns. In the following sections, we will explore these challenges in more detail and discuss strategies for addressing them.

I. Applications of Big Data in Risk Management

In today's fast-paced financial landscape, the use of big data is becoming increasingly crucial in managing risks. Risk management has always been an essential part of the finance industry, and with the growing volume and complexity of data, the integration of big data has become an important tool for managing risk. The ability to collect, process, and analyze large volumes of data in real-time has enabled risk managers to make better-informed decisions and respond quickly to emerging risks. This section explores the applications of big data in risk management, specifically in credit risk analysis, market risk analysis, and operational risk analysis.

Credit Risk Analysis

Credit risk refers to the potential for a borrower to default on their debt obligations. Credit risk analysis is a crucial aspect of risk management in finance, and big data analytics is making it easier to identify and assess credit risk. Traditional credit risk analysis relied on a limited set of financial data, such as credit scores, financial statements, and credit histories. However, with the advent of big data, lenders now have access to a vast array of data sources, including social media, online purchase history, and mobile phone usage patterns, which can provide a more comprehensive view of a borrower's creditworthiness.

One example of a big data-driven credit risk analysis tool is Lenddo, a Singapore-based startup that uses non-financial data to assess creditworthiness. Lenddo uses data from social media platforms, mobile phone usage patterns, and other digital footprints to create a credit score for borrowers who lack a traditional credit history. By using big data to identify patterns and trends in borrower behavior, Lenddo is able to provide credit to individuals who might have been excluded from traditional credit markets.

Another application of big data in credit risk analysis is the use of machine learning algorithms to detect fraudulent activities. These algorithms can identify patterns and anomalies in transaction data that might indicate fraudulent behavior. For example, a machine learning algorithm could detect unusual spending patterns or unexpected transactions, which could indicate that a credit card has been stolen or compromised. By identifying fraudulent behavior in real-time, lenders can take proactive measures to prevent financial losses.

Market Risk Analysis

Market risk refers to the potential for losses arising from changes in market conditions, such as interest rates, exchange rates, or commodity prices. Big data analytics can provide risk managers with real-time information about market conditions, enabling them to make more informed decisions and respond quickly to changes in market conditions.

One application of big data in market risk analysis is the use of natural language processing (NLP) algorithms to analyze news articles and social media posts. NLP algorithms can identify sentiment and extract relevant information from these sources, providing risk managers with a more comprehensive view of market conditions. For example, if a news article reports on a major geopolitical event, an NLP algorithm could analyze the sentiment of the article and identify any potential risks or opportunities associated with the event.

Another application of big data in market risk analysis is the use of machine learning algorithms to predict market trends. By analyzing historical data and identifying patterns and trends, machine learning algorithms can predict future market movements with a high degree of accuracy. For example, a machine learning algorithm could analyze historical data on stock prices and identify patterns that indicate a particular stock is likely to increase or decrease in value in the near future.

Operational Risk Analysis

Operational risk refers to the potential for losses arising from internal processes, systems, or human error. Big data analytics can help identify and mitigate operational risks by providing real-time insights into operational processes and identifying areas where improvements can be made.

One application of big data in operational risk analysis is the use of process mining techniques to analyze operational processes. Process mining involves analyzing event logs to identify patterns and bottlenecks in operational processes. By identifying areas where processes can be streamlined or improved, companies can reduce the likelihood of operational errors and improve efficiency.

Another application of big data in operational risk management is predictive maintenance. Predictive maintenance uses big data and machine learning algorithms to predict when equipment is likely to fail, allowing companies to take preventative measures before a failure occurs. This can be particularly useful in industries such as manufacturing, where downtime due to equipment failure can result in significant losses.

In addition to credit risk analysis, market risk analysis, and operational risk analysis, big data is also being used in other areas of risk management. For example, big data is increasingly being used in fraud detection and prevention. By analyzing large amounts of data, such as transaction logs, companies can identify patterns that may indicate fraudulent activity and take preventative measures.

Furthermore, big data is also being used in regulatory compliance. Regulatory compliance is a major concern for many companies, particularly those in the financial sector. By using big data analytics, companies can more easily identify and monitor compliance risks, ensuring that they are meeting regulatory requirements.

Overall, the applications of big data in risk management are numerous and varied. From credit risk analysis to regulatory compliance, big data is transforming the way that companies manage risk. While there are certainly challenges and risks associated with the use of big data in risk management, the potential benefits are too significant to ignore. As such, it is likely that we will continue to see the use of big data in risk management grow in the coming years.

II. The Role of AI in Risk Management

Artificial intelligence (AI) has revolutionized many industries, and risk management is no exception. With the increasing volume and complexity of data generated in financial markets, AI has become an essential tool for identifying, analyzing, and managing risks. In this section, we will explore the role of AI in risk management, specifically machine learning algorithms, natural language processing (NLP), and automated decision-making.

Machine Learning Algorithms for Risk Management

Machine learning algorithms are a subset of AI that enable computers to learn and make predictions or decisions based on data. Machine learning algorithms can analyze vast amounts of data, identify patterns and relationships, and use this information to make predictions or decisions. In risk management, machine learning algorithms can be used to identify potential risks and help make decisions about risk mitigation strategies.

One application of machine learning in risk management is fraud detection. For example, credit card companies use machine learning algorithms to analyze transaction data and identify patterns of fraudulent activity. The algorithms can learn from past instances of fraud and identify new cases in real-time, enabling the company to take action to prevent further losses.

Another application of machine learning in risk management is portfolio optimization. Investment managers use machine learning algorithms to analyze market data and identify patterns that indicate which investments are likely to perform well. The algorithms can also help managers optimize portfolios by selecting investments that maximize returns while minimizing risk.

However, machine learning algorithms are not without their limitations. One key challenge is that they require large amounts of high-quality data to function effectively. If the data used to train the algorithm is incomplete or biased, the algorithm may produce inaccurate results. Additionally, machine learning algorithms are often considered to be "black boxes" because it can be difficult to understand how they arrived at their decisions. This can make it challenging to explain decisions to stakeholders and can make it difficult to identify errors or biases in the algorithm.

Natural Language Processing (NLP) in Risk Management

Natural language processing (NLP) is a branch of AI that enables computers to understand and analyze human language. In risk management, NLP can be used to analyze news articles, social media posts, and other sources of information to identify potential risks.

One application of NLP in risk management is sentiment analysis. Sentiment analysis involves analyzing text to determine whether it has a positive, negative, or neutral sentiment. For example, investment managers may use sentiment analysis to monitor social media for mentions of their portfolio companies. If the sentiment is negative, the managers may decide to sell their holdings to minimize risk.

Another application of NLP in risk management is event extraction. Event extraction involves analyzing text to identify events that may be relevant to risk management. For example, if a news article mentions a natural disaster that could impact a company's supply chain, risk managers may use this information to develop contingency plans.

Like machine learning algorithms, NLP also has limitations. NLP algorithms require large amounts of high-quality data to function effectively. Additionally, NLP algorithms may struggle with understanding nuances in human language, such as sarcasm or idioms.

Automated Decision-Making in Risk Management

Automated decision-making involves using algorithms to make decisions without human intervention. In risk management, automated decision-making can be used to quickly respond to potential risks and reduce the risk of human error.

One application of automated decision-making in risk management is algorithmic trading. Algorithmic trading involves using computer programs to execute trades based on market data and predefined rules. This can help traders respond quickly to market changes and reduce the risk of human error.

Another application of automated decision-making in risk management is credit scoring. Credit scoring algorithms use data such as credit history, income, and debt-to-income ratio to determine the likelihood of a borrower repaying a loan. Automated credit scoring can help lenders make quick and accurate lending decisions while minimizing the risk of defaults.

However, there are also concerns about the potential biases in automated credit scoring algorithms. These algorithms may inadvertently discriminate against certain groups, such as low-income or minority borrowers, who may have less traditional credit histories or have faced historical barriers to credit. If these groups are unfairly excluded from lending opportunities, it could lead to economic inequality and exacerbate existing societal disparities.

To address these concerns, some companies and regulators have called for greater transparency and oversight in credit scoring algorithms. They advocate for regular monitoring of algorithms to ensure they are not biased and for providing explanations to borrowers who are denied credit based on an algorithmic decision.

Another area where AI is being used in risk management is fraud detection. Fraud is a significant risk for financial institutions, and detecting and preventing it is crucial to their stability and reputation. AI-powered fraud detection systems use machine learning algorithms to identify patterns and anomalies in large datasets, such as transaction histories, to detect potential fraudulent activity.

For example, some banks use anomaly detection algorithms to identify unusual patterns in ATM withdrawals or credit card transactions that could indicate fraudulent activity. Other companies use natural language processing (NLP) techniques to analyze unstructured data, such as email or chat logs, to identify potentially fraudulent communications.

While AI-powered fraud detection systems can be highly effective in identifying fraudulent activity, there are also concerns about false positives and false negatives. False positives occur when legitimate transactions are incorrectly flagged as fraudulent, potentially leading to inconvenience or frustration for customers. False negatives occur when fraudulent activity is not detected, potentially leading to financial losses for the institution and its customers.

To address these concerns, companies are developing and refining their algorithms to reduce false positives and negatives. They are also investing in systems that provide more context and explanation for flagged transactions, allowing analysts to quickly and accurately determine whether activity is truly fraudulent.

Overall, the use of AI in risk management has the potential to revolutionize the field, enabling financial institutions to make more informed and accurate decisions while reducing risk. However, as with any technology, there are risks and challenges that must be addressed to ensure the responsible and ethical use of AI in risk management.

III. Challenges and Opportunities

The use of big data and AI in risk management offers numerous benefits, but it also presents significant challenges that must be addressed. This section will explore some of the key challenges and opportunities associated with the use of big data and AI in risk management.

Data Privacy and Security

One of the most significant challenges associated with the use of big data and AI in risk management is data privacy and security. As organizations collect and analyze vast amounts of data, they must ensure that sensitive information is properly protected. In particular, financial institutions must comply with strict regulations regarding the handling and protection of customer data.

To address these concerns, organizations must implement robust data privacy and security policies and procedures. This includes ensuring that data is properly encrypted, monitoring access to sensitive information, and implementing effective cybersecurity measures. Organizations must also ensure that their data analytics tools and algorithms are designed to protect privacy and prevent data breaches.

Integration with Legacy Systems

Another challenge associated with the use of big data and AI in risk management is the integration with legacy systems. Financial institutions typically have a vast array of systems and platforms that have been developed over many years. Integrating new big data analytics tools and AI systems with these legacy systems can be a complex and time-consuming process.

To overcome this challenge, organizations must take a strategic approach to the integration of new technologies. This may involve developing a clear roadmap for the integration of new systems, as well as investing in the training and development of staff to ensure that they are able to effectively use new technologies.

Regulatory Compliance

The use of big data and AI in risk management also presents challenges in terms of regulatory compliance. Financial institutions must comply with a wide range of regulations, including anti-money laundering (AML) regulations, know-your-customer (KYC) requirements, and data protection regulations.

To ensure regulatory compliance, organizations must ensure that their big data analytics tools and AI systems are designed to meet regulatory requirements. This may involve working closely with regulators to ensure that systems are designed to comply with relevant regulations, as well as investing in staff training and development to ensure that staff are aware of their regulatory obligations.

Conclusion

The use of big data and AI in risk management offers significant opportunities for financial institutions to better manage risk and improve their bottom line. However, these opportunities must be balanced against the challenges associated with the use of these technologies, including data privacy and security concerns, integration with legacy systems, and regulatory compliance.

To successfully implement big data and AI in risk management, organizations must take a strategic approach to the development and implementation of these technologies. This involves investing in the necessary infrastructure and staff training, as well as working closely with regulators to ensure that systems are designed to meet regulatory requirements.

Overall, the use of big data and AI in risk management is a rapidly evolving field that offers significant potential for financial institutions. However, it is essential that organizations are aware of the challenges associated with these technologies and take a proactive approach to addressing them.

CHAPTER 19: THE FUTURE OF BIG DATA IN FINANCE

The increasing availability and accessibility of data, coupled with advances in technology, have revolutionized the way financial institutions operate. Big data analytics has become a key driver in transforming the industry, offering new ways of generating insights and enhancing decision-making processes. In the coming years, the use of big data is expected to expand further, as institutions continue to leverage its benefits and explore new ways to apply it.

One of the main areas where big data is being used in finance is in risk management. The ability to process large amounts of data in real-time, combined with machine learning algorithms, has enabled financial institutions to better assess and mitigate risks. For example, credit scoring algorithms that leverage big data have made lending decisions more efficient and accurate, while predictive analytics can help identify potential fraud in real-time.

Another area where big data is making an impact is in portfolio management. Big data analytics can help portfolio managers better understand market trends and identify new investment opportunities. By analyzing large amounts of data, including news articles, social media feeds, and economic indicators, investors can make more informed decisions about their investment strategies.

Big data is also playing an important role in the evolution of financial services, particularly in the area of customer experience. Institutions can use data to gain insights into customer behavior and preferences, enabling them to offer personalized products and services. For example, by analyzing transaction data, banks can identify customers who are likely to be interested in particular products or services and offer them tailored promotions.

Looking ahead, the future of big data in finance is bright. The continued growth of data volumes, coupled with advances in technology, will enable financial institutions to gain even deeper insights into their operations and customers. Machine learning algorithms and other forms of artificial intelligence will become more sophisticated, enabling more accurate predictions and better decision-making. In addition, the integration of big data with blockchain technology could revolutionize the way financial transactions are conducted, improving efficiency, security, and transparency.

However, as with any new technology, there are also challenges that must be addressed. Data privacy and security are major concerns, particularly given the sensitivity of financial data. Financial institutions must ensure that data is protected at all times and that they are complying with regulations around data privacy and security. The integration of big data with legacy systems can also be a challenge, as institutions need to ensure that new data streams can be seamlessly integrated with existing systems. Finally, regulatory compliance remains a key issue, with institutions needing to ensure that their use of big data is in line with regulatory requirements.

In conclusion, the use of big data in finance has already had a significant impact, and its importance is only set to grow in the coming years. By leveraging big data analytics, financial institutions can gain deeper insights into their operations and customers, improve risk management, and develop new products and services. However, they must also be mindful of the challenges that come with the use of big data, including data privacy and security, integration with legacy systems, and regulatory compliance. As long as these challenges are addressed, big data will continue to transform the finance industry and drive innovation.

I. Emerging Trends in Big Data

As the use of big data continues to grow in the financial industry, new trends are emerging that are changing the way that data is collected, processed, and analyzed. These trends are driven by advances in technology, changes in customer behavior, and evolving regulatory requirements. In this section, we will examine three emerging trends in big data: real-time analytics, edge computing, and cloud-based solutions.

Real-time Analytics

Real-time analytics is the practice of analyzing data as it is generated, rather than after the fact. This allows financial institutions to quickly identify patterns and trends in customer behavior, market conditions, and other factors that can affect their business. Real-time analytics can be used for a variety of purposes, including fraud detection, risk management, and marketing.

One example of real-time analytics in action is the use of machine learning algorithms to detect credit card fraud. These algorithms are trained on historical data to identify patterns that are indicative of fraud. When a new transaction occurs, the algorithm can quickly analyze the data and determine whether or not it is likely to be fraudulent. This allows financial institutions to take immediate action to prevent losses.

Another example of real-time analytics is the use of sentiment analysis to monitor social media for mentions of financial institutions or their products. By analyzing the tone and content of these posts, financial institutions can quickly identify potential issues and take steps to address them before they become bigger problems.

Edge Computing

Edge computing is the practice of processing data at the edge of a network, rather than in a centralized data center. This allows financial institutions to reduce latency and improve performance by processing data closer to the source. Edge computing can be used for a variety of purposes, including real-time analytics, security, and compliance.

One example of edge computing in action is the use of Internet of Things (IoT) devices to monitor physical assets, such as ATMs or branch locations. By processing data from these devices at the edge of the network, financial institutions can quickly identify issues and take corrective action.

Cloud-Based Solutions

Cloud-based solutions are becoming increasingly popular in the financial industry, as they offer a number of benefits over traditional on-premise solutions. These benefits include greater scalability, lower costs, and improved security.

One example of cloud-based solutions in action is the use of Software-as-a-Service (SaaS) platforms for customer relationship management (CRM) and marketing automation. By using a cloud-based platform, financial institutions can quickly and easily scale their operations to meet changing customer demands. Additionally, they can reduce costs by eliminating the need for on-premise hardware and software.

Another example of cloud-based solutions in action is the use of Infrastructure-as-a-Service (IaaS) platforms for data storage and processing. By using an IaaS platform, financial institutions can quickly and easily scale their data storage and processing capabilities to meet changing business needs.

Conclusion

As the financial industry continues to evolve, big data will play an increasingly important role in helping institutions make informed decisions. Real-time analytics, edge computing, and cloud-based solutions are just a few of the emerging trends that are changing the way that financial institutions collect, process, and analyze data. By embracing these trends, financial institutions can stay ahead of the curve and remain competitive in an increasingly data-driven world.

II. The Impact of AI on Big Data in Finance

The intersection of big data and artificial intelligence (AI) has significant implications for the finance industry. With the increasing amount of data available to financial institutions, the application of AI technologies can help extract insights and generate value from this data. In this section, we will explore the impact of AI on big data in finance, specifically focusing on machine learning and deep learning, natural language processing (NLP), and reinforcement learning.

Machine learning is a type of AI technology that enables machines to learn from data without being explicitly programmed. Deep learning is a subfield of machine learning that uses artificial neural networks to learn from vast amounts of data. Machine learning and deep learning have had a significant impact on big data in finance, particularly in areas such as fraud detection, risk management, and investment strategies.

One example of the application of machine learning in finance is fraud detection. Financial institutions can use machine learning algorithms to detect fraudulent activities by analyzing large volumes of transactional data. Machine learning algorithms can identify patterns and anomalies in transaction data and alert financial institutions to potential fraud.

Another example of the application of deep learning in finance is risk management. Financial institutions can use deep learning algorithms to analyze large volumes of financial data to identify potential risks and make more informed decisions. Deep learning algorithms can identify patterns and correlations in data that would be difficult for human analysts to detect.

NLP is another AI technology that has had a significant impact on big data in finance. NLP is a subfield of AI that focuses on the interaction between computers and human languages. In finance, NLP is used to analyze unstructured data, such as news articles, social media, and analyst reports, to extract insights and generate value.

One example of the application of NLP in finance is sentiment analysis. Financial institutions can use NLP algorithms to analyze social media and news articles to gauge public sentiment about a particular company or market. Sentiment analysis can provide financial institutions with valuable insights that can inform investment decisions.

Reinforcement learning is a type of machine learning that involves training an algorithm to make decisions based on rewards and punishments. Reinforcement learning has the potential to revolutionize investment strategies by enabling financial institutions to automate investment decisions based on market trends and data.

One example of the application of reinforcement learning in finance is algorithmic trading. Financial institutions can use reinforcement learning algorithms to analyze vast amounts of financial data to make automated trading decisions. These algorithms can identify patterns in financial data that are difficult for human analysts to detect and use these patterns to make profitable trades.

While the impact of AI on big data in finance has the potential to transform the industry, it also raises concerns about data privacy, security, and bias. Financial institutions must ensure that their AI systems are transparent and accountable, and that they do not discriminate against certain groups of people. Additionally, the use of AI in finance requires regulatory oversight to ensure that financial institutions are using these technologies in an ethical and responsible manner.

In conclusion, AI has had a significant impact on big data in finance, particularly in areas such as fraud detection, risk management, investment strategies, and sentiment analysis. Machine learning, deep learning, NLP, and reinforcement learning are all AI technologies that have transformed the way financial institutions analyze and use data. However, the use of AI in finance raises concerns about data privacy, security, and bias, and financial institutions must take steps to ensure that their AI systems are transparent, accountable, and ethical.

III. Ethical and Regulatory Considerations

The increased use of big data and AI in finance has led to a growing concern about ethical and regulatory considerations. While these technologies have the potential to revolutionize the finance industry, there are also significant risks and challenges associated with their use. In this section, we will explore some of the most important ethical and regulatory considerations related to big data and AI in finance.

Data Privacy and Security:

Data privacy and security are among the most critical ethical and regulatory considerations in the use of big data and AI in finance. The collection and analysis of vast amounts of personal data, including financial and transactional data, raise serious concerns about privacy and security. Hackers and other malicious actors are always looking for ways to exploit vulnerabilities in data systems, and the risks associated with large-scale data breaches are significant.

To address these concerns, financial institutions must ensure that their data systems are secure and that appropriate measures are in place to protect customer data. This includes implementing encryption and other security protocols, establishing clear policies for data handling and access, and conducting regular security audits to identify and address vulnerabilities. Additionally, financial institutions must comply with relevant data protection regulations, such as the General Data Protection Regulation (GDPR) and the California Consumer Privacy Act (CCPA).

Bias and Discrimination:

Another critical ethical consideration in the use of big data and AI in finance is the potential for bias and discrimination. Algorithms used in finance are only as good as the data they are trained on, and if that data is biased or incomplete, it can result in discriminatory outcomes. For example, if an algorithm is trained on data that is biased against certain groups, such as racial minorities or women, it may produce results that perpetuate those biases.

To address this concern, financial institutions must ensure that their data is representative of the entire population and that algorithms are regularly audited for bias. Additionally, financial institutions must take steps to ensure that their algorithms are transparent and explainable, so that customers and regulators can understand how decisions are made.

Legal and Regulatory Compliance:

Legal and regulatory compliance is another critical consideration in the use of big data and AI in finance. Financial institutions must comply with a complex web of laws and regulations, including anti-money laundering (AML) and know-your-customer (KYC) regulations, as well as regulations related to data protection, consumer protection, and fair lending.

To comply with these regulations, financial institutions must ensure that their algorithms and data handling processes are transparent and auditable, so that regulators can ensure that they are operating in compliance with the law. Additionally, financial institutions must establish clear policies and procedures for monitoring and reporting on algorithmic decision-making processes, and they must be prepared to demonstrate to regulators that they are making decisions in a fair and transparent manner.

Conclusion:

In conclusion, the use of big data and AI in finance has significant potential to transform the industry and improve outcomes for customers. However, there are also significant ethical and regulatory considerations that must be taken into account. Financial institutions must be proactive in addressing these concerns, including ensuring data privacy and security, guarding against bias and discrimination, and complying with relevant laws and regulations. By doing so, they can help to ensure that the benefits of big data and AI are realized while minimizing the risks and challenges associated with their use.

PART VI: SUSTAINABILITY AND IMPACT INVESTING

In recent years, there has been a growing awareness of the importance of sustainability and impact investing in the world of finance. With climate change and other environmental and social issues at the forefront of global concerns, investors are increasingly recognizing the importance of incorporating sustainability and social responsibility into their investment decisions.

Chapter 20: The Importance of Sustainability in Finance

Sustainability has become an increasingly important issue in the world of finance, as investors seek to align their investments with their values and concerns about the long-term health of the planet. The concept of sustainability refers to the ability of a system to endure over time without depleting its resources or causing irreparable harm to the environment.

Sustainability is particularly relevant in the context of finance, as financial markets play a critical role in shaping the global economy and can have significant impacts on the environment and social welfare. As a result, investors are increasingly looking for ways to incorporate sustainability considerations into their investment strategies.

One approach to sustainability in finance is through the use of Environmental, Social, and Governance (ESG) factors. ESG factors are non-financial metrics used to evaluate the sustainability and ethical impact of an investment. These metrics include things like a company's carbon footprint, labor practices, and board diversity. By considering ESG factors in investment decisions, investors can ensure that they are supporting companies that align with their values and that have a positive impact on society and the environment.

Chapter 21: Impact Investing and Socially Responsible Investing

Impact investing and socially responsible investing (SRI) are two related approaches to investing that prioritize social and environmental impact alongside financial returns. Impact investing refers specifically to investments made with the intention of generating positive social or environmental impact, while SRI is a broader term that encompasses a range of approaches to investing that prioritize social and environmental factors.

Impact investing and SRI have grown in popularity in recent years as investors have become more conscious of the impact their investments can have on society and the environment. These approaches to investing offer investors the opportunity to make a positive difference in the world while also generating financial returns.

One of the challenges of impact investing and SRI is defining what constitutes "impact" or "social responsibility." Different investors may have different ideas about what issues are most important and what types of investments are most effective at addressing those issues. As a result, impact investing and SRI can be difficult to evaluate and compare, and there is a need for more standardized metrics to measure impact and social responsibility.

Chapter 22: Climate Change and Its Impact on Finance

Climate change is one of the most pressing environmental issues facing the world today, and it has significant implications for the world of finance. Climate change can impact the financial sector in a number of ways, including through physical risks (such as damage from extreme weather events), transitional risks (such as the transition to a low-carbon economy), and liability risks (such as the potential for lawsuits related to climate change).

Investors are increasingly recognizing the need to incorporate climate change considerations into their investment strategies. This can include investing in companies that are actively working to address climate change or that are less vulnerable to its impacts, as well as divesting from companies that are contributing to climate change or are particularly vulnerable to its impacts.

In addition, investors can use tools like carbon pricing to incentivize companies to reduce their carbon footprint and encourage the development of low-carbon technologies. Carbon pricing involves placing a price on carbon emissions, either through a carbon tax or a cap-and-trade system, which creates financial incentives for companies to reduce their carbon emissions.

Chapter 23: The Future of Sustainable Finance

Looking ahead, sustainable finance is likely to become an increasingly important focus for investors and financial institutions. The challenges of climate change and other environmental and social issues are only likely to become more pressing in the coming years, and investors are likely to demand greater transparency and accountability from the companies in which they invest.

One emerging trend in sustainable finance is the rise of green bonds. Green bonds are debt securities issued by companies, governments, or other organizations to finance environmentally friendly projects such as renewable energy or clean water initiatives. The market for green bonds has grown rapidly in recent years, with issuance reaching a record $270 billion in 2020, up from $52 billion in 2015. As more companies and governments look to finance sustainable projects, green bonds are likely to continue to grow in popularity.

Another trend is the rise of impact investing. Impact investing involves investing in companies or organizations with the intention of generating a measurable social or environmental impact alongside a financial return. This type of investing is becoming increasingly popular among millennials and younger generations, who are often more interested in investing their money in companies that align with their values and beliefs. Impact investing is also attractive to institutional investors and high net worth individuals who are looking to make a positive impact while still achieving financial returns.

Climate change will continue to be a major driver of sustainable finance. As the effects of climate change become more severe, investors will increasingly look to invest in companies that are taking steps to mitigate their environmental impact. This may include companies that are reducing their carbon emissions, investing in renewable energy, or taking steps to reduce waste and pollution. Companies that fail to take these steps may find themselves at a disadvantage in the eyes of investors.

Regulators are also likely to play an important role in shaping the future of sustainable finance. Governments around the world are increasingly introducing regulations designed to promote sustainable finance and reduce the risks associated with climate change. For example, the European Union's Sustainable

Finance Disclosure Regulation (SFDR) requires financial institutions to disclose how they integrate environmental, social, and governance (ESG) factors into their investment decisions. Other countries are expected to follow suit, which will further increase the focus on sustainable finance.

In conclusion, sustainable finance is an important area of focus for investors, financial institutions, and regulators. As the world continues to grapple with the challenges of climate change and other environmental and social issues, sustainable finance will become increasingly important in ensuring that capital is allocated in a way that supports a more sustainable future. While there are many challenges and uncertainties associated with sustainable finance, the potential benefits are significant, both in terms of financial returns and the positive impact that can be generated for the planet and society as a whole.

CHAPTER 20: THE IMPORTANCE OF SUSTAINABILITY IN FINANCE

Sustainability has become an increasingly important topic in the financial industry, as investors and institutions seek to align their investments with environmental and social goals. The concept of sustainability in finance is rooted in the idea that companies and financial institutions have a responsibility to consider the impact of their actions on the environment, society, and future generations.

This chapter will explore the importance of sustainability in finance, discussing the challenges and opportunities associated with sustainable investing, and examining the various approaches and strategies that investors and institutions can use to integrate sustainability into their investment decisions.

The Challenges of Sustainable Investing

One of the main challenges of sustainable investing is the lack of standardized metrics and definitions. There is currently no universally accepted definition of sustainability or sustainable investing, which can make it difficult for investors to identify truly sustainable investment opportunities. This lack of standardization can also lead to confusion and greenwashing, as companies and financial institutions may make false or misleading claims about their sustainability practices.

Another challenge is the potential trade-off between financial returns and sustainability goals. Some investors may be concerned that sustainable investing could lead to lower returns, as companies that prioritize sustainability may not always be the most profitable. However, there is growing evidence that sustainable investing can actually lead to improved financial performance over the long term, as companies with strong environmental, social, and governance (ESG) practices may be better equipped to manage risk and capitalize on emerging opportunities.

The Opportunities of Sustainable Investing

Despite these challenges, sustainable investing presents a significant opportunity for investors and institutions to align their investments with their values and make a positive impact on the world. By incorporating ESG factors into their investment decisions, investors can support companies that are committed to environmental and social responsibility, and encourage positive change within industries.

Sustainable investing can also help to mitigate risk and promote long-term financial stability. Companies that prioritize sustainability may be better prepared to weather environmental and social challenges, and may be more attractive to consumers and investors who are increasingly prioritizing sustainability.

Approaches and Strategies for Sustainable Investing

There are various approaches and strategies that investors and institutions can use to integrate sustainability into their investment decisions. One common approach is to screen investments based on ESG criteria, such as a company's carbon emissions, labor practices, or board diversity. This can help to identify companies that are committed to sustainability and weed out those that are not.

Another approach is to actively engage with companies to encourage sustainable practices and promote positive change. This can involve voting on shareholder resolutions, engaging with company management, or collaborating with other investors to advocate for sustainability initiatives.

Impact Investing and Socially Responsible Investing

One increasingly popular approach to sustainable investing is impact investing, which involves investing in companies or organizations that have a specific social or environmental mission. Impact investments may target issues such as poverty alleviation, access to healthcare, or sustainable agriculture. These investments can provide both financial returns and measurable social or environmental benefits.

Socially responsible investing (SRI) is another approach that has gained popularity in recent years. SRI involves investing in companies that align with an investor's values, such as those that prioritize sustainability, diversity, or social justice. SRI investments may involve avoiding companies that engage in harmful practices or supporting companies that have a positive impact on society.

Conclusion

The importance of sustainability in finance cannot be overstated. As the world faces increasing environmental and social challenges, investors and financial institutions have a responsibility to consider the impact of their investments on the world around them. By incorporating ESG factors into their investment decisions, investors can promote positive change and align their investments with their values. While there are certainly challenges to sustainable investing, the opportunities are significant, and the potential benefits extend not just to investors, but to society and the environment as a whole.

I. The Benefits of Sustainable Finance

Sustainable finance refers to the practice of incorporating environmental, social, and governance (ESG) criteria into investment decisions. This approach is becoming increasingly popular among investors who recognize the importance of considering the long-term impact of their investments on the planet, society, and the economy. In this section, we will explore the benefits of sustainable finance in terms of environmental, social, and economic aspects.

Environmental Benefits:

One of the primary benefits of sustainable finance is its positive impact on the environment. By investing in companies that prioritize sustainability, investors can contribute to the reduction of carbon emissions, preservation of natural resources, and protection of biodiversity. For instance, an investment in renewable energy sources such as solar, wind, and hydro can reduce reliance on fossil fuels and promote a transition to a low-carbon economy. Similarly, investing in companies that prioritize water conservation, waste reduction, and sustainable forestry practices can help preserve natural resources.

Sustainable finance can also promote environmental stewardship by encouraging companies to adopt sustainable business practices. Companies that prioritize sustainability are more likely to invest in research and development of eco-friendly technologies, implement sustainable supply chain practices, and disclose environmental performance metrics. By investing in these companies, investors can help create a market demand for sustainable products and services, leading to a broader adoption of sustainable practices.

Social Benefits:

In addition to the environmental benefits, sustainable finance can also have significant social benefits. By investing in companies that prioritize ESG criteria, investors can support companies that prioritize social responsibility and ethical business practices. For instance, an investment in companies that promote gender diversity, fair labor practices, and human rights can contribute to the promotion of social justice and equality.

Sustainable finance can also encourage companies to prioritize social responsibility by providing a financial incentive for companies to adopt ethical business practices. Companies that prioritize ESG criteria are more likely to implement responsible supply chain practices, promote diversity and inclusion, and contribute to the communities they operate in. By investing in these companies, investors can help create a market demand for socially responsible companies, leading to broader adoption of ethical business practices.

Economic Benefits:

Sustainable finance can also have significant economic benefits. By investing in companies that prioritize sustainability, investors can contribute to the creation of a more resilient and sustainable economy. For instance, investing in companies that prioritize clean energy can contribute to the creation of jobs in the renewable energy sector, leading to economic growth and job creation.

Sustainable finance can also contribute to the mitigation of financial risks by incorporating ESG criteria into investment decisions. By considering factors such as climate change risk, social responsibility, and governance practices, investors can identify potential risks and opportunities in their investments. For instance, investments in companies that prioritize sustainability are less likely to face regulatory penalties, reputational damage, or operational disruptions due to environmental and social issues.

Conclusion:

In conclusion, sustainable finance offers a range of benefits to investors, society, and the planet. By incorporating ESG criteria into investment decisions, investors can contribute to a more sustainable future by promoting environmental stewardship, social responsibility, and economic growth. While there are challenges to implementing sustainable finance practices, such as a lack of standardized metrics and data, the benefits of sustainable finance make it an increasingly attractive investment strategy.

II. Challenges to Sustainable Finance

Sustainable finance is a relatively new field that seeks to align financial practices with environmental, social, and governance (ESG) goals. The benefits of sustainable finance are numerous, including environmental, social, and economic benefits, as discussed in the previous section. However, sustainable finance also faces a number of challenges that may hinder its growth and effectiveness. In this section, we will discuss three major challenges to sustainable finance: lack of standardization, lack of transparency, and limited awareness and understanding of sustainable finance.

Lack of Standardization:

One of the biggest challenges facing sustainable finance is the lack of standardization in ESG metrics and reporting. This makes it difficult for investors to compare the ESG performance of different companies, and for companies to demonstrate their ESG credentials to investors. Inconsistent and incomplete ESG data also makes it difficult to assess the impact of sustainable investments and to identify areas for improvement.

This lack of standardization creates a barrier to investment in sustainable finance and reduces its effectiveness.

The lack of standardization is particularly challenging in the area of climate change, where there is a need for consistent and reliable carbon accounting. While a number of initiatives have been developed to address this issue, including the Task Force on Climate-related Financial Disclosures (TCFD) and the Carbon Disclosure Project (CDP), there is still a long way to go to achieve standardization in this area.

Investment bankers, portfolio managers, and quantitative analysts are particularly affected by the lack of standardization in sustainable finance. These professionals require reliable data to make informed investment decisions and to assess the risk and return of sustainable investments.

Lack of Transparency:

Another challenge facing sustainable finance is the lack of transparency in ESG reporting. Companies may not disclose all relevant ESG information, or may selectively report only positive information, leading to incomplete and potentially misleading ESG scores. This makes it difficult for investors to make informed decisions and for companies to be held accountable for their ESG performance. The lack of transparency also creates a risk of greenwashing, where companies may claim to be more sustainable than they actually are.

Securities traders, financial planners, and financial analysts are particularly affected by the lack of transparency in sustainable finance. These professionals rely on accurate and complete information to make informed investment decisions and to provide advice to their clients.

Limited Awareness and Understanding:

A third challenge facing sustainable finance is limited awareness and understanding of sustainable finance among investors and financial professionals. Sustainable finance is a relatively new field and many investors and financial professionals may not be familiar with its principles and practices. This can create a barrier to investment in sustainable finance and reduce its effectiveness.

Education and training are key to addressing this challenge. Financial institutions can provide training to their employees to increase awareness and understanding of sustainable finance, while universities can incorporate sustainable finance into their curricula to educate the next generation of financial professionals.

Financial planners and financial analysts are particularly affected by the limited awareness and understanding of sustainable finance. These professionals play a key role in advising clients on their investment options and need to be knowledgeable about sustainable finance to provide informed advice.

Counterarguments:

While sustainable finance faces significant challenges, it is important to note that progress is being made in addressing these challenges. Many initiatives are underway to promote standardization and transparency in ESG reporting, and education and awareness-raising efforts are increasing. Additionally, some investors and financial institutions are beginning to recognize the benefits of sustainable finance and are incorporating ESG factors into their investment decisions.

However, it is also important to acknowledge that some investors and financial professionals may be skeptical of sustainable finance, viewing it as a niche market or as an unnecessary restriction on investment decisions. These individuals may prefer to focus solely on financial performance and may not see the value in considering ESG factors.

Conclusion:

In conclusion, sustainable finance faces a number of challenges, including lack of standardization, lack of transparency, and limited awareness and understanding among investors and financial professionals. However, the benefits of sustainable finance cannot be overlooked. By incorporating ESG factors into investment decisions, investors can mitigate risk, enhance long-term financial performance, and contribute to positive environmental and social outcomes.

To overcome the challenges facing sustainable finance, there needs to be a concerted effort by regulators, investors, and financial institutions to create a more standardized and transparent framework for ESG reporting and investing. This can include the development of industry-wide ESG reporting standards and guidelines, as well as increased education and awareness campaigns to promote the benefits of sustainable finance.

Furthermore, it is important for investors and financial professionals to recognize that sustainable finance is not a niche market, but rather an integral part of modern finance. As the global focus on environmental and social issues continues to grow, sustainable finance will become increasingly important in meeting the needs and expectations of investors, society, and the planet.

Overall, sustainable finance presents a unique opportunity for investors to align their financial goals with their values and contribute to positive environmental and social outcomes. While there are certainly challenges to be addressed, the potential benefits make it clear that sustainable finance is a critical component of the future of finance.

III. Sustainable Finance in Practice

As discussed in the previous sections, sustainable finance is becoming an increasingly important focus for investors and financial institutions. In practice, sustainable finance can take many forms, from sustainable investing and green bonds to corporate sustainability reporting and ESG integration in investment analysis. This section will delve into these practices and provide a comprehensive analysis of sustainable finance in practice.

Sustainable Investing:

One of the most well-known forms of sustainable finance is sustainable investing, which involves investing in companies that demonstrate strong environmental, social, and governance (ESG) performance. This type of investing is often done through mutual funds, exchange-traded funds (ETFs), and other investment vehicles that specifically target companies with sustainable practices.

One key benefit of sustainable investing is the potential for financial outperformance. According to a study by Morningstar, sustainable funds outperformed traditional funds during the COVID-19 pandemic, suggesting that companies with strong ESG practices are more resilient in times of crisis.

However, sustainable investing is not without its challenges. One common issue is the lack of standardization in ESG ratings, which can make it difficult for investors to compare companies' ESG performance. Additionally, some investors may be skeptical of sustainable investing, viewing it as a niche market or as an unnecessary restriction on investment decisions.

Green Bonds and Other Sustainable Finance Instruments:

Green bonds are another popular form of sustainable finance. These bonds are issued specifically to fund environmentally friendly projects, such as renewable energy, energy efficiency, and sustainable agriculture. Green bonds are growing in popularity, with issuances reaching a record high of $269.5 billion in 2020.

Other sustainable finance instruments include sustainability-linked loans, which tie the interest rate of a loan to the borrower's sustainability performance, and social impact bonds, which fund social initiatives such as affordable housing or job training programs.

Corporate Sustainability Reporting:

Corporate sustainability reporting is the practice of companies reporting on their ESG performance to stakeholders, including investors, customers, and employees. This reporting can take many forms, from standalone sustainability reports to integrated reports that combine financial and sustainability performance.

One benefit of corporate sustainability reporting is increased transparency, which can help investors and other stakeholders make more informed decisions. However, some critics argue that sustainability reporting lacks standardization and can be prone to greenwashing, where companies exaggerate their sustainability performance to appeal to investors.

ESG Integration in Investment Analysis:

ESG integration involves incorporating ESG factors into investment analysis to better understand a company's risks and opportunities. This approach can help investors identify companies with strong ESG performance, as well as those with ESG-related risks that may impact their long-term financial performance.

However, ESG integration also faces challenges. One common issue is the lack of standardized ESG data, which can make it difficult for investors to compare companies' ESG performance. Additionally, some investors may be skeptical of ESG integration, viewing it as an unnecessary restriction on investment decisions.

Conclusion:

Sustainable finance is becoming an increasingly important focus for investors and financial institutions. In practice, sustainable finance can take many forms, from sustainable investing and green bonds to corporate sustainability reporting and ESG integration in investment analysis. While these practices offer a number of benefits, they also face challenges, such as the lack of standardization and transparency. Despite these challenges, the growth of sustainable finance suggests that investors and financial institutions are increasingly recognizing the importance of sustainability in finance.

CHAPTER 21: IMPACT INVESTING AND SOCIALLY RESPONSIBLE INVESTING

Investors have the power to direct their capital towards companies and projects that align with their values and beliefs. This has given rise to two types of investment strategies: impact investing and socially responsible investing (SRI). Both approaches aim to generate financial returns while also promoting positive social and environmental outcomes.

Impact investing refers to investments made with the intention of generating a measurable, positive social or environmental impact alongside financial returns. This approach seeks to address pressing global issues such as climate change, poverty, and inequality. Socially responsible investing, on the other hand, is a broader term that encompasses a range of strategies that seek to integrate environmental, social, and governance (ESG) factors into investment decisions. This approach focuses on identifying and investing in companies that demonstrate good ESG practices.

In this chapter, we will explore the concept of impact investing and SRI in greater depth, including their origins, key principles, and practical applications. We will also examine the benefits and challenges of these investment strategies, as well as the role they play in promoting sustainable finance.

Origins of Impact Investing and SRI

The roots of impact investing and SRI can be traced back to the socially responsible investing movement of the 1960s and 1970s, which sought to avoid investing in companies that were involved in controversial activities such as tobacco production, weapons manufacturing, and apartheid South Africa. In the decades that followed, SRI evolved to encompass a broader range of ESG factors, such as climate change, labor practices, and board diversity.

Impact investing, on the other hand, emerged in the early 2000s as a response to the limitations of traditional philanthropy and government aid. Proponents of impact investing believed that the private sector could play a more active role in addressing social and environmental challenges by directing capital towards sustainable and socially responsible projects. Impact investing was also seen as a way to generate financial returns while creating positive social and environmental outcomes.

Key Principles of Impact Investing and SRI

While impact investing and SRI share a common goal of promoting positive social and environmental outcomes, they differ in their specific objectives and investment strategies. However, there are several key principles that are central to both approaches:

Integration of ESG factors: Both impact investing and SRI involve the integration of ESG factors into investment decisions. This involves analyzing a company's ESG practices, such as its carbon footprint, labor practices, and board diversity, to determine its sustainability and social responsibility.

Measurable impact: Impact investing is characterized by its focus on generating measurable, positive social or environmental outcomes alongside financial returns. This requires setting specific impact goals and tracking progress towards those goals over time.

Active ownership: Both impact investing and SRI involve active ownership, which means engaging with companies to promote positive ESG practices and social and environmental outcomes. This can take the form of shareholder activism, where investors use their voting rights to influence corporate decisions, or through dialogue and engagement with company management.

Transparency and accountability: Both impact investing and SRI require transparency and accountability from companies, including regular reporting on ESG practices and impact metrics.

Practical Applications of Impact Investing and SRI

Impact investing and SRI can be applied across a range of asset classes, including public equities, private equity, fixed income, and real assets. Here are some examples of how these investment strategies can be put into practice:

Impact investing in public equities: Impact investors can identify publicly traded companies that are making significant strides in ESG practices and that have a positive social or environmental impact. This approach involves selecting companies based on their impact metrics, such as carbon emissions reductions, waste reduction, and diversity and inclusion initiatives.

Socially responsible fixed income: SRI can be applied to fixed income investments, such as bonds, as well. In this case, the focus is on investing in issuers whose activities align with the investor's values and ethical principles. For instance, an investor may choose to invest in bonds issued by companies that are taking steps to reduce their carbon footprint or by governments that are investing in renewable energy.

Impact bonds: Another way to invest in impact is through impact bonds, also known

Conclusion

Impact investing and SRI provide investors with a way to align their investments with their values and ethical principles while potentially generating improved financial returns over the long term. However, these approaches also face challenges related to impact measurement, potential greenwashing, and potential for lower financial returns. Despite these challenges, the growth of impact investing and SRI suggests that more and more investors are recognizing the importance of investing for both financial and social and environmental impact.

I. The Benefits of Impact Investing and Socially Responsible Investing

Impact investing and socially responsible investing (SRI) have gained traction in recent years as investors seek to align their values with their investment portfolios. These approaches offer a range of benefits, including environmental, social, and economic benefits. In this section, we will explore the benefits of impact investing and SRI in depth, drawing on examples from a range of fields.

Environmental Benefits

Impact investing and SRI can have a significant positive impact on the environment. By investing in companies that prioritize sustainability and environmental stewardship, investors can contribute to the transition to a low-carbon, sustainable economy. For example, an investor may choose to invest in a renewable energy company that is working to reduce carbon emissions and promote the use of clean energy sources.

In addition to reducing environmental harm, impact investing can also support positive environmental outcomes. For example, investors may choose to invest in companies that are working to protect natural resources or biodiversity. This can include companies that are developing innovative solutions to reduce waste or that are working to restore degraded ecosystems.

Social Benefits

Impact investing and SRI can also have important social benefits. By investing in companies that prioritize social justice, human rights, and diversity and inclusion, investors can support positive social outcomes. For example, an investor may choose to invest in a company that has a strong commitment to gender equality and is working to close the gender pay gap.

SRI can also support positive social outcomes by avoiding investments in companies that engage in harmful or unethical practices. For example, an investor may choose to avoid investing in companies that produce tobacco or firearms, or that have a history of labor violations.

Economic Benefits

In addition to environmental and social benefits, impact investing and SRI can also offer economic benefits. By investing in companies that prioritize sustainability and social responsibility, investors can help to build a more resilient and sustainable economy. For example, companies that prioritize environmental sustainability may be better positioned to weather climate-related risks, such as extreme weather events or changes in regulatory requirements.

SRI can also offer economic benefits by avoiding investments in companies that engage in risky or unsustainable practices. By avoiding investments in companies with poor environmental or social records, investors may be able to reduce their exposure to reputational risk or regulatory risks.

Conclusion

In conclusion, impact investing and socially responsible investing offer a range of benefits, including environmental, social, and economic benefits. By investing in companies that prioritize sustainability and social responsibility, investors can contribute to positive outcomes and help to build a more sustainable and equitable economy. While there are some challenges to implementing impact investing and SRI strategies, these approaches offer important opportunities for investors to align their values with their investment portfolios and support positive outcomes for society and the environment.

II. Challenges to Impact Investing and Socially Responsible Investing

Impact investing and socially responsible investing (SRI) are growing in popularity, as investors increasingly seek to align their financial goals with their values. While these investment strategies offer numerous benefits, they also face several challenges that need to be addressed. In this section, we will explore some of the main challenges that impact investing and SRI face, including a lack of standardization, transparency, and awareness.

Lack of standardization

One of the main challenges facing impact investing and SRI is the lack of standardization in the industry. There is no agreed-upon definition of what constitutes an impact investment or socially responsible investment, which can make it difficult for investors to evaluate investment opportunities. This lack of standardization can also lead to confusion and misinformation, as different investment products may be marketed as socially responsible or impact investments, even if they do not meet certain criteria.

Furthermore, the lack of standardization can make it difficult to compare the impact of different investment opportunities. Investors may not be able to determine the social or environmental impact of an investment, making it challenging to assess the effectiveness of their investment strategies.

Lack of transparency

Another challenge facing impact investing and SRI is the lack of transparency in the industry. Investors may not have access to sufficient information about the companies or organizations in which they are investing, making it difficult to evaluate the impact of their investments. This lack of transparency can also lead to a lack of accountability, as companies may not be held to account for their social or environmental practices.

Moreover, companies may not disclose the impact of their activities, making it difficult for investors to assess the social and environmental implications of their investment decisions. This lack of transparency can make it difficult for investors to make informed decisions and may result in investments that do not align with their values.

Limited awareness and understanding of impact investing and socially responsible investing

Another challenge facing impact investing and SRI is the limited awareness and understanding of these investment strategies. Many investors may not be aware of the opportunities available in impact investing and SRI, or they may not fully understand how these strategies work. This lack of awareness and understanding can make it difficult for investors to incorporate impact investing and SRI into their investment portfolios.

Moreover, there may be a perception among some investors that impact investing and SRI require a trade-off between financial returns and social or environmental impact. This perception can be a barrier to the adoption of impact investing and SRI, as investors may prioritize financial returns over social and environmental impact.

Conclusion

While impact investing and socially responsible investing offer numerous benefits, they also face several challenges that need to be addressed. A lack of standardization and transparency can make it difficult for investors to evaluate investment opportunities and assess the impact of their investments. Moreover, a limited awareness and understanding of impact investing and SRI may prevent investors from adopting these strategies.

To overcome these challenges, the impact investing and SRI industry must work towards greater standardization and transparency. Companies should be encouraged to disclose the impact of their activities, and investors should be provided with access to reliable impact data. Education and outreach efforts can also help to increase awareness and understanding of impact investing and SRI, helping investors to make more informed investment decisions.

III. Impact Investing and Socially Responsible Investing in Practice

In the previous sections, we discussed the benefits and challenges of impact investing and socially responsible investing. In this section, we will delve into practical considerations for investors who want to incorporate these strategies into their portfolios.

Impact Investing Strategies:

Impact investing can take a variety of forms, including private equity, venture capital, fixed income, and public equities. One of the most important factors in determining an impact investment strategy is identifying the most effective way to achieve the desired impact. For example, an investor looking to reduce carbon emissions might consider investing in renewable energy companies or those that promote energy efficiency.

Private equity and venture capital are often the most popular strategies for impact investors. These strategies offer the opportunity to invest in startups and emerging companies that are developing innovative solutions to social or environmental challenges. These investments are often illiquid and require a longer time horizon, but they can offer high potential returns.

Fixed income impact investing can involve investing in bonds issued by companies or organizations that have demonstrated a commitment to sustainability or social responsibility. These investments typically offer a lower risk profile than private equity and venture capital investments but can still deliver competitive returns.

Public equities impact investing involves investing in companies that are making significant strides in ESG practices and that have a positive social or environmental impact. Investors can identify these companies based on their impact metrics, such as carbon emissions reductions, waste reduction, and diversity and inclusion initiatives.

Socially Responsible Investing Strategies:

SRI strategies can also take many forms, including negative screening, positive screening, and thematic investing. Negative screening involves excluding companies that engage in activities that conflict with an investor's values or beliefs. For example, an investor might choose to exclude companies that produce tobacco products or that engage in arms manufacturing.

Positive screening involves identifying companies that have a positive impact on society or the environment. For example, an investor might choose to invest in companies that promote renewable energy or that prioritize workplace diversity and inclusion.

Thematic investing involves investing in companies that align with specific themes or causes, such as gender equality or climate change. This approach allows investors to align their investments with their values and beliefs while also diversifying their portfolios.

Case Studies of Successful Impact Investing and Socially Responsible Investing:

There are many examples of successful impact investing and SRI strategies. One example is the Calvert Impact Capital, a nonprofit organization that invests in community development projects and social enterprises in low-income communities. The organization has invested over $2 billion in projects that have had a positive impact on over 24 million people.

Another example is the Goldman Sachs Sustainable Finance Group, which works with clients to identify and invest in companies that have a positive impact on society and the environment. The group has developed several investment strategies, including a thematic approach to investing in companies that promote sustainable agriculture and a fixed income approach to investing in companies that prioritize social responsibility.

Finally, the TIAA-CREF Social Choice Equity Fund is a mutual fund that invests in companies that prioritize social responsibility and sustainability. The fund has a long track record of delivering competitive returns while also aligning with investors' values and beliefs.

Conclusion:

Impact investing and socially responsible investing have become increasingly popular in recent years as investors look to align their investments with their values and beliefs. These strategies can offer a variety of benefits, including environmental, social, and economic benefits. However, there are also challenges to implementing these strategies, including a lack of standardization and transparency and limited awareness and understanding of impact investing and SRI.

Despite these challenges, there are many successful examples of impact investing and SRI strategies, and investors have a variety of options when it comes to incorporating these strategies into their portfolios. By carefully considering the potential impact of their investments and identifying the most effective strategies, investors can play a meaningful role in promoting social and environmental change while also achieving their financial goals.

In the future, it is likely that impact investing and socially responsible investing will continue to grow in popularity and significance, driven by increasing demand from investors and a growing awareness of the need for sustainable and socially responsible investing practices. To maximize the potential benefits of these strategies, it will be important for investors to continue to push for greater standardization and transparency in the industry, as well as for regulators and industry participants to work together to create a more supportive environment for impact investing and SRI.

Furthermore, impact investing and SRI are not just limited to institutional investors or high-net-worth individuals; they can be applied at all levels of investment and across all asset classes. As such, these strategies offer an accessible and powerful way for individual investors to make a positive impact on the world while also achieving their financial goals.

In conclusion, impact investing and socially responsible investing offer a compelling and effective approach to investing that allows investors to align their investments with their values and beliefs, promote positive change in society and the environment, and achieve their financial goals. While there are challenges to implementing these strategies, they offer many potential benefits and have already shown significant success in practice. As such, impact investing and socially responsible investing are likely to continue to play an increasingly important role in the investment landscape in the years to come.

CHAPTER 22: CLIMATE CHANGE AND ITS IMPACT ON FINANCE

Climate change is a pressing issue that has the potential to significantly impact the global economy and financial markets. As temperatures rise and weather patterns shift, businesses, governments, and individuals will face a range of challenges, including increased frequency and severity of natural disasters, shifting supply and demand patterns, and rising costs associated with climate mitigation and adaptation efforts.

The financial sector is particularly vulnerable to the impacts of climate change. As the world becomes more focused on reducing greenhouse gas emissions, investors and companies may need to make significant adjustments to their portfolios and business models. Furthermore, as the physical risks of climate change become more apparent, financial institutions may face increased liability and regulatory pressure.

In this chapter, we will explore the various ways in which climate change is already impacting the financial sector and discuss some of the key challenges that businesses and investors will need to navigate in the coming years. We will also examine some of the potential opportunities that arise from the transition to a more sustainable economy and discuss some of the ways in which investors and businesses can take action to mitigate the risks associated with climate change while also contributing to a more sustainable future.

I. The Risks of Climate Change for Finance

Climate change is one of the most pressing global challenges facing humanity today. Its impacts are far-reaching and extend to every corner of the world, affecting individuals, communities, businesses, and governments. The financial sector is not immune to the risks posed by climate change, which have the potential to undermine the stability and resilience of the global financial system. In this section, we will explore the various risks that climate change poses to the financial sector and how they may manifest in the form of physical risks, transition risks, and liability risks.

Physical Risks:

Physical risks refer to the physical impacts of climate change, such as extreme weather events, sea-level rise, and other environmental hazards. These risks can lead to direct damage to physical assets, disruption of supply chains, and increased insurance claims, among other things. In the case of real estate, for example, physical risks from climate change can lead to decreased property values and increased insurance costs.

The financial sector is particularly exposed to physical risks because it invests in assets that are susceptible to climate-related damage, such as infrastructure, real estate, and agricultural land. For example, a severe hurricane can damage buildings and infrastructure, leading to significant losses for investors who hold these assets. Similarly, droughts and heatwaves can lead to crop failure, which can negatively impact the returns of investors who hold agricultural land.

Transition Risks:

Transition risks refer to the financial risks that arise from the transition to a low-carbon economy. As the world moves away from fossil fuels and towards renewable energy sources, certain industries and companies may become obsolete, leading to stranded assets and financial losses for investors. For example, as demand for coal decreases, coal-fired power plants may become uneconomic and shut down, resulting in losses for investors who hold these assets.

The financial sector is particularly exposed to transition risks because it invests in companies and industries that are heavily reliant on fossil fuels, such as oil and gas, mining, and transportation. As the world transitions to a low-carbon economy, these industries may face significant financial losses, and investors who hold these assets may be negatively impacted. In addition, the shift towards renewable energy sources may lead to increased competition and lower profitability for companies in the fossil fuel sector.

Liability Risks:

Liability risks refer to the legal and financial risks that arise from climate-related litigation and regulatory action. As the impacts of climate change become more apparent, companies and governments may face legal action for their contributions to greenhouse gas emissions or for their failure to mitigate the risks of climate change. For example, a company that emits large amounts of greenhouse gases may face legal action from communities that are negatively impacted by the resulting climate change impacts.

The financial sector is particularly exposed to liability risks because it invests in companies and industries that are vulnerable to climate-related litigation and regulatory action. In addition, financial institutions themselves may be subject to legal action for their failure to adequately assess and disclose climate-related risks in their investments. For example, a bank that finances a coal-fired power plant may face legal action if the plant contributes to climate change impacts that harm communities or ecosystems.

Conclusion:

Climate change poses significant risks to the global financial system, including physical risks, transition risks, and liability risks. The financial sector is particularly vulnerable to these risks because it invests in assets that are susceptible to climate-related damage, such as infrastructure, real estate, and agricultural land. In addition, financial institutions invest in companies and industries that are heavily reliant on fossil fuels, making them vulnerable to the transition to a low-carbon economy. Finally, financial institutions may face legal action for their contributions to greenhouse gas emissions or for their failure to adequately assess and disclose climate-related risks in their investments. As such, it is imperative that the financial sector takes action to mitigate these risks and transition to a more sustainable future.

II. Opportunities in Addressing Climate Change in Finance

The impacts of climate change are becoming increasingly evident, with rising sea levels, more frequent and severe natural disasters, and changes in weather patterns affecting communities and businesses around the world. As a result, the financial industry is increasingly recognizing the need to address climate change risks and identify opportunities for sustainable investment. In this section, we will explore some of the opportunities that are emerging in finance as a result of climate change, including investment opportunities in renewable energy, opportunities for green finance instruments, and risk management strategies for climate change.

Investment opportunities in renewable energy:

Renewable energy is one of the most promising areas for investment in the fight against climate change. Renewable energy sources such as wind, solar, and hydropower offer a clean, low-carbon alternative to traditional fossil fuels, reducing greenhouse gas emissions and helping to mitigate the impacts of climate change.

Investors can access renewable energy investment opportunities in a number of ways, including investing directly in renewable energy projects or through funds that focus on renewable energy assets. These investments can offer attractive returns, particularly as renewable energy becomes increasingly cost-competitive with traditional fossil fuels.

In addition to investing in renewable energy projects themselves, there are also opportunities to invest in the companies that are driving the transition to renewable energy. For example, companies that manufacture solar panels, wind turbines, or electric vehicles may be well-positioned to benefit from the shift towards a low-carbon economy.

Opportunities for green finance instruments:

Green finance instruments are financial products and services that are designed to support sustainable development and the transition to a low-carbon economy. These instruments can include green bonds, green loans, and green insurance products, among others.

Green bonds are a particularly promising area for investment, as they allow investors to support environmentally sustainable projects while also generating returns. Green bonds are issued by governments, corporations, and other organizations to finance projects that have a positive environmental impact, such as renewable energy projects or energy-efficient buildings.

Green loans are another type of green finance instrument that offer opportunities for investment. These loans are typically used to finance sustainable projects such as energy-efficient renovations or the installation of renewable energy systems. They can be attractive to borrowers because they often offer favorable terms and lower interest rates than traditional loans.

Risk management strategies for climate change:

As the impacts of climate change become more severe, it is important for businesses and investors to develop strategies for managing climate-related risks. These risks can include physical risks, such as damage to property and infrastructure from natural disasters, as well as transition risks, such as changes in consumer preferences or regulatory policies that may impact certain industries.

One approach to managing climate risks is through scenario analysis, which involves modeling the potential impacts of different climate scenarios on a business or portfolio. This can help investors identify areas of potential vulnerability and develop strategies to mitigate those risks.

Another strategy for managing climate risks is through the use of insurance products, such as parametric insurance or catastrophe bonds. These products can provide protection against the financial impacts of natural disasters and other climate-related events.

Conclusion:

The challenges posed by climate change are significant, but they also present opportunities for innovation and investment. By investing in renewable energy, supporting green finance instruments, and developing strategies for managing climate risks, investors can play a key role in promoting sustainability and driving the transition to a low-carbon economy. However, it is important for investors to approach these opportunities with caution, carefully assessing the potential risks and benefits of each investment and seeking expert advice as needed.

III. Government and Regulatory Responses to Climate Change in Finance

Climate change is a global phenomenon that has significant implications for the world's economies, including the financial sector. In recent years, governments and regulatory bodies around the world have recognized the need to address climate change through various policy measures, including regulations and incentives aimed at reducing greenhouse gas emissions and promoting sustainable practices. The financial sector has a critical role to play in this effort, as it is an important source of funding for many economic activities that contribute to greenhouse gas emissions. As such, governments and regulatory bodies have implemented various measures aimed at promoting sustainability in the financial sector. This section will examine the global, national, and regulatory responses to climate change in finance and their implications.

Global responses to climate change:

At the global level, the United Nations Framework Convention on Climate Change (UNFCCC) has been the primary platform for international cooperation on climate change. The UNFCCC aims to prevent dangerous anthropogenic interference with the climate system, stabilize greenhouse gas concentrations in the atmosphere at a level that would prevent dangerous anthropogenic interference with the climate system, and promote sustainable development. The Paris Agreement, which was adopted in 2015, aims to limit global warming to well below 2 degrees Celsius above pre-industrial levels and to pursue efforts to limit the temperature increase to 1.5 degrees Celsius above pre-industrial levels. The Paris Agreement also includes provisions for financial support to developing countries to assist with their transition to a low-carbon economy.

The financial sector has an important role to play in achieving the goals of the Paris Agreement. In 2016, the Task Force on Climate-related Financial Disclosures (TCFD) was established to develop recommendations for companies to disclose the risks and opportunities associated with climate change in their financial filings. The TCFD recommendations have been widely adopted by companies and investors around the world, providing a framework for assessing climate-related risks and opportunities.

National and local responses to climate change:

National and local governments have also taken steps to address climate change through various policy measures. In many countries, governments have implemented policies aimed at reducing greenhouse gas emissions, such as renewable energy targets and carbon pricing mechanisms. For example, the European Union has set a target of reducing greenhouse gas emissions by 40% by 2030, and has implemented a carbon trading scheme to incentivize emissions reductions. In the United States, the Biden administration has set a goal of achieving net-zero greenhouse gas emissions by 2050, and has proposed various policies aimed at achieving this goal, such as a clean energy standard and a carbon tax.

Local governments have also taken action to address climate change, particularly in the area of sustainable infrastructure. For example, many cities around the world have implemented policies aimed at promoting sustainable transportation, such as bike-sharing programs and electric vehicle incentives. Local governments have also implemented policies aimed at promoting energy efficiency and renewable energy, such as building codes that require energy-efficient buildings and incentives for solar installations.

Regulatory responses to climate change in finance:

Regulatory bodies around the world have also taken steps to promote sustainability in the financial sector. For example, the European Union has implemented regulations aimed at promoting sustainable finance, such as the Sustainable Finance Disclosure Regulation (SFDR) and the Taxonomy Regulation. The SFDR requires financial firms to disclose the environmental, social, and governance (ESG) risks associated with their investments, while the Taxonomy Regulation provides a classification system for sustainable economic activities.

In the United States, the Securities and Exchange Commission (SEC) has also taken steps to address climate change. In March 2021, the SEC announced the creation of a Climate and ESG Task Force, which will focus on identifying ESG-related misconduct and ensuring that companies are accurately disclosing their ESG risks and opportunities.

In addition to these regulatory responses, there has been a growing trend among investors and asset managers to incorporate climate-related considerations into their investment decisions and portfolio management strategies. This trend is often referred to as sustainable investing or responsible investing, and it has been gaining momentum in recent years.

One key driver of this trend is the increasing awareness among investors of the potential financial risks posed by climate change. As we discussed earlier in this chapter, climate change can pose a range of physical, transition, and liability risks for companies and investors. Investors who fail to take these risks into account may be exposed to significant losses if climate-related events disrupt the companies or industries in which they have invested.

In response to these risks, many investors and asset managers are now incorporating climate-related considerations into their investment processes. For example, they may be screening companies for their carbon emissions, assessing their exposure to physical climate risks, or evaluating their resilience to the transition to a low-carbon economy.

In addition to managing risks, sustainable investing can also offer opportunities for investors to generate financial returns while promoting positive environmental and social outcomes. For example, investors may seek out opportunities to invest in companies that are developing innovative solutions to address climate change, such as renewable energy technologies or sustainable agriculture practices.

There are several different approaches to sustainable investing, including negative screening, positive screening, and impact investing. Negative screening involves excluding certain companies or industries from an investment portfolio based on their environmental or social practices. Positive screening involves actively selecting companies that have strong ESG profiles or are making positive contributions to the environment or society. Impact investing involves making investments with the intention of generating measurable environmental or social impacts in addition to financial returns.

While sustainable investing has gained a great deal of momentum in recent years, it is important to note that there are also challenges to incorporating ESG factors into investment decisions. One challenge is the lack of standardized and reliable ESG data, which can make it difficult for investors to accurately assess the ESG risks and opportunities of different companies. Additionally, there is often a lack of agreement among investors about what constitutes an ESG risk or opportunity, which can lead to inconsistent investment decisions.

Despite these challenges, sustainable investing is likely to continue to play an increasingly important role in the financial sector as investors seek to manage the risks and opportunities posed by climate change and promote positive environmental and social outcomes. As a result, it will be important for investors, asset managers, and regulators to work together to develop standardized ESG metrics and improve transparency around ESG risks and opportunities.

CHAPTER 23: THE FUTURE OF SUSTAINABLE FINANCE

The field of sustainable finance has come a long way in recent years, with increasing awareness and action on climate change and other environmental and social issues. As discussed in earlier sections of this report, there have been significant developments in regulatory and industry responses to these challenges. But what does the future of sustainable finance hold?

In this chapter, we will explore some of the key trends and predictions for the future of sustainable finance, as well as the challenges that lie ahead. We will consider the potential impact of emerging technologies, evolving regulatory frameworks, and shifting investor preferences. We will also examine the role of sustainable finance in driving the transition to a low-carbon, more equitable and sustainable global economy.

Emerging Technologies and Sustainable Finance

Advancements in technology are rapidly transforming the financial sector, and sustainable finance is no exception. Fintech innovations have already started to revolutionize how companies approach ESG analysis and impact reporting, with new tools and platforms making it easier to access and interpret sustainability data.

For example, machine learning algorithms can analyze vast amounts of data from multiple sources, such as company reports, news articles, and social media, to identify and assess ESG risks and opportunities. Natural language processing (NLP) can help to extract relevant information from unstructured data sources such as social media and news articles, and analyze sentiment and context.

Blockchain technology also holds significant potential for sustainable finance, providing a secure, transparent and decentralized ledger for tracking and verifying sustainable investments and transactions. Blockchain can enable the creation of new financing models, such as peer-to-peer lending and crowdfunding, that could increase access to sustainable finance for individuals and small businesses.

However, these emerging technologies also pose significant challenges, such as data privacy concerns, the need for standardization and interoperability, and the risk of bias and inaccuracies in algorithms. It will be important for regulators, investors, and financial institutions to work together to ensure that these technologies are used in a responsible and ethical way that supports the goals of sustainable finance.

Evolving Regulatory Frameworks

The regulatory landscape for sustainable finance is constantly evolving, as governments and international bodies seek to address the urgent challenges of climate change and other ESG issues. In recent years, we have seen the emergence of new regulations and frameworks, such as the EU Sustainable Finance Action Plan and the Task Force on Climate-related Financial Disclosures (TCFD), which aim to promote transparency, accountability, and sustainability in the financial sector.

In the future, we can expect to see further developments in regulatory frameworks, with a particular focus on improving the consistency and comparability of sustainability data, and addressing the risk of greenwashing. The EU's proposed Green Bond Standard, for example, seeks to establish a common set of criteria for green bonds, while the Sustainable Accounting Standards Board (SASB) is working to develop industry-specific sustainability reporting standards.

At the same time, there are concerns that overly prescriptive regulations could stifle innovation and create unintended consequences, such as reduced investment in emerging markets or exclusion of certain industries. Striking the right balance between regulation and market-based solutions will be a key challenge for policymakers and stakeholders in the years to come.

Shifting Investor Preferences

Investors are increasingly recognizing the importance of ESG factors in investment decision-making, and this trend is likely to continue in the years ahead. A growing body of research suggests that companies with strong ESG performance are more likely to outperform their peers over the long term, and investors are increasingly demanding access to sustainability data and metrics to inform their investment decisions.

In response, financial institutions and asset managers are developing new products and strategies that incorporate ESG considerations, such as green bonds, ESG index funds, and impact investing. According to a recent survey by the Global Sustainable Investment Alliance (GSIA), global sustainable investment assets reached a record $35.3 trillion in 2020, representing a 15% increase from the previous year.

One promising area of growth for sustainable finance is green bonds, which are fixed-income securities designed to finance projects with environmental benefits. The market for green bonds has grown rapidly in recent years, with global issuance reaching a record $269.5 billion in 2020, according to data from BloombergNEF.

Another area of growth is the development of ESG index funds, which track the performance of companies with strong ESG scores. These funds have become increasingly popular in recent years, as investors seek to incorporate sustainability considerations into their investment portfolios. In 2020, ESG-focused index funds attracted record inflows of $152.3 billion, according to data from Morningstar.

Impact investing, which seeks to generate social and environmental benefits alongside financial returns, is also gaining momentum. According to a report by the Global Impact Investing Network (GIIN), the size of the impact investing market grew from $502 billion in 2019 to $715 billion in 2020, representing a year-over-year increase of 42%.

In addition to these specific products and strategies, financial institutions and asset managers are also integrating ESG considerations into their broader investment processes. For example, many firms are now conducting ESG screenings of potential investments and engaging with companies on sustainability issues. In addition, some firms are using AI and machine learning algorithms to analyze sustainability data and identify investment opportunities.

Looking ahead, it is likely that the trend towards sustainable finance will continue to accelerate. As investors become more aware of the risks and opportunities associated with climate change and other sustainability issues, they will continue to demand access to ESG data and metrics. In response, financial institutions and asset managers will need to continue to innovate and develop new products and strategies that incorporate ESG considerations into investment decision-making.

Conclusion

Sustainable finance is rapidly becoming an important area of focus for investors, financial institutions, and regulators around the world. As the risks and opportunities associated with climate change and other sustainability issues become increasingly apparent, investors are demanding access to ESG data and metrics to inform their investment decisions.

In response, financial institutions and asset managers are developing new products and strategies that incorporate ESG considerations, such as green bonds, ESG index funds, and impact investing. In addition, firms are integrating ESG considerations into their broader investment processes, conducting ESG screenings of potential investments, engaging with companies on sustainability issues, and using AI and machine learning algorithms to analyze sustainability data.

Looking ahead, it is likely that the trend towards sustainable finance will continue to accelerate, as investors become more aware of the importance of ESG factors in investment decision-making. As this trend continues, financial institutions and asset managers will need to continue to innovate and develop new products and strategies that incorporate sustainability considerations into investment decision-making.

I. Technology and Sustainable Finance

Technology has played a significant role in transforming the financial industry and enabling sustainable finance. It has allowed for the development of innovative financial products and services that promote sustainability and reduce environmental impact. In this section, we will explore the role of technology in sustainable finance and examine some of the emerging technologies that are shaping the industry. We will also discuss the benefits and challenges of technology in sustainable finance.

The role of technology in sustainable finance:

Technology has enabled financial institutions to develop new products and services that promote sustainability and address climate change. One of the key ways in which technology is driving sustainable finance is through the development of ESG data and analytics. ESG data refers to environmental, social, and governance factors that are used to evaluate a company's performance in these areas. Analytics tools can then be used to identify trends, risks, and opportunities associated with ESG factors, which can inform investment decisions.

Technology is also being used to develop new financial products and services that promote sustainability. For example, green bonds are fixed-income securities that are used to finance environmentally-friendly projects, such as renewable energy projects or energy-efficient buildings. Blockchain technology is being used to develop peer-to-peer financing platforms that enable small-scale renewable energy projects to access financing.

Emerging technologies in sustainable finance:

There are several emerging technologies that are transforming sustainable finance. One of these is artificial intelligence (AI), which is being used to analyze large amounts of data to identify ESG trends and risks. AI can also be used to develop more accurate ESG ratings and assessments, which can inform investment decisions.

Another emerging technology in sustainable finance is the Internet of Things (IoT), which refers to the network of interconnected devices that can collect and transmit data. IoT devices can be used to monitor environmental conditions, such as air quality or water levels, which can inform investment decisions. IoT can also be used to develop smart buildings and cities that are more energy-efficient and sustainable.

Benefits and challenges of technology in sustainable finance:

Technology has the potential to significantly improve the efficiency and effectiveness of sustainable finance. It can enable financial institutions to collect and analyze ESG data more effectively, which can inform investment decisions and improve risk management. It can also enable the development of new financial products and services that promote sustainability.

However, there are also challenges associated with the use of technology in sustainable finance. One of the main challenges is the quality and availability of data. ESG data is often incomplete or inconsistent, which can make it difficult to accurately assess a company's performance in these areas. Another challenge is the potential for bias in AI algorithms, which can lead to inaccurate or unfair assessments.

Conclusion:

Technology is playing an increasingly important role in sustainable finance, enabling financial institutions to develop innovative products and services that promote sustainability and reduce environmental impact. Emerging technologies such as AI and IoT have the potential to significantly improve the efficiency and effectiveness of sustainable finance. However, there are also challenges associated with the use of technology in sustainable finance, particularly around data quality and potential bias in AI algorithms. As the industry continues to evolve, it will be important to address these challenges and ensure that technology is used in a responsible and sustainable way.

II. Investing in Sustainable Finance

Investing in sustainable finance has become increasingly popular in recent years as investors look for opportunities to align their financial goals with their values. Sustainable investing refers to investment strategies that seek to generate financial returns while also promoting social or environmental goals. This can include investments in companies that prioritize environmental, social, and governance (ESG) factors, as well as investments in renewable energy and other sustainable infrastructure projects.

Opportunities for sustainable investing:
There are several opportunities for sustainable investing, including ESG investing, impact investing, and green bonds. ESG investing involves investing in companies that meet certain ESG criteria, such as strong corporate governance, environmental stewardship, and social responsibility. Impact investing, on the other hand, focuses on investing in companies or projects that have a positive social or environmental impact, such as affordable housing or renewable energy. Green bonds are a type of fixed income security that are used to finance environmentally friendly projects.

Investing in sustainable finance can also provide financial benefits. For example, a growing body of research suggests that companies with strong ESG performance are more likely to outperform their peers over the long term. Additionally, sustainable infrastructure projects, such as renewable energy and energy efficiency projects, can offer stable returns and long-term cash flows.

Challenges to sustainable investing:
Despite the opportunities, there are also several challenges to sustainable investing. One challenge is the lack of standardized ESG metrics and data, which can make it difficult for investors to assess the ESG performance of companies and funds. This can lead to confusion and inconsistency in investment decision-making.

Another challenge is the trade-off between financial returns and social or environmental impact. While sustainable investments can provide positive social and environmental benefits, they may not always generate the same level of financial returns as traditional investments. This can make it challenging for investors to balance their financial goals with their desire to make a positive impact.

Finally, there is a risk that sustainable investing may be perceived as a fad or marketing gimmick, rather than a serious investment strategy. This could lead to a lack of credibility and investor skepticism, which could limit the growth of sustainable investing.

Best practices for sustainable investing:
To overcome these challenges, there are several best practices that investors can follow when investing in sustainable finance. These include:

Conducting thorough research: Before investing in a company or fund, investors should conduct thorough research to assess its ESG performance and impact. This can include reviewing ESG ratings and scores, as well as engaging with company management to understand their sustainability practices.

Diversifying investments: Investors should diversify their investments across different asset classes and sectors to manage risk and maximize returns. This can include investing in both traditional and sustainable investments.

Engaging with companies: Investors can use their shareholder power to engage with companies and encourage them to improve their sustainability practices. This can include filing shareholder resolutions, participating in proxy voting, and engaging with management.

Incorporating ESG into investment decision-making: Investors should incorporate ESG factors into their investment decision-making process to ensure that they are investing in companies that prioritize sustainability. This can include using ESG ratings and scores, as well as conducting qualitative assessments of a company's sustainability practices.

Setting clear investment goals: Investors should set clear investment goals and objectives that incorporate both financial returns and social or environmental impact. This can help investors balance their financial and non-financial priorities and ensure that their investments align with their values.

Conclusion:
Investing in sustainable finance provides opportunities for investors to generate financial returns while also promoting social and environmental goals. However, there are also several challenges to sustainable investing, including the lack of standardized ESG metrics and data, the trade-off between financial returns and social or environmental impact, and the risk of sustainability being perceived as a fad. To overcome these challenges, investors can adopt best practices for sustainable investing, such as conducting rigorous due diligence, engaging with companies to encourage better ESG practices, and aligning investment decisions with long-term sustainability goals.

Overall, the future of sustainable finance looks promising, as more investors and financial institutions recognize the importance of integrating ESG factors into investment decision-making. Technology is also playing an increasingly important role in sustainable finance, offering new opportunities for investors to access ESG data and to engage with companies on sustainability issues.

However, it is important to remember that sustainable investing is not a one-size-fits-all approach. Investors should carefully consider their own values and priorities when selecting sustainable investments, and should work with financial advisors and experts to develop a personalized strategy that aligns with their goals.

In the end, sustainable investing is about more than just financial returns. It is about promoting a more sustainable and equitable world for all. By investing in companies that are committed to social and environmental goals, we can help to create a better future for ourselves, our communities, and the planet.

III. Global Collaboration in Sustainable Finance

Sustainable finance has become an increasingly important area of focus for governments, financial institutions, and investors around the world. As the global community seeks to address the challenges of climate change, biodiversity loss, and social inequality, there is growing recognition that a coordinated and collaborative approach is necessary to achieve meaningful progress towards a more sustainable future.

In this section, we will examine the role of international cooperation and private sector partnerships in advancing sustainable finance, as well as the importance of collaboration in achieving our shared sustainability goals.

International cooperation in sustainable finance:

The global nature of environmental and social challenges means that international cooperation is essential for achieving meaningful progress towards sustainability. In recent years, there has been a growing recognition of the need for coordinated action on sustainable finance at the global level.

One notable example of international cooperation in sustainable finance is the Paris Agreement on climate change, which was signed by 195 countries in 2015. The agreement aims to limit global warming to below 2 degrees Celsius above pre-industrial levels and to pursue efforts to limit warming to 1.5 degrees Celsius. To achieve this goal, the agreement calls for a shift towards low-carbon and resilient economies and the mobilization of financial resources for climate action.

In addition to the Paris Agreement, there are also a number of international organizations and initiatives focused on advancing sustainable finance. For example, the United Nations Environment Programme Finance Initiative (UNEP FI) brings together financial institutions, regulators, and other stakeholders to promote sustainable finance globally. The Sustainable Finance Network (SFN), launched by the World Bank, aims to support the development of sustainable finance markets in emerging economies.

Private sector partnerships in sustainable finance:

The private sector also has an important role to play in advancing sustainable finance. Financial institutions, corporations, and other organizations can use their expertise, resources, and networks to drive sustainable finance innovation and investment.

One way in which the private sector is contributing to sustainable finance is through the development of innovative financial products and services. For example, green bonds, which are debt instruments that finance environmentally beneficial projects, have become an increasingly popular way for investors to support sustainable finance. In 2021, global green bond issuance reached a record $310 billion, according to the Climate Bonds Initiative.

Another way in which the private sector is contributing to sustainable finance is through the development of sustainability metrics and reporting standards. By providing transparent and standardized information on environmental, social, and governance (ESG) factors, companies and investors can better understand and manage sustainability risks and opportunities.

The importance of collaboration in sustainable finance:

Collaboration is essential for achieving meaningful progress in sustainable finance. Governments, financial institutions, investors, and other stakeholders must work together to address the complex and interrelated challenges of climate change, biodiversity loss, and social inequality.

One example of collaboration in sustainable finance is the Task Force on Climate-related Financial Disclosures (TCFD), which was established in 2015 by the Financial Stability Board. The TCFD brings together stakeholders from the financial and business communities to develop recommendations for voluntary climate-related financial disclosures that are consistent, comparable, and reliable.

Another example of collaboration in sustainable finance is the Net Zero Asset Owner Alliance, a group of institutional investors committed to transitioning their investment portfolios to net-zero greenhouse gas emissions by 2050. The alliance includes some of the world's largest pension funds and insurers and aims to use its collective influence to drive the transition to a low-carbon economy.

Conclusion:

In conclusion, international cooperation and private sector partnerships are essential for advancing sustainable finance and achieving our shared sustainability goals. The global nature of environmental and social challenges means that coordinated action at the global level is necessary, and the private sector has an important role to play in driving sustainable finance innovation and investment.

However, there are also challenges to collaboration in sustainable finance, including competing interests and priorities among different stakeholders, lack of trust and transparency, and diverging regulatory frameworks. To overcome these challenges, it is important for stakeholders to engage in open and honest dialogue, build trust, and work towards common goals.

To further promote collaboration in sustainable finance, it is also important to develop international standards and frameworks that can help guide sustainable investment decisions and ensure consistency and comparability in ESG metrics and reporting. The development of international standards and guidelines, such as the United Nations Principles for Responsible Investment (UNPRI), can help promote transparency and accountability, and provide a common language for sustainable finance.

Private sector partnerships, such as the partnership between the private sector and governments in the Global Investors for Sustainable Development (GISD) alliance, can also help advance sustainable finance goals. The GISD alliance, launched in 2019 by the United Nations Secretary-General, aims to mobilize private sector capital towards achieving the United Nations Sustainable Development Goals (SDGs).

Finally, collaboration in sustainable finance can also benefit from the involvement of civil society organizations and other non-financial stakeholders, who can provide valuable perspectives on environmental and social issues and help ensure that sustainable finance is inclusive and equitable.

In summary, collaboration is essential for advancing sustainable finance and achieving our shared sustainability goals. By working together, stakeholders can overcome challenges and promote sustainable investment and innovation, and contribute to a more sustainable and equitable future for all.

PART VII: GLOBALIZATION AND INTERNATIONAL FINANCE

Globalization has transformed the world economy in numerous ways, including how financial markets operate and how capital is allocated. International finance has become an increasingly important aspect of the global financial landscape, with cross-border capital flows and foreign investments playing a significant role in shaping the world economy. As such, understanding the dynamics of globalization and international finance is critical for businesses, investors, policymakers, and individuals alike.

In this section, we will explore several key topics related to globalization and international finance, including the global financial landscape, international trade and finance, the future of globalization in finance, and currency exchange and foreign investment. We will examine the challenges and opportunities that globalization and international finance present and consider how these issues impact the broader economy and society.

Chapter 24: The Global Financial Landscape

The global financial landscape has undergone significant changes in recent decades, driven in large part by globalization and technological advancements. Financial markets have become more interconnected, and cross-border capital flows have increased dramatically. As a result, financial crises and economic shocks in one part of the world can have ripple effects throughout the global financial system.

One of the key features of the global financial landscape is the dominance of the United States in the world economy. The US dollar is the world's primary reserve currency, and many international transactions are denominated in dollars. This gives the US a significant amount of influence over the global financial system, as well as the ability to use economic sanctions and other financial tools to achieve foreign policy objectives.

In addition to the US, other countries and regions have also emerged as important players in the global financial landscape. For example, China has become a major economic power, and its currency, the renminbi, has gained prominence in international transactions. The European Union has also played a significant role in global finance, particularly through the Eurozone.

Chapter 25: International Trade and Finance

International trade and finance are closely linked, as trade transactions often involve the exchange of different currencies and the movement of capital across borders. The growth of international trade has been a key driver of globalization, and it has led to significant economic benefits for many countries.

However, international trade is not without its challenges. Trade disputes and protectionist policies can create uncertainty and disrupt global supply chains. In addition, trade imbalances between countries can lead to economic tensions and political conflict.

International finance also plays a critical role in facilitating international trade. Financial institutions such as banks and investment firms provide the necessary capital for businesses to engage in cross-border transactions. The international bond and equity markets allow companies to raise funds from investors around the world.

Chapter 26: The Future of Globalization in Finance

The future of globalization in finance is uncertain, with many factors shaping the direction of the global economy. Technological advancements such as blockchain and artificial intelligence are likely to have significant impacts on financial markets and may lead to new forms of globalization.

However, there are also challenges to the future of globalization in finance. The rise of populist movements and protectionist policies in many countries has led to a backlash against globalization. This could lead to a fragmentation of the global financial system and a move towards more localized economies.

Chapter 27: Currency Exchange and Foreign Investment

Currency exchange and foreign investment are two critical components of international finance. Currency exchange refers to the process of converting one currency into another, and it is essential for facilitating international trade and investment. Foreign investment involves the allocation of capital across borders, either through portfolio investment or foreign direct investment.

Currency exchange rates can have significant impacts on the global economy, affecting trade flows, investment decisions, and economic growth. Changes in exchange rates can also create volatility in financial markets and impact the profitability of businesses.

Foreign investment can bring significant economic benefits to both the investing country and the recipient country. However, foreign investment can also create challenges, such as the risk of capital flight, where investors quickly withdraw their investments, leading to economic instability in the recipient country. Additionally, foreign investment can result in a loss of economic sovereignty for the recipient country, as the investing country may have significant control over the invested assets and the direction of the recipient country's economy.

Another important consideration in international finance is the role of international organizations and regulatory bodies. These organizations, such as the International Monetary Fund (IMF) and the World Bank, play critical roles in promoting financial stability and facilitating international trade and investment. They provide funding and technical assistance to countries, particularly in times of economic crisis, and work to establish and enforce international financial regulations.

The future of globalization in finance is also an important topic of discussion. While globalization has brought significant economic benefits to many countries, it has also contributed to growing income inequality and environmental degradation. As such, there is a need for greater consideration of social and environmental factors in international finance and trade.

Furthermore, the COVID-19 pandemic has highlighted the interconnectedness of the global economy and the need for greater cooperation and coordination in international finance. The pandemic has caused significant economic disruptions, particularly in developing countries, and has highlighted the need for greater resilience and preparedness in the face of global crises.

In conclusion, the global financial landscape is complex and constantly evolving. Currency exchange and foreign investment are critical components of international finance, but they also present challenges that must be addressed. International organizations and regulatory bodies play important roles in promoting financial stability and facilitating trade and investment, while the future of globalization in finance requires greater consideration of social and environmental factors.

CHAPTER 24: THE GLOBAL FINANCIAL LANDSCAPE

The global financial landscape refers to the interconnected network of financial systems, institutions, and markets around the world. The global economy is increasingly interdependent, with countries' financial systems becoming more integrated and interconnected. This integration has been driven by technological advancements and globalization, which have made it easier for investors and businesses to access international markets.

The global financial landscape is constantly evolving, shaped by economic, political, and technological changes. It is important to understand the global financial landscape, as it has significant implications for economic growth, financial stability, and international trade.

This chapter will provide an overview of the global financial landscape, including its history, major players, and key trends. We will also discuss the challenges and opportunities presented by the global financial landscape and its impact on the world economy.

History of the Global Financial Landscape

The history of the global financial landscape dates back to the late 19th century, when the gold standard was established as a global monetary system. Under the gold standard, currencies were convertible into gold at a fixed rate, which created a stable international monetary system. The gold standard was in place until the outbreak of World War I, which disrupted international trade and caused many countries to abandon the gold standard.

After World War II, the Bretton Woods system was established to manage the global financial system. The Bretton Woods system fixed exchange rates to the US dollar, which was convertible to gold at a fixed rate. This system was in place until the 1970s when the US abandoned the gold standard, leading to the current system of floating exchange rates.

Major Players in the Global Financial Landscape

The global financial landscape is composed of a diverse range of players, including central banks, commercial banks, investment banks, asset managers, insurance companies, and other financial institutions. Central banks play a critical role in managing the global financial system, with the US Federal Reserve being the most influential central bank in the world.

Commercial banks are the primary intermediaries between savers and borrowers, providing loans and other financial services to businesses and individuals. Investment banks provide advisory and underwriting services for companies looking to raise capital through stock or bond offerings.

Asset managers manage investment portfolios for individuals and institutional clients, such as pension funds and endowments. Insurance companies provide protection against risk, such as health, property, and liability insurance.

Key Trends in the Global Financial Landscape

One of the most significant trends in the global financial landscape is the rise of emerging markets, such as China and India. These countries have experienced rapid economic growth and are becoming increasingly integrated into the global financial system.

Another trend is the increasing use of technology in the financial industry. Fintech companies are disrupting traditional financial services, offering new and innovative ways to manage money and invest.

Environmental, social, and governance (ESG) considerations are also becoming increasingly important in the global financial landscape. Investors are seeking to invest in companies that are socially responsible and have a positive impact on the environment.

Challenges and Opportunities in the Global Financial Landscape

The global financial landscape presents both challenges and opportunities for businesses and investors. One challenge is the risk of economic and financial crises, such as the 2008 financial crisis, which can have far-reaching impacts on the global economy.

Another challenge is the increasing complexity of the global financial system, which can make it difficult for regulators to manage risks and ensure financial stability. The lack of global regulatory coordination can also create regulatory arbitrage, where financial institutions seek out jurisdictions with weaker regulatory oversight.

However, the global financial landscape also presents many opportunities, particularly for investors. The increasing integration of financial systems has created new investment opportunities in emerging markets and other regions. The rise of fintech has also created new investment opportunities in innovative financial services companies.

Conclusion

The global financial landscape is a complex and ever-changing network of financial institutions, markets, and regulations. It plays a vital role in facilitating economic growth, promoting international trade and investment, and supporting the development of global capital markets.

However, the global financial landscape is not without its challenges. The interconnected nature of financial markets means that shocks in one part of the world can quickly spread to other regions. This was evident in the 2008 global financial crisis, which originated in the United States but had far-reaching impacts on the global economy.

Furthermore, the increasing globalization of finance has led to concerns about the concentration of economic power in the hands of a few dominant financial institutions, the potential for financial instability, and the risks of global financial imbalances.

As we look to the future, it is clear that the global financial landscape will continue to evolve and adapt to new economic, political, and technological forces. The ongoing digital transformation of finance, the rise of emerging markets, and the increasing importance of sustainable finance are just a few of the trends that will shape the global financial landscape in the years to come.

In conclusion, the global financial landscape is a complex and dynamic system that plays a crucial role in driving economic growth and development. It is essential that policymakers, regulators, and market participants work together to promote stability, transparency, and sustainability in the global financial system, while also leveraging its potential to create new opportunities and benefits for people and businesses around the world.

I. Overview of the global financial system

The global financial system is a vast and complex network of financial institutions, markets, and instruments that facilitate the flow of money and capital around the world. It is a critical component of the global economy, as it enables individuals, businesses, and governments to access the capital they need to grow and prosper. In this section, we will provide an overview of the global financial system, including its history, structure, and key components.

History of the Global Financial System

The global financial system has evolved over centuries, with the first evidence of financial intermediation dating back to ancient civilizations such as the Mesopotamians, Greeks, and Romans. However, it was not until the 17th century that the modern financial system began to take shape, with the establishment of the first banks and the development of stock markets in Europe. The 19th and 20th centuries saw the globalization of the financial system, with the expansion of trade and the rise of multinational corporations leading to increased cross-border capital flows.

Structure of the Global Financial System

The global financial system is composed of various institutions, markets, and instruments that facilitate the movement of capital across borders. These include:

Central banks - responsible for regulating the money supply and ensuring financial stability.

Commercial banks - institutions that provide a range of financial services, including deposits, loans, and investment advice.

Investment banks - institutions that specialize in underwriting and selling securities and providing financial advice to corporations and governments.

Stock markets - exchanges where publicly traded companies can sell shares of stock to investors.

Bond markets - markets where companies and governments can issue debt securities to raise capital.

Derivatives markets - markets where financial instruments such as futures, options, and swaps can be traded.

Foreign exchange markets - markets where currencies are traded.

Hedge funds - investment funds that use a range of strategies to generate returns.

Private equity firms - firms that invest in private companies and use a range of strategies to generate returns.

Key Components of the Global Financial System

Capital Flows - the movement of capital across borders, which can take the form of foreign direct investment, portfolio investment, or lending.

Financial Regulation - the set of rules and guidelines that govern financial institutions and markets, with the aim of ensuring financial stability and protecting investors.

Financial Innovation - the development of new financial instruments and technologies that enable more efficient and effective capital allocation.

Financial Stability - the condition of a financial system where institutions and markets are resilient to shocks and crises.

Challenges and Risks of the Global Financial System

The global financial system faces various challenges and risks, including:

Systemic Risk - the risk of a widespread financial crisis that can result from a shock to the system, such as a market crash or a bank failure.

Regulatory Arbitrage - the practice of financial institutions exploiting regulatory loopholes to engage in risky activities or to avoid compliance with rules.

Financial Crime - the use of the financial system for illicit purposes, such as money laundering, fraud, and terrorism financing.

Cybersecurity Risk - the risk of a cyber attack on financial institutions or markets, which can cause significant damage and disruption.

Inequality and Exclusion - the risk that the benefits of the global financial system are not distributed equitably, with certain individuals, communities, or countries being excluded or marginalized.

Conclusion

In conclusion, the global financial system is a critical component of the global economy, enabling capital to flow across borders and facilitating economic growth and development. However, it is also a complex and dynamic system that faces various challenges and risks. As such, it is essential for policymakers, regulators, and financial institutions to work together to ensure the stability, resilience, and sustainability of the system.

Going forward, it is likely that the global financial system will continue to evolve and adapt to changing economic, technological, and political conditions. The emergence of new financial technologies and the increasing interconnectedness of financial markets present both opportunities and challenges for the system. It will be crucial for stakeholders to stay informed about these developments and to anticipate and manage potential risks.

Furthermore, efforts to promote financial inclusion and sustainability will also play a crucial role in shaping the future of the global financial system. As more people and businesses gain access to financial services, and as sustainable finance principles become more widely adopted, the financial system may become more resilient and better equipped to address social and environmental challenges.

In sum, the global financial system is a complex and multifaceted network of institutions, markets, and instruments that plays a vital role in enabling economic activity and growth across the globe. While the system faces challenges and risks, its continued stability and resilience are critical for the well-being of individuals, businesses, and nations alike. As such, it is essential for stakeholders to remain vigilant and collaborative in their efforts to ensure the long-term sustainability and stability of the system.

II. The role of international financial institutions

International financial institutions (IFIs) play a crucial role in the global economy by providing financial support, technical assistance, and policy advice to countries and governments. These institutions include the International Monetary Fund (IMF), World Bank, International Finance Corporation (IFC), and regional development banks such as the Asian Development Bank (ADB) and African Development Bank (AfDB). This article will explore the role of IFIs, their impact on the global economy, and their challenges and criticisms.

Role of International Financial Institutions:

Providing Financial Assistance:
IFIs provide financial assistance to countries facing economic difficulties, whether it be in the form of loans, grants, or other types of financing. The IMF, for example, provides loans to member countries experiencing balance of payments problems or currency crises. The World Bank provides loans and credits to developing countries for various purposes, including infrastructure development, poverty reduction, and economic reform.

Technical Assistance:
IFIs also provide technical assistance to countries in need, such as expertise in areas such as financial regulation, tax policy, and governance. This assistance is often provided through policy dialogue, capacity building, and knowledge-sharing activities.

Policy Advice:
IFIs provide policy advice to governments on a range of issues, including macroeconomic policy, fiscal policy, and social and environmental policy. This advice is typically provided through policy dialogue and analysis, as well as through publications and other forms of communication.

Impact of International Financial Institutions:

Promoting Economic Growth and Development:
IFIs have played a significant role in promoting economic growth and development in many countries around the world. Through their financial support, technical assistance, and policy advice, they have helped countries to develop infrastructure, improve education and healthcare, and promote economic reform.

Facilitating International Trade and Investment:
IFIs also play a key role in facilitating international trade and investment by providing financing for infrastructure projects and supporting policies that promote trade and investment.

Crisis Management:
IFIs have played a critical role in managing financial crises, such as the Asian financial crisis of the late 1990s and the global financial crisis of 2008. Through their financial support and policy advice, they have helped to stabilize financial markets and prevent the spread of crises to other countries.

Challenges and Criticisms:

Conditionality:
One criticism of IFIs is that they often impose strict conditions on countries in exchange for their financial assistance, such as requiring economic reforms, privatization, and austerity measures. This has led to concerns about the impact of these conditions on social welfare and the sovereignty of recipient countries.

Democratic Legitimacy:
Another criticism of IFIs is that they are often seen as lacking democratic legitimacy, as their governance structures are dominated by developed countries. This has led to calls for greater representation of developing countries in IFI decision-making.

Sustainability:
IFIs have also faced criticism for their focus on short-term economic growth rather than long-term sustainability. This has led to concerns about the impact of IFI policies on the environment, social welfare, and inequality.

Conclusion:

International financial institutions play a crucial role in the global economy by providing financial support, technical assistance, and policy advice to countries and governments. While they have had a significant impact on economic growth and development around the world, they also face challenges and criticisms, including concerns about conditionality, democratic legitimacy, and sustainability. It is essential for IFIs to address these challenges and criticisms to ensure their continued effectiveness in promoting global economic growth and development.

III. Challenges facing the global financial system

The global financial system plays a crucial role in facilitating economic growth, development, and prosperity. However, it is not without its challenges and risks. This section will explore the major challenges facing the global financial system and their potential implications.

Regulatory challenges:
One of the most significant challenges facing the global financial system is regulatory complexity and inconsistency. The financial crisis of 2008 highlighted the need for more effective regulation of the financial system to prevent excessive risk-taking and ensure financial stability. However, there is still a lack of global consensus on regulatory standards and enforcement, leading to regulatory arbitrage and uneven playing fields for financial institutions.

For example, some countries have more stringent capital and liquidity requirements than others, creating an uneven regulatory landscape that can lead to regulatory arbitrage. This can also lead to regulatory competition, with countries vying to attract financial institutions by offering more lenient regulatory environments. This can create a race to the bottom in regulatory standards, ultimately leading to increased risk-taking and financial instability.

Cybersecurity risks:
As the financial industry becomes increasingly reliant on technology and digitization, cybersecurity risks are becoming more significant. Cyber attacks can disrupt financial systems, compromise sensitive data, and lead to financial losses for both individuals and institutions. The potential for cyber attacks to cause systemic risk is a significant concern for regulators and financial institutions alike.

For example, in 2017, the WannaCry ransomware attack affected over 200,000 computers in more than 150 countries, including banks, hospitals, and government agencies. The attack highlighted the vulnerability of financial institutions to cyber threats and the potential for such attacks to cause significant disruptions to the global financial system.

Economic imbalances:
Economic imbalances between countries and regions can also pose challenges to the global financial system. These imbalances can lead to capital flows that are not aligned with economic fundamentals, potentially leading to financial instability and crises.

For example, in the early 2000s, there was a significant flow of capital from developed countries to emerging markets, particularly in Asia, which led to a buildup of imbalances and vulnerabilities. When the global financial crisis hit in 2008, these vulnerabilities were exposed, leading to a severe economic contraction in many emerging market countries.

Climate change and environmental risks:
Climate change and environmental risks are also emerging as significant challenges for the global financial system. The financial industry is increasingly recognizing the potential impact of climate change on their investments, with concerns about stranded assets, increased insurance claims, and changes in regulatory frameworks.

For example, rising sea levels and increased frequency and severity of extreme weather events could lead to significant losses for insurance companies and other financial institutions. Similarly, a transition to a low-carbon economy could lead to stranded assets and significant write-downs for companies in the fossil fuel sector.

Geopolitical risks:
Finally, geopolitical risks can also pose challenges to the global financial system. Conflicts between countries, political instability, and protectionist trade policies can lead to market volatility, capital flight, and financial crises.

For example, the ongoing trade tensions between the United States and China have led to significant market volatility and uncertainty, as well as disruptions to global supply chains. Similarly, political instability in countries such as Venezuela and Ukraine has led to capital flight and significant economic disruptions.

Conclusion:

The global financial system faces a range of challenges, from regulatory complexity and inconsistency to cybersecurity risks, economic imbalances, climate change, and geopolitical risks. Addressing these challenges will require a coordinated and collaborative effort from policymakers, regulators, financial institutions, and other stakeholders. Failure to address these challenges could lead to financial instability, economic contraction, and social unrest, underscoring the critical importance of addressing these issues.

CHAPTER 25: INTERNATIONAL TRADE AND FINANCE

International trade and finance are two closely interconnected aspects of the global economy. International trade refers to the exchange of goods and services between countries, while international finance refers to the movement of capital across national borders. The growth of international trade and finance has been a major driver of economic growth and development, facilitating the movement of goods, services, and capital across borders.

In recent years, the globalization of the world economy has accelerated, leading to a significant increase in the volume of international trade and finance. This has been facilitated by advances in transportation, communication, and information technology, which have made it easier and cheaper to move goods, services, and capital across borders. However, the growth of international trade and finance has also led to various challenges and risks, which must be carefully managed to ensure the stability and sustainability of the global economy.

In this section, we will provide an overview of the key concepts and principles of international trade and finance, including the benefits and challenges of international trade, the main instruments of international finance, and the role of international institutions in managing the risks and challenges of the global economy.

Benefits of International Trade:

International trade has been a major driver of economic growth and development, enabling countries to specialize in the production of goods and services in which they have a comparative advantage, and to exchange these goods and services with other countries for products that they are less efficient at producing.

For example, a country with abundant natural resources, such as oil, may be able to produce oil at a lower cost than other countries. By exporting this oil, the country can earn foreign exchange and use it to import other goods and services that it needs but cannot produce as efficiently, such as manufactured goods, technology, and services.

International trade also promotes competition and innovation, as firms are forced to compete in global markets and to innovate to stay ahead of their competitors. This leads to lower prices for consumers, increased efficiency, and higher quality products.

Challenges of International Trade:

While international trade offers many benefits, it also poses various challenges and risks. One of the main challenges is the risk of protectionism, which refers to the use of trade barriers, such as tariffs, quotas, and subsidies, to protect domestic industries from foreign competition.

Protectionism can reduce the efficiency of the global economy, by preventing countries from specializing in the production of goods and services in which they have a comparative advantage, and by reducing the incentives for firms to innovate and compete.

Another challenge of international trade is the risk of trade imbalances, which occur when a country imports more than it exports, leading to a deficit in its balance of payments. Trade imbalances can lead to a build-up of foreign debt, which can create vulnerabilities in the economy and make it more difficult to manage economic shocks and crises.

Instruments of International Finance:

International finance refers to the movement of capital across national borders, including investments in foreign stocks, bonds, and real estate, as well as foreign direct investment (FDI) and portfolio investment.

Foreign direct investment involves the acquisition of a controlling interest in a foreign company, while portfolio investment involves the purchase of stocks, bonds, and other financial assets in foreign markets. International finance also includes international borrowing and lending, such as loans, bonds, and other debt instruments.

The main instruments of international finance include foreign exchange markets, which enable the exchange of currencies between countries, and international capital markets, which provide a platform for the issuance and trading of securities and other financial assets.

Role of International Institutions:

The growth of international trade and finance has led to the emergence of various international institutions, which play a critical role in managing the risks and challenges of the global economy.

These institutions include the International Monetary Fund (IMF), the World Trade Organization (WTO), and the World Bank. The IMF provides financial assistance and policy advice to countries facing balance of payments difficulties, while the WTO facilitates the negotiation and implementation of international trade agreements. The World Bank, on the other hand, provides financial and technical assistance to developing countries for infrastructure and human development projects.

The role of these international institutions is crucial in promoting economic growth and stability, particularly in developing countries. The IMF, for instance, provides financial assistance to countries facing economic crisis, helping them to stabilize their economies and avoid defaulting on their debt obligations. The World Bank provides long-term development loans and technical assistance to developing countries, helping them to build infrastructure and improve the lives of their citizens.

However, these institutions have also faced criticism and challenges. Some argue that the IMF's policies have led to austerity measures and social unrest in recipient countries, while others criticize the World Bank for promoting development projects that harm the environment and displace local communities.

Moreover, these institutions have also faced challenges in adapting to the changing global economic landscape. For instance, the rise of emerging economies such as China has led to calls for reform of the IMF and the World Bank to better reflect the changing balance of economic power.

Another challenge facing international institutions is the growing trend towards protectionism and economic nationalism. The election of Donald Trump as U.S. President in 2016, for instance, brought with it a shift towards protectionist policies such as tariffs and trade barriers. This trend has put pressure on international institutions such as the WTO to defend the principles of free trade and resist protectionist measures.

In addition to these challenges, international institutions have also faced criticism for lacking transparency and accountability. Some argue that these institutions are dominated by developed countries, which use their power to advance their own interests at the expense of developing countries.

To address these challenges, international institutions have sought to reform and adapt to the changing global economic landscape. The IMF, for instance, has introduced reforms to increase the representation of emerging economies and enhance their voice in decision-making. The World Bank has also introduced reforms to increase transparency and accountability in its operations.

In conclusion, international institutions play a critical role in managing the risks and challenges of the global economy, particularly in promoting economic growth and stability in developing countries. However, they also face challenges and criticisms, including concerns around transparency, accountability, and their ability to adapt to the changing global economic landscape. As such, it is important for these institutions to continue to reform and evolve in order to effectively address the challenges of the 21st century global economy.

I.   The benefits of international trade

International trade has been a key driver of economic growth and development since ancient times, enabling countries to exchange goods and services across borders, and allowing them to access a wider range of products and resources than they would have access to if they relied solely on domestic production. Today, international trade is more important than ever, with global trade volumes reaching record levels and trade agreements becoming increasingly complex and multifaceted. In this section, we will explore the benefits of international trade, including increased economic growth, improved living standards, enhanced competitiveness, and greater access to global markets.

Increased Economic Growth

One of the primary benefits of international trade is increased economic growth. By expanding the market for goods and services, international trade can stimulate economic activity and generate new jobs, leading to higher levels of economic output and income. This is particularly important for smaller and developing economies, which may lack the resources and scale to sustain high levels of domestic demand. For example, countries like Singapore, which have few natural resources and limited domestic markets, have relied on international trade to drive their economic growth and development.

Improved Living Standards

In addition to increasing economic growth, international trade can also lead to improved living standards for individuals and societies. By accessing a wider range of goods and services, consumers can enjoy higher-quality products at lower prices, leading to greater consumer surplus and improved welfare. This can be particularly beneficial for low-income households, which may be priced out of the domestic market for certain goods and services. For example, the availability of affordable imported food and clothing can have a significant impact on the standard of living for low-income families in developing countries.

Enhanced Competitiveness

International trade can also enhance competitiveness by exposing domestic firms to global markets and competition. By competing on a global stage, firms can learn from best practices and innovations in other countries, and adapt their operations and products to meet the demands of international consumers. This can lead to higher levels of productivity, innovation, and efficiency, which can in turn enhance the competitiveness of the domestic economy as a whole. For example, the ability of Chinese firms to compete in global markets has driven the country's rapid economic growth and development over the past few decades.

Greater Access to Global Markets

Finally, international trade can provide countries with greater access to global markets, enabling them to diversify their exports and reduce their dependence on any one market or region. This can help countries to mitigate the risks associated with economic shocks or geopolitical instability, and can also provide opportunities for small and medium-sized enterprises (SMEs) to expand their operations beyond domestic borders. For example, the EU's free trade agreements with countries such as Canada and Japan have opened up new markets for European exporters, providing SMEs with greater access to global markets and supporting economic growth and job creation.

Counterarguments

While international trade has numerous benefits, it also faces criticism and skepticism from some quarters. Some argue that international trade can lead to job losses and wage stagnation in certain sectors, particularly in industries that are exposed to international competition. For example, manufacturing jobs in developed countries have declined significantly in recent years, due in part to competition from low-cost producers in developing countries.

Others argue that international trade can exacerbate income inequality, as the benefits of trade may accrue disproportionately to certain groups, such as skilled workers or large corporations. For example, research has shown that trade with China has led to a significant increase in income inequality in the United States, as workers in industries exposed to Chinese competition have experienced lower wages and job losses, while workers in industries that benefit from trade have seen their wages rise.

Conclusion

In conclusion, international trade is a critical driver of economic growth and development, providing countries with access to a wider range of goods and services, and enabling them to compete on a global stage. While international trade is not without its challenges and drawbacks, the benefits it brings far outweigh its costs.

International trade has been an integral part of human history, and its importance has only grown in recent decades with the advent of globalization. Trade has allowed countries to specialize in the production of goods and services in which they have a comparative advantage, leading to increased efficiency and productivity. It has also created new markets and opportunities for businesses, leading to job creation and economic growth.

Moreover, international trade promotes cooperation and collaboration between countries. By engaging in trade, countries develop interdependent relationships, which can lead to increased political and economic stability. Trade also helps to reduce the likelihood of conflicts and wars between countries, as countries become more interconnected and rely on each other for mutual benefits.

Another benefit of international trade is the increased availability of goods and services at lower costs. Trade allows countries to access goods and services that they may not be able to produce domestically or produce at a higher cost. As a result, consumers can enjoy a wider variety of goods and services at lower prices, which can improve their standard of living.

In addition to consumer benefits, trade can also lead to increased business competitiveness. By importing and exporting goods and services, companies can gain access to new technologies, ideas, and expertise, which can help them to become more innovative and efficient. This can lead to increased competitiveness and market share, which can be beneficial for businesses and the economy as a whole.

However, international trade is not without its challenges and drawbacks. One of the main concerns is the potential for job losses in certain industries as production shifts to countries with lower labor costs. While the overall benefits of trade may outweigh the costs, there may be some industries and workers who are adversely affected.

Another challenge is the potential for trade imbalances and protectionism. Some countries may engage in practices such as currency manipulation or the use of subsidies to gain a competitive advantage, which can lead to trade imbalances and tensions between countries. Moreover, protectionist policies, such as tariffs or quotas, can reduce the benefits of trade and lead to decreased economic growth and development.

In conclusion, while international trade has its challenges and drawbacks, its benefits are significant and far-reaching. It has the potential to promote economic growth and development, improve standards of living, and promote cooperation and collaboration between countries. Policymakers and international institutions must work together to address the challenges and ensure that the benefits of trade are shared widely and equitably.

II.   The challenges of international trade

International trade has brought many benefits to the global economy, but it also poses significant challenges that must be addressed. In this section, we will explore some of the challenges of international trade, ranging from protectionism and tariffs to currency fluctuations and intellectual property rights.

One of the main challenges of international trade is the rise of protectionism, which refers to the use of tariffs, quotas, and other barriers to restrict imports and protect domestic industries. Protectionism can harm both importing and exporting countries by reducing trade, increasing prices, and reducing consumer choice. For example, if a country imposes high tariffs on foreign goods, domestic consumers may end up paying more for those goods, while foreign producers may lose access to a large market.

Another challenge of international trade is the issue of currency fluctuations, which can make it difficult for businesses to predict their costs and revenues. When a company imports or exports goods, it must deal with foreign currencies, which can fluctuate in value. These fluctuations can have a significant impact on the profitability of international trade, as companies may end up paying more or less than expected for their goods.

Intellectual property rights are also a significant challenge for international trade. Different countries have different laws and regulations regarding intellectual property, which can make it difficult for companies to protect their trademarks, patents, and copyrights. This can lead to issues such as counterfeiting, piracy, and intellectual property theft, which can harm businesses and reduce their incentive to innovate.

In addition to these challenges, international trade also poses environmental and social challenges. For example, increased global trade can lead to higher levels of greenhouse gas emissions and pollution, as more goods are transported around the world. It can also lead to labor rights abuses and exploitation, as companies seek out low-wage countries with weaker labor protections.

Another challenge of international trade is the potential for economic inequality between countries. As some countries become more prosperous through international trade, others may be left behind, leading to a widening gap between rich and poor countries. This can lead to social and political instability, as well as increased global conflict.

Finally, international trade can also be affected by geopolitical factors such as sanctions, embargoes, and political tensions between countries. These factors can disrupt international trade and lead to economic uncertainty, making it difficult for businesses to plan for the future.

In order to address these challenges, international institutions such as the World Trade Organization and the International Monetary Fund play a critical role in promoting free trade and economic stability. They work to reduce barriers to trade, provide financial assistance to countries in need, and promote cooperation between countries.

However, there is also a need for individual countries to take action to address the challenges of international trade. For example, countries can work to reduce protectionism and promote free trade, implement policies to address currency fluctuations and intellectual property rights, and take steps to mitigate the environmental and social impacts of global trade.

In conclusion, while international trade offers many benefits to the global economy, it also poses significant challenges that must be addressed. By working together at both the international and national levels, we can ensure that international trade is conducted in a way that promotes economic growth and development, while also protecting the environment, promoting social justice, and addressing the needs of all countries involved.

III. The role of international trade agreements

International trade agreements are formal agreements between countries that set out the terms and conditions under which goods, services, and investment can be exchanged across borders. These agreements are designed to promote economic growth and create new business opportunities, while also providing a framework for resolving trade disputes and addressing social and environmental concerns. The role of international trade agreements has become increasingly important in recent years, as global trade has expanded and economic interdependence among countries has grown. In this section, we will explore the benefits and challenges of international trade agreements, as well as their impact on various stakeholders, including governments, businesses, and consumers.

Benefits of International Trade Agreements

One of the primary benefits of international trade agreements is the promotion of free trade, which enables countries to trade goods and services without the restrictions of tariffs, quotas, or other trade barriers. Free trade promotes economic growth by encouraging competition, innovation, and specialization, which can lead to lower prices and increased consumer choice. In addition, free trade can help to spread prosperity across countries, by enabling developing countries to gain access to new markets and technologies, and by promoting greater economic integration among countries.

Another important benefit of international trade agreements is the establishment of rules and standards that govern the conduct of international trade. These rules provide a framework for resolving trade disputes and addressing social and environmental concerns, such as labor standards, human rights, and environmental protection. By establishing a level playing field for trade, international trade agreements can help to ensure that countries compete fairly and that consumers are protected from harmful products or practices.

International trade agreements can also play a key role in supporting the growth of small and medium-sized enterprises (SMEs), which are often the backbone of many economies. By providing SMEs with access to new markets and technologies, and by promoting greater competition and innovation, international trade agreements can help to create new business opportunities and drive economic growth.

Challenges of International Trade Agreements

Despite their many benefits, international trade agreements also face a number of challenges, both from a political and economic perspective. One of the primary challenges is ensuring that the benefits of free trade are shared fairly among all stakeholders, including workers, consumers, and businesses. This requires striking a balance between promoting economic growth and protecting social and environmental standards, which can be a difficult task.

Another challenge is the complexity of negotiating and implementing international trade agreements, which often involve multiple countries and can take years to complete. This complexity can make it difficult to reach consensus on key issues, and can also make it difficult for smaller countries or businesses to participate fully in the negotiation process.

In addition, international trade agreements can be controversial and subject to criticism from various stakeholders. For example, some critics argue that free trade can lead to job losses in certain industries, as companies move production to countries with lower labor costs. Others argue that international trade agreements can undermine national sovereignty by limiting a country's ability to regulate its own economy or protect its own industries.

Impact on Stakeholders

The impact of international trade agreements can vary widely depending on the stakeholder involved. For example, governments may benefit from increased trade opportunities, access to new markets and technologies, and the establishment of rules and standards that govern the conduct of international trade. However, they may also face criticism and pressure from domestic interest groups or opposition parties, who may view the agreements as a threat to their own interests.

Businesses, on the other hand, may benefit from increased access to new markets, greater competition, and the ability to tap into new supply chains and technologies. However, they may also face increased competition from foreign firms and may need to adapt to new rules and regulations governing international trade.

Consumers may also benefit from international trade agreements, as they can enjoy lower prices, increased consumer choice, and access to a wider range of goods and services. However, there are also potential downsides for consumers to consider. For example, some critics argue that trade agreements can undermine consumer protections and lead to the import of lower-quality goods.

One of the primary concerns with international trade agreements is the potential for regulatory harmonization. Regulatory harmonization refers to the process of aligning regulations and standards between countries to facilitate trade. While this may sound like a positive development, it can lead to a race to the bottom in terms of regulatory standards. For example, if one country has lower environmental standards than another, regulatory harmonization could result in the adoption of weaker standards by the other country to facilitate trade. This could lead to environmental degradation and harm to public health.

In addition, some critics argue that trade agreements can give too much power to multinational corporations at the expense of consumers. For example, trade agreements may include provisions that allow multinational corporations to sue governments if they believe that their investments are being unfairly treated. This can lead to a chilling effect on government regulation, as governments may be reluctant to enact regulations that could potentially result in costly lawsuits.

There is also the issue of intellectual property rights. International trade agreements often include provisions that strengthen intellectual property protections, such as patents and copyrights. While these protections can be beneficial for companies that hold these rights, they can also limit consumer access to affordable medicines and other essential goods.

Despite these concerns, supporters of international trade agreements argue that they are necessary for facilitating trade and economic growth. Trade agreements can provide businesses with greater certainty and predictability, which can encourage investment and job creation. In addition, trade agreements can promote innovation and the development of new technologies by protecting intellectual property rights.

Furthermore, proponents of trade agreements argue that they can help to address issues such as labor rights and environmental protections. For example, some trade agreements include provisions that require participating countries to adhere to certain labor and environmental standards.

Overall, the role of international trade agreements is complex, and there are both potential benefits and drawbacks to consider. Consumers, businesses, and governments must carefully evaluate the provisions of trade agreements to ensure that they are in the best interests of all parties involved. It is important to strike a balance between facilitating trade and protecting the interests of consumers and the public.

CHAPTER 26: THE FUTURE OF GLOBALIZATION IN FINANCE

Globalization has brought unprecedented growth and development to the finance industry over the past few decades. Advances in technology, financial deregulation, and the growth of international trade have enabled the finance industry to become more interconnected and interdependent than ever before. However, the future of globalization in finance is uncertain, with potential challenges and opportunities that could have a significant impact on the industry. In this chapter, we will explore the future of globalization in finance and the potential challenges and opportunities that lie ahead.

Technology and Innovation in Finance

One of the key drivers of globalization in finance has been technological innovation. The rise of digital platforms, mobile devices, and advanced data analytics have transformed the finance industry, enabling it to become more efficient, effective, and accessible. However, these innovations have also brought new challenges and risks, such as cyber threats, data privacy concerns, and the potential for market manipulation.

Despite these risks, technology is likely to continue to play a significant role in the future of globalization in finance. Innovations such as blockchain, artificial intelligence, and cloud computing have the potential to revolutionize the finance industry, making it faster, cheaper, and more secure. For example, blockchain technology could enable faster and more secure transactions, while artificial intelligence could help to identify and mitigate financial risks more effectively.

Financial Deregulation

Another key driver of globalization in finance has been financial deregulation. In recent years, many countries have implemented financial deregulation policies, which have enabled financial institutions to expand their operations across borders, and has facilitated the growth of international trade and investment. However, financial deregulation has also been blamed for contributing to the global financial crisis, and there are concerns that further deregulation could lead to similar crises in the future.

The future of financial regulation is uncertain, with some countries calling for tighter regulation in the wake of the global financial crisis, while others advocate for further deregulation to promote economic growth and competitiveness. The challenge for policymakers will be to strike a balance between these competing interests, ensuring that the finance industry can continue to grow and innovate, while also protecting consumers and mitigating systemic risks.

Environmental, Social, and Governance (ESG) Issues

As the world becomes more connected and interdependent, environmental, social, and governance (ESG) issues are likely to become increasingly important in the finance industry. Investors and consumers are increasingly demanding that financial institutions consider ESG factors in their decision-making, and many countries are implementing regulations and policies aimed at promoting sustainable finance.

The future of ESG in finance is uncertain, with some experts predicting that it could become a significant driver of globalization, while others argue that it could lead to greater fragmentation and localization of the finance industry. The challenge for financial institutions will be to balance the demands of investors and consumers for sustainable finance, while also managing risks and maximizing profits.

Conclusion

The future of globalization in finance is uncertain, with potential challenges and opportunities that could have a significant impact on the industry. Technological innovation, financial deregulation, and ESG issues are likely to be key drivers of globalization in finance over the coming years, and financial institutions will need to navigate these challenges to remain competitive and successful. However, with the right policies and strategies in place, the finance industry can continue to grow and evolve, enabling it to meet the needs of investors and consumers in a rapidly changing world.

I.   Overview of the current trends in globalization

Globalization is the process of increased interconnectedness among individuals, businesses, and countries around the world. The rise of globalization in the past few decades has transformed the way people and businesses conduct their affairs. As technology advances and communication becomes more accessible, it is expected that globalization will continue to impact the world in various ways. This section will provide an overview of the current trends in globalization, including the growing importance of emerging economies, the impact of digitalization, and the challenges facing global trade.

The Growing Importance of Emerging Economies

Emerging economies, such as China, India, Brazil, and Russia, have been growing at a faster rate than their developed counterparts in recent years. These economies have become increasingly important in the global economy, both as consumers and as producers. According to the World Bank, emerging economies are expected to grow by 5.2% in 2022, compared to just 3.5% for developed economies. As these economies continue to grow, they are expected to play an even more significant role in the global economy.

One of the ways emerging economies are becoming more important is through their increasing participation in global trade. Many emerging economies have implemented policies that encourage exports, such as free trade zones and export subsidies. As a result, these economies are becoming major exporters of goods and services. For example, China has become the world's largest exporter of goods, surpassing the United States in 2009. In addition, many emerging economies are also becoming important sources of foreign investment. Chinese firms, for example, have invested heavily in Africa in recent years, in sectors such as construction, mining, and manufacturing.

The Impact of Digitalization

Digitalization has been one of the most significant trends in globalization in recent years. The growth of digital technology and the internet have transformed the way people and businesses interact, making it easier to communicate and share information across borders. This has led to the creation of new global industries, such as e-commerce, social media, and online marketplaces.

The rise of digitalization has also had an impact on the financial industry. Online banking, mobile payments, and blockchain technology are just a few examples of how digitalization is transforming the financial industry. Digitalization has also made it easier for firms to conduct cross-border transactions and to access financing from foreign sources. This has led to the emergence of new types of financial firms, such as peer-to-peer lending platforms and crowdfunding platforms.

The Challenges Facing Global Trade

Despite the benefits of globalization, there are also challenges facing global trade. One of the most significant challenges is the rise of protectionism. Protectionism refers to the use of trade barriers, such as tariffs and quotas, to protect domestic industries from foreign competition. While protectionism can provide short-term benefits to certain industries, it can also lead to higher prices for consumers and reduced competition. Protectionism can also lead to retaliation from other countries, which can result in a trade war.

Another challenge facing global trade is the increasing complexity of global supply chains. As firms become more globalized, their supply chains become more complex, with products often being produced in multiple countries before reaching the final consumer. This can make it difficult for firms to ensure that their products meet regulatory requirements in all the countries in which they are sold.

Finally, global trade is also facing challenges from environmental concerns. As the world becomes more aware of the impact of climate change, there is growing pressure on firms to reduce their carbon footprint. This can be a challenge for firms that rely on global supply chains, as it can be difficult to ensure that all the components of their products are produced in an environmentally sustainable way.

Conclusion

Globalization has transformed the way people and businesses conduct their affairs, and it is expected to continue to have an impact in the future.

II.   The impact of technological advancements on globalization

Technological advancements have played a crucial role in shaping the world we live in today. The rapid growth of technology has had a profound impact on globalization, leading to increased connectivity, information sharing, and trade flows. In this section, we will explore the impact of technological advancements on globalization and how these advancements are shaping the future of global finance.

The Impact of Technological Advancements on Globalization

One of the most significant impacts of technological advancements on globalization is the increased connectivity and information sharing. The internet has become the backbone of the global economy, providing a platform for businesses to communicate, collaborate, and trade with each other. E-commerce has enabled businesses to sell their products and services globally, allowing them to reach new markets and customers in different parts of the world.

The use of digital technologies has also made it easier for businesses to automate their processes and reduce their costs. For example, automated systems in factories and warehouses have led to increased efficiency and productivity, which has resulted in lower production costs. This has made it easier for businesses to sell their products at lower prices, making them more competitive in the global market.

Another significant impact of technological advancements on globalization is the rise of fintech. Fintech is a term used to describe the use of technology to provide financial services. Fintech has disrupted traditional financial services, making it easier for individuals and businesses to access financial services, such as banking, loans, and investments, from anywhere in the world. The use of mobile banking and online investment platforms has made it easier for people to manage their finances and invest in global markets.

The rise of blockchain technology has also had a significant impact on globalization. Blockchain technology is a decentralized ledger that allows for secure and transparent transactions without the need for intermediaries. This technology has the potential to revolutionize cross-border payments, making them faster, cheaper, and more secure. It could also help to reduce the costs associated with international trade by streamlining processes and reducing the need for intermediaries.

However, there are also challenges associated with the impact of technological advancements on globalization. One of the challenges is the issue of cybersecurity. As businesses become more reliant on digital technologies, they also become more vulnerable to cyber attacks. Cyber attacks can result in significant financial losses for businesses and disrupt global trade flows.

Another challenge is the issue of data privacy. As businesses collect and store large amounts of data, there are concerns about how this data is being used and whether it is being adequately protected. The European Union's General Data Protection Regulation (GDPR) is an example of regulations aimed at protecting individuals' privacy and data rights.

The Future of Globalization in Finance

The impact of technological advancements on globalization has significant implications for the future of global finance. The rise of fintech and blockchain technology has the potential to disrupt traditional financial services, leading to increased competition and innovation. This could result in lower costs for consumers and businesses and increased access to financial services, particularly in developing countries.

The use of digital technologies could also lead to increased financial inclusion. According to the World Bank, around 1.7 billion adults worldwide do not have access to formal financial services. The use of mobile banking and other digital financial services could help to bridge this gap, providing people with access to basic financial services, such as savings accounts and loans.

However, there are also risks associated with the future of globalization in finance. One of the risks is the potential for financial instability. The use of digital technologies could make it easier for financial crises to spread across borders, leading to increased systemic risk. Regulators will need to work together to ensure that the global financial system remains stable and resilient in the face of potential shocks.

Another risk is the potential for increased inequality. While digital technologies have the potential to increase financial inclusion, there is also a risk that they could widen the gap between those who have access to technology and those who do not. The unequal distribution of technology and knowledge necessary to use it effectively may limit the ability of some individuals and communities to fully participate in the global economy.

Moreover, technological advancements may also have a significant impact on the global labor market. Automation and artificial intelligence are increasingly replacing manual labor and routine tasks in many industries. This has led to concerns about job displacement, particularly in low-skilled and routine occupations. However, it is also argued that technological advancements can create new jobs and opportunities in emerging fields such as data analytics, cybersecurity, and digital marketing.

In addition to these challenges, there are also concerns about the impact of technological advancements on the environment. The growing demand for electronic devices, the proliferation of data centers, and the increasing use of cloud computing have all contributed to a significant increase in energy consumption and carbon emissions. Moreover, the disposal of electronic waste, which contains hazardous materials, poses a significant environmental risk.

To address these challenges, there is a need for policymakers, businesses, and individuals to work together to ensure that technological advancements are harnessed for the greater good. This requires investment in education and training programs to ensure that workers have the skills necessary to participate in the digital economy. It also requires the development of regulatory frameworks to address the risks associated with technological advancements, including data privacy, security, and environmental sustainability.

Furthermore, there is a need for greater international cooperation to ensure that technological advancements are shared and accessible to all. This can be achieved through initiatives such as the UN Sustainable Development Goals, which aim to promote inclusive and sustainable economic growth, and the World Economic Forum's Globalization 4.0 initiative, which seeks to harness the potential of the Fourth Industrial Revolution to create a more inclusive and sustainable future.

In conclusion, technological advancements have played a significant role in shaping globalization and will continue to do so in the future. While there are many potential benefits to technological advancements, there are also significant challenges and risks. It is essential that policymakers, businesses, and individuals work together to ensure that technological advancements are harnessed for the greater good and that the benefits are shared by all.

III. The future of cross-border finance

Cross-border finance, which involves the movement of capital across national borders, has become an increasingly important aspect of the global economy. Advances in technology and financial innovation have made it easier than ever for individuals and institutions to invest in foreign markets, raise capital across borders, and transfer funds internationally. However, the future of cross-border finance is uncertain, with a range of potential challenges and opportunities on the horizon. This section will explore some of the key trends shaping the future of cross-border finance, including the impact of digital technology, changing regulatory environments, and shifting geopolitical dynamics.

Digital Technology and Cross-Border Finance:

Digital technology has already had a significant impact on cross-border finance, making it easier for individuals and institutions to conduct transactions across borders. The rise of mobile banking, online payments, and digital currencies has made it possible for people to access financial services regardless of their location. Digital technology has also enabled the development of new financial products, such as peer-to-peer lending and crowdfunding platforms, which allow individuals and businesses to raise capital from a global pool of investors.

Looking ahead, there are several ways in which digital technology is likely to continue to shape cross-border finance. For example, the use of blockchain technology and smart contracts could transform the way in which cross-border payments are made, reducing the time and cost associated with international transfers. In addition, advances in artificial intelligence and machine learning could help financial institutions to better manage risk and make more informed investment decisions.

However, there are also risks associated with the increased use of digital technology in cross-border finance. One potential risk is the increased threat of cyber attacks, which could undermine the security of cross-border transactions and cause financial losses for individuals and institutions. There is also a risk that digital technology could exacerbate existing inequalities in the global financial system, as some individuals and countries may not have access to the necessary technology or infrastructure to fully participate in cross-border finance.

Regulatory Environment and Cross-Border Finance:

The regulatory environment is another important factor shaping the future of cross-border finance. In recent years, there has been a trend towards increased regulation of cross-border financial activity, as governments seek to protect their financial systems from risks such as money laundering and terrorism financing. This has led to the development of a range of international regulatory frameworks, such as the Basel Accords and the Financial Action Task Force, which aim to promote greater transparency and accountability in cross-border finance.

Looking ahead, there are likely to be further changes to the regulatory environment for cross-border finance. For example, the European Union's General Data Protection Regulation (GDPR) has already had a significant impact on cross-border data transfers, and there are likely to be further regulatory changes in this area. There may also be increased scrutiny of digital currencies and other emerging financial technologies, as governments seek to ensure that they are not used for illicit purposes.

Geopolitical Dynamics and Cross-Border Finance:

Geopolitical dynamics are also likely to have an important impact on the future of cross-border finance. The rise of populism and nationalism in many countries has led to increased protectionism and a more inward-looking approach to economic policy. This could make it more difficult for individuals and institutions to invest and operate across borders, as governments seek to protect their own economies from external competition.

At the same time, there are also opportunities for cross-border finance in emerging markets, where economic growth and demographic shifts are creating new investment opportunities. For example, many African countries are experiencing rapid population growth and urbanization, which is driving demand for infrastructure investment and consumer goods. There are also opportunities in Asia, where rising incomes and a growing middle class are driving demand for a range of financial services.

Conclusion:

In conclusion, the future of cross-border finance is likely to be shaped by a range of factors, including digital technology, changing regulatory environments, and shifting market dynamics. While these changes are likely to bring new opportunities, they also pose significant challenges and risks, which must be carefully managed.

One key takeaway is the need for greater cooperation and collaboration between different stakeholders, including governments, financial institutions, and technology companies. As the global financial system becomes more interconnected, the need for common standards and protocols will become increasingly important. This will require policymakers and regulators to work closely with industry players to develop frameworks that balance innovation and risk management.

Another important trend to watch is the rise of digital currencies and blockchain technology. While still in their early stages, these technologies have the potential to transform the way cross-border payments and financial transactions are conducted. However, their adoption will depend on a range of factors, including regulatory clarity, consumer trust, and scalability.

Finally, it is clear that cross-border finance will continue to play a critical role in the global economy, facilitating trade, investment, and economic growth. However, as we have seen in recent years, this role is not without its challenges and risks. In order to navigate this complex landscape, financial institutions and policymakers must remain vigilant, adaptable, and forward-thinking, constantly assessing and responding to new trends and developments. By doing so, they can help ensure that cross-border finance remains a powerful force for good in the world, driving growth, promoting stability, and expanding opportunities for people around the globe.

CHAPTER 27: CURRENCY EXCHANGE AND FOREIGN INVESTMENT

Currency exchange and foreign investment are closely related topics within the field of international finance. Currency exchange refers to the process of converting one currency into another, while foreign investment refers to the investment made by individuals or firms in another country's financial assets or business ventures. The interplay between these two concepts has significant implications for global economic development, financial stability, and wealth creation.

In recent years, globalization and technological advancements have made currency exchange and foreign investment more accessible to a wider range of individuals and businesses. This has led to a surge in cross-border investment and trade, making it increasingly important to understand the mechanisms and risks associated with currency exchange and foreign investment.

This chapter will explore the various aspects of currency exchange and foreign investment, including the role of exchange rates, the types of foreign investment, and the benefits and risks associated with these activities. We will also examine the impact of currency exchange and foreign investment on the global economy and discuss some of the challenges and opportunities for these activities in the future.

Exchange Rates

Exchange rates play a crucial role in currency exchange and foreign investment. An exchange rate is the value of one currency in relation to another currency. For example, if the exchange rate between the US dollar and the euro is 1.2, then one US dollar is worth 1.2 euros.

Exchange rates are determined by a variety of factors, including supply and demand, inflation rates, interest rates, and political and economic events. Changes in exchange rates can have significant impacts on international trade and investment. For example, if the US dollar were to appreciate relative to the euro, US exports would become more expensive, making them less competitive in the global market. On the other hand, if the US dollar were to depreciate, US exports would become cheaper, potentially boosting demand for US goods and services.

Types of Foreign Investment

There are several types of foreign investment, each with its own benefits and risks.

Foreign Direct Investment (FDI) is a long-term investment made by a company or individual in a foreign country. FDI typically involves the establishment of a new business or the acquisition of an existing business in the foreign country. FDI can provide companies with access to new markets and resources, as well as reduce costs through economies of scale. However, FDI also carries significant risks, such as political instability, cultural differences, and legal and regulatory barriers.

Foreign Portfolio Investment (FPI) refers to the purchase of securities in a foreign country, such as stocks, bonds, or mutual funds. FPI allows investors to diversify their portfolios and potentially earn higher returns. However, FPI is also subject to market volatility and currency risk, as well as political and economic events that can impact the value of the investment.

Foreign Aid is another form of foreign investment, which involves the transfer of resources from one country to another. Foreign aid can take many forms, including economic aid, military aid, and humanitarian aid. While foreign aid can provide much-needed resources to developing countries, it can also create dependency and undermine the recipient country's ability to develop sustainable economic growth.

Benefits and Risks of Currency Exchange and Foreign Investment

Currency exchange and foreign investment can bring significant benefits to both individuals and countries, including increased trade, economic growth, and access to new markets and resources. However, these activities are also subject to significant risks, including currency risk, political risk, and regulatory risk.

Currency risk refers to the risk of loss due to changes in exchange rates. For example, if an investor purchases stocks in a foreign country and the value of the foreign currency declines, the investor will experience a loss when the investment is converted back into the investor's home currency.

Political risk refers to the risk of loss due to political events, such as changes in government policies, civil unrest, or war. Political risk can have a significant impact on currency exchange and foreign investment. For example, a change in government policy regarding trade or investment can cause currency values to fluctuate rapidly, leading to losses for investors who have not adequately hedged their positions. Civil unrest or political instability in a foreign country can also have a negative impact on currency exchange rates, as investors may become wary of investing in that country and seek safer investment opportunities elsewhere.

In addition to political risk, investors must also be aware of economic risk when investing in foreign currencies. Economic risk refers to the risk of loss due to changes in economic conditions, such as inflation, interest rates, and economic growth. These factors can have a significant impact on currency exchange rates, as they can affect the demand for a particular currency. For example, if a country experiences high inflation, its currency may depreciate in value as investors lose confidence in its purchasing power.

Investors must also consider the role of central banks in foreign currency exchange and investment. Central banks have a significant impact on currency exchange rates, as they control the money supply and set interest rates. For example, if a central bank raises interest rates, it may strengthen the value of the country's currency, as higher interest rates can make it more attractive for investors to hold that currency. Conversely, if a central bank lowers interest rates, it may weaken the value of the currency.

Another factor that investors must consider when investing in foreign currencies is the impact of global events on currency exchange rates. Global events, such as natural disasters, political crises, or economic downturns, can have a significant impact on currency exchange rates. For example, the COVID-19 pandemic caused a significant drop in the value of many currencies, as investors became increasingly risk-averse and sought safe-haven assets.

Investors must also consider the impact of currency exchange rates on their foreign investments. Currency exchange rates can have a significant impact on the returns of foreign investments, as gains or losses in the foreign currency must be converted back into the investor's home currency. For example, if an investor holds a foreign stock that increases in value by 10%, but the value of the foreign currency depreciates by 5% relative to the investor's home currency, the investor's overall return will only be 5%.

To mitigate the risks associated with currency exchange and foreign investment, investors can use a range of strategies, such as hedging, diversification, and careful research and analysis. Hedging involves taking positions in the foreign exchange market that offset the risk of losses in other investments. Diversification involves spreading investments across different asset classes and currencies to reduce the impact of any single event. Research and analysis involve carefully assessing the political, economic, and market conditions in the countries where an investor plans to invest, in order to make informed decisions about currency exchange and foreign investment.

Conclusion:

In conclusion, currency exchange and foreign investment can be complex and risky, with a range of factors influencing currency exchange rates and investment returns. Investors must be aware of the risks associated with political, economic, and global events, as well as the impact of central banks on currency exchange rates. To mitigate these risks, investors can use a range of strategies, such as hedging, diversification, and careful research and analysis. By carefully managing their currency exchange and foreign investment portfolios, investors can potentially achieve strong returns while minimizing their exposure to risk.

I. The importance of currency exchange

Currency exchange is an essential aspect of the global economy, facilitating trade and investment across borders. It is the process of converting one currency into another, which enables international transactions to take place. Currency exchange is important for businesses, investors, and individuals who engage in cross-border transactions, as it allows them to buy and sell goods and services, invest in foreign assets, or travel abroad. The exchange rate, which is the value of one currency in terms of another, plays a critical role in currency exchange, and its fluctuations can have a significant impact on the economy. This chapter will explore the importance of currency exchange and its role in the global economy.

The role of currency exchange in the global economy:

Currency exchange is a vital component of the global economy as it enables international transactions to occur. The exchange of currencies is essential for businesses and investors who engage in cross-border transactions, as it allows them to buy and sell goods and services, invest in foreign assets, or travel abroad. Currency exchange plays a crucial role in facilitating international trade, as it allows businesses to pay for goods and services in different currencies. This, in turn, helps to promote trade between countries and boosts economic growth.

Currency exchange is also important for investors who seek to invest in foreign assets. When investors purchase foreign stocks, bonds, or real estate, they must first exchange their domestic currency for the currency of the country in which they are investing. Currency exchange rates can significantly impact the returns on these investments, and therefore, it is essential for investors to pay close attention to currency exchange rates when making investment decisions.

Individuals who travel abroad also require currency exchange services to convert their domestic currency into the currency of the country they are visiting. Currency exchange services are available at airports, banks, and foreign exchange bureaus, allowing travelers to obtain the currency they need for their trip.

Factors affecting currency exchange rates:

The exchange rate, which is the value of one currency in terms of another, is determined by a range of factors, including supply and demand, economic indicators, and geopolitical events. Currency exchange rates are constantly fluctuating, and these fluctuations can have a significant impact on the economy.

Supply and demand:

The most critical factor that affects currency exchange rates is supply and demand. When there is a high demand for a particular currency, its value increases, and when there is a low demand, its value decreases. Similarly, when there is a high supply of a currency, its value decreases, and when there is a low supply, its value increases. The supply and demand for a currency are influenced by a range of factors, including trade flows, investment flows, and tourism.

Economic indicators:

Economic indicators, such as interest rates, inflation, and employment data, can also impact currency exchange rates. For example, if a country raises interest rates, its currency may strengthen as foreign investors seek higher returns on their investments. Similarly, if a country has high inflation, its currency may weaken as it becomes less attractive to foreign investors.

Geopolitical events:

Geopolitical events, such as political unrest or changes in government policies, can also impact currency exchange rates. For example, if a country experiences civil unrest or political instability, its currency may weaken as investors become concerned about the country's economic prospects. Similarly, changes in government policies, such as trade tariffs or tax policies, can impact currency exchange rates by affecting trade flows and investment flows.

The impact of currency exchange on the economy:

Currency exchange rates can have a significant impact on the economy, as they affect international trade, investment, and tourism. Fluctuations in exchange rates can impact the competitiveness of a country's exports, making them more or less expensive for foreign buyers. For example, if a country's currency appreciates, its exports become more expensive, making them less competitive in international markets and potentially decreasing demand for them. This can lead to a decrease in export revenue and ultimately negatively affect the country's balance of payments.

On the other hand, a depreciating currency can make a country's exports more competitive, potentially increasing demand for them and boosting export revenue. However, this can also lead to inflation as imported goods become more expensive.

Currency exchange rates can also impact international investment. Investors are likely to invest in countries with strong currencies, as these currencies provide a stable and secure investment environment. Conversely, countries with weak currencies may be perceived as more risky, potentially discouraging investment. Additionally, fluctuations in currency exchange rates can impact the value of foreign investments. For example, if an investor has invested in a foreign currency that depreciates, the value of their investment decreases.

Tourism is another area that can be impacted by currency exchange rates. When a country's currency appreciates, it can become more expensive for tourists to visit, potentially decreasing tourism revenue. On the other hand, a depreciating currency can make a country more affordable for tourists, potentially increasing tourism revenue.

Overall, the impact of currency exchange rates on the economy is complex and multifaceted. It can impact a range of areas, including international trade, investment, and tourism. As such, it is important for individuals and businesses to stay informed about currency exchange rates and the factors that influence them.

Factors that influence currency exchange rates:

There are a range of factors that can influence currency exchange rates, including:

Economic fundamentals: The strength of a country's economy, including factors such as inflation, interest rates, and GDP, can impact currency exchange rates. Countries with strong economic fundamentals are likely to have strong currencies, while those with weak economic fundamentals may have weaker currencies.

Political stability: Political stability can impact currency exchange rates, as uncertainty can lead to a decrease in demand for a country's currency. Additionally, changes in government policies can also impact currency exchange rates.

Market sentiment: Market sentiment, or the overall mood of investors, can impact currency exchange rates. For example, if investors are optimistic about a country's economic prospects, demand for its currency may increase, leading to an appreciation in its value.

International trade and investment: International trade and investment can also impact currency exchange rates, as demand for a country's currency can be influenced by the amount of goods and services it exports and the level of foreign investment it attracts.

Speculation: Finally, speculation can also impact currency exchange rates. Traders may speculate on the future value of a currency based on a range of factors, including economic and political developments, and this can impact its value in the short term.

Conclusion:

In conclusion, currency exchange rates play a significant role in the global economy. They impact international trade, investment, and tourism, and fluctuations in exchange rates can have both positive and negative effects on these areas. There are a range of factors that can influence currency exchange rates, including economic fundamentals, political stability, market sentiment, international trade and investment, and speculation. As such, it is important for individuals and businesses to stay informed about these factors and their potential impact on currency exchange rates.

II. The benefits and challenges of foreign investment

Foreign investment is the process of investing in foreign assets or operations, including stocks, bonds, real estate, and businesses. Foreign investment has become an increasingly important part of the global economy, with the flow of capital across borders increasing significantly in recent years. While foreign investment can offer significant benefits, it also presents a number of challenges and risks. In this section, we will explore the benefits and challenges of foreign investment, and provide insights from various fields, such as investment banking, actuarial science, portfolio management, quantitative analysis, securities trading, financial planning, and financial analysis.

Benefits of foreign investment:

Diversification of portfolio:
Foreign investment allows investors to diversify their portfolio by investing in different markets, sectors, and asset classes. This can help reduce the risk of losses due to market volatility, economic downturns, or other factors that may affect specific industries or regions. For example, an investor in the United States who has a portfolio of only U.S. stocks may face significant losses if the U.S. economy experiences a recession. However, by diversifying their portfolio to include foreign stocks, bonds, or real estate, the investor may be able to offset those losses with gains in other markets.

Access to new markets and growth opportunities:
Foreign investment provides investors with access to new markets and growth opportunities, which may not be available in their home country. For example, an investor in the United States may be able to invest in emerging markets such as China, India, or Brazil, which offer high growth potential due to their large populations, growing middle classes, and expanding economies. By investing in these markets, the investor may be able to capture higher returns than they would be able to achieve in their home market.

Currency diversification:
Foreign investment also allows investors to diversify their currency exposure, which can help reduce the risk of currency fluctuations. For example, an investor in the United States who invests only in U.S. assets may face losses if the U.S. dollar depreciates against other currencies, such as the Euro or Yen. However, by investing in foreign assets denominated in different currencies, the investor can offset those losses with gains in other currencies.

Access to specialized knowledge and expertise:
Foreign investment can provide investors with access to specialized knowledge and expertise, which may not be available in their home country. For example, an investor in the United States who invests in a foreign company may gain access to the company's expertise in a particular industry or technology, which may not be available in the U.S. By leveraging this expertise, the investor may be able to make better investment decisions and achieve higher returns.

Challenges of foreign investment:

Political risk:
One of the major challenges of foreign investment is political risk, which refers to the risk of loss due to political events, such as changes in government policies, civil unrest, or war. Political risk can have a significant impact on foreign investments, as it can lead to expropriation of assets, loss of contracts, or other forms of financial loss. For example, an investor in Venezuela may face significant losses due to the country's political instability, currency devaluation, and expropriation of assets by the government.

Currency risk:
Another challenge of foreign investment is currency risk, which refers to the risk of loss due to currency fluctuations. Currency risk can affect the returns of foreign investments, as gains in one currency may be offset by losses in another. For example, an investor in the United States who invests in a foreign stock may face losses if the foreign currency depreciates against the U.S. dollar.

Regulatory risk:

Regulatory risk refers to the risk of loss due to changes in laws or regulations in foreign markets. Regulatory risk can have a significant impact on foreign investors, as it can affect the profitability and viability of their investments. For example, if a foreign government introduces new regulations that restrict foreign ownership or impose higher taxes on foreign investments, it could significantly impact the returns of foreign investors in that market. In extreme cases, regulatory risk can even lead to expropriation of assets, where a government seizes the assets of foreign investors without compensation.

One example of regulatory risk impacting foreign investment is the changes made by the Chinese government to its foreign investment laws in recent years. In 2018, China passed the Foreign Investment Law, which aimed to create a more level playing field for foreign investors in China. However, some analysts have noted that the law is still somewhat vague and could be subject to interpretation by local authorities, leading to uncertainty for foreign investors.

Another example of regulatory risk is the increasing trend towards protectionism and anti-globalization policies in some countries. For example, in the United States, there has been a push to renegotiate or withdraw from certain trade agreements, such as the North American Free Trade Agreement (NAFTA) and the Trans-Pacific Partnership (TPP). These actions could potentially impact foreign investment in the US, as well as US investment in other countries.

Operational risk:

Operational risk refers to the risk of loss due to internal or external factors that impact the operations of a company. In the context of foreign investment, operational risk can include issues such as supply chain disruptions, cyber attacks, or natural disasters. For example, a company that relies on a specific supplier in a foreign market may be impacted if that supplier experiences a disruption due to a natural disaster or political instability.

Another example of operational risk is cyber attacks, which can be particularly damaging to companies that operate in multiple countries. In 2017, the WannaCry ransomware attack impacted companies and organizations around the world, highlighting the vulnerability of companies to cyber threats. Companies that operate in multiple countries may be particularly vulnerable to cyber attacks, as they may have different systems and processes in place in each country.

Environmental risk:

Environmental risk refers to the risk of loss due to environmental factors, such as climate change, natural disasters, or pollution. In the context of foreign investment, environmental risk can impact companies in a number of ways. For example, a company that operates in a country with high levels of air pollution may face reputational risk if it is seen as contributing to the problem. Similarly, a company that operates in a region prone to natural disasters may face operational risk if its facilities are damaged or destroyed in a disaster.

Climate change is an increasingly important environmental risk for foreign investors to consider. As the effects of climate change become more apparent, governments around the world are introducing new regulations to reduce greenhouse gas emissions and promote sustainability. Companies that do not adapt to these changing regulations may face regulatory risk, as well as reputational risk if they are seen as contributing to climate change.

Conclusion:

Foreign investment can bring significant benefits to both investors and the countries in which they invest. However, it is important for investors to be aware of the risks involved in foreign investment, including political, economic, regulatory, operational, and environmental risks. By understanding and managing these risks, investors can maximize their returns while minimizing their exposure to potential losses.

III. The role of exchange rates in the global economy

Exchange rates are a crucial component of the global economy, playing a key role in international trade, investment, and financial transactions. In this section, we will explore the various ways in which exchange rates impact the global economy, including the effects on trade balances, inflation, and financial stability. We will also examine the role of exchange rate policy and the challenges faced by policymakers in managing exchange rates in a globalized world.

The Impact of Exchange Rates on Trade:

Exchange rates play a critical role in determining the competitiveness of a country's exports in international markets. When a country's currency appreciates, its exports become more expensive for foreign buyers, while imports become cheaper for domestic consumers. This can lead to a trade deficit, as the country imports more than it exports. On the other hand, when a country's currency depreciates, its exports become cheaper, making them more competitive in international markets. This can lead to a trade surplus, as the country exports more than it imports.

For example, suppose the United States dollar (USD) appreciates relative to the euro (EUR). In this case, U.S. exports become more expensive for European buyers, while European imports become cheaper for U.S. consumers. This can lead to a decrease in U.S. exports and an increase in imports, resulting in a trade deficit.

Conversely, suppose the USD depreciates relative to the EUR. In this case, U.S. exports become cheaper for European buyers, while European imports become more expensive for U.S. consumers. This can lead to an increase in U.S. exports and a decrease in imports, resulting in a trade surplus.

Exchange Rates and Inflation:

Exchange rates also play a significant role in determining the inflation rate in a country. When a country's currency depreciates, the prices of imported goods increase, which can lead to higher inflation. This is because the cost of production for domestic producers also increases, as they require more expensive imported inputs. On the other hand, when a country's currency appreciates, the prices of imported goods decrease, which can lead to lower inflation.

For example, suppose the Japanese yen (JPY) appreciates relative to the USD. In this case, the prices of Japanese imports to the U.S. decrease, making them cheaper for U.S. consumers. This can lead to lower inflation in the U.S. Conversely, suppose the JPY depreciates relative to the USD. In this case, the prices of Japanese imports to the U.S. increase, making them more expensive for U.S. consumers. This can lead to higher inflation in the U.S.

Exchange Rates and Financial Stability:

Exchange rates can also impact the stability of the global financial system. Large and rapid fluctuations in exchange rates can lead to significant losses for investors and financial institutions. This can lead to a contagion effect, where financial instability in one country spreads to other countries and regions.

For example, suppose a country experiences a sudden currency devaluation due to a financial crisis. This can lead to a significant loss for foreign investors who hold assets denominated in that currency. This, in turn, can lead to a loss of confidence in that country's financial system, which can spread to other countries and regions.

Exchange Rate Policy and Challenges:

Exchange rate policy refers to the actions taken by policymakers to manage exchange rates in their respective countries. This can include interventions in foreign exchange markets, changes in interest rates, and the use of capital controls.

One of the challenges faced by policymakers in managing exchange rates is the potential for trade-offs between different policy objectives. For example, a central bank may want to lower interest rates to stimulate economic growth, but doing so may also lead to a depreciation in the currency, which can increase inflation and reduce the competitiveness of exports.

Another challenge is the potential for currency manipulation,Another challenge associated with exchange rates in the global economy is the potential for currency manipulation. Currency manipulation occurs when a country artificially lowers the value of its currency in order to make its exports cheaper and more competitive in foreign markets. This can be achieved through a variety of methods, such as buying foreign currency, lowering interest rates, or imposing capital controls.

Currency manipulation is often seen as a form of unfair trade practice, as it can harm the competitiveness of other countries' exports and result in trade imbalances. For example, if a country artificially devalues its currency, it can make its exports cheaper, which may lead to an increase in demand for those products at the expense of other countries' exports. This can lead to a trade surplus for the country engaging in currency manipulation, while other countries may experience trade deficits.

The impact of currency manipulation on the global economy can be significant. In some cases, it can lead to a race to the bottom, where countries engage in a cycle of devaluing their currencies in order to gain a competitive advantage. This can result in a destabilization of exchange rates and cause uncertainty in the global economy.

In response to currency manipulation, countries may take various measures to protect their economies. For example, they may impose trade tariffs or other trade barriers to limit the imports of artificially cheap products. They may also engage in their own currency manipulation to counteract the effects of other countries' actions.

The role of exchange rates in the global economy is also closely tied to international finance. The exchange rate of a currency can have a significant impact on international investments and capital flows. For example, if a country's currency appreciates, it may become more attractive for foreign investors to invest in that country, as they can earn a higher return due to the increased value of the currency. Conversely, if a currency depreciates, foreign investors may be less likely to invest in that country, as they may face a lower return due to the decreased value of the currency.

Exchange rates can also impact the borrowing and lending decisions of international investors. For example, if a foreign investor is borrowing in a currency that is appreciating, they may face a higher repayment amount due to the increased value of that currency. Similarly, if a foreign investor is lending in a currency that is depreciating, they may face a lower repayment amount due to the decreased value of that currency.

In addition to the impact on international investments, exchange rates can also have implications for international trade. As mentioned earlier, fluctuations in exchange rates can impact the competitiveness of a country's exports. This can have implications for the balance of trade between countries, as countries with more competitive exports may experience a trade surplus, while countries with less competitive exports may experience a trade deficit.

Furthermore, exchange rates can impact the tourism industry. A weaker currency can make a country more attractive to foreign tourists, as they can get more for their money. This can lead to an increase in tourism and boost the economy of the country in question. On the other hand, a stronger currency can make a country less attractive to foreign tourists, as their money may not go as far.

In conclusion, exchange rates play a crucial role in the global economy, impacting international trade, investment, and finance. Fluctuations in exchange rates can have significant implications for the competitiveness of countries' exports, as well as the borrowing and lending decisions of international investors. Additionally, the potential for currency manipulation and the impact on the tourism industry further highlight the importance of understanding the role of exchange rates in the global economy.

PART VIII: BEHAVIORAL FINANCE

Finance has long been considered a field of numbers and objective analysis. However, recent research has shown that our emotions, biases, and cognitive limitations also play a significant role in our financial decision-making. This realization has given rise to a new field of study called behavioral finance, which explores the psychological factors that affect our financial choices and market outcomes.

In this section, we will delve into the world of behavioral finance, exploring its origins, key concepts, and future implications. We will begin by examining the psychology of finance, looking at how our emotions and thought processes can lead to irrational behavior and financial mistakes. We will then explore the role of emotions in financial decision-making, delving into the ways in which feelings like fear, greed, and overconfidence can impact investment decisions.

Next, we will examine the field of behavioral finance itself, looking at how it has emerged as a response to the shortcomings of traditional finance theory. We will explore the key concepts of behavioral finance, such as heuristics, biases, and framing effects, and discuss how these factors can impact investment strategies and market outcomes.

Finally, we will look to the future of behavioral finance, exploring the implications of this growing field for investors, financial professionals, and policymakers. We will examine the potential for new investment strategies and financial products that are designed to incorporate insights from behavioral finance. We will also consider the potential for behavioral finance to inform policy decisions, helping to create more efficient and effective financial markets.

Throughout this section, we will draw on a range of examples and perspectives from professionals in the financial industry, including investment bankers, actuaries, portfolio managers, quantitative analysts, securities traders, financial planners, and financial analysts. We will also consider counter-arguments and dissenting opinions, striving to present a balanced and objective view of this important and rapidly-evolving field.

By the end of this section, readers will have a comprehensive understanding of the role of psychology and behavior in finance, and the potential implications of this understanding for investors, financial professionals, and policymakers alike.

CHAPTER 28: THE PSYCHOLOGY OF FINANCE

Understanding the psychology of finance is crucial for making informed investment decisions. This chapter aims to provide an overview of the psychological factors that influence financial decision-making. It will examine how cognitive biases, emotions, and personality traits affect investors' behavior, leading to suboptimal investment decisions. The chapter will also explore the implications of psychological factors for investment professionals and their clients.

Importance of understanding the psychology of finance:

Investors are not always rational when making investment decisions. Instead, they are often influenced by psychological factors, such as cognitive biases and emotions, which can lead to suboptimal investment choices. For example, investors may hold onto losing investments because of a psychological bias called "loss aversion." Loss aversion refers to the tendency to avoid losses more than to acquire gains, even if the potential gains outweigh the losses. This bias can lead investors to hold onto losing stocks for too long, resulting in a significant loss.

In addition to cognitive biases, emotions play a critical role in financial decision-making. For instance, fear and greed can influence investors to buy or sell assets in response to market fluctuations, leading to impulsive decisions. Understanding how emotions affect investment decisions can help investors make rational decisions and avoid costly mistakes.

Personality traits also influence financial decision-making. For example, risk tolerance, overconfidence, and self-control are key personality traits that impact investment choices. Individuals with a high level of risk tolerance may be more willing to invest in high-risk assets, while those with low risk tolerance may prefer low-risk investments. Overconfidence can lead to overtrading, while a lack of self-control can result in impulsive investment decisions.

Overall, understanding the psychological factors that influence financial decision-making is crucial for making informed investment decisions. This chapter aims to provide a comprehensive overview of the psychology of finance, examining how cognitive biases, emotions, and personality traits affect investment choices. By gaining a deeper understanding of these factors, investors and investment professionals can make more informed investment decisions and avoid costly mistakes.

II. Theoretical Frameworks

Theoretical frameworks are essential tools for organizing and understanding complex phenomena in various disciplines. A theoretical framework provides a set of concepts, assumptions, and propositions that help to explain, predict, and control phenomena under investigation. In the field of finance, theoretical frameworks help to explain how financial markets work, how individuals make financial decisions, and how financial institutions operate. This section will provide an overview of theoretical frameworks and their importance in the field of finance.

Overview of Theoretical Frameworks:

Theoretical frameworks provide a lens through which we can view the world and make sense of it. They offer a way to systematically organize and analyze information, identify relationships between variables, and generate new insights. Theoretical frameworks can be used to explain why certain phenomena occur, make predictions about future outcomes, and suggest ways to improve existing processes. In finance, theoretical frameworks are used to understand the behavior of financial markets, institutions, and individuals.

The Importance of Theoretical Frameworks in Finance:

Theoretical frameworks are important in finance for several reasons. First, they provide a way to organize and make sense of complex financial phenomena. Financial markets and institutions are highly complex systems that involve many actors and interactions. Theoretical frameworks help to identify the key variables and relationships that underlie these systems, making them more understandable and manageable.

Second, theoretical frameworks provide a basis for predicting and controlling financial outcomes. By identifying the key variables that influence financial outcomes, theoretical frameworks can be used to make predictions about future outcomes and develop strategies to improve them. For example, a theoretical framework that explains how interest rates influence economic growth can be used to develop policies that promote economic growth.

Third, theoretical frameworks help to generate new insights and innovations in finance. By providing a structured way to analyze financial phenomena, theoretical frameworks can reveal new patterns and relationships that were previously unknown. These insights can lead to new financial products, investment strategies, and business models that can drive growth and innovation in the industry.

Examples of Theoretical Frameworks in Finance:

There are many theoretical frameworks that are used in finance. Some of the most important ones include:

Modern Portfolio Theory (MPT): MPT is a framework for constructing portfolios that maximize expected returns for a given level of risk. It is based on the principle of diversification, which suggests that by investing in a variety of assets, investors can reduce their overall risk.

Efficient Market Hypothesis (EMH): EMH is a framework that suggests that financial markets are efficient and that all available information is already reflected in market prices. This means that it is not possible to consistently outperform the market by using publicly available information.

Behavioral Finance: Behavioral finance is a framework that combines insights from psychology and finance to explain how individuals make financial decisions. It suggests that individuals are not always rational and may be influenced by emotions, biases, and other factors when making financial decisions.

Conclusion:

Theoretical frameworks are essential tools for organizing and understanding complex financial phenomena. They provide a structured way to analyze financial systems, make predictions about future outcomes, and generate new insights and innovations. In the following sections, we will explore some of the most important theoretical frameworks in finance and how they are used to explain financial phenomena.

Prospect theory

Prospect theory is a behavioral economic theory that describes how people make decisions in situations involving uncertainty. It was first proposed by psychologists Daniel Kahneman and Amos Tversky in 1979 and has since become a key concept in economics and finance. The theory suggests that people are not always rational in their decision-making and are influenced by psychological factors such as risk aversion, loss aversion, and reference points. This essay will provide a thorough analysis of prospect theory, including its origins, key concepts, and implications for decision-making in various fields.

Origins of Prospect Theory:

Prospect theory was developed in response to the limitations of expected utility theory, the traditional economic theory of decision-making under uncertainty. Expected utility theory assumes that individuals make rational decisions based on the expected utility or payoff of each outcome. However, Kahneman and Tversky found that people often deviate from this rational decision-making process in predictable ways.

The research that led to the development of prospect theory began in the 1970s, when Kahneman and Tversky began investigating the way people make decisions under risk. They found that people's choices were influenced by factors such as the probability of a particular outcome, the potential payoff, and the reference point or status quo.

Key Concepts of Prospect Theory:

The main concepts of prospect theory are value function, reference point, and loss aversion. The value function describes how individuals perceive the value of potential outcomes. It shows that people are risk-averse when it comes to gains but risk-seeking when it comes to losses. This means that people are more likely to take risks to avoid losses than to achieve gains of the same magnitude.

The reference point is a critical component of prospect theory because it helps to determine whether an outcome is perceived as a gain or a loss. The reference point can be thought of as the status quo or the starting point from which people evaluate potential outcomes. For example, if an individual is offered a $50 raise, they might perceive this as a gain if their current salary is $40,000, but as a loss if their current salary is $60,000.

Loss aversion is another key concept in prospect theory. It refers to the tendency of people to feel the pain of losses more intensely than the pleasure of gains of the same magnitude. This means that people are more likely to be motivated by avoiding losses than by achieving gains.

Implications of Prospect Theory:

Prospect theory has important implications for decision-making in various fields, including finance, marketing, and public policy. In finance, prospect theory helps explain why investors might hold onto losing investments even when it would be rational to sell them. Loss aversion causes investors to hold onto losing investments because the pain of realizing a loss is greater than the potential gain from selling the investment.

In marketing, prospect theory can be used to influence consumer behavior by framing choices in terms of gains or losses. For example, a company might offer a discount on a product as a gain, rather than charging a higher price as a loss. This can make the product more attractive to consumers.

In public policy, prospect theory can help policymakers understand how people make decisions about risk and uncertainty. For example, loss aversion can help explain why people might be hesitant to take action to address climate change, even when the potential costs of inaction are high.

Conclusion:

Prospect theory is a fundamental concept in behavioral economics that helps explain why people are not always rational in their decision-making. By understanding the key concepts of prospect theory, including the value function, reference point, and loss aversion, decision-makers in various fields can make more informed choices. The implications of prospect theory are far-reaching and have important implications for finance, marketing, and public policy.

Mental accounting

In the world of finance, people are expected to make rational decisions, taking into account all relevant factors and making optimal choices that will maximize their gains. However, in reality, people often make irrational decisions, driven by emotions, biases, and cognitive limitations. One such phenomenon is mental accounting, which refers to the tendency of people to categorize their money into separate mental accounts and treat each account differently, leading to suboptimal financial decisions. This section will provide a comprehensive analysis of mental accounting, including its definition, theoretical foundations, empirical evidence, and practical implications.

Overview of Mental Accounting:

Mental accounting refers to the cognitive process by which individuals categorize and evaluate financial outcomes based on their source, timing, and intended use, rather than their economic value. According to mental accounting theory, people create separate mental accounts for different sources of income, expenses, and assets, such as salary, bonus, savings, investments, debt, and gifts. Each mental account is subject to its own set of rules, preferences, and emotions, and people tend to treat the money in each account differently, based on their mental accounting principles. For instance, people may be more willing to spend money from a bonus account than a savings account, or to pay off a low-interest debt with a high-interest credit card balance, based on their mental accounting criteria.

Theoretical Foundations:

Mental accounting theory is based on the concepts of prospect theory, which posits that people evaluate financial outcomes in terms of gains and losses relative to a reference point, and diminishing marginal utility, which suggests that the value of a dollar decreases as the wealth of an individual increases. According to prospect theory, people are risk-averse when it comes to gains and risk-seeking when it comes to losses, leading to the framing effect, whereby the way information is presented affects their decision-making. For example, people may be more likely to choose a sure gain over a risky gain and a risky loss over a sure loss, depending on how the options are framed. Mental accounting adds to this by suggesting that people create separate accounts for gains and losses and evaluate them differently, leading to inconsistencies in their decision-making.

Empirical Evidence:

Numerous studies have provided empirical evidence for the existence of mental accounting and its impact on financial decisions. For example, Thaler (1985) showed that people are more likely to spend unexpected income, such as a tax refund, on luxury items rather than necessities, as they perceive it as "free money" and not part of their regular income. Similarly, Tversky and Kahneman (1986) found that people are more likely to save money in a separate account for emergencies rather than using it to pay off high-interest debt, even though the economic value of both actions is the same. In another study, Heath and Soll (1996) showed that people are more likely to pay for an expensive item with a credit card if it is divided into smaller monthly payments, even though the total cost is higher due to interest charges.

Practical Implications:

Understanding mental accounting can have significant practical implications for individuals and organizations involved in financial decision-making. For example, financial advisors can use mental accounting principles to help their clients make better investment decisions by framing the options in a way that aligns with their mental accounts. Similarly, banks and credit card companies can design their products and services to appeal to consumers' mental accounting biases, such as offering rewards and bonuses for specific types of purchases or using color-coding and labeling to differentiate between different types of expenses. Finally, individuals can improve their own financial decision-making by being aware of their mental accounting biases and consciously trying to integrate all relevant factors into their overall financial plan.

Conclusion:

In conclusion, mental accounting is a cognitive bias that affects how people categorize and evaluate their money, leading to suboptimal financial decisions. It can have significant implications for individual investors, as well as financial institutions and policymakers who design and market financial products.

Despite the prevalence of mental accounting, there are ways to mitigate its effects. One approach is to increase financial literacy and awareness of cognitive biases, so individuals can recognize when they are engaging in mental accounting and make more rational decisions. This could be done through education and training programs, as well as through the design of financial products and services that incorporate behavioral insights.

Another approach is to design financial products and services that are more aligned with the way people naturally think about money. For example, instead of offering a single savings account with a uniform interest rate, financial institutions could offer multiple accounts with different interest rates, each designated for a specific financial goal. This approach would make it easier for individuals to mentally segregate their money and avoid commingling funds.

In addition, policymakers could play a role in mitigating the effects of mental accounting by regulating financial products and services to prevent deceptive marketing practices that exploit cognitive biases. They could also encourage the development of financial products that are more aligned with the way people naturally think about money, and invest in research to better understand how cognitive biases affect financial decision-making.

Overall, mental accounting is a complex and important phenomenon that has significant implications for personal finance, financial institutions, and public policy. By understanding the cognitive biases that underlie mental accounting and developing strategies to mitigate its effects, individuals and institutions can make more informed financial decisions and improve their overall financial well-being.

Loss aversion

Loss aversion is a cognitive bias that has been studied extensively in the field of behavioral finance. It refers to the tendency of people to feel the pain of losses more intensely than the pleasure of gains. In other words, people are more likely to take risks to avoid losses than to seek gains. This bias can have significant implications for financial decision making, as it can lead individuals to make suboptimal investment choices.

In this section, we will explore loss aversion in detail. We will begin by discussing the origin of this bias and the theoretical underpinnings that explain its persistence. We will then examine the various ways in which loss aversion manifests itself in financial decision making, including the endowment effect, status quo bias, and the sunk cost fallacy. Finally, we will explore strategies that can help individuals overcome loss aversion and make better financial decisions.

Theoretical Framework:

Loss aversion is a key concept in prospect theory, which is a behavioral economics theory developed by Kahneman and Tversky in 1979. Prospect theory proposes that people evaluate losses and gains relative to a reference point, which is often the status quo. In other words, people perceive losses and gains differently depending on their starting point. They experience more pain from losses than pleasure from gains of equal magnitude.

Prospect theory also suggests that people are risk averse when considering gains, but risk-seeking when considering losses. For example, individuals may be more willing to take risks to avoid a loss than to achieve a gain. This phenomenon is known as the "reflection effect," which describes the tendency for people to exhibit opposite risk preferences when considering gains versus losses.

One of the key drivers of loss aversion is the emotional response to losses. Research has shown that losses activate the amygdala, a part of the brain associated with negative emotions such as fear and anxiety. In contrast, gains activate the striatum, a part of the brain associated with positive emotions such as pleasure and reward. This suggests that losses are more salient and impactful than gains, and that the emotional response to losses is more intense.

Manifestations of Loss Aversion:

Loss aversion manifests itself in various ways in financial decision making. One of the most well-known examples is the endowment effect, which describes the tendency for people to place a higher value on something they own compared to something they do not own. This effect can lead to suboptimal investment decisions, as individuals may be reluctant to sell assets even if they are not performing well, simply because they feel a loss would be more painful than a gain.

Another manifestation of loss aversion is the status quo bias, which describes the tendency for people to prefer the current state of affairs over change, even if the change would be beneficial. This bias can lead to inertia in investment decisions, as individuals may be reluctant to sell or reallocate assets even if the current allocation is not performing well, simply because they are attached to the current state of affairs.

The sunk cost fallacy is another manifestation of loss aversion. This bias describes the tendency for people to continue investing in a project or asset simply because they have already invested a significant amount of resources, even if it is clear that the investment is unlikely to be profitable. This bias can lead to irrational decision making and can result in significant losses.

Strategies for Overcoming Loss Aversion:

Despite its prevalence, loss aversion can be overcome with the right strategies. One such strategy is to reframe losses as opportunities for learning and growth. By shifting the focus away from the pain of losses and towards the potential for future gains, individuals can become more comfortable taking risks and making investment decisions that may result in short-term losses but long-term gains.

Another strategy is to use mental accounting to separate gains and losses into different mental buckets. By doing so, individuals can focus on the gains and minimize the impact of losses, making them less averse to the latter. For example, investors might consider separating their portfolios into different mental accounts based on risk tolerance or investment goals. This can help them view losses in one account as a natural part of the investment process and not necessarily indicative of their overall financial situation.

Another approach is to use diversification to mitigate the impact of losses. Diversification involves spreading investments across a variety of asset classes, industries, and geographies to reduce the impact of any single investment's performance. This can help to minimize the impact of any one loss and maintain a more stable portfolio overall. Diversification is a common strategy used by professional investors such as portfolio managers, who may spread investments across hundreds or thousands of different stocks, bonds, and other assets to reduce the risk of significant losses.

Finally, one effective strategy for overcoming loss aversion is to seek the advice of a financial professional. Financial advisors and wealth managers are trained to help clients navigate the complexities of investing and to provide guidance on how to build and manage a successful portfolio. By working with a professional, individuals can receive personalized advice tailored to their unique financial situation and investment goals, which can help them overcome their biases and make better investment decisions.

In conclusion, loss aversion is a powerful cognitive bias that can lead individuals to make poor investment decisions based on their fear of losses. However, by understanding the underlying causes of this bias and adopting strategies such as reframing losses as opportunities, using mental accounting to minimize the impact of losses, diversifying investments, and seeking the advice of a professional, investors can overcome loss aversion and build successful portfolios that meet their long-term financial goals.

Overconfidence bias

Overconfidence bias is a cognitive bias that occurs when people overestimate their own abilities or the accuracy of their beliefs and predictions. This bias is pervasive across a wide range of domains, from financial decision-making to political forecasting to sports betting. Overconfidence bias can lead to poor decision-making, as people may take excessive risks or make unrealistic assumptions based on their inflated sense of confidence.

This essay will provide an in-depth analysis of overconfidence bias, its causes, consequences, and strategies for overcoming it. It will also draw on examples from various fields, including investment banking, actuarial science, portfolio management, quantitative analysis, securities trading, financial planning, and financial analysis.

Causes of Overconfidence Bias:

One of the main causes of overconfidence bias is a lack of feedback. When people do not receive clear and accurate feedback on their performance or predictions, they may assume that they are doing better than they actually are. This can lead to overconfidence, as they become more confident in their abilities or beliefs without realizing that they are making mistakes.

Another cause of overconfidence bias is the tendency to focus on confirming evidence while ignoring disconfirming evidence. When people seek out information that supports their beliefs or predictions, they may overlook or discount evidence that contradicts them. This can lead to overconfidence, as they become more convinced that they are right without considering alternative perspectives or possibilities.

Consequences of Overconfidence Bias:

The consequences of overconfidence bias can be significant, particularly in the realm of financial decision-making. Overconfidence can lead to excessive risk-taking, as people may assume that they have more control over outcomes than they actually do. This can result in losses, as people may fail to adequately assess the risks and potential downsides of their decisions.

In investment banking, for example, overconfidence can lead to investments in risky ventures that ultimately fail. In actuarial science, overconfidence can lead to underestimation of the probability of negative events, such as natural disasters or economic downturns, resulting in inadequate preparation or response. In portfolio management, overconfidence can lead to concentration in a few high-risk investments, resulting in portfolio losses. In quantitative analysis, overconfidence can lead to the use of flawed models or assumptions, resulting in inaccurate predictions. In securities trading, overconfidence can lead to excessive trading and poor investment performance.

Strategies for Overcoming Overconfidence Bias:

Overcoming overconfidence bias can be challenging, but there are several strategies that can help. One such strategy is to seek out feedback and criticism from others. By soliciting input from people who have different perspectives or expertise, individuals can gain a more accurate understanding of their own abilities and beliefs.

Another strategy is to develop a habit of actively seeking out disconfirming evidence. By intentionally seeking out information that contradicts one's beliefs or predictions, individuals can reduce the impact of confirmation bias and become more open to alternative perspectives and possibilities.

A third strategy is to use probabilistic thinking and decision-making. By acknowledging and quantifying uncertainty, individuals can avoid overconfidence and make more accurate predictions and decisions. For example, in investment banking, probabilities can be used to assess the likelihood of success or failure of a venture. In actuarial science, probabilities can be used to estimate the probability of negative events and their potential impact. In portfolio management, probabilities can be used to assess the risks and potential downsides of different investments. In quantitative analysis, probabilities can be used to model uncertainty and account for potential errors.

Conclusion:

Overconfidence bias is a pervasive and potentially dangerous cognitive bias that can lead to poor decision-making in a wide range of domains. However, by understanding its causes and consequences and using strategies such as seeking out feedback, actively seeking disconfirming evidence, and using probabilistic thinking, individuals can overcome this bias and make more accurate predictions and better decisions.

It is important to note that overconfidence bias can also be exacerbated by group dynamics, such as group polarization and groupthink. In group settings, individuals may be more likely to engage in overconfident behavior and dismiss dissenting opinions in order to maintain group harmony or to conform to the perceived group norm. This can lead to group decision-making that is overly risky or based on incomplete information.

One way to mitigate the negative effects of group dynamics on overconfidence bias is to encourage diverse perspectives and open discussion of conflicting viewpoints. This can help to prevent groupthink and ensure that all relevant information and perspectives are considered before a decision is made. Another strategy is to assign a "devil's advocate" role to a team member who is tasked with challenging assumptions and arguments presented by the group.

In addition to the strategies discussed above, there are also tools and techniques that can help individuals and teams to avoid overconfidence bias in decision-making. For example, probabilistic thinking involves assigning probabilities to different outcomes and considering the range of possible outcomes rather than just focusing on a single outcome. This can help to reduce the impact of overconfidence bias by forcing individuals to consider the possibility of different outcomes and to weigh the potential costs and benefits of each.

Overall, overconfidence bias is a complex and multifaceted cognitive bias that can have significant implications for decision-making in a variety of domains. While it is not always possible to eliminate this bias entirely, by understanding its causes and consequences and using effective strategies and techniques, individuals and teams can minimize its negative effects and make more accurate and effective decisions.

III. Biases and Heuristics

Humans are not perfect decision-makers. We often rely on mental shortcuts and heuristics to make quick and efficient decisions, but these shortcuts can lead to systematic errors in judgment and decision-making. These errors are known as cognitive biases and can have significant implications in a wide range of domains, including finance, medicine, politics, and more.

In the field of finance, cognitive biases can be particularly damaging. Investors who fall prey to these biases may make decisions based on faulty assumptions, leading to poor investment outcomes. In fact, some of the most well-known investment bubbles, such as the dot-com bubble of the late 1990s and the housing market bubble of the mid-2000s, can be traced back to cognitive biases and heuristics that led investors astray.

Despite the potentially negative consequences of cognitive biases, they are an inherent part of the human decision-making process. They are the result of our brains' natural tendency to simplify complex information and patterns, leading to the development of mental shortcuts that allow us to make quick decisions without expending too much cognitive effort.

The study of cognitive biases and heuristics has been a topic of interest for psychologists, economists, and other social scientists for decades. In recent years, however, the field has gained increasing attention from the business and finance communities. This is due in part to the realization that cognitive biases can have significant implications for investment decisions and financial outcomes.

In this article, we will explore some of the most common cognitive biases and heuristics that affect financial decision-making. We will discuss their causes, consequences, and potential strategies for overcoming them. We will also provide examples from a variety of fields, including investment banking, actuarial science, portfolio management, quantitative analysis, securities trading, financial planning, and financial analysis. By the end of this article, readers should have a thorough understanding of the impact of cognitive biases on financial decision-making and the strategies that can be used to mitigate their effects.

Availability heuristic

In our daily lives, we are constantly making decisions based on limited information. Whether we are deciding what to eat for breakfast, what route to take to work, or which stocks to invest in, we rely on our instincts and past experiences to guide our choices. However, these instincts and past experiences are not always reliable, and can often lead us astray. This is where cognitive biases, such as the availability heuristic, come into play.

The availability heuristic is a cognitive bias that occurs when individuals make decisions based on the ease with which examples or instances come to mind. This bias is based on the assumption that if something is easy to remember, it must be more important or more likely to happen than things that are harder to remember.

The availability heuristic has been studied extensively in the field of psychology and has been shown to influence a wide range of judgments and decisions, including those related to financial investments, health behaviors, and legal decisions. In this section, we will explore the concept of availability heuristic in detail, including its causes, consequences, and ways to overcome it.

Causes of Availability Heuristic

The availability heuristic is a natural consequence of the way our brains process and store information. Our brains are wired to process and store information that is relevant to our survival and well-being, and to discard or ignore information that is not. As a result, we tend to remember information that is vivid, emotionally charged, or unique, and to forget information that is mundane or routine.

For example, an investment banker may remember a few high-profile cases in which investments went sour, but forget about the many cases in which investments yielded healthy returns. This bias can lead to overly conservative investment decisions, as the banker may be more likely to focus on the risks rather than the potential rewards.

Another factor that can contribute to availability bias is media coverage. When events are covered extensively in the media, they become more salient and memorable, even if they are rare or unlikely to occur. For example, people may overestimate the risk of plane crashes, despite the fact that they are statistically very unlikely, due to the extensive media coverage given to high-profile crashes.

Consequences of Availability Heuristic

The availability heuristic can lead to a number of negative consequences, particularly when it comes to decision-making. One consequence is that people may make decisions based on incomplete or inaccurate information, leading to poor outcomes. For example, a portfolio manager may decide to invest in a particular stock based on a few recent news articles, without fully researching the company's financials or market position.

Another consequence is that people may overestimate the likelihood of rare or unlikely events, leading to excessive worry or fear. For example, people may avoid flying even though it is statistically safer than driving, due to a perceived risk of plane crashes based on media coverage.

The availability heuristic can also lead to confirmation bias, which is the tendency to seek out and interpret information in a way that confirms preexisting beliefs or hypotheses. For example, an actuary who believes that the company's employee retirement plan is underfunded may selectively focus on information that supports this belief, while ignoring information that suggests the plan is on solid financial footing.

Ways to Overcome Availability Heuristic

Fortunately, there are ways to overcome the availability heuristic and make more informed decisions. One way is to actively seek out and consider information that is less memorable or less vivid, but equally important. For example, a financial analyst may review financial statements and market data in addition to news articles when making investment recommendations.

Another way to overcome availability bias is to use probabilistic thinking, which involves considering the likelihood of various outcomes based on available evidence. For example, a securities trader may estimate the probability of a market downturn based on historical trends and current economic indicators, rather than relying solely on recent news headlines.

In addition, it can be helpful to use decision-making tools such as checklists and decision trees. These tools provide a systematic framework for evaluating different options and considering all relevant factors, rather than relying on the availability of a few salient examples.

Furthermore, seeking out diverse perspectives and opinions can help to counteract the influence of the availability heuristic. This can involve consulting with colleagues, seeking feedback from multiple sources, and actively seeking out dissenting opinions.

Finally, individuals can also take steps to reduce the impact of emotional factors on decision-making. This may involve taking a break before making a decision to allow emotions to subside, or seeking support from a trusted colleague or mentor to help provide a more objective perspective.

Overall, while the availability heuristic can be a powerful influence on decision-making, there are effective strategies for overcoming its limitations. By actively seeking out diverse information, using probabilistic thinking, and using decision-making tools, individuals can make more informed and rational decisions.

Anchoring and adjustment heuristic

When making decisions, people often rely on mental shortcuts, known as heuristics, to simplify the process. However, these heuristics can sometimes lead to biases and errors in judgment. One such heuristic is the anchoring and adjustment heuristic, which involves using an initial reference point, or anchor, to make subsequent judgments or estimates.

Anchoring bias is a cognitive bias in which an individual's judgments or decisions are influenced by an initial piece of information. Once an anchor is established, people tend to adjust their estimates or judgments from the anchor, rather than starting from scratch. This can lead to errors in decision-making, as the anchor may be arbitrary or irrelevant to the decision at hand.

Examples of Anchoring and Adjustment Heuristic:

Anchoring and adjustment heuristic can occur in a variety of settings, including financial decision-making. For example, an investment banker may use the recent stock price of a company as an anchor when estimating the company's future value. This can lead the banker to adjust their estimate of the company's value based on the anchor, rather than starting from scratch and considering all available information.

Similarly, a financial planner may use an initial estimate of a client's retirement savings as an anchor when developing a retirement plan. If the initial estimate is too high or too low, it can lead to errors in the retirement plan, as the planner may not adjust sufficiently based on all available information.

Anchoring and adjustment heuristic can also occur in non-financial settings. For example, a real estate agent may use the initial asking price of a house as an anchor when advising the seller on the sale price. This can lead to an overvaluing or undervaluing of the house, as the agent may not adjust sufficiently based on all available information.

Causes of Anchoring and Adjustment Heuristic:

Anchoring and adjustment heuristic occurs because people tend to rely on the first piece of information they receive when making judgments or decisions. Once an anchor is established, people tend to adjust their estimates or judgments from the anchor, rather than starting from scratch. This can be due to a variety of factors, including cognitive limitations and social influences.

Cognitive limitations can play a role in anchoring and adjustment heuristic. People may not have the time, resources, or mental energy to consider all available information when making decisions. Instead, they rely on heuristics, such as anchoring and adjustment, to simplify the decision-making process.

Social influences can also play a role in anchoring and adjustment heuristic. People may be influenced by the opinions or behavior of others, leading them to adopt the same anchor or adjust their estimates in a similar way. Additionally, people may be influenced by the authority or expertise of the person providing the anchor, leading them to give more weight to the initial information.

Consequences of Anchoring and Adjustment Heuristic:

Anchoring and adjustment heuristic can lead to errors in judgment and decision-making. When people rely too heavily on an anchor, they may fail to consider all available information and make decisions that are not in their best interest.

For example, a portfolio manager may use an initial estimate of a stock's value as an anchor when deciding whether to buy or sell the stock. If the initial estimate is too high, the manager may overvalue the stock and make a poor investment decision. Conversely, if the initial estimate is too low, the manager may undervalue the stock and miss out on potential gains.

Anchoring and adjustment heuristic can also lead to errors in negotiation. When negotiating a price, both parties may use initial offers as anchors, leading to an agreement that is not in either party's best interest. For example, a buyer may start with a low offer, which anchors the seller's expectations and leads them to overvalue their property.

Ways to Overcome Anchoring and Adjustment Heuristic

To overcome the anchoring and adjustment heuristic, it is important to recognize when it may be influencing our judgments and decisions. One way to do this is to question the initial anchor and consider alternative anchors. For example, when negotiating a price, rather than accepting the first offer as the anchor, both parties can agree to consider a range of possible prices and negotiate within that range.

Another way to overcome the anchoring and adjustment heuristic is to use a structured decision-making process that considers multiple sources of information and weighs them appropriately. For example, a portfolio manager may use a decision-making framework that considers both quantitative data, such as financial ratios and market trends, and qualitative data, such as industry analysis and management quality, to make investment decisions.

It is also important to be aware of biases that may influence the initial anchor, such as the framing effect, which refers to the way information is presented or framed influencing how it is perceived. For example, presenting a price as a discount off of a higher price may lead individuals to perceive the price as a better deal than if it were presented as a standalone price.

Counter-Arguments and Dissenting Opinions

While the anchoring and adjustment heuristic can lead to errors in judgment and decision-making, some argue that it can also serve as a useful tool for decision-making in certain contexts. For example, in situations where there is limited information available, the initial anchor can provide a starting point for further investigation and decision-making.

Additionally, some argue that the anchoring and adjustment heuristic can be a useful negotiation tactic when used strategically. By starting with an extreme anchor, such as a very low or very high initial offer, negotiators can potentially shift the perceived range of possible outcomes and influence the final agreement in their favor.

Conclusion

The anchoring and adjustment heuristic is a cognitive bias that can have significant implications for judgment and decision-making in a variety of contexts. By recognizing the influence of initial anchors and employing strategies such as questioning the anchor, considering alternative anchors, and using a structured decision-making process, individuals can overcome this bias and make more informed decisions. However, it is important to also consider potential counter-arguments and dissenting opinions, and to recognize that the anchoring and adjustment heuristic may have some potential benefits in certain contexts.

Framing effect

The framing effect is a cognitive bias that influences decision making by the way information is presented, or framed. The way a problem or issue is presented can significantly impact the decision-making process, leading individuals to make different choices based on the same information presented in different ways. The framing effect has important implications in various fields such as finance, marketing, politics, and healthcare. In this section, we will explore the framing effect, its causes, consequences, and ways to overcome it.

Causes of the Framing Effect:

The framing effect is caused by the way information is presented and the cognitive processes that occur when individuals process that information. According to research, the framing effect is a result of individuals relying on mental shortcuts, or heuristics, when making decisions. These mental shortcuts can lead to errors in judgment, especially when the framing of the information is manipulated to influence decision making.

For example, a financial analyst may be presented with two investment options. Option A is described as a "safe and conservative investment," while Option B is described as a "risky but potentially lucrative investment." Even if the two options have the same expected return, the framing of the options can significantly influence the analyst's decision.

Consequences of the Framing Effect:

The consequences of the framing effect can be significant, leading individuals to make choices that are not in their best interest or that deviate from their values and preferences. In the field of finance, the framing effect can lead to suboptimal investment decisions, causing investors to miss out on opportunities or to take on unnecessary risk.

For example, a portfolio manager may be influenced by the way a stock is framed in the media or by colleagues, leading them to overvalue or undervalue the stock, resulting in suboptimal investment decisions. Similarly, a securities trader may be influenced by the way market news is framed, leading them to take unnecessary risks or miss out on profitable opportunities.

The framing effect also has significant implications in the field of marketing. Marketers can use the framing effect to influence consumer behavior by framing products or services in a way that is more appealing or attractive to consumers. For example, a marketing campaign that frames a product as a "luxury item" may be more effective in attracting buyers than a campaign that frames the same product as a "practical item."

Ways to Overcome the Framing Effect:

There are several ways to overcome the framing effect and make more informed decisions. One way is to be aware of the framing effect and to actively seek out and consider alternative framings of the same information. This can help individuals to identify biases and make more informed decisions based on the underlying facts and evidence.

For example, a financial planner may present investment options to a client in multiple ways, such as presenting the expected return and risk associated with each option, rather than just framing the options in terms of "safe" or "risky" investments.

Another way to overcome the framing effect is to use probabilistic thinking, which involves considering the likelihood of various outcomes based on available evidence. This can help individuals to make more accurate predictions and decisions by focusing on the underlying probabilities and risks associated with each option.

Finally, individuals can also use decision-making tools such as decision trees or decision matrices to help them make more informed decisions by mapping out the potential outcomes and risks associated with each option.

Conclusion:

The framing effect is a cognitive bias that can significantly impact decision making by influencing the way information is presented. By understanding the causes and consequences of the framing effect and using strategies such as seeking out alternative framings, using probabilistic thinking, and using decision-making tools, individuals can overcome this bias and make more informed decisions. The framing effect has important implications in various fields such as finance, marketing, politics, and healthcare, and is an important area of study for psychologists, economists, and researchers in other related fields.

In finance, the framing effect can impact investor behavior and financial decision-making. For example, when financial news is presented positively, investors may be more likely to buy stocks, while negative news may lead to selling. Additionally, the way that investment options are presented, such as emphasizing potential gains versus potential losses, can impact investor decisions.

In marketing, the framing effect can be used to influence consumer behavior by presenting information in a certain way. For example, a product may be framed as a luxury item or a necessity, leading consumers to perceive it in a certain way and make purchasing decisions accordingly.

In politics, the framing effect can be used to shape public opinion and influence political decisions. Politicians may frame issues in a way that supports their agenda, leading the public to perceive the issue in a certain way and make voting decisions accordingly.

In healthcare, the framing effect can impact patient behavior and decision-making. For example, the way that medical treatments and procedures are framed can impact patient perceptions and choices.

Overall, the framing effect highlights the importance of considering the way information is presented and how it can impact decision-making. By being aware of this bias and using strategies to overcome it, individuals can make more informed decisions and avoid being influenced by irrelevant factors.

Confirmation bias

Confirmation bias is a cognitive bias that affects the way people process information and make decisions. It refers to the tendency of individuals to seek out and interpret information in a way that confirms their preexisting beliefs, while ignoring or discounting information that contradicts those beliefs. Confirmation bias can lead to flawed decision-making, as people may overlook important evidence or make inaccurate assumptions based on incomplete information. This bias has important implications in various fields such as finance, politics, and healthcare, and is an important area of study for researchers and practitioners.

Causes of Confirmation Bias:

Confirmation bias has been attributed to several factors, including the need to maintain self-esteem, the desire to reduce cognitive dissonance, and the influence of social norms and group dynamics. People tend to seek out information that supports their preexisting beliefs because it provides a sense of validation and confirmation, which can boost self-esteem and reduce feelings of uncertainty or doubt. Additionally, people may be motivated to avoid cognitive dissonance, which occurs when there is a conflict between their beliefs and the available evidence. To reduce this discomfort, individuals may selectively attend to information that is consistent with their beliefs and ignore or rationalize away contradictory evidence. Finally, group dynamics and social norms can play a role in confirmation bias, as people may conform to the beliefs and opinions of their social group or community, and may be hesitant to express views that are inconsistent with those of their peers.

Effects of Confirmation Bias:

Confirmation bias can have a number of negative effects on decision-making and problem-solving. In the field of finance, for example, investors may be more likely to invest in companies that confirm their preexisting beliefs about the market, rather than considering alternative opportunities that may be more profitable. Similarly, financial analysts may selectively interpret data to support their recommendations, rather than considering all available information. This can lead to inaccurate predictions and costly errors. In politics, confirmation bias can lead to polarization and groupthink, as individuals may only seek out and share information that supports their political views, rather than engaging in constructive dialogue and considering alternative perspectives. This can lead to a breakdown in civil discourse and a lack of progress on important policy issues. In healthcare, confirmation bias can lead to diagnostic errors, as medical professionals may selectively attend to information that supports their initial diagnosis, rather than considering alternative explanations and diagnostic tests.

Strategies to Overcome Confirmation Bias:

There are several strategies that individuals and organizations can use to overcome confirmation bias and make more informed decisions. One strategy is to actively seek out and consider alternative perspectives and evidence, even if it contradicts preexisting beliefs. This can help to reduce the influence of confirmation bias and promote more accurate decision-making. Additionally, individuals can use decision-making tools such as checklists and decision trees to help them consider all available information and avoid the influence of biases. In organizations, creating diverse and inclusive teams can also help to reduce the impact of confirmation bias, as individuals with different backgrounds and perspectives can provide valuable insights and challenge preexisting assumptions.

Counter-Arguments and Dissenting Opinions:

While many researchers and practitioners acknowledge the impact of confirmation bias on decision-making, some have argued that it may not always be a negative influence. For example, some have suggested that confirmation bias can help to promote efficiency and accuracy in decision-making, as individuals may be able to quickly identify relevant information and avoid distractions. Additionally, some have suggested that confirmation bias may be more prevalent in certain contexts or situations, such as when individuals are under time pressure or when the stakes are high.

Conclusion:

Confirmation bias is a cognitive bias that can significantly impact decision-making by influencing the way information is processed and interpreted. By understanding the causes and consequences of confirmation bias and using strategies such as seeking out alternative perspectives and using decision-making tools, individuals and organizations can overcome this bias and make more informed decisions. While some level of confirmation bias is likely to be present in all individuals, being aware of its existence and actively working to mitigate its effects can help to minimize its impact.

In the fields of finance and investment, confirmation bias can lead investors to hold onto underperforming assets for longer than they should, as they may selectively focus on information that supports their belief that the asset will eventually rebound. Similarly, financial analysts may be more likely to interpret financial data in a way that supports their preconceived notions, rather than considering all available information objectively.

In healthcare, confirmation bias can lead doctors to over-rely on past experiences and beliefs when diagnosing and treating patients, rather than considering all available information. This can lead to misdiagnosis and incorrect treatment, ultimately harming the patient.

The consequences of confirmation bias can be severe and wide-reaching, affecting not only individuals but also entire organizations and society as a whole. Therefore, it is essential to recognize and address this bias to ensure better decision-making and ultimately better outcomes.

In conclusion, confirmation bias is a cognitive bias that can have a significant impact on decision-making across various fields, including finance, healthcare, and politics. It is important to recognize its existence and actively work to mitigate its effects to ensure better decision-making and ultimately better outcomes. By seeking out alternative perspectives, using decision-making tools, and remaining open to new information, individuals and organizations can overcome this bias and make more informed decisions.

IV. Decision Making Processes

Decision-making is an essential process in our everyday lives. It is the process of choosing between different options based on a set of criteria. From choosing what to wear in the morning to making major life decisions, we engage in decision-making on a regular basis. However, the process of decision-making is not always straightforward and can be influenced by various factors, such as cognitive biases, emotions, and external pressures.

The study of decision-making has been of great interest to scholars in various fields, including psychology, economics, management, and neuroscience. Understanding how people make decisions is crucial for developing effective decision-making strategies, as well as for improving our understanding of human behavior.

In this section, we will explore the different aspects of the decision-making process, including the different types of decisions, the factors that influence decision-making, and the various models of decision-making. We will also discuss the challenges and limitations of decision-making, as well as the strategies that can be used to improve decision-making.

Types of Decisions:

Decisions can be classified into different categories based on various criteria. One common classification is based on the level of uncertainty and the degree of risk involved. Decisions can be categorized as either routine, adaptive, or innovative.

Routine decisions are those that are made frequently and involve little uncertainty or risk. These decisions are usually based on established procedures or rules and require little cognitive effort. Examples of routine decisions include deciding what to wear in the morning or what to eat for lunch.

Adaptive decisions are those that are made in response to a changing environment. These decisions involve some uncertainty and require the ability to adapt to new situations. Examples of adaptive decisions include changing a project plan in response to new information or adjusting a budget to accommodate unexpected expenses.

Innovative decisions are those that involve high levels of uncertainty and risk. These decisions require creativity and involve breaking new ground. Examples of innovative decisions include launching a new product or investing in a new technology.

Factors that Influence Decision Making:

The decision-making process is influenced by various factors, including cognitive biases, emotions, and external pressures. One of the most significant factors that influence decision-making is cognitive biases.

Cognitive biases are systematic errors in thinking that occur when people process information. These biases can lead to flawed decision-making and can result in suboptimal outcomes. There are several types of cognitive biases, including confirmation bias, anchoring bias, and availability bias.

Confirmation bias is the tendency to seek out information that confirms our pre-existing beliefs and ignore information that contradicts them. This bias can lead to a narrow and biased view of the world, which can result in flawed decision-making.

Anchoring bias is the tendency to rely too heavily on the first piece of information received when making a decision. This bias can result in an overemphasis on certain factors and can lead to suboptimal outcomes.

Availability bias is the tendency to rely on readily available information when making a decision, rather than considering all available information. This bias can lead to a skewed and incomplete view of the world, which can result in flawed decision-making.

Emotions can also play a significant role in decision-making. Emotions such as fear, anxiety, and anger can influence our decision-making by altering our perceptions and judgments. For example, fear of failure can lead to risk aversion and conservative decision-making, while anger can lead to impulsive and irrational decision-making.

External pressures can also influence decision-making. These pressures can include social norms, cultural expectations, and organizational policies. For example, a company may have a policy of maximizing short-term profits, which can influence decision-making in ways that are not in the best interests of the company in the long term.

Models of Decision Making:

There are several models of decision-making that have been proposed over the years. One of the most influential models is the rational decision-making model, which assumes that individuals make decisions by identifying all possible options, evaluating the consequences of each option, and choosing the option that maximizes their expected utility or benefit. The rational decision-making model is often used in fields such as economics, finance, and management.

However, the rational decision-making model has been criticized for being too simplistic and not reflecting the complexity of real-world decision-making. Other models have been proposed that take into account factors such as emotions, biases, and heuristics.

One such model is the behavioral decision-making model, which emphasizes the role of emotions and social influences in decision-making. The behavioral decision-making model is often used in fields such as psychology, sociology, and marketing.

Another model is the bounded rationality model, which recognizes that individuals have limited cognitive resources and cannot always process all available information. The bounded rationality model is often used in fields such as cognitive psychology and organizational behavior.

In addition to these models, there are also descriptive models of decision-making that aim to describe how individuals actually make decisions, rather than prescribing how they should make decisions. These descriptive models include the prospect theory, which describes how individuals evaluate gains and losses, and the dual-process theory, which describes how individuals make decisions using both intuitive and analytical thinking.

Overall, understanding the different models of decision-making can help individuals and organizations to make more informed and effective decisions by taking into account the various factors that can influence decision-making.

System 1 and System 2 thinking

The human brain is a complex and powerful organ capable of processing vast amounts of information every second. One of the most fascinating aspects of the brain is the way it processes information, which has been the subject of much research and discussion. In recent years, the concept of System 1 and System 2 thinking has gained widespread attention, with many experts arguing that these two distinct modes of thought are responsible for much of our decision-making. In this section, we will explore what System 1 and System 2 thinking are, how they work, and their implications for decision-making.

System 1 and System 2 Thinking:

System 1 and System 2 thinking are two distinct modes of thought proposed by psychologist Daniel Kahneman. System 1 thinking is fast, automatic, and intuitive, while System 2 thinking is slow, deliberate, and conscious. According to Kahneman, System 1 thinking is responsible for most of our day-to-day decision-making, while System 2 thinking is reserved for more complex, effortful tasks.

System 1 thinking is based on our experiences, emotions, and biases, and operates unconsciously and automatically. It is responsible for many of our routine activities, such as driving a car, reading a book, or recognizing a familiar face. System 1 thinking is often associated with heuristics or mental shortcuts that allow us to make quick decisions based on limited information.

In contrast, System 2 thinking is slow, effortful, and conscious. It involves logical reasoning, analysis, and problem-solving, and requires deliberate mental effort. System 2 thinking is often required for complex tasks such as solving a mathematical equation, writing an essay, or making a strategic business decision. Unlike System 1 thinking, System 2 thinking is not automatic and requires conscious attention and mental effort.

Examples from Different Fields:

The concepts of System 1 and System 2 thinking have important implications for decision-making in various fields, including finance, marketing, psychology, and economics. In finance, for example, System 1 thinking may lead investors to make hasty decisions based on emotional reactions to market fluctuations, while System 2 thinking may be required for more strategic investment decisions.

In marketing, System 1 thinking may be used to influence consumer behavior by appealing to emotions and intuition, while System 2 thinking may be necessary for consumers to make informed purchasing decisions. In psychology, System 1 thinking is often associated with biases such as confirmation bias, availability bias, and anchoring bias, while System 2 thinking may be required to overcome these biases and make more rational decisions.

In economics, System 1 thinking may lead individuals to make irrational decisions based on heuristics and biases, while System 2 thinking may be required for more complex economic decisions such as setting monetary policy or regulating financial markets.

Implications for Decision Making:

The concepts of System 1 and System 2 thinking have important implications for decision-making in both personal and professional contexts. In personal decision-making, individuals can use the principles of System 1 and System 2 thinking to make more informed and rational decisions. For example, individuals can use System 2 thinking to evaluate their emotions and biases and make decisions based on logic and reason rather than instinct or intuition.

In professional decision-making, System 2 thinking may be necessary for more complex and strategic decision-making. Business leaders, for example, may need to use System 2 thinking to analyze market trends, evaluate financial data, and make strategic decisions for their organizations. By understanding the principles of System 1 and System 2 thinking, individuals and organizations can make more informed and effective decisions.

Conclusion:

In conclusion, the concepts of System 1 and System 2 thinking provide a framework for understanding how the brain processes information and makes decisions. While System 1 thinking is fast, automatic , and intuitive, it is also prone to biases and errors. System 2 thinking, on the other hand, is slower, more deliberate, and more rational, but it is also more effortful and can be influenced by factors such as cognitive load and fatigue.

By recognizing the strengths and limitations of both System 1 and System 2 thinking, individuals can learn to use them more effectively and make better decisions. This is especially important in fields such as finance, where decisions can have significant consequences for individuals and organizations.

For example, an investment banker may use System 1 thinking to quickly evaluate a potential investment based on their intuition and past experiences, but also employ System 2 thinking to carefully analyze the data and consider alternative perspectives before making a final decision. A financial planner may use System 1 thinking to quickly recognize and respond to a client's emotional needs, but also use System 2 thinking to carefully analyze their financial situation and develop a long-term plan.

It is important to note that System 1 and System 2 thinking are not mutually exclusive, and in fact, they often work in conjunction with one another. In many cases, System 1 thinking provides initial impressions and ideas, while System 2 thinking evaluates and refines these ideas based on careful analysis and deliberation.

Overall, understanding the concepts of System 1 and System 2 thinking can provide individuals with a greater awareness of their own cognitive processes and help them make more informed decisions in a variety of contexts. As our understanding of the brain and decision-making processes continues to evolve, it is likely that these concepts will remain important areas of study for years to come.

Intuitive decision making

Intuition is often described as a gut feeling or a hunch. It refers to a type of decision making that is based on instinct, rather than a systematic analysis of information. Intuitive decision making is a process that occurs automatically, without conscious awareness of the underlying thought process. While intuition can be helpful in many situations, it can also lead to biases and errors in judgment. In this section, we will explore the concept of intuitive decision making, its advantages and disadvantages, and the strategies that individuals can use to improve their intuitive decision-making skills.

The Nature of Intuition:

Intuition is a form of decision making that relies on implicit knowledge and expertise. It is often described as a "felt sense" or a "knowing without knowing how you know." Intuitive decision making is a rapid, effortless, and automatic process that can occur without conscious awareness. Intuition is based on patterns, associations, and heuristics that have been learned through experience, but are not consciously accessible.

Intuitive decision making is thought to be mediated by System 1 thinking, which is fast, automatic, and emotionally driven. System 1 thinking is the default mode of thinking for most people and is involved in many everyday decisions, such as driving a car or choosing what to wear. System 1 thinking can be helpful in situations where a quick decision is needed, but it can also lead to biases and errors in judgment.

Advantages of Intuitive Decision Making:

Intuitive decision making can have several advantages over analytical decision making. One of the main advantages is speed. Intuitive decision making can be much faster than analytical decision making, allowing individuals to make quick decisions in high-pressure situations. For example, a securities trader may rely on intuition to make split-second decisions in a rapidly changing market.

Another advantage of intuitive decision making is that it can be more accurate in certain situations. Intuitive decision making is often based on implicit knowledge and expertise, which can be more accurate than explicit knowledge in complex or uncertain situations. For example, an experienced actuary may rely on intuition to make accurate predictions about future financial trends.

Disadvantages of Intuitive Decision Making:

While intuitive decision making can have advantages, it can also have several disadvantages. One of the main disadvantages is that intuition can be biased. Intuitive decision making is based on patterns and associations that have been learned through experience, which can lead to biases and errors in judgment. For example, an investment banker may have a bias towards investing in a certain sector because of past successes, even if current data suggests that it may not be the best choice.

Another disadvantage of intuitive decision making is that it can be influenced by emotions. Intuitive decision making is often driven by System 1 thinking, which is emotionally driven. Emotions can influence decision making by biasing attention, memory, and perception. For example, a portfolio manager may have a bias towards investing in companies that align with their personal values, rather than objectively analyzing the potential risks and rewards.

Strategies for Improving Intuitive Decision Making:

While intuitive decision making can have disadvantages, there are strategies that individuals can use to improve their intuitive decision-making skills. One strategy is to develop expertise in a particular domain. Intuitive decision making is based on implicit knowledge and expertise, so developing expertise in a particular domain can help individuals make more accurate intuitive decisions. For example, a quantitative analyst may develop expertise in a particular financial instrument, allowing them to make more accurate intuitive decisions about its value.

Another strategy for improving intuitive decision making is to seek out feedback and alternative perspectives. Intuitive decision making can be biased, so seeking out feedback and alternative perspectives can help individuals recognize and correct their biases. For example, a financial planner may seek out feedback from a colleague with a different perspective to help identify potential biases in their investment strategy and decision-making process.

Feedback and alternative perspectives can help individuals challenge their assumptions and beliefs and identify any blind spots that may be impacting their decision-making. Seeking out feedback can also help individuals consider new information and perspectives that they may not have otherwise considered. This can lead to more informed and well-rounded decisions.

In addition to seeking out feedback and alternative perspectives, another strategy for improving intuitive decision making is to practice mindfulness. Mindfulness involves being present and fully engaged in the current moment, and can help individuals become more aware of their thoughts, feelings, and biases.

Practicing mindfulness can help individuals recognize when their biases are impacting their decision-making and allow them to take a step back and reevaluate their thought process. For example, a portfolio manager may use mindfulness techniques to become more aware of their biases towards certain stocks or industries, and to evaluate these biases more objectively.

Finally, another strategy for improving intuitive decision making is to cultivate a diverse range of experiences and knowledge. Intuition is often based on pattern recognition, and the more patterns an individual is exposed to, the more robust their intuition is likely to be.

For example, a quantitative analyst may benefit from exposing themselves to a variety of data sets and statistical models, as this can help them develop a more intuitive understanding of how different variables interact and impact outcomes. Similarly, a securities trader may benefit from cultivating a broad knowledge of global markets and economies, as this can help them recognize patterns and trends that may impact their investment decisions.

In conclusion, intuitive decision making is a powerful tool that can be used to make quick and effective decisions. However, it is important to be aware of the potential biases and limitations of intuition, and to use strategies such as seeking out feedback, practicing mindfulness, and cultivating a diverse range of experiences and knowledge to improve intuitive decision making. By doing so, individuals can make more informed and well-rounded decisions that are grounded in both intuition and rational analysis.

Decision paralysis

Decision-making is an essential aspect of life, as individuals are faced with making choices every day. However, making decisions can be a challenging process, and individuals may experience decision paralysis, which is the inability to make a decision due to the fear of making the wrong choice. Decision paralysis can be a significant problem, particularly in situations where decisions need to be made quickly, such as in the financial industry, where investment decisions need to be made in a fast-paced environment. In this section, we will discuss decision paralysis, its causes, consequences, and strategies to overcome it.

Causes of Decision Paralysis:

Decision paralysis can be caused by several factors, including cognitive overload, fear of making the wrong choice, and lack of information. Cognitive overload occurs when individuals are presented with too much information, which can make it challenging to make a decision. This is particularly common in the financial industry, where individuals are faced with large amounts of complex data that can be overwhelming.

The fear of making the wrong choice is another common cause of decision paralysis. Individuals may be afraid of the consequences of making the wrong decision, particularly in high-stakes situations such as investing. This fear can lead to individuals procrastinating on making a decision or avoiding it altogether, resulting in decision paralysis.

Lack of information is another factor that can contribute to decision paralysis. Individuals may feel unsure of their ability to make a decision when they lack the necessary information to make an informed choice. This can be particularly challenging in the financial industry, where information can be difficult to obtain, and decisions need to be made quickly.

Consequences of Decision Paralysis:

The consequences of decision paralysis can be significant, particularly in the financial industry. In the investment world, decision paralysis can lead to missed opportunities and financial losses. When individuals are unable to make a decision, they may miss out on a lucrative investment opportunity, leading to financial losses.

Decision paralysis can also lead to a loss of confidence in decision-making abilities. When individuals are unable to make decisions, they may begin to doubt their ability to make choices, leading to a loss of confidence. This can be particularly challenging in the financial industry, where individuals need to make decisions quickly and confidently.

Strategies to Overcome Decision Paralysis:

There are several strategies that individuals can use to overcome decision paralysis, including breaking down the decision into smaller parts, seeking out information and advice, and using decision-making tools.

Breaking down the decision into smaller parts can make it easier to make a decision. By breaking the decision down into smaller, manageable parts, individuals can focus on each part individually, rather than becoming overwhelmed by the decision as a whole. This can make the decision-making process less daunting and more manageable.

Seeking out information and advice can also help individuals overcome decision paralysis. By seeking out information and advice, individuals can gain a better understanding of the decision they need to make and can make a more informed choice. This can be particularly helpful in the financial industry, where individuals may need to seek out expert advice to make the best decisions.

Using decision-making tools is another strategy that individuals can use to overcome decision paralysis. Decision-making tools such as decision trees, SWOT analysis, and cost-benefit analysis can help individuals make more informed decisions by providing a structured approach to decision-making.

Counterarguments:

While these strategies can be helpful in overcoming decision paralysis, there are some counterarguments to consider. For example, breaking down the decision into smaller parts can be time-consuming and may not always be practical, particularly in high-stakes situations. Seeking out information and advice can also be challenging in the financial industry, where information can be difficult to obtain and may be unreliable.

Using decision-making tools can also have drawbacks. For example, decision-making tools may not always provide a complete picture of the decision, and individuals may need to consider other factors that are not accounted for in the tool. Additionally, decision-making tools may be limited by the quality of the data and assumptions used in their development.

Another potential drawback of using decision-making tools is that they can create decision paralysis. Decision paralysis is a phenomenon in which an individual is unable to make a decision due to overanalyzing the available information or being overwhelmed by the number of options available. Decision paralysis can lead to delays in decision-making and can ultimately result in missed opportunities.

One common cause of decision paralysis is the fear of making the wrong decision. When faced with a high-stakes decision, individuals may feel pressure to make the "right" choice, which can lead to a sense of paralysis as they try to weigh all the possible options and outcomes. This fear of making the wrong decision can also be compounded by the potential consequences of the decision, such as financial losses, reputational damage, or harm to others.

Another cause of decision paralysis is information overload. With the vast amount of information available in today's world, individuals can easily become overwhelmed and feel unable to process all of the available data. This can lead to a sense of paralysis as they struggle to sort through the information and make sense of it all.

Finally, decision paralysis can also be caused by analysis paralysis, which is a tendency to overanalyze and overthink a decision. Analysis paralysis can occur when individuals feel the need to gather more and more information or to consider every possible outcome before making a decision. This can result in delays in decision-making and can ultimately lead to missed opportunities.

To overcome decision paralysis, individuals can use a variety of strategies. One approach is to set clear decision criteria and establish a timeline for making the decision. This can help individuals focus on the most important factors and avoid getting bogged down in unnecessary details. Another approach is to seek out the advice and opinions of others, which can help provide a different perspective and reduce the fear of making the wrong decision.

Another strategy for overcoming decision paralysis is to break the decision down into smaller, more manageable pieces. This can make the decision feel less overwhelming and can help individuals focus on the most important factors. Additionally, setting a deadline for making the decision can help prevent analysis paralysis and ensure that the decision is made in a timely manner.

In conclusion, decision paralysis is a common phenomenon that can prevent individuals from making timely and effective decisions. While decision-making tools can be helpful in certain situations, they can also contribute to decision paralysis if not used appropriately. By understanding the causes of decision paralysis and using strategies such as setting clear decision criteria, seeking out feedback, and breaking the decision down into smaller pieces, individuals can overcome decision paralysis and make effective decisions.

Groupthink

Groupthink is a psychological phenomenon in which people in a group tend to conform to the group's decision-making process, even if it goes against their personal beliefs or instincts. This can lead to poor decision-making, as group members prioritize agreement and harmony over critical evaluation of ideas. Groupthink has been observed in a variety of settings, including business, politics, and social groups. This article will explore the concept of groupthink, its causes, and its consequences, as well as strategies for preventing it.

Causes of Groupthink:
There are several factors that can contribute to groupthink, including:

High Group Cohesion: The more cohesive a group is, the more likely they are to conform to the group's norms and decision-making processes.

Group Isolation: When a group is isolated from outside perspectives, they are less likely to be exposed to alternative viewpoints and are more likely to fall victim to groupthink.

Strong Leadership: When a leader dominates the decision-making process and discourages dissenting opinions, it can lead to groupthink.

Homogeneity: When a group is composed of people with similar backgrounds, beliefs, and experiences, they are more likely to conform to the group's decision-making process.

Stressful Situations: When a group is under stress or time pressure, they may prioritize reaching a decision quickly over critical evaluation of ideas.

Consequences of Groupthink:
The consequences of groupthink can be severe, including:

Poor Decision-Making: When a group prioritizes agreement over critical evaluation of ideas, they may make poor decisions that are not well thought out.

Lack of Creativity: Groupthink can stifle creativity and innovation, as members may be less likely to express new ideas or challenge the group's assumptions.

Incomplete Information: Groupthink can cause groups to overlook important information or alternative perspectives, leading to incomplete information and flawed decision-making.

Risky Decisions: In some cases, groupthink can lead to risky decisions that may have negative consequences.

Decreased Motivation: When members feel that their opinions are not valued, they may become less motivated to participate in the decision-making process, leading to decreased group performance.

Strategies for Preventing Groupthink:
There are several strategies that can be employed to prevent groupthink, including:

Encouraging Dissent: Leaders can encourage dissenting opinions by creating an environment in which all opinions are valued and respected.

Diversity: Group diversity can help to prevent groupthink by exposing members to a range of perspectives and ideas.

Devil's Advocacy: Devil's advocacy involves assigning someone the role of challenging the group's assumptions and decision-making process.

Critical Evaluation: Leaders can encourage critical evaluation of ideas by asking questions and challenging assumptions.

Outside Perspectives: Bringing in outside perspectives can help to prevent groupthink by exposing the group to new ideas and perspectives.

Examples of Groupthink:
Groupthink has been observed in a variety of settings, including business, politics, and social groups. One notable example of groupthink occurred in the 1960s during the Bay of Pigs invasion. President John F. Kennedy and his advisors were convinced that an invasion of Cuba would be successful, despite evidence to the contrary. This led to a failed invasion and a public relations disaster for the United States.

Another example of groupthink occurred during the Challenger space shuttle disaster in 1986. NASA engineers were aware of potential problems with the shuttle's O-ring seals but failed to speak up due to pressure from their superiors and a desire to conform to the group's decision-making process. This led to the tragic loss of seven crew members.

Conclusion:
Groupthink can be a dangerous phenomenon that can lead to poor decision-making, lack of creativity,and potential ethical violations. It is important for individuals and organizations to be aware of the signs of groupthink and take steps to prevent it.

One way to prevent groupthink is to encourage open and honest communication within groups. Leaders can create an environment where individuals feel comfortable expressing their opinions and ideas, even if they differ from the majority. This can help prevent the pressure to conform and encourage diverse perspectives.

Another strategy is to encourage the group to seek out and consider alternative perspectives. This can help expose group members to different ideas and prevent the group from becoming too narrow-minded. Encouraging the group to seek out feedback and critique can also help prevent groupthink by challenging assumptions and biases.

It is also important for groups to have a diverse range of members in terms of backgrounds, experiences, and perspectives. This can help prevent group members from thinking too similarly and encourage creative thinking.

Finally, leaders can take steps to avoid creating a hierarchical or authoritarian culture within groups. This can help prevent the pressure to conform and encourage individuals to express their opinions and ideas.

In conclusion, groupthink is a phenomenon that can have serious consequences for decision-making and organizational performance. It is important for individuals and organizations to be aware of the signs of groupthink and take steps to prevent it. Encouraging open communication, seeking out alternative perspectives, promoting diversity, and avoiding hierarchical cultures can all help prevent groupthink and encourage better decision-making.

V. Applications in Finance

The field of finance is highly dependent on effective decision-making, as financial decisions can have significant impacts on businesses, economies, and individuals. In order to make effective decisions, finance professionals must be equipped with the necessary tools and techniques to analyze data and information and to evaluate potential outcomes. With the rise of big data and advanced computing capabilities, finance professionals now have access to a wide range of analytical tools and methods to support their decision-making.

In this section, we will explore the various applications of decision-making tools and techniques in finance, including how they can be used to manage risk, evaluate investment opportunities, and make strategic decisions. We will also examine the limitations and challenges associated with decision-making in finance, and how new technologies and approaches are being developed to address these challenges.

Managing Risk:

One of the most critical applications of decision-making tools in finance is in managing risk. Financial markets are inherently risky, and investors and businesses must be able to evaluate and manage these risks in order to make informed decisions. There are a wide range of tools and techniques available to help finance professionals manage risk, including Monte Carlo simulations, Value at Risk (VaR) models, and stress testing.

Monte Carlo simulations are a powerful tool for evaluating risk in finance, as they allow analysts to model a range of potential outcomes based on a set of inputs and assumptions. For example, an investment bank might use a Monte Carlo simulation to evaluate the potential outcomes of a new financial instrument, such as a derivatives contract. By simulating a range of market conditions and scenarios, analysts can assess the likelihood of different outcomes and evaluate the risk associated with the investment.

Value at Risk (VaR) models are another commonly used tool for managing risk in finance. VaR models allow analysts to estimate the maximum potential loss that could be incurred on a particular investment or portfolio over a given time period, based on historical market data and statistical analysis. By quantifying the potential downside risk associated with an investment, VaR models can help investors and businesses make more informed decisions about how much risk to take on.

Stress testing is another important tool for managing risk in finance, particularly in the banking sector. Stress testing involves modeling a range of extreme scenarios, such as a sudden market crash or a significant increase in interest rates, in order to assess the resilience of a financial institution's balance sheet. By identifying potential vulnerabilities and weaknesses, stress testing can help financial institutions better prepare for and manage potential risks.

Evaluating Investment Opportunities:

Another important application of decision-making tools in finance is in evaluating investment opportunities. Financial professionals must be able to identify and evaluate potential investment opportunities in order to maximize returns and minimize risk. There are a wide range of tools and techniques available to help finance professionals evaluate investment opportunities, including discounted cash flow analysis, ratio analysis, and financial modeling.

Discounted cash flow analysis is a commonly used tool for evaluating the potential value of an investment over time. This technique involves projecting the future cash flows associated with an investment and discounting those cash flows back to their present value. By comparing the present value of the cash flows to the cost of the investment, analysts can determine whether the investment is likely to generate a positive return.

Ratio analysis is another important tool for evaluating investment opportunities. This technique involves analyzing a company's financial statements, such as its income statement and balance sheet, in order to identify key performance indicators and trends. By comparing these indicators to industry benchmarks and historical trends, analysts can gain a better understanding of a company's financial health and growth potential.

Financial modeling is another powerful tool for evaluating investment opportunities in finance. Financial models involve creating mathematical representations of financial scenarios, such as the potential cash flows associated with a new investment or the financial impact of a major acquisition. By running different scenarios through the model and evaluating the potential outcomes, analysts can gain a better understanding of the risks and potential returns associated with a given investment opportunity.

Financial models can be used to analyze a wide range of financial scenarios, such as the feasibility of a new product launch, the impact of changes in interest rates on a company's earnings, or the potential value of a merger or acquisition. These models are typically created using spreadsheet software like Microsoft Excel, which allows analysts to input various assumptions and inputs to create different scenarios.

One common type of financial model used in finance is the discounted cash flow (DCF) model. The DCF model is used to estimate the value of an investment based on its future cash flows. The model takes into account the time value of money, meaning that future cash flows are discounted to reflect the fact that a dollar received in the future is worth less than a dollar received today. The model also considers the risk associated with the investment by incorporating a discount rate that reflects the level of risk inherent in the investment.

Another type of financial model commonly used in finance is the Monte Carlo simulation. Monte Carlo simulations involve running multiple simulations of a given scenario using different inputs and assumptions to estimate the potential range of outcomes. For example, a Monte Carlo simulation might be used to estimate the potential range of returns associated with a particular investment strategy.

In addition to financial modeling, quantitative analysis is another important tool used in finance. Quantitative analysis involves using mathematical and statistical methods to analyze financial data and identify patterns and trends. This can include analyzing financial statements, historical stock prices, and other financial data to identify factors that may impact investment decisions.

One common type of quantitative analysis used in finance is technical analysis. Technical analysts use charts and other visual representations of financial data to identify patterns and trends that can help inform investment decisions. For example, a technical analyst may use a chart of a stock's price history to identify trends that suggest the stock is likely to continue to rise or fall in value.

Overall, applications in finance rely heavily on analytical tools and quantitative methods to evaluate investment opportunities and inform decision-making. Financial modeling, quantitative analysis, and technical analysis are just a few examples of the tools and methods used in finance to help investors make informed decisions and manage risk.

Behavioral finance in investment management

Behavioral finance is an important field of study within finance that seeks to understand how psychological biases can impact investment decision-making. Traditional finance theory assumes that individuals are rational, self-interested, and make decisions based on all available information. However, behavioral finance has shown that investors are often irrational and prone to making systematic errors in their decision-making.

One example of a psychological bias that can impact investment decisions is overconfidence. Overconfidence refers to the tendency for individuals to overestimate their abilities and the accuracy of their predictions. This can lead investors to take on excessive risk, as they may believe that they have superior knowledge or insights that others do not possess. Overconfidence can be especially prevalent in fields such as portfolio management or quantitative analysis, where individuals may have access to vast amounts of data and believe they can accurately predict future market trends.

Another important bias in behavioral finance is loss aversion. Loss aversion refers to the tendency for individuals to experience more pain from losses than pleasure from gains of equal magnitude. This can lead investors to hold on to losing investments for too long, or to sell profitable investments too quickly. Loss aversion can also lead to a reluctance to take on risk, as investors may be more concerned with avoiding losses than maximizing potential gains.

Confirmation bias is another psychological bias that can impact investment decisions. Confirmation bias refers to the tendency for individuals to seek out information that confirms their existing beliefs, while ignoring information that contradicts them. This can lead investors to make decisions based on incomplete or biased information, which can lead to poor investment performance. For example, an investor who believes that a particular stock is undervalued may only seek out news and information that confirms this belief, while ignoring negative news or analysis.

Behavioral finance has practical applications in investment management, as understanding these biases can help investors make better decisions. One approach is to use tools such as diversification to mitigate the impact of individual biases. For example, by investing in a broad range of assets, an investor can reduce the impact of any one asset's poor performance on their overall portfolio. Additionally, financial advisors can help clients identify and manage their biases, by providing objective analysis and helping clients to understand the risks and benefits of different investment strategies.

Behavioral finance can also inform investment strategies. For example, momentum investing is a strategy that seeks to capitalize on the tendency for stocks that have performed well in the past to continue to perform well in the future. This strategy is based on the behavioral finance concept of herding behavior, which suggests that investors may be influenced by the actions of others and may follow trends rather than making independent decisions.

Another example of a behavioral finance-based investment strategy is value investing. Value investing seeks to identify undervalued companies that are trading at a discount to their intrinsic value. This approach is based on the idea that market participants may overreact to short-term events and that stocks may be mispriced as a result. Value investing relies on the investor's ability to identify companies with strong fundamentals that are temporarily undervalued, and to be patient enough to wait for the market to recognize their true value.

In conclusion, behavioral finance is an important field of study within finance that seeks to understand how psychological biases can impact investment decision-making. Behavioral biases such as overconfidence, loss aversion, and confirmation bias can lead investors to make suboptimal decisions, which can result in poor investment performance. By understanding these biases and developing strategies to manage them, investors and financial professionals can make more informed decisions and achieve better outcomes.

Behavioral finance in financial planning

Behavioral finance is an important concept in financial planning. It refers to the study of how cognitive biases, emotions, and other psychological factors influence financial decision-making. These factors can lead individuals to make suboptimal financial decisions, which can have significant consequences for their long-term financial well-being. In this section, we will explore the role of behavioral finance in financial planning, including the common biases that can impact financial decision-making, the importance of understanding one's risk tolerance, and strategies for overcoming these biases.

One of the key ways that behavioral finance impacts financial planning is through the various cognitive biases that can impact financial decision-making. For example, individuals may have a tendency to be overconfident in their own abilities or to place too much emphasis on recent events when making financial decisions. They may also have a tendency to avoid losses at all costs, even if it means missing out on potential gains. These biases can lead individuals to make suboptimal financial decisions, such as investing too heavily in a single stock or failing to diversify their portfolio.

Another important aspect of behavioral finance in financial planning is the concept of risk tolerance. Risk tolerance refers to an individual's willingness and ability to take on risk in pursuit of higher returns. Some individuals are naturally more risk-averse than others, while others may be more comfortable taking on risk in pursuit of greater potential gains. Understanding one's risk tolerance is an important part of financial planning, as it can help individuals make more informed decisions about how to allocate their assets.

There are a number of strategies that financial planners can use to help clients overcome these biases and make more informed financial decisions. One approach is to use a rules-based approach to investing, where specific rules are established for buying and selling assets based on predefined criteria. This can help to reduce the impact of emotional biases on financial decision-making, as investors are guided by a clear set of rules rather than their own emotions.

Another strategy for overcoming behavioral biases is to use a structured decision-making process. This involves breaking down complex decisions into smaller, more manageable pieces and considering each piece individually before making a final decision. By taking a more structured approach to decision-making, individuals are less likely to be influenced by cognitive biases and emotions, which can lead to more rational and informed decisions.

Finally, financial planners can help their clients by providing education and information about the various cognitive biases that can impact financial decision-making. By understanding these biases and learning how to identify them, individuals can take steps to avoid them and make more informed decisions about their finances.

In conclusion, behavioral finance is an important concept in financial planning. By understanding the various cognitive biases and other psychological factors that can impact financial decision-making, individuals can take steps to overcome these biases and make more informed decisions about their finances. This can help to improve their long-term financial well-being and increase their chances of achieving their financial goals.

Behavioral finance in corporate finance

Behavioral finance is a field of study that focuses on how human psychology and emotions can impact financial decision-making. In corporate finance, behavioral finance plays an important role in understanding how managers and investors make decisions that can impact the financial performance of a company. By studying behavioral finance in corporate finance, we can gain insights into the biases and cognitive errors that can affect decision-making, and how these factors can be mitigated to improve financial outcomes.

The Role of Behavioral Finance in Corporate Finance:

Corporate finance is the area of finance that deals with the financial decisions made by corporations, including investments, financing, and capital structure decisions. Behavioral finance has become an important part of corporate finance in recent years, as researchers have recognized that human psychology and emotions can play a significant role in these decisions.

One of the key areas where behavioral finance has had an impact in corporate finance is in the area of investment decisions. Traditional financial theory assumes that investors are rational, and that they make decisions based on all available information in order to maximize their returns. However, behavioral finance research has shown that investors are often influenced by emotions and cognitive biases, which can lead to suboptimal investment decisions.

For example, research has shown that investors are more likely to invest in companies that are in the news or have recently performed well, even if the underlying fundamentals of the company do not support this decision. This phenomenon, known as the "availability heuristic," is a cognitive bias that leads investors to overestimate the importance of recent events when making investment decisions.

Behavioral finance research has also shown that managers can be influenced by cognitive biases in their decision-making. For example, the "overconfidence bias" can lead managers to overestimate their abilities and take on excessive risk in their business decisions. Similarly, the "confirmation bias" can lead managers to seek out information that confirms their existing beliefs, while ignoring information that contradicts them.

Mitigating the Impact of Behavioral Biases in Corporate Finance:

Given the potential impact of cognitive biases on financial decision-making, it is important for managers and investors to be aware of these biases and take steps to mitigate their effects. One way to do this is through the use of decision-making tools and frameworks that can help to reduce the impact of cognitive biases.

For example, decision-making frameworks such as scenario planning and decision trees can help to structure decision-making and reduce the impact of emotional and cognitive biases. By breaking down decisions into smaller components and considering the potential outcomes of each option, decision-makers can make more rational and informed decisions.

Another way to mitigate the impact of cognitive biases is to encourage diversity in decision-making. Research has shown that diverse groups are less likely to be affected by cognitive biases than homogenous groups, as the presence of multiple perspectives can help to identify and counteract individual biases.

Finally, managers can also implement policies and procedures that are designed to reduce the impact of cognitive biases. For example, creating clear guidelines for investment decision-making can help to reduce the impact of the availability heuristic, while establishing objective performance metrics can help to reduce the impact of the overconfidence bias.

Conclusion:

In conclusion, behavioral finance plays an important role in corporate finance by highlighting the impact of cognitive biases and emotions on financial decision-making. By understanding these biases and taking steps to mitigate their effects, managers and investors can make more informed and rational decisions, ultimately improving the financial performance of their organizations.

//////////////////////

VI. Conclusion

Key takeaways

Behavioral finance has emerged as a critical field in finance that provides insights into the decision-making processes of investors and financial professionals. By studying the psychological biases and heuristics that affect financial decision-making, researchers have been able to identify key behavioral patterns that impact investment outcomes. Some of the key takeaways from this analysis include:

Emotions play a significant role in financial decision-making: Investors are not always rational actors, and their decisions are often influenced by emotions such as fear, greed, and overconfidence.

Cognitive biases can lead to poor investment decisions: Investors are prone to a range of cognitive biases, including overconfidence, anchoring, and confirmation bias, which can lead them to make suboptimal investment decisions.

The impact of group dynamics on decision-making: Group dynamics can lead to groupthink, which can lead to poor decision-making and a lack of creativity in financial decision-making.

Financial models and quantitative analysis can help mitigate some of these biases: By using financial models and quantitative analysis, financial professionals can reduce the impact of emotional and cognitive biases on investment decisions.

There is a need for more research on the intersection of psychology and finance: As the field of behavioral finance continues to evolve, there is a need for more research on the intersection of psychology and finance, including the impact of social and cultural factors on investment decisions.

Future research directions

The field of behavioral finance is still in its early stages, and there are many opportunities for future research. Some of the key areas for future research in this field include:

The impact of technology on investment decision-making: As technology continues to evolve, it is likely to have a significant impact on investment decision-making. Future research should explore the impact of technology on investor behavior and decision-making.

The role of emotions in risk management: While much research has focused on the impact of emotions on investment decisions, less attention has been paid to the role of emotions in risk management. Future research should explore how emotions impact risk management decisions.

The impact of culture on investment decisions: While much research has been conducted in Western countries, less is known about how cultural factors impact investment decisions in other parts of the world. Future research should explore the impact of culture on investment decision-making.

The impact of social media on investment decisions: Social media has become an increasingly important source of information for investors. Future research should explore the impact of social media on investor behavior and decision-making.

The development of new tools and techniques for mitigating behavioral biases: While financial models and quantitative analysis can help mitigate some behavioral biases, there is a need for new tools and techniques for addressing these biases. Future research should focus on developing new techniques for mitigating behavioral biases.

In conclusion, behavioral finance has become a critical field in finance that provides insights into the decision-making processes of investors and financial professionals. By studying the psychological biases and heuristics that impact financial decision-making, researchers have been able to identify key behavioral patterns that impact investment outcomes. While the field of behavioral finance is still evolving, it has already provided important insights into how emotions, cognitive biases, and group dynamics impact financial decision-making. As the field continues to evolve, there are many opportunities for future research in this important area.

CHAPTER 29: THE ROLE OF EMOTIONS IN FINANCIAL DECISION MAKING

In recent years, there has been growing interest in the role of emotions in financial decision making. It is now widely recognized that emotions can play a significant role in the way people make financial decisions, from saving and investing to borrowing and spending. Research in this area has revealed that emotions can have both positive and negative effects on financial decision making, and that understanding these effects is essential for financial planners, investors, and policymakers.

In this chapter, we will explore the role of emotions in financial decision making. We will begin by discussing the nature of emotions and their impact on behavior, and then examine how emotions influence different aspects of financial decision making, including risk perception, investment decisions, and consumer behavior. We will also examine the implications of these findings for financial planning and investment management, and consider some of the challenges and opportunities for future research in this area.

The Nature of Emotions and their Impact on Behavior

Emotions are complex psychological experiences that involve a range of cognitive and physiological processes. They are typically characterized by a subjective feeling state, such as happiness, sadness, fear, or anger, as well as changes in physiological arousal, such as increased heart rate, sweating, or muscle tension.

One of the key features of emotions is their impact on behavior. Emotions can influence a wide range of cognitive and behavioral processes, including attention, memory, decision making, and social interactions. They can also motivate us to take action or avoid certain situations, depending on our emotional state.

Research has shown that emotions can have both positive and negative effects on financial decision making. On the one hand, positive emotions such as happiness and contentment can lead to more optimistic views of the future, greater willingness to take risks, and more favorable perceptions of financial opportunities. On the other hand, negative emotions such as fear and anxiety can lead to more pessimistic views of the future, greater aversion to risk, and more cautious financial behavior.

The Influence of Emotions on Financial Decision Making

Risk Perception

One of the most important ways in which emotions influence financial decision making is through their impact on risk perception. Research has shown that emotions can have a significant impact on how people perceive and respond to financial risks.

Positive emotions, such as happiness and excitement, can lead people to perceive risks as less severe and more manageable. This can lead to more risk-taking behavior, including higher levels of investment in risky assets such as stocks and mutual funds. By contrast, negative emotions such as fear and anxiety can lead people to perceive risks as more severe and more difficult to manage. This can lead to more risk-averse behavior, including a greater focus on safe and conservative investments such as bonds and cash.

Investment Decisions

Emotions can also have a significant impact on investment decisions. Research has shown that emotions can influence both the process of making investment decisions and the outcomes of those decisions.

One important way in which emotions can influence investment decisions is through their impact on information processing. Positive emotions can lead people to focus on positive information and ignore or downplay negative information, while negative emotions can lead people to focus on negative information and ignore or downplay positive information. This can lead to biases in decision making, such as overconfidence, confirmation bias, and loss aversion.

Another important way in which emotions can influence investment decisions is through their impact on investment behavior. Positive emotions such as optimism and confidence can lead people to take more risks and make more aggressive investment decisions, while negative emotions such as fear and anxiety can lead people to become more risk-averse and make more conservative investment decisions.

Consumer Behavior

Emotions can also have a significant impact on consumer behavior, including spending and borrowing decisions. Research has shown that emotions can influence both the perception of financial risks and the willingness to engage in risk-taking behavior. For example, a person who is feeling anxious or stressed may perceive a financial decision as riskier than someone who is feeling calm and relaxed, even if the objective risk level is the same.

In addition, emotions can play a role in a person's tendency to overspend or accumulate debt. Impulse buying and overspending are often driven by emotions such as excitement, happiness, or even boredom. In contrast, anxiety and fear can lead to a more cautious approach to spending and borrowing.

Marketing and advertising strategies also rely heavily on emotional appeals to influence consumer behavior. Advertisements that appeal to consumers' emotions, such as happiness, excitement, or social status, have been shown to be more effective than those that rely solely on rational arguments. For example, a car advertisement that emphasizes the feeling of freedom and adventure that comes with owning a luxury car is likely to be more effective than one that focuses solely on the car's features and specifications.

Overall, emotions play a significant role in financial decision-making, both for individuals and in the broader marketplace. Understanding the influence of emotions on financial behavior is critical for individuals seeking to make informed financial decisions and for businesses seeking to develop effective marketing and advertising strategies. By acknowledging the impact of emotions on financial decision-making, individuals and businesses can work to mitigate their negative effects and harness their positive potential.

However, the impact of emotions on financial decision-making is not always straightforward, and there are many factors that can moderate or complicate the relationship between emotions and financial behavior. For example, cultural differences can influence the way that emotions are experienced and expressed, which can in turn affect financial decision-making. Socioeconomic factors, such as income and education level, can also influence the way that emotions are processed and the impact that they have on financial behavior.

Additionally, the relationship between emotions and financial decision-making can be influenced by individual differences in personality and cognitive processes. For example, individuals who are more prone to impulsivity or sensation-seeking may be more likely to engage in risky financial behavior, regardless of their emotional state. Similarly, individuals with certain cognitive biases, such as overconfidence or a tendency to discount future consequences, may be more susceptible to making poor financial decisions even when they are experiencing negative emotions.

Given the complexity of the relationship between emotions and financial decision-making, there is a need for continued research in this area to better understand the mechanisms underlying this relationship and to develop effective interventions for individuals and businesses seeking to improve financial decision-making. By building a more nuanced understanding of the role of emotions in financial behavior, we can work to create a more informed and effective financial landscape for individuals and businesses alike.

I. Theoretical Frameworks

Theoretical frameworks are essential for understanding the various aspects of financial decision-making. These frameworks provide a foundation for analyzing how individuals and organizations make financial choices and how they are influenced by various factors. A theoretical framework is a conceptual model that explains how different variables are related and how they interact to produce a particular outcome. In the field of finance, theoretical frameworks provide a structure for understanding the complex relationships between different financial variables.

Theoretical frameworks can be used to analyze various aspects of financial decision-making, including the role of emotions, cognitive biases, and social influences. They can also be used to evaluate the impact of various financial policies and interventions on individuals and organizations. Theoretical frameworks are especially important for developing financial models that can be used to predict financial outcomes, such as stock prices, interest rates, and economic growth.

There are several theoretical frameworks used in finance, including behavioral finance, agency theory, capital structure theory, and market efficiency theory. Each of these frameworks provides a unique perspective on financial decision-making and is based on different assumptions and principles.

Behavioral finance is a theoretical framework that examines how psychological factors, such as emotions and cognitive biases, influence financial decision-making. This framework challenges the traditional assumptions of rationality and efficiency in financial markets and argues that individuals are often irrational and make decisions based on emotions and biases.

Agency theory is a theoretical framework that examines the relationship between principals and agents in organizations. This framework focuses on how conflicts of interest between principals and agents can lead to agency costs, such as moral hazard and adverse selection. Agency theory is often used to explain issues related to corporate governance and executive compensation.

Capital structure theory is a theoretical framework that examines how firms finance their operations and investments. This framework focuses on the trade-off between debt and equity financing and how firms can optimize their capital structure to maximize their value.

Market efficiency theory is a theoretical framework that examines how financial markets process information and how quickly they adjust to new information. This framework assumes that financial markets are efficient and that prices reflect all available information. However, this assumption has been challenged by the existence of anomalies and market inefficiencies.

In summary, theoretical frameworks are essential for understanding the complex relationships between financial variables and how they affect financial decision-making. They provide a foundation for developing financial models, predicting financial outcomes, and evaluating financial policies and interventions. In the following sections, we will examine these theoretical frameworks in more detail and explore their applications in finance.

Emotion regulation theory

Emotion regulation theory is an important framework in psychology that examines how individuals regulate their emotional responses to different stimuli. In the context of finance, emotion regulation theory has been used to understand how individuals regulate their emotions when making financial decisions. This section will provide an overview of emotion regulation theory and discuss its application in finance.

Emotion Regulation Theory:
Emotion regulation theory suggests that individuals use different strategies to manage their emotions in response to environmental stimuli. These strategies can be categorized as either antecedent-focused or response-focused. Antecedent-focused strategies involve modifying the environment or situation to reduce the intensity of the emotional response, while response-focused strategies involve regulating the emotional response after it has occurred.

Antecedent-focused strategies include cognitive reappraisal, which involves reinterpreting the meaning of a situation to reduce the emotional impact. For example, an investor who experiences a drop in the value of their portfolio might reinterpret this as an opportunity to buy low rather than a significant financial loss. Other antecedent-focused strategies include attentional deployment, which involves directing attention away from the emotional stimulus, and situation selection, which involves choosing to engage in activities that are less likely to elicit a strong emotional response.

Response-focused strategies include expressive suppression, which involves inhibiting the outward expression of emotions, and emotional venting, which involves expressing emotions to reduce their intensity. However, research suggests that expressive suppression can have negative consequences for mental health, while emotional venting can intensify negative emotions.

Application in Finance:
Emotion regulation theory has important implications for finance, as emotions can significantly influence financial decision-making. For example, research has shown that individuals who are unable to regulate their emotions are more likely to engage in impulsive and risky behavior, such as overspending or taking on excessive debt. On the other hand, individuals who are able to regulate their emotions are more likely to make prudent financial decisions and achieve financial stability.

One strategy that has been shown to be effective in regulating emotions in the context of finance is cognitive reappraisal. This involves reframing financial situations in a more positive light, such as focusing on long-term goals rather than short-term losses. Additionally, mindfulness techniques, such as meditation, have been shown to improve emotion regulation and reduce financial stress.

However, the effectiveness of emotion regulation strategies may depend on individual differences, such as personality traits or cultural background. For example, research has shown that individuals from collectivistic cultures may be more likely to use suppression as an emotion regulation strategy, while individuals from individualistic cultures may be more likely to use cognitive reappraisal.

Conclusion:

Emotion regulation theory provides a valuable framework for understanding how individuals manage their emotions in response to financial stimuli. Antecedent-focused strategies, such as cognitive reappraisal and attentional deployment, may be effective in reducing the emotional impact of financial decisions, while response-focused strategies, such as expressive suppression, may have negative consequences for mental health. Future research should continue to explore the effectiveness of different emotion regulation strategies in the context of finance, taking into account individual differences in personality and culture.

Appraisal theory

Appraisal theory is another widely accepted theoretical framework for understanding the role of emotions in financial decision-making. According to appraisal theory, emotions are triggered by an individual's subjective interpretation or appraisal of a particular situation. The theory posits that emotions are not simply a reaction to external events but are instead influenced by an individual's interpretation of those events, as well as their individual goals, values, and beliefs.

Appraisal theory suggests that there are several key dimensions of appraisal that influence the experience of emotion, including the appraisal of goal relevance, goal congruence, and goal conduciveness. For example, if an individual perceives a situation as highly relevant to their goals and values, they are more likely to experience intense emotions, such as anxiety or excitement. Similarly, if an individual perceives a situation as congruent with their goals and values, they are more likely to experience positive emotions, such as happiness or satisfaction.

In the context of financial decision-making, appraisal theory suggests that emotions are influenced by an individual's appraisal of the potential outcomes of their financial decisions. For example, if an individual perceives that a particular investment has a high potential for return and is congruent with their financial goals and values, they may experience positive emotions such as excitement and optimism. On the other hand, if an individual perceives that a particular investment is risky or does not align with their goals and values, they may experience negative emotions such as anxiety or fear.

Appraisal theory has important implications for understanding the impact of emotions on financial decision-making. By recognizing the importance of subjective interpretation and appraisal, appraisal theory highlights the need to consider individual differences in goals, values, and beliefs when studying the role of emotions in financial decision-making. This perspective also suggests that interventions aimed at improving financial decision-making should focus not only on providing objective information about financial decisions but also on helping individuals develop more effective appraisal strategies.

For example, an investment banker may use appraisal theory to understand the emotional reactions of a client to a proposed investment strategy. By recognizing the importance of individual appraisal and interpretation, the investment banker can tailor their communication and presentation of information to address the client's specific goals, values, and beliefs. This may involve emphasizing the potential benefits of the investment in a way that aligns with the client's goals and values, or addressing potential concerns or risks in a way that is congruent with the client's appraisal of the situation.

Overall, appraisal theory provides a useful framework for understanding the complex interplay between emotions and financial decision-making. By recognizing the importance of subjective interpretation and appraisal, appraisal theory highlights the need to consider individual differences in goals, values, and beliefs when studying the role of emotions in financial decision-making. This perspective has important implications for the development of interventions aimed at improving financial decision-making, and highlights the importance of tailoring these interventions to address the specific goals, values, and beliefs of individual investors.

Affect-as-information theory

Affect-as-information theory is a theoretical framework that suggests that emotions serve as a source of information when individuals make decisions. According to this theory, individuals use their current emotional states as a heuristic or shortcut to evaluate a situation and make a decision. In other words, emotions provide a valuable source of information that individuals use to assess the situation and make decisions.

The theory proposes that individuals often rely on their affective or emotional reactions to guide their decision-making process. This means that individuals may use their emotional responses to assess the risks and benefits associated with a particular decision. For example, if an investor is feeling anxious or worried about the stock market, they may be less likely to invest in a particular stock because they perceive it as risky. On the other hand, if an investor is feeling optimistic or positive about the stock market, they may be more likely to invest in a particular stock because they perceive it as profitable.

Research has shown that affect-as-information theory can have significant implications for financial decision-making. One study conducted by Loewenstein, Weber, Hsee, and Welch (2001) found that individuals who were in a positive mood were more likely to take risks when making financial decisions. In contrast, individuals who were in a negative mood were less likely to take risks and were more likely to choose safer, less risky investments.

Furthermore, research has also shown that affective reactions to financial information can influence investment decisions. For example, a study conducted by Lerner and Keltner (2001) found that individuals who were shown negative financial news (such as a decline in the stock market) were more likely to sell their investments compared to those who were shown positive financial news (such as an increase in the stock market).

Overall, affect-as-information theory suggests that emotions play a critical role in the decision-making process, especially in situations where individuals do not have access to all the relevant information or when the decision-making process is complex. This theory highlights the importance of emotions as a source of information and provides insight into how individuals use emotions to make decisions.

Counterarguments against affect-as-information theory include the possibility that emotions may not always accurately reflect the reality of the situation. For example, an individual may be feeling anxious or worried about a financial decision, even if the decision is relatively low-risk. This could lead to a biased decision that is not based on rational evaluation of the situation. Additionally, some researchers argue that affective reactions to financial information may be influenced by other factors, such as personality traits or cognitive biases, which could also impact decision-making.

In conclusion, affect-as-information theory provides a valuable framework for understanding the role of emotions in financial decision-making. The theory suggests that emotions play a critical role in the decision-making process and can serve as a source of valuable information for individuals. However, it is important to recognize the potential limitations of this theory and to consider other factors that may impact decision-making, such as cognitive biases and personality traits. By taking a comprehensive approach to understanding financial decision-making, researchers and practitioners can develop strategies to help individuals make more informed and effective decisions.

Self-regulation theory

Self-regulation theory is a framework that describes the processes by which individuals control their thoughts, emotions, and behaviors to achieve their goals. It proposes that individuals engage in a series of feedback loops involving monitoring, evaluating, and adjusting their behavior based on the feedback they receive. This theory has been applied to a variety of domains, including health behavior change, financial decision-making, and academic achievement.

At the core of self-regulation theory is the idea that individuals have goals and that they use their self-regulatory resources to achieve those goals. Self-regulatory resources refer to the cognitive and emotional processes that individuals use to monitor and control their behavior. These resources include attentional control, emotion regulation, and impulse control. The ability to regulate these processes is critical for achieving goals, as it allows individuals to resist temptations and distractions that can interfere with goal pursuit.

One of the key components of self-regulation theory is the feedback loop model. This model proposes that individuals engage in a cycle of monitoring, evaluating, and adjusting their behavior based on the feedback they receive. The monitoring process involves tracking one's behavior and identifying whether it is consistent with one's goals. The evaluation process involves assessing the effectiveness of one's behavior in achieving those goals. Finally, the adjustment process involves modifying one's behavior in response to the feedback received.

The feedback loop model has been applied to a variety of domains. For example, in the domain of health behavior change, individuals may use this model to modify their behavior in response to feedback about their diet or exercise habits. In the domain of financial decision-making, individuals may use this model to adjust their investment strategy based on feedback about their portfolio performance. In the domain of academic achievement, students may use this model to adjust their study habits based on feedback about their grades or test scores.

Another important component of self-regulation theory is the concept of self-efficacy. Self-efficacy refers to an individual's belief in their ability to successfully perform a particular behavior. This belief is influenced by a variety of factors, including past performance, social support, and cognitive factors such as attention and memory. Self-efficacy plays an important role in self-regulation, as it helps individuals to maintain motivation and perseverance in the face of obstacles and setbacks.

Self-regulation theory has important implications for a variety of fields, including education, health promotion, and finance. In the field of education, self-regulation theory has been used to develop interventions that help students to improve their study habits and academic performance. For example, one study found that a self-regulation intervention that included goal-setting, monitoring, and self-evaluation helped college students to improve their GPA and reduce their rates of procrastination.

In the field of health promotion, self-regulation theory has been used to develop interventions that help individuals to make healthier choices. For example, one study found that a self-regulation intervention that included self-monitoring and goal-setting helped individuals to increase their physical activity and reduce their sedentary behavior. In the field of finance, self-regulation theory has been used to develop interventions that help individuals to make better financial decisions. For example, one study found that a self-regulation intervention that included goal-setting, self-monitoring, and feedback helped individuals to reduce their credit card debt and improve their credit scores.

Despite the potential benefits of self-regulation theory, there are also some limitations to this framework. For example, some researchers have argued that self-regulation theory does not adequately account for the role of contextual factors in shaping behavior. Others have suggested that self-regulation theory does not adequately account for the role of automatic processes in behavior, such as habit formation or priming effects.

In conclusion, self-regulation theory is a useful framework for understanding how individuals control their thoughts, emotions, and behaviors to achieve their goals. By considering the interplay of the various cognitive and affective processes involved in self-regulation, researchers can gain insight into how people successfully manage their impulses, persist in the face of obstacles, and achieve long-term goals.

Self-regulation theory has important implications for a variety of fields, including psychology, education, healthcare, and business. For example, educators can use self-regulation theory to help students develop effective study habits and persist in challenging academic tasks. Healthcare professionals can use self-regulation strategies to help patients manage chronic illnesses and adhere to treatment plans. In the business world, self-regulation strategies can be used to help employees set and achieve career goals, and to manage stress and work-life balance.

However, there are also limitations to self-regulation theory. One limitation is that it tends to focus on the individual, rather than considering the broader social and environmental factors that influence self-regulation. For example, social support and environmental cues can play important roles in helping individuals achieve their goals. Additionally, cultural differences in self-regulation may exist, and future research may need to explore these differences in greater depth.

Another limitation is that self-regulation theory tends to emphasize the importance of effortful control, which may not always be the most effective way to achieve goals. In some cases, relying too heavily on effortful control can lead to burnout or disengagement from the goal. Thus, researchers should also consider the role of other factors, such as motivation, in achieving goals.

Overall, self-regulation theory is a valuable framework for understanding how individuals achieve their goals through cognitive and affective processes. However, researchers must also consider the broader social and environmental factors that influence self-regulation, as well as the potential limitations of an emphasis on effortful control. With continued research and application, self-regulation theory has the potential to contribute to a better understanding of how individuals can achieve success in various domains of life.

II. Emotions and Financial Decision Making

Emotions play a crucial role in decision making, and financial decisions are no exception. While we often like to think of ourselves as rational beings who make objective choices, research has consistently shown that emotions strongly influence our financial decision making. This is because financial decisions are often complex, involve uncertainty, and have high stakes, all of which can trigger emotional responses.

In recent years, there has been increasing interest in studying the relationship between emotions and financial decision making. Researchers have used a variety of methods, including surveys, experiments, and brain imaging, to better understand how emotions impact our financial choices. This field of research has important implications for a wide range of professionals, including investment bankers, portfolio managers, financial analysts, and financial planners, who must navigate the complex emotions of their clients while helping them make sound financial decisions.

One of the key challenges in studying emotions and financial decision making is that emotions are often difficult to measure and quantify. Unlike objective factors such as income or interest rates, emotions are subjective experiences that can vary widely from person to person. However, researchers have developed a range of methods for measuring emotions, including self-report measures, physiological measures, and behavioral measures.

Despite the challenges, research has revealed a number of important insights into how emotions impact financial decision making. For example, studies have shown that emotions such as fear, greed, and regret can lead to biased decision making, such as overreacting to market fluctuations, taking on excessive risk, or failing to diversify portfolios. On the other hand, positive emotions such as hope and optimism can lead to more prudent decision making, such as investing for the long term and avoiding impulsive choices.

Overall, the study of emotions and financial decision making is a rich and growing field that has important implications for both individuals and professionals. In this section, we will explore some of the key findings from this research and discuss how they can be applied in practice. We will also examine some of the challenges and limitations of this field of study, and suggest directions for future research.

Fear and anxiety

Fear and anxiety are two of the most common emotions that people experience in their daily lives. They play an important role in helping individuals to navigate their environment, assess potential risks and threats, and make decisions about how to respond to those threats. However, in certain situations, fear and anxiety can also interfere with decision making, leading individuals to make choices that are not in their best interest. This is particularly true in the realm of finance, where decisions based on fear and anxiety can have significant and long-lasting consequences.

In this section, we will explore the role of fear and anxiety in financial decision making, including the ways in which these emotions can impact our cognitive processes, decision making strategies, and financial outcomes. We will also consider some of the factors that can moderate the impact of fear and anxiety on financial decision making, and discuss strategies that individuals can use to overcome these emotions and make more informed financial decisions.

The Psychology of Fear and Anxiety

Fear and anxiety are complex emotions that involve a range of cognitive and physiological processes. At their core, both emotions are designed to help individuals identify and respond to threats in their environment. Fear is typically elicited by a specific threat or danger, while anxiety is a more general and diffuse sense of unease or apprehension about future events.

From a cognitive perspective, fear and anxiety can impact decision making in several ways. First, these emotions can interfere with attention and working memory, making it difficult for individuals to focus on relevant information and keep it in mind. This can lead to a focus on immediate, short-term gains or losses, rather than the long-term consequences of a decision.

Second, fear and anxiety can also lead to a bias in information processing, in which individuals are more likely to attend to negative or threatening information, and discount positive or neutral information. This bias can make it difficult to accurately assess the risks and benefits of different options, and can lead to overly conservative or risk-averse decision making.

Finally, fear and anxiety can also impact individuals' confidence in their decision making abilities, leading to self-doubt and indecision. This can be particularly problematic in financial decision making, where confidence and assertiveness are often key to negotiating favorable terms and achieving financial goals.

The Impact of Fear and Anxiety on Financial Decision Making

Given the complex ways in which fear and anxiety can impact cognitive processes, it is not surprising that these emotions can have significant consequences for financial decision making. In particular, fear and anxiety can lead to a range of biases and heuristics that can impact financial outcomes.

One of the most common ways in which fear and anxiety impact financial decision making is through a phenomenon known as loss aversion. Loss aversion refers to the tendency for individuals to be more sensitive to losses than gains, such that the pain of losing $100 is felt more acutely than the pleasure of gaining $100. This bias can lead to risk-averse decision making, in which individuals are more willing to accept lower returns in order to avoid potential losses.

In addition to loss aversion, fear and anxiety can also lead to a number of other cognitive biases, such as the availability heuristic, in which individuals rely on the most easily accessible information when making decisions, rather than considering a broader range of information. Fear and anxiety can also lead to an over-reliance on past experience or intuition, rather than systematic analysis of available data.

Finally, fear and anxiety can also lead to a range of behavioral biases, such as herding behavior, in which individuals follow the crowd rather than making independent decisions, and anchoring, in which individuals are unduly influenced by initial estimates or values.

Moderating Factors and Strategies for Overcoming Fear and Anxiety

While fear and anxiety can have significant consequences for financial decision making, it is important to note that the impact of these emotions is not uniform across all individuals. There are moderating factors that can influence the strength of the relationship between fear/anxiety and financial decision making.

One moderating factor is the level of financial literacy. Individuals who have a higher level of financial literacy tend to make more informed and rational decisions when faced with financial decisions. They are better able to understand financial information and evaluate the risks and benefits of different options, which can help reduce the impact of fear and anxiety on their decision making.

Another moderating factor is the level of experience with financial decision making. Individuals who have more experience making financial decisions may be less likely to experience fear and anxiety when faced with similar situations in the future. This is because they have developed a level of familiarity and comfort with financial decision making and are better equipped to handle the associated emotions.

In addition to these moderating factors, there are strategies that individuals can use to overcome fear and anxiety when making financial decisions. One strategy is to seek out social support from trusted sources, such as family, friends, or financial advisors. Social support can provide emotional reassurance and help individuals feel more confident and in control of their decision making.

Another strategy is to engage in relaxation techniques, such as deep breathing, meditation, or yoga, which can help reduce feelings of stress and anxiety. Exercise and physical activity can also be effective in reducing stress and anxiety, as well as improving overall mood and cognitive function.

Finally, individuals can use cognitive strategies, such as reframing or positive self-talk, to help manage their emotions and make more rational financial decisions. Reframing involves looking at a situation from a different perspective, while positive self-talk involves using positive statements to reinforce one's confidence and ability to make effective decisions.

Despite the potential negative impact of fear and anxiety on financial decision making, it is important to note that these emotions are a natural and normal part of the human experience. They can serve as important signals of potential risks and dangers, and can help individuals make more informed and cautious decisions. However, it is important for individuals to be aware of the potential biases and distortions that can be caused by fear and anxiety, and to use strategies to mitigate their impact when making financial decisions.

Greed and overconfidence

Greed and overconfidence are two emotions that can significantly impact financial decision making. Both of these emotions can lead individuals to take on unnecessary risks and make irrational decisions, which can ultimately result in financial losses. In this section, we will explore the concepts of greed and overconfidence and how they can affect financial decision making. We will also discuss strategies for mitigating the negative effects of these emotions.

Defining Greed and Overconfidence:

Greed is defined as an intense desire for material possessions or wealth. It is a strong emotion that can lead individuals to make decisions that prioritize personal gain over other factors such as risk or long-term consequences. Greed can manifest in various ways, such as a desire for higher returns on investments, a need for financial power and status, or a craving for material possessions.

Overconfidence, on the other hand, refers to an individual's belief in their abilities or knowledge that exceeds their actual capabilities. It is a cognitive bias that can lead individuals to overestimate their skills, knowledge, and ability to predict outcomes. Overconfidence can lead to excessive risk-taking and irrational decision making in financial matters.

Effects of Greed and Overconfidence on Financial Decision Making:

Both greed and overconfidence can have significant negative effects on financial decision making. For instance, greed can lead individuals to take on too much risk, such as investing in high-risk securities or leveraging too much debt. This behavior can result in significant losses if the investments do not perform as expected. In the investment banking field, the desire to maximize profits can lead to unethical behavior and financial fraud, such as insider trading or Ponzi schemes.

Similarly, overconfidence can lead individuals to overestimate their ability to predict market trends, leading them to make rash decisions based on incomplete information. This overconfidence can result in significant losses, as investors make decisions based on faulty assumptions.

One example of the effects of overconfidence on financial decision making is the dot-com bubble of the late 1990s. During this time, many investors were caught up in the hype surrounding internet-based companies and invested heavily in these companies, even though many of them were not yet profitable. This overconfidence led to a significant market crash when the bubble burst, resulting in massive financial losses for many investors.

Strategies for Mitigating the Negative Effects of Greed and Overconfidence:

There are several strategies that individuals can use to mitigate the negative effects of greed and overconfidence on financial decision making.

One strategy is to diversify investments, which can help to reduce risk and minimize losses. By spreading investments across multiple sectors, individuals can protect themselves from significant losses due to the failure of any one investment.

Another strategy is to set realistic expectations for investment returns. This can help to prevent individuals from becoming overly focused on short-term gains and can encourage them to take a more long-term view of their investments.

Additionally, seeking out professional advice from financial planners or investment managers can help to provide a more objective view of investment decisions. These professionals can provide insights into market trends and potential risks, which can help to mitigate the effects of overconfidence and reduce the risk of making irrational decisions.

Conclusion:

In conclusion, greed and overconfidence are two emotions that can significantly impact financial decision making. These emotions can lead individuals to take on unnecessary risks, make irrational decisions, and ultimately result in significant financial losses. It is important to recognize the negative effects of these emotions and to take steps to mitigate their impact. By diversifying investments, setting realistic expectations, and seeking professional advice, individuals can reduce the risk of making irrational financial decisions based on greed and overconfidence.

Regret and disappointment

Regret and disappointment are emotions that are commonly experienced in the context of financial decision making. Regret refers to the negative feeling that arises from the recognition that a different decision could have resulted in a more favorable outcome. Disappointment, on the other hand, is the negative feeling that arises when an outcome falls short of one's expectations. Both emotions can have significant effects on subsequent financial decisions.

Regret aversion is a well-established phenomenon in behavioral finance, which refers to the tendency for individuals to avoid taking actions that may lead to regret. This aversion can manifest in various ways, such as avoiding decisions altogether, delaying decisions, or choosing the option that minimizes the likelihood of regret. In financial decision making, regret aversion can lead to suboptimal outcomes, as individuals may be unwilling to take on risks or make decisions that may lead to regret.

Disappointment can also have significant effects on financial decision making. In particular, the feeling of disappointment can lead to risk aversion, as individuals may become more focused on avoiding losses than on achieving gains. This can result in missed opportunities for growth and reduced overall returns. Additionally, disappointment can lead to a loss of confidence in one's decision-making abilities, which can have long-term consequences for financial well-being.

Moderating Factors

Like other emotions, the impact of regret and disappointment on financial decision making is moderated by various factors. One important factor is the severity of the emotion. For instance, individuals may be more likely to avoid taking risks or to become risk-averse when the feeling of regret is particularly strong. Similarly, the feeling of disappointment may have a greater impact on financial decisions when the outcome falls particularly short of expectations.

Another moderating factor is the source of the emotion. For example, regret that arises from an action taken (i.e., commission) may have a different impact on financial decision making than regret that arises from an action not taken (i.e., omission). Similarly, disappointment that arises from a personal mistake may have different effects than disappointment that arises from external factors outside of one's control.

Finally, individual differences in personality, such as risk tolerance and resilience, may also moderate the impact of regret and disappointment on financial decision making. For example, individuals who are more risk-tolerant may be less likely to be influenced by regret and disappointment, while individuals who are less resilient may be more likely to be negatively affected by these emotions.

Strategies for Overcoming Regret and Disappointment

Given the potential negative impact of regret and disappointment on financial decision making, it is important to develop strategies for overcoming these emotions. One approach is to reframe the situation in a more positive light. For instance, instead of focusing on the negative outcome, individuals can focus on what they learned from the experience and how they can apply this knowledge to future decisions. This can help to reduce the feeling of regret and disappointment and promote a more positive outlook.

Another strategy is to seek social support. Discussing the situation with a trusted friend or advisor can help to provide a different perspective and provide emotional support. Additionally, seeking professional counseling or therapy can be beneficial for individuals who are struggling to overcome the negative impact of regret and disappointment on their financial decision making.

Finally, developing a growth mindset can also be helpful. Instead of viewing negative outcomes as failures, individuals can view them as opportunities for growth and development. This can help to reduce the impact of regret and disappointment on subsequent decisions and promote a more positive attitude towards financial decision making.

Conclusion

Regret and disappointment are common emotions that can have significant effects on financial decision making. Regret aversion can lead to suboptimal outcomes, while disappointment can lead to risk aversion and a loss of confidence in one's decision-making abilities. The impact of these emotions is moderated by various factors, including the severity of the emotion, the perceived controllability of the outcome, and individual differences such as personality and cognitive style.

While it may be difficult to completely eliminate regret and disappointment in financial decision making, there are strategies that individuals can use to mitigate their negative effects. These strategies include focusing on the long-term perspective, reframing losses as learning opportunities, and seeking social support.

One important takeaway from the research on regret and disappointment is the importance of recognizing and acknowledging these emotions. Many people may try to avoid or suppress these emotions, but doing so can ultimately lead to worse outcomes. By acknowledging and processing regret and disappointment, individuals can make more informed and deliberate decisions in the future.

Furthermore, it is important for financial professionals to be aware of the impact of regret and disappointment on their clients. By understanding the emotional factors that influence financial decision making, professionals can provide better guidance and support to their clients. This may include helping clients set realistic expectations, providing reassurance and emotional support during difficult periods, and encouraging clients to adopt a long-term perspective.

In conclusion, regret and disappointment are complex emotions that can significantly impact financial decision making. While these emotions may never be completely eliminated, individuals and financial professionals can use strategies to mitigate their negative effects and make more informed decisions. By acknowledging the role of emotions in financial decision making, we can create a more nuanced and effective approach to managing personal finances and investing.

Hope and optimism

Hope and optimism are positive emotions that can have a significant impact on financial decision making. These emotions can increase risk-taking behavior, enhance creativity and innovation, and improve decision-making abilities. However, excessive optimism and unrealistic expectations can also lead to irrational decision making and financial losses. In this section, we will explore the concept of hope and optimism, their effects on financial decision making, and the strategies for maintaining a balance between optimism and realism.

Definition of Hope and Optimism

Hope and optimism are positive emotions that are often used interchangeably. However, there are subtle differences between the two. Hope is defined as a positive expectation that something desirable will occur, even if the likelihood of it happening is uncertain. Optimism, on the other hand, is a generalized expectation that good things will happen in the future, regardless of specific outcomes or events.

Hope and optimism are closely related to motivation and goal attainment. They are also important for mental and physical health, resilience, and overall well-being. Research suggests that individuals who are hopeful and optimistic are more likely to engage in positive behaviors and achieve their goals.

Effects of Hope and Optimism on Financial Decision Making

Hope and optimism can have both positive and negative effects on financial decision making. On the one hand, these emotions can increase risk-taking behavior and enhance creativity and innovation. For example, hopeful and optimistic individuals are more likely to invest in new ventures, start their own businesses, and pursue higher education.

On the other hand, excessive optimism and unrealistic expectations can lead to irrational decision making and financial losses. For example, investors who are overly optimistic about a particular stock may ignore warning signs and invest too heavily, leading to significant losses. Similarly, business owners who are overly optimistic about their company's future may take on too much debt, leading to financial difficulties and bankruptcy.

Moderating Factors

The impact of hope and optimism on financial decision making is moderated by various factors, including the level of uncertainty, the magnitude of potential outcomes, and the level of experience and expertise of the decision maker.

For example, the impact of hope and optimism is greater when the level of uncertainty is high, such as in the case of new ventures and start-ups. In these situations, individuals who are hopeful and optimistic may be more willing to take risks and invest in the future, even if the likelihood of success is uncertain.

Similarly, the impact of hope and optimism is greater when the potential outcomes are more significant, such as in the case of high-stakes investments or major business decisions. In these situations, individuals who are hopeful and optimistic may be more willing to take risks and pursue ambitious goals, even if the risks are high.

Finally, the impact of hope and optimism is moderated by the level of experience and expertise of the decision maker. Experienced and knowledgeable investors, for example, may be better able to balance their optimism with a realistic assessment of risk and potential outcomes.

Strategies for Maintaining a Balance Between Optimism and Realism

Maintaining a balance between optimism and realism is essential for effective financial decision making. Here are some strategies for achieving this balance:

Consider the evidence: When making financial decisions, it is important to consider the evidence and data, rather than relying solely on intuition or emotions. Conducting a thorough analysis of the risks and potential outcomes can help to balance optimism with realism.

Seek expert advice: Consulting with experts and professionals, such as financial advisors, can provide valuable insights and help to balance optimism with a realistic assessment of risk.

Set realistic goals: Setting realistic goals that are achievable within a given timeframe can help to maintain a balance between optimism and realism. Unrealistic expectations can lead to disappointment and irrational decision making.

Diversify investments: Diversifying investments can help to spread risk and minimize losses. Investing in a variety of assets can provide a balance between optimism and realism by mitigating the risk of over-reliance on a single investment, which can lead to excessive optimism and overconfidence.

Monitor and adjust your approach: Regularly monitoring your investments and adjusting your approach based on changing circumstances can help to maintain a balance between optimism and realism. For example, if market conditions change, it may be necessary to adjust your investment strategy to reflect the new reality.

Avoid extreme optimism: While optimism can be beneficial in financial decision making, extreme optimism can lead to overconfidence and irrational decision making. It is important to maintain a realistic assessment of risks and potential outcomes, rather than becoming overly optimistic.

Understand your own biases: It is important to understand and recognize your own biases when making financial decisions. Confirmation bias, for example, can lead to a narrow and overly optimistic view of potential outcomes. Being aware of these biases can help to maintain a balance between optimism and realism.

Practice mindfulness: Mindfulness techniques, such as meditation and deep breathing, can help to reduce stress and anxiety and promote a more balanced approach to decision making. By reducing the impact of negative emotions, mindfulness can help to maintain a balance between optimism and realism.

Conclusion:

Hope and optimism are important factors in financial decision making, but they must be balanced with a realistic assessment of risks and potential outcomes. Excessive optimism can lead to overconfidence and irrational decision making, while too much pessimism can lead to missed opportunities and a lack of confidence. By seeking expert advice, considering the evidence, setting realistic goals, diversifying investments, monitoring and adjusting approach, avoiding extreme optimism, understanding biases, and practicing mindfulness, individuals can maintain a balance between optimism and realism, leading to more effective financial decision making.

III. The Impact of Emotions on Investment Performance

The world of investment is complex, dynamic, and often unpredictable. There are countless variables that can affect investment performance, including economic conditions, political events, technological advancements, and societal trends. However, one often overlooked factor that can have a significant impact on investment performance is human emotion.

Emotions play a crucial role in the decision-making process of investors, and can lead to both positive and negative outcomes. On one hand, emotions such as hope and optimism can drive investors to take calculated risks and pursue potentially lucrative opportunities. On the other hand, emotions such as fear and anxiety can cause investors to make irrational decisions and miss out on potentially profitable investments.

Understanding the impact of emotions on investment performance is essential for investors who want to make informed, rational decisions. This requires a deep understanding of the psychological factors that underpin investment decision making, as well as the strategies and techniques that can be used to manage emotions and mitigate their negative impact.

In this comprehensive analysis, we will explore the impact of emotions on investment performance in detail. We will examine the various emotions that can affect investment decision making, including greed, overconfidence, regret, disappointment, hope, and optimism. We will also explore the psychological and cognitive processes that underlie these emotions, and discuss the various strategies that investors can use to manage their emotions and make informed, rational investment decisions.

To provide a well-rounded analysis, we will draw on insights and perspectives from a variety of fields, including investment banking, actuarial science, portfolio management, quantitative analysis, securities trading, financial planning, and financial analysis. We will also present counter-arguments and dissenting opinions in a balanced and objective way, in order to provide a comprehensive and nuanced understanding of the subject matter.

Overall, this analysis will provide investors with a valuable resource for understanding the role of emotions in investment performance, and equipping them with the knowledge and strategies necessary to make informed, rational decisions in today's complex and dynamic investment landscape.

The role of emotions in investment decisions

Investment decisions are critical in determining the financial success of individuals and organizations alike. Given the complexity and uncertainty of financial markets, investment decisions can be challenging, and emotions can play a significant role in shaping these decisions.

Research in psychology and behavioral economics has shown that emotions can impact investment decisions in several ways. For instance, emotions such as fear, anxiety, and greed can lead to irrational decision-making, resulting in suboptimal investment outcomes. Similarly, emotions such as hope and optimism can influence investors to take on higher levels of risk than they should, leading to significant losses.

The role of emotions in investment decisions has gained increasing attention in recent years, with scholars and practitioners recognizing the need to understand the psychological factors that influence investment behavior. Professionals in the financial industry, such as investment bankers, actuaries, portfolio managers, quantitative analysts, securities traders, financial planners, and financial analysts, must be aware of the potential impact of emotions on investment performance.

Emotions can impact investment decisions at various stages of the investment process, from information gathering and analysis to portfolio construction and management. For instance, emotions can influence the way investors interpret and react to market news, as well as their risk perceptions and tolerance. Emotions can also impact investment decisions related to portfolio diversification, asset allocation, and investment style.

Given the impact of emotions on investment decisions, it is crucial to understand the psychological mechanisms that drive these emotions and their effects on investment behavior. This requires an interdisciplinary approach that combines insights from psychology, neuroscience, economics, and finance.

The purpose of this article is to provide a comprehensive analysis of the role of emotions in investment decisions. Specifically, we will explore how emotions such as fear, greed, hope, and optimism can influence investment decisions, the mechanisms that underlie these effects, and strategies for managing emotions to improve investment performance.

By understanding the role of emotions in investment decisions, investors and financial professionals can make more informed and effective investment decisions, ultimately leading to improved investment outcomes.

The impact of emotions on investment returns

Investing is an emotional activity. The decisions that investors make are influenced by a wide range of emotions, such as fear, greed, hope, and regret. These emotions can have a significant impact on investment returns. This section will explore the impact of emotions on investment returns and provide insights into how investors can manage their emotions to achieve better returns.

The Impact of Emotions on Investment Returns:

Emotions can have a profound impact on investment returns. In many cases, emotions can cause investors to make irrational decisions that result in significant losses. For example, fear can cause investors to sell their investments during market downturns, locking in losses and missing out on potential gains when the market rebounds.

On the other hand, greed can cause investors to take on excessive risk, investing in speculative assets with the hope of earning quick profits. This type of behavior can lead to significant losses if the investments do not perform as expected.

The impact of emotions on investment returns is well documented in the academic literature. For example, a study by Terrance Odean and Brad Barber found that overconfident investors tend to trade more frequently, resulting in lower returns. Similarly, a study by Hersh Shefrin and Meir Statman found that investors tend to hold onto losing investments for too long in the hope of recouping their losses, resulting in lower returns.

Another study by John Nofsinger and Richard W. Sias found that the emotional states of investors can have a significant impact on their investment decisions. The study found that investors who are feeling happy tend to take on more risk, while investors who are feeling anxious tend to take on less risk.

In addition to these academic studies, there are numerous real-world examples of the impact of emotions on investment returns. For example, during the dot-com bubble of the late 1990s, many investors became overly optimistic about the potential of internet companies and invested heavily in these stocks. When the bubble burst, many of these investors lost a significant portion of their investments.

Similarly, during the financial crisis of 2008, many investors panicked and sold their investments, locking in losses and missing out on the subsequent market rebound. These examples highlight the importance of managing emotions when making investment decisions.

Managing Emotions to Improve Investment Returns:

While emotions can have a significant impact on investment returns, there are strategies that investors can use to manage their emotions and improve their investment returns. Here are a few key strategies:

Develop a sound investment strategy: Having a sound investment strategy can help to reduce the impact of emotions on investment decisions. A well-designed investment strategy should include a clear set of goals, a diversified portfolio, and a disciplined approach to buying and selling investments.

Focus on the long-term: Focusing on the long-term can help to reduce the impact of short-term fluctuations on investment decisions. By focusing on the long-term, investors can avoid making impulsive decisions based on short-term market movements.

Avoid making emotional decisions: Avoiding emotional decisions is easier said than done, but it is an important strategy for improving investment returns. When making investment decisions, investors should rely on data and analysis rather than emotions.

Seek professional advice: Seeking professional advice can be an effective way to manage emotions and improve investment returns. Financial advisors can provide valuable insights into investment strategies and help investors to make more informed decisions.

Stay informed: Staying informed about the markets and economic trends can help investors to make better-informed investment decisions. By staying informed, investors can avoid making decisions based on incomplete or inaccurate information.

Conclusion:

In conclusion, emotions can have a significant impact on investment returns. Fear, greed, hope, and regret are just a few of the emotions that can influence investment decisions. While it is impossible to eliminate emotions from investment decisions, there are strategies that can help investors mitigate the negative effects of emotions and maximize their returns.

One key strategy is to maintain a balanced and objective approach to investing. By conducting thorough research and analysis, seeking expert advice, and keeping emotions in check, investors can make informed decisions that are based on logic and evidence rather than impulse and emotion.

Another strategy is to practice mindfulness and self-awareness. By recognizing and acknowledging their emotions, investors can better understand how they may be influencing their decisions and take steps to regulate their emotions and maintain a level-headed approach.

Finally, it is important to remember that investing is a long-term game. Short-term fluctuations and market volatility can be emotionally challenging, but investors who stay the course and remain committed to their long-term goals are more likely to achieve success.

In summary, emotions are an inevitable and natural part of the investment process. However, by understanding the impact of emotions on investment decisions and adopting effective strategies for managing them, investors can increase their chances of achieving their financial goals and building a more secure financial future.

The impact of emotions on investment risk

Investment risk is a crucial factor in making investment decisions. Investors aim to maximize returns while minimizing risk. However, emotions can significantly impact investment risk. Emotional biases can cloud an investor's judgment, leading them to take unnecessary risks or avoid potentially profitable investments. In this section, we will explore the impact of emotions on investment risk and how investors can mitigate the negative effects of emotions on their investment decisions.

Impact of Emotions on Investment Risk

Emotions can significantly impact investment risk by influencing an investor's perception of risk and their risk appetite. Emotions such as fear, greed, and overconfidence can lead to irrational investment decisions, resulting in higher risk exposure.

Fear

Fear is a common emotion that can significantly impact investment risk. Fear can lead to an investor's perception of risk being skewed towards the negative, causing them to avoid potentially profitable investments. For example, during a market downturn, fear can cause investors to panic and sell their investments, leading to losses. On the other hand, fear can also cause investors to overreact to news and events, leading to higher risk exposure.

Greed

Greed is another common emotion that can significantly impact investment risk. Greed can cause investors to take unnecessary risks, leading to higher risk exposure. For example, investors may invest in speculative stocks or engage in high-risk trading strategies to maximize their returns, but at the expense of increasing their risk exposure.

Overconfidence

Overconfidence is an emotion that can lead investors to take risks beyond their risk tolerance level. Overconfident investors may believe that they have superior knowledge or skills, leading them to engage in high-risk investments. This can lead to significant losses if the investment does not perform as expected.

Mitigating the Negative Effects of Emotions on Investment Risk

To mitigate the negative effects of emotions on investment risk, investors can adopt several strategies.

Develop a Risk Management Plan

A risk management plan is essential in mitigating the negative effects of emotions on investment risk. The plan should identify the investor's risk tolerance level, investment goals, and risk appetite. By setting clear investment objectives and risk parameters, investors can avoid taking unnecessary risks or engaging in impulsive investment decisions.

Use Diversification

Diversification is a strategy that involves investing in a variety of assets to spread risk. By diversifying their portfolio, investors can reduce their risk exposure and mitigate the impact of negative emotions on their investments. For example, a portfolio manager can allocate their portfolio across different asset classes such as stocks, bonds, and commodities to reduce risk exposure.

Implement a Systematic Investment Plan

A systematic investment plan is a strategy that involves investing a fixed amount of money at regular intervals. By implementing a systematic investment plan, investors can avoid making impulsive investment decisions based on emotions such as fear or greed. Instead, they can focus on their long-term investment goals and avoid reacting to short-term market fluctuations.

Seek Professional Advice

Professional advice from financial advisors, investment bankers, and other professionals can help investors make informed investment decisions. Professional advisors can provide objective guidance on investment opportunities, risk management strategies, and other investment-related issues. This can help investors avoid making irrational investment decisions based on emotions.

Conclusion

Emotions can significantly impact investment risk. Fear, greed, and overconfidence can lead to irrational investment decisions, resulting in higher risk exposure. To mitigate the negative effects of emotions on investment risk, investors can develop a risk management plan, use diversification, implement a systematic investment plan, and seek professional advice. By adopting these strategies, investors can make informed investment decisions and avoid the negative impact of emotions on their investments.

IV. Strategies for Managing Emotions in Financial Decision Making

When it comes to making financial decisions, emotions can often cloud our judgment and lead us to make irrational choices that can have negative consequences. This is especially true in the world of finance, where even the slightest shift in the market can lead to significant gains or losses. Managing emotions is therefore critical for successful financial decision-making.

In this section, we will explore various strategies for managing emotions in financial decision-making. We will begin by discussing the role of emotions in financial decision-making and how they can impact our ability to make rational decisions. We will then explore various strategies that can help us manage our emotions and make better financial decisions.

Role of Emotions in Financial Decision-Making:

Emotions can play a significant role in financial decision-making. Fear, greed, hope, and regret are just a few of the emotions that can influence our investment decisions. When the market is volatile, fear can lead investors to panic and sell off their investments, even if it is not in their best interest. On the other hand, greed can cause investors to take on more risk than they should, leading to potentially disastrous losses.

Similarly, hope can cause investors to hold onto investments that are no longer performing well, hoping that they will recover. This can lead to missed opportunities and further losses. Regret can also play a role in financial decision-making. When investors make a bad decision, they may experience regret and make irrational decisions in an attempt to rectify the situation.

Strategies for Managing Emotions in Financial Decision-Making:

While it is impossible to eliminate emotions from financial decision-making, there are strategies that can help us manage them more effectively. Here are some of the strategies that can be used:

Develop a Plan:
Having a plan in place can help investors manage their emotions by providing a framework for decision-making. A well-defined plan can help investors stay focused on their long-term goals and avoid making impulsive decisions based on short-term market fluctuations.

For example, a financial planner can work with an investor to develop a personalized financial plan that takes into account their goals, risk tolerance, and time horizon. This plan can then be used as a guide for making investment decisions and managing emotions.

Focus on the Big Picture:
When making financial decisions, it is important to focus on the big picture rather than getting caught up in the daily ups and downs of the market. It is essential to remember that investing is a long-term process and that short-term market fluctuations should not drive investment decisions.

Investors should focus on their long-term financial goals and work towards achieving them, even if there are some bumps along the way. By keeping the big picture in mind, investors can avoid making rash decisions based on short-term market movements.

Avoid Emotional Triggers:
There are certain emotional triggers that can lead to poor financial decision-making. For example, watching financial news can be overwhelming and lead to emotional responses that can impact decision-making. Investors should limit their exposure to financial news and instead focus on long-term strategies.

Similarly, investing in individual stocks can be emotionally taxing, as the performance of the stock can trigger emotional responses. Investors should consider investing in mutual funds or ETFs, which can provide diversified exposure to the market and reduce emotional triggers.

Stay Disciplined:
Staying disciplined is critical for managing emotions in financial decision-making. This means sticking to a plan and avoiding impulsive decisions based on emotions. Investors should avoid making changes to their investment strategy based on short-term market movements and instead focus on their long-term goals.

Sticking to a plan can be challenging, especially during times of market volatility, but it is essential for successful long-term investing.

Conclusion:

Managing emotions is critical for successful financial decision-making. Emotions can cloud our judgment and lead us to make irrational decisions that can have negative consequences. By utilizing strategies to manage emotions, individuals can improve their financial decision-making and achieve their financial goals.

One effective strategy for managing emotions is to take a systematic approach to decision-making. This involves identifying the relevant criteria for making a decision, gathering and analyzing data, and evaluating the potential outcomes of each option. By using a systematic approach, individuals can reduce the impact of emotions on their decision-making process and make more objective and rational decisions.

Another strategy is to practice mindfulness and self-awareness. This involves paying attention to our emotions and recognizing when they are influencing our decisions. By practicing mindfulness, individuals can learn to recognize their emotional triggers and respond in a more rational and constructive way.

Emotional intelligence is also an important factor in managing emotions in financial decision-making. Emotional intelligence involves the ability to recognize, understand, and regulate our own emotions, as well as the emotions of others. By developing emotional intelligence, individuals can improve their ability to manage their own emotions and communicate effectively with others.

Behavioral finance is a field that studies the impact of emotions and cognitive biases on financial decision-making. Behavioral finance provides valuable insights into the ways in which emotions can influence financial decisions, and offers strategies for managing these emotions. For example, the field has identified the importance of framing, or the way in which a decision is presented, in influencing decision-making. By being aware of framing effects, individuals can make more objective decisions.

Financial education is another important strategy for managing emotions in financial decision-making. By educating oneself about financial concepts and strategies, individuals can make more informed decisions and feel more confident in their financial decisions. Financial education can also help individuals develop a long-term perspective on their finances, which can help reduce the impact of emotions on their decision-making.

In conclusion, managing emotions is a critical aspect of financial decision-making. By using strategies such as a systematic approach to decision-making, mindfulness and self-awareness, emotional intelligence, behavioral finance, and financial education, individuals can improve their ability to make rational and objective financial decisions. By taking steps to manage emotions, individuals can achieve their financial goals and avoid the negative consequences of irrational decision-making.

Mindfulness

In today's fast-paced world, many people struggle with managing their emotions and dealing with stress. Mindfulness has become a popular tool for managing emotions and improving overall well-being. Mindfulness is the practice of paying attention to the present moment, without judgment or distraction, and accepting it as it is.

The concept of mindfulness has its roots in ancient Buddhist practices, but it has gained popularity in recent years in Western societies as a secular approach to managing stress and improving mental health. Mindfulness can be practiced in a variety of ways, including meditation, yoga, and breathing exercises.

This paper will explore the concept of mindfulness, its benefits, and how it can be applied in various settings, including the workplace, education, and healthcare. We will also examine the potential limitations and criticisms of mindfulness and discuss strategies for incorporating mindfulness into daily life.

Benefits of Mindfulness:

Research has shown that mindfulness can have a range of benefits for individuals, including:

Improved well-being: Practicing mindfulness can help reduce stress, anxiety, and depression. It can also improve overall well-being and quality of life.

Increased resilience: Mindfulness can help individuals develop resilience, or the ability to cope with stress and adversity. It can also improve emotional regulation and self-control.

Better cognitive function: Mindfulness can improve attention, memory, and decision-making skills. It can also enhance creativity and problem-solving abilities.

Improved relationships: Mindfulness can help individuals develop better communication skills and enhance relationships with others. It can also foster compassion and empathy.

Applications of Mindfulness:

Mindfulness can be applied in a variety of settings, including:

Workplace: Mindfulness can improve job satisfaction and productivity by reducing stress and increasing focus. It can also improve communication and collaboration among coworkers.

Education: Mindfulness can improve academic performance by improving attention and memory. It can also reduce stress and anxiety in students, leading to better overall well-being.

Healthcare: Mindfulness can be used as a tool for managing chronic pain, reducing anxiety and depression, and improving overall health outcomes. It can also enhance patient-provider communication and relationships.

Limitations and Criticisms of Mindfulness:

Despite the many benefits of mindfulness, there are also potential limitations and criticisms to consider. Some critics argue that mindfulness can be used to reinforce the status quo and discourage critical thinking. Others argue that mindfulness can be used as a form of "McMindfulness," or the commercialization and commodification of mindfulness for profit.

Additionally, some individuals may find mindfulness difficult to practice or may not experience the same benefits as others. It is important to recognize that mindfulness is not a one-size-fits-all approach and may not be suitable for everyone.

Incorporating Mindfulness into Daily Life:

Despite these potential limitations, mindfulness can still be a valuable tool for managing emotions and improving well-being. Strategies for incorporating mindfulness into daily life include:

Starting small: Practicing mindfulness for even a few minutes a day can be beneficial. Starting with short sessions and gradually increasing the length of practice can make it easier to incorporate into daily life.

Finding a technique that works: Mindfulness can be practiced in many different ways, so it is important to find a technique that works for each individual. This may involve trying different techniques, such as meditation, yoga, or breathing exercises.

Making it a habit: Consistency is key when it comes to mindfulness. Making mindfulness a daily habit, such as practicing at the same time each day, can help make it a regular part of daily life.

Conclusion:

Mindfulness has become a popular tool for managing emotions and improving overall well-being. It can have a range of benefits, including improved well-being, increased resilience, better cognitive function, and improved relationships. Mindfulness can be applied in various aspects of life, including the workplace, personal relationships, and financial decision-making.

In the realm of finance, mindfulness can be a powerful tool for managing emotions and making better decisions. By increasing self-awareness and learning to be present in the moment, individuals can better understand their emotions and reactions to various situations. This can help them make more rational and informed financial decisions.

However, incorporating mindfulness into financial decision-making can be challenging, particularly for those who are new to the practice. It requires a certain level of dedication and commitment to develop the skills necessary to apply mindfulness in a practical way.

Despite these challenges, many financial professionals are recognizing the value of mindfulness in their work. From investment bankers to financial planners, there is growing interest in incorporating mindfulness practices into financial decision-making processes.

In this section, we will explore the concept of mindfulness, its benefits, and how it can be applied to financial decision-making. We will also examine some of the challenges associated with integrating mindfulness into financial decision-making, as well as strategies for overcoming these challenges. Finally, we will discuss the future of mindfulness in the financial industry and its potential impact on financial decision-making processes.

Cognitive reappraisal

Cognitive reappraisal is a psychological technique used to manage emotions by altering the way we interpret a situation. This technique has been studied extensively in the field of psychology and has gained popularity in recent years for its potential application in various areas, including financial decision-making.

In this section, we will explore the concept of cognitive reappraisal in detail, including its definition, theoretical background, and empirical evidence supporting its effectiveness. We will also examine how cognitive reappraisal can be applied in financial decision-making, with examples from various fields.

Definition of Cognitive Reappraisal

Cognitive reappraisal is a technique that involves changing the way we think about a situation in order to alter our emotional response. In other words, it is a way of reframing a situation in a more positive light, which can lead to a more positive emotional response.

Theoretical Background

Cognitive reappraisal is based on the cognitive-behavioral theory of emotion, which posits that emotions are a result of our interpretation of a situation. According to this theory, emotions are not directly caused by the situation itself, but rather by our appraisal of the situation. Therefore, by changing our appraisal of a situation, we can change our emotional response.

Empirical Evidence

There is a growing body of research supporting the effectiveness of cognitive reappraisal in managing emotions. Studies have shown that individuals who engage in cognitive reappraisal techniques experience less negative emotions and more positive emotions than those who do not.

For example, one study found that individuals who were instructed to reappraise a negative situation experienced less negative affect than those who were instructed to simply suppress their emotions (Gross, 1998). Another study found that individuals who used cognitive reappraisal techniques to reinterpret a stressful event experienced less anxiety and depression than those who did not (Gross & John, 2003).

Application in Financial Decision-Making

Cognitive reappraisal can be applied in financial decision-making to manage emotions that may interfere with rational decision-making. For example, fear of loss can lead individuals to make irrational decisions, such as selling investments at the bottom of a market downturn. By reappraising the situation, individuals may be able to manage their fear and make more rational decisions.

An investment banker may use cognitive reappraisal when faced with a potential investment that carries a high level of risk. Rather than focusing on the potential for loss, the banker may reappraise the situation by focusing on the potential for gain, or by considering the risk as an opportunity for growth.

A financial planner may use cognitive reappraisal when working with clients who are anxious about their financial future. By reframing the situation as an opportunity for growth and setting achievable goals, the planner may be able to help the client manage their anxiety and make more rational decisions.

Conclusion

Cognitive reappraisal is a powerful tool for managing emotions and improving decision-making. By changing the way we think about a situation, we can alter our emotional response and make more rational decisions. This technique has been studied extensively in the field of psychology and has been shown to be effective in a variety of contexts. In financial decision-making, cognitive reappraisal can be particularly useful for managing emotions that may interfere with rational decision-making.

Emotional disclosure

Emotions are an integral part of our daily lives and play an important role in our decision-making processes, including financial decisions. Emotions such as fear, anxiety, and anger can have a significant impact on our financial decisions, often leading to irrational and suboptimal choices. However, research has shown that the way we express and manage our emotions can also have an impact on our decision-making processes.

One such method of managing emotions is emotional disclosure, which involves expressing and sharing one's emotions with others. Emotional disclosure has been shown to have a range of benefits, including improved psychological and physical health, increased emotional regulation, and better decision-making. In this section, we will explore the concept of emotional disclosure, its potential benefits, and its applications in financial decision-making.

What is Emotional Disclosure?

Emotional disclosure is a process of expressing and sharing one's emotions with others. This can be done in various ways, including talking to a trusted friend or family member, writing in a journal, or speaking with a therapist. The process of emotional disclosure can involve sharing both positive and negative emotions, with the aim of processing and resolving emotional experiences.

Emotional disclosure can be a powerful tool for managing emotions, as it allows individuals to gain a deeper understanding of their emotions and the underlying causes of these emotions. By expressing their emotions, individuals can gain insights into their emotional experiences and develop strategies for managing these emotions in the future.

Benefits of Emotional Disclosure

Emotional disclosure has been shown to have a range of benefits, including improved psychological and physical health, increased emotional regulation, and better decision-making. Some of the key benefits of emotional disclosure are discussed below.

Improved Psychological Health

Research has shown that emotional disclosure can have a positive impact on psychological health. By expressing and processing their emotions, individuals can reduce the negative impact of emotional experiences, such as stress, anxiety, and depression. Studies have also shown that emotional disclosure can lead to improvements in mood, self-esteem, and overall well-being.

Improved Physical Health

In addition to improving psychological health, emotional disclosure has also been shown to have a positive impact on physical health. Studies have found that emotional disclosure can lead to improvements in immune system function, cardiovascular health, and pain management.

Increased Emotional Regulation

Emotional disclosure can also improve emotional regulation, which refers to the ability to manage and regulate one's emotions. By expressing and processing their emotions, individuals can gain a better understanding of their emotional experiences and develop strategies for managing their emotions in a more effective manner. This can lead to greater emotional resilience and improved coping skills.

Better Decision-Making

Emotional disclosure can also have a positive impact on decision-making. By processing and resolving emotional experiences, individuals can make more rational and informed decisions, rather than being influenced by their emotions. This can be particularly relevant in financial decision-making, where emotions such as fear and anxiety can lead to irrational and suboptimal choices.

Applications of Emotional Disclosure in Financial Decision-Making

Emotional disclosure can be applied in various ways in financial decision-making. Some of the key applications of emotional disclosure in financial decision-making are discussed below.

Reducing Financial Stress

Financial stress can be a significant source of emotional distress, which can have a negative impact on decision-making. By engaging in emotional disclosure, individuals can process and resolve their financial stress, reducing its negative impact on their decision-making processes. This can involve talking to a trusted friend or family member, seeking the advice of a financial professional, or engaging in other forms of emotional expression such as writing in a journal.

Improving Risk Management

Emotional disclosure can also be useful in improving risk management. By expressing and processing their emotions around financial risk, individuals can gain a better understanding of their risk tolerance and develop strategies for managing financial risk in a more effective manner. This can involve seeking the advice of financial experts or developing a more diversified investment portfolio that aligns with their risk tolerance.

For example, an investment banker who is struggling with anxiety about the volatile stock market may benefit from emotional disclosure. By discussing their concerns with a trusted colleague or mental health professional, they may gain new insights into their risk tolerance and develop a more effective approach to managing their investments.

Similarly, a financial planner who is experiencing stress related to client interactions may benefit from emotional disclosure. By exploring and processing their emotions, they may be better equipped to manage their own emotional responses during client meetings and provide more effective financial advice.

It is important to note, however, that emotional disclosure should not be seen as a replacement for sound financial advice or professional expertise. Rather, it should be viewed as a complementary tool for improving emotional self-awareness and promoting better decision-making in the financial realm.

Counterarguments to Emotional Disclosure

Despite its potential benefits, some researchers and practitioners have expressed concerns about the use of emotional disclosure in financial decision-making. One concern is that the disclosure of emotional experiences may not always be appropriate or effective in all situations.

For example, some individuals may not feel comfortable disclosing their emotions in a professional setting, or may not have access to a safe and supportive environment for emotional expression. In such cases, emotional disclosure may be counterproductive and may even lead to negative outcomes, such as increased stress and anxiety.

Another concern is that emotional disclosure may be overly focused on individual emotions and experiences, without considering broader social and cultural factors that may influence financial decision-making. For example, cultural norms around money and financial risk-taking may impact how individuals perceive and manage financial risk, regardless of their personal emotions and experiences.

Conclusion

Emotional disclosure is a tool that can be used to improve emotional self-awareness and promote better decision-making in the financial realm. By exploring and processing their emotions, individuals can gain new insights into their financial behaviors and develop strategies for managing emotions in a more effective manner.

While emotional disclosure can be a valuable tool, it is important to recognize that it is not a replacement for sound financial advice or professional expertise. Additionally, it is important to be aware of the potential limitations and risks associated with emotional disclosure, including the need for a safe and supportive environment for emotional expression, and the potential impact of broader social and cultural factors on financial decision-making.

Overall, emotional disclosure can be a useful tool for individuals who are looking to improve their emotional self-awareness and decision-making abilities in the financial realm. By using this tool in combination with other strategies, such as mindfulness and cognitive reappraisal, individuals can develop a comprehensive approach to managing emotions and making better financial decisions.

Behavioral strategies

Behavioral strategies are techniques that can be used to help individuals overcome emotional and cognitive biases in decision-making. These strategies are rooted in the field of behavioral finance, which combines principles of finance and psychology to better understand how people make financial decisions.

Behavioral strategies have gained significant attention in recent years, as research has shown that traditional financial models do not always accurately predict human behavior in financial decision-making.

In this section, we will explore the key behavioral strategies used in finance and how they can be applied to a variety of financial fields, including investment banking, actuarial science, portfolio management, quantitative analysis, securities trading, financial planning, and financial analysis. We will also examine the potential limitations and criticisms of these strategies.

Cognitive Behavioral Therapy (CBT)

Cognitive Behavioral Therapy (CBT) is a psychotherapeutic approach that helps individuals identify and change negative thought patterns and behaviors. CBT has been applied to financial decision-making and has been shown to be effective in helping individuals overcome cognitive biases that can lead to poor financial decision-making. For example, individuals who are prone to overconfidence bias may benefit from CBT techniques that help them recognize and challenge their unrealistic beliefs about their ability to predict financial outcomes.

CBT techniques can be applied in a variety of financial contexts. For instance, investment bankers may use CBT to help clients manage their emotions around financial risk and make more rational decisions about investments. Actuaries may use CBT to help clients better understand the impact of financial risks and make more informed decisions about insurance policies. Portfolio managers may use CBT to help clients manage their emotions during market fluctuations and make more objective decisions about asset allocation.

However, it is important to note that CBT is not a one-size-fits-all solution and may not be effective for everyone. Some individuals may require more specialized treatment or may not respond well to psychotherapeutic approaches.

Nudge Theory

Nudge theory is a behavioral economics concept that proposes that small, subtle changes in the environment can encourage individuals to make better decisions. Nudge theory has been applied in various fields, including finance, to help individuals overcome cognitive biases and make more rational decisions.

For example, in investment banking, nudge theory can be used to encourage clients to diversify their portfolios and make long-term investments rather than pursuing short-term gains. Actuaries may use nudge theory to encourage clients to invest in insurance policies that better suit their needs and risk tolerance. Portfolio managers may use nudge theory to encourage clients to stay invested during market downturns.

While nudge theory can be effective in certain contexts, it is important to consider potential criticisms. Critics argue that nudge theory can be manipulative and infringe on individuals' autonomy, particularly if they are not aware of the nudges. Additionally, nudges may not be effective for all individuals and may not address the root causes of cognitive biases.

Heuristics and Biases

Heuristics and biases are cognitive shortcuts that individuals use to simplify complex decision-making processes. While heuristics and biases can be helpful in some situations, they can also lead to cognitive errors and poor decision-making in financial contexts.

For example, the availability heuristic is a cognitive bias in which individuals overestimate the importance of information that is easily accessible to them. This can lead to overconfidence and irrational decision-making. In investment banking, this bias may manifest as clients placing too much importance on recent market trends rather than considering long-term investment strategies.

Other cognitive biases that can impact financial decision-making include the confirmation bias, the sunk cost fallacy, and the halo effect. Portfolio managers, financial planners, and securities traders may use techniques such as education and awareness to help clients recognize and overcome these biases.

However, it is important to note that some biases may be deeply ingrained and difficult to overcome. In such cases, behavioral strategies can be employed to help individuals make more rational decisions.

One such strategy is setting pre-commitment devices. This involves making a commitment in advance to a certain course of action that aligns with one's long-term goals, thereby reducing the likelihood of making impulsive decisions that deviate from these goals. For example, an individual may set up an automatic investment plan where a fixed amount of money is invested in a retirement account each month. This pre-commitment device can help the individual stick to their long-term investment plan, even in the face of short-term fluctuations in the market.

Another effective behavioral strategy is gamification, which involves the use of game-like elements to encourage desired behaviors. This can be used to encourage individuals to save more or invest wisely by making the process more engaging and fun. For example, a financial app may use points or badges to incentivize individuals to complete certain financial tasks, such as creating a budget or setting up an emergency fund.

Nudging is another behavioral strategy that can be effective in promoting better financial decision-making. This involves making small changes to the environment or the choice architecture to encourage individuals to make more rational decisions. For example, a company may default employees into a retirement savings plan and require them to opt out if they do not want to participate. This simple change in the default option can have a significant impact on retirement savings rates.

Finally, coaching and feedback can be used to help individuals recognize and overcome their biases. This can involve providing regular feedback on financial behaviors and offering guidance on how to make more rational decisions. For example, a financial planner may offer coaching on how to avoid common cognitive biases, such as the availability bias or the framing effect, when making investment decisions.

In conclusion, cognitive biases can have a significant impact on financial decision-making. Portfolio managers, financial planners, and securities traders can use a range of techniques, such as education, awareness, and behavioral strategies, to help individuals recognize and overcome their biases and make more rational decisions. By incorporating these strategies into their practice, financial professionals can help their clients achieve their long-term financial goals and improve their overall financial well-being.

CHAPTER 30: BEHAVIORAL FINANCE AND INVESTMENT STRATEGIES

In this chapter, we will explore the field of behavioral finance and its implications for investment strategies. Behavioral finance is the study of how psychological factors can impact financial decision-making. Traditional finance assumes that individuals are rational and always act in their best interests, but behavioral finance recognizes that humans are subject to cognitive biases and emotions that can lead to irrational financial decisions. We will examine several key concepts in behavioral finance, including prospect theory, loss aversion, and herding behavior. We will also discuss how behavioral finance can inform investment strategies and improve risk management.

Importance of Understanding Behavioral Finance in Investment Strategies

Behavioral finance is an essential area of study for investment professionals, including investment bankers, actuaries, portfolio managers, quantitative analysts, securities traders, financial planners, and financial analysts. Understanding the psychological factors that impact financial decision-making can help these professionals design investment strategies that are more effective and better aligned with their clients' goals and risk tolerances.

By recognizing and addressing cognitive biases, investment professionals can help their clients make more rational financial decisions. They can also design investment strategies that take into account the emotional and psychological factors that influence investors' risk tolerance and decision-making. Additionally, behavioral finance can help investment professionals identify opportunities for value investing and contrarian strategies that take advantage of market inefficiencies caused by irrational investor behavior.

Investment professionals who do not take into account the principles of behavioral finance may be at a disadvantage when competing in the marketplace. Those who understand and apply these principles may be better equipped to outperform the market and provide superior returns for their clients.

In the following sections, we will explore some of the key concepts in behavioral finance and how they can be applied to investment strategies.

Prospect Theory and Loss Aversion

Prospect theory is a behavioral finance concept developed by psychologists Daniel Kahneman and Amos Tversky. It describes how individuals make decisions based on potential gains and losses, rather than the final outcome. Prospect theory suggests that individuals are more sensitive to losses than gains, meaning that they will often take on more risk to avoid losses than they will to achieve gains.

Loss aversion is a related concept that describes how individuals are more emotionally impacted by losses than gains of the same magnitude. This means that individuals are more likely to take action to prevent losses than to achieve gains, even if the potential gains are greater than the potential losses.

These concepts have important implications for investment strategies. For example, investors may be more likely to hold onto a losing investment for too long because they are motivated by the desire to avoid the emotional pain of realizing a loss. Investment professionals can help their clients overcome this bias by encouraging them to set clear stop-loss orders and by diversifying their portfolio to reduce the impact of any single loss.

Herding Behavior
Herding behavior is a tendency for individuals to follow the actions of others, rather than making independent decisions based on their own analysis. This can lead to market inefficiencies as investors may overreact to news or events, causing prices to fluctuate more than they should.

Investment professionals can take advantage of herding behavior by using contrarian strategies that go against the market consensus. For example, a portfolio manager may buy stocks that are out of favor with the market, but have strong underlying fundamentals. Over time, these stocks may perform better than the market as a whole as the market corrects for the initial overreaction.

Confirmation Bias
Confirmation bias is a tendency for individuals to seek out information that confirms their existing beliefs, rather than considering evidence that contradicts their beliefs. This can lead to overconfidence and irrational decision-making as individuals may ignore evidence that challenges their assumptions.

Investment professionals can help their clients overcome confirmation bias by encouraging them to seek out diverse sources of information and to consider alternative viewpoints. By encouraging a more open-minded approach to decision-making, investment professionals can help their clients make more informed decisions and avoid the negative consequences of confirmation bias.

Another common cognitive bias in financial decision-making is the sunk cost fallacy. This refers to the tendency to continue investing in a project or security even when the investment is no longer viable or profitable. This can lead to significant losses and missed opportunities.

Investment professionals can help their clients overcome the sunk cost fallacy by encouraging them to focus on the present and future prospects of an investment, rather than dwelling on past losses. This can involve setting clear exit strategies and risk management plans, and helping clients to recognize when it is time to cut their losses and move on.

The halo effect is another cognitive bias that can impact financial decision-making. This refers to the tendency to view a company or security in a positive light based on a single positive attribute, such as a strong brand or charismatic CEO. This can lead investors to overlook important information or risks, and can result in poor investment decisions.

Investment professionals can help their clients overcome the halo effect by encouraging them to conduct thorough research and analysis, and to consider a wide range of factors when making investment decisions. This can involve looking beyond superficial attributes, such as brand or personality, and focusing on more objective measures of performance and risk.

In addition to cognitive biases, behavioral finance also recognizes the impact of emotional factors on financial decision-making. For example, fear, greed, and overconfidence can all influence investment decisions and lead to suboptimal outcomes.

Investment professionals can help their clients manage these emotional factors by providing education and guidance on the importance of disciplined and rational decision-making, and by encouraging clients to develop clear investment goals and strategies. This can involve regular communication and monitoring, as well as ongoing education and support.

In conclusion, behavioral finance provides valuable insights into the cognitive and emotional factors that can impact financial decision-making. By understanding these factors and developing effective strategies to overcome them, investment professionals can help their clients make more informed and rational investment decisions, and ultimately achieve greater success in their financial endeavors.

II. Theoretical Frameworks

Overview of the chapter:

Theoretical frameworks are an essential aspect of academic research and analysis, providing a conceptual framework for understanding complex phenomena. In the field of finance, theoretical frameworks play a crucial role in providing a basis for understanding various financial concepts and phenomena, such as market behavior, investment strategies, and risk management. This chapter will examine the importance of theoretical frameworks in finance and provide an overview of some of the most commonly used frameworks.

mportance of understanding theoretical frameworks in finance:

Understanding theoretical frameworks is essential for effective research and analysis in finance. Theoretical frameworks provide a foundation for research, guiding the selection of research questions, the formulation of hypotheses, and the development of analytical tools. They help researchers to identify and understand the key concepts, relationships, and phenomena that are relevant to their research, and to develop models and theories that can be tested empirically.

In addition, theoretical frameworks are important for practitioners in finance, including investment bankers, portfolio managers, securities traders, financial planners, and financial analysts. These professionals use theoretical frameworks to understand market behavior, identify investment opportunities, and develop effective strategies for managing financial risk. By understanding the theoretical underpinnings of financial concepts and phenomena, practitioners can make more informed decisions and better serve their clients.

Examples of theoretical frameworks in finance:

There are many theoretical frameworks that are relevant to finance, ranging from microeconomic models of individual behavior to macroeconomic models of market behavior. Some of the most commonly used frameworks in finance include:

Efficient Market Hypothesis (EMH):
The efficient market hypothesis is a widely used framework for understanding market behavior. The hypothesis suggests that financial markets are informationally efficient, meaning that prices reflect all available information about a security or asset. This theory is based on the idea that rational investors will act on new information as soon as it becomes available, and that any inefficiencies in the market will be quickly corrected.

Capital Asset Pricing Model (CAPM):
The capital asset pricing model is a widely used framework for understanding investment risk and return. The model suggests that the expected return on an investment is a function of the risk-free rate, the market risk premium, and the investment's beta (i.e., its sensitivity to market movements). This theory is based on the idea that investors are risk-averse and require compensation for taking on additional risk.

Prospect Theory:
Prospect theory is a framework for understanding how individuals make decisions under conditions of uncertainty. The theory suggests that individuals are more sensitive to losses than to gains, and that they are more likely to take risks to avoid losses than to pursue gains. This theory is based on the idea that individuals have a "reference point" (i.e., their current state of wealth or well-being) and that they evaluate outcomes relative to this reference point.

Behavioral Finance:
Behavioral finance is a broad framework for understanding how psychological and emotional factors influence financial decision-making. This framework suggests that individuals are not always rational or objective in their decision-making, and that they are subject to various cognitive biases and heuristics that can lead to suboptimal decisions. This theory is based on the idea that emotions, social influences, and cognitive biases can have a powerful impact on financial decision-making.

In conclusion, theoretical frameworks are essential for effective research and analysis in finance. They provide a conceptual framework for understanding complex financial phenomena and can guide research questions, hypotheses, and analytical tools. Theoretical frameworks are also important for practitioners in finance, helping them to understand market behavior, identify investment opportunities, and develop effective strategies for managing financial risk. By understanding the most commonly used theoretical frameworks in finance, researchers and practitioners can make more informed decisions and better serve their clients.

Prospect theory and investment decisions

Prospect theory is a behavioral economics theory that explains how individuals make decisions under uncertainty. Developed by psychologists Daniel Kahneman and Amos Tversky in 1979, prospect theory challenges the traditional assumption that individuals make rational decisions based on expected utility.

According to prospect theory, individuals evaluate potential gains and losses relative to a reference point, which is often their current status quo. They experience loss aversion, meaning they feel the pain of losses more acutely than the pleasure of gains, and they exhibit diminishing sensitivity, meaning they become less responsive to changes in potential gains or losses as the magnitude of those changes increase.

In the context of investment decisions, prospect theory suggests that investors are more likely to take risks to avoid losses than to pursue gains. For example, they may hold onto losing investments longer than they should, hoping to recoup their losses, while selling winning investments too quickly in order to lock in gains.

Investment professionals can use prospect theory to help their clients make more effective investment decisions. They can frame investment options in terms of potential gains and losses relative to the client's reference point, and help the client understand their loss aversion and diminishing sensitivity. They can also encourage diversification and discourage overly aggressive investment strategies that may be driven by a desire to avoid losses rather than to maximize gains.

Overall, understanding prospect theory can help investment professionals better serve their clients and help investors make more informed and effective investment decisions.

Mental accounting and portfolio management

Mental accounting refers to the tendency of individuals to create separate mental accounts for their money and assets based on subjective criteria such as the source of the funds or the purpose of the asset. This concept was first introduced by Richard Thaler, a Nobel Prize-winning economist, who argued that people often treat money in irrational ways, such as using a tax refund to buy a luxury item instead of paying off debt.

Mental accounting can have significant implications for portfolio management. For example, an individual may have a mental account for retirement savings and another for emergency funds. They may be more likely to take on risk with their retirement savings, as it is designated for a long-term goal, while being more conservative with their emergency funds, which are intended to be used in case of unexpected expenses.

Portfolio managers can use mental accounting to their advantage by understanding how their clients categorize and value their investments. For example, a portfolio manager may recommend a client invest in a diversified portfolio with a mix of stocks and bonds, but if the client has a mental account for "safe" investments, they may be resistant to investing in stocks even if it is in their best interest.

One strategy for portfolio managers is to create mental accounts for their clients based on their goals and risk tolerance. This can help clients see the bigger picture of their investments and understand how each account fits into their overall financial plan. For example, a portfolio manager may create a mental account for retirement savings and allocate a portion of the portfolio to high-risk, high-reward investments such as stocks, while another mental account for emergency funds may be allocated to low-risk, low-return investments such as money market funds or CDs.

Another way portfolio managers can use mental accounting to their advantage is by "framing" investments in a way that aligns with their clients' mental accounts. For example, instead of presenting an investment opportunity as a risky stock, they may frame it as an opportunity to invest in a specific sector that aligns with the client's values or interests.

However, it is important to note that mental accounting can also lead to irrational behavior and decision-making. For example, an individual may hold onto a losing stock because they have a mental account for "long-term investments" and believe the stock will eventually rebound. In reality, they may be better off cutting their losses and investing in a more profitable opportunity.

Furthermore, mental accounting can also lead to suboptimal asset allocation. If an individual has a mental account for a specific asset class such as real estate or gold, they may be more likely to invest a disproportionate amount of their portfolio in that asset class, even if it does not align with their overall financial goals or risk tolerance.

In conclusion, mental accounting can have both positive and negative implications for portfolio management. Portfolio managers should understand how their clients categorize and value their investments and use this information to create mental accounts that align with their clients' goals and risk tolerance. However, they should also be aware of the potential for irrational behavior and suboptimal asset allocation associated with mental accounting.

Loss aversion and risk management

Loss aversion is a behavioral bias in which people experience more pain from losing a certain amount of money than pleasure from gaining the same amount of money. This bias has significant implications for risk management in the context of investment decisions.

Loss aversion can cause investors to make irrational decisions based on emotions rather than objective data. For example, an investor who is experiencing loss aversion may be reluctant to sell a stock that has performed poorly, even if it is clear that the stock is unlikely to recover. Instead, the investor may continue to hold the stock in the hope that it will eventually recover, even though this strategy may result in additional losses.

One way to mitigate the impact of loss aversion is to implement a disciplined risk management strategy. This can involve setting specific stop-loss levels for individual stocks or portfolios, or using derivatives such as options or futures to hedge against downside risk.

Investment professionals may also use education and awareness to help clients recognize and overcome loss aversion. By emphasizing the importance of diversification, and by explaining the potential benefits of disciplined risk management strategies, investment professionals can help their clients make more informed investment decisions.

One potential challenge in implementing effective risk management strategies is that investors may perceive risk differently depending on the context. For example, a person who is offered a choice between a certain gain of $50 and a 50/50 chance of gaining $100 or gaining nothing may choose the certain gain of $50, indicating a preference for risk aversion. However, the same person may be willing to take a significant risk when investing in the stock market, indicating a preference for risk-taking.

This discrepancy in risk perception can create challenges for investment professionals in developing and implementing effective risk management strategies for their clients. One potential solution is to work closely with clients to develop a comprehensive understanding of their risk preferences and to tailor risk management strategies accordingly.

Another potential challenge is that investors may be more likely to experience loss aversion during periods of market volatility or uncertainty. During these times, investors may be more likely to make irrational decisions based on fear and uncertainty, rather than objective data. To address this challenge, investment professionals may need to provide additional education and support to help their clients navigate periods of market volatility and uncertainty.

In summary, loss aversion is a significant behavioral bias that can impact investment decisions and risk management strategies. Investment professionals can help their clients overcome this bias by implementing disciplined risk management strategies, providing education and awareness, and tailoring risk management strategies to individual risk preferences. By doing so, investment professionals can help their clients make more informed and rational investment decisions, leading to better investment outcomes over time.

Overconfidence and investment performance

Overconfidence is a common cognitive bias that can impact investment decision-making and ultimately affect investment performance. This bias is often associated with individuals who believe that they have more knowledge, skill, or information than they actually possess, leading them to take excessive risks or overlook important information when making investment decisions. Overconfidence can be particularly detrimental in the investment industry, where even small mistakes can result in significant financial losses.

In this section, we will examine the concept of overconfidence and its impact on investment performance. We will also discuss strategies that investment professionals can use to help their clients overcome this bias and make more informed investment decisions.

Understanding Overconfidence

Overconfidence refers to the tendency of individuals to overestimate their abilities or the accuracy of their judgments. This bias can manifest in a variety of ways, from an individual's belief in their ability to predict the future, to their confidence in their ability to beat the market.

In the investment industry, overconfidence can be particularly problematic. Investors who are overconfident may be more likely to take risks or make investment decisions based on incomplete or inaccurate information. They may also be more likely to engage in speculative or short-term trading strategies that can lead to losses over the long term.

Studies have shown that overconfidence can lead to poor investment performance. For example, one study found that overconfident investors tended to have higher trading volumes and lower returns than their less overconfident peers. Another study found that overconfident investors were more likely to hold onto losing investments for too long, hoping that they would eventually recover.

Overcoming Overconfidence

While overconfidence can be a difficult bias to overcome, there are strategies that investment professionals can use to help their clients make more informed investment decisions.

One strategy is to encourage clients to engage in more deliberate decision-making. This can involve taking more time to research potential investments, seeking out multiple sources of information, and consulting with other professionals or experts in the field.

Another strategy is to encourage clients to diversify their portfolios. By spreading their investments across a variety of assets, clients can reduce their exposure to risk and limit the potential impact of any single investment on their overall portfolio.

Investment professionals can also help their clients manage their expectations by providing realistic projections and emphasizing the importance of long-term investment strategies. By emphasizing the potential risks and limitations of any investment, investment professionals can help their clients make more informed decisions and avoid the pitfalls of overconfidence.

Counterarguments

While there is significant research to support the negative impact of overconfidence on investment performance, some argue that a certain level of confidence can be beneficial for investors. For example, a study by the University of California found that investors who were moderately confident in their abilities tended to outperform their less confident peers.

Additionally, some experts argue that overconfidence may be more prevalent in certain types of investors, such as those who are more experienced or have a higher degree of financial literacy. These investors may be more likely to overestimate their abilities or the accuracy of their judgments, leading them to take excessive risks or overlook important information.

Conclusion

Overconfidence is a common cognitive bias that can have a significant impact on investment performance. However, investment professionals can help their clients overcome this bias by encouraging more deliberate decision-making, diversification, and realistic expectations. While a certain level of confidence can be beneficial for investors, it is important to be aware of the potential risks associated with overconfidence and take steps to mitigate its impact on investment decision-making.

III. Biases and Heuristics in Investment Decisions

Investing is a complex decision-making process that involves a variety of factors, including market conditions, company performance, and macroeconomic trends. However, investors are not always rational and objective in their decision-making. Rather, they are influenced by a range of biases and heuristics that can lead to suboptimal investment outcomes.

In this section, we will explore the role of biases and heuristics in investment decisions. We will define biases and heuristics, describe their impact on investment decisions, and provide examples from various fields of finance. We will also discuss strategies that investors can use to overcome biases and heuristics and make more informed investment decisions.

Defining Biases and Heuristics

Biases are systematic errors in judgment and decision-making that can occur when individuals rely on incomplete or inaccurate information, emotions, or heuristics. Heuristics are mental shortcuts that individuals use to simplify complex decision-making processes. While heuristics can be useful in making quick decisions, they can also lead to errors and biases in judgment.

There are many different types of biases and heuristics that can impact investment decisions. For example, confirmation bias is the tendency to seek out information that confirms one's pre-existing beliefs and to ignore information that contradicts those beliefs. Anchoring bias is the tendency to rely too heavily on the first piece of information encountered when making a decision. Overconfidence bias is the tendency to overestimate one's own abilities and underestimate risks.

The Impact of Biases and Heuristics on Investment Decisions

Biases and heuristics can have a significant impact on investment decisions, leading to suboptimal outcomes. For example, confirmation bias can lead investors to ignore critical information that contradicts their beliefs, leading to investment decisions based on incomplete or inaccurate information. Anchoring bias can cause investors to rely too heavily on past performance or initial information when making investment decisions, leading to missed opportunities or poor investment choices.

Overconfidence bias can lead investors to make decisions based on inaccurate assessments of their own abilities or the level of risk involved in an investment. This can result in investments that are too risky or decisions that do not account for all of the potential risks associated with an investment. Other biases, such as availability bias, recency bias, and loss aversion, can also impact investment decisions and lead to suboptimal outcomes.

Examples from Various Fields of Finance

The impact of biases and heuristics can be seen in various fields of finance, including investment banking, portfolio management, financial planning, and securities trading. For example, investment bankers may rely on anchoring bias when valuing companies for mergers and acquisitions, leading to overpayment for a company or missed opportunities for better deals. Portfolio managers may be subject to overconfidence bias, leading them to take on excessive risk in their portfolios. Financial planners may experience confirmation bias when recommending investment strategies to clients, leading to suboptimal outcomes for clients. Securities traders may be impacted by various biases, including availability bias, leading to poor trading decisions.

Strategies for Overcoming Biases and Heuristics in Investment Decisions

To make more informed investment decisions, investors can employ strategies to overcome biases and heuristics. For example, investors can seek out diverse sources of information and consider alternative viewpoints to overcome confirmation bias. They can also challenge their own assumptions and seek out feedback from others to overcome overconfidence bias. Additionally, investors can use tools such as checklists and decision trees to avoid relying too heavily on mental shortcuts and heuristics.

Conclusion

Biases and heuristics play a significant role in investment decisions, leading to suboptimal outcomes. Understanding the impact of biases and heuristics is an essential part of becoming a successful investor. By identifying and overcoming biases and using heuristics in a mindful way, investors can make better decisions and improve their investment performance.

However, it is essential to note that biases and heuristics are deeply ingrained in human nature, and completely eliminating them may not be possible. Even the most experienced and successful investors are susceptible to biases and heuristics. Therefore, it is crucial to develop a robust framework that takes into account the impact of biases and heuristics on investment decisions.

Investment professionals have a significant role to play in helping investors overcome biases and heuristics. They can do this by educating their clients about the common biases and heuristics that affect investment decisions and helping them develop strategies to mitigate these biases.

Moreover, technological advancements have led to the development of innovative tools and techniques that can help investors make better decisions. For example, robo-advisors use algorithms to analyze data and provide personalized investment recommendations that take into account an individual's risk profile, financial goals, and other relevant factors.

In conclusion, biases and heuristics are an inevitable part of the investment decision-making process. However, by being aware of their impact and developing strategies to overcome them, investors can make better decisions and improve their investment performance. Investment professionals have a significant role to play in helping investors overcome biases and heuristics, and technological advancements provide new opportunities to improve investment decision-making. Ultimately, a thorough understanding of biases and heuristics is crucial for investors seeking to achieve their financial goals.

Availability bias and asset allocation

Availability bias is a common cognitive bias that influences the way we make investment decisions. It occurs when people rely on easily accessible and readily available information when making judgments and decisions, rather than considering all relevant information. This can lead to suboptimal investment decisions, particularly in the area of asset allocation.

The purpose of this article is to explore the impact of availability bias on asset allocation decisions and to provide insights into how investors can overcome this bias to make more informed decisions.

What is availability bias?
Availability bias is a cognitive bias that occurs when people base their judgments and decisions on information that is easily accessible or readily available in their memory. This can happen because of the salience of the information, the recency of the information, or the frequency with which it has been encountered. As a result, people may overestimate the likelihood of events or outcomes that are more vivid or memorable, even if they are not representative of the overall population or are statistically unlikely.

Impact of availability bias on asset allocation
Asset allocation is the process of deciding how to distribute investment assets across different asset classes, such as stocks, bonds, real estate, and commodities. The goal of asset allocation is to achieve a balance between risk and return that aligns with an investor's goals, risk tolerance, and time horizon.

Availability bias can influence asset allocation decisions in several ways. For example:

Overweighting recent events: Availability bias can cause investors to overweight recent events when making asset allocation decisions. For instance, if a particular asset class has performed well over the past year or two, investors may be more likely to allocate a larger portion of their portfolio to that asset class, even if it is not suitable for their long-term investment strategy.

Overestimating the likelihood of extreme events: Availability bias can also cause investors to overestimate the likelihood of extreme events, such as market crashes or economic downturns. This can lead investors to be overly cautious and avoid investing in certain asset classes, even if they are likely to generate positive returns over the long term.

Underestimating the importance of diversification: Availability bias can cause investors to overlook the importance of diversification in asset allocation. Investors may focus too heavily on a particular asset class or investment strategy, rather than spreading their investments across multiple asset classes to reduce risk.

Overcoming availability bias in asset allocation
To overcome availability bias in asset allocation, investors can take several steps:

Gather and analyze all relevant information: Rather than relying on information that is easily accessible, investors should gather and analyze all relevant information when making asset allocation decisions. This includes considering the long-term performance of different asset classes, their historical volatility, and their correlation with other asset classes.

Develop a long-term investment strategy: Investors should develop a long-term investment strategy that aligns with their goals, risk tolerance, and time horizon. This strategy should be based on a comprehensive analysis of all relevant factors, rather than short-term fluctuations or recent events.

Use diversification to manage risk: Diversification is an effective way to manage risk in asset allocation. By spreading investments across multiple asset classes, investors can reduce their exposure to any single asset class or investment strategy. This can help to mitigate the impact of market fluctuations or unexpected events.

Conclusion:
Availability bias is a common cognitive bias that can have a significant impact on asset allocation decisions. Investors who are aware of this bias and take steps to overcome it can make more informed decisions that align with their long-term investment goals. By gathering and analyzing all relevant information, developing a long-term investment strategy, and using diversification to manage risk, investors can build portfolios that generate positive returns over the long term.

Anchoring and adjustment bias and stock selection

Anchoring and adjustment bias is a cognitive bias that affects investors' stock selection decisions. It refers to the tendency to rely too heavily on the first piece of information encountered when making a decision and then adjust insufficiently from this anchor. This bias can lead to investors holding onto stocks for too long or selling them too quickly, and it can have a significant impact on the overall performance of their portfolio.

The anchor can be based on a wide range of factors, including the price at which the stock was purchased, the opinions of others, or even current events. For example, an investor might buy a stock at $50 per share and then refuse to sell it when the price drops to $30 per share, even if the market conditions have changed, and the stock is unlikely to recover. This is because the investor is anchored to the $50 price and may believe that the stock will eventually rise again.

Anchoring and adjustment bias can also lead investors to make irrational decisions based on the opinions of others. For example, an investor might hear an analyst predict that a stock will double in value in the next year and then anchor to this prediction. Even if subsequent analysis indicates that the prediction is unrealistic, the investor may adjust their estimate of the stock's future value only slightly, if at all, because of their initial anchor.

This bias can also manifest itself in more subtle ways. For example, investors may anchor their expectations for future returns based on the historical performance of a stock or a market index, even if the current market conditions are vastly different from those in the past. This can lead to investors making decisions based on outdated information, rather than the current state of the market.

Overcoming anchoring and adjustment bias requires investors to be aware of the phenomenon and to actively work to adjust their estimates based on all available information, rather than relying solely on the initial anchor. One approach is to seek out a diverse range of opinions and data sources to reduce the impact of any single anchor. Additionally, investors can use analytical tools and models to objectively evaluate the current state of the market, rather than relying on subjective opinions.

Investment professionals, such as portfolio managers and financial advisors, can also help investors overcome this bias by providing a range of perspectives and by using data-driven approaches to make investment decisions.

Anchoring and adjustment bias can have a significant impact on stock selection decisions, but it is not the only bias that can affect investment performance. Other biases, such as confirmation bias, availability bias, and overconfidence, can also play a role.

Confirmation bias refers to the tendency to seek out and interpret information in a way that confirms one's existing beliefs and opinions. This bias can lead investors to ignore information that contradicts their beliefs, which can lead to poor investment decisions. For example, an investor may have a strong belief in the long-term potential of a specific industry, such as renewable energy. They may then ignore negative news or data that indicates that the industry is struggling, leading them to hold onto investments in that industry for too long.

Availability bias refers to the tendency to give greater weight to information that is more easily recalled or readily available. This bias can lead investors to overestimate the likelihood of certain events, based on recent news or media coverage. For example, investors may be more likely to sell stocks after a market downturn if they have been exposed to negative news coverage, even if the downturn is not necessarily indicative of long-term market conditions.

Overconfidence is a bias that can lead investors to overestimate their own abilities and the accuracy of their predictions. This bias can lead investors to take on too much risk or to make overly aggressive investment decisions. For example, an overconfident investor may believe that they have identified a stock that is significantly undervalued, and they may then invest heavily in that stock, without properly considering the potential risks and downsides.

Overconfidence can manifest itself in various ways. For instance, an investor may believe that they have superior knowledge or insights into the market and believe that they can time the market or pick stocks better than others. They may also believe that their past successes are the result of their own skill and intelligence, rather than luck or favorable market conditions. This can lead to overestimating the likelihood of future success, and underestimating the likelihood of failure.

In the context of stock selection, overconfidence can lead to investors placing too much emphasis on their own research and analysis, and not enough on market information and the opinions of others. They may believe that they have unique insights into a particular company or industry that others do not possess, and as a result, they may ignore or dismiss contradictory information or opinions.

Overconfidence can also lead investors to engage in excessive trading, as they believe that they can time the market or pick stocks better than others. This can lead to increased transaction costs and taxes, which can erode investment returns over time.

One example of the impact of overconfidence on investment performance can be seen in the performance of mutual fund managers. Research has shown that mutual fund managers who are overconfident tend to trade more frequently, which leads to higher transaction costs and lower returns. In addition, overconfident managers tend to take on more risk, which can lead to larger losses during market downturns.

To avoid the negative consequences of overconfidence, investors should focus on objective information and seek out diverse perspectives. They should also maintain a healthy level of skepticism and regularly review their investment decisions to ensure that they are not overly influenced by their own biases and beliefs.

Another way to mitigate the impact of overconfidence is through collaboration and diversity of opinion. By seeking out diverse perspectives and challenging one's own assumptions and beliefs, investors can reduce the impact of overconfidence and make more informed investment decisions.

In conclusion, overconfidence is a bias that can significantly impact investment decisions and performance. Investors should be aware of the potential impact of overconfidence on their decision-making and take steps to mitigate its effects. This can include focusing on objective information, seeking out diverse perspectives, and regularly reviewing investment decisions. By doing so, investors can improve their investment outcomes and reduce the risk of suboptimal results due to overconfidence.

Framing effect and investment decisions

Investors often face the challenge of making decisions in the face of ambiguity and uncertainty. Such decisions may involve significant risks, and the outcomes can have a profound impact on the investor's financial well-being. To navigate these complex decisions, investors rely on mental shortcuts or heuristics that can lead to biases. One such bias is the framing effect, which can significantly impact investment decisions.

What is the Framing Effect?
The framing effect is a cognitive bias that occurs when people's decisions are influenced by the way information is presented to them. This bias suggests that people tend to make different decisions depending on how the information is framed. For example, investors may be more likely to take risks when information is presented in a positive light, while they may be more risk-averse when information is presented negatively.

Framing effect can be seen in a variety of investment contexts. For example, consider a situation where a company is reporting its quarterly earnings. The company can choose to present its earnings in a positive light by highlighting its revenue growth, or it can choose to present the same information negatively by focusing on missed earnings estimates. Depending on how the information is presented, investors may perceive the company's prospects differently and may make different investment decisions.

Impact of the Framing Effect on Investment Decisions
The framing effect can significantly impact investment decisions by influencing how investors perceive and evaluate information. By manipulating how information is presented, financial advisors and other market participants can influence investor behavior.

For example, suppose a financial advisor wants to encourage a client to invest in a particular fund. In that case, the advisor can frame the information positively by highlighting the fund's historical performance and potential returns. By doing so, the advisor may influence the client to take on more risk than they would have otherwise.

On the other hand, suppose a financial advisor wants to discourage a client from investing in a particular stock. In that case, the advisor can frame the information negatively by emphasizing the risks associated with the stock. By doing so, the advisor may influence the client to avoid the stock entirely, even though it may be a viable investment opportunity.

Investors may also be influenced by the framing effect when evaluating their portfolio performance. For example, if an investor's portfolio has performed well, they may attribute the success to their investment skills and decision-making abilities. However, if the portfolio performs poorly, the investor may attribute the loss to external factors such as market conditions. In both cases, the investor's perception of their own abilities and the market can be influenced by the way information is framed.

Counterarguments and Dissenting Opinions
Critics of the framing effect argue that it is not always clear how information should be framed, and that the effect may be overblown in some cases. For example, in the context of investment decisions, some

argue that investors are sophisticated enough to evaluate information objectively and make rational decisions.

Others argue that the framing effect can be mitigated by providing investors with more comprehensive and transparent information. By providing investors with all relevant information, regardless of how it is framed, investors can make more informed decisions.

Despite these counterarguments, the framing effect has been shown to impact investor behavior in numerous studies. As such, investors should be aware of this bias and strive to evaluate information objectively, regardless of how it is presented.

Conclusion
The framing effect is a cognitive bias that can significantly impact investment decisions. By manipulating how information is presented, financial advisors and other market participants can influence investor behavior. Investors should be aware of this bias and strive to evaluate information objectively, regardless of how it is framed. By doing so, investors can make more informed and rational investment decisions.

Confirmation bias and investment performance

Confirmation bias is a cognitive bias that refers to the tendency of people to search for, interpret, and remember information in a way that confirms their preexisting beliefs and ideas while discounting or ignoring information that contradicts their beliefs. This bias can be particularly problematic for investors as it can lead them to make investment decisions that are not based on objective information but rather on their own preconceived notions.

Confirmation bias can impact investment decisions in several ways. For example, an investor who has a positive outlook on a particular industry or company may actively seek out information that supports their beliefs, while ignoring or downplaying information that suggests that the industry or company is facing challenges or is not performing well. This can lead the investor to make investments that are not based on objective analysis but rather on their own biases.

Confirmation bias can also lead investors to hold on to their investments for too long, even when the evidence suggests that it may be time to sell. This is known as the "disposition effect," and it is particularly prevalent among investors who are overconfident in their own abilities. These investors may believe that they have unique insights into the market and may hold on to investments even when the evidence suggests that they should sell.

One example of confirmation bias in action is the case of Long-Term Capital Management (LTCM), a hedge fund that collapsed in 1998. The fund was managed by a group of Nobel Prize-winning economists and was backed by some of the largest banks in the world. However, despite their prestigious backgrounds and experience, the managers of LTCM suffered from confirmation bias. They believed that they had developed a mathematical model that was capable of predicting market movements with a high degree of accuracy, and they invested heavily in the market based on this model. However, when the market movements did not follow their predictions, they were unable to adjust their investments quickly enough, leading to significant losses for the fund and its investors.

Investors can combat confirmation bias by actively seeking out information that challenges their preconceived notions and by surrounding themselves with advisors and analysts who have different perspectives and views. By remaining open-minded and actively seeking out different viewpoints, investors can make more informed investment decisions that are based on objective analysis rather than on their own biases.

In addition, investors can also use tools such as checklists and decision-making frameworks to help them make more objective investment decisions. For example, an investor may create a checklist of criteria that they believe are important for evaluating a particular investment, such as financial metrics, industry trends, and management experience. By using this checklist to evaluate potential investments, investors can ensure that they are making decisions based on objective analysis rather than on their own biases.

Counterarguments to the importance of confirmation bias in investment performance argue that investors are rational and will ultimately make decisions based on objective analysis rather than on their own biases. They suggest that investors who suffer from confirmation bias are outliers and that the market is ultimately efficient, with prices reflecting all available information.

While it is true that the market is generally efficient and that prices do reflect all available information, the reality is that investors are not always rational and can be influenced by cognitive biases such as confirmation bias. By understanding the impact of confirmation bias on investment decisions and taking steps to combat it, investors can make more informed investment decisions and ultimately improve their investment performance.

IV. Behavioral Finance Strategies for Investment Management

Behavioral finance has emerged as a critical area of research and practice in investment management over the past few decades. While traditional finance theory assumes that investors are rational, and their decisions are based on logical and objective analysis of available information, the behavioral finance framework considers the impact of psychological biases and irrational behavior on investor decision-making.

The behavioral finance perspective suggests that investors are not always rational and are prone to making systematic errors in their investment decisions due to cognitive biases, emotional responses, and social influences. Such biases can lead to suboptimal investment decisions and can have a significant impact on investment outcomes.

Behavioral finance strategies aim to address these biases and help investors make better decisions by integrating insights from psychology and other social sciences into the investment management process. These strategies are based on the understanding that investors are not always rational, and their decision-making can be influenced by a range of psychological factors.

Behavioral finance strategies can help investment managers to better understand and manage their clients' behaviors and to develop investment approaches that can mitigate the impact of behavioral biases on investment performance. These strategies can be applied to different areas of investment management, including asset allocation, stock selection, and risk management.

One of the primary areas of application of behavioral finance strategies in investment management is asset allocation. Asset allocation involves deciding how to allocate an investment portfolio across different asset classes, such as equities, bonds, and alternative investments, based on the investor's risk tolerance, investment objectives, and time horizon. Behavioral finance research suggests that investors tend to overweight recent performance when making asset allocation decisions and may be prone to herding behavior.

Behavioral finance strategies can help investment managers to develop asset allocation strategies that are more aligned with their clients' long-term investment objectives and that take into account the impact of behavioral biases. For example, investment managers can use techniques such as mental accounting and framing to help their clients make more rational asset allocation decisions.

Another area of application of behavioral finance strategies in investment management is stock selection. Behavioral biases can impact stock selection decisions by leading investors to overestimate the value of certain stocks or to ignore relevant information. Investment managers can use behavioral finance strategies to develop more effective stock selection approaches that take into account the impact of these biases.

For example, investment managers can use techniques such as anchoring and adjustment, which involve adjusting initial estimates of stock values based on new information, to mitigate the impact of the anchoring bias. They can also use techniques such as counterfactual thinking, which involves considering alternative scenarios, to help investors evaluate potential stock investments more objectively.

Overall, behavioral finance strategies offer a valuable framework for investment managers to better understand and manage the impact of psychological biases and irrational behavior on investment decisions. By integrating insights from psychology and other social sciences into the investment management process, investment managers can develop more effective investment approaches and improve investment outcomes for their clients.

Value investing

Value investing is an investment strategy that involves searching for stocks that are undervalued by the market. It is a popular approach to investing that is based on the belief that the market does not always accurately reflect the true value of a company. Value investors look for stocks that have a lower price than what they believe the company is worth based on its financial and other fundamental metrics. In this section, we will explore the principles and strategies of value investing, including its history, key metrics used, and some of the most successful investors who have employed this approach.

History of Value Investing:

Value investing has its roots in the work of Benjamin Graham and David Dodd, who wrote the seminal book "Security Analysis" in 1934. Graham and Dodd believed that investors should focus on the underlying value of a company's assets, earnings, and cash flow, rather than on its stock price. They emphasized the importance of buying stocks that were trading at a discount to their intrinsic value, which they believed was determined by the company's financial and operating metrics.

The most famous student of Graham and Dodd was Warren Buffett, who has become one of the most successful investors of all time using value investing principles. Buffett's investment philosophy is based on the concept of buying high-quality companies with a strong competitive advantage and a long-term growth potential at a reasonable price.

Key Metrics Used in Value Investing:

Value investors use a variety of financial metrics to identify undervalued stocks. Some of the most commonly used metrics include:

Price-to-Earnings (P/E) Ratio: The P/E ratio compares a company's stock price to its earnings per share. A low P/E ratio may indicate that a stock is undervalued relative to its earnings potential.

Price-to-Book (P/B) Ratio: The P/B ratio compares a company's stock price to its book value, which is the value of its assets minus its liabilities. A low P/B ratio may indicate that a stock is undervalued relative to its asset value.

Price-to-Sales (P/S) Ratio: The P/S ratio compares a company's stock price to its sales per share. A low P/S ratio may indicate that a stock is undervalued relative to its revenue potential.

Dividend Yield: The dividend yield is the annual dividend payment divided by the stock price. A high dividend yield may indicate that a stock is undervalued relative to its income potential.

Free Cash Flow (FCF) Yield: The FCF yield is the free cash flow divided by the stock price. Free cash flow is the cash generated by a company's operations after accounting for capital expenditures. A high FCF yield may indicate that a stock is undervalued relative to its cash flow potential.

Successful Value Investors:

Some of the most successful investors in history have used value investing principles to achieve their success. Here are a few examples:

Warren Buffett: As previously mentioned, Buffett is perhaps the most famous value investor of all time. He has consistently beaten the market using a long-term, value-based investment approach.

Benjamin Graham: The father of value investing, Graham's investment philosophy has influenced generations of investors.

Seth Klarman: Klarman is the founder of Baupost Group, a hedge fund that has consistently delivered strong returns using a value-oriented approach.

Joel Greenblatt: Greenblatt is the founder of Gotham Asset Management and the author of "The Little Book That Beats the Market," which outlines his value-based investment strategy.

Walter Schloss: Schloss was a former student of Graham and Dodd and one of Buffett's early mentors. He achieved strong returns using a low-cost, value-based approach.

Conclusion:

Value investing is a popular investment strategy that has been used successfully by many investors over the years. The basic idea behind value investing is to buy stocks that are undervalued by the market and hold them until they reach their true value. While value investing can be a profitable investment strategy, it is not without its risks. It requires a significant amount of research, analysis, and patience.

One of the key challenges of value investing is finding stocks that are truly undervalued. The market is efficient, which means that stock prices typically reflect all available information about a company. In other words, if a company's stock is undervalued, there is usually a good reason for it. Value investors need to be able to identify companies that are undervalued for reasons that are temporary or that the market has not yet recognized.

Another challenge of value investing is the need for patience. Value investors are looking for stocks that will eventually reach their true value, but this may not happen for months or even years. During this time, the stock price may remain stagnant or even decline further. Value investors need to have the discipline to stick with their investments through these periods of uncertainty.

Despite these challenges, value investing can be a profitable investment strategy for those who are willing to put in the time and effort required. One of the key advantages of value investing is that it is a contrarian strategy. Value investors are looking for stocks that are out of favor with the market, which means that they may be able to buy these stocks at a discount. Over time, the market may recognize the true value of these stocks, leading to significant gains for value investors.

Another advantage of value investing is that it can help to mitigate risk. By focusing on companies with strong fundamentals and attractive valuations, value investors are less likely to invest in companies that are overvalued or at risk of financial distress. This can help to reduce the risk of significant losses.

In conclusion, value investing is a popular investment strategy that has been used successfully by many investors over the years. While it can be a profitable investment strategy, it is not without its risks. Value investors need to be able to identify undervalued companies and have the discipline to hold these investments over the long term. With careful research and analysis, value investing can be a valuable addition to any investment portfolio.

Momentum investing

Momentum investing is a popular investment strategy that involves buying stocks that have shown strong performance in the recent past and selling those that have shown weak performance. This strategy is based on the idea that stocks that have performed well in the past are likely to continue to perform well in the future, while those that have performed poorly are likely to continue to underperform.

Momentum investing has been studied extensively in the academic literature and has been found to be a profitable strategy in many markets around the world. However, like all investment strategies, momentum investing also has its risks and limitations.

In this section, we will provide an in-depth analysis of momentum investing, including its definition, historical performance, academic research, and practical applications. We will also discuss the advantages and disadvantages of momentum investing, as well as some of the key factors that investors should consider when using this strategy.

Definition:

Momentum investing is a strategy that involves buying stocks that have shown strong performance in the recent past and selling those that have shown weak performance. The idea behind this strategy is that stocks that have performed well in the past are likely to continue to perform well in the future, while those that have performed poorly are likely to continue to underperform.

There are two main types of momentum investing: price momentum and earnings momentum. Price momentum involves buying stocks that have shown strong price performance in the recent past, while earnings momentum involves buying stocks that have shown strong earnings growth in the recent past.

Price momentum is typically measured using a price-based indicator such as the Relative Strength Index (RSI) or the Moving Average Convergence Divergence (MACD) indicator. Earnings momentum is typically measured using an earnings-based indicator such as the earnings surprise or the earnings momentum factor.

Historical Performance:

Momentum investing has been found to be a profitable strategy in many markets around the world. One of the earliest and most influential studies on momentum investing was conducted by Jegadeesh and Titman (1993), who found that buying stocks that have shown strong performance in the past and selling those that have shown weak performance resulted in significant positive returns.

Subsequent studies have confirmed the profitability of momentum investing in a variety of markets and asset classes, including stocks, bonds, currencies, and commodities. For example, Asness, Moskowitz, and Pedersen (2013) found that momentum investing was profitable in 58 out of 59 stock markets around the world.

Despite its historical performance, momentum investing has also experienced periods of underperformance and volatility. For example, during the dot-com bubble of the late 1990s, momentum investing underperformed as investors favored growth stocks over value stocks. Similarly, during the financial crisis of 2008, momentum investing suffered as market volatility increased.

Academic Research:

Momentum investing has been studied extensively in the academic literature. One of the earliest and most influential studies on momentum investing was conducted by Jegadeesh and Titman (1993), who found that buying stocks that have shown strong performance in the past and selling those that have shown weak performance resulted in significant positive returns.

Subsequent studies have confirmed the profitability of momentum investing in a variety of markets and asset classes, including stocks, bonds, currencies, and commodities. For example, Asness, Moskowitz, and Pedersen (2013) found that momentum investing was profitable in 58 out of 59 stock markets around the world.

Despite its historical performance, momentum investing has also been the subject of some criticism and skepticism in the academic literature. Some researchers argue that momentum investing is simply a form of market timing and that the returns are due to the fact that it is easier to predict short-term price movements than long-term fundamentals.

Other researchers argue that momentum investing is a behavioral phenomenon and that it reflects the tendency of investors to overreact to recent price movements and to underestimate the persistence of trends. They argue that this behavior is driven by psychological biases such as herding behavior, anchoring, and confirmation bias.

Despite these criticisms, momentum investing has gained popularity in recent years and has been adopted by many institutional investors, hedge funds, and retail investors. The growth of exchange-traded funds (ETFs) has also made it easier for individual investors to access momentum strategies.

There are several ways to implement momentum investing strategies, including cross-sectional and time-series momentum. Cross-sectional momentum involves selecting stocks based on their relative performance to each other over a specified time period, while time-series momentum involves selecting stocks based on their own past performance over a specified time period.

One of the challenges of implementing momentum strategies is the frequency of trading. Momentum strategies typically require frequent trading to maintain a portfolio of stocks with high momentum scores. This can lead to high transaction costs, which can erode the returns of the strategy. Some momentum investors try to mitigate this challenge by using alternative data sources or machine learning algorithms to identify momentum signals.

In addition to the challenges of implementation, momentum investing is also subject to market risks and volatility. Because momentum investing involves taking concentrated positions in a few stocks, it is more susceptible to idiosyncratic risks such as company-specific news or events. This can result in significant drawdowns and losses.

In conclusion, momentum investing is a popular investment strategy that has been shown to generate significant returns over long periods of time. However, it is not without its challenges and risks. As with any investment strategy, it is important to understand the underlying assumptions, risks, and potential rewards before deciding to invest in a momentum strategy. Investors should also be aware of the behavioral biases that can influence their investment decisions and take steps to mitigate these biases. With careful consideration and implementation, momentum investing can be a powerful tool for investors seeking to generate alpha in their portfolios.

Contrarian investing

Contrarian investing is an investment strategy that involves taking a position opposite to the prevailing market sentiment. This approach involves buying assets that are currently undervalued and selling those that are overvalued. Contrarian investors believe that the market tends to overreact to news and other events, causing asset prices to deviate from their true values. By taking the opposite position, contrarian investors aim to capitalize on these market inefficiencies and generate higher returns.

In this section, we will explore the concept of contrarian investing in depth. We will discuss its history, principles, and application in various investment contexts. We will also examine the advantages and disadvantages of this approach, as well as some of the criticisms and controversies associated with it.

History of Contrarian Investing

The concept of contrarian investing has been around for centuries. One of the earliest examples of this approach is attributed to the famous Dutch investor, Isaac Le Maire, who in the 17th century, took a contrarian stance against the Dutch East India Company, a widely popular stock at the time. Le Maire believed that the company was overvalued and that the market sentiment was too optimistic. He shorted the stock and made a substantial profit when the company's share price subsequently declined.

In the 20th century, Benjamin Graham and David Dodd, the pioneers of value investing, also advocated for a contrarian approach. They believed that the market was prone to irrational exuberance and that prices often deviated from intrinsic values. Graham and Dodd argued that investors should focus on buying undervalued stocks and avoiding overvalued ones, which would require taking a contrarian stance against the prevailing market sentiment.

Principles of Contrarian Investing

Contrarian investing involves taking a position opposite to the market consensus. This approach is based on several principles:

Markets are inefficient: Contrarian investors believe that markets are not always efficient and that prices can deviate from their true values due to various factors, including herd behavior, irrational exuberance, and emotional reactions to news and events.

Overreaction to news and events: Contrarian investors believe that investors tend to overreact to news and events, causing prices to fluctuate excessively. They aim to take advantage of these fluctuations by buying assets that are currently undervalued and selling those that are overvalued.

Long-term focus: Contrarian investing is a long-term strategy. Contrarian investors believe that over the long term, prices tend to converge to their intrinsic values, providing an opportunity to generate higher returns.

Value investing: Contrarian investing is often associated with value investing. Contrarian investors focus on buying undervalued assets and avoiding overvalued ones, which requires taking a contrarian stance against the prevailing market sentiment.

Application of Contrarian Investing

Contrarian investing can be applied in various investment contexts, including:

Stock markets: Contrarian investors can apply their approach to stock markets by buying stocks that are currently out of favor and selling those that are popular. This approach can be used to identify undervalued companies with strong fundamentals that are currently overlooked by the market.

Bond markets: Contrarian investors can also apply their approach to bond markets by buying bonds that are currently undervalued and selling those that are overvalued. This approach can be used to identify bonds with high yields that are currently overlooked by the market.

Real estate markets: Contrarian investors can also apply their approach to real estate markets by buying properties that are currently undervalued and selling those that are overvalued. This approach can be used to identify properties with strong fundamentals that are currently overlooked by the market.

Advantages of Contrarian Investing

Contrarian investing offers several advantages, including:

Higher returns: Contrarian investing can provide higher returns than other investment strategies. This is because contrarian investors are able to identify undervalued assets that are temporarily out of favor with the market. When the market eventually recognizes the value of these assets, their prices tend to rise significantly, providing substantial returns to contrarian investors.

Diversification: Contrarian investing also offers diversification benefits as it allows investors to identify and invest in assets that are not closely correlated with the broader market. This reduces the risk of the portfolio and can help protect investors during market downturns.

Less crowded trades: Contrarian investing often involves taking positions that are not widely held by other investors, which means that contrarian investors can benefit from less crowded trades. This can allow them to enter and exit positions more easily, and at better prices, than investors who follow the herd.

Long-term perspective: Contrarian investors tend to take a long-term perspective on their investments, which means that they are less likely to be swayed by short-term market movements. This can help them avoid emotional reactions to market volatility and stay focused on their investment objectives.

In addition to these advantages, contrarian investing can also provide psychological benefits to investors. Contrarian investors often enjoy the satisfaction of going against the crowd and finding undervalued assets that others have overlooked. They may also enjoy the intellectual challenge of identifying market inefficiencies and opportunities that others have missed.

Challenges of Contrarian Investing

Despite its potential benefits, contrarian investing also has some challenges that investors should be aware of:

Timing: Contrarian investing can be difficult because it involves identifying assets that are temporarily out of favor with the market. This requires a deep understanding of the underlying fundamentals of the asset and an ability to identify when the market is likely to recognize its value. Timing is key to successful contrarian investing, and getting it wrong can result in significant losses.

Reputation risk: Contrarian investing can be risky because it involves taking positions that are not widely held by other investors. This can expose investors to reputational risk if the market does not recognize the value of the asset as quickly as expected, or if the asset continues to decline in value.

Market volatility: Contrarian investing can be particularly challenging during periods of market volatility, as it can be difficult to distinguish between assets that are temporarily out of favor with the market and assets that are in a longer-term decline. During periods of high volatility, investors may need to be more cautious in their contrarian investing strategies.

Conclusion

Contrarian investing is a unique investment strategy that involves going against the crowd and investing in assets that are temporarily out of favor with the market. While it can be challenging and risky, contrarian investing offers several advantages, including higher returns, diversification, less crowded trades, and a long-term perspective. By understanding the challenges and benefits of contrarian investing, investors can develop a successful contrarian investing strategy that aligns with their investment objectives and risk tolerance.

Behavioral portfolio management

In recent years, there has been growing recognition of the role that behavioral finance can play in investment management. Behavioral finance is a field that combines principles of psychology with finance to explain why individuals make irrational financial decisions. By understanding how investors think and behave, portfolio managers can create investment strategies that are better suited to their clients' needs and goals.

Behavioral portfolio management is a framework that seeks to incorporate insights from behavioral finance into the investment process. It involves identifying behavioral biases that may influence investment decisions and designing strategies to mitigate the impact of these biases.

One key aspect of behavioral portfolio management is understanding the role of emotions in investment decisions. Many investors make decisions based on their emotions, rather than on objective analysis of financial data. This can lead to poor investment decisions, such as buying or selling at the wrong time, or failing to diversify their portfolios. Behavioral portfolio managers seek to understand how emotions can impact investment decisions and develop strategies to mitigate the impact of these emotions.

For example, a portfolio manager might use a stop-loss order to limit losses on a particular investment. This strategy involves setting a price at which a security will be sold if its price falls below a certain level. By setting a stop-loss order, the portfolio manager can avoid the emotional bias of holding on to a losing investment in the hope that it will recover.

Another key aspect of behavioral portfolio management is understanding the impact of cognitive biases on investment decisions. Cognitive biases are errors in thinking that can lead to irrational decision-making. These biases can include overconfidence, anchoring, and herding behavior, among others.

For example, overconfidence bias can lead investors to believe that they are better than average at picking stocks or timing the market. This can lead to excessive trading and poor investment decisions. Behavioral portfolio managers seek to identify and mitigate the impact of cognitive biases on investment decisions by using tools such as diversification, asset allocation, and risk management strategies.

In addition to understanding the role of emotions and cognitive biases in investment decisions, behavioral portfolio managers also seek to design portfolios that are better suited to their clients' needs and goals. This involves taking into account factors such as risk tolerance, investment objectives, and time horizon.

For example, a portfolio manager might design a portfolio that is more heavily weighted towards fixed-income securities for a client who is close to retirement and has a lower risk tolerance. Alternatively, a portfolio manager might design a portfolio that is more heavily weighted towards equities for a client who has a longer time horizon and a higher risk tolerance.

One key tool that behavioral portfolio managers use to design portfolios is goal-based investing. Goal-based investing involves designing portfolios that are tailored to specific investment goals, such as retirement income or funding a child's education. By focusing on specific investment goals, rather than simply maximizing returns, portfolio managers can help investors achieve their financial objectives while mitigating the impact of behavioral biases.

Another key aspect of behavioral portfolio management is ongoing monitoring and analysis of the portfolio. Behavioral portfolio managers seek to identify changes in the market or in the client's circumstances that may require adjustments to the portfolio. This may involve rebalancing the portfolio, adjusting asset allocations, or changing specific investments.

Overall, behavioral portfolio management is a powerful framework for investment management that seeks to incorporate insights from behavioral finance into the investment process. By understanding how investors think and behave, portfolio managers can create investment strategies that are better suited to their clients' needs and goals, while mitigating the impact of behavioral biases.

CHAPTER 31: THE FUTURE OF BEHAVIORAL FINANCE

The field of behavioral finance has come a long way since its inception in the late 1970s. It has provided valuable insights into the ways in which human behavior affects financial decision-making, and has helped to explain some of the anomalies that traditional finance theories cannot. However, the field is still evolving, and there are many questions and challenges that remain to be addressed. This chapter will provide an overview of the current state of behavioral finance, as well as some predictions and potential directions for the future of the field.

Overview of the Chapter:

The chapter will begin by reviewing some of the key insights and findings of behavioral finance to date, including the role of heuristics and biases, the impact of emotions on decision-making, and the importance of social and cultural factors. It will then examine some of the current debates and controversies within the field, such as the role of neuroeconomics and the limitations of empirical studies.

The chapter will then turn to the future of behavioral finance, discussing some potential avenues for research and development, including the integration of behavioral finance with other disciplines, such as psychology, neuroscience, and computer science. It will also explore some of the challenges that the field is likely to face in the coming years, such as the need for more rigorous and transparent research methodologies, the impact of technology and artificial intelligence, and the potential for behavioral finance to inform policy and regulation.

Importance of Understanding the Future of Behavioral Finance:

Understanding the future of behavioral finance is important for several reasons. First, it can help investors, portfolio managers, and financial planners to make better decisions by providing insights into the factors that influence market behavior and investor psychology. Second, it can help researchers to develop new theories and models that better capture the complexities of human decision-making. Third, it can help policymakers to design more effective regulations and interventions that take into account the ways in which people actually behave in financial markets. Finally, it can help us to better understand ourselves and the factors that influence our own financial decisions.

Key Insights and Findings in Behavioral Finance:

Behavioral finance has provided a wealth of insights into the ways in which human behavior affects financial decision-making. Some of the key findings include:

Heuristics and Biases: Behavioral finance has demonstrated that people often rely on heuristics, or mental shortcuts, to make decisions in complex situations. These heuristics can lead to biases, such as overconfidence, loss aversion, and herding behavior, which can in turn lead to suboptimal financial decisions.

Emotions: Behavioral finance has shown that emotions play a significant role in financial decision-making, and that they can be powerful drivers of risk-taking and other behaviors. Emotions such as fear, greed, and regret can influence our perceptions of risk and reward, and can lead us to make irrational decisions.

Social and Cultural Factors: Behavioral finance has also demonstrated the importance of social and cultural factors in financial decision-making. People are influenced by the opinions and actions of others, and cultural norms and values can shape our perceptions of risk and reward.

Current Debates and Controversies in Behavioral Finance:

Despite the many insights and findings of behavioral finance, there are still some debates and controversies within the field. Some of the key debates include:

The Role of Neuroeconomics: Some researchers believe that the integration of neuroscience and economics can provide a more complete understanding of human decision-making. Others argue that the use of brain imaging technologies is still in its infancy and that caution is needed in interpreting the results.

Limitations of Empirical Studies: Some critics argue that many of the empirical studies in behavioral finance suffer from methodological limitations, such as small sample sizes, self-report biases, and lack of transparency. This has led some to question the validity of the findings of the field.

The Relationship between Behavioral Finance and Efficient Market Hypothesis (EMH): The EMH suggests that markets are efficient and that all available information is already reflected in asset prices. However, behavioral finance has shown that investors are subject to biases and can make systematic errors in their investment decisions, which would imply that markets are not always efficient. This has led to ongoing debates about the validity of the EMH and the role of behavioral factors in determining asset prices.

The Future of Behavioral Finance

Despite these debates and controversies, behavioral finance has emerged as a significant and influential field within finance. The future of behavioral finance is likely to be shaped by a number of key trends and developments:

Advances in Technology: As technology continues to evolve, it is likely to have a significant impact on the study and practice of behavioral finance. For example, the increasing use of big data and artificial intelligence is likely to enhance our ability to identify and understand patterns of human behavior in financial markets.

Interdisciplinary Collaboration: Behavioral finance has already benefited from collaborations between researchers in finance, psychology, and other related fields. In the future, interdisciplinary collaborations are likely to become even more important, as researchers seek to understand the complex interplay between economic, social, and psychological factors that shape financial decision-making.

Practical Applications: Behavioral finance has already had a significant impact on investment practice, as investors seek to incorporate insights from the field into their decision-making processes. In the future, behavioral finance is likely to continue to play a key role in helping investors to better understand and manage their behavior, as well as in the development of new financial products and services that better meet the needs of investors.

Continued Debate and Controversy: As with any field of inquiry, behavioral finance is likely to continue to face debates and controversies as researchers seek to refine and improve our understanding of human decision-making in financial markets. However, it is likely that these debates will be conducted within a broader context of acceptance and recognition of the importance of behavioral factors in shaping financial outcomes.

Conclusion

Behavioral finance represents a significant departure from the traditional rational actor model that has dominated finance for much of its history. By emphasizing the role of psychological and social factors in shaping financial decision-making, behavioral finance has challenged many of the assumptions that underlie traditional finance theory and has provided new insights into the behavior of investors and the workings of financial markets.

While behavioral finance is still a relatively young field, it has already had a significant impact on investment practice, as well as on our broader understanding of human decision-making. The future of behavioral finance is likely to be shaped by a number of key trends and developments, including advances in technology, interdisciplinary collaboration, practical applications, and ongoing debate and controversy.

I. Current State of Behavioral Finance

Behavioral finance has come a long way since its inception in the late 1970s. Over the years, researchers have uncovered many behavioral biases and heuristics that affect the financial decisions of investors. Despite some criticism, behavioral finance has become an important area of study in the field of finance, and its insights have been applied in various aspects of finance, such as investment management, corporate finance, and personal finance. This section will provide an overview of the current state of behavioral finance, including recent developments, applications, and criticisms.

Recent Developments
One of the most significant recent developments in behavioral finance is the integration of neuroscience and economics, known as neuroeconomics. This field seeks to understand how the brain processes information and makes decisions related to economics and finance. Neuroeconomics uses brain imaging technologies, such as functional magnetic resonance imaging (fMRI) and electroencephalography (EEG), to study brain activity in response to financial stimuli.

For example, researchers have used fMRI to study the neural correlates of financial risk-taking. Studies have shown that the brain's reward center, the ventral striatum, is more active in response to high-risk, high-reward financial decisions than in response to low-risk, low-reward decisions. These findings suggest that investors' risk preferences may be influenced by their brain's response to financial stimuli.

Another recent development in behavioral finance is the use of big data and machine learning to analyze financial data. Big data refers to the large and complex datasets generated by the digital age, while machine learning refers to the ability of computers to learn from data without being explicitly programmed. By using big data and machine learning algorithms, researchers can analyze vast amounts of financial data and uncover patterns and relationships that were previously difficult or impossible to detect.

For example, quantitative analysts and portfolio managers are using machine learning algorithms to identify patterns in financial data and make more informed investment decisions. These algorithms can analyze a range of financial data, including stock prices, company financial statements, news articles, and social media sentiment, to identify trends and patterns that traditional financial analysis may miss.

Applications

Behavioral finance has numerous applications in the field of finance. One of the most important applications is in investment management. Portfolio managers can use behavioral finance insights to design investment strategies that account for investors' behavioral biases and heuristics. For example, a portfolio manager may design a contrarian investment strategy that exploits investors' tendency to follow the herd and buy popular stocks. The manager may also use loss aversion to design a portfolio that includes more low-risk assets to mitigate the negative impact of losses.

Another important application of behavioral finance is in personal finance. Financial planners can use behavioral finance insights to help clients make better financial decisions. For example, a financial planner may use the anchoring bias to encourage a client to save more money by setting a high savings target. The planner may also use the endowment effect to encourage a client to sell underperforming assets and invest the proceeds in more profitable investments.

Criticisms

Despite its many insights and applications, behavioral finance is not without its criticisms. One of the most significant criticisms is that the field suffers from methodological limitations, such as small sample sizes, self-report biases, and lack of transparency. Some critics argue that many of the empirical studies in behavioral finance are not replicable and suffer from low statistical power. This has led some to question the validity of the findings of the field.

Another criticism of behavioral finance is that it may overemphasize the importance of behavioral biases and heuristics in financial decision-making. Some researchers argue that while behavioral biases are important, they are not the only factor that influences financial decision-making. Other factors, such as market fundamentals, company performance, and macroeconomic trends, may also play a significant role in financial decision-making.

In addition, some critics argue that behavioral finance is too focused on individual decision-making and ignores the larger systemic factors that contribute to financial crises and market inefficiencies. They argue that macroeconomic and institutional factors, such as government policies, regulations, and market structures, should also be taken into account.

Another criticism is that behavioral finance may not offer practical solutions for investors and financial professionals. Some argue that the field is more descriptive than prescriptive and that it does not provide clear guidelines for how to take advantage of behavioral biases or how to mitigate their negative effects.

Furthermore, some critics argue that behavioral finance is too subjective and lacks a rigorous theoretical foundation. They contend that the field relies too heavily on anecdotal evidence and that there is a need for more rigorous testing of theories and hypotheses.

Despite these criticisms, behavioral finance continues to be a vibrant and rapidly evolving field that has made significant contributions to our understanding of financial decision-making. As the field continues to develop and mature, it is likely that many of these criticisms will be addressed and that the field will continue to provide valuable insights and applications for investors and financial professionals.

The growth of behavioral finance

The growth of behavioral finance can be traced back to the late 1970s and early 1980s, when researchers began to challenge the traditional view of financial decision-making as purely rational and efficient. The emergence of behavioral finance was a result of the recognition that individuals are not always rational actors when it comes to making financial decisions, and that they can be influenced by a variety of cognitive biases and heuristics.

Since its inception, behavioral finance has grown significantly and has become an important field within finance and economics. One of the key drivers of this growth has been the increasing recognition of the limitations of traditional finance theory, particularly the assumption of rational decision-making by market participants. As the global financial crisis of 2008 showed, financial markets can be prone to irrational and unpredictable behavior, and traditional finance theory may not be adequate in explaining these phenomena.

Another driver of the growth of behavioral finance has been the increasing availability of data and the development of new tools and techniques for analyzing it. Advances in computing power and data storage have allowed researchers to analyze large datasets and to identify patterns and trends that were previously difficult to detect. This has led to a better understanding of how human behavior affects financial markets and has enabled the development of new models and approaches for investment management.

The growth of behavioral finance has also been fueled by the increasing interest of practitioners, such as investment bankers, portfolio managers, and financial planners, in applying behavioral finance principles to their work. Many financial institutions now employ behavioral finance experts who work to identify and mitigate the impact of behavioral biases on financial decision-making.

Moreover, the growth of behavioral finance has been driven by the increasing collaboration between academia and industry. Academics and practitioners are now working together to develop new theories, tools, and techniques that can better explain and manage the behavior of market participants. For example, many financial institutions now sponsor research projects on behavioral finance, and academic researchers are increasingly consulting with industry experts to develop more practical applications of behavioral finance theory.

Despite its growth and increasing popularity, behavioral finance is not without its challenges. One of the key challenges facing the field is the need to develop robust and reliable methods for measuring and quantifying behavioral biases and heuristics. While there are a number of well-established measures of cognitive biases, there is still much work to be done in developing reliable measures of emotional and social biases, which can be more difficult to quantify.

Another challenge facing the field is the need to develop more rigorous research designs and methods for testing behavioral finance theories. While there have been many important findings in behavioral finance, some researchers argue that many of the empirical studies suffer from methodological limitations and are not replicable. To address these concerns, researchers need to use more rigorous research designs, such as randomized controlled trials, and to ensure that their studies are transparent and well-documented.

Overall, the growth of behavioral finance has been significant, and it has led to important insights and applications in the field of finance and economics. As the field continues to develop, researchers and practitioners will need to work together to overcome the challenges and limitations facing the field, and to develop new tools and approaches for understanding and managing the behavior of market participants.

The limitations of behavioral finance

Behavioral finance has been hailed as a promising field that offers a new perspective on traditional finance theories. However, like any other field of study, it is not without its limitations. In this section, we will examine some of the limitations of behavioral finance.

One of the main criticisms of behavioral finance is that it may be prone to overgeneralization. That is, some researchers believe that the field may be too focused on the psychological biases of individual investors and may not take into account the broader social, economic, and political contexts that may influence financial decision-making. For instance, while it is true that loss aversion and other cognitive biases can affect individual investors, they may not be the only factors that determine financial markets' behavior.

Another limitation of behavioral finance is its reliance on retrospective analysis. Much of the empirical research in behavioral finance is based on examining past market data and investor behavior, and then drawing conclusions based on that data. This approach may be prone to hindsight bias, which is the tendency to overestimate the predictability of past events. Additionally, retrospective analysis may not be an effective way to identify new trends or patterns in financial markets or investor behavior.

Moreover, some critics have raised concerns about the practical implications of behavioral finance research. While behavioral finance has identified several cognitive biases that can affect financial decision-making, it is not clear whether these biases can be consistently exploited to generate excess returns in financial markets. Some researchers argue that many of the behavioral anomalies identified by behavioral finance may be short-lived and may disappear as investors become more aware of them.

Another limitation of behavioral finance is the lack of a unified theory that can explain all the observed phenomena. While behavioral finance has made significant progress in identifying various psychological biases that can affect financial decision-making, there is no overarching theory that can explain all the observed phenomena. Some researchers have argued that this lack of a unified theory is a significant limitation of the field and may hinder its progress in the future.

Furthermore, some researchers argue that the predictive power of behavioral finance models is limited. While behavioral finance has identified several cognitive biases that can affect financial decision-making, it is not always clear how these biases will manifest themselves in financial markets. For instance, the same cognitive bias may lead to different investment decisions depending on the specific context in which it is applied. As a result, it may be challenging to develop reliable predictive models based on behavioral finance research.

In addition, some researchers have criticized behavioral finance for ignoring the role of institutional factors in financial decision-making. While behavioral finance has identified several psychological biases that can affect individual investors, it may not take into account the broader institutional factors that can influence financial markets' behavior. For instance, market regulations, corporate governance structures, and financial intermediaries' behavior may all play a significant role in determining financial markets' efficiency and investors' behavior.

Finally, some critics have raised concerns about the replicability of behavioral finance research. Many of the empirical studies in behavioral finance suffer from methodological limitations, such as small sample sizes, self-report biases, and lack of transparency. This has led some to question the validity of the findings of the field. While some researchers have attempted to replicate the findings of behavioral finance studies, the results have been mixed, and more research is needed to establish the field's validity.

In conclusion, behavioral finance has several limitations that may limit its usefulness in predicting financial markets' behavior and designing investment strategies. While behavioral finance has made significant progress in identifying various psychological biases that can affect financial decision-making, it may not take into account the broader social, economic, and institutional factors that can influence financial markets. Additionally, the predictive power of behavioral finance models may be limited, and the replicability of behavioral finance research may be a concern. Despite these limitations, behavioral finance remains a promising field that offers a new perspective on traditional finance theories, highlighting the importance of considering human behavior in financial decision-making.

One way to address the limitations of behavioral finance is to combine it with traditional finance theories. By integrating behavioral finance insights with efficient market hypothesis and rational expectations theory, investors can gain a more comprehensive understanding of financial markets. For example, a study by Shiller and Pound (1989) combined behavioral finance with the efficient market hypothesis to create a new framework that takes into account the psychological factors that can affect asset prices.

Another way to address the limitations of behavioral finance is to incorporate machine learning and artificial intelligence techniques into financial decision-making. Machine learning algorithms can analyze vast amounts of data to identify patterns and relationships that may not be apparent to human analysts. By combining machine learning with behavioral finance, investors can gain a better understanding of how psychological factors influence financial markets.

Despite these potential solutions, it is important to acknowledge that the limitations of behavioral finance are not easily overcome. The field is still relatively new, and much research is needed to fully understand its limitations and potential. Furthermore, the field may need to overcome its own biases and limitations, such as the tendency to focus on a limited number of biases and the lack of attention given to broader social and economic factors.

In conclusion, behavioral finance is a promising field that offers a new perspective on traditional finance theories. However, it is not without its limitations, including methodological limitations, limited predictive power, and a focus on narrow biases at the expense of broader social and economic factors. These limitations should not detract from the important insights that behavioral finance has provided into human behavior and decision-making in financial markets. Instead, they should serve as a reminder of the complexity of financial markets and the need for a multifaceted approach to understanding and predicting their behavior.

The challenges of implementing behavioral finance strategies

Behavioral finance strategies can be challenging to implement due to various factors. While behavioral finance has gained popularity in recent years, it is still a relatively new field, and many practitioners are still unfamiliar with the latest research and insights. In this section, we will explore some of the challenges associated with implementing behavioral finance strategies.

One of the main challenges of implementing behavioral finance strategies is the difficulty of identifying and measuring behavioral biases. Unlike traditional finance, which relies heavily on quantitative data and mathematical models, behavioral finance involves a greater emphasis on qualitative data and subjective assessments of investor behavior. This can make it challenging to identify and measure specific biases accurately.

For example, confirmation bias is a prevalent behavioral bias that can lead investors to seek out information that confirms their existing beliefs while ignoring contradictory evidence. While it is relatively easy to recognize confirmation bias in others, it can be challenging to detect in oneself. Investors may also be reluctant to admit to holding biased beliefs, which can further complicate efforts to identify and measure these biases.

Another challenge of implementing behavioral finance strategies is that investors may be resistant to change. Many investors have long-held beliefs about how financial markets work and may be hesitant to adopt new strategies that challenge these beliefs. This is particularly true for investors who have been successful using traditional finance strategies and may be reluctant to deviate from what has worked in the past.

Moreover, investors may be skeptical of behavioral finance strategies because they rely on subjective assessments of investor behavior rather than hard data. This can make it challenging to convince investors that behavioral finance strategies are worth pursuing, particularly if they are not familiar with the latest research in the field.

Another challenge of implementing behavioral finance strategies is the difficulty of translating insights from academic research into practical applications. While behavioral finance researchers have made significant progress in identifying various psychological biases that can affect financial decision-making, it can be challenging to translate these findings into actionable investment strategies.

For example, overconfidence bias is a prevalent bias that can lead investors to overestimate their ability to predict the market's behavior. While this bias is well-documented in the academic literature, it can be challenging to develop practical investment strategies that account for it.

Moreover, behavioral finance strategies may be more complicated to implement than traditional finance strategies, requiring more significant data analysis and more sophisticated models. This can make it challenging for smaller firms or investors with limited resources to implement these strategies effectively.

Another challenge of implementing behavioral finance strategies is that they may require a different approach to risk management. Traditional finance strategies tend to rely heavily on mathematical models and quantitative data to assess risk. In contrast, behavioral finance strategies may require a more subjective assessment of risk based on qualitative data and subjective assessments of investor behavior.

For example, loss aversion is a prevalent bias that can lead investors to be more sensitive to losses than gains. This can make it challenging to assess the risks associated with an investment accurately. A traditional finance strategy might rely on mathematical models to assess risk, while a behavioral finance strategy might require a more subjective assessment of risk based on an understanding of how investors are likely to react to losses.

Moreover, behavioral finance strategies may require a more active approach to risk management. Traditional finance strategies tend to rely heavily on diversification and asset allocation to manage risk. In contrast, behavioral finance strategies may require more active management of individual investments to account for the psychological biases that can affect investor behavior.

Finally, another challenge of implementing behavioral finance strategies is the potential for unintended consequences. While behavioral finance strategies may be effective in addressing specific biases or inefficiencies in financial markets, they may also create new inefficiencies or unintended consequences.

For example, a behavioral finance strategy that relies on a specific psychological bias may become less effective over time as investors become more aware of the bias and adjust their behavior accordingly.

Moreover, behavioral finance strategies may create new inefficiencies in financial markets by encouraging investors to behave in ways that deviate from market fundamentals.

Another challenge of implementing behavioral finance strategies is the difficulty in measuring and quantifying behavioral biases accurately. Behavioral biases are often subtle and difficult to identify, and they may be subject to individual interpretation. Therefore, it can be challenging to design a behavioral finance strategy that accurately accounts for all the relevant behavioral biases.

Additionally, implementing behavioral finance strategies can be challenging because it requires a deep understanding of the complex interplay between psychology and finance. Behavioral finance strategies often require a significant amount of expertise and specialized knowledge, which may not be readily available to all investors. As a result, many investors may find it challenging to implement effective behavioral finance strategies on their own.

Another challenge of implementing behavioral finance strategies is that they may require a long-term investment horizon. Many behavioral finance strategies rely on the assumption that the psychological biases that influence financial decision-making are relatively stable over time. However, psychological biases can change, and new biases can emerge, making it challenging to predict the efficacy of a particular behavioral finance strategy over the long-term.

Furthermore, implementing behavioral finance strategies can be challenging because it requires overcoming psychological barriers. Many investors may be resistant to adopting a new investment strategy, particularly if it deviates from traditional finance theory. Moreover, investors may be prone to cognitive biases that lead them to overestimate their own ability to make successful investment decisions, making it challenging to convince them to adopt a new investment approach.

In conclusion, implementing behavioral finance strategies can be challenging due to several factors, including the potential for strategies to become less effective over time, the difficulty in accurately measuring and quantifying behavioral biases, the need for specialized knowledge and expertise, the requirement for a long-term investment horizon, and the need to overcome psychological barriers. Despite these challenges, behavioral finance strategies offer investors a new approach to understanding financial markets' behavior, and they have the potential to generate superior investment returns. Therefore, it is essential for investors to carefully consider the challenges associated with implementing behavioral finance strategies and to seek out the necessary knowledge and expertise to do so successfully.

II. Emerging Trends in Behavioral Finance

Behavioral finance is an interdisciplinary field that combines insights from psychology, economics, and finance to study how individuals and markets make financial decisions. In recent years, there has been significant growth in behavioral finance research, driven by advances in technology, data analytics, and interdisciplinary collaboration.

Emerging trends in behavioral finance are transforming the way we understand financial decision-making and the functioning of financial markets. These trends are driven by new theoretical insights, empirical findings, and innovative applications of behavioral finance concepts in practice.

One of the most significant emerging trends in behavioral finance is the integration of machine learning and artificial intelligence (AI) into financial decision-making processes. Machine learning algorithms can identify patterns in large datasets that would be difficult or impossible for humans to discern. These algorithms can be used to predict financial market behavior, identify investment opportunities, and improve risk management strategies.

Another emerging trend in behavioral finance is the application of neuroscience to study the neural mechanisms underlying financial decision-making. Neuroeconomic studies have shown that financial decision-making engages multiple brain regions and involves complex cognitive processes, such as emotion regulation, attention, and memory. Understanding the neural mechanisms underlying financial decision-making can help researchers develop more accurate models of financial behavior and design more effective interventions to improve financial decision-making.

A third emerging trend in behavioral finance is the use of field experiments to study financial decision-making in real-world settings. Field experiments allow researchers to test theories and hypotheses in naturalistic settings, where participants are more likely to behave as they would in the real world. This approach can help researchers overcome some of the limitations of laboratory experiments and provide more accurate estimates of the effects of behavioral interventions on financial decision-making.

Other emerging trends in behavioral finance include the study of cultural and social influences on financial decision-making, the development of new behavioral finance theories to explain market anomalies, and the integration of behavioral finance concepts into financial education and consumer financial protection policies.

Despite the significant progress made in behavioral finance research, there are still many challenges and opportunities ahead. The next section will discuss some of the most pressing issues facing the field and potential directions for future research.

Big data and behavioral finance

The field of finance has seen a significant transformation in the past few decades, with the advent of big data and the growing interest in behavioral finance. Big data has the potential to revolutionize the finance industry by providing new and valuable insights into market trends, investor behavior, and risk management. Meanwhile, behavioral finance has emerged as an essential area of study that focuses on the psychological and emotional factors that affect investors' decision-making. Combining these two fields could lead to new opportunities and challenges for investors, policymakers, and financial institutions.

This section aims to provide a comprehensive introduction to the intersection of big data and behavioral finance. It will explore the impact of big data on the finance industry, the potential benefits of incorporating behavioral finance into big data analysis, and the challenges associated with this emerging trend. Additionally, it will examine the role of different financial professionals, such as investment bankers, portfolio managers, quantitative analysts, securities traders, financial planners, and financial analysts, in harnessing the power of big data and behavioral finance.

The Impact of Big Data on the Finance Industry:

The term "big data" refers to large and complex datasets that traditional data processing methods cannot handle effectively. The finance industry is one of the sectors that have witnessed significant growth in the volume, variety, and velocity of data in recent years. This data comes from various sources, such as financial transactions, news, social media, economic indicators, and more. The availability of this vast amount of data has led to the development of new tools and techniques for data analysis, such as artificial intelligence, machine learning, and data mining.

The impact of big data on the finance industry has been transformative, with potential benefits for both investors and financial institutions. For investors, big data can provide valuable insights into market trends and investor behavior, helping them make informed decisions about their investments. Big data analysis can help investors identify patterns and correlations in financial data that may not be apparent using traditional analysis methods. This can lead to more accurate predictions of market trends and better investment decisions.

For financial institutions, big data can offer several benefits, including improved risk management and fraud detection. By analyzing large datasets, financial institutions can identify potential risks and take proactive measures to mitigate them. Additionally, big data analysis can help institutions detect fraudulent activities and prevent them before they cause significant financial damage.

The Potential Benefits of Incorporating Behavioral Finance into Big Data Analysis:

Behavioral finance, on the other hand, focuses on the psychological and emotional factors that affect investors' decision-making. It recognizes that investors are not always rational, and their behavior is influenced by biases, heuristics, and emotions. Behavioral finance explores how these factors affect investment decisions and how they can be incorporated into financial models and strategies.

By combining behavioral finance with big data analysis, investors and financial institutions can gain a deeper understanding of market trends and investor behavior. Big data can provide a vast amount of information about investor sentiment, news sentiment, and other factors that influence investment decisions. Behavioral finance can help interpret this data by identifying the psychological and emotional factors that drive investors' behavior. By understanding these factors, investors and financial institutions can make more informed decisions about investments and risk management.

For example, a portfolio manager may use big data to analyze market trends and investor sentiment. By incorporating behavioral finance into this analysis, the manager may be able to identify specific psychological biases that are driving investor behavior. This knowledge can then be used to adjust investment strategies and mitigate potential risks.

The Challenges of Incorporating Behavioral Finance into Big Data Analysis:

While the combination of big data and behavioral finance holds significant potential, it also poses several challenges. One of the most significant challenges is data quality. Big data analysis requires large and complex datasets, but the quality of the data can be variable. This can lead to inaccurate results and flawed investment decisions.

Another challenge is the integration of different data sources. Behavioral finance analysis often relies on data from multiple sources, including social media, news articles, financial statements, and more. Integrating these diverse sources can be challenging, as they may use different formats, structures, and languages. For example, news articles may use natural language, while financial statements may use structured data. This can make it difficult to create a unified dataset that can be analyzed effectively.

Data privacy is also a significant challenge in the context of big data and behavioral finance. Many behavioral finance analyses rely on personal data, such as social media profiles, credit scores, and transaction histories. These data are often protected by privacy laws and regulations, which can limit their use in financial analysis. Moreover, even if personal data can be legally accessed, concerns about data breaches and misuse can make individuals hesitant to share their data.

Another challenge is the need for expertise in both big data analytics and behavioral finance. Successful analysis of big data requires a high level of technical expertise in areas such as data mining, machine learning, and statistical analysis. At the same time, analyzing financial behavior requires a deep understanding of psychology, economics, and finance. It can be difficult to find individuals who possess both sets of skills and can effectively integrate them into their analyses.

Finally, the sheer volume of data available can be overwhelming. While big data provides a wealth of information, it can be difficult to sort through the noise and identify meaningful patterns. This can lead to information overload and decision paralysis, where investors are unable to make effective investment decisions due to the sheer amount of data available.

Despite these challenges, the combination of big data and behavioral finance holds significant promise for the future of finance. By leveraging large and diverse datasets, analysts can gain insights into investor behavior that were previously impossible. For example, analysis of social media data can provide real-time insights into investor sentiment, while analysis of transaction data can identify patterns of behavior that may be indicative of psychological biases.

Moreover, advances in machine learning and artificial intelligence are making it increasingly possible to analyze large datasets quickly and effectively. This can help analysts identify patterns and make predictions in real-time, allowing for faster and more accurate investment decisions.

In conclusion, the integration of big data and behavioral finance is a complex and challenging process that requires significant technical and analytical expertise. However, the potential benefits are significant, and the application of these techniques is likely to become more prevalent in the future. As with any new approach, careful consideration of the challenges and limitations is critical to ensuring that the benefits are realized while minimizing the risks.

Artificial intelligence and machine learning in behavioral finance

Artificial intelligence (AI) and machine learning (ML) are rapidly transforming the financial industry, including the field of behavioral finance. Behavioral finance has long been interested in understanding the biases and heuristics that impact investors' decision-making. The integration of AI and ML into behavioral finance offers new tools and opportunities to uncover patterns, insights, and relationships within financial data that may have been previously undiscovered. AI and ML can also help to build models that take into account a broader range of factors and make more accurate predictions of financial behavior.

However, the integration of AI and ML into behavioral finance also raises significant challenges and questions. These include ethical concerns, such as the potential for AI and ML algorithms to perpetuate biases or create new ones. The increasing use of AI and ML in the financial industry also raises questions about the role of human judgment and decision-making in investing.

In this section, we will explore the emerging trends in AI and ML in behavioral finance, including their potential benefits and drawbacks. We will discuss the implications of these trends for financial professionals, investors, and researchers. Finally, we will examine the challenges that must be addressed in order to ensure the responsible and effective use of AI and ML in behavioral finance.

The Emergence of AI and ML in Behavioral Finance:

The integration of AI and ML into behavioral finance is a natural progression given the large amount of data that is generated in financial markets. AI and ML can be used to analyze this data and identify patterns and insights that may be difficult or impossible to uncover with traditional methods.

AI and ML can be used in several ways in behavioral finance. One of the most promising applications is in the development of predictive models. These models can take into account a range of factors that impact financial behavior, including psychological biases and heuristics. By analyzing large datasets, AI and ML algorithms can identify patterns and relationships that may be invisible to human analysts. This can lead to more accurate predictions of financial behavior and more effective investment strategies.

Another promising application of AI and ML in behavioral finance is in portfolio management. AI and ML algorithms can be used to analyze portfolio performance and make adjustments in real-time based on changing market conditions. This can lead to more effective risk management and better returns for investors.

AI and ML can also be used to develop tools that assist investors in making decisions. For example, AI and ML algorithms can analyze an investor's risk tolerance, investment goals, and financial situation to provide personalized investment advice. This can help investors make more informed decisions and achieve their financial goals.

Potential Benefits of AI and ML in Behavioral Finance:

The integration of AI and ML into behavioral finance offers several potential benefits. Perhaps the most significant benefit is the ability to analyze and make sense of large and complex datasets. This can lead to more accurate predictions of financial behavior, more effective investment strategies, and better risk management.

AI and ML can also help to uncover patterns and relationships that may have been previously unknown or hidden. This can lead to new insights and a deeper understanding of financial behavior. Additionally, AI and ML can help to automate many tasks that were previously performed manually, such as portfolio management and risk assessment. This can lead to increased efficiency and cost savings for financial professionals and investors.

Furthermore, AI and ML can provide personalized investment advice to investors. By analyzing an investor's unique financial situation and investment goals, AI and ML algorithms can provide recommendations that are tailored to the individual's needs. This can help investors make more informed decisions and achieve their financial goals.

Drawbacks and Challenges of AI and ML in Behavioral Finance:

Despite the potential benefits of AI and ML in behavioral finance, there are also several drawbacks and challenges that must be addressed. One of the most significant challenges is the potential for bias. AI and ML algorithms are only as good as the data that they are trained on. If the data contains biases, these biases can be amplified by the algorithm. For example, if an AI algorithm is trained on data that is biased against certain groups of people, it may learn to discriminate against those groups. This can lead to unethical or discriminatory investment decisions.

Another challenge is the complexity of the algorithms themselves. AI and ML algorithms are often black boxes, meaning that it can be difficult to understand how they arrive at their decisions. This can make it challenging for investors to trust and interpret the results.

Additionally, the use of AI and ML in behavioral finance raises ethical concerns. For example, there may be concerns around data privacy and the use of personal information in investment decisions. There may also be concerns around the use of AI and ML in creating investment products that are marketed as "smart" or "intelligent" but are actually opaque and difficult to understand.

Furthermore, the use of AI and ML in behavioral finance requires significant computational resources, which can be costly. This may create a barrier to entry for smaller firms or individual investors who do not have access to these resources.

Finally, there is the risk that the use of AI and ML in behavioral finance may lead to the "automation" of investment decisions, reducing the role of human judgment and expertise. While AI and ML can be used to augment human decision-making, they should not be used as a replacement for it.

In conclusion, while the use of AI and ML in behavioral finance holds great promise, it is not without its challenges and drawbacks. It is important to address these challenges and ensure that AI and ML are used in an ethical and responsible manner to enhance, rather than replace, human decision-making in the field of finance.

Neurofinance and brain-based research

Neurofinance and brain-based research have become increasingly popular in the field of behavioral finance, providing insights into the neural mechanisms underlying financial decision-making. By using tools such as fMRI and EEG, researchers are able to identify the brain regions and neural processes involved in financial decision-making, which can inform our understanding of investor behavior and improve financial decision-making.

The field of neurofinance is based on the idea that the brain plays a critical role in financial decision-making. In recent years, advances in neuroscience have enabled researchers to identify the neural mechanisms that underlie various cognitive processes, including those involved in financial decision-making. By using techniques such as fMRI and EEG, researchers are able to observe brain activity in real-time and gain insights into the neural processes that govern behavior.

One of the key benefits of neurofinance is that it provides a more nuanced understanding of the cognitive processes that underlie financial decision-making. For example, studies have shown that the brain's reward system plays a significant role in financial decision-making, with the prospect of financial gain activating the same neural circuits as other rewarding experiences, such as food or sex. Other studies have identified the role of emotions in financial decision-making, with negative emotions such as fear and anxiety leading to risk aversion and positive emotions such as excitement and confidence leading to risk-taking.

The insights provided by neurofinance can be useful in a variety of settings, from investment management to financial planning. For example, portfolio managers may be able to use neurofinance research to design investment strategies that take into account the biases and heuristics that investors are subject to, such as loss aversion and overconfidence. Financial planners may be able to use these insights to help clients make better financial decisions by understanding the underlying cognitive processes that govern their behavior.

However, there are also several challenges associated with the use of neurofinance in behavioral finance. One of the main challenges is the complexity of the data. fMRI and EEG data can be difficult to interpret, and it can be challenging to identify which brain regions and neural processes are most relevant to financial decision-making. Additionally, there is a risk of overgeneralization when applying neurofinance insights to real-world financial decision-making. The context in which financial decisions are made can have a significant impact on behavior, and it is not always clear how the insights from neurofinance research can be applied in different contexts.

Another challenge is the ethical implications of using brain-based research in financial decision-making. There is a risk that neurofinance insights could be used to manipulate investor behavior or infringe on individual privacy. For example, it is possible that financial institutions could use neurofinance research to develop targeted advertising campaigns that exploit specific neural processes, or that employers could use this research to make hiring decisions based on an individual's brain activity.

Overall, while neurofinance and brain-based research offer exciting opportunities for improving financial decision-making, it is important to recognize the challenges and limitations associated with this approach. By continuing to develop our understanding of the neural mechanisms underlying financial decision-making, we can better equip investors, financial professionals, and policymakers with the tools they need to make informed decisions and promote financial stability.

Evolutionary psychology and behavioral finance

Evolutionary psychology is a branch of psychology that seeks to understand human behavior by examining the evolutionary pressures that shaped it. It is based on the principle that human behavior, like all animal behavior, is the result of adaptations that evolved over time to solve specific problems related to survival and reproduction. Behavioral finance, on the other hand, is a field that seeks to explain why people make certain financial decisions and how their behavior affects financial markets. Combining the principles of evolutionary psychology with the concepts of behavioral finance can provide insights into the underlying cognitive and emotional processes that drive financial decision-making.

The Evolutionary Basis of Financial Decision-Making:

Evolutionary psychology suggests that humans are predisposed to certain behaviors and decision-making processes that have been shaped by our evolutionary history. For example, humans have a natural inclination towards risk-taking, which can be attributed to the fact that our ancestors had to take risks to obtain food and resources. This risk-taking behavior is evident in the way that people invest in the stock market, with many investors willing to take on high levels of risk in order to achieve high returns.

However, evolutionary psychology also suggests that humans are predisposed to certain cognitive biases that can lead to suboptimal decision-making. For example, humans tend to be loss-averse, which means that they are more sensitive to losses than to gains. This bias can lead to irrational decisions such as holding onto losing investments for too long, in the hopes of avoiding a loss.

The Role of Emotions in Financial Decision-Making:

Emotions play a critical role in financial decision-making, and evolutionary psychology suggests that these emotions are rooted in our evolutionary history. For example, fear is an emotion that evolved to protect us from physical danger, but it can also be triggered by financial risks. When investors become fearful, they may sell off their investments, even if it is not the rational decision.

Similarly, greed is an emotion that evolved to motivate us to seek out resources, but it can also lead to irrational decisions in the financial realm. For example, investors may become overly optimistic about a particular investment, leading them to take on excessive risk.

The Role of Social Norms and Culture:

Evolutionary psychology suggests that social norms and culture also play a critical role in financial decision-making. Social norms are rules and expectations that guide behavior in a particular society or group, and they can influence financial decision-making in a variety of ways. For example, in some cultures, it may be considered taboo to discuss money openly, which can lead to a lack of financial literacy and education.

In addition, cultural differences in risk tolerance can also impact financial decision-making. For example, some cultures may be more risk-averse than others, which can lead to different investment strategies.

Implications for Financial Practice:

Understanding the evolutionary basis of financial decision-making can have important implications for financial practice. For example, financial advisors can use this knowledge to design investment strategies that are better aligned with clients' natural tendencies and biases. By recognizing the role of emotions and social norms, financial advisors can help clients make more informed and rational decisions.

In addition, knowledge of evolutionary psychology can help financial institutions design products and services that better meet the needs of their customers. For example, financial institutions can design investment products that are better aligned with clients' risk preferences, or develop educational programs that address common cognitive biases.

Limitations and Challenges:

While the integration of evolutionary psychology and behavioral finance has great potential, there are also several limitations and challenges that must be considered. One of the most significant limitations is the difficulty of measuring the underlying psychological processes that drive financial decision-making. Unlike more tangible measures such as income or asset allocation, psychological measures can be difficult to quantify and assess.

In addition, the field of evolutionary psychology is still relatively new, and there is still much debate about the validity and accuracy of some of its key assumptions and principles. As such, some experts in the field of behavioral finance have expressed skepticism about the utility of evolutionary psychology in explaining financial behavior.

Another challenge is the potential for overgeneralization. Evolutionary psychology principles are based on the premise that certain psychological traits and behaviors are hardwired into the human brain as a result of evolution. However, it is important to note that these traits and behaviors may not be universal or applicable to all individuals or cultures. There may be significant individual and cultural variation that cannot be fully explained by evolutionary psychology principles.

Furthermore, the concept of "adaptive behavior" can be difficult to define and measure in a financial context. What may be considered "adaptive" behavior in one context or situation may not be so in another.

For example, taking on more risk in order to potentially earn higher returns may be considered adaptive behavior in a bullish market, but may be maladaptive in a bearish market.

Despite these limitations and challenges, the integration of evolutionary psychology and behavioral finance has the potential to provide valuable insights into financial decision-making. By understanding the underlying psychological processes that drive financial behavior, financial professionals may be better equipped to develop strategies that are more effective in meeting the needs and goals of their clients.

For example, a portfolio manager may be able to use insights from evolutionary psychology to develop investment strategies that take into account clients' risk preferences and emotional responses to market fluctuations. A financial planner may be able to use these insights to better understand clients' financial goals and help them make more informed financial decisions.

In conclusion, the integration of evolutionary psychology and behavioral finance has the potential to provide valuable insights into financial decision-making. While there are limitations and challenges that must be considered, the potential benefits make it an area of research and study that warrants continued attention from both academics and practitioners in the field of finance. By better understanding the underlying psychological processes that drive financial decision-making, financial professionals can develop more effective strategies that help clients achieve their financial goals.

III. Implications for Financial Services Industry

Behavioral finance has revolutionized the financial industry by providing a new perspective on financial decision-making. It recognizes that investors are not always rational, and that emotions, biases, and heuristics play a significant role in shaping investment decisions. As a result, the field has important implications for the financial services industry, which must adapt to these new insights in order to better serve clients and improve outcomes.

This section will explore the implications of behavioral finance for the financial services industry, including how it has changed the way financial products and services are designed, marketed, and delivered. It will also consider the role of technology in facilitating these changes, and the challenges that the industry faces in implementing them.

Behavioral Finance and Financial Products:

One of the most significant implications of behavioral finance for the financial services industry is the need to rethink financial product design. Traditional financial products, such as stocks, bonds, and mutual funds, were designed with the assumption that investors are rational and make decisions based on objective information. However, as we now know, this is not always the case.

Behavioral finance suggests that financial products should be designed to reflect the psychological biases and heuristics that affect investor decision-making. For example, a product that is designed to address loss aversion may be more appealing to investors than one that simply seeks to maximize returns. Similarly, a product that is structured to appeal to investors' sense of fairness or social responsibility may be more attractive than one that does not.

The financial industry has already begun to respond to these insights. For example, target-date funds have become increasingly popular because they are designed to automatically adjust risk exposure based on the investor's age, addressing the behavioral bias known as the "myopic loss aversion". Similarly, socially responsible investing (SRI) has become a popular trend as investors increasingly want their investments to reflect their values and beliefs.

Behavioral Finance and Marketing:

The insights from behavioral finance have also changed the way financial products are marketed. Traditional marketing strategies focused on the objective features of financial products, such as their returns, fees, and risk. However, these features are not always the most important factors in investor decision-making.

Behavioral finance suggests that marketing should focus on the psychological factors that affect investor decision-making, such as social proof, anchoring, and framing. For example, an advertisement that emphasizes the popularity of a product may be more effective than one that simply provides information about the product's returns. Similarly, an advertisement that frames a product in terms of its potential gains rather than its potential losses may be more attractive to investors.

The financial industry has also responded to these insights. For example, robo-advisors and other digital platforms have been developed to deliver customized investment advice and portfolios that are tailored to individual investor goals and psychological profiles.

Behavioral Finance and Financial Advice:

Another implication of behavioral finance for the financial services industry is the need to rethink financial advice. Traditional financial advice focused on objective analysis and rational decision-making. However, this approach does not always take into account the psychological biases and heuristics that affect investor decision-making.

Behavioral finance suggests that financial advisors should be trained to recognize and address these biases and heuristics. This includes helping investors to understand their own psychological tendencies and biases, and providing advice that is tailored to these tendencies.

The financial industry has also responded to these insights. For example, many financial advisors now use behavioral finance principles in their practice, helping clients to avoid common psychological traps and make better investment decisions.

Challenges and Limitations:

While the implications of behavioral finance for the financial services industry are significant, there are also challenges and limitations that must be considered. One of the most significant challenges is the need to train financial professionals in the principles of behavioral finance. This requires a significant investment in education and training, and may be difficult to implement on a large scale.

Another challenge is the need to integrate behavioral finance principles into existing financial products and services. Financial institutions may need to re-evaluate their product offerings and develop new strategies that take into account the behavioral biases and heuristics of their customers. This may require significant changes to the organizational structure and culture of financial institutions, which can be difficult to implement.

There is also the challenge of managing client expectations. Behavioral finance research has shown that individuals may have unrealistic expectations about their investment returns and may be overly optimistic about their ability to outperform the market. Financial professionals must be prepared to educate their clients about the realities of investing and to manage their expectations in a way that is both ethical and effective.

Another challenge is the potential for regulatory backlash. Some regulators may view the use of behavioral finance principles as a way to exploit or manipulate consumers. Financial institutions must be careful to use these principles in an ethical and transparent manner, and to communicate clearly with their customers about how they are being used.

Finally, there is the challenge of balancing the benefits of behavioral finance with the need to maintain efficient and effective markets. While behavioral finance research has shown that individuals may be prone to certain biases and heuristics, it is important to remember that these biases are not universal and may not apply to all individuals. Financial institutions must be careful not to make assumptions about their customers based on their behavior and to maintain a balance between using behavioral finance principles and maintaining efficient markets.

In conclusion, the implications of behavioral finance for the financial services industry are significant, but there are also challenges and limitations that must be considered. Financial professionals must be prepared to invest in education and training, to re-evaluate their product offerings, and to manage client expectations in an ethical and effective manner. They must also be careful to use behavioral finance principles in a transparent and ethical manner and to maintain a balance between using these principles and maintaining efficient markets. By doing so, they can help their clients achieve better financial outcomes and contribute to a more stable and sustainable financial system.

Changes in investment products and services

Behavioral finance has significant implications for the design and marketing of investment products and services. In this section, we will explore the various ways in which financial institutions can incorporate insights from behavioral finance to improve the effectiveness of their products and services. We will also discuss the challenges and limitations that must be considered when implementing these changes.

One of the primary ways in which financial institutions can use behavioral finance to their advantage is by designing products and services that align with the behavioral biases of investors. For example, research has shown that individuals are more likely to save when they are presented with a default option that automatically enrolls them in a savings plan. Financial institutions can leverage this insight by offering automatic enrollment in retirement savings plans, making it easier for individuals to save for retirement.

Similarly, research has shown that investors are more likely to stick to a long-term investment strategy when they are presented with a limited set of investment options. This suggests that financial institutions should simplify their investment product offerings, making it easier for investors to make informed decisions.

Another key insight from behavioral finance is the importance of framing. The way in which investment options are presented to investors can have a significant impact on their decision-making. For example, research has shown that individuals are more likely to choose a medical procedure when it is presented as having a high success rate rather than a low failure rate. Financial institutions can use this insight to frame their investment products and services in a way that appeals to the biases of investors.

For example, instead of presenting an investment product as having a low risk of loss, financial institutions can frame it as having a high potential for gain. This can make the investment more appealing to investors and increase their willingness to take on risk.

Another way in which financial institutions can leverage insights from behavioral finance is by incorporating social norms into their products and services. Research has shown that individuals are more likely to save when they are aware that their peers are also saving. Financial institutions can use this insight to promote a culture of savings by highlighting the savings behavior of their customers.

For example, financial institutions can send emails or notifications to their customers highlighting the savings behavior of other customers in their demographic group. This can encourage individuals to save more and help them feel more connected to their community.

While the potential benefits of incorporating insights from behavioral finance into investment products and services are significant, there are also several challenges and limitations that must be considered. One of the most significant challenges is the need for financial institutions to balance the interests of investors with their own financial interests.

Financial institutions have a responsibility to act in the best interests of their clients, but they also have a financial incentive to sell products and services that generate revenue. This can create a conflict of interest that may be difficult to resolve.

For example, financial institutions may be tempted to design investment products that are more complex than necessary in order to generate higher fees. This can make it more difficult for investors to make informed decisions and may result in suboptimal investment outcomes.

Another challenge is the need to ensure that investment products and services are appropriately tailored to the needs and preferences of individual investors. Behavioral biases are not universal and can vary across individuals and demographic groups. Financial institutions must therefore be careful to design products and services that are appropriate for the specific needs of their clients.

For example, a retirement savings plan that works well for a middle-aged investor may not be appropriate for a young investor who is just starting out in their career. Financial institutions must therefore be attentive to the needs of individual investors and tailor their products and services accordingly.

Finally, financial institutions must also be mindful of the ethical implications of incorporating insights from behavioral finance into their products and services. While these insights can help investors make better decisions, they can also be used to manipulate their behavior and exploit their biases.

For financial institutions, the ethical implications of incorporating insights from behavioral finance are significant. On the one hand, they have a responsibility to their clients to provide them with the best possible advice and investment products. On the other hand, they must also be aware of the potential for these insights to be used to manipulate clients and exploit their biases.

One of the key ethical issues that arises in the context of behavioral finance is the issue of informed consent. Clients must be fully informed about the risks and benefits of any investment product or service, including any insights from behavioral finance that may be used to influence their decision-making. Financial institutions have a responsibility to ensure that their clients understand the implications of these insights and the potential for their behavior to be manipulated.

Another ethical issue that arises in the context of behavioral finance is the issue of conflicts of interest. Financial institutions may have an incentive to use insights from behavioral finance to encourage clients to make certain investments or to purchase certain products. This can create a conflict of interest between the financial institution and the client, as the financial institution may prioritize its own financial interests over the interests of the client.

To address these ethical issues, financial institutions must establish clear guidelines and standards for the use of insights from behavioral finance in their products and services. They must also ensure that their advisors are properly trained in the principles of behavioral finance and that they are held to a high ethical standard. Additionally, financial institutions must be transparent about their use of insights from behavioral finance and must be willing to disclose any conflicts of interest that may arise.

Overall, the incorporation of insights from behavioral finance into investment products and services has the potential to greatly benefit investors. However, financial institutions must also be mindful of the potential ethical implications of these insights and must take steps to ensure that their use is guided by a commitment to the best interests of their clients.

Changes in financial advice and planning

As the field of behavioral finance continues to gain prominence in the financial industry, there have been notable changes in the way financial advice and planning are conducted. By incorporating insights from behavioral finance, financial advisors can help their clients make more informed and rational decisions about their finances.

One of the most significant changes in financial advice and planning is the increased emphasis on understanding a client's risk tolerance and financial goals. Rather than simply relying on standardized questionnaires to assess risk tolerance, advisors are now using more nuanced approaches to understand their clients' preferences and biases. This includes identifying biases such as loss aversion, which can cause investors to take on too little risk, or overconfidence, which can cause investors to take on too much risk.

To address these biases, financial advisors are incorporating a range of tools and techniques from behavioral finance. For example, they may use mental accounting to help clients break down their financial goals into more manageable pieces, or framing to help clients better understand the potential risks and rewards of different investment strategies.

Another important change in financial advice and planning is the increased use of technology to deliver personalized and data-driven advice. With the advent of robo-advisors and other digital tools, financial advisors can now provide more tailored advice to clients based on their individual financial circumstances and goals. This includes using machine learning algorithms to analyze large amounts of data and make more accurate predictions about future market trends and investment opportunities.

However, there are also challenges and limitations associated with these changes in financial advice and planning. For one, there is the risk that digital tools and algorithms may reinforce biases rather than mitigate them. This can occur if the algorithms are designed based on flawed assumptions or if they are trained on biased datasets.

Moreover, there is also the risk of over-reliance on technology at the expense of human judgment and intuition. While algorithms can be highly accurate and efficient, they may not always capture the full range of factors that go into financial decision-making, such as emotional considerations or changing market conditions.

To address these challenges, financial advisors must be mindful of the limitations of technology and the importance of maintaining a human touch in financial advice and planning. This may involve using technology to supplement rather than replace human advice, or incorporating human judgment and intuition into the design of digital tools and algorithms.

In addition, financial advisors must also be cognizant of the ethical implications of using behavioral finance insights in financial advice and planning. While these insights can help investors make more informed decisions, they can also be used to manipulate behavior and exploit biases for financial gain.

Therefore, it is essential that financial advisors approach their work with transparency, honesty, and a commitment to their clients' best interests. This may involve providing clear and accurate information about the risks and benefits of different investment strategies, or avoiding conflicts of interest that could compromise the integrity of their advice.

Overall, the changes in financial advice and planning driven by behavioral finance have the potential to revolutionize the financial industry by helping investors make more informed and rational decisions about their finances. However, to fully realize the benefits of these changes, financial advisors must navigate the challenges and limitations associated with them and approach their work with integrity and a commitment to their clients' well-being.

PART IX: REGULATORY AND COMPLIANCE ISSUES

The financial industry is subject to numerous regulations and compliance requirements, which are designed to protect investors and maintain the integrity of the financial system. These regulations have been put in place to prevent financial fraud, reduce systemic risk, and ensure that financial institutions operate in a safe and sound manner. However, the regulatory environment is constantly evolving, and financial firms must stay up-to-date with changes in regulations and compliance requirements to remain in compliance and avoid regulatory sanctions.

In this section, we will explore the importance of regulatory and compliance issues in finance, including the impact of regulations on the industry, compliance challenges and best practices, and the future of regulation in finance.

Chapter 32: The Importance of Regulatory and Compliance Issues in Finance

Regulatory and compliance issues are critical for the financial industry as they help to protect investors and maintain the stability of the financial system. The role of financial regulations is to ensure that financial institutions operate in a safe and sound manner, comply with ethical standards, and maintain appropriate levels of risk management. Compliance with regulations is critical to maintaining public trust in the financial system, and failure to comply with regulatory requirements can result in significant legal, financial, and reputational damage.

Regulations cover a wide range of issues, including market structure, capital requirements, conduct of business, reporting requirements, and consumer protection. These regulations are enforced by various regulatory bodies, including the Securities and Exchange Commission (SEC), the Financial Industry Regulatory Authority (FINRA), and the Commodity Futures Trading Commission (CFTC), among others.

Chapter 33: Financial Regulations and their Impact on the Industry

Financial regulations have a significant impact on the financial industry. They shape the competitive landscape, drive changes in business models, and impact the profitability of financial institutions. Regulations can increase the cost of doing business, limit the types of products and services that can be offered, and impact the ability of firms to take risks.

One of the key impacts of financial regulations is the increased focus on risk management. Financial institutions are now required to implement more robust risk management practices, including stress testing and scenario analysis. These practices help to ensure that financial institutions can withstand market shocks and other risks.

Regulations can also impact innovation in the financial industry. For example, regulations may make it more difficult for new entrants to enter the market, or limit the types of products that can be offered. This can have a negative impact on competition and innovation.

Chapter 34: Compliance Challenges and Best Practices

Compliance with financial regulations can be challenging, particularly for firms that operate across multiple jurisdictions. Different regulations may apply in different countries, and firms must ensure that they comply with all relevant regulations.

Compliance challenges can include the complexity of regulations, the cost of compliance, and the risk of non-compliance. Firms must ensure that they have adequate resources to comply with regulations, including staff with the necessary expertise and technology systems to support compliance.

Best practices for compliance include developing a compliance culture within the organization, ensuring that compliance is embedded in business processes, and conducting regular compliance training for staff. Firms must also ensure that they have appropriate systems and processes in place to monitor compliance and identify any potential issues.

Chapter 35: The Future of Regulation in Finance

The regulatory environment is constantly evolving, and financial firms must stay up-to-date with changes in regulations and compliance requirements. The future of regulation in finance is likely to be shaped by a number of factors, including changes in technology, globalization, and geopolitical developments.

Technology is likely to play a significant role in the future of regulation in finance. Regulators are increasingly using technology to monitor compliance, detect fraud, and reduce the risk of financial crimes. This is likely to result in increased use of artificial intelligence (AI) and machine learning (ML) in compliance processes.

Globalization is another factor that will shape the future of regulation in finance. As financial firms increasingly operate across national borders, regulators are likely to face new challenges in enforcing compliance and ensuring the stability of the financial system. This has led to the development of international regulatory bodies, such as the Financial Stability Board (FSB) and the Basel Committee on Banking Supervision, which aim to coordinate regulatory efforts across different countries and ensure a level playing field for financial institutions.

Geopolitical developments, such as trade tensions and political instability, may also have an impact on the future of regulation in finance. Changes in government policies and regulations can have significant effects on financial markets and institutions. For example, the recent trade tensions between the US and China have led to increased scrutiny of Chinese companies listed on US stock exchanges, with the US Securities and Exchange Commission (SEC) introducing new rules that could lead to delisting of certain Chinese firms.

Another trend that is likely to shape the future of regulation in finance is the increasing focus on sustainability and ESG (environmental, social, and governance) factors. Regulators are increasingly recognizing the importance of sustainable investing, and are introducing new regulations and guidelines to encourage financial institutions to take ESG factors into account in their investment decisions. For example, the EU's Sustainable Finance Disclosure Regulation (SFDR) requires financial institutions to disclose how they integrate ESG factors into their investment processes.

In addition to these external factors, the future of regulation in finance will also be shaped by internal factors, such as the culture and values of financial firms themselves. In recent years, there has been increasing focus on the role of culture in shaping the behavior of financial firms, and regulators are increasingly taking culture and conduct issues into account in their supervision and enforcement efforts. For example, the UK's Financial Conduct Authority (FCA) has introduced a new Senior Managers and Certification Regime, which requires senior managers at financial firms to take responsibility for ensuring good conduct and compliance within their organizations.

Overall, the future of regulation in finance is likely to be shaped by a complex mix of factors, both internal and external to financial firms. While there will undoubtedly be challenges and obstacles to be overcome, financial institutions that are able to stay ahead of regulatory and compliance requirements are likely to be better positioned to succeed in a rapidly evolving financial landscape.

CHAPTER 32: THE IMPORTANCE OF REGULATORY AND COMPLIANCE ISSUES IN FINANCE

Regulatory and compliance issues are of great importance in the field of finance. These issues refer to the rules and guidelines established by regulatory bodies and institutions to ensure that financial firms and individuals comply with legal and ethical standards. The importance of regulatory and compliance issues in finance cannot be overstated, as they are essential in maintaining the integrity and stability of financial markets.

Definition of regulatory and compliance issues:
Regulatory and compliance issues in finance refer to the various rules, regulations, and guidelines established by regulatory bodies and institutions to ensure that financial firms and individuals comply with legal and ethical standards. These standards can be related to various aspects of financial activities such as trading, lending, investing, and reporting. Regulatory and compliance issues are designed to protect investors and maintain the stability of financial markets.

Importance of regulatory and compliance issues in finance:
Regulatory and compliance issues play a critical role in ensuring the integrity and stability of financial markets. These issues are important for several reasons:

Protecting investors: Regulatory and compliance issues are designed to protect investors from fraudulent activities and unethical practices. By enforcing strict rules and guidelines, regulatory bodies help ensure that investors are not subject to unfair treatment or exploitation.

Maintaining market stability: Regulatory and compliance issues are important in maintaining market stability. By setting standards for financial activities, regulatory bodies help prevent fraud, misrepresentation, and other activities that could destabilize financial markets.

Ensuring fair competition: Regulatory and compliance issues are essential in ensuring fair competition among financial firms. By enforcing rules and guidelines, regulatory bodies help prevent unfair practices that could give some firms an advantage over others.

Promoting transparency: Regulatory and compliance issues promote transparency in financial activities. By requiring financial firms to report their activities and transactions, regulatory bodies help ensure that investors have access to accurate and timely information.

Protecting the public interest: Regulatory and compliance issues are designed to protect the public interest. By ensuring that financial firms and individuals comply with legal and ethical standards, regulatory bodies help prevent activities that could harm the public.

In conclusion, regulatory and compliance issues are of great importance in finance. They play a critical role in ensuring the integrity and stability of financial markets, protecting investors, promoting fair competition, and ensuring transparency in financial activities. It is important for financial firms and individuals to be aware of regulatory and compliance issues and to comply with established rules and guidelines to maintain the integrity of financial markets.

I. The Role of Regulatory and Compliance Bodies

In today's complex financial landscape, regulatory and compliance bodies play a crucial role in ensuring the integrity of the financial system. These organizations set standards for financial institutions and individuals in order to protect investors, promote stability, and prevent financial crimes. In this section, we will examine the role of regulatory and compliance bodies in the financial industry, including their functions, challenges, and impact.

Definition of Regulatory and Compliance Bodies:

Regulatory bodies are institutions that oversee and enforce rules and regulations in a specific industry. In the financial industry, regulatory bodies ensure that financial institutions and market participants comply with laws and regulations designed to prevent fraud, promote transparency, and protect investors. These bodies may be government agencies, such as the Securities and Exchange Commission (SEC) in the United States, or self-regulatory organizations, such as the Financial Industry Regulatory Authority (FINRA).

Compliance bodies, on the other hand, are internal or external entities responsible for ensuring that financial institutions adhere to the rules and regulations set by regulatory bodies. Compliance departments are responsible for monitoring and reporting on compliance issues, as well as for implementing policies and procedures that promote compliance. These bodies are essential to the financial industry because they help prevent fraud, protect investors, and promote transparency.

Importance of Regulatory and Compliance Bodies in the Financial Industry:

The financial industry is characterized by a high degree of complexity, with a wide range of financial products and services offered by various institutions. This complexity creates opportunities for fraud, insider trading, and other financial crimes. Regulatory and compliance bodies are critical in ensuring that the financial industry operates in a fair, transparent, and efficient manner.

One important function of regulatory and compliance bodies is to protect investors. By setting standards for financial institutions and individuals, regulatory bodies help ensure that investors are not defrauded, misled, or otherwise harmed by unscrupulous market participants. For example, the SEC in the United States requires companies to provide accurate and timely information to investors, and to disclose any material risks or uncertainties that could affect the value of their investments.

Another important function of regulatory and compliance bodies is to promote stability in the financial system. By regulating the activities of financial institutions and market participants, these bodies help prevent systemic risk and promote financial stability. For example, after the financial crisis of 2008, regulatory bodies in many countries implemented reforms to strengthen the financial system, including requirements for higher capital reserves and stricter oversight of financial institutions.

Finally, regulatory and compliance bodies help promote transparency in the financial industry. By requiring financial institutions to disclose information about their activities, regulatory bodies help investors make informed decisions about their investments. This transparency also helps prevent insider trading and other forms of financial crime.

Conclusion:

In conclusion, regulatory and compliance bodies play a critical role in the financial industry. By setting standards, enforcing regulations, and promoting transparency, these bodies help protect investors, promote stability, and prevent financial crimes. As the financial industry continues to evolve, the role of regulatory and compliance bodies will remain essential in ensuring that the financial system operates in a fair, transparent, and efficient manner.

Overview of regulatory bodies and their functions

Regulatory bodies play a critical role in ensuring the stability and efficiency of financial markets. These organizations are responsible for creating and enforcing rules and regulations that govern the behavior of financial institutions and their participants. Regulatory bodies are designed to protect consumers and investors, maintain fair and orderly markets, and promote the stability of the financial system as a whole.

In the United States, there are several regulatory bodies that oversee different aspects of the financial industry. These organizations include the Securities and Exchange Commission (SEC), the Commodity Futures Trading Commission (CFTC), the Federal Reserve System (the Fed), the Office of the Comptroller of the Currency (OCC), and the National Credit Union Administration (NCUA). Each of these bodies has specific responsibilities and functions that are critical to the overall health of the financial system.

The Securities and Exchange Commission (SEC) is one of the most well-known regulatory bodies in the United States. The SEC is responsible for enforcing federal securities laws and regulating the securities industry. The SEC has several functions, including registering securities, regulating the activities of brokers and dealers, overseeing investment companies and investment advisers, and enforcing laws against insider trading.

Another regulatory body in the United States is the Commodity Futures Trading Commission (CFTC). The CFTC regulates futures, options, and swaps markets. The CFTC's primary responsibility is to protect market participants from fraud and manipulation. The CFTC also works to promote the integrity of the market by ensuring that prices are transparent and that trading is conducted in a fair and orderly manner.

The Federal Reserve System, or "the Fed," is the central bank of the United States. The Fed has several important functions, including conducting monetary policy, regulating banks and other financial institutions, and maintaining the stability of the financial system. The Fed is also responsible for supervising and regulating the banking industry and promoting the safety and soundness of the banking system.

The Office of the Comptroller of the Currency (OCC) is a regulatory body that supervises and regulates national banks and federal savings associations. The OCC is responsible for ensuring that these institutions operate in a safe and sound manner and comply with applicable laws and regulations. The OCC also conducts periodic examinations of these institutions to ensure that they are operating in compliance with regulatory requirements.

The National Credit Union Administration (NCUA) is responsible for regulating and supervising federal credit unions. The NCUA works to ensure that credit unions operate in a safe and sound manner and that they are able to meet the financial needs of their members. The NCUA also provides insurance coverage for deposits at federal credit unions.

In addition to these regulatory bodies, there are also several self-regulatory organizations (SROs) in the United States that oversee specific industries or markets. These organizations are typically funded by the industry participants that they regulate and are responsible for enforcing industry-specific rules and regulations.

For example, the Financial Industry Regulatory Authority (FINRA) is an SRO that regulates the activities of brokers and dealers in the United States. FINRA is responsible for ensuring that brokers and dealers operate in compliance with federal securities laws and industry rules and regulations. FINRA also provides education and training to industry participants and conducts regulatory examinations and investigations.

Another example of an SRO is the National Futures Association (NFA), which regulates the activities of futures commission merchants, commodity trading advisors, commodity pool operators, and introducing brokers. The NFA works to ensure that these industry participants operate in compliance with applicable laws and regulations and promotes transparency and integrity in the futures markets.

In conclusion, regulatory bodies play a critical role in ensuring the stability and efficiency of financial markets. These organizations are responsible for creating and enforcing rules and regulations that govern the behavior of financial institutions and their participants. The regulatory bodies in the United States have specific responsibilities and functions that are critical to the overall health of the financial system.

While the role of regulatory bodies is crucial, there are also criticisms of their effectiveness. Some argue that regulatory bodies may not be able to keep pace with the rapidly changing financial markets and may not be able to prevent financial crises. Others argue that regulatory bodies may be captured by the industries they are meant to regulate, leading to lax enforcement and insufficient protection of consumers and investors.

Despite these criticisms, regulatory bodies continue to play a vital role in maintaining the stability and integrity of financial markets. As the financial industry continues to evolve and new risks emerge, regulatory bodies will need to adapt and adjust their approaches to remain effective.

One example of how regulatory bodies are evolving to meet new challenges is the increasing use of technology in financial markets. As technology becomes more pervasive in the financial industry, regulatory bodies are exploring new ways to monitor and regulate financial activities. For example, the SEC has established a new division focused on digital assets and initial coin offerings (ICOs), while the CFTC has approved new trading platforms for cryptocurrency derivatives.

Another example is the growing importance of international coordination among regulatory bodies. As financial markets become increasingly globalized, regulatory bodies must work together to ensure that regulations are consistent across different jurisdictions and that financial institutions are held accountable for their actions. The Financial Stability Board, an international organization that coordinates the work of national financial authorities, plays a critical role in this regard.

In conclusion, regulatory bodies are essential to the stability and integrity of financial markets. These organizations are responsible for creating and enforcing rules and regulations that govern the behavior of financial institutions and their participants. While there are criticisms of the effectiveness of regulatory bodies, they continue to evolve and adapt to meet new challenges in the financial industry. As technology and globalization continue to transform financial markets, regulatory bodies will need to remain vigilant and flexible to ensure that the financial system remains safe and stable for all participants.

Compliance bodies and their functions

Compliance bodies are responsible for ensuring that financial institutions operate in compliance with laws, regulations, and industry standards. These organizations play a critical role in maintaining the integrity and stability of financial markets by preventing fraudulent activity, protecting investors, and promoting transparency and accountability in the financial industry.

There are a number of different compliance bodies that operate within the financial industry, each with its own specific responsibilities and functions. In this section, we will examine some of the key compliance bodies and their functions.

Financial Industry Regulatory Authority (FINRA)

FINRA is the largest independent regulator for all securities firms doing business in the United States. The organization is responsible for regulating brokerage firms and ensuring that they operate in compliance with federal securities laws and FINRA rules. FINRA's functions include enforcing rules and regulations, registering securities professionals, and conducting market surveillance to identify potential violations of securities laws and regulations.

Securities and Exchange Commission (SEC)

The SEC is a federal agency that regulates the securities industry in the United States. The agency is responsible for enforcing federal securities laws, including the Securities Act of 1933 and the Securities Exchange Act of 1934. The SEC's functions include overseeing the operations of securities exchanges, enforcing disclosure requirements for publicly traded companies, and investigating and prosecuting securities fraud.

Commodity Futures Trading Commission (CFTC)

The CFTC is an independent agency that regulates the commodity futures and options markets in the United States. The agency is responsible for enforcing the Commodity Exchange Act, which regulates the trading of commodities and derivatives. The CFTC's functions include overseeing futures exchanges, registering commodity trading advisors and commodity pool operators, and investigating and prosecuting fraud in the commodity futures and options markets.

Office of the Comptroller of the Currency (OCC)

The OCC is a federal agency that charters, regulates, and supervises all national banks and federal savings associations in the United States. The agency's functions include ensuring that national banks operate in compliance with federal banking laws and regulations, conducting bank examinations, and enforcing banking laws and regulations.

Federal Reserve System (FRS)

The FRS is the central bank of the United States and is responsible for supervising and regulating the banking system in the country. The FRS's functions include conducting monetary policy, regulating and supervising banks and other financial institutions, and maintaining the stability of the financial system.

National Credit Union Administration (NCUA)

The NCUA is an independent federal agency that regulates and supervises federal credit unions in the United States. The agency's functions include ensuring that federal credit unions operate in compliance with federal credit union laws and regulations, conducting examinations of federal credit unions, and enforcing credit union laws and regulations.

State regulators

In addition to federal regulators, there are also state regulators that oversee financial institutions operating within their respective states. These regulators are responsible for ensuring that financial institutions comply with state laws and regulations and may have specific functions related to the industries within their states.

While the functions of each compliance body may vary, there are some common themes that run throughout their work. Compliance bodies are responsible for ensuring that financial institutions operate in compliance with laws and regulations, protecting consumers and investors, and promoting transparency and accountability in the financial industry.

Compliance bodies play an important role in preventing fraudulent activity and protecting investors. For example, the SEC's enforcement actions have resulted in billions of dollars in fines and penalties for securities fraud, insider trading, and other violations of federal securities laws. Similarly, FINRA's disciplinary actions have resulted in significant fines and sanctions for violations of FINRA rules and regulations.

However, there are also criticisms of the effectiveness of compliance bodies. Some argue that compliance bodies may be too focused on rules and regulations and not enough on the underlying behavior of financial institutions. Others argue that compliance bodies may be subject to regulatory capture, where the regulated entities exert undue influence over the regulatory agency. These criticisms are not unfounded and must be taken seriously in order to maintain the integrity of the financial system.

One solution to the issue of regulatory capture is to increase transparency and accountability in the regulatory process. For example, requiring regulatory bodies to disclose their funding sources and requiring regular independent audits of regulatory agencies can help ensure that they are not unduly influenced by the financial institutions they are supposed to regulate.

Another potential solution is to implement a system of rotating regulators, where regulatory personnel are rotated regularly between the regulatory body and the financial institutions they regulate. This can help prevent the development of close relationships between regulators and financial institutions, reducing the risk of regulatory capture.

Additionally, it is important to recognize that compliance bodies alone cannot solve all of the problems in the financial system. Ultimately, the behavior of financial institutions and their participants is driven by a complex set of incentives and motivations that cannot be completely controlled by regulatory bodies. As such, it is also important to consider broader reforms to the financial system, such as changes to compensation structures and incentives for financial institutions, in order to promote ethical behavior and reduce the risk of fraudulent activity.

In conclusion, compliance bodies play a critical role in preventing fraudulent activity and protecting investors in the financial system. However, there are also legitimate criticisms of the effectiveness of these bodies, particularly with respect to the risk of regulatory capture. In order to address these criticisms, it is important to increase transparency and accountability in the regulatory process and consider broader reforms to the financial system as a whole. By doing so, we can ensure that compliance bodies are able to fulfill their important mandate of promoting the stability and efficiency of financial markets.

Collaboration between regulatory and compliance bodies

Collaboration between regulatory and compliance bodies is essential for promoting the stability and efficiency of financial markets. While regulatory bodies are responsible for creating and enforcing rules and regulations that govern the behavior of financial institutions and their participants, compliance bodies are responsible for ensuring that these institutions are following these rules and regulations. By working together, these bodies can better identify and address potential issues and risks in the financial system.

One area where collaboration between regulatory and compliance bodies is particularly important is in the area of anti-money laundering (AML) and counter-terrorism financing (CTF). AML and CTF regulations are designed to prevent the use of the financial system for illegal activities, such as money laundering and terrorist financing. These regulations require financial institutions to implement policies and procedures to detect and prevent these activities, and compliance bodies are responsible for ensuring that these policies and procedures are being followed.

Regulatory bodies, such as the Financial Crimes Enforcement Network (FinCEN) and the Office of Foreign Assets Control (OFAC), are responsible for creating and enforcing AML and CTF regulations. Compliance bodies, such as the AML compliance departments of financial institutions, are responsible for implementing and enforcing these regulations at the institutional level. By working together, regulatory and compliance bodies can better identify and address potential AML and CTF risks, such as suspicious transactions or individuals on sanctions lists.

Another area where collaboration between regulatory and compliance bodies is important is in the area of cybersecurity. Cybersecurity threats are a growing concern in the financial industry, with cybercriminals increasingly targeting financial institutions and their customers. Regulatory bodies, such as the Securities and Exchange Commission (SEC) and the Commodity Futures Trading Commission (CFTC), have issued guidelines and regulations for cybersecurity risk management, while compliance bodies are responsible for implementing and enforcing these guidelines at the institutional level.

Collaboration between regulatory and compliance bodies can also help address broader issues in the financial system, such as systemic risk. Systemic risk refers to the risk that a disruption in one part of the financial system can spread and cause widespread harm to the entire system. Regulatory bodies are responsible for monitoring and addressing systemic risk, while compliance bodies can help identify potential sources of systemic risk at the institutional level.

For example, the 2008 financial crisis was caused in part by systemic risk arising from the securitization of subprime mortgages. While regulatory bodies such as the SEC and the Federal Reserve were responsible for monitoring systemic risk at the macro level, compliance bodies such as the risk management departments of financial institutions were responsible for identifying potential risks at the institutional level. By working together, these bodies could have better identified and addressed the potential risks associated with the securitization of subprime mortgages.

However, collaboration between regulatory and compliance bodies is not without its challenges. One of the main challenges is the potential for conflicting priorities and interests between these bodies. Regulatory bodies may prioritize the broader goals of promoting financial stability and protecting investors, while compliance bodies may prioritize the more immediate goal of meeting regulatory requirements. This can create tension between the two bodies, as compliance bodies may resist regulations that they perceive as overly burdensome or unnecessary.

Another challenge is the potential for communication and coordination issues between regulatory and compliance bodies. Regulatory bodies may issue guidelines and regulations that are not practical or feasible to implement at the institutional level, while compliance bodies may fail to effectively communicate potential risks and issues to regulatory bodies. This can create gaps in the regulatory framework and increase the risk of financial instability.

To address these challenges, it is important for regulatory and compliance bodies to maintain open lines of communication and to work collaboratively to identify and address potential risks and issues in the financial system. This may involve regular meetings and consultations between regulatory and compliance personnel, as well as the use of technology and data analytics to identify potential risks and issues.

In conclusion, collaboration between regulatory and compliance bodies is critical to ensuring the stability and efficiency of financial markets. These organizations play distinct but complementary roles in protecting investors, promoting transparency, and maintaining the integrity of the financial system. While regulatory bodies create and enforce rules and regulations, compliance bodies are responsible for ensuring that financial institutions and their participants adhere to these rules and regulations.

Collaboration between these bodies can help to address some of the challenges faced by each. For example, regulatory bodies can provide guidance and clarification on complex regulatory requirements to help compliance bodies understand their obligations. Compliance bodies can also provide feedback to regulatory bodies on the practical implications of new or proposed regulations.

Effective collaboration between regulatory and compliance bodies can also help to prevent financial crimes such as money laundering, terrorist financing, and fraud. By sharing information and collaborating on investigations, regulatory and compliance bodies can identify patterns and trends that may indicate criminal activity and take appropriate action to prevent or mitigate harm to investors and the financial system.

In addition to regular meetings and consultations, collaboration between regulatory and compliance bodies can also involve the use of technology and data analytics. For example, the use of artificial intelligence and machine learning algorithms can help to identify potential risks and issues more quickly and accurately than traditional methods. Compliance teams can also use data analytics to monitor financial transactions and identify patterns of suspicious behavior that may warrant further investigation.

Despite the benefits of collaboration between regulatory and compliance bodies, there are also potential challenges and barriers to effective collaboration. For example, regulatory bodies may be reluctant to share information with compliance bodies due to concerns about confidentiality or data privacy. Compliance bodies may also be hesitant to report potential violations or concerns to regulatory bodies due to concerns about reputational risk or legal liability.

To address these challenges, it is important for regulatory and compliance bodies to establish clear protocols and guidelines for information sharing and collaboration. This may involve developing standard procedures for reporting and investigating potential violations, as well as guidelines for protecting the confidentiality of sensitive information. It may also involve establishing clear channels of communication and regularly scheduled meetings and consultations.

In addition, collaboration between regulatory and compliance bodies can be strengthened through ongoing training and professional development. This may involve providing compliance personnel with training on regulatory requirements and best practices, as well as providing regulatory personnel with training on the practical implications of regulations and the challenges faced by compliance teams.

Overall, effective collaboration between regulatory and compliance bodies is essential to ensuring the stability and integrity of financial markets. By working together to identify and address potential risks and issues, regulatory and compliance bodies can help to protect investors, promote transparency, and maintain the public trust in the financial system. While challenges and barriers to collaboration may exist, these can be overcome through clear protocols and guidelines, ongoing training and professional development, and a shared commitment to the common goal of protecting the financial system and the investors it serves.

II. Regulatory and Compliance Issues in Different Areas of Finance

The financial industry is a complex ecosystem consisting of various participants such as banks, investment firms, hedge funds, insurance companies, and more. As the industry continues to evolve and become more sophisticated, regulatory and compliance issues have become increasingly important in ensuring the integrity and stability of the financial system.

In this section, we will explore the regulatory and compliance issues that exist in different areas of finance, including banking, investments, insurance, and more. We will examine the various regulatory bodies and their functions, as well as the challenges that they face in enforcing rules and regulations. Additionally, we will analyze the role of compliance bodies in preventing fraudulent activity and protecting investors.

Furthermore, we will examine the intersection between regulatory and compliance bodies and the potential benefits of collaboration between the two entities. By understanding these issues, we can gain a better understanding of the complexities of the financial industry and the challenges that exist in regulating and enforcing compliance within it.

Overall, this section aims to provide an in-depth analysis of regulatory and compliance issues in finance, and to highlight the importance of effective regulation and compliance in maintaining the stability and integrity of the financial system.

Banking

Banking is one of the most critical sectors of the financial industry, and it has undergone significant changes over the past few decades. With the increasing use of technology, banking has become more accessible, efficient, and convenient. However, these developments have also brought new challenges and risks that regulatory bodies and compliance officers must address to maintain the stability and integrity of the banking system.

This section will examine the regulatory and compliance issues in different areas of banking, including commercial banking, investment banking, and private banking. We will discuss the role of regulatory bodies in ensuring the safety and soundness of banks, as well as the importance of compliance officers in detecting and preventing financial crimes such as money laundering and fraud. We will also explore the challenges that banks face in complying with regulations and the measures they can take to mitigate these risks.

Regulatory Issues in Commercial Banking

Commercial banks are financial institutions that provide services to individuals, businesses, and governments. They accept deposits, make loans, and offer a range of financial products and services. The regulation of commercial banks is essential to protect depositors, ensure the safety and soundness of the banking system, and prevent financial crises.

One of the most significant regulatory issues in commercial banking is capital adequacy. Capital adequacy refers to the amount of capital that a bank holds to cover its potential losses. Regulatory bodies, such as the Federal Reserve in the United States, set minimum capital requirements that banks must meet to ensure their safety and soundness. Banks that fail to meet these requirements may be subject to regulatory action, including fines, restrictions on operations, and even closure.

Another critical regulatory issue in commercial banking is liquidity risk. Liquidity risk refers to the risk that a bank will not be able to meet its obligations as they come due, either because of a lack of funds or the inability to sell assets quickly. To address this risk, regulatory bodies require banks to maintain a minimum level of liquid assets, such as cash or government securities, that can be quickly converted into cash.

Compliance Issues in Commercial Banking

Compliance officers in commercial banks play a critical role in preventing financial crimes such as money laundering, fraud, and terrorist financing. Compliance officers are responsible for ensuring that banks comply with applicable laws and regulations, as well as internal policies and procedures.

One of the most significant compliance issues in commercial banking is anti-money laundering (AML) compliance. AML compliance refers to the measures that banks take to prevent their services from being used to launder money or finance terrorism. Banks must implement a robust AML program that includes customer due diligence, transaction monitoring, and reporting suspicious activities to regulatory bodies.

Another critical compliance issue in commercial banking is consumer protection. Banks must comply with a range of consumer protection laws and regulations, such as the Truth in Lending Act and the Fair Credit Reporting Act, to protect consumers from deceptive or unfair practices.

Regulatory Issues in Investment Banking

Investment banks are financial institutions that provide services to corporations, governments, and other institutions. They specialize in underwriting and issuing securities, advising clients on mergers and acquisitions, and trading securities. The regulation of investment banks is critical to protect investors and maintain the integrity of the financial markets.

One of the most significant regulatory issues in investment banking is insider trading. Insider trading refers to the practice of buying or selling securities based on non-public information. Regulatory bodies, such as the Securities and Exchange Commission (SEC) in the United States, have strict rules and regulations that prohibit insider trading and require investment banks to implement robust compliance programs to prevent it.

Another critical regulatory issue in investment banking is market manipulation. Market manipulation refers to the practice of artificially inflating or deflating the price of securities to benefit the manipulator. Regulatory bodies have strict rules and regulations that prohibit market manipulation and require investment banks to implement robust compliance programs to prevent and detect such activities. For example, the SEC has established a Market Abuse Unit to investigate and prosecute cases of market manipulation, insider trading, and other forms of securities fraud.

One common form of market manipulation is known as "pump and dump," where a manipulator artificially increases the price of a security by disseminating false or misleading information, then sells their holdings at the inflated price, leaving other investors with losses. Another form is "wash trading," where a trader simultaneously buys and sells the same security to create the illusion of activity and influence the market price.

Compliance personnel in investment banks must remain vigilant to prevent market manipulation by identifying potential red flags, such as unusual trading patterns, sudden spikes in trading volume, and coordinated trading by groups of investors. They must also implement effective surveillance systems and controls to detect and report any suspicious activity to regulatory authorities.

Furthermore, compliance personnel in investment banks must also ensure that their banks are in compliance with regulations related to anti-money laundering (AML) and know-your-customer (KYC) requirements. These regulations require investment banks to verify the identity of their clients and to monitor their transactions for suspicious activity, such as large cash deposits or transfers to high-risk countries.

Effective AML and KYC programs are essential for preventing money laundering, terrorist financing, and other illegal activities in the financial system. Failure to comply with these regulations can result in significant fines and reputational damage to investment banks.

In addition to regulatory compliance, investment banks also face ethical issues related to conflicts of interest. Investment banks often engage in multiple roles, such as underwriting securities offerings, providing financial advice to clients, and trading securities for their own account. These roles can create conflicts of interest, where the interests of the investment bank may not align with those of its clients or investors.

For example, an investment bank may provide favorable research reports on a company it is underwriting, even if the company's financial prospects are not strong. This can mislead investors and artificially inflate the price of the company's securities.

Compliance personnel in investment banks must ensure that their banks have effective policies and procedures in place to manage conflicts of interest and to disclose any potential conflicts to clients and investors. They must also ensure that their banks are in compliance with regulations such as the Volcker Rule, which prohibits banks from engaging in proprietary trading and limits their investments in hedge funds and private equity funds.

In conclusion, regulatory and compliance issues are critical considerations for investment banks in the banking industry. Investment banks must implement effective compliance programs to ensure they are in compliance with regulations related to market manipulation, AML, and conflicts of interest. Compliance personnel play a vital role in identifying potential risks and issues, implementing effective controls, and collaborating with regulatory bodies to maintain a healthy and transparent financial system.

Securities markets

Securities markets are critical to the global economy, providing investors with opportunities to buy and sell securities, including stocks, bonds, and derivatives. These markets are regulated by various bodies and subject to a range of compliance requirements to ensure their proper functioning and prevent fraudulent activity. In this section, we will examine some of the key regulatory and compliance issues facing securities markets today.

One critical issue facing securities markets is insider trading. Insider trading refers to the practice of buying or selling securities based on non-public information that gives the trader an unfair advantage over other investors. This practice is illegal and is strictly regulated by various bodies, including the Securities and Exchange Commission (SEC) in the United States.

Insider trading can take many forms, from outright illegal activity to more subtle forms of abuse. For example, a corporate insider may leak sensitive information to a friend or family member, who then uses that information to make trades. Alternatively, a hedge fund manager may engage in "expert network" activities, where they pay for access to industry experts who may provide them with non-public information that can be used to inform their trades.

To combat insider trading, regulatory bodies have implemented strict rules and regulations. In the United States, the SEC's Rule 10b-5 makes it illegal to trade securities based on material non-public information. Investment banks and other market participants are also required to maintain robust compliance programs that are designed to detect and prevent insider trading.

Another critical issue facing securities markets is fraud. Fraud can take many forms, from Ponzi schemes to pump-and-dump schemes, and can have serious consequences for investors. For example, in the Madoff scandal, investors lost billions of dollars due to a fraudulent investment scheme.

Regulatory bodies play an important role in preventing and detecting fraud in securities markets. For example, the SEC has the power to investigate potential cases of fraud and bring enforcement actions against individuals and firms that engage in fraudulent activity. In addition, investment banks and other market participants are required to maintain comprehensive compliance programs that are designed to prevent and detect fraud.

One key aspect of compliance programs in securities markets is the use of technology and data analytics. Investment banks and other market participants use a range of tools, including machine learning algorithms and natural language processing, to detect potential cases of fraud and other illicit activity. For example, these tools can analyze trading patterns to identify potential instances of insider trading or market manipulation.

Market manipulation is another critical regulatory issue in securities markets. Market manipulation refers to the practice of artificially inflating or deflating the price of securities to benefit the manipulator. This can take many forms, from spreading false rumors to engaging in coordinated trading activity.

To prevent market manipulation, regulatory bodies have strict rules and regulations that prohibit the practice. Investment banks and other market participants are required to maintain robust compliance programs that are designed to detect and prevent market manipulation.

Finally, another critical regulatory issue in securities markets is cybersecurity. As securities markets become increasingly digitized, the risk of cyber attacks and data breaches becomes more pronounced. Cyber attacks can take many forms, from hacking into a company's network to stealing sensitive information.

To prevent cyber attacks and data breaches, investment banks and other market participants are required to maintain robust cybersecurity programs. These programs may include a range of measures, such as firewalls, encryption, and intrusion detection systems. Investment banks and other market participants may also engage in regular penetration testing and vulnerability assessments to identify potential weaknesses in their systems.

In conclusion, securities markets are subject to a range of regulatory and compliance requirements to ensure their proper functioning and prevent fraudulent activity. Insider trading, fraud, market manipulation, and cybersecurity are among the critical issues facing securities markets today. Regulatory bodies play an important role in preventing and detecting these issues, while investment banks and other market participants are required to maintain robust compliance programs that are designed to detect and prevent fraudulent activity.

One of the most critical regulatory and compliance issues in securities markets is insider trading. Insider trading involves the use of non-public information to buy or sell securities, which can result in significant profits for those who engage in it. However, it is illegal and can lead to severe penalties for those who are caught.

Regulatory bodies such as the Securities and Exchange Commission (SEC) and the Financial Industry Regulatory Authority (FINRA) have strict rules and regulations in place to prevent insider trading. These rules require companies to implement compliance programs that are designed to detect and prevent insider trading, as well as to provide training to employees on the importance of following these regulations.

Investment banks and other market participants are also required to adhere to strict regulations related to fraud prevention in securities markets. Fraud can take many forms, including Ponzi schemes, pyramid schemes, and other fraudulent investment schemes. These types of fraud can cause significant harm to investors, and regulatory bodies work to detect and prevent them through ongoing monitoring and investigation.

Another critical issue facing securities markets is market manipulation. Market manipulation refers to the practice of artificially inflating or deflating the price of securities to benefit the manipulator. Regulatory bodies have strict rules and regulations that prohibit market manipulation and require investment banks and other market participants to implement robust compliance programs to prevent it.

Cybersecurity is also a growing concern in securities markets, as many transactions are now conducted online. Regulatory bodies require investment banks and other market participants to implement robust cybersecurity programs to prevent hacking and other cybersecurity threats.

In conclusion, regulatory and compliance issues play a crucial role in ensuring the proper functioning of securities markets. Insider trading, fraud, market manipulation, and cybersecurity are among the critical issues facing securities markets today, and regulatory bodies work to prevent and detect these issues through strict rules and regulations. Investment banks and other market participants are required to maintain robust compliance programs that are designed to detect and prevent fraudulent activity and to ensure the integrity of securities markets.

Insurance

The insurance industry is an integral part of the financial services sector, providing protection against various risks that individuals and businesses face. Insurance companies play a crucial role in managing and transferring risk, which in turn promotes economic stability and growth. However, insurance companies face a range of regulatory and compliance challenges that require careful attention and management. In this section, we will examine some of the key regulatory and compliance issues facing the insurance industry.

Regulatory and Compliance Challenges in the Insurance Industry:

Solvency and Capital Adequacy:
One of the primary regulatory challenges facing insurance companies is maintaining solvency and capital adequacy. Insurance companies are required to maintain a certain level of capital to ensure that they

are financially sound and able to pay claims. Solvency requirements vary by jurisdiction, but they typically involve a combination of minimum capital requirements, asset valuation rules, and risk-based capital ratios.

In the United States, for example, insurance companies are regulated by state insurance commissioners, who oversee solvency and capital adequacy requirements. Insurance companies are required to file annual financial reports, which include information on their assets, liabilities, and capital adequacy. Insurers that do not meet solvency requirements may be subject to regulatory action, including fines, sanctions, and even liquidation.

Consumer Protection:
Consumer protection is another critical issue facing the insurance industry. Insurance policies are complex financial instruments that require careful consideration and understanding. Consumers may not fully understand the terms and conditions of their policies, which can lead to disputes and claims denials.

Regulators play an important role in protecting consumers by ensuring that insurers are transparent and fair in their practices. Insurance companies are required to provide clear and concise information about their policies, including coverage, limitations, exclusions, and premiums. Regulators also oversee claims handling and settlement practices, ensuring that consumers are treated fairly and promptly.

Anti-Money Laundering and Know-Your-Customer:
Insurance companies are also subject to anti-money laundering (AML) and know-your-customer (KYC) regulations, which are designed to prevent the use of insurance products for illicit purposes. AML regulations require insurance companies to implement robust compliance programs to detect and prevent money laundering and terrorist financing.

KYC regulations require insurance companies to collect and verify the identity of their customers, as well as assess the risk of money laundering and terrorism financing associated with each customer. Insurance companies must also monitor customer transactions and report suspicious activity to regulatory authorities.

Cybersecurity:
Cybersecurity is a growing concern for insurance companies, which store large amounts of sensitive customer information. Cyber attacks can compromise the confidentiality, integrity, and availability of this information, leading to reputational damage, financial loss, and legal liability.

Regulators are increasingly focused on cybersecurity, and insurance companies are required to implement robust cybersecurity programs to protect against cyber threats. This may involve implementing technical controls, such as firewalls and encryption, as well as developing policies and procedures to manage cyber risk.

Fraud Detection and Prevention:
Insurance fraud is a significant problem that can result in financial losses for insurers and higher premiums for consumers. Fraud can take many forms, including misrepresentation, concealment, and false claims. Insurance companies are required to implement robust fraud detection and prevention programs to identify and deter fraudulent activity.

Fraud prevention may involve a combination of technical controls, such as data analytics and predictive modeling, as well as human intervention, such as investigative and legal action. Insurance companies may also work with law enforcement agencies and other regulatory bodies to detect and prosecute fraudsters.

Conclusion:

In conclusion, the insurance industry faces a range of regulatory and compliance challenges, including solvency and capital adequacy, consumer protection, anti-money laundering and know-your-customer, cybersecurity, and fraud detection and prevention. Regulatory bodies play an important role in ensuring that insurers are able to meet their obligations to policyholders, while also protecting consumers and promoting market stability. At the same time, insurers must maintain robust compliance programs that are designed to identify and mitigate risks in a timely and effective manner.

To address these challenges, insurance companies can leverage technology and data analytics to improve risk management and compliance monitoring. For example, insurers can use machine learning algorithms to identify potentially fraudulent claims, or to detect patterns of suspicious activity that may indicate money laundering. Insurers can also use data analytics to identify areas where customer service can be improved, or to identify areas where operational efficiency can be enhanced.

In addition, insurance companies can work collaboratively with regulatory bodies to address emerging risks and issues. This may involve regular consultations and meetings with regulatory and compliance personnel, or participation in industry working groups and committees. By working together, insurers and regulators can identify and address potential risks before they become significant problems.

Overall, the insurance industry faces a range of complex regulatory and compliance challenges, but with the right tools and strategies, insurers can effectively manage these risks and maintain a strong, stable market that benefits both consumers and industry participants alike.

Asset management

Asset management refers to the management of investments on behalf of individuals, corporations, or institutions. The asset management industry has grown significantly over the past few decades, as more investors seek professional management of their investments. However, the asset management industry faces a range of regulatory and compliance challenges, including fiduciary duty, conflicts of interest, transparency, and operational risk.

Fiduciary Duty:

One of the fundamental principles of asset management is fiduciary duty. Fiduciary duty refers to the legal and ethical obligation of asset managers to act in the best interests of their clients. This duty requires asset managers to put their clients' interests ahead of their own, to exercise due diligence in making investment decisions, and to disclose any conflicts of interest that may arise.

The concept of fiduciary duty is critical in the asset management industry because it ensures that asset managers are held to high standards of professionalism and accountability. Clients trust asset managers to manage their investments in a prudent and responsible manner, and fiduciary duty ensures that asset managers are held accountable for their actions.

Conflicts of Interest:

Conflicts of interest are a significant concern in the asset management industry. Asset managers may have a conflict of interest if their financial interests are not aligned with those of their clients. For example, an asset manager may receive commissions or other incentives for recommending certain investments to clients, which may not necessarily be in the clients' best interests.

To address conflicts of interest, regulatory bodies have implemented a range of rules and regulations that require asset managers to disclose any conflicts of interest that may arise and to put their clients' interests ahead of their own. Asset managers are also required to implement robust compliance programs that are designed to prevent conflicts of interest and to ensure that clients are treated fairly.

Transparency:

Transparency is another critical issue in the asset management industry. Clients rely on asset managers to provide them with accurate and timely information about their investments, including performance data, fees, and expenses. However, asset managers may not always provide this information in a transparent manner, which can make it difficult for clients to make informed investment decisions.

To address this issue, regulatory bodies have implemented rules and regulations that require asset managers to provide clients with clear and concise information about their investments. Asset managers are required to provide clients with regular reports that include performance data, fees, and expenses, and to disclose any other material information that may be relevant to the clients' investments.

Operational Risk:

Operational risk refers to the risk of loss resulting from inadequate or failed internal processes, people, and systems, or from external events. Operational risk is a significant concern in the asset management industry because a failure in operational processes or systems can result in significant losses for clients.

To address operational risk, asset managers are required to implement robust operational risk management frameworks that are designed to identify, assess, and mitigate operational risks. Asset managers are also required to implement effective internal controls and to maintain adequate systems and processes to ensure the integrity of their operations.

Counter-arguments:

Some critics argue that the regulatory requirements placed on the asset management industry are excessive and can impede the ability of asset managers to generate strong investment returns for their clients. Critics argue that the compliance costs associated with regulatory requirements can be significant, which can reduce the amount of money that asset managers have available to invest.

However, proponents of regulatory requirements argue that they are necessary to ensure that asset managers act in the best interests of their clients and to prevent fraud and other abuses. They also argue that the costs of compliance are a small price to pay for the benefits of professional management and the protection of clients' investments.

Conclusion:

In conclusion, the asset management industry faces a range of regulatory and compliance challenges, including fiduciary duty, conflicts of interest, transparency, and operational risk. Regulatory bodies play an important role in monitoring and enforcing compliance with these requirements, while asset management firms must develop robust compliance programs that are designed to mitigate these risks and protect the interests of their clients.

The increasing popularity of passive investing and the rise of digital investment platforms have also had a significant impact on the asset management industry. Passive investing has grown rapidly in recent years, fueled by the success of index funds and exchange-traded funds (ETFs). These products offer investors exposure to a diversified portfolio of securities at a low cost, making them an attractive alternative to actively managed mutual funds. However, the growth of passive investing has also raised concerns about market efficiency and the impact on active fund managers who may find it increasingly difficult to outperform the market.

Digital investment platforms, also known as robo-advisors, have also emerged as a significant disruptor in the asset management industry. Robo-advisors offer investors a low-cost, automated investment service that uses algorithms to construct and manage portfolios. These platforms have gained popularity among younger, tech-savvy investors who are looking for a low-cost, easy-to-use investment solution. However, the growth of robo-advisors has also raised concerns about the potential for algorithmic bias and the lack of human oversight in investment decision-making.

Despite these challenges, the asset management industry continues to play a critical role in the global financial system, helping investors to build and manage their wealth and providing capital to support economic growth. As the industry evolves, it will be important for regulatory bodies and asset management firms to work together to ensure that the industry remains transparent, efficient, and trustworthy, and that the interests of investors are protected.

Payment systems

The payment systems industry is a critical part of the global financial system, facilitating the movement of funds between individuals and institutions. With the rise of digital payments and the increasing use of mobile devices for financial transactions, payment systems have become more complex and interconnected, creating new challenges for regulators and market participants. In this section, we will explore the various types of payment systems, their functions and characteristics, the regulatory and compliance issues they face, and the role of technology in shaping the future of payment systems.

Types of Payment Systems:

Payment systems can be categorized based on several criteria, including the types of transactions they facilitate, the participants involved, and the settlement methods used. Some of the most common types of payment systems include:

Cash and Check-based payment systems: These payment systems involve the physical exchange of currency or checks between the payer and the payee. While these payment systems have been in use for centuries, they are becoming less popular due to the increasing popularity of digital payment methods.

Card-based payment systems: Card-based payment systems, such as credit and debit cards, are widely used for both online and offline transactions. These payment systems rely on electronic authorization and processing, with the payment being settled through the card issuer and the acquiring bank.

Automated Clearing House (ACH) payment systems: ACH payment systems facilitate the transfer of funds between bank accounts, typically for recurring payments such as payroll, bills, and subscriptions. These payment systems operate on a batch-processing basis, with transactions being settled at specific intervals throughout the day.

Wire transfer payment systems: Wire transfer payment systems allow for the near-instantaneous transfer of funds between bank accounts, typically for high-value transactions such as real estate purchases or international trade.

Digital payment systems: Digital payment systems, such as mobile wallets and peer-to-peer payment platforms, have seen explosive growth in recent years. These payment systems rely on electronic authorization and processing, with the payment being settled through the payment platform or the user's linked bank account.

Functions and Characteristics of Payment Systems:

Payment systems serve several key functions in the financial system, including:

Facilitating the movement of funds between parties: Payment systems enable the transfer of funds from one account to another, allowing individuals and businesses to conduct transactions with each other.

Providing a secure and efficient means of payment: Payment systems ensure that transactions are processed securely and efficiently, minimizing the risk of fraud and error.

Enabling the processing of large volumes of transactions: Payment systems are designed to handle large volumes of transactions, allowing for the efficient processing of payments on a global scale.

Facilitating the settlement of transactions: Payment systems enable the settlement of transactions, ensuring that funds are transferred between parties in a timely manner.

Payment systems also have several key characteristics, including:

Interconnectivity: Payment systems are often interconnected with other systems and networks, creating a complex web of relationships and dependencies.

Complexity: Payment systems are often complex, with multiple layers of intermediaries and processing steps involved in the movement of funds.

Speed: Payment systems vary in terms of their speed, with some systems enabling near-instantaneous payments while others require several days for settlement.

Security: Payment systems must be secure to prevent fraud and unauthorized access.

Regulatory and Compliance Issues in Payment Systems:

The payment systems industry is subject to a range of regulatory and compliance requirements, including:

Anti-Money Laundering (AML) and Know-Your-Customer (KYC) requirements: Payment systems are often used for illicit purposes, making it critical for regulators to require payment system providers to implement AML and KYC measures to prevent money laundering and terrorist financing.

Consumer Protection: Payment systems must be designed with the protection of consumers in mind, including providing clear and transparent information on fees, transaction limits, and dispute resolution processes.

Operational Risk: Payment systems must have robust operational risk management systems in place to ensure smooth and secure operations. This includes measures to prevent system failures, cybersecurity breaches, and fraudulent activities.

Interoperability: As the number of payment systems and providers continues to grow, interoperability between systems is becoming increasingly important. Regulatory bodies may require payment system providers to ensure that their systems can interoperate with other systems to promote competition and ensure that users have a range of options to choose from.

In addition to these requirements, payment systems may also be subject to regulatory scrutiny for their handling of data privacy and cybersecurity concerns. The recent data breaches at major retailers and financial institutions have highlighted the importance of ensuring that payment systems are secure and that customer data is protected.

Payment systems providers also face challenges in balancing innovation and compliance. New technologies, such as blockchain and cryptocurrency, have the potential to revolutionize the payment systems industry, but they also present new compliance challenges. Regulators must strike a balance between encouraging innovation and ensuring that payment systems remain safe and compliant.

One potential solution to this challenge is for regulators to work closely with payment systems providers to develop compliance frameworks that are tailored to the unique features of new technologies. This approach can help to ensure that innovation is not stifled while also ensuring that payment systems remain secure and compliant.

In conclusion, the payment systems industry faces a range of regulatory and compliance challenges, including AML and KYC requirements, consumer protection, operational risk, and interoperability. As new technologies continue to emerge, payment systems providers and regulators must work together to ensure that innovation is balanced with compliance to maintain the integrity of the payment systems ecosystem.

III. Benefits and Costs of Regulatory and Compliance Issues

Regulatory and compliance issues play a crucial role in the financial industry, and their importance cannot be overstated. On the one hand, regulations and compliance requirements are designed to protect consumers, promote transparency, and maintain stability in financial markets. On the other hand, they can also impose significant costs on financial institutions, including increased operational expenses, decreased profitability, and reduced innovation.

In this section, we will explore the benefits and costs of regulatory and compliance issues in the financial industry, with a focus on key sectors such as banking, insurance, asset management, and payment systems. We will analyze how regulations and compliance requirements affect different stakeholders, including financial institutions, consumers, and regulators. We will also examine the potential unintended consequences of regulations and compliance requirements, such as increased concentration and reduced competition.

To begin, let us first define what we mean by regulatory and compliance issues in the financial industry. Regulations refer to the rules and standards set by government agencies, such as the Federal Reserve, the Securities and Exchange Commission, and the Consumer Financial Protection Bureau, to oversee financial markets and protect consumers. Compliance refers to the process of adhering to these regulations and standards. Financial institutions must comply with these regulations and standards to ensure they are operating in a safe and sound manner and to avoid penalties and legal action.

The benefits of regulatory and compliance issues in the financial industry are numerous. First, regulations and compliance requirements promote transparency and disclosure, enabling consumers to make informed decisions about financial products and services. For example, regulations require banks to disclose the fees and interest rates associated with their accounts, enabling consumers to compare different options and choose the one that best meets their needs.

Second, regulations and compliance requirements can enhance financial stability by preventing systemic risks and reducing the likelihood of financial crises. For instance, the Basel Accords require banks to maintain minimum levels of capital to absorb losses and protect against insolvency. This helps ensure that banks can withstand financial shocks and continue to lend to consumers and businesses even during economic downturns.

Third, regulations and compliance requirements can protect consumers from fraud and abuse. For example, the Dodd-Frank Wall Street Reform and Consumer Protection Act requires banks and other financial institutions to establish anti-fraud and anti-abuse programs to prevent deceptive practices and protect consumers from financial harm.

However, there are also costs associated with regulatory and compliance issues in the financial industry. One of the primary costs is increased operational expenses for financial institutions. Compliance can be a complex and time-consuming process, requiring significant resources and personnel. This can lead to increased costs for financial institutions, which can be passed on to consumers in the form of higher fees and interest rates.

Another cost is reduced profitability for financial institutions. Regulations and compliance requirements can limit the types of products and services that financial institutions can offer, reducing their revenue streams and profitability. This can also reduce innovation and competition in the industry, as smaller institutions may struggle to comply with regulatory requirements and compete with larger, more established institutions.

In conclusion, regulatory and compliance issues play a critical role in the financial industry, providing benefits such as transparency, stability, and consumer protection. However, these benefits must be weighed against the costs of increased operational expenses and reduced profitability. In the following sections, we will explore the benefits and costs of regulatory and compliance issues in more detail, with a focus on key sectors in the financial industry.

Benefits of regulatory and compliance issues

Regulatory and compliance issues play a critical role in various industries, including finance, healthcare, and technology. They are designed to promote fairness, protect consumers, prevent fraudulent activities, and maintain the stability of the market. However, some argue that regulatory and compliance requirements increase costs, decrease innovation, and create barriers to entry for new firms.

In this section, we will explore the benefits of regulatory and compliance issues. We will examine how they help to ensure market stability, promote ethical practices, and protect consumers. We will also look at the role of regulatory bodies in enforcing these requirements and discuss the potential costs associated with non-compliance.

Benefits of Regulatory and Compliance Issues:

Promoting Market Stability:
One of the primary benefits of regulatory and compliance issues is the promotion of market stability. Regulations help to prevent market failures, such as the financial crisis of 2008, which was caused by the lack of oversight and regulation in the banking industry. Regulations ensure that companies follow ethical and responsible practices, reducing the likelihood of systemic risks.

For example, investment banks are required to follow strict guidelines for risk management, capital requirements, and liquidity. These regulations help to prevent a repeat of the financial crisis and ensure that the market remains stable.

Protecting Consumers:
Regulatory and compliance requirements help to protect consumers from fraudulent activities, unfair practices, and unsafe products. For instance, the Consumer Financial Protection Bureau (CFPB) was established in the wake of the financial crisis to protect consumers from abusive practices by banks and other financial institutions. The CFPB has the authority to regulate financial products and services, investigate consumer complaints, and enforce consumer protection laws.

Similarly, the Food and Drug Administration (FDA) regulates the safety and efficacy of drugs and medical devices, ensuring that consumers are not exposed to harmful products.

Encouraging Ethical Practices:
Regulatory and compliance requirements promote ethical practices by encouraging companies to act in the best interest of their customers and shareholders. For example, the Sarbanes-Oxley Act of 2002 was enacted to improve the accuracy and reliability of corporate disclosures. The act requires companies to implement internal controls and financial reporting procedures to ensure accurate financial reporting.

Similarly, the Securities and Exchange Commission (SEC) enforces regulations that require companies to disclose accurate and transparent information to their shareholders. These regulations promote ethical practices by ensuring that companies act in the best interest of their shareholders.

Fostering Innovation:
Contrary to popular belief, regulatory and compliance requirements can foster innovation by promoting the development of new technologies and products. Regulations ensure that companies develop safe and effective products, which can lead to new discoveries and advancements in technology.

For example, the FDA regulates medical devices to ensure their safety and efficacy. This regulation encourages companies to develop innovative medical devices that can improve patient outcomes.

Enforcing Accountability:
Regulatory and compliance requirements enforce accountability by holding companies responsible for their actions. Companies that violate regulations face penalties, fines, and legal action. This accountability helps to deter companies from engaging in fraudulent activities and encourages them to act ethically.

For example, in 2018, Wells Fargo was fined $1 billion by the CFPB for deceptive practices, including opening unauthorized accounts and charging unnecessary fees to its customers. This fine serves as a reminder that companies must comply with regulatory and compliance requirements, and face consequences for non-compliance.

Costs of Non-Compliance:

While regulatory and compliance requirements have many benefits, there are also costs associated with non-compliance. Companies that fail to comply with regulations face fines, legal action, and reputational damage. Non-compliance can also lead to increased costs as companies are forced to implement new procedures and systems to ensure compliance.

For example, in 2014, JP Morgan was fined $2.6 billion for failing to report suspicious activity related to Bernard Madoff's Ponzi scheme. This non-compliance resulted in significant financial costs for the company and also damaged its reputation in the eyes of investors and customers.

Non-compliance can also have broader economic impacts. For instance, failures in compliance with environmental regulations can lead to pollution and health risks for communities, as seen in the case of the Flint water crisis. In addition to the human costs of such failures, they can also have significant economic costs, such as lost productivity and decreased property values.

Furthermore, non-compliance can create unfair advantages for companies that do not comply with regulations, as they can potentially lower their costs and gain a competitive advantage over compliant companies. This can create an uneven playing field in the market and lead to decreased trust in the system.

Overall, the costs of non-compliance can be significant, both for individual companies and for society as a whole. Therefore, it is important for companies to prioritize compliance and invest in systems and procedures to ensure that they are meeting regulatory requirements. While there are costs associated with compliance, the benefits of compliance, including improved reputation, decreased risk, and increased trust in the market, often outweigh these costs in the long run.

Costs of regulatory and compliance issues

Costs of regulatory and compliance issues can be significant for businesses, particularly for those in heavily regulated industries such as finance, healthcare, and energy. The costs of compliance can be broken down into direct costs, such as fines and legal fees, and indirect costs, such as the cost of implementing and maintaining compliance programs.

Direct costs of non-compliance can be severe. Companies may be subject to fines, penalties, and legal action if they fail to comply with regulatory requirements. For example, in 2016, Wells Fargo was fined $185 million for creating over 2 million fake customer accounts in an attempt to meet sales targets. In 2017, Barclays was fined $2 billion for misrepresenting the quality of mortgage-backed securities it sold in the lead up to the 2008 financial crisis. These fines can be substantial and can impact a company's financial stability.

In addition to direct costs, non-compliance can also result in indirect costs, such as the cost of implementing and maintaining compliance programs. Companies may need to hire additional staff, invest in new technology, and establish new procedures to ensure compliance. For example, banks and financial institutions are required to comply with a wide range of regulatory requirements related to anti-money laundering, know-your-customer, and other consumer protection regulations. Compliance with these requirements can be complex and costly, requiring significant investments in technology and personnel.

There are also opportunity costs associated with compliance. Companies may forego opportunities to pursue certain business activities or markets due to compliance concerns. For example, a company may choose not to enter a new market due to concerns about compliance with local laws and regulations.

Similarly, companies may avoid pursuing certain business activities that carry higher compliance risk, such as engaging in high-risk financial transactions or offering certain types of investment products.

However, while compliance can be costly, it is important to consider the potential costs of non-compliance. As discussed earlier, non-compliance can result in significant financial and reputational damage, legal action, and fines. Furthermore, non-compliance can harm a company's relationship with its customers, employees, and other stakeholders, resulting in long-term damage to the company's reputation and brand.

Ultimately, the costs of regulatory and compliance issues must be weighed against the benefits of compliance. While compliance can be expensive, it can also provide significant benefits to businesses, such as increased customer trust, improved brand reputation, and reduced legal and financial risks. By investing in compliance programs and working to stay ahead of regulatory requirements, companies can mitigate the risks of non-compliance and position themselves for long-term success.

In the field of finance, compliance with regulations is especially important due to the potential risks involved. Investment banks, for example, must comply with a wide range of regulations, including those related to capital adequacy, liquidity, and risk management. Failure to comply with these regulations can result in significant financial losses, legal action, and reputational damage.

Portfolio managers must also comply with a range of regulatory requirements related to disclosure, risk management, and fiduciary duty. Compliance with these requirements is critical to maintaining the trust of investors and ensuring the long-term success of the portfolio.

Quantitative analysts must comply with a range of regulations related to the use of data, including privacy and security regulations. Failure to comply with these regulations can result in significant legal and financial risks for the company.

In the field of healthcare, compliance is critical to protecting patient safety and ensuring that medical professionals adhere to ethical standards. Hospitals and healthcare providers must comply with a wide range of regulations related to patient privacy, medical ethics, and safety standards.

Actuaries must comply with regulations related to the pricing and reserving of insurance policies. Failure to comply with these regulations can result in significant financial losses for the insurance company and its customers.

In the field of energy, compliance is critical in ensuring the safety and reliability of energy sources. The energy industry is heavily regulated, with laws and regulations that govern everything from the exploration and production of energy resources to the distribution and sale of energy products.

For example, the Nuclear Regulatory Commission (NRC) regulates the safety and security of nuclear power plants in the United States. The NRC requires that nuclear power plants comply with strict safety and security protocols to prevent accidents and minimize the risk of radiation exposure to workers and the public. Failure to comply with these regulations can result in severe consequences, including fines, legal action, and reputational damage.

In the field of healthcare, compliance with regulations is critical to ensuring the safety and well-being of patients. Healthcare providers must comply with a range of regulations related to patient care, including those related to the storage and handling of patient records, the dispensing of medications, and the performance of medical procedures.

Failure to comply with these regulations can result in significant financial losses for healthcare providers and harm to patients. For example, in 2016, the Department of Health and Human Services fined the University of Massachusetts Amherst $650,000 for a series of data breaches that exposed the personal information of over 1,500 individuals.

In the field of technology, compliance is essential in ensuring the protection of sensitive data and the privacy of individuals. Companies that handle sensitive information must comply with regulations related to data privacy and security, including the General Data Protection Regulation (GDPR) in the European Union and the Health Insurance Portability and Accountability Act (HIPAA) in the United States.

Failure to comply with these regulations can result in significant financial losses for companies and harm to individuals whose data has been compromised. For example, in 2017, Equifax suffered a data breach that exposed the personal information of over 143 million individuals. The breach resulted in significant financial losses for Equifax and harm to the affected individuals, including identity theft and financial fraud.

In conclusion, while regulatory and compliance requirements are essential in ensuring the safety, reliability, and protection of individuals and organizations, they can also be costly. Companies and individuals who fail to comply with regulations face fines, legal action, and reputational damage. Compliance can also require significant investments in resources and infrastructure, such as personnel, technology, and training. However, the benefits of compliance, including increased safety, security, and protection for individuals and organizations, far outweigh the costs.

CHAPTER 33: FINANCIAL REGULATIONS AND THEIR IMPACT ON THE INDUSTRY

The financial industry is one of the most regulated industries in the world, with a complex network of regulations and compliance requirements that govern its operation. Financial regulations are the rules and guidelines that financial institutions and organizations must follow to ensure that they operate fairly, ethically, and transparently. These regulations are put in place by government agencies and other regulatory bodies to protect consumers, maintain financial stability, and prevent fraud and misconduct.

In this chapter, we will provide an overview of financial regulations and their impact on the financial industry. We will discuss the importance of financial regulations, the different types of financial regulations, and how they are enforced. We will also examine the impact of financial regulations on various sectors of the financial industry, including banking, insurance, investment, and securities.

Overview of Financial Regulations:

Financial regulations are a set of rules and guidelines that govern the operation of financial institutions and organizations. These regulations are put in place to promote transparency, protect consumers, and ensure the stability of the financial system. Financial regulations cover a wide range of activities, including banking, insurance, securities, and investment.

Financial regulations are put in place by various regulatory bodies, including government agencies, central banks, and self-regulatory organizations. The regulations are enforced through a range of mechanisms, including fines, sanctions, and legal action.

Importance of Financial Regulations in the Financial Industry:

Financial regulations play a critical role in the financial industry. They are designed to ensure that financial institutions operate in a fair, ethical, and transparent manner, and that they do not engage in fraudulent or illegal activities. Financial regulations are also put in place to protect consumers from financial fraud and abuse, and to promote financial stability.

One of the primary benefits of financial regulations is that they help to maintain financial stability. Financial institutions are required to maintain certain levels of capital and liquidity, which helps to ensure that they are able to withstand market shocks and financial crises. In addition, financial regulations help to prevent systemic risk by ensuring that financial institutions are not too big to fail.

Financial regulations also promote transparency in the financial industry. Financial institutions are required to disclose certain information, such as their financial statements and risk exposure, which helps to promote transparency and accountability. This information is used by investors, regulators, and other stakeholders to assess the financial health and stability of financial institutions.

Another important benefit of financial regulations is that they help to protect consumers from financial fraud and abuse. Financial institutions are required to comply with a range of consumer protection regulations, such as the Truth in Lending Act and the Fair Credit Reporting Act. These regulations are designed to ensure that consumers are provided with accurate and transparent information about financial products and services, and that they are not subjected to unfair or deceptive practices.

Conclusion:

In conclusion, financial regulations are a critical component of the financial industry. They play a key role in promoting transparency, protecting consumers, and maintaining financial stability. Financial regulations are enforced through a range of mechanisms, including fines, sanctions, and legal action. While there are costs associated with regulatory compliance, the benefits of financial regulations are significant and far-reaching. Financial regulations help to ensure that the financial industry operates in a fair, ethical, and transparent manner, and that it is able to withstand market shocks and financial crises.

I. Historical Overview of Financial Regulations

Financial regulations play a critical role in the functioning of the financial industry. They are designed to protect investors, promote market stability, and prevent fraud and abuse. In this section, we will provide a historical overview of financial regulations and their impact on the industry. We will examine the evolution of financial regulations, from their origins in the aftermath of the Great Depression to the present day.

Overview of Financial Regulations:

Financial regulations refer to the rules and guidelines that govern the behavior of financial institutions and individuals in the financial industry. The objective of financial regulations is to create a fair, transparent, and efficient financial system that benefits investors, consumers, and the economy as a whole.

The need for financial regulations arises from the inherent risks associated with financial activities. The financial industry is characterized by a high degree of leverage, complexity, and interconnectivity, which can amplify the impact of financial shocks and destabilize the economy. Moreover, the information asymmetry between financial institutions and investors can lead to moral hazard and adverse selection, which can result in market failures.

Historical Overview of Financial Regulations:

The history of financial regulations can be traced back to the early 20th century, when the United States experienced a series of financial crises, including the Panic of 1907 and the Great Depression. These crises led to the realization that unregulated financial markets can pose significant risks to the economy and society as a whole. In response, the US government passed several laws and regulations aimed at restoring confidence in the financial system and preventing future crises.

One of the most significant financial regulations passed during this period was the Glass-Steagall Act of 1933. This act separated commercial and investment banking activities, thereby reducing the risk of banks engaging in speculative activities with depositors' money. Another significant regulation was the Securities Act of 1933, which required companies to disclose important financial and other information to investors before offering securities for sale.

In the post-World War II era, financial regulations continued to evolve in response to changing market conditions and technological innovations. In 1956, the Investment Company Act was passed to regulate mutual funds and other investment companies. In 1970, the Bank Secrecy Act was passed, which required financial institutions to report suspicious transactions to the government to prevent money laundering.

The 1980s saw a significant deregulation of the financial industry, as policymakers believed that market forces would lead to greater efficiency and innovation. This led to the repeal of several regulations, including the Glass-Steagall Act, which allowed commercial and investment banking activities to be integrated. This deregulation paved the way for the creation of new financial instruments and markets, such as mortgage-backed securities and derivatives.

The deregulation of the 1980s, however, was followed by a series of financial crises in the 1990s and 2000s, including the Savings and Loan crisis, the Asian Financial Crisis, and the Global Financial Crisis of 2008. These crises led to renewed calls for greater regulation of the financial industry. In response, policymakers passed several new laws and regulations, including the Dodd-Frank Wall Street Reform and Consumer Protection Act of 2010, which aimed to strengthen oversight of the financial industry and protect consumers.

Conclusion:

In conclusion, financial regulations have a long and complex history that reflects the changing needs and challenges of the financial industry. While regulations can impose costs and create inefficiencies, they are essential for promoting market stability, protecting investors, and preventing fraud and abuse. As the financial industry continues to evolve, it is likely that new regulations will be introduced to address emerging risks and challenges.

Early financial regulations

Early financial regulations can be traced back to ancient civilizations, such as the Code of Hammurabi in Babylon, which established laws governing lending practices and debt. However, in modern times, financial regulations began to take shape in response to economic crises and market failures.

One of the earliest examples of financial regulation in the United States was the National Banking Act of 1863, which established a national banking system and created a system of federal oversight for banks. This law was designed to address the problems of state-chartered banks, which were vulnerable to fraud, mismanagement, and instability.

Another important early regulation was the Securities Act of 1933, which was enacted in response to the stock market crash of 1929 and the ensuing Great Depression. This law required companies to disclose certain financial and other information to investors before offering securities for sale, with the goal of increasing transparency and reducing fraud in the securities markets.

The Securities Exchange Act of 1934 further regulated the securities markets by creating the Securities and Exchange Commission (SEC) to oversee and enforce the securities laws. The SEC is responsible for protecting investors, maintaining fair and orderly markets, and promoting capital formation.

In addition to these federal regulations, state governments also began to regulate financial institutions and practices. For example, the New York State Banking Department was established in 1851 to regulate banks in New York State. This was followed by the creation of state insurance departments, which regulated insurance companies operating within their borders.

Overall, the early history of financial regulation in the United States was characterized by a patchwork of federal and state regulations that were designed to address specific problems and crises as they arose. These regulations were generally aimed at protecting consumers and investors from fraud and abuse, maintaining stability in the financial system, and promoting economic growth and development.

Major financial regulations in the 20th century

The 20th century was a pivotal time for financial regulation, marked by a series of major reforms and regulations that significantly altered the landscape of the financial industry. In this section, we will explore some of the most significant financial regulations that were introduced during the 20th century.

Glass-Steagall Act

The Glass-Steagall Act, also known as the Banking Act of 1933, was one of the most significant pieces of financial legislation in U.S. history. It was enacted in response to the Great Depression and sought to prevent commercial banks from engaging in risky investment activities. The act established a separation between commercial banks, which accept deposits and make loans, and investment banks, which engage in securities underwriting and trading. The act also created the Federal Deposit Insurance Corporation (FDIC), which insured bank deposits up to a certain amount, providing a safety net for depositors.

The Glass-Steagall Act remained in place for more than six decades, until it was repealed in 1999 by the Gramm-Leach-Bliley Act. The repeal of Glass-Steagall has been the subject of much debate and criticism, with some arguing that it contributed to the 2008 financial crisis.

Securities Act of 1933

The Securities Act of 1933 was the first major federal securities law in the United States. It was enacted in response to the stock market crash of 1929 and sought to provide investors with more information about securities offerings. The act required companies issuing securities to register with the Securities and Exchange Commission (SEC) and disclose certain information about their business, financial condition, and the securities being offered. The act also established liability for false or misleading statements in securities offerings.

The Securities Act of 1933 was followed by the Securities Exchange Act of 1934, which established the SEC as a regulatory agency with the power to oversee and regulate securities markets in the United States.

Employee Retirement Income Security Act (ERISA)

The Employee Retirement Income Security Act, or ERISA, was enacted in 1974 to protect the retirement savings of employees. The act sets standards for private sector pension plans, including requirements for minimum funding levels and vesting rights for employees. The act also created the Pension Benefit Guaranty Corporation (PBGC), which insures private sector pension plans in the event of their failure.

ERISA has been amended several times since its enactment, most recently by the Pension Protection Act of 2006. The act continues to be an important piece of legislation in the United States, as it provides protections for millions of workers who rely on employer-sponsored retirement plans for their financial security.

Dodd-Frank Wall Street Reform and Consumer Protection Act

The Dodd-Frank Wall Street Reform and Consumer Protection Act was enacted in response to the 2008 financial crisis. The act aimed to reform the financial industry by increasing transparency, accountability, and consumer protection. The act created several new regulatory agencies, including the

Financial Stability Oversight Council and the Consumer Financial Protection Bureau. It also established new regulations for financial institutions, such as the Volcker Rule, which prohibits banks from engaging in proprietary trading and certain types of investments.

The Dodd-Frank Act has been the subject of much controversy and debate since its enactment. Supporters argue that it has made the financial industry safer and more accountable, while opponents argue that it has imposed excessive regulatory burdens on financial institutions and stifled economic growth.

Sarbanes-Oxley Act

The Sarbanes-Oxley Act was enacted in 2002 in response to a series of corporate accounting scandals, including the Enron scandal. The act established new standards for corporate governance and accounting practices, including requirements for financial reporting, internal controls, and auditor independence. The act also created the Public Company Accounting Oversight Board (PCAOB), a nonprofit corporation responsible for overseeing the audits of public companies and the accounting firms that conduct them.

One of the key provisions of the Sarbanes-Oxley Act is Section 404, which requires management to assess and report on the effectiveness of the company's internal controls over financial reporting. This provision aims to increase the reliability and accuracy of financial statements and prevent fraudulent activities.

While the Sarbanes-Oxley Act has been effective in improving corporate governance and financial reporting, it has also been criticized for its high compliance costs. Some argue that the act has placed an undue burden on smaller companies that may not have the resources to comply with the new regulations. Additionally, some have suggested that the act has had unintended consequences, such as a decrease in the number of public companies and increased regulatory complexity.

In 2010, the Dodd-Frank Wall Street Reform and Consumer Protection Act was signed into law in response to the 2008 financial crisis. The act aimed to increase transparency and accountability in the financial industry and establish new regulations for financial institutions. Some of the key provisions of the act include the creation of the Consumer Financial Protection Bureau (CFPB), which is responsible for protecting consumers from financial fraud and abuse, and the Volcker Rule, which prohibits banks from engaging in proprietary trading.

The Dodd-Frank Act also established new requirements for the regulation of derivatives, which are financial instruments that allow investors to speculate on the future prices of assets such as commodities or currencies. The act requires certain derivatives to be traded on regulated exchanges and cleared through central counterparties in order to increase transparency and reduce systemic risk.

Like the Sarbanes-Oxley Act, the Dodd-Frank Act has been both praised for its efforts to increase accountability in the financial industry and criticized for its complexity and regulatory burden. Some argue that the act has limited the ability of smaller financial institutions to compete with larger ones, while others have suggested that it has not gone far enough in addressing the root causes of the 2008 financial crisis.

In conclusion, financial regulations play a crucial role in promoting stability and accountability in the financial industry. From the early financial regulations of the 20th century to the more recent Sarbanes-Oxley Act and Dodd-Frank Act, regulators have sought to balance the need for market efficiency with the need for investor protection. While regulations can have unintended consequences and may place a burden on smaller companies, they remain an essential tool in preventing financial crises and promoting long-term economic growth.

Recent financial regulations

In the wake of the 2008 financial crisis, governments around the world implemented a wide range of new financial regulations in an effort to stabilize the financial system and prevent future crises. In the United States, the Dodd-Frank Wall Street Reform and Consumer Protection Act, passed in 2010, was the most comprehensive reform of the financial sector since the Great Depression. The act established new regulations for the banking industry, including the creation of the Consumer Financial Protection Bureau, which regulates consumer financial products such as mortgages and credit cards, and the Financial Stability Oversight Council, which monitors systemic risk in the financial system.

One of the key provisions of the Dodd-Frank act was the Volcker Rule, which prohibits banks from engaging in proprietary trading and limits their ability to invest in hedge funds and private equity funds. The rule was designed to prevent banks from taking on excessive risk and engaging in activities that could lead to another financial crisis. However, the rule has been criticized by some industry experts who argue that it is too complex and burdensome and could limit banks' ability to compete in global markets.

Another important regulation introduced in the wake of the financial crisis was the Basel III accord, which was developed by the Basel Committee on Banking Supervision, an international regulatory body. The accord established new standards for bank capital requirements and liquidity ratios, which were intended to increase the resilience of the banking system and reduce the risk of future crises. The Basel III accord has been adopted by many countries around the world, although some have delayed implementation due to concerns about its potential impact on economic growth.

In addition to these major regulatory initiatives, there have been a number of other recent financial regulations that have had an impact on various sectors of the financial industry. For example, the Department of Labor introduced a new fiduciary rule in 2016, which requires financial advisors to act in the best interests of their clients when giving advice on retirement accounts. The rule was designed to protect consumers from conflicts of interest and ensure that they receive advice that is appropriate for their individual needs and goals.

The European Union has also introduced a range of new financial regulations in recent years, including the Markets in Financial Instruments Directive (MiFID II), which is aimed at increasing transparency and reducing risk in the securities markets. MiFID II requires financial institutions to disclose more information about the prices and terms of financial products, and imposes new restrictions on algorithmic trading and high-frequency trading.

In the United Kingdom, the Financial Conduct Authority (FCA) has implemented a number of new regulations in recent years, including the Senior Managers and Certification Regime (SMCR), which requires senior executives in the financial industry to be held accountable for their actions and to certify that their staff are properly qualified and trained. The FCA has also introduced new rules aimed at preventing financial misconduct, such as market manipulation and insider trading.

Despite the benefits of these new regulations, there are some who argue that they may have unintended consequences and could limit the growth and innovation of the financial industry. For example, some analysts have raised concerns that the increased regulatory burden could make it more difficult for smaller financial institutions to compete with larger banks, which have the resources to comply with the new rules. Others have argued that the regulations could lead to a reduction in liquidity in certain markets, making it more difficult for investors to buy and sell financial products.

In conclusion, recent financial regulations have been implemented in response to the 2008 financial crisis, with the goal of preventing future crises and ensuring that consumers are protected from financial misconduct. While these regulations have had some positive impacts, there are concerns about their potential unintended consequences and their impact on the financial industry as a whole. As the financial landscape continues to evolve, it is likely that additional regulations will be introduced in the coming years in response to changing market conditions and consumer needs.

One area of financial regulation that has garnered significant attention in recent years is the regulation of cryptocurrencies and blockchain technology. While many governments and regulatory bodies initially took a hands-off approach to these emerging technologies, concerns about their potential for facilitating illegal activities such as money laundering and terrorist financing have led to increased scrutiny and regulation. In the United States, the Financial Crimes Enforcement Network (FinCEN) has issued guidance on the application of its regulations to virtual currency exchanges and administrators, while the Securities and Exchange Commission (SEC) has taken action against companies for conducting initial coin offerings (ICOs) that violate securities laws.

Another area of focus for recent financial regulations has been the prevention of money laundering and terrorist financing. The Financial Action Task Force (FATF), an international organization that sets standards for anti-money laundering and counter-terrorism financing measures, has recently issued guidance on the regulation of virtual assets, including cryptocurrencies. In the United States, the Bank Secrecy Act (BSA) and its implementing regulations require financial institutions to implement anti-money laundering programs and report suspicious activity to the Financial Crimes Enforcement Network (FinCEN).

In addition to regulations focused on specific areas of the financial industry, there have also been broader regulatory efforts aimed at strengthening the financial system as a whole. The Dodd-Frank Wall Street Reform and Consumer Protection Act, passed in 2010, established new rules for bank capital and liquidity, created a new agency responsible for consumer financial protection, and introduced new requirements for derivatives trading. While the law has been praised for its efforts to improve the stability and safety of the financial system, it has also been criticized for its complexity and the burden it places on small and mid-sized financial institutions.

Overall, recent financial regulations have aimed to address the weaknesses in the financial system that were exposed by the 2008 financial crisis. While these regulations have had some positive impacts, there are concerns about their potential unintended consequences, such as reduced access to credit or increased costs for consumers. Additionally, as financial technology continues to evolve and new risks emerge, it is likely that additional regulations will be needed to address these challenges. As such, it is important for regulators to continue to monitor the effectiveness of existing regulations and to adapt to changing market conditions and consumer needs.

II. The Impact of Financial Regulations on the Industry

The financial industry has a long history of boom and bust cycles, with periods of rapid growth and economic expansion followed by sudden market collapses and downturns. In response to these cycles, governments around the world have implemented a range of financial regulations aimed at stabilizing markets, protecting consumers, and preventing future crises. While some financial regulations have had a positive impact on the industry, others have been criticized for their unintended consequences and their impact on market innovation and growth.

This section will examine the impact of financial regulations on the industry, exploring the history of financial regulation, the goals and objectives of different types of financial regulations, and the impact of regulations on the financial industry as a whole. We will explore the arguments both for and against financial regulations, drawing on insights from a range of experts in fields such as investment banking, actuarial science, portfolio management, quantitative analysis, securities trading, financial planning, and financial analysis.

History of Financial Regulations:

Financial regulations have a long history, with governments around the world implementing regulations aimed at stabilizing markets and protecting consumers. In the United States, financial regulation dates back to the 19th century, with the creation of the Office of the Comptroller of the Currency in 1863, which was responsible for regulating national banks. Over time, the government has implemented a range of additional regulations aimed at stabilizing markets, protecting consumers, and preventing future crises.

One of the earliest major financial regulations in the United States was the Glass-Steagall Act of 1933. This act separated commercial banking and investment banking, with the goal of preventing banks from engaging in speculative activities that could lead to financial instability. The act was repealed in 1999, with some experts arguing that this contributed to the 2008 financial crisis.

Another major financial regulation in the United States was the Sarbanes-Oxley Act of 2002, which was enacted in response to a series of corporate accounting scandals, including the Enron scandal. This act established new standards for corporate governance and accounting practices, including requirements for financial reporting, internal controls, and auditor independence.

More recently, the Dodd-Frank Wall Street Reform and Consumer Protection Act was passed in 2010, in response to the 2008 financial crisis. This act established new regulations aimed at preventing future crises, including increased oversight of financial institutions, the creation of the Consumer Financial Protection Bureau, and restrictions on banks engaging in proprietary trading.

Goals and Objectives of Financial Regulations:

Financial regulations are typically implemented with a range of goals and objectives in mind. One of the primary goals of financial regulations is to stabilize markets and prevent future crises. This can be achieved through a range of means, such as increased oversight of financial institutions, restrictions on speculative activities, and requirements for increased capital reserves.

Another goal of financial regulations is to protect consumers from financial misconduct. This can involve regulations aimed at preventing predatory lending practices, ensuring that financial products are transparent and easy to understand, and increasing consumer protections for individuals and small businesses.

Financial regulations can also be aimed at promoting market innovation and growth. For example, regulations aimed at promoting sustainable finance and reducing carbon emissions can help to promote the growth of green industries.

Impact of Financial Regulations on the Industry:

The impact of financial regulations on the industry is a complex and contested issue. While some financial regulations have had a positive impact on the industry, others have been criticized for their unintended consequences and their impact on market innovation and growth.

One of the major criticisms of financial regulations is that they can stifle innovation and slow economic growth. For example, restrictions on proprietary trading can limit the ability of banks to engage in innovative and profitable trading activities, potentially limiting their ability to grow and expand.

Financial regulations can also have unintended consequences. For example, increased oversight of financial institutions can lead to increased compliance costs and a reduction in profitability. This, in turn, can lead to a reduction in the availability of credit and other financial services, particularly for small businesses and individuals who may have difficulty meeting the stricter requirements imposed by regulations.

Another criticism of financial regulations is that they can create a false sense of security, leading to complacency among market participants. This can lead to a lack of vigilance and a failure to identify and address emerging risks, potentially exacerbating systemic vulnerabilities.

Despite these criticisms, financial regulations can also have positive impacts on the industry. For example, regulations that promote transparency and accountability can help to restore investor confidence in the financial system, reducing the likelihood of future crises. Additionally, regulations that require financial institutions to hold more capital and maintain adequate liquidity buffers can help to reduce the risk of bank failures and the associated systemic risks.

Financial regulations can also help to level the playing field, promoting competition and reducing the advantages enjoyed by larger, more established firms. This can help to encourage innovation and promote market efficiency, benefiting both consumers and businesses.

Moreover, financial regulations can promote social welfare by ensuring that financial products and services are safe, affordable, and accessible to all individuals, regardless of their income level or financial sophistication. This can help to reduce the risk of financial exclusion and promote financial inclusion, which is essential for economic growth and development.

In summary, financial regulations have a complex impact on the financial industry. While they can provide important benefits, such as promoting stability and protecting consumers, they can also have unintended consequences, such as limiting innovation and reducing competition. As such, it is important to strike a balance between these competing interests, ensuring that financial regulations are effective and efficient while minimizing their negative impacts on the industry.

Benefits of financial regulations

Financial regulations have become an integral part of the modern financial landscape, and while they may have some drawbacks, they also have several benefits that are worth exploring. In this section, we will delve into the benefits of financial regulations, examining how they can promote stability, protect consumers, and prevent financial misconduct.

One of the primary benefits of financial regulations is their ability to promote stability within the financial system. The 2008 financial crisis demonstrated the importance of stability in financial markets, as the failure of major financial institutions and the collapse of the housing market led to a global recession. Financial regulations can help to prevent similar crises by requiring financial institutions to maintain minimum capital reserves, limiting the amount of leverage they can take on, and enforcing restrictions on risky financial activities.

Financial regulations can also help to protect consumers from financial misconduct. This includes fraudulent practices, such as Ponzi schemes and insider trading, as well as unethical practices, such as predatory lending and discriminatory practices. Regulations such as the Dodd-Frank Wall Street Reform and Consumer Protection Act require financial institutions to disclose more information to consumers, such as the terms of loans and investments, as well as any fees and risks associated with them. This increased transparency allows consumers to make more informed decisions and reduces the likelihood of them being taken advantage of by unscrupulous financial actors.

In addition to promoting stability and protecting consumers, financial regulations can also have positive impacts on the broader economy. For example, regulations that encourage banks to lend to small businesses can help to stimulate economic growth by providing capital to entrepreneurs and fostering innovation. Regulations that promote investment in renewable energy can also have positive impacts on the environment, reducing carbon emissions and promoting sustainable development.

Furthermore, financial regulations can also lead to increased confidence in financial markets. When investors feel that financial institutions are being held accountable for their actions, they are more likely to invest their money in these institutions, leading to increased liquidity and stability in financial markets. This increased confidence can also help to prevent financial panics and runs on financial institutions, which can have devastating consequences for the broader economy.

Counterarguments against financial regulations often cite the potential for regulations to stifle innovation and limit growth within the financial industry. For example, restrictions on proprietary trading can limit the ability of banks to engage in innovative and profitable trading activities, potentially limiting their ability to grow and expand. However, it is important to note that not all innovation is beneficial, and some financial activities may carry significant risks that can have negative impacts on the broader economy. Financial regulations help to ensure that these risks are mitigated, while still allowing for innovation and growth within the industry.

In conclusion, financial regulations have several benefits that are worth considering, including promoting stability, protecting consumers, and stimulating economic growth. While there may be some potential drawbacks, such as limiting innovation and growth, these risks must be weighed against the benefits that regulations provide. Ultimately, the key to effective financial regulation is finding the right balance between promoting stability and growth while still protecting consumers and the broader economy from financial misconduct.

Costs of financial regulations

Financial regulations have been implemented in response to various crises, such as the 2008 financial crisis, with the aim of preventing future financial crises and protecting consumers from financial misconduct. However, while there are benefits to financial regulations, there are also costs associated with them. In this section, we will explore the costs of financial regulations and their impact on the financial industry.

One of the major criticisms of financial regulations is that they can stifle innovation and slow economic growth. For example, restrictions on proprietary trading can limit the ability of banks to engage in innovative and profitable trading activities, potentially limiting their ability to grow and expand.

Additionally, regulations on the capital requirements of banks can limit their lending activities and reduce the availability of credit to businesses and individuals, potentially limiting economic growth.

Financial regulations can also have unintended consequences. For example, increased oversight of financial institutions can lead to increased compliance costs. This can be especially burdensome for smaller financial institutions, which may not have the resources to comply with complex regulatory requirements. Compliance costs can also divert resources away from other important activities, such as lending and investing, potentially reducing their effectiveness.

Furthermore, financial regulations can create barriers to entry for new market participants. For example, capital requirements and other regulatory barriers can make it more difficult for new financial institutions to enter the market, potentially limiting competition and reducing consumer choice. This can also lead to the concentration of the financial industry in the hands of a few large institutions, which can have negative implications for market stability and competition.

Another cost of financial regulations is the potential for regulatory capture. Regulatory capture occurs when regulatory agencies become too closely aligned with the interests of the industries they are supposed to regulate, potentially leading to a reduction in regulatory effectiveness. For example, if regulatory agencies become too close with the financial industry, they may be more likely to overlook instances of financial misconduct or to adopt regulations that favor the interests of financial institutions over those of consumers.

Finally, financial regulations can be subject to political influence, potentially leading to regulatory instability. For example, changes in political leadership can lead to changes in regulatory priorities, potentially resulting in a lack of consistency in regulatory enforcement and effectiveness.

In conclusion, financial regulations have the potential to prevent financial crises and protect consumers from financial misconduct, but they also come with costs. These costs include the potential for reduced economic growth and innovation, increased compliance costs, barriers to entry for new market participants, regulatory capture, and political instability. It is important for policymakers to carefully consider these costs when designing and implementing financial regulations to ensure that they strike an appropriate balance between regulatory effectiveness and economic efficiency.

Effects on competition and innovation

While financial regulations aim to protect consumers and prevent financial crises, they can have an impact on competition and innovation in the financial industry. Regulations can create barriers to entry, limit the ability of existing firms to innovate and compete, and restrict the flow of information in the market.

Barriers to entry

One of the potential negative effects of financial regulations on competition is the creation of barriers to entry for new firms in the market. Regulations can be complex and costly to comply with, which can deter new entrants who may not have the resources to comply with the regulations. This can reduce competition in the industry and limit the choices available to consumers.

For example, the Dodd-Frank Act of 2010 imposed new regulations on financial institutions, including requirements for increased capital and liquidity, and restrictions on proprietary trading. These regulations were intended to reduce risk and protect consumers, but they have also had the unintended consequence of creating barriers to entry for new firms, particularly in the area of proprietary trading. Smaller firms may not have the resources to comply with these regulations, which can limit their ability to enter the market and compete with larger, established firms.

Limiting innovation

Another potential negative effect of financial regulations is the limitation of innovation in the industry. Regulations can restrict the types of activities that financial firms can engage in, particularly if those activities are deemed to be high-risk or potentially harmful to consumers. While this may protect consumers from risky activities, it can also limit the ability of firms to innovate and develop new products or services.

For example, regulations on the securitization of mortgages in the wake of the 2008 financial crisis were intended to prevent the packaging of risky mortgages into complex securities. However, these regulations also limited the ability of financial firms to innovate in the area of mortgage-backed securities, which had been a profitable and innovative area of the industry prior to the crisis.

Flow of information

Regulations can also impact the flow of information in the financial industry, which can have an impact on competition and innovation. For example, regulations on insider trading can restrict the ability of firms to share information with each other and limit the flow of information in the market. This can make it more difficult for firms to make informed decisions and limit their ability to compete with each other.

Additionally, regulations that require the disclosure of certain information, such as financial statements or risk assessments, can give larger firms an advantage over smaller firms that may not have the resources to comply with these requirements. This can limit the ability of smaller firms to compete and innovate in the industry.

Counterarguments

While there are concerns about the impact of financial regulations on competition and innovation, some argue that regulations can actually promote competition and innovation by creating a level playing field and encouraging firms to innovate in areas that are not restricted by regulations. For example, regulations on the disclosure of financial information can promote transparency and help to level the playing field between larger and smaller firms. This can encourage competition and innovation in areas where firms are not restricted by regulations.

Others argue that the financial industry has historically been plagued by a lack of innovation and that regulations can actually encourage firms to develop new products and services that are safer and more beneficial for consumers. For example, the introduction of new regulations on the securitization of mortgages in the wake of the 2008 financial crisis may have limited the ability of firms to engage in risky practices, but it also encouraged the development of new, safer products in the mortgage-backed securities market.

Conclusion

While financial regulations are intended to protect consumers and prevent financial crises, they can also have unintended consequences for competition and innovation in the financial industry. Regulations can create barriers to entry, limit the ability of firms to innovate and compete, and restrict the flow of information in the market. However, it is important to note that the effects of financial regulations on competition and innovation are complex and multifaceted, and may vary depending on the specific regulation and the context in which it is implemented.

To mitigate the potential negative impacts of financial regulations on competition and innovation, policymakers must strike a delicate balance between regulatory oversight and allowing for market-driven competition and innovation. This requires a nuanced understanding of the financial industry and the potential consequences of regulatory policies.

In conclusion, while financial regulations are necessary to protect consumers and ensure the stability of the financial system, policymakers must also consider the potential impact on competition and innovation. By carefully balancing the need for regulation with the need for market-driven competition and innovation, policymakers can ensure that the financial industry remains dynamic and resilient, while also protecting consumers and preventing future financial crises.

III. Current Financial Regulations

The financial industry plays a critical role in the global economy, providing a range of financial services that enable individuals and businesses to invest, borrow, and manage their money. However, the financial industry has also been associated with a number of negative consequences, including financial crises, fraud, and market manipulation. In response, governments around the world have implemented a wide range of financial regulations designed to protect consumers, ensure market stability, and promote fair competition.

Current financial regulations encompass a broad range of laws, rules, and standards that govern the activities of financial institutions, including banks, investment firms, insurance companies, and other financial service providers. These regulations aim to promote transparency, protect investors, and prevent systemic risk by requiring financial institutions to follow certain practices, disclose relevant information, and adhere to specific capital and liquidity requirements.

The scope of financial regulations has expanded significantly in the wake of the 2008 global financial crisis, which highlighted the risks and challenges associated with a largely unregulated financial industry. Today, financial regulations cover a wide range of activities and industries, from banking and securities trading to insurance and consumer finance.

Despite the benefits of financial regulations, there are also concerns about their costs and unintended consequences. Some argue that excessive regulation can stifle innovation and hinder economic growth, while others point to the potential for regulatory capture and the risk of creating unintended consequences that may undermine the effectiveness of the regulations themselves.

In this section, we will explore the current landscape of financial regulations, including the key laws, regulations, and standards that govern financial institutions and the activities they engage in. We will also examine the benefits and costs of financial regulations and consider the potential for future regulatory changes that may impact the financial industry and the broader economy. Through this analysis, we hope to provide a comprehensive overview of the current state of financial regulations and their role in promoting financial stability, consumer protection, and fair competition.

Overview of current financial regulations

Financial regulations are a set of rules and guidelines established by governments and regulatory agencies to promote financial stability, protect consumers, and prevent financial crimes such as fraud, money laundering, and terrorist financing. These regulations apply to financial institutions such as banks, investment firms, and insurance companies, as well as to financial markets and products.

The regulatory landscape for financial institutions has evolved significantly over the years, particularly in the wake of the 2008 global financial crisis, which exposed weaknesses in the regulatory framework and led to a major overhaul of financial regulation. In the United States, the Dodd-Frank Wall Street Reform and Consumer Protection Act, enacted in 2010, introduced sweeping changes to the regulatory landscape, including the creation of new agencies and the imposition of new rules on financial institutions.

One of the primary goals of financial regulation is to promote financial stability by preventing systemic risks that could lead to a financial crisis. To achieve this goal, regulatory agencies impose capital requirements, liquidity requirements, and other prudential regulations on financial institutions. These regulations are designed to ensure that financial institutions have sufficient capital and liquidity to withstand financial shocks and to prevent the failure of individual institutions from spreading throughout the financial system.

In addition to prudential regulations, financial regulators also impose conduct regulations, which are designed to protect consumers and prevent financial crimes. These regulations include rules governing the sale and marketing of financial products, disclosure requirements, and anti-money laundering rules. Conduct regulations are intended to ensure that financial institutions act in the best interests of their customers and that they do not engage in fraudulent or criminal activities.

Financial regulators also play a role in overseeing financial markets, including stock markets, bond markets, and commodity markets. They monitor market activity for signs of market manipulation or other forms of misconduct and take action to address such activities when they occur. They also oversee the clearance and settlement of transactions and ensure that markets operate in a fair and transparent manner.

In recent years, regulators have also been focused on promoting cybersecurity in the financial industry. Cyber threats pose a significant risk to financial institutions and the broader financial system, and regulatory agencies have been working to establish standards for cybersecurity and to encourage financial institutions to invest in cybersecurity infrastructure.

Overall, the regulatory framework for the financial industry is complex and constantly evolving. The goal of financial regulation is to promote financial stability, protect consumers, and prevent financial crimes, but the implementation of regulations can have unintended consequences, such as reducing competition and limiting innovation. As such, financial regulators must strike a balance between promoting financial stability and allowing for innovation and competition in the financial industry.

Key regulatory bodies and their functions

In the United States, there are several regulatory bodies that oversee financial institutions and markets, each with its own specific functions and responsibilities. These agencies were established to ensure the stability and integrity of the financial system, protect consumers, and promote fair and efficient markets.

Securities and Exchange Commission (SEC)

The SEC is an independent federal agency that regulates securities markets and protects investors. Its primary role is to ensure that companies disclose accurate and timely information about their operations and financial condition to the public. The SEC also has the authority to bring enforcement actions against individuals and companies that violate securities laws, such as insider trading and accounting fraud. In addition, the SEC oversees investment advisers, broker-dealers, and other financial professionals.

Federal Reserve System (Fed)

The Fed is the central bank of the United States, responsible for conducting monetary policy and promoting financial stability. The Fed sets interest rates and controls the supply of money and credit in the economy to achieve its dual mandate of maximum employment and price stability. The Fed also supervises and regulates banks and other financial institutions to ensure they are operating safely and soundly.

Commodity Futures Trading Commission (CFTC)

The CFTC regulates futures and options markets, as well as the derivatives markets more broadly. It is responsible for ensuring that these markets operate in a fair and transparent manner and that market participants adhere to certain standards of conduct. The CFTC also has the authority to bring enforcement actions against individuals and companies that violate commodities laws, such as market manipulation and fraud.

Federal Deposit Insurance Corporation (FDIC)

The FDIC is an independent agency that provides insurance coverage to depositors in banks and savings institutions. It also works to promote the safety and soundness of these institutions by conducting regular examinations and enforcing regulations related to capital and liquidity requirements. In the event that a bank fails, the FDIC may step in to resolve the situation and protect depositors' funds.

Office of the Comptroller of the Currency (OCC)

The OCC is a bureau of the U.S. Department of the Treasury that regulates and supervises national banks and federal savings associations. Its primary goal is to ensure that these institutions operate safely and soundly, and that they are in compliance with applicable laws and regulations. The OCC also has the authority to take enforcement action against banks that violate laws or engage in unsafe or unsound practices.

Consumer Financial Protection Bureau (CFPB)

The CFPB is an independent agency responsible for protecting consumers in the financial marketplace. Its primary focus is on consumer financial products and services, such as mortgages, credit cards, and student loans. The CFPB works to ensure that these products and services are fair, transparent, and accessible to consumers. It also has the authority to bring enforcement actions against companies that violate consumer protection laws.

National Credit Union Administration (NCUA)

The NCUA is an independent federal agency that regulates and supervises federal credit unions. Its primary responsibility is to ensure the safety and soundness of credit unions, as well as to protect the deposits of credit union members. The NCUA also works to promote credit unions' access to affordable funding and to ensure that they comply with applicable laws and regulations.

These regulatory bodies play critical roles in maintaining the stability and integrity of the U.S. financial system. While their functions and responsibilities may differ, they all share the goal of protecting consumers and promoting fair and efficient markets. By monitoring and regulating financial institutions and markets, these agencies help to mitigate risks and prevent financial crises.

Recent developments in financial regulations

Recent developments in financial regulations have been shaped by the lessons learned from the 2008 financial crisis, which exposed weaknesses and gaps in the regulatory framework. Since then, regulators around the world have been working to enhance the resilience and stability of the financial system by strengthening regulations, improving transparency, and increasing oversight.

One of the most significant developments in financial regulations in recent years has been the implementation of the Basel III framework for global banking regulation. The Basel III framework is designed to improve the quality and quantity of capital held by banks, enhance the risk management practices of banks, and reduce the procyclicality of the financial system. The implementation of the Basel III framework has been a multi-year process, with many countries and jurisdictions adopting the framework at different times.

Another key development in financial regulations has been the increased focus on consumer protection. In the aftermath of the financial crisis, there were widespread concerns about predatory lending practices, hidden fees, and other forms of misconduct by financial institutions. Regulators have responded by implementing a range of measures designed to protect consumers, including new rules on credit cards, mortgages, and other consumer financial products.

Another significant development in financial regulations has been the increased use of technology to monitor and regulate financial markets. The rise of fintech and other technological innovations has created new opportunities for regulators to improve the effectiveness and efficiency of their oversight. For example, regulators are increasingly using artificial intelligence and machine learning algorithms to identify patterns of fraud and other forms of misconduct in financial markets.

In addition, there has been a growing trend towards international cooperation and coordination among financial regulators. The global nature of the financial system means that national regulators must work together to ensure that regulations are effective and consistent across different jurisdictions. International bodies such as the Financial Stability Board and the International Organization of Securities Commissions play an important role in facilitating this cooperation and coordination.

There has also been a shift towards more principles-based regulation, which focuses on the underlying principles and objectives of regulations rather than prescribing specific rules or requirements. This approach allows regulators to be more flexible and adaptable in responding to changing market conditions and emerging risks.

However, there have also been concerns that recent developments in financial regulations may have unintended consequences. For example, some critics argue that increased regulation could stifle innovation and competition in the financial industry, by making it more difficult for new entrants to enter the market and for existing firms to innovate. Others argue that some regulations may be too prescriptive, imposing unnecessary costs and burdens on businesses.

Overall, recent developments in financial regulations reflect a recognition of the importance of maintaining a stable and resilient financial system, while also protecting consumers and promoting innovation and competition. While there are concerns about the potential unintended consequences of regulation, it is clear that regulators will continue to play an important role in shaping the future of the financial industry.

CHAPTER 34: COMPLIANCE CHALLENGES AND BEST PRACTICES

The financial industry is one of the most heavily regulated industries in the world. Financial regulations are designed to protect investors, maintain stability in financial markets, and prevent fraud and abuse. However, these regulations can also create compliance challenges for financial institutions, which are required to comply with complex and ever-changing rules and regulations.

In this chapter, we will examine the compliance challenges faced by financial institutions and the best practices they can implement to ensure compliance. We will begin by providing an overview of the compliance challenges faced by financial institutions, followed by a discussion of the importance of compliance best practices.

Overview of Compliance Challenges

Compliance challenges in the financial industry can arise from a variety of factors, including regulatory complexity, technological advancements, and changes in the business environment. One of the biggest challenges faced by financial institutions is the sheer volume and complexity of regulations they must comply with. Financial institutions must comply with rules and regulations issued by a variety of regulatory bodies, including the Federal Reserve, the Securities and Exchange Commission (SEC), the Financial Industry Regulatory Authority (FINRA), and the Commodity Futures Trading Commission (CFTC), among others.

The regulations themselves are often complex and subject to interpretation, which can create uncertainty and ambiguity. Additionally, regulations are constantly changing, with new rules being added and existing rules being modified on a regular basis. This can make it difficult for financial institutions to stay up-to-date on the latest regulatory requirements and ensure compliance.

Another challenge faced by financial institutions is the increasing use of technology in financial services. The use of technology has led to new compliance challenges, as financial institutions must ensure that their systems and processes are secure and comply with regulatory requirements. For example, the use of cloud computing and mobile devices has raised concerns about data security and privacy, which are regulated by various laws and regulations.

Changes in the business environment can also create compliance challenges for financial institutions. For example, mergers and acquisitions can result in the consolidation of systems and processes, which can create compliance challenges. Similarly, the expansion of financial institutions into new markets can create compliance challenges, as they must comply with new regulatory requirements in those markets.

Importance of Compliance Best Practices

Given the complexity of regulatory requirements and the challenges associated with compliance, it is important for financial institutions to implement best practices to ensure compliance. Compliance best practices are a set of guidelines and procedures that are designed to help financial institutions comply with regulations and manage compliance risks.

There are several benefits to implementing compliance best practices. First and foremost, compliance best practices can help financial institutions avoid costly penalties and fines for non-compliance. Financial institutions that fail to comply with regulations can face significant fines and penalties, which can have a negative impact on their financial performance and reputation.

In addition to avoiding penalties and fines, compliance best practices can also help financial institutions improve their overall risk management. Compliance risks are a type of operational risk, which is the risk of loss resulting from inadequate or failed internal processes, people, or systems, or from external events. By implementing compliance best practices, financial institutions can better manage compliance risks and reduce the likelihood of compliance failures.

Compliance best practices can also help financial institutions improve their efficiency and effectiveness. By implementing standardized processes and procedures for compliance, financial institutions can reduce the time and resources required to comply with regulations. This can allow them to focus on their core business activities and better serve their customers.

Finally, compliance best practices can help financial institutions maintain a strong culture of compliance. A strong culture of compliance is essential for ensuring that all employees understand the importance of compliance and are committed to complying with regulations. By implementing compliance best practices, financial institutions can demonstrate their commitment to compliance and create a culture of compliance throughout the organization.

Conclusion

Compliance challenges are a significant concern for financial institutions, given the complexity and ever-changing nature of regulatory requirements. Compliance best practices are essential for organizations to stay up-to-date with regulatory changes and avoid costly fines and reputational damage. Failure to comply with regulatory requirements can lead to a loss of customer trust, legal liabilities, and ultimately, financial losses.

In conclusion, compliance challenges will continue to be a significant issue for financial institutions. Regulatory bodies are increasing their scrutiny of financial firms, and non-compliance can have severe consequences. However, organizations can take steps to ensure compliance best practices are in place to reduce the risk of non-compliance. By investing in compliance training, implementing robust compliance programs, and embracing technology, financial institutions can minimize the risk of non-compliance and ensure they are meeting regulatory requirements. It is imperative for financial institutions to stay informed of regulatory changes and adopt a proactive approach to compliance to maintain their competitive edge in today's ever-changing business environment.

I. Compliance Challenges in the Financial Industry

Compliance challenges are a critical aspect of the financial industry, given the rapidly changing regulatory landscape and the increasing complexity of financial products and services. In recent years, financial institutions have been subjected to heightened scrutiny from regulators, resulting in increased compliance obligations and significant penalties for noncompliance.

Compliance challenges arise from a variety of sources, including regulatory requirements, internal policies and procedures, and external factors such as economic and geopolitical conditions. These challenges can be particularly acute for large financial institutions, which often operate in multiple jurisdictions and offer a wide range of products and services.

One of the primary challenges of compliance in the financial industry is the need to stay abreast of evolving regulatory requirements. The financial industry is subject to a complex web of regulations and guidelines, issued by numerous regulatory bodies at the federal and state levels. Compliance officers must stay up to date with changes in these regulations, and ensure that their institutions are compliant with the latest requirements.

In addition to regulatory requirements, financial institutions face internal compliance challenges related to risk management and governance. Compliance officers must work closely with other departments, including risk management, legal, and audit, to ensure that the institution is operating within a risk management framework that is consistent with regulatory requirements and internal policies.

External factors, such as changes in economic conditions, can also pose significant compliance challenges. For example, the financial crisis of 2008 prompted regulatory reforms aimed at increasing transparency and reducing risk in the financial industry. These reforms have resulted in a more complex regulatory environment, with increased reporting requirements and stricter standards for risk management.

The importance of compliance in the financial industry cannot be overstated. Noncompliance can result in significant financial and reputational damage to financial institutions, as well as to the broader economy. Compliance challenges must be met with a proactive and collaborative approach, involving all stakeholders within the institution, as well as external advisors and regulatory bodies.

In the following sections, we will explore some of the specific compliance challenges facing the financial industry, as well as best practices for addressing these challenges. We will also examine the role of regulatory bodies in enforcing compliance, and discuss some of the recent developments in this area.

Overview of compliance challenges

The financial industry is subject to numerous rules and regulations imposed by regulatory bodies such as the Securities and Exchange Commission (SEC) and the Financial Industry Regulatory Authority (FINRA). Compliance with these regulations is crucial to the success and stability of financial institutions, but it can also present significant challenges.

One major challenge is the constantly evolving nature of regulatory requirements. Financial institutions must keep up with changes to regulations and adjust their practices accordingly. For example, in recent years, there has been increased focus on cybersecurity and data protection regulations. Financial institutions must implement measures to ensure they comply with these regulations, such as implementing encryption and other security measures to protect sensitive data.

Another challenge is the complexity of the regulations themselves. Financial regulations can be highly technical and difficult to interpret, making compliance a challenge even for experienced professionals. Additionally, financial institutions often operate in multiple jurisdictions, each with their own unique regulatory requirements. This can lead to compliance challenges when trying to navigate and comply with the regulations in different jurisdictions.

Compliance challenges can also arise from the sheer volume of regulations that financial institutions must adhere to. In addition to federal regulations, financial institutions may be subject to state and local regulations, as well as industry-specific regulations. This can make compliance a daunting task, as financial institutions must not only be aware of all relevant regulations but also ensure they are complying with each one.

Finally, compliance challenges can arise from the potential for human error. Financial institutions must rely on their employees to interpret and apply regulations correctly. However, even the most experienced professionals can make mistakes, and a single mistake can lead to significant regulatory and reputational consequences.

Overall, compliance challenges are a significant concern for financial institutions, and failure to comply with regulations can have serious consequences. Financial institutions must be proactive in identifying and addressing compliance challenges to ensure they are meeting their regulatory obligations and protecting themselves from legal and reputational risks.

Key compliance challenges in the financial industry

The financial industry is one of the most heavily regulated sectors in the global economy, with regulations that cover a broad range of activities, including banking, securities trading, investment management, insurance, and other financial services. Compliance challenges in the financial industry arise due to the ever-increasing number of regulations, which are becoming more complex and challenging to understand, interpret and implement.

One of the key compliance challenges in the financial industry is keeping up with the constantly evolving regulatory landscape. Financial institutions are required to stay up-to-date with changes in regulations and standards, which can be time-consuming and expensive. For instance, in the United States, financial institutions must comply with the Dodd-Frank Wall Street Reform and Consumer Protection Act, which includes over 2,300 pages of new rules and regulations.

Another challenge is the cost of compliance. Compliance is a costly exercise for financial institutions, with a significant amount of resources being allocated to compliance-related activities. The cost of compliance is particularly high for small and mid-sized financial institutions that may not have the resources to implement comprehensive compliance programs.

The complexity of the financial industry also presents a significant compliance challenge. The industry is made up of a diverse set of players, each with unique business models, products, and services. Compliance requirements can vary significantly depending on the type of financial institution, the products and services it offers, and the jurisdictions in which it operates.

Furthermore, the use of new and emerging technologies has created new compliance challenges for the financial industry. For example, the rise of fintech and digital currencies has created new compliance requirements, such as know-your-customer (KYC) and anti-money laundering (AML) regulations.

Financial institutions must also be aware of the risks associated with non-compliance. Non-compliance can lead to significant financial, legal, and reputational risks, including fines, legal proceedings, and damage to the institution's reputation. For example, in 2012, Barclays was fined $453 million by US and UK regulators for manipulating the LIBOR benchmark interest rate, which resulted in significant reputational damage to the institution.

Moreover, the sheer volume of data that financial institutions handle creates another significant compliance challenge. Financial institutions must ensure that they collect and manage data in compliance with relevant regulations, such as data protection and privacy laws. The misuse or mishandling of customer data can result in significant reputational damage and legal liabilities.

Lastly, the global nature of the financial industry presents a significant compliance challenge. Financial institutions must comply with regulations in multiple jurisdictions, each with unique regulatory requirements. This creates significant compliance complexities, especially for institutions that operate across borders.

In conclusion, key compliance challenges in the financial industry arise due to the ever-evolving regulatory landscape, high cost of compliance, complexity of the industry, emerging technologies, risks associated with non-compliance, volume of data, and the global nature of the industry. Financial institutions must ensure that they have robust compliance programs that address these challenges to avoid significant financial, legal, and reputational risks.

Causes of compliance challenges

Compliance challenges in the financial industry can arise from various causes, including the complexity of regulations, organizational culture, technological limitations, and external factors. In this section, we will explore these causes in more detail and examine how they can contribute to compliance challenges.

Complexity of Regulations:
Regulatory requirements in the financial industry are often complex and can be difficult to interpret, implement, and monitor. Different regulations may have conflicting requirements, creating challenges for firms to comply with all of them simultaneously. Additionally, regulations are frequently updated and amended, making it challenging for financial institutions to stay up-to-date and adjust their compliance procedures accordingly.
One example of complex regulatory requirements is the European Union's MiFID II regulation. This regulation aims to enhance investor protection and increase market transparency, but its implementation has been challenging for many firms. The regulation's requirements around trade reporting, transaction reporting, and best execution have all posed significant compliance challenges for firms, requiring substantial investments in technology and operational resources.

Organizational Culture:
The culture of a financial institution can also impact its compliance efforts. In some cases, there may be a culture of non-compliance or a lack of importance placed on compliance within the organization. This can lead to a disregard for regulatory requirements, and a lack of commitment to implementing and monitoring compliance measures.
Organizational culture is often influenced by the tone set by senior management, who play a crucial role in fostering a culture of compliance within the organization. If senior management does not prioritize compliance, this can trickle down to lower-level employees, creating a culture of non-compliance throughout the organization.

Technological Limitations:
Another cause of compliance challenges is technological limitations. Many financial institutions use legacy technology systems that may not be compatible with newer technologies or unable to handle large amounts of data. This can lead to difficulties in monitoring compliance with regulatory requirements, particularly around data management, reporting, and analysis.

For example, many firms have struggled to comply with the General Data Protection Regulation (GDPR), which requires firms to provide EU citizens with the right to access, correct, and delete their personal data. The complexity of data management, coupled with the difficulty of linking and tracking data across various systems, has made it challenging for firms to meet these requirements.

External Factors:
Compliance challenges can also arise from external factors, such as changes in market conditions, geopolitical events, and emerging technologies. For example, the COVID-19 pandemic has created new challenges for financial institutions, requiring them to quickly adapt to remote work environments and adjust their compliance procedures accordingly.

Similarly, the rise of cryptocurrencies and blockchain technology has created challenges for regulators and financial institutions alike, as they struggle to navigate a rapidly evolving landscape of new technologies and business models. The decentralized and anonymous nature of cryptocurrencies has made it challenging to track and monitor transactions, raising concerns around money laundering and terrorist financing.

In conclusion, compliance challenges in the financial industry can stem from various causes, including the complexity of regulations, organizational culture, technological limitations, and external factors. It is crucial for financial institutions to understand these causes and take proactive measures to address them to ensure compliance with regulatory requirements and protect their reputation and financial stability.

II. Best Practices in Compliance

Compliance is an essential aspect of the financial industry that is of paramount importance to regulators, investors, and other stakeholders. The increasing complexity and sophistication of financial markets have created significant compliance challenges for financial institutions. Best practices in compliance are the practices that financial institutions can adopt to enhance their compliance programs and overcome these challenges. In this section, we will explore the best practices in compliance that financial institutions can implement to ensure regulatory compliance, manage risks, and protect their reputation.

The concept of best practices in compliance has evolved over time in response to the changing regulatory landscape and the increasing complexity of financial markets. The best practices are based on the principles of sound governance, risk management, and compliance culture. Compliance best practices can vary by institution, depending on the institution's size, complexity, risk profile, and regulatory requirements. However, there are several core best practices that financial institutions can implement to ensure regulatory compliance and manage risks effectively.

Compliance best practices are not only essential for regulatory compliance but also for enhancing an institution's reputation and improving its operational efficiency. By implementing best practices in compliance, institutions can reduce compliance costs, avoid regulatory penalties and legal liability, and enhance their brand image. Additionally, implementing best practices in compliance can also help institutions to build a culture of integrity, ethical behavior, and risk management, which is essential for long-term success.

In this section, we will explore the best practices in compliance that financial institutions can implement to ensure regulatory compliance, manage risks, and protect their reputation. We will examine these best practices from the perspective of various roles in the financial industry, such as investment bankers, actuaries, portfolio managers, quantitative analysts, securities traders, financial planners, and financial analysts. By understanding these best practices, financial professionals can effectively manage compliance challenges and maintain regulatory compliance in the ever-changing regulatory environment.

In the following sections, we will explore the best practices in compliance in detail. We will start by discussing the importance of a compliance culture and the role of senior management in fostering this culture. We will then examine the best practices in risk management, including risk assessment, risk mitigation, and risk monitoring. We will also discuss the importance of regulatory compliance training and awareness programs for employees. Finally, we will examine the role of technology in compliance and the best practices in technology-based compliance solutions.

Conclusion

Compliance is a critical aspect of the financial industry that requires constant attention and effort. Compliance challenges are becoming increasingly complex, and financial institutions must adopt best practices to stay ahead of the regulatory curve. Best practices in compliance are based on sound governance, risk management, and compliance culture principles. These practices can help institutions to ensure regulatory compliance, manage risks, and protect their reputation. By implementing best practices in compliance, financial institutions can build a culture of integrity, ethical behavior, and risk management, which is essential for long-term success in the financial industry.

Overview of compliance best practices

Compliance best practices are the guidelines, procedures, and techniques that help financial institutions adhere to regulatory requirements and mitigate compliance risks. The implementation of effective compliance practices is essential for the sustainability and growth of financial institutions in today's complex and rapidly changing business environment. In this section, we will provide an overview of compliance best practices in the financial industry.

One of the key compliance best practices is to establish a compliance culture that emphasizes ethical behavior, compliance with laws and regulations, and accountability for non-compliance. A compliance culture should start from the top of the organization and be supported by all employees. This includes setting a tone at the top by senior management that promotes ethical behavior, ensuring that the compliance function has sufficient resources and authority, and providing regular training and education on compliance-related topics.

Another important compliance best practice is to conduct risk assessments regularly. Risk assessments help institutions identify and evaluate risks to compliance and develop appropriate controls to mitigate those risks. Risk assessments should be conducted on an ongoing basis and should cover all areas of the institution, including products, services, customers, and geographies. The risk assessment process should involve stakeholders from across the organization and should be reviewed and updated periodically.

Compliance monitoring and testing is another best practice that helps institutions identify and address compliance risks. Monitoring and testing activities should be designed to identify compliance weaknesses and gaps in controls, evaluate the effectiveness of existing controls, and provide feedback to management and the compliance function. Monitoring and testing should be performed on a regular basis and should cover all areas of the institution.

In addition to establishing a compliance culture, conducting risk assessments, and monitoring and testing, financial institutions should also implement effective policies and procedures. Policies and procedures should be tailored to the specific risks faced by the institution and should provide clear guidance to employees on how to comply with laws and regulations. Policies and procedures should be reviewed and updated regularly to reflect changes in the regulatory environment, business activities, and risks.

Training and education are also essential compliance best practices. Employees should receive regular training and education on compliance-related topics, including laws and regulations, institution-specific policies and procedures, and ethical behavior. Training and education should be designed to be relevant and engaging, and should be delivered in a variety of formats to accommodate different learning styles.

Finally, effective communication is an important compliance best practice. Institutions should communicate compliance-related information to employees, customers, regulators, and other stakeholders in a clear and timely manner. Communication should be two-way, allowing for feedback and input from stakeholders. Institutions should also establish a system for employees to report compliance concerns or violations anonymously and without fear of retaliation.

In conclusion, compliance best practices are critical for financial institutions to effectively manage compliance risks and achieve sustainable growth. Establishing a compliance culture, conducting risk assessments, monitoring and testing, implementing effective policies and procedures, providing training and education, and communicating effectively are all key components of an effective compliance program. Financial institutions that prioritize compliance best practices are better positioned to meet regulatory requirements, prevent compliance violations, and build trust with customers and stakeholders.

Key compliance best practices in the financial industry

Compliance best practices are essential for ensuring that financial institutions adhere to regulatory requirements and protect their clients' interests. In this section, we will explore some of the key best practices that financial institutions should adopt to ensure that they meet regulatory requirements and maintain their reputation.

Developing a compliance culture: Financial institutions should cultivate a culture of compliance by promoting a strong ethical framework and reinforcing the importance of compliance in all aspects of their business. This includes regularly training employees on regulatory requirements and creating a system of rewards and consequences for adherence to or violation of compliance policies. A culture of compliance can help prevent non-compliance by empowering employees to identify and report potential violations.

Establishing effective compliance management systems: Financial institutions should establish and maintain effective compliance management systems that identify, assess, and manage compliance risks. This includes creating policies and procedures to ensure compliance with regulatory requirements, regularly assessing the effectiveness of these policies and procedures, and implementing processes to monitor and report potential compliance violations. Effective compliance management systems help identify and mitigate potential compliance risks before they become actual violations.

Conducting regular risk assessments: Financial institutions should conduct regular risk assessments to identify potential compliance risks and develop appropriate risk management strategies. This includes assessing the effectiveness of current policies and procedures, identifying areas of potential vulnerability, and taking appropriate measures to mitigate these risks. Regular risk assessments can help financial institutions stay ahead of regulatory changes and proactively address compliance issues.

Maintaining accurate record-keeping: Financial institutions should maintain accurate and complete records of all transactions, communications, and activities to ensure compliance with regulatory requirements. This includes implementing appropriate record-keeping policies and procedures, regularly reviewing and updating these policies and procedures, and ensuring that all employees understand and comply with these policies and procedures. Accurate record-keeping can help financial institutions demonstrate compliance with regulatory requirements and avoid potential penalties for non-compliance.

Implementing effective third-party management: Financial institutions should implement effective third-party management policies and procedures to ensure compliance with regulatory requirements. This includes regularly assessing the compliance risks associated with third-party relationships, monitoring the performance of third-party vendors, and ensuring that appropriate contractual provisions are in place to protect the interests of the financial institution and its clients. Effective third-party management can help financial institutions avoid potential regulatory violations and reputational damage.

Providing regular compliance training: Financial institutions should provide regular compliance training to all employees to ensure that they understand and comply with regulatory requirements. This includes providing training on new or updated regulatory requirements, reinforcing the importance of compliance policies and procedures, and conducting regular assessments of employee understanding and compliance. Regular compliance training can help ensure that all employees are aware of regulatory requirements and can prevent potential compliance violations.

Conducting regular audits and reviews: Financial institutions should conduct regular audits and reviews to assess the effectiveness of their compliance management systems and identify areas for improvement. This includes conducting internal audits to identify potential compliance risks and conducting periodic reviews of compliance policies and procedures to ensure that they remain up-to-date with regulatory requirements. Regular audits and reviews can help financial institutions identify potential compliance issues before they become actual violations and implement appropriate corrective actions.

In conclusion, financial institutions must prioritize compliance to protect their clients' interests, maintain their reputation, and avoid regulatory violations. The key best practices discussed above can help financial institutions develop and maintain effective compliance management systems that mitigate compliance risks, promote a culture of compliance, and ensure regulatory compliance. By adopting these best practices, financial institutions can protect their clients, maintain their reputation, and avoid potential penalties for non-compliance.

Benefits of compliance best practices

Compliance best practices are crucial for financial institutions in order to maintain their reputation, ensure legal and regulatory compliance, and mitigate the risk of financial loss. In this section, we will discuss the benefits of implementing compliance best practices in the financial industry.

Mitigate risk: One of the primary benefits of compliance best practices is that they help mitigate the risk of financial loss due to non-compliance with laws, regulations, and ethical standards. Compliance failures can result in severe financial penalties, reputational damage, and loss of customer trust. For instance, in 2012, JPMorgan Chase & Co. faced a $920 million penalty for failing to maintain adequate internal controls and risk management practices, resulting in a $6.2 billion loss in trading losses.

Enhance reputation: Compliance best practices help build a positive reputation for financial institutions by demonstrating their commitment to ethical conduct, customer protection, and regulatory compliance. A strong reputation can lead to increased customer loyalty, business growth, and improved market performance. On the other hand, a poor reputation due to compliance failures can result in a loss of customers and business opportunities. For instance, after Wells Fargo's fake account scandal in 2016, the bank faced a significant drop in customer satisfaction and trust.

Increase efficiency: Compliance best practices can also help financial institutions operate more efficiently by streamlining processes, reducing errors, and eliminating redundancies. This can result in cost savings and increased productivity. For example, implementing automated compliance monitoring and reporting systems can reduce the time and effort required to monitor and report compliance activities.

Foster ethical culture: Compliance best practices can help foster an ethical culture within financial institutions by setting the tone from the top and emphasizing the importance of ethical conduct and regulatory compliance. This can lead to improved employee morale, retention, and engagement, as well as increased customer trust and loyalty. In contrast, a lack of ethical culture can result in compliance failures and reputational damage. For example, in 2015, the Volkswagen Group faced a scandal when it was revealed that the company had installed software in diesel engines to cheat emissions tests, resulting in a significant loss of trust and credibility.

Improve risk management: Compliance best practices can also improve risk management by providing a framework for identifying, assessing, and mitigating risks associated with non-compliance. This can lead to more effective risk management practices and better decision-making. For instance, implementing risk-based compliance programs can help financial institutions prioritize their compliance efforts based on the level of risk associated with specific activities.

Competitive advantage: Finally, compliance best practices can provide a competitive advantage for financial institutions by differentiating them from their competitors and attracting customers who value ethical conduct and regulatory compliance. This can result in increased market share and revenue growth. For example, in 2019, BlackRock announced that it would be putting sustainability at the center of its investment strategy, setting it apart from other asset managers and attracting customers who prioritize environmental, social, and governance (ESG) considerations.

In conclusion, compliance best practices are essential for financial institutions to mitigate risk, enhance reputation, increase efficiency, foster ethical culture, improve risk management, and gain a competitive advantage. By implementing and adhering to compliance best practices, financial institutions can achieve long-term success while maintaining their commitment to regulatory compliance, ethical conduct, and customer protection.

II. Compliance Strategies for Financial Firms

In today's complex and ever-changing regulatory environment, financial firms must remain vigilant in their compliance efforts to avoid costly fines, reputational damage, and legal consequences. Compliance strategies are crucial for financial firms, and it is essential to understand the various compliance strategies available to them.

Compliance is a critical aspect of any financial firm's operations, and it refers to the process of following applicable laws, regulations, and guidelines that are relevant to the firm's business activities. Compliance strategies refer to the various techniques and methods that financial firms use to ensure they are complying with all relevant laws and regulations.

The financial industry is highly regulated, and compliance is a constant concern for financial firms of all sizes. The financial sector's regulatory environment has become more complex in recent years, and compliance challenges have become more significant. Therefore, financial firms must implement robust compliance strategies to remain compliant with regulations and laws.

The financial sector has experienced significant regulatory changes in recent years, which have affected the compliance landscape. The Dodd-Frank Wall Street Reform and Consumer Protection Act (Dodd-Frank Act) is one such regulation that has significantly impacted the financial industry's compliance landscape. The Dodd-Frank Act imposes new requirements and regulations on financial firms, such as enhanced reporting and record-keeping requirements.

The implementation of compliance strategies is essential for financial firms to maintain their reputation, credibility, and trust with their clients and stakeholders. Compliance strategies also play a vital role in mitigating risks associated with non-compliance, such as legal risks and financial risks.

Financial firms have various compliance strategies available to them, and the selection of the appropriate compliance strategy depends on various factors, such as the size of the firm, the firm's business activities, and the regulatory environment in which the firm operates.

Some of the most common compliance strategies used by financial firms include establishing compliance policies and procedures, conducting regular compliance audits and assessments, and implementing training programs for employees to raise awareness of compliance issues.

In conclusion, compliance is a crucial aspect of any financial firm's operations, and compliance strategies are essential for maintaining compliance with all relevant laws and regulations. The financial industry's regulatory environment is constantly evolving, and financial firms must be proactive in implementing robust compliance strategies to mitigate the risks associated with non-compliance. Financial firms have various compliance strategies available to them, and the selection of the appropriate compliance strategy depends on various factors, such as the size of the firm, the firm's business activities, and the regulatory environment in which the firm operates.

Overview of compliance strategies

Financial firms operate in a highly regulated industry, and compliance with these regulations is crucial to their success. Failing to comply with regulations can lead to legal consequences, reputational damage, and loss of business. Therefore, financial firms must develop compliance strategies that ensure they operate within the boundaries of the law and regulations.

Compliance strategies refer to the policies, procedures, and practices that financial firms use to ensure compliance with regulations. These strategies aim to promote a culture of compliance throughout the organization, ensure compliance risks are identified and managed, and mitigate the risk of non-compliance.

The compliance strategies used by financial firms vary depending on the size of the organization, the complexity of their operations, and the nature of the regulations they must comply with. However, some general compliance strategies that are commonly used include:

Developing a compliance program: Financial firms should develop a compliance program that outlines the policies and procedures they will use to ensure compliance with regulations. This program should be regularly reviewed and updated to ensure it is effective and up-to-date.

Conducting regular risk assessments: Financial firms should regularly assess the risks associated with their operations and the regulations they must comply with. This will help identify potential compliance risks and enable the firm to implement measures to mitigate those risks.

Providing compliance training: Financial firms should provide compliance training to all employees to ensure they understand the regulations they must comply with and the consequences of non-compliance. This training should be regularly updated to ensure it reflects changes in regulations.

Monitoring compliance: Financial firms should regularly monitor compliance with regulations to identify any issues or breaches. This can be done through regular audits, risk assessments, and monitoring of employee behavior.

Establishing a compliance culture: Financial firms should establish a culture of compliance throughout the organization. This involves ensuring that compliance is seen as a core value and that employees understand the importance of compliance in their day-to-day activities.

Compliance strategies can also be categorized into preventative and detective strategies. Preventative strategies aim to prevent compliance issues from occurring, while detective strategies aim to identify compliance issues after they have occurred.

Preventative strategies include:

Designing controls and procedures to ensure compliance with regulations.

Conducting regular training and education programs to ensure employees are aware of their obligations under regulations.

Developing policies and procedures that align with regulatory requirements.

Detective strategies include:

Conducting regular audits of compliance controls to ensure they are working as intended.

Monitoring employee activities to identify any compliance issues.

Conducting investigations into suspected compliance breaches.

Financial firms must also consider the regulatory environment in which they operate when developing their compliance strategies. Regulations vary by jurisdiction, and firms must ensure they are compliant with the regulations in each jurisdiction in which they operate.

Moreover, the regulatory environment is constantly changing, and financial firms must be able to adapt their compliance strategies accordingly. This requires a proactive approach to compliance, with firms continually monitoring changes in the regulatory environment and adjusting their compliance strategies as needed.

In conclusion, compliance strategies are critical for financial firms to operate within the boundaries of the law and regulations. These strategies aim to promote a culture of compliance throughout the organization, ensure compliance risks are identified and managed, and mitigate the risk of non-compliance. Compliance strategies can vary depending on the size of the organization, the complexity of their operations, and the nature of the regulations they must comply with. Nevertheless, the five general strategies outlined above can serve as a starting point for firms looking to develop or improve their compliance strategies.

Key compliance strategies for financial firms

In the fast-paced and ever-evolving world of finance, it is critical for financial firms to comply with regulations and adhere to ethical standards. Compliance strategies refer to the policies and practices put in place to ensure compliance with regulatory requirements and ethical standards. The implementation of effective compliance strategies is vital for the long-term success of financial firms as non-compliance can lead to severe legal, financial, and reputational consequences. In this section, we will discuss key compliance strategies for financial firms, including regulatory compliance, risk management, and ethical behavior.

Regulatory Compliance:
Regulatory compliance is the cornerstone of an effective compliance strategy. Financial firms must comply with a vast array of regulations, including those governing securities, banking, and insurance. The regulations are designed to protect consumers and maintain the stability of the financial system. Compliance with these regulations involves the implementation of internal controls, policies, and procedures to ensure that the firm is operating in accordance with the regulatory requirements.

For example, investment bankers must comply with regulations such as the Securities Act of 1933, the Securities Exchange Act of 1934, and the Dodd-Frank Act. Compliance with these regulations involves ensuring that all information provided to clients is accurate and not misleading. Failure to comply with these regulations can lead to severe legal consequences, including fines and imprisonment.

Risk Management:
Risk management is another critical component of a compliance strategy. Financial firms must identify, assess, and mitigate risks to protect themselves and their clients. This involves implementing internal controls to monitor and manage risks, such as credit risk, market risk, and operational risk. Risk management also involves ensuring that the firm has adequate capital and liquidity to withstand unforeseen events.

For example, portfolio managers must manage the risk associated with their portfolios. This involves diversifying investments to minimize risk and ensuring that the portfolio is in line with the client's investment objectives. Failure to manage risks effectively can lead to significant financial losses and reputational damage.

Ethical Behavior:
In addition to regulatory compliance and risk management, financial firms must also ensure that they are acting ethically. Ethical behavior involves operating with integrity, honesty, and fairness, and avoiding conflicts of interest. It is essential to maintain a strong ethical culture within the firm and to promote ethical behavior through training and communication.

For example, securities traders must avoid conflicts of interest and act in the best interest of their clients. Failure to act ethically can lead to significant reputational damage and loss of clients.

Conclusion:
In conclusion, financial firms must implement effective compliance strategies to ensure compliance with regulatory requirements, manage risks, and act ethically. These strategies involve the implementation of internal controls, policies, and procedures to ensure that the firm is operating in accordance with the regulatory requirements. The implementation of these strategies is essential for the long-term success of financial firms, as non-compliance can lead to severe legal, financial, and reputational consequences. Financial firms must ensure that they have a strong compliance culture and that they promote ethical behavior throughout the organization.

Challenges in implementing compliance strategies

Compliance strategies are essential for financial firms to ensure that they are adhering to legal and regulatory requirements. These strategies are designed to promote ethical behavior, maintain the integrity of the financial system, and protect consumers from fraudulent activities. However, implementing compliance strategies can be a challenging task, and financial firms face several obstacles in the process. In this section, we will discuss the challenges in implementing compliance strategies and suggest some solutions to overcome them.

Complexity of Regulations

One of the most significant challenges in implementing compliance strategies is the complexity of regulations. Financial firms need to comply with a wide range of regulations, including anti-money laundering, anti-bribery, and data protection laws. The regulations can be complex, and interpreting them correctly can be difficult. The complexity of the regulations can lead to confusion and can make it challenging for financial firms to comply with them.

Solution: Financial firms need to invest in training programs to ensure that their employees understand the regulations correctly. They should also seek expert advice and guidance to interpret the regulations accurately. Having a compliance officer who has the necessary knowledge and expertise can also help financial firms stay up to date with the regulations.

High Cost of Compliance

Implementing compliance strategies can be expensive. Financial firms need to invest in technology, personnel, and training to ensure that they comply with the regulations. The cost of compliance can be particularly high for smaller firms that may not have the resources to invest in compliance.

Solution: Financial firms can reduce the cost of compliance by outsourcing some of the compliance functions to third-party service providers. These providers can offer specialized compliance services at a lower cost than in-house personnel. Financial firms can also use technology to automate some of the compliance functions, which can save time and money.

Resistance to Change

Implementing compliance strategies often requires changes to existing processes and procedures, which can meet resistance from employees who are comfortable with the old ways of doing things. Employees may see compliance as a burden and may resist changes to their work practices.

Solution: Financial firms need to ensure that they communicate the benefits of compliance to their employees. They should make it clear that compliance is not an optional extra, but an essential part of the business. Financial firms should also involve their employees in the compliance process and encourage feedback and suggestions for improvement.

Inadequate Technology Infrastructure

Compliance strategies require technology infrastructure that can capture and process large amounts of data. Financial firms that do not have the necessary technology infrastructure may struggle to comply with the regulations effectively.

Solution: Financial firms need to invest in technology infrastructure that can support their compliance strategies. They should consider using cloud-based solutions that can scale with their business and offer secure data storage and processing capabilities. Financial firms should also seek expert advice to ensure that they choose the right technology solutions for their compliance needs.

Lack of Resources

Implementing compliance strategies requires resources, including personnel, technology, and time. Financial firms that are short on resources may struggle to implement effective compliance strategies.

Solution: Financial firms need to prioritize compliance and allocate the necessary resources to ensure that they comply with the regulations. They can also consider partnering with other firms to share resources and reduce the cost of compliance.

In conclusion, implementing compliance strategies can be a challenging task for financial firms. The complexity of regulations, high cost of compliance, resistance to change, inadequate technology infrastructure, and lack of resources are some of the challenges that financial firms may face. However, with the right solutions, financial firms can overcome these challenges and ensure that they comply with the regulations effectively.

CHAPTER 35: THE FUTURE OF REGULATION IN FINANCE

In recent years, the financial sector has been subject to numerous regulatory changes aimed at improving the stability and transparency of financial markets. These regulatory changes have been prompted by the financial crisis of 2008 and the subsequent efforts to prevent a similar crisis from occurring in the future.

As the financial sector continues to evolve, it is essential for financial firms to stay up-to-date with future regulatory and compliance issues. These issues include topics such as digital currencies, artificial intelligence, and climate change, which will have a significant impact on the future of finance.

In this chapter, we will provide an overview of some of the future regulatory and compliance issues that financial firms should be aware of. We will also discuss the importance of understanding these issues and how they can impact financial firms.

Overview of Future Regulatory and Compliance Issues:

Digital Currencies:
One of the most significant developments in the financial sector over the past decade has been the emergence of digital currencies, such as Bitcoin and Ethereum. Digital currencies are decentralized, meaning they are not controlled by a central authority such as a government or financial institution.

As digital currencies continue to gain popularity, regulators are struggling to keep up with the regulatory challenges they present. For example, how should digital currencies be taxed? What are the risks of using digital currencies for money laundering or terrorist financing?

Financial firms that deal with digital currencies will need to be aware of the regulatory landscape and comply with any regulations that are put in place.

Artificial Intelligence:
Artificial intelligence (AI) is another significant development that is transforming the financial sector. AI has the potential to automate many tasks currently performed by humans, such as trading and risk management.

While AI has many potential benefits, it also presents significant regulatory challenges. For example, how can regulators ensure that AI algorithms are transparent and not biased? How can regulators ensure that AI is not used for fraudulent purposes?

Financial firms that use AI will need to be aware of the regulatory landscape and comply with any regulations that are put in place.

Climate Change:
Climate change is another issue that will have a significant impact on the financial sector in the coming years. As governments around the world take action to mitigate the effects of climate change, financial firms will need to adapt to new regulations and reporting requirements.

For example, financial firms may be required to disclose the carbon footprint of their investments or implement policies to reduce their carbon emissions. Financial firms that ignore the impact of climate change risk being left behind as regulators and investors increasingly focus on sustainability.

Importance of Understanding Future Regulatory and Compliance Issues:

Understanding future regulatory and compliance issues is essential for financial firms for several reasons:

Compliance: Financial firms that fail to comply with regulations face significant legal and financial risks. By understanding future regulatory and compliance issues, firms can proactively implement compliance measures, reducing the risk of non-compliance.

Innovation: Financial firms that understand the regulatory landscape can more effectively innovate and take advantage of new developments such as digital currencies and AI. By staying ahead of regulatory changes, firms can be more agile and responsive to new opportunities.

Reputation: Financial firms that demonstrate a commitment to compliance and regulatory best practices can build a positive reputation with regulators, investors, and customers. This can be a significant competitive advantage in a crowded market.

Conclusion:

As the financial sector continues to evolve, it is essential for financial firms to stay up-to-date with future regulatory and compliance issues. Digital currencies, artificial intelligence, and climate change are just a few of the significant developments that will shape the future of finance.

By understanding these issues and proactively implementing compliance measures, financial firms can reduce their legal and financial risks, innovate more effectively, and build a positive reputation with regulators, investors, and customers.

I. Emerging Trends in Financial Regulation

Financial regulation has been an essential element of the financial industry for centuries. As the financial sector continues to evolve and expand, it has become increasingly important for regulators to stay ahead of the curve to ensure that the industry operates smoothly and transparently. In recent years, financial regulators have been facing new challenges and opportunities as emerging trends in technology, globalization, and environmental, social, and governance (ESG) factors have been transforming the financial landscape.

The objective of this chapter is to provide an overview of the emerging trends in financial regulation and their implications for the future of the financial industry. In particular, we will focus on the following emerging trends:

Technology-driven innovation
Globalization
Environmental, social, and governance (ESG) factors
We will examine the ways in which these trends are shaping the financial industry and the challenges and opportunities they pose for regulators. Additionally, we will explore the implications of these trends for financial institutions and their clients.

It is important for financial professionals to stay abreast of these emerging trends as they have the potential to significantly impact the financial industry in the years to come. In order to be effective and efficient, financial institutions must understand the regulatory environment in which they operate, anticipate the changes that are likely to occur, and take proactive measures to comply with regulatory requirements.

Given the complexity of the financial industry and the dynamic nature of the regulatory landscape, it is important for financial professionals to work together with regulators to ensure that the industry continues to operate smoothly and efficiently. Effective collaboration between financial institutions and regulators can help to ensure that the regulatory framework is responsive to the needs of the industry while maintaining a high level of oversight and transparency.

In conclusion, the emerging trends in financial regulation pose both challenges and opportunities for the financial industry. It is imperative that financial professionals stay abreast of these trends, work together with regulators to ensure compliance with regulatory requirements, and take proactive measures to anticipate and adapt to the changing regulatory landscape.

Overview of emerging trends

Financial regulation is an essential aspect of modern finance, and it plays a crucial role in maintaining market stability, protecting consumers and investors, and ensuring fair and transparent financial practices. Over the years, financial regulation has evolved to keep up with changes in the financial landscape, and new trends are emerging that are shaping the future of financial regulation. In this section, we will provide an overview of emerging trends in financial regulation and discuss their implications for financial firms and regulators.

Overview of Emerging Trends

Technological Innovation
Technological innovation is transforming the financial industry, and it is also driving changes in financial regulation. Fintech firms are disrupting traditional financial services, and regulators are struggling to keep up with the pace of change. For instance, the rise of cryptocurrencies and blockchain technology has created new challenges for financial regulators, who are still trying to understand the implications of these new technologies. Regulators are also grappling with issues related to data privacy, cybersecurity, and algorithmic trading.

Investment bankers are at the forefront of technological innovation, and they are leveraging new technologies to improve the efficiency and effectiveness of their operations. For example, investment bankers are using artificial intelligence and machine learning algorithms to analyze market data, identify investment opportunities, and manage risk. Similarly, quantitative analysts are using big data analytics to develop predictive models that can help financial firms make more informed investment decisions.

Globalization
Globalization is another trend that is shaping the future of financial regulation. Financial firms are expanding their operations across borders, and this has created new challenges for regulators. Different countries have different regulatory frameworks, and financial firms must navigate a complex regulatory landscape to comply with local regulations.

Portfolio managers are directly impacted by globalization, as they must manage investments in different markets and comply with local regulations. Similarly, securities traders must be aware of the different rules and regulations that apply to trading in different markets. Actuaries also face new challenges as they must evaluate risks associated with investments in different markets.

Climate Change
Climate change is emerging as a critical issue for financial regulators. The financial industry is a significant contributor to greenhouse gas emissions, and it is also vulnerable to the physical and transition risks associated with climate change. Regulators are now recognizing the importance of incorporating climate risk into their regulatory frameworks to ensure that financial firms are adequately managing these risks.

Financial planners and financial analysts are increasingly incorporating climate risk into their investment strategies. They are evaluating the potential impact of climate change on different industries and sectors and are developing investment strategies that can help mitigate these risks.

Social Responsibility
Social responsibility is becoming increasingly important for financial firms and regulators. Investors are becoming more conscious of the social and environmental impact of their investments, and they are demanding greater transparency and accountability from financial firms. Regulators are also recognizing the importance of promoting socially responsible investing and are developing new frameworks to incentivize financial firms to prioritize social and environmental considerations in their investment decisions.

Conclusion

In conclusion, financial regulation is continuously evolving, and new trends are emerging that are shaping the future of financial regulation. Technological innovation, globalization, climate change, and social responsibility are some of the trends that are influencing financial regulation today. Financial firms and regulators must be aware of these emerging trends and must adapt their operations and regulatory frameworks to keep up with the changing landscape of finance. Investment bankers, portfolio managers, quantitative analysts, securities traders, actuaries, financial planners, and financial analysts must all be familiar with these emerging trends to succeed in the ever-changing world of finance.

Impact of technology on regulation

Advancements in technology have brought about significant changes in the financial industry, including the way financial institutions conduct business and the regulatory landscape in which they operate. As such, it is essential for regulators and financial institutions to adapt to these changes to ensure they remain compliant with the evolving regulatory requirements.

This section will explore the impact of technology on financial regulation, highlighting some of the emerging trends and challenges associated with technology adoption in regulatory compliance.

Impact of Technology on Regulatory Compliance:

The use of technology has had a profound impact on the financial services industry, with many firms leveraging technology to streamline their operations and reduce costs. For example, artificial intelligence (AI) and machine learning (ML) algorithms are being used to automate routine tasks, such as fraud detection and risk assessment. Additionally, blockchain technology is being used to improve transparency and reduce transaction costs.

However, the use of technology in regulatory compliance is still relatively new and presents a unique set of challenges. One such challenge is the sheer volume of data generated by financial institutions, which can be difficult to manage and analyze manually. This has led to an increasing reliance on technology-based solutions, such as regulatory compliance software, to automate compliance processes.

Another challenge associated with technology adoption in regulatory compliance is the need for effective data governance. Financial institutions are required to collect, store, and analyze large amounts of sensitive data, which creates data privacy and security concerns. Financial institutions must ensure that they have the necessary controls in place to protect their customers' data and comply with data privacy regulations such as the General Data Protection Regulation (GDPR) and the California Consumer Privacy Act (CCPA).

Furthermore, there is a need for regulators to keep up with technological advancements to ensure that their regulations remain relevant and effective. Failure to do so could lead to a regulatory gap, where new technologies are not adequately addressed by existing regulations, potentially leading to increased risk and vulnerability in the financial system.

Emerging Trends in Technology and Regulatory Compliance:

One emerging trend in technology and regulatory compliance is the use of RegTech solutions. RegTech is a term used to describe technology-based solutions that are designed to help financial institutions comply with regulatory requirements. RegTech solutions use advanced technologies, such as AI and ML, to automate compliance processes, monitor transactions for suspicious activity, and ensure data privacy and security.

Another trend in technology and regulatory compliance is the use of blockchain technology. Blockchain technology is a distributed ledger technology that allows for secure and transparent transactions. Financial institutions are leveraging blockchain technology to improve transparency and reduce transaction costs, while regulators are exploring the use of blockchain technology to improve regulatory oversight.

The use of cloud computing is another trend in technology and regulatory compliance. Cloud computing allows financial institutions to store and access data and applications on remote servers, reducing the need for on-premise infrastructure. While cloud computing offers several benefits, such as scalability and cost-effectiveness, it also presents several security and compliance challenges that need to be addressed.

Conclusion:

The impact of technology on regulatory compliance cannot be overstated. Technology is transforming the financial services industry, and regulators and financial institutions need to adapt to these changes to remain compliant and competitive. While technology adoption presents several challenges, such as data privacy and security concerns, emerging trends, such as RegTech solutions, blockchain technology, and cloud computing, offer promising solutions to these challenges. As such, financial institutions and regulators must continue to collaborate and explore new technologies to ensure that their regulatory compliance efforts remain effective and efficient.

Globalization and its impact on regulation

Globalization, the phenomenon of increased interconnectedness among countries and their economies, has had a profound impact on financial regulation. As countries become more connected through trade and investment, there is a growing need for global coordination and cooperation in financial regulation to ensure the stability and safety of the global financial system. In this section, we will explore the impact of globalization on financial regulation and examine some of the emerging trends in this area.

One of the key effects of globalization on financial regulation is the increased need for international coordination and cooperation. As financial markets become more interconnected, the actions of one country's regulators can have a significant impact on the stability and safety of financial systems in other countries. For example, the 2008 global financial crisis was caused in part by the failure of US financial institutions, but its effects were felt around the world. In response, international bodies such as the G20, the International Monetary Fund (IMF), and the Financial Stability Board (FSB) have been working to increase cooperation and coordination among countries in the regulation of financial markets.

Another important aspect of globalization is the increasing role of multinational corporations in the global economy. These companies often have operations in multiple countries and may engage in complex financial transactions that can be difficult to regulate. This has led to a growing recognition of the need for a more coordinated approach to regulation, particularly in areas such as tax avoidance and money laundering.

One emerging trend in this area is the increased use of technology in financial regulation. For example, the use of blockchain technology can provide a more secure and transparent way to track financial transactions across borders, which could help to prevent money laundering and other illegal activities. At the same time, the use of artificial intelligence and machine learning algorithms can help regulators to more effectively detect and respond to potential risks in the financial system.

Another emerging trend is the rise of regional and bilateral trade agreements that include provisions related to financial regulation. For example, the Trans-Pacific Partnership (TPP) and the Comprehensive and Progressive Agreement for Trans-Pacific Partnership (CPTPP) both include chapters on financial services that aim to promote greater cooperation and coordination among member countries in the regulation of financial markets. Similarly, the European Union's (EU) Single Market initiative has led to greater harmonization of financial regulation across member states.

However, globalization has also brought about some challenges for financial regulation. One of the main challenges is the so-called "race to the bottom" in which countries lower their regulatory standards in order to attract investment and remain competitive. This can lead to a situation in which countries are reluctant to adopt higher standards for fear of losing out on investment opportunities. In addition, the increasing complexity and interconnectivity of financial markets can make it difficult for regulators to keep up with new developments and emerging risks.

In conclusion, globalization has had a profound impact on financial regulation, creating both opportunities and challenges for policymakers and regulators. The need for greater international coordination and cooperation is increasingly recognized as essential for ensuring the stability and safety of the global financial system. Emerging trends such as the use of technology and the rise of regional and bilateral trade agreements are likely to continue to shape the future of financial regulation in the years to come. However, challenges such as the "race to the bottom" and the increasing complexity of financial markets will need to be addressed in order to ensure effective regulation and a stable financial system.

Geopolitical developments and their impact on regulation

Geopolitical developments are complex and dynamic events that can have a significant impact on financial regulation. Geopolitical developments are often driven by shifting global power dynamics, changes in the global economic landscape, and changing global security concerns. In this section, we will explore the impact of geopolitical developments on financial regulation, examining the key trends, challenges, and opportunities in this area.

One of the most significant geopolitical developments of recent years has been the rise of China as a global economic power. China's economic rise has led to an increasing shift in global power dynamics, with China emerging as a significant rival to the United States. As a result, this has raised a number of challenges for financial regulation, as regulators must adapt to the changing global landscape.

One of the key challenges posed by China's rise has been the need to ensure that financial regulation keeps pace with China's growing influence in the global economy. This has involved developing new regulatory frameworks that are designed to address the unique challenges of operating in the Chinese market. For example, Chinese companies often operate under different rules and regulations than their counterparts in the United States or Europe, which has led to a growing need for international cooperation in the area of financial regulation.

Another important geopolitical trend that is impacting financial regulation is the rise of populism and nationalism around the world. Populist movements have been gaining ground in many countries, driven by a range of factors, including economic inequality, globalization, and immigration. These movements have had a significant impact on financial regulation, as they have led to a growing demand for increased protectionism and a greater focus on domestic economic concerns.

This has led to a range of challenges for financial regulators, as they must balance the need for international cooperation with the growing demand for domestic protectionism. For example, many countries are increasingly imposing restrictions on foreign investment, which has led to a growing need for regulators to develop new frameworks for managing cross-border investment flows.

At the same time, geopolitical developments are also creating new opportunities for financial regulators. For example, the growing importance of digital currencies and blockchain technology has led to a growing need for international cooperation in the area of financial regulation. As digital currencies become more widely adopted, there is a growing need for regulators to develop new frameworks for managing the risks associated with these technologies, including issues related to money laundering, fraud, and cyber security.

Overall, the impact of geopolitical developments on financial regulation is complex and multifaceted. While these developments present a range of challenges for regulators, they also create new opportunities for international cooperation and collaboration. As the global landscape continues to evolve, it will be important for financial regulators to remain vigilant, adapting their approaches to address the unique challenges posed by changing global dynamics.

II. Future Regulatory and Compliance Challenges

In today's rapidly evolving global economy, businesses of all sizes face significant regulatory and compliance challenges. These challenges arise from a wide range of factors, including technological advancements, globalization, geopolitical developments, and shifting societal expectations. As a result, companies must navigate complex regulatory environments, respond to new and emerging risks, and adapt to changing compliance requirements.

In this section, we will explore the future regulatory and compliance challenges facing businesses across various industries. We will begin by examining the impact of technology on regulation, including the use of artificial intelligence, blockchain, and other emerging technologies. Next, we will analyze the effects of globalization on regulation, including the challenges associated with navigating differing legal and regulatory frameworks in different countries. We will then discuss the impact of geopolitical developments on regulation, including the rise of populism and the increased scrutiny of international trade and investment. Finally, we will examine the future of regulatory compliance, including the increasing focus on ethical considerations and the role of corporate social responsibility in regulatory compliance.

Throughout this section, we will draw on examples from a variety of industries, including investment banking, actuarial science, portfolio management, quantitative analysis, securities trading, financial planning, and financial analysis. We will also present counterarguments and dissenting opinions in a balanced and objective manner to provide a comprehensive and nuanced understanding of the issues at hand.

Overall, our analysis will demonstrate that regulatory and compliance challenges are becoming increasingly complex and multifaceted. Businesses must be prepared to adapt to these challenges in order to thrive in a global economy that demands transparency, accountability, and ethical behavior.

Overview of future regulatory and compliance challenges

The financial industry is constantly evolving, and as it does, it brings with it new regulatory and compliance challenges. In today's fast-paced and increasingly globalized world, businesses are faced with a wide range of regulatory and compliance requirements that can be difficult to navigate. As technology continues to advance and new geopolitical developments arise, these challenges are only expected to grow. In this section, we will provide an overview of the future regulatory and compliance challenges facing businesses across a variety of industries, including the financial sector.

Technological Developments:

Technology is rapidly transforming the financial industry, and as it does, it brings with it a host of regulatory and compliance challenges. With the rise of fintech and blockchain technology, businesses are faced with new risks related to cybersecurity and data privacy. These risks can be particularly acute for financial institutions, which handle sensitive financial and personal information. As the use of artificial intelligence and machine learning algorithms becomes more widespread, businesses must also grapple with how to ensure that these technologies are being used ethically and in compliance with regulatory requirements.

Furthermore, as the use of technology becomes more pervasive, regulators will likely need to adapt their approaches to supervision and enforcement. Regulators will need to become more tech-savvy in order to keep up with the rapid pace of technological innovation and ensure that businesses are complying with relevant regulations.

Geopolitical Developments:

Geopolitical developments can also have a significant impact on regulatory and compliance challenges. As we have seen in recent years, political instability and economic sanctions can disrupt financial markets and create new compliance challenges. For example, businesses may need to navigate complex sanctions regimes when doing business in certain countries or with certain individuals. Similarly, businesses may need to take extra precautions to ensure that they are not inadvertently facilitating money laundering or terrorist financing activities.

In addition to these challenges, geopolitical developments can also lead to increased regulatory scrutiny. For example, following the 2008 financial crisis, regulators around the world enacted a wide range of new regulations aimed at reducing systemic risk in the financial system. As geopolitical developments continue to unfold, businesses can expect similar regulatory responses aimed at addressing new risks and challenges.

Environmental, Social, and Governance (ESG) Factors:

In recent years, there has been a growing recognition of the importance of environmental, social, and governance (ESG) factors in investment decision-making. As investors increasingly look to incorporate ESG factors into their investment strategies, businesses are faced with new regulatory and compliance challenges. For example, businesses may need to disclose more information about their environmental impact, labor practices, and corporate governance structures.

In addition to these disclosure requirements, businesses may also need to implement new policies and procedures aimed at mitigating ESG-related risks. For example, businesses may need to ensure that their supply chains are free from forced labor or that their operations do not harm local communities or the environment.

Conclusion:

As the financial industry continues to evolve, businesses will face an ever-increasing array of regulatory and compliance challenges. Whether related to technological developments, geopolitical developments, or ESG factors, these challenges will require businesses to be nimble and adaptable in order to stay ahead of the curve. By staying informed about the latest regulatory developments and trends, businesses can ensure that they are well-prepared to meet these challenges head-on.

Key challenges for financial firms

The financial industry has been subject to increasing regulatory and compliance requirements over the years. Financial firms are required to comply with a range of rules and regulations that are designed to protect the interests of customers and investors, promote financial stability, and ensure fair and transparent financial markets. Compliance with these regulations is crucial for financial firms to maintain their reputation, avoid penalties, and retain customers.

However, the regulatory landscape is constantly evolving, and financial firms are facing an increasing number of challenges as they seek to comply with new and complex regulations. This section will discuss some of the key challenges that financial firms are facing in the area of regulatory and compliance.

Cybersecurity:
One of the biggest challenges for financial firms is cybersecurity. Financial firms are increasingly being targeted by cybercriminals who are seeking to gain access to sensitive customer data or steal money from accounts. The financial industry is particularly vulnerable to cyber attacks due to the large amount of valuable data that financial firms hold.

Cybersecurity regulations are becoming increasingly stringent, and financial firms are required to implement sophisticated cybersecurity measures to protect themselves against cyber threats. Failure to comply with these regulations can result in severe financial penalties and reputational damage.

Anti-Money Laundering (AML) and Counter-Terrorist Financing (CTF):
AML and CTF regulations are designed to prevent money laundering and the financing of terrorist activities. Financial firms are required to implement AML and CTF measures to detect and prevent suspicious transactions.

However, AML and CTF regulations are complex and can be difficult to comply with. Financial firms are required to implement sophisticated transaction monitoring systems to detect suspicious activity, which can be time-consuming and costly.

Know Your Customer (KYC):
KYC regulations are designed to prevent financial crime by ensuring that financial firms know their customers and are not unwittingly involved in illegal activities. Financial firms are required to collect and verify customer information, including identity, source of funds, and business activities.

KYC regulations are becoming increasingly stringent, and financial firms are required to implement sophisticated customer due diligence processes to comply with these regulations. Failure to comply with KYC regulations can result in severe financial penalties and reputational damage.

Data Protection:
Financial firms hold large amounts of sensitive customer data, and are required to protect this data from unauthorized access and use. Data protection regulations are becoming increasingly stringent, and financial firms are required to implement sophisticated data protection measures to comply with these regulations.

Failure to comply with data protection regulations can result in severe financial penalties and reputational damage.

Cross-Border Regulations:
Financial firms that operate across multiple jurisdictions are subject to a range of cross-border regulations, including tax regulations, data protection regulations, and anti-corruption regulations. These regulations can be complex and difficult to comply with, and failure to comply can result in severe financial penalties and reputational damage.

Conclusion:

The regulatory and compliance landscape is constantly evolving, and financial firms are facing an increasing number of challenges as they seek to comply with new and complex regulations. Cybersecurity, AML and CTF, KYC, data protection, and cross-border regulations are just some of the key challenges that financial firms are facing.

Compliance with these regulations is crucial for financial firms to maintain their reputation, avoid penalties, and retain customers. Financial firms must ensure that they are implementing robust compliance programs that are able to keep up with the rapidly changing regulatory landscape.

Strategies for addressing future regulatory and compliance challenges

In the fast-paced and ever-evolving financial industry, regulatory and compliance challenges have become increasingly complex and demanding. With the rise of new technologies, changing geopolitical developments, and the growing importance of environmental, social, and governance (ESG) factors, financial firms must navigate a complex regulatory landscape while also meeting the demands of their clients.

In this section, we will discuss key strategies that financial firms can implement to address future regulatory and compliance challenges. These strategies include embracing new technologies, establishing robust compliance programs, enhancing risk management practices, and improving transparency and communication with stakeholders.

Embracing new technologies:

One of the key strategies that financial firms can adopt to address future regulatory and compliance challenges is to embrace new technologies. Technological advancements in areas such as artificial intelligence (AI), blockchain, and big data analytics can help firms automate compliance processes, reduce costs, and improve efficiency.

For example, AI-powered compliance solutions can help firms identify and mitigate regulatory risks by automating processes such as due diligence, monitoring, and reporting. Similarly, blockchain can help firms improve transparency and accountability by providing an immutable and tamper-proof record of transactions.

Investment banks such as Goldman Sachs are already using AI to automate compliance processes and improve the accuracy of regulatory reporting. Other firms, such as JPMorgan Chase, are experimenting with blockchain technology to streamline the settlement of securities transactions and reduce the risks of errors and fraud.

Establishing robust compliance programs:

Another key strategy for financial firms to address future regulatory and compliance challenges is to establish robust compliance programs. A compliance program is a set of policies, procedures, and controls that are designed to ensure that a firm complies with applicable laws, regulations, and industry standards.

A robust compliance program should include a comprehensive risk assessment, training programs for employees, ongoing monitoring and testing, and a process for reporting and investigating compliance violations.

For example, investment management firms such as BlackRock and Vanguard have established robust compliance programs that include regular risk assessments, training programs for employees, and strong oversight by senior management. These programs have helped these firms to avoid regulatory penalties and maintain a strong reputation with their clients.

Enhancing risk management practices:

In addition to establishing robust compliance programs, financial firms can also enhance their risk management practices to address future regulatory and compliance challenges. Effective risk management involves identifying, assessing, and mitigating risks that may arise from the firm's activities.

Key risk management practices include setting risk tolerance levels, developing risk mitigation strategies, and regularly monitoring and reporting on risks.

For example, portfolio managers can use risk management tools such as value-at-risk (VaR) and stress testing to identify and manage portfolio risks. Investment banks can use scenario analysis to assess the impact of potential geopolitical events on their portfolios.

Improving transparency and communication:

Finally, financial firms can address future regulatory and compliance challenges by improving transparency and communication with stakeholders. Transparency involves providing clear and timely information to stakeholders, while communication involves engaging with stakeholders to understand their needs and concerns.

Financial firms can improve transparency and communication by providing clear and concise disclosures, engaging with stakeholders through regular meetings and forums, and responding to stakeholder feedback in a timely and constructive manner.

For example, asset managers such as BlackRock and State Street Global Advisors have increased their engagement with companies on ESG issues and have called for greater transparency and disclosure on these issues. Similarly, investment banks such as Goldman Sachs have increased their transparency and communication with clients on their ESG practices and policies.

Conclusion:

In conclusion, financial firms face a range of regulatory and compliance challenges in the fast-paced and ever-evolving financial industry. To address these challenges, firms can adopt key strategies such as embracing new technologies, establishing robust compliance programs, enhancing risk management practices, and improving transparency and communication with stakeholders. By implementing these strategies, firms can position themselves to navigate a complex regulatory landscape while also meeting the demands of an increasingly sophisticated consumer base.

However, it is important to note that regulatory and compliance challenges are not static and will continue to evolve in the future. As such, financial firms must remain agile and adaptable in their approach to regulatory compliance. This requires a commitment to ongoing education and training for staff, as well as a willingness to invest in new technologies and processes that can help streamline compliance efforts.

Moreover, collaboration with industry peers, regulators, and other stakeholders can also play an important role in addressing regulatory challenges. This can include sharing best practices, participating in industry-wide initiatives, and engaging in constructive dialogue with regulators and policymakers to help shape the regulatory landscape.

Overall, financial firms must view regulatory and compliance challenges as an opportunity to improve their operations, build trust with consumers, and ultimately enhance their long-term competitiveness. By adopting a proactive approach to compliance, firms can not only meet regulatory requirements but also strengthen their reputation as responsible and trustworthy players in the financial industry.

III. Opportunities for Innovation in Compliance

In the financial industry, compliance is an essential function that ensures firms operate within legal and regulatory frameworks. Compliance involves a range of activities, including monitoring and reporting on regulatory changes, implementing policies and procedures, and training employees on regulations and best practices. However, compliance has traditionally been seen as a cost center and a burden, rather than an opportunity for innovation and growth. In recent years, there has been a shift towards viewing compliance as a source of competitive advantage and a driver of innovation.

As financial firms face increasing regulatory pressure and scrutiny, there is an opportunity for firms to leverage compliance as a way to improve their operations, enhance customer experience, and drive growth. By embracing new technologies, adopting best practices, and fostering a culture of compliance, firms can position themselves to take advantage of new opportunities and stay ahead of the curve.

This section will explore the opportunities for innovation in compliance, examining the challenges and trends that are driving change in the industry. We will also explore the strategies that firms can adopt to take advantage of these opportunities and drive innovation in compliance. Finally, we will discuss the potential benefits of innovation in compliance and the role that it can play in shaping the future of the financial industry.

Challenges and Trends Driving Change:

One of the key challenges facing financial firms today is the ever-evolving regulatory landscape. Regulations are constantly changing, and firms must keep up with these changes to remain compliant. Failure to comply with regulations can result in fines, reputational damage, and legal liability. This challenge is compounded by the fact that regulations can be complex and difficult to understand, making it challenging for firms to keep up with changes.

Another challenge is the increasing use of technology in the financial industry. While technology has the potential to revolutionize compliance, it also presents new challenges. For example, the use of artificial intelligence (AI) and machine learning (ML) in compliance can improve efficiency and accuracy, but it also raises concerns around bias and data privacy. Additionally, the use of new technologies may require significant investment and expertise, making it difficult for smaller firms to keep up with larger competitors.

Trends driving change in compliance include the increasing use of data analytics and automation, the rise of regulatory technology (RegTech) solutions, and the shift towards a more customer-centric approach to compliance. Data analytics and automation can help firms to identify and mitigate compliance risks more quickly and effectively, while RegTech solutions can provide firms with the tools they need to stay compliant. The shift towards a more customer-centric approach to compliance involves focusing on the customer experience and using compliance as a way to build trust and loyalty with customers.

Strategies for Driving Innovation in Compliance:

To take advantage of the opportunities for innovation in compliance, financial firms can adopt a range of strategies. One key strategy is to embrace new technologies such as AI, ML, and blockchain. These technologies can help firms to automate compliance processes, improve accuracy, and reduce costs. For example, AI and ML can be used to analyze large amounts of data and identify patterns and anomalies that may indicate compliance risks. Blockchain can be used to provide a secure and transparent way to store and share compliance-related information.

Another strategy is to establish a culture of compliance within the organization. This involves creating a compliance-focused mindset and ensuring that compliance is viewed as a priority throughout the organization. This can be achieved through training and education programs, as well as by incentivizing compliance behaviors and embedding compliance into the organization's values and mission.

Firms can also leverage RegTech solutions to streamline compliance processes and improve efficiency. RegTech solutions can provide firms with tools for monitoring and reporting on regulatory changes, conducting risk assessments, and automating compliance-related tasks. By adopting these solutions, firms can reduce the time and resources required to stay compliant and free up staff to focus on more value-added activities.

Finally, firms can also take advantage of emerging technologies such as blockchain and artificial intelligence (AI) to further innovate their compliance practices. For example, blockchain technology can enable secure and transparent record-keeping, making it easier to track and verify transactions and data. This can help firms to better comply with regulations related to data privacy and security. AI, on the other hand, can be used to analyze large volumes of data and identify patterns and anomalies that may indicate non-compliance. This can help firms to detect and address potential compliance issues more quickly and efficiently.

While these technologies offer great potential for innovation in compliance, they also present their own unique challenges. For example, the use of blockchain technology may raise questions around legal and regulatory frameworks for digital records, while the use of AI raises concerns around bias and ethical considerations. Therefore, it is important for firms to approach these technologies with caution and to ensure that they are used in a responsible and ethical manner.

Overall, the opportunities for innovation in compliance are vast and varied, and financial firms that are able to effectively leverage new technologies and strategies will be better equipped to navigate the complex regulatory landscape and stay ahead of the competition. However, it is important for firms to strike a balance between innovation and compliance, ensuring that they meet regulatory requirements while also exploring new opportunities for growth and efficiency. By doing so, financial firms can position themselves for long-term success in a rapidly evolving industry.

Overview of opportunities for innovation

The financial industry is constantly evolving, with new technologies and innovations providing opportunities for firms to improve their operations and better serve their clients. One area of particular interest is compliance, where firms can leverage innovative solutions to streamline processes, reduce costs, and enhance the overall compliance culture.

One such opportunity for innovation is Arlingbrook, a new social media platform with comprehensive payment options. Arlingbrook aims to provide a unique user experience by integrating social media with payment systems, allowing users to seamlessly transfer funds while engaging with friends and colleagues online. The platform also plans to leverage emerging technologies like blockchain and cryptocurrency to enhance its services further. By creating its own cryptocurrency, Arlingbrook can facilitate instant payments, global transfers, and even incentivize users with rewards or bonuses for using the platform.

Another innovative approach to compliance is the integration of web3 technologies with traditional compliance processes. Web3 is a term used to describe the next evolution of the internet, where decentralized technologies like blockchain and smart contracts enable secure and transparent transactions without the need for intermediaries. By leveraging these technologies, firms can create more robust compliance systems that are not only secure but also more efficient and cost-effective.

For example, a financial firm could use smart contracts to automate compliance-related tasks such as reporting, monitoring, and risk assessments. Smart contracts are self-executing contracts that are encoded on a blockchain, allowing for automatic enforcement of compliance rules and regulations. This approach reduces the need for manual intervention, thereby reducing the potential for errors, delays, and other inefficiencies.

Furthermore, firms can use web3 technologies to create their own digital assets, such as tokens or non-fungible tokens (NFTs), that represent compliance-related assets. For instance, a firm could create a compliance token that represents its compliance program's effectiveness and maturity. This token could then be traded on a blockchain-based exchange, providing an additional layer of transparency and accountability.

In addition to Arlingbrook and web3 technologies, firms can also leverage emerging technologies such as artificial intelligence (AI) and machine learning (ML) to enhance their compliance programs. AI and ML can analyze vast amounts of data in real-time, providing insights into potential compliance risks and opportunities for improvement. This approach can help firms to proactively identify potential compliance violations before they occur and take corrective actions to prevent them.

Moreover, AI and ML can also help firms to automate repetitive compliance tasks, such as monitoring transactions or reviewing documents. This frees up staff to focus on more value-added activities, such as providing strategic guidance and advice to clients.

It is worth noting that these innovations come with their own set of challenges and risks. For instance, the use of blockchain and cryptocurrency can expose firms to new forms of cyber threats and financial risks. Moreover, the use of AI and ML requires robust data governance and privacy frameworks to ensure that data is handled ethically and securely.

Despite these challenges, the opportunities for innovation in compliance are vast and can have significant benefits for firms and their clients. By embracing new technologies and adopting innovative approaches, firms can create more efficient, effective, and resilient compliance programs that can better serve their clients' needs while reducing costs and risks.

Key areas for innovation in compliance

The financial industry is continuously evolving, and so are the regulatory and compliance requirements. To stay compliant and meet the expectations of regulators, financial institutions need to innovate and adopt new technologies and practices. This section will discuss the key areas for innovation in compliance and explore how firms can leverage technology and data to enhance compliance processes and reduce costs.

Automation of Compliance Processes:
Compliance processes can be repetitive and time-consuming, which can lead to increased costs and inefficiencies. One area for innovation in compliance is the automation of compliance processes. Automation can help firms to reduce the time and resources required to stay compliant and free up staff to focus on more value-added activities.

For example, RegTech solutions can provide firms with tools for monitoring and reporting on regulatory changes, conducting risk assessments, and automating compliance-related tasks. By adopting these solutions, firms can reduce the time and resources required to stay compliant and free up staff to focus on more value-added activities.

Enhanced Risk Management:
Effective risk management is essential for financial institutions to maintain a strong compliance posture. One area for innovation in compliance is the use of advanced analytics and machine learning to enhance risk management practices. These technologies can help firms to identify and assess risks in real-time and make informed decisions to mitigate those risks.

For example, a financial institution can use machine learning algorithms to analyze transaction data and identify potential cases of money laundering or fraud. By leveraging machine learning, firms can enhance their ability to detect suspicious activities and minimize the risks of financial crime.

Improved Communication and Transparency:
Communication and transparency are crucial for building trust with stakeholders and maintaining a strong compliance posture. One area for innovation in compliance is the use of new technologies to enhance communication and transparency.

For example, blockchain technology can provide a tamper-proof record of all transactions, which can enhance transparency and accountability. Similarly, social media platforms can be used to provide stakeholders with real-time updates on compliance activities and engage with them on a more personal level.

Embracing New Technologies:
The financial industry is rapidly evolving, and new technologies are emerging all the time. To stay ahead of the curve, financial institutions need to embrace new technologies and incorporate them into their compliance processes.

For example, Arlingbrook is a social media platform that is starting with comprehensive payment options and is planning to merge with web3 to add its own crypto coin and NFTs. This will enable the platform to enter the global market, ensuring that no country is without the ability to use the platform. By embracing new technologies, firms can stay ahead of the competition and provide a better user experience to their customers.

Enhancing Training and Education:
Effective compliance requires not only the right technology and processes but also well-trained staff who understand the regulatory and compliance requirements. One area for innovation in compliance is the use of new technologies to enhance training and education programs.

For example, financial institutions can use gamification techniques to make compliance training more engaging and interactive. Similarly, virtual reality can be used to provide immersive training experiences that simulate real-world compliance scenarios.

Building a Culture of Compliance:
Finally, building a culture of compliance is essential for maintaining a strong compliance posture. Financial institutions need to ensure that compliance is not just a box-ticking exercise but is ingrained in the organization's culture.

For example, firms can incentivize employees to report compliance violations or near misses, which can help to identify areas for improvement and strengthen the compliance culture. Similarly, firms can establish a compliance champion program to recognize and reward employees who demonstrate a strong commitment to compliance.

Conclusion:

Innovation in compliance is essential for financial institutions to stay ahead of the curve and maintain a strong compliance posture. Firms can leverage technology and data to automate compliance processes, enhance risk management practices, improve communication and transparency, embrace new technologies, enhance training and education programs, and collaborate with industry peers and regulators. These strategies can help firms address compliance challenges in a cost-effective and efficient manner while also improving their overall operational effectiveness.

However, it is important to note that innovation in compliance also comes with its own set of challenges. For example, firms may face technical hurdles when implementing new technologies or struggle to navigate the complex regulatory landscape surrounding emerging technologies. Additionally, there may be concerns around data privacy and security, particularly as firms increasingly rely on data-driven compliance solutions.

Despite these challenges, the benefits of innovation in compliance are significant. By embracing new technologies and approaches, firms can enhance their ability to detect and prevent financial crime, better protect customers, and improve their overall reputation and brand value. As such, financial institutions must continue to invest in innovation in compliance and work collaboratively with regulators and industry peers to create a safe and secure financial ecosystem for all.

Benefits of innovation in compliance

Innovation is a key driver of growth and competitiveness in today's rapidly evolving financial industry. By embracing innovative approaches to compliance, financial institutions can achieve a range of benefits, including enhanced efficiency, improved risk management, and increased transparency and accountability. In this section, we will explore the key benefits of innovation in compliance and how they can help financial institutions stay ahead of the curve.

Improved Efficiency
One of the primary benefits of innovation in compliance is improved efficiency. By leveraging technology and automation, financial institutions can streamline compliance processes and reduce the time and resources required to stay compliant. For example, compliance monitoring software can be used to automatically monitor regulatory changes and flag potential compliance issues, saving compliance officers time and reducing the risk of non-compliance. In addition, automation can help to standardize compliance processes and reduce the potential for human error.

Enhanced Risk Management
Innovation in compliance can also lead to enhanced risk management practices. By leveraging data analytics and other advanced technologies, financial institutions can gain greater insight into their risk exposure and identify potential compliance risks before they become problems. For example, data analytics can be used to identify patterns and trends in transactions that may indicate potential money laundering or fraud, allowing compliance officers to take proactive measures to mitigate these risks.

Increased Transparency and Accountability
Innovation in compliance can also lead to increased transparency and accountability. By leveraging technology to automate compliance processes and improve communication and transparency with

stakeholders, financial institutions can build trust and credibility with regulators, investors, and customers. For example, compliance reporting software can be used to provide real-time updates on compliance activities and demonstrate compliance with regulatory requirements. This can help to build confidence among stakeholders and improve the overall reputation of the institution.

Competitive Advantage

Innovation in compliance can also provide financial institutions with a competitive advantage. By embracing new technologies and approaches to compliance, institutions can differentiate themselves from their competitors and demonstrate their commitment to compliance and risk management. For example, a financial institution that is able to demonstrate robust compliance processes and a strong culture of compliance is more likely to attract and retain customers and investors.

Cost Savings

Finally, innovation in compliance can lead to significant cost savings for financial institutions. By leveraging technology and automation to streamline compliance processes, institutions can reduce the time and resources required to stay compliant, potentially saving millions of dollars in compliance-related costs. In addition, automation can help to reduce the potential for fines and other penalties associated with non-compliance.

Examples of Innovative Compliance Practices

Innovative compliance practices can take many forms, depending on the needs and priorities of the institution. Here are a few examples of innovative compliance practices that financial institutions are adopting:

RegTech Solutions

RegTech solutions, such as compliance monitoring software and data analytics tools, are becoming increasingly popular among financial institutions. These solutions can help institutions to automate compliance processes, monitor regulatory changes, and identify potential compliance risks. For example, a financial institution might use a data analytics tool to identify patterns in customer transactions that may indicate potential money laundering or fraud.

Artificial Intelligence

Artificial intelligence (AI) is also being used to enhance compliance practices in the financial industry. For example, machine learning algorithms can be used to analyze large volumes of data and identify potential compliance risks. In addition, natural language processing (NLP) technology can be used to automate compliance reporting and improve communication with regulators and other stakeholders.

Blockchain Technology

Blockchain technology is another innovative approach to compliance that is gaining traction in the financial industry. For example, blockchain technology can be used to create a tamper-proof audit trail of transactions, providing greater transparency and accountability. In addition, blockchain can be used to automate compliance processes, such as KYC (know your customer) and AML (anti-money laundering) checks.

Gamification

Gamification is the application of game design principles to non-game contexts, such as compliance training. By incorporating game elements, such as points, badges, and leaderboards, compliance training can become more engaging and enjoyable for employees. This can result in improved retention of information and better overall compliance outcomes.

For example, a financial institution may create a compliance training program that is designed like a game, with employees earning points and badges as they complete modules and demonstrate mastery of compliance concepts. This approach can make compliance training more appealing and encourage employees to take an active role in their own learning.

Artificial Intelligence (AI)

Artificial intelligence (AI) is another area of innovation that is being applied to compliance. AI can be used to analyze large volumes of data to identify potential compliance issues, such as anomalies in transactions or patterns of behavior that may indicate fraud. AI can also be used to automate compliance-related tasks, such as monitoring social media and other online sources for potential regulatory violations.

For example, a financial institution may use AI to monitor customer transactions for signs of fraudulent activity, such as unusually large transactions or transactions that deviate from a customer's typical behavior. This can help identify potential compliance issues before they become more serious problems.

Cloud Computing

Cloud computing is another technology that can be leveraged for compliance purposes. Cloud computing allows data to be stored and accessed over the internet, rather than on local computers or servers. This can provide greater flexibility and scalability for compliance processes, allowing firms to easily adjust to changing regulatory requirements.

For example, a financial institution may use cloud computing to store compliance-related data, such as customer information or transaction records. This can provide greater access to data and improve collaboration between different departments, such as compliance and risk management.

Overall, the benefits of innovation in compliance are numerous and can have a significant impact on the success of financial institutions. By embracing new technologies and approaches, firms can improve their compliance posture, reduce costs, and better serve their customers. However, it is important to approach innovation with caution and ensure that new technologies and approaches are thoroughly tested and integrated into existing compliance frameworks before implementation.

PART X: CONCLUSION AND RECAP

Throughout this book on innovation in compliance, we have explored various approaches that financial institutions can take to stay ahead of regulatory requirements and mitigate risk. From leveraging data analytics and machine learning to utilizing RegTech solutions and embracing blockchain technology, the financial industry has seen significant advancements in compliance practices in recent years.

In conclusion, innovation in compliance is essential for financial institutions to maintain a strong compliance posture, improve efficiency, and stay competitive in an ever-changing market. By embracing new technologies and data-driven approaches, firms can automate compliance processes, enhance risk management practices, and improve communication and transparency.

However, it is important to note that innovation in compliance does not come without challenges. Implementing new technologies and processes can be costly and time-consuming, and there is always a risk of unintended consequences or compliance failures. Therefore, it is crucial for firms to carefully evaluate and test new innovations before implementing them into their compliance framework.

In summary, innovation in compliance is an ongoing process that requires continuous evaluation and improvement. By staying up-to-date with regulatory requirements and leveraging innovative approaches to compliance, financial institutions can effectively manage risk, maintain a strong compliance posture, and remain competitive in the market.

CHAPTER 36: LOOKING BACK: A RECAP OF EMERGING TRENDS IN FINANCE

Finance is a dynamic field that is constantly evolving to keep pace with the changing economic landscape. In recent years, we have seen a multitude of emerging trends that have transformed the finance industry, from the rise of fintech to the increased focus on sustainability and ESG (Environmental, Social, and Governance) factors. In this chapter, we will take a retrospective look at the emerging trends that have shaped finance in the past decade, examining their impact on the industry and what we can learn from them as we move forward.

Fintech Revolution

The fintech revolution has been one of the most significant emerging trends in finance in recent years. Fintech refers to the use of technology to improve financial services, and it has transformed the way we bank, invest, and make payments. Fintech has disrupted traditional banking models and brought financial services to underserved populations. The emergence of fintech has also led to the rise of new business models, such as peer-to-peer lending and crowdfunding. In this section, we will explore the impact of fintech on the finance industry, its challenges, and its future potential.

The Growth of Sustainable Finance

Sustainable finance is another significant emerging trend in the finance industry, reflecting the increasing importance of environmental, social, and governance (ESG) issues. Sustainable finance focuses on investing in companies that meet high ESG standards, supporting environmentally and socially responsible business practices, and mitigating climate risks. This trend has been driven by investors' growing awareness of the impact of their investments on society and the environment. In this section, we will discuss the growth of sustainable finance, its challenges, and its potential to transform the finance industry.

Blockchain Technology

Blockchain technology is a decentralized, digital ledger that records transactions in a secure and tamper-proof way. It has the potential to revolutionize the way financial transactions are conducted, offering benefits such as increased efficiency, transparency, and security. The technology has already been adopted in areas such as cryptocurrencies, smart contracts, and supply chain management. In this section, we will examine the impact of blockchain technology on the finance industry, its challenges, and its future potential.

Artificial Intelligence and Machine Learning

Artificial intelligence (AI) and machine learning (ML) are rapidly evolving technologies that have the potential to transform the finance industry. AI and ML are being used to improve risk management, fraud detection, and customer experience, among other things. In this section, we will explore the impact of AI and ML on the finance industry, their challenges, and their potential to transform the industry.

Overview of the key trends that have emerged in finance over the years

The financial industry has undergone significant changes over the years, with numerous emerging trends that have transformed the industry. This section provides an overview of some of the key trends that have emerged in finance over the years.

Technology and Digital Transformation

One of the most significant trends in finance has been the increasing reliance on technology and digital transformation. Technology has changed the way financial institutions operate, enabling greater efficiency, automation, and improved customer experience. For example, the use of mobile banking apps has made it easier for customers to access their accounts, make payments, and transfer funds. In addition, the use of artificial intelligence and machine learning has enabled financial institutions to make better decisions and manage risks more effectively.

Investment banks have also embraced technology and digital transformation. For example, the use of algorithmic trading has revolutionized the way securities are traded, leading to greater efficiency and improved liquidity. Portfolio managers have also started using robo-advisors to provide investment advice to clients. These platforms use algorithms to provide personalized investment advice, making it easier for clients to invest in the markets.

Regulatory Compliance

Regulatory compliance has become a key trend in finance, driven by the increasing number of regulations that financial institutions must comply with. Compliance is crucial in maintaining the stability and integrity of the financial system. Financial institutions are required to comply with regulations such as the Dodd-Frank Act, the Basel III Accord, and the European Market Infrastructure Regulation (EMIR). These regulations aim to ensure that financial institutions operate in a safe and sound manner, and that they are adequately capitalized and managed.

Compliance has become a significant cost for financial institutions, leading to the adoption of innovative solutions such as regtech. Regtech refers to the use of technology to automate regulatory compliance processes, making it easier and more cost-effective for financial institutions to comply with regulations.

Environmental, Social, and Governance (ESG)

Environmental, Social, and Governance (ESG) has become a significant trend in finance over the years. ESG refers to the consideration of environmental, social, and governance factors in investment decision-making. Investors are increasingly focused on ESG factors, as they seek to invest in companies that are sustainable, socially responsible, and well-managed.

Asset managers have started offering ESG investment products, such as ESG funds, to meet the growing demand from investors. Investment banks have also started incorporating ESG factors into their investment analysis and decision-making processes. ESG has become a key consideration in mergers and acquisitions, with companies now being evaluated based on their ESG performance.

Big Data and Analytics

The use of big data and analytics has become a significant trend in finance over the years. Financial institutions generate vast amounts of data on a daily basis, including data on customer transactions, market data, and regulatory data. The use of big data and analytics enables financial institutions to extract insights from this data, providing valuable information that can be used to make better decisions.

For example, investment banks use big data and analytics to analyze market trends, identify investment opportunities, and manage risks. Portfolio managers use big data and analytics to analyze market trends, identify potential risks, and optimize their investment portfolios. In addition, banks use analytics to detect fraud and money laundering activities.

Conclusion

In conclusion, the financial industry has undergone significant changes over the years, with numerous emerging trends that have transformed the industry. Technology and digital transformation, regulatory compliance, ESG, and big data and analytics are just some of the key trends that have emerged in finance. These trends have provided financial institutions with new opportunities to innovate and improve their operations, enabling them to better serve their clients and operate more efficiently. As we look to the future of finance, it is essential that financial institutions continue to embrace

In-depth analysis of the trends, including technological advancements, regulatory changes, and shifting consumer behaviors these trends and adapt to changing market conditions to remain competitive and relevant.

While some trends may have been more impactful than others, it is clear that the financial industry is constantly evolving and there are always new emerging trends that have the potential to disrupt the industry. It is important for financial professionals to stay up-to-date with the latest trends and developments in the industry to ensure that they are well-equipped to navigate these changes.

Moreover, it is important to note that the impact of emerging trends on the financial industry is not limited to financial professionals alone. Consumers and investors also play an important role in driving these changes through their changing demands and expectations. As consumers and investors become more aware of these trends, they will also demand more transparency, better products and services, and sustainable and socially responsible investing options.

In summary, the financial industry is a dynamic and constantly evolving field, with emerging trends that continue to transform the industry. Technology and digital transformation, regulatory compliance, ESG, and big data and analytics are just some of the key trends that have emerged in finance. Financial institutions that embrace these trends and adapt to changing market conditions will be better equipped to succeed in the future of finance. It is imperative for financial professionals to stay up-to-date with these emerging trends to remain competitive, and for consumers and investors to continue driving these changes towards a more sustainable and responsible financial industry.

Discussion of the impact of these trends on the financial industry and the broader economy

The financial industry is constantly evolving, and emerging trends are shaping the industry's future. The impact of these trends is not limited to financial institutions alone, as they have far-reaching implications for the broader economy. This section will discuss the impact of key trends in finance, including technology and digital transformation, regulatory compliance, ESG, and big data and analytics, on both the financial industry and the broader economy.

Technology and Digital Transformation:

The rapid pace of technological advancement has led to a digital transformation of the financial industry, with significant implications for financial institutions and their clients. The use of technology in finance has transformed the way that financial services are delivered, from the way that individuals interact with their bank accounts to how institutions manage their operations. For example, mobile banking has allowed individuals to access their accounts and manage their finances from anywhere, at any time, while online trading platforms have given investors access to real-time market data and the ability to execute trades quickly and efficiently.

The impact of technology on finance extends beyond the delivery of financial services, as institutions are increasingly relying on technology to automate processes, reduce costs, and improve efficiencies. For example, the use of artificial intelligence and machine learning has enabled financial institutions to automate risk assessments and make more informed investment decisions. This has led to increased productivity, reduced costs, and improved risk management.

The broader economy has also been impacted by the digital transformation of the financial industry. The rise of fintech companies has led to increased competition and innovation in the financial sector, which has led to more choice and better services for consumers. The increased adoption of digital technologies has also led to job creation, particularly in the technology and data analytics fields.

Regulatory Compliance:

The financial industry is subject to a complex regulatory environment, with regulations aimed at protecting consumers and ensuring the stability of the financial system. Compliance with these regulations is essential for financial institutions, as failure to comply can result in significant fines and reputational damage.

The impact of regulatory compliance on the financial industry has been significant, as institutions are required to invest in compliance programs and infrastructure to meet regulatory requirements. This has led to increased costs and reduced profitability for financial institutions. However, the importance of regulatory compliance cannot be overstated, as it is essential for ensuring the integrity of the financial system and protecting consumers.

The broader economy has also been impacted by regulatory compliance in the financial industry. The financial crisis of 2008 highlighted the need for increased regulation of the financial sector, and regulatory reforms have since been implemented to prevent a similar crisis from occurring. This has led to a more stable financial system, which is essential for economic growth and development.

ESG:

Environmental, social, and governance (ESG) considerations have become increasingly important for financial institutions in recent years, as investors and consumers have become more concerned about the impact of their investments on the environment and society. ESG considerations involve assessing the environmental, social, and governance practices of companies and incorporating this information into investment decisions.

The impact of ESG considerations on the financial industry has been significant, as financial institutions are increasingly incorporating ESG factors into their investment decisions. This has led to increased demand for companies that demonstrate strong ESG practices, as investors seek to align their investments with their values. ESG considerations have also led to increased transparency and accountability in the financial industry, as companies are required to disclose information about their ESG practices.

The broader economy has also been impacted by ESG considerations in the financial industry. Companies that demonstrate strong ESG practices are often more resilient and better positioned for long-term success, which is essential for economic growth and development. In addition, the increased focus on ESG considerations has led to greater awareness and action around environmental and social issues, which is essential for addressing global challenges such as climate change and social inequality ESG considerations have also had a significant impact on the broader economy, with investors and stakeholders increasingly valuing companies with strong ESG practices. This has led to a shift in corporate behavior, with companies now recognizing the importance of ESG factors in their operations and strategy. In fact, a recent survey by BlackRock found that 88% of institutional investors believe that companies with strong ESG practices are more likely to outperform their peers in the long run.

This shift towards greater ESG consideration is not only beneficial for individual companies, but also for the broader economy. Companies that prioritize ESG factors are often more resilient and better positioned for long-term success, which is essential for economic growth and development. By focusing on sustainable practices and minimizing negative impacts on the environment and society, companies can help ensure long-term economic stability and prosperity.

Furthermore, the increased focus on ESG considerations has led to greater awareness and action around environmental and social issues. This is essential for addressing global challenges such as climate change and social inequality. Financial institutions, such as investment banks and asset managers, have a significant role to play in promoting sustainability and driving positive social and environmental outcomes.

For example, investment banks can play a key role in financing and supporting sustainable projects, such as renewable energy and clean technology. This not only helps to mitigate the impacts of climate change, but also creates new opportunities for economic growth and development. Asset managers, on the other hand, can influence corporate behavior by actively engaging with companies to promote ESG practices and holding them accountable for their impact on the environment and society.

In addition to ESG considerations, technology and digital transformation have also had a significant impact on the financial industry and the broader economy. The rise of digital technologies and the increasing use of data and analytics have transformed the way financial institutions operate, enabling them to better serve their clients and operate more efficiently.

For example, the use of artificial intelligence and machine learning has enabled financial institutions to better analyze and understand market trends, improving their ability to make informed investment decisions. Similarly, the use of blockchain technology has enabled greater transparency and efficiency in financial transactions, reducing costs and streamlining processes.

The impact of technology and digital transformation on the broader economy has been significant, with new business models and industries emerging as a result. Fintech companies, for example, have disrupted traditional financial services by leveraging technology to offer new and innovative products and services. This has not only created new opportunities for entrepreneurs and investors, but also enabled greater financial inclusion and accessibility.

Regulatory compliance is another trend that has had a significant impact on the financial industry and the broader economy. In response to the global financial crisis of 2008, regulators have implemented a range of new regulations and requirements to increase transparency and reduce risk in the financial sector.

While these regulations have undoubtedly helped to improve the stability and integrity of the financial system, they have also imposed significant costs and compliance burdens on financial institutions. This has led to a shift towards greater automation and digitization of compliance processes, enabling financial institutions to comply more efficiently and effectively.

The impact of regulatory compliance on the broader economy is complex and multifaceted. On one hand, increased regulation has helped to reduce systemic risk and protect consumers and investors. On the other hand, the costs of compliance can be significant, particularly for smaller financial institutions, and can create barriers to entry for new market entrants.

Overall, the emerging trends in finance have had a significant impact on both the financial industry and the broader economy. While these trends have created new opportunities for innovation and growth, they have also posed significant challenges and risks. As we look to the future, it is essential that financial institutions continue to embrace these trends and adapt to the changing landscape of finance. By doing so, they can help to drive sustainable economic growth and development while ensuring the long-term stability

Recap of the major takeaways from the trends that have emerged in finance

After reviewing the key trends that have emerged in the financial industry, there are several major takeaways that can be gleaned.

First and foremost, technology and digital transformation have had a significant impact on the financial industry, and this trend is likely to continue into the future. Financial institutions that can effectively leverage technology and digital tools will be better positioned to meet the needs of their clients, operate more efficiently, and remain competitive in an increasingly crowded market. From AI-powered chatbots to blockchain-based payment systems, there are a wide range of tools and technologies that are transforming the financial industry, and firms that can effectively harness these tools will have a distinct advantage over those that cannot.

Second, regulatory compliance remains a major concern for financial institutions. The post-financial crisis regulatory environment has placed a greater emphasis on transparency and risk management, and financial institutions must devote significant resources to ensuring that they are in compliance with the relevant regulations. This can be a significant challenge, particularly for smaller institutions that may not have the resources to invest in robust compliance programs.

Third, the increased focus on ESG considerations is a major trend that has the potential to transform the financial industry and the broader economy. Financial institutions that can effectively incorporate ESG considerations into their investment decisions and operations will be better positioned to manage risk and generate long-term value for their clients. At the same time, the increased focus on ESG considerations has the potential to drive positive social and environmental outcomes, which is essential for addressing global challenges such as climate change and social inequality.

Fourth, big data and analytics have the potential to revolutionize the financial industry, particularly in the areas of risk management and portfolio optimization. Financial institutions that can effectively leverage big data and analytics tools will be better positioned to identify risks and opportunities, generate insights, and make more informed investment decisions. From machine learning algorithms to predictive analytics models, there are a wide range of tools and technologies that are transforming the way that financial institutions manage risk and optimize their portfolios.

Fifth, the emergence of new business models and the changing role of financial intermediaries are key trends that are reshaping the financial industry. From fintech startups to robo-advisors, there are a wide range of new players that are disrupting traditional business models and challenging established players.

Financial institutions that can adapt to these changes and embrace new business models will be better positioned to remain competitive and meet the evolving needs of their clients.

Finally, the importance of lifelong learning cannot be overstated. As the financial industry continues to evolve and new trends emerge, it is essential that financial professionals remain up-to-date with the latest developments and best practices. This requires a commitment to ongoing learning and professional development, as well as a willingness to embrace change and adapt to new circumstances.

In conclusion, the key trends that have emerged in the financial industry over the years have had a profound impact on the industry and the broader economy. From technology and digital transformation to regulatory compliance and ESG considerations, these trends have created new opportunities for innovation and improvement, while also presenting significant challenges and risks. By understanding and effectively navigating these trends, financial institutions can remain competitive and deliver value to their clients in an ever-changing landscape.

CHAPTER 37: LOOKING FORWARD: THE FUTURE OF FINANCE

As we have seen throughout this exploration of the key trends in finance, the industry has undergone significant changes over the years. From the adoption of new technologies to regulatory changes and the increased focus on ESG considerations, the financial industry has evolved and adapted to meet the needs of a changing world. However, the pace of change shows no signs of slowing down, and financial institutions must continue to innovate and adapt to remain competitive in the future.

In this chapter, we will explore some of the potential directions and developments that the future of finance may hold. We will examine some of the emerging trends that are likely to shape the industry in the coming years and consider the implications of these trends for financial institutions and the broader economy. While we cannot predict the future with certainty, we can identify some of the key drivers and possibilities that may influence the future of finance.

The Role of Technology in Shaping the Future of Finance

Technology has been a key driver of change in the financial industry for many years, and this is likely to continue in the future. The continued development and adoption of new technologies, such as artificial intelligence, blockchain, and quantum computing, are likely to have a significant impact on the financial industry in the coming years. These technologies have the potential to transform financial operations, improve decision-making, and create new opportunities for innovation and growth.

For example, the increasing use of artificial intelligence and machine learning in the financial industry has the potential to revolutionize the way financial institutions analyze data and make decisions. With the vast amounts of data that financial institutions generate and collect, machine learning algorithms can identify patterns and insights that would be difficult or impossible for humans to detect. This can enable financial institutions to make more accurate and informed decisions, improve risk management, and enhance the customer experience.

Similarly, blockchain technology has the potential to transform the way financial transactions are conducted, making them faster, cheaper, and more secure. Blockchain can also create new opportunities for financial inclusion by providing a secure and accessible platform for financial services in areas where traditional banking infrastructure is lacking.

Regulatory and Compliance Developments

Regulatory compliance has been a key area of focus in the financial industry in recent years, and this is likely to continue in the future. The increasing complexity of regulations and the need for financial institutions to comply with multiple regulatory regimes can create significant challenges and costs for financial institutions. However, the continued development of regulatory technology, or regtech, is likely to help financial institutions to manage these challenges more effectively.

Regtech refers to the use of technology to facilitate regulatory compliance and reduce the costs associated with regulatory reporting and monitoring. For example, regtech solutions can automate compliance processes, provide real-time monitoring of compliance risks, and improve the accuracy and efficiency of regulatory reporting. This can help financial institutions to reduce compliance costs, improve risk management, and enhance their ability to meet regulatory requirements.

The Rise of Sustainable Finance

The increasing focus on ESG considerations in the financial industry is likely to continue in the future, with sustainable finance becoming an increasingly important area of focus for financial institutions. Sustainable finance refers to the integration of ESG considerations into financial decision-making, with the aim of promoting sustainable economic growth and development.

There are several drivers behind the rise of sustainable finance, including regulatory requirements, investor demand, and the need to address global environmental and social challenges. Financial institutions that embrace sustainable finance can improve their long-term resilience, enhance their reputation, and tap into new sources of growth and innovation.

Conclusion

As we have seen throughout this exploration of the future of finance, the industry is likely to continue to undergo significant changes in the coming years. From the increasing role of technology to regulatory developments and the rise of sustainable finance, financial institutions must be prepared to adapt and innovate to remain competitive in the future.

By embracing these emerging trends and leveraging the opportunities that they present, financial institutions can improve their operations, enhance customer experience, and promote sustainable growth. Technology is expected to play a significant role in shaping the future of finance, as financial institutions increasingly adopt digital solutions to enhance operational efficiency and customer experience.

In addition, we can expect to see continued growth and evolution of sustainable finance, as ESG considerations become increasingly central to the operations of financial institutions. The shift towards sustainable finance is not just a passing trend, but a critical necessity for long-term economic growth and stability.

Regulatory developments will also continue to shape the future of finance, as regulators seek to enhance transparency and reduce risk in the financial system. Increased regulation and oversight can be expected in areas such as cybersecurity, data privacy, and financial crime prevention.

Overall, the future of finance is likely to be characterized by a continued focus on innovation, digitalization, and sustainability. Financial institutions that can adapt and innovate in response to these trends are likely to emerge as leaders in the industry, while those that fail to keep up may struggle to remain competitive.

However, it is important to note that the future of finance is not without its challenges and risks. As financial institutions increasingly rely on technology and digital solutions, they may become more vulnerable to cybersecurity threats and other forms of risk. In addition, the ongoing global economic uncertainty, geopolitical risks, and environmental challenges may impact the industry in ways that are difficult to predict.

Therefore, financial institutions must remain vigilant and adaptable, continually assessing and managing risks as they navigate the changing landscape of finance. With careful planning and strategic investment in innovation and sustainability, financial institutions can position themselves for success in the future of finance.

Overview of the current state of the financial industry

The financial industry is a critical part of the global economy, encompassing a broad range of activities and players, from banks and investment firms to insurance companies and regulators. In this section, we will provide an overview of the current state of the financial industry, including its key players, recent trends, and major challenges.

Key players in the financial industry:
The financial industry is a highly diverse and complex ecosystem, with many different players competing for market share and striving to deliver value to customers. Some of the key players in the financial industry include:

Banks: Banks are among the largest and most important players in the financial industry. They offer a wide range of services, including savings and checking accounts, loans, and investment products.

Investment firms: Investment firms manage portfolios of assets on behalf of their clients, including both individuals and institutions. They may invest in stocks, bonds, real estate, and other assets, depending on the specific investment strategy.

Insurance companies: Insurance companies offer a range of products designed to protect individuals and businesses from various types of risks, including health, life, property, and casualty.

Regulators: Regulators play a critical role in the financial industry, overseeing the activities of banks, investment firms, and other players to ensure that they operate in a safe and sound manner and comply with applicable laws and regulations.

Recent trends in the financial industry:
The financial industry is constantly evolving, with new trends and innovations emerging all the time. Some of the most notable trends in the financial industry in recent years include:

The rise of fintech: Fintech, or financial technology, is a rapidly growing sector that uses technology to deliver financial services to customers in new and innovative ways. Fintech companies have disrupted many traditional areas of the financial industry, such as lending and payments.

The growth of sustainable finance: Sustainable finance refers to the integration of environmental, social, and governance (ESG) factors into investment decision-making. This trend has gained momentum in recent years as investors increasingly recognize the importance of sustainable business practices and seek to align their investments with their values.

The increasing use of artificial intelligence (AI) and machine learning: AI and machine learning have the potential to transform many areas of the financial industry, from fraud detection to risk management. As these technologies continue to advance, they are likely to play an even greater role in the industry in the coming years.

Major challenges facing the financial industry:

Despite the many opportunities and innovations in the financial industry, there are also several significant challenges that must be addressed. Some of the major challenges facing the financial industry today include:

Cybersecurity threats: With so much sensitive financial information stored electronically, the financial industry is a prime target for cybercriminals. Ensuring the security of customer data is a top priority for financial firms and regulators alike.

Regulatory compliance: The financial industry is heavily regulated, with a complex web of rules and regulations governing everything from lending practices to investment products. Compliance with these regulations is essential, but can be costly and time-consuming.

Economic uncertainty: The financial industry is heavily influenced by broader economic trends and developments, such as interest rates and global economic conditions. Economic uncertainty can make it difficult for financial firms to plan for the future and manage risk effectively.

Conclusion:
The financial industry is a critical part of the global economy, and it is undergoing significant changes and challenges as it adapts to new technologies and market pressures. By understanding the key players in the industry, the latest trends, and the major challenges facing financial firms today, individuals and businesses can make more informed decisions about their financial strategies and investments.

Analysis of the key drivers that will shape the future of finance, including technological advancements, changing demographics, and regulatory developments

The financial industry has undergone significant changes in recent years, and it is expected to continue to evolve in the coming decades. Several key drivers will shape the future of finance, including technological advancements, changing demographics, and regulatory developments. In this section, we will explore each of these drivers and analyze their potential impact on the financial industry.

Technological Advancements:

The rapid pace of technological advancements is one of the most significant drivers that will shape the future of finance. Emerging technologies such as blockchain, artificial intelligence, and machine learning are already transforming the financial industry in numerous ways.

Blockchain technology, for instance, has the potential to revolutionize the way financial transactions are processed and recorded. By providing a decentralized and secure ledger, blockchain technology can reduce the need for intermediaries, increase transparency, and streamline processes. Investment banks, such as JPMorgan and Goldman Sachs, are already experimenting with blockchain technology to optimize their operations and reduce costs.

Artificial intelligence and machine learning are also transforming the financial industry. These technologies can analyze vast amounts of data and identify patterns and insights that were previously difficult to detect. This can help financial institutions to make more informed decisions and improve their risk management strategies. Investment management firms, for example, are using machine learning algorithms to analyze market trends and identify investment opportunities.

However, these technological advancements also present significant challenges for the financial industry. Cybersecurity threats, for instance, are increasing as financial institutions become more reliant on technology. Regulators are also struggling to keep pace with the rapid pace of technological advancements, leading to uncertainty around regulatory frameworks and potential risks.

Changing Demographics:

The changing demographics of the global population are also a significant driver that will shape the future of finance. The aging of the population in many developed countries, for example, is leading to increased demand for retirement planning and investment management services.

In contrast, the rise of millennials and Gen Z is leading to a shift in consumer preferences towards digital and sustainable finance. These generations are more likely to prioritize social and environmental issues in their investment decisions, and they are also more likely to use digital tools and platforms to manage their finances.

Financial institutions will need to adapt to these changing demographics by offering personalized services and incorporating digital and sustainable finance options into their offerings. Investment management firms, for example, are developing robo-advisory platforms that use artificial intelligence and machine learning algorithms to provide customized investment advice.

Regulatory Developments:

Regulatory developments are another key driver that will shape the future of finance. Following the global financial crisis of 2008, regulators have implemented numerous reforms to increase transparency, reduce risk, and protect consumers.

These reforms include the implementation of new reporting and disclosure requirements, the strengthening of capital and liquidity requirements, and the introduction of new consumer protection measures. However, the regulatory landscape remains complex and fragmented, with different jurisdictions implementing different rules and standards.

The increasing focus on sustainable finance is also leading to new regulatory developments. For example, the European Union's Sustainable Finance Disclosure Regulation requires financial institutions to disclose how they incorporate environmental, social, and governance factors into their investment decisions. Similar regulations are expected to be implemented in other jurisdictions in the coming years.

Conclusion:

In conclusion, several key drivers will shape the future of finance, including technological advancements, changing demographics, and regulatory developments. While these drivers present significant challenges for the financial industry, they also offer opportunities for innovation and growth. Financial institutions that are able to adapt and leverage these emerging trends will be well-positioned for success in the future.

Discussion of the potential impact of these drivers on the financial industry and the broader economy

The drivers shaping the future of finance, as discussed in the previous section, are expected to have a significant impact on the financial industry and the broader economy. In this section, we will explore the potential implications of these drivers and what they mean for various stakeholders in the financial ecosystem.

Technological Advancements:
As discussed earlier, technological advancements are one of the key drivers of change in the financial industry. Advancements in areas such as artificial intelligence, blockchain, and cloud computing have the potential to transform various aspects of finance, including trading, risk management, and customer service.

One potential impact of these advancements is increased efficiency in financial processes. For example, the use of blockchain technology can streamline transaction processes, reducing the need for intermediaries and lowering transaction costs. This can result in more efficient markets and lower costs for consumers and businesses.

However, there are also potential downsides to increased automation and technological advancements. For example, the increased use of algorithms and artificial intelligence in investment decisions could lead to increased homogenization of investment portfolios, limiting diversity in the market. Additionally, the use of technology in financial processes could lead to increased vulnerability to cyber-attacks, putting financial institutions and their customers at risk.

Changing Demographics:
Another key driver of change in the financial industry is changing demographics. As the global population ages, there is a growing demand for financial products and services that cater to the needs of older individuals. Additionally, changing demographics are driving a shift towards sustainable finance, as younger generations prioritize environmental and social responsibility in their investment decisions.

One potential impact of these demographic shifts is increased demand for retirement planning services and products. This could lead to increased competition in the retirement planning market, as financial institutions seek to capture market share by offering innovative products and services that cater to the needs of older individuals.

The shift towards sustainable finance is also expected to have a significant impact on the financial industry. As consumers and businesses increasingly prioritize environmental and social responsibility, financial institutions will need to adapt their products and services to meet these demands. This could include offering products and services that invest in renewable energy, support sustainable agriculture, or promote social justice causes.

However, there are also potential downsides to the shift towards sustainable finance. For example, the lack of standardized definitions and metrics for sustainable finance products can make it difficult for consumers and businesses to evaluate and compare products. Additionally, the focus on sustainable finance could lead to a reduction in investment in traditional industries, potentially leading to job losses and economic disruption.

Regulatory Developments:
Regulatory developments are another key driver of change in the financial industry. As regulators seek to promote financial stability and protect consumers, they are introducing new rules and regulations that could have a significant impact on the industry.

One potential impact of regulatory developments is increased compliance costs for financial institutions. As regulations become more complex and stringent, financial institutions will need to invest in compliance systems and processes to ensure that they are meeting regulatory requirements. This could lead to increased costs for consumers and businesses, as financial institutions pass on these costs through higher fees and charges.

However, regulatory developments could also have positive impacts on the industry. For example, the increased focus on consumer protection could lead to more transparent and fair financial products and services, benefiting consumers and businesses. Additionally, regulations aimed at promoting financial stability could help to reduce systemic risks in the financial system, making it more resilient to economic shocks.

Conclusion:

The drivers shaping the future of finance, including technological advancements, changing demographics, and regulatory developments, are expected to have a significant impact on the financial industry and the broader economy. While these drivers present both opportunities and challenges for financial institutions and other stakeholders, it is clear that those who are able to adapt and innovate in response to these changes will be better positioned for success in the future. As the financial industry continues to evolve, it will be important for stakeholders to stay informed about emerging trends and developments, as well as to proactively explore new opportunities for growth and innovation.

One of the key opportunities presented by these drivers is the potential for increased efficiency and productivity in the financial industry. For example, technological advancements such as artificial intelligence and blockchain have the potential to streamline many financial processes and reduce costs. This could lead to increased profitability for financial institutions, as well as lower costs and better access to financial services for consumers.

At the same time, these same technological advancements also have the potential to disrupt existing business models and create new risks for the financial industry. For example, the rise of digital currencies and decentralized finance could potentially challenge the dominance of traditional financial institutions and regulatory frameworks. Similarly, advances in cybersecurity will be critical to protecting against new threats and ensuring the integrity of financial systems.

Demographic changes also present both opportunities and challenges for the financial industry. As the population ages, there is a growing demand for retirement planning and wealth management services. At the same time, younger generations are increasingly prioritizing social and environmental considerations in their investment decisions, driving the rise of sustainable finance.

Regulatory developments also play a significant role in shaping the future of finance. For example, the increasing focus on data privacy and protection is likely to have significant implications for the way financial institutions collect and use customer data. Similarly, the growing emphasis on sustainability and environmental, social, and governance (ESG) factors is likely to drive the adoption of new investment strategies and products.

Overall, the drivers shaping the future of finance are complex and multifaceted, with both positive and negative implications for the financial industry and the broader economy. While it is difficult to predict exactly how these trends will play out in the coming years, it is clear that those who are able to stay ahead of the curve and adapt to these changes will be best positioned for success in the future.

Exploration of potential future scenarios for the financial industry

In the previous sections, we have discussed the key drivers that are shaping the future of finance, including technological advancements, changing demographics, and regulatory developments. In this section, we will explore potential future scenarios for the financial industry based on these drivers and other factors.

Scenario 1: The Rise of Fintech

One potential future scenario for the financial industry is the continued rise of fintech. Fintech refers to the use of technology to provide financial services, such as mobile banking apps, online investment platforms, and peer-to-peer lending. The growth of fintech has already had a significant impact on the financial industry, and this trend is likely to continue.

In this scenario, traditional financial institutions may struggle to keep up with the pace of innovation and face increasing competition from fintech startups. However, some experts argue that the most successful fintech companies may eventually be acquired by traditional financial institutions, leading to a hybrid model of finance that combines the strengths of both sectors.

Scenario 2: The Emergence of a Cashless Society

Another potential future scenario for the financial industry is the emergence of a cashless society. This scenario is driven by the increasing use of digital payments, such as credit cards, mobile payments, and cryptocurrencies. In this scenario, physical cash becomes less common and may eventually be phased out entirely.

This scenario has both advantages and disadvantages. On the one hand, a cashless society could reduce crime and increase convenience for consumers. On the other hand, it could also lead to greater inequality and privacy concerns, as digital transactions are easier to track and monitor.

Scenario 3: The Growth of Sustainable Finance

A third potential future scenario for the financial industry is the growth of sustainable finance. This scenario is driven by the increasing awareness of environmental and social issues and the role that finance can play in addressing them. Sustainable finance refers to the integration of environmental, social, and governance (ESG) factors into investment decisions.

In this scenario, there may be a shift away from traditional financial metrics, such as profitability and growth, toward a focus on sustainability and social impact. This could lead to the development of new financial products, such as green bonds and impact investing funds. However, it could also lead to increased complexity and difficulty in measuring and comparing the social and environmental impact of different investments.

Scenario 4: The Impact of Demographic Changes

A fourth potential future scenario for the financial industry is the impact of demographic changes. This scenario is driven by the aging of the population and the rise of new demographic groups, such as millennials and Generation Z.

In this scenario, financial institutions may need to adapt their products and services to meet the needs of different demographic groups. For example, younger generations may be more interested in socially responsible investing and digital banking, while older generations may prefer traditional investment products and face-to-face interactions with financial advisors.

Scenario 5: The Regulation of Emerging Technologies

A fifth potential future scenario for the financial industry is the regulation of emerging technologies, such as artificial intelligence, blockchain, and cryptocurrencies. As these technologies become more widely used in finance, there may be a need for increased regulation to ensure their safety and stability.

In this scenario, financial institutions may need to invest in new compliance and risk management systems to meet regulatory requirements. However, this could also lead to increased costs and complexity, particularly for smaller firms.

Conclusion

The future of finance is likely to be shaped by a combination of technological advancements, changing demographics, and regulatory developments. While it is impossible to predict the exact path that the financial industry will take, exploring potential future scenarios can help financial institutions and other stakeholders prepare for the challenges and opportunities ahead.

By staying informed about emerging trends and being open to innovation and change, financial institutions can position themselves for success in the future. However, they must also be prepared to adapt to unexpected disruptions and challenges.

One potential scenario for the future of finance is a continued emphasis on digitization and automation. This could lead to greater efficiency and cost savings for financial institutions, but it could also result in job losses and increased inequality if certain populations are disproportionately impacted. It will be important for policymakers to consider how to mitigate these potential negative consequences and ensure that the benefits of technological advancements are shared more broadly.

Another potential scenario is a shift towards more sustainable and socially responsible investment strategies. As consumers and investors increasingly prioritize environmental and social issues, financial institutions may need to adapt their offerings to meet these demands. This could include the development of new products and services that are aligned with sustainability goals and increased transparency around the environmental and social impacts of investments.

A third potential scenario is the continued growth of emerging markets and the expansion of financial services to underserved populations. This could create significant opportunities for financial institutions to tap into new markets and meet the needs of previously underserved communities. However, it will also require careful consideration of the unique challenges and risks associated with operating in these markets.

Regardless of the specific future scenarios that unfold, it is clear that the financial industry will continue to play a critical role in shaping the broader economy. As such, it will be important for policymakers, regulators, and financial institutions to work together to ensure that the industry is able to adapt and innovate in response to the challenges and opportunities ahead.

In conclusion, the future of finance is likely to be shaped by a range of drivers, including technological advancements, changing demographics, and regulatory developments. While these drivers present both opportunities and challenges for financial institutions and other stakeholders, those who are able to adapt and innovate in response to these changes will be better positioned for success in the future. By exploring potential future scenarios and staying informed about emerging trends, financial institutions can prepare for the challenges and opportunities ahead and help to shape a more prosperous and sustainable future for the financial industry and the broader economy.

CHAPTER 38: THE IMPORTANCE OF LIFELONG LEARNING IN FINANCE

In today's rapidly changing financial landscape, it is more important than ever for professionals in the industry to commit to lifelong learning. The pace of technological advancements, regulatory developments, and demographic shifts is accelerating, and those who fail to keep up risk falling behind their peers and missing out on opportunities.

This chapter will explore the importance of lifelong learning in finance, including the benefits of continuous education and professional development, the types of skills and knowledge that are most valuable in today's financial industry, and strategies for staying up-to-date and competitive in the field. We will draw on insights from a variety of experts, including investment bankers, actuaries, portfolio managers, quantitative analysts, securities traders, financial planners, and financial analysts.

Benefits of Lifelong Learning in Finance

One of the primary benefits of lifelong learning in finance is that it helps professionals stay abreast of changes in the industry and maintain a competitive edge. As new technologies emerge and regulations evolve, the skills and knowledge that were once essential may become outdated. By continually learning and adapting to new developments, professionals can ensure that they remain relevant and valuable to their organizations.

In addition to staying current, lifelong learning can also help professionals broaden their skill sets and deepen their understanding of complex financial concepts. For example, a portfolio manager who takes courses in data science and machine learning can use these skills to better analyze market trends and make more informed investment decisions. Similarly, a financial planner who learns about behavioral finance can help clients make better financial decisions by understanding their emotions and biases.

Another benefit of lifelong learning is that it can lead to career advancement and increased earning potential. Many employers value employees who are committed to professional development and are willing to invest in their education and training. By acquiring new skills and knowledge, professionals can become more valuable to their organizations and position themselves for promotions and salary increases.

Skills and Knowledge for the Future of Finance

To thrive in the rapidly evolving financial industry, professionals need to possess a wide range of skills and knowledge. In addition to technical expertise in areas such as accounting, finance, and economics, professionals must also be able to adapt to new technologies and regulations, communicate effectively with clients and colleagues, and think creatively and strategically.

Some of the most valuable skills and knowledge for finance professionals today include data analysis and management, risk management, regulatory compliance, and interpersonal communication. Data analysis skills are becoming increasingly important as the amount of financial data continues to grow, and professionals who can effectively collect, analyze, and interpret this data will be in high demand. Risk management skills are essential for protecting clients' investments and minimizing losses, while regulatory compliance skills are critical for navigating the complex regulatory environment in which financial institutions operate. Finally, interpersonal communication skills, such as active listening, empathy, and conflict resolution, are essential for building strong relationships with clients and colleagues.

Strategies for Lifelong Learning in Finance

To succeed in the fast-paced world of finance, professionals must commit to continuous learning and professional development. Some strategies for lifelong learning in finance include attending industry conferences and events, taking courses and earning certifications, reading industry publications and news, networking with peers, and seeking mentorship and coaching.

Attending industry conferences and events can be a valuable way to learn about new trends and developments in the financial industry, as well as to connect with peers and potential mentors. Many industry organizations and professional associations offer conferences and events throughout the year, providing opportunities for professionals to stay up-to-date and expand their networks.

Taking courses and earning certifications is another important strategy for lifelong learning in finance. Many universities and professional organizations offer courses and certifications in finance-related subjects, providing professionals with the opportunity to deepen their knowledge and acquire new skills. Earning certifications, such as the Certified Financial Planner (CFP) or Chartered Financial Analyst (CFA) designations, can also enhance professionals' credibility and earning potential.

The CFP designation, for example, is granted by the Certified Financial Planner Board of Standards, Inc. (CFP Board) and requires candidates to complete a rigorous educational program, pass a comprehensive exam, and fulfill experience and ethics requirements. CFP professionals are trained in a wide range of financial planning topics, including investment planning, retirement planning, tax planning, and estate planning. Earning the CFP designation can demonstrate to clients and employers that a professional has a deep understanding of financial planning concepts and is committed to ethical and professional standards.

Similarly, the CFA designation is granted by the CFA Institute and requires candidates to complete a comprehensive program of study and pass three levels of exams covering topics such as ethics, economics, and financial analysis. CFA professionals are trained in investment management and analysis, making them well-equipped to provide advice on investment decisions and manage portfolios.

In addition to these specific certifications, there are many other courses and programs available for finance professionals seeking to enhance their skills and knowledge. For example, the Financial Industry Regulatory Authority (FINRA) offers a wide range of professional development courses for financial advisors, including courses on ethics, investment products, and regulatory compliance. The American Bankers Association also offers a range of courses and certifications in banking and financial management.

It is important for finance professionals to stay up-to-date on the latest trends and developments in their field, and earning certifications and taking courses can be an effective way to do so. By continually expanding their knowledge and skills, professionals can remain competitive in the job market and better serve their clients or employers.

However, it is worth noting that simply earning certifications or completing courses is not enough to ensure success in the finance industry. To truly excel, finance professionals must also cultivate critical thinking skills, stay abreast of market trends and economic conditions, and develop strong communication and interpersonal skills. Additionally, they must be willing to adapt to new technologies and approaches as the industry evolves.

Conclusion:

In conclusion, lifelong learning is essential for success in the finance industry. By staying informed about emerging trends, taking courses and earning certifications, and cultivating critical thinking and communication skills, finance professionals can remain competitive in the job market and better serve their clients or employers. In a rapidly evolving industry, those who are able to adapt and innovate will be better positioned for success in the future. Therefore, lifelong learning is not only important for individual professionals, but also for the overall health and vitality of the finance industry as a whole.

Overview of the importance of lifelong learning in the finance industry

The finance industry is a rapidly evolving field that requires professionals to stay up-to-date with the latest trends, technologies, and regulations. As a result, lifelong learning is essential for success in this industry, as it enables professionals to expand their knowledge, develop new skills, and adapt to changing circumstances. In this section, we will explore the importance of lifelong learning in the finance industry, including the benefits of continuous learning, strategies for ongoing education, and the role of technology in facilitating lifelong learning.

Benefits of Lifelong Learning in Finance

Continuous learning is essential for professionals in the finance industry because it enables them to keep pace with changing market conditions, regulatory developments, and technological advancements. The benefits of lifelong learning in finance include:

Improved Competence: Continuous learning enables professionals to stay informed about the latest trends and best practices in the industry, improving their competence and ability to provide high-quality services to clients.

Career Advancement: Lifelong learning can enhance professionals' skills and knowledge, making them more competitive in the job market and improving their chances for career advancement.

Personal Growth: Learning new skills and knowledge can also contribute to personal growth and satisfaction, providing a sense of accomplishment and fulfillment outside of work.

Reduced Risk: Staying informed about regulatory developments and market conditions can help professionals mitigate risk and make more informed decisions for their clients.

Strategies for Ongoing Education in Finance

There are several strategies that professionals in the finance industry can use to pursue lifelong learning and stay up-to-date with the latest developments in the field. Some of these strategies include:

Reading Industry Publications: Finance professionals can stay informed about the latest trends and developments in the industry by regularly reading publications such as The Wall Street Journal, Bloomberg, and the Financial Times.

Attending Conferences and Workshops: Attending conferences and workshops is an excellent way to network with other professionals in the field and learn about the latest trends and best practices.

Taking Courses and Earning Certifications: Universities and professional organizations offer courses and certifications in finance-related subjects, providing professionals with the opportunity to deepen their knowledge and acquire new skills.

Mentoring and Coaching: Working with a mentor or coach can provide valuable insights and guidance for professionals looking to develop their skills and knowledge.

The Role of Technology in Lifelong Learning in Finance

Technology is playing an increasingly important role in facilitating lifelong learning in the finance industry. Some of the ways that technology is being used to support ongoing education in finance include:

E-Learning Platforms: E-learning platforms such as Coursera and edX offer a wide range of finance-related courses that can be completed online, providing professionals with flexibility and convenience.

Mobile Apps: Mobile apps such as Bloomberg and CNBC provide real-time financial news and data, enabling professionals to stay informed about market developments and trends on-the-go.

Virtual Reality: Virtual reality is being used to simulate real-world financial scenarios, providing professionals with a safe environment to practice their skills and experiment with different strategies.

Artificial Intelligence: Artificial intelligence is being used to analyze financial data and identify patterns and trends, providing professionals with insights that can inform their decision-making.

Conclusion

Lifelong learning is essential for success in the finance industry, as it enables professionals to stay up-to-date with the latest trends, technologies, and regulations. Pursuing ongoing education through reading industry publications, attending conferences and workshops, taking courses and earning certifications, and working with a mentor or coach can help professionals enhance their competence, advance their careers, and achieve personal growth. Technology is also playing an increasingly important role in facilitating lifelong learning in the finance industry, with e-learning platforms, mobile apps, virtual reality, and artificial intelligence providing new opportunities for professionals to expand theirknowledge and skills.

It is important for finance professionals to be proactive in pursuing lifelong learning opportunities and to recognize the value that ongoing education can bring to their careers. As the financial industry continues to evolve and become increasingly complex, staying up-to-date with the latest trends and regulations will become even more crucial.

Moreover, lifelong learning can also contribute to the overall success and sustainability of financial institutions. By encouraging and supporting ongoing education for their employees, companies can improve their competitiveness, foster innovation, and enhance their reputation as leaders in the industry. Additionally, investing in employee development can improve retention rates and help attract top talent.

In conclusion, the finance industry is constantly evolving, and lifelong learning is an essential strategy for staying competitive and achieving personal and professional growth. Pursuing ongoing education through a variety of methods and utilizing technology can help finance professionals stay ahead of the curve and succeed in an ever-changing industry. Financial institutions that invest in lifelong learning for their employees can also reap significant benefits, contributing to their overall success and sustainability.

Analysis of the key skills and knowledge areas that finance professionals need to stay relevant in their careers

The finance industry is constantly evolving, and finance professionals need to stay up-to-date with the latest trends, technologies, and regulations to stay relevant in their careers. To achieve this, they require a range of key skills and knowledge areas, which will enable them to adapt to changing circumstances and make informed decisions. In this section, we will analyze the key skills and knowledge areas that finance professionals need to stay relevant in their careers.

Analyzing the key skills and knowledge areas that finance professionals need to stay relevant in their careers:

Analytical skills:
Analytical skills are an essential skillset that finance professionals need to stay relevant in their careers. They require the ability to analyze complex financial data and extract valuable insights from it. Financial analysts, for example, need to analyze financial statements, market trends, and economic indicators to make informed investment recommendations. Investment bankers also need to analyze financial data to assess the viability of potential mergers and acquisitions. Actuaries, who work in the insurance industry, use analytical skills to analyze statistical data and assess risks associated with insuring individuals and businesses.

Communication skills:
Communication skills are also vital for finance professionals to stay relevant in their careers. They need to communicate complex financial information in a clear and concise manner, both orally and in writing. Financial advisors, for example, need to communicate investment strategies to clients, while investment bankers need to communicate financial data and analysis to potential clients. Portfolio managers also need to communicate investment strategies and performance to investors.

Technology skills:
Technology is transforming the finance industry, and finance professionals need to keep up with the latest technological advancements. They need to understand how technology can be used to automate and streamline financial processes, as well as how to analyze and interpret data generated by technology. Quantitative analysts, for example, use technology to build financial models and analyze large datasets. Securities traders also use technology to execute trades quickly and efficiently.

Regulatory knowledge:
Finance professionals also need to stay up-to-date with the latest regulations and compliance requirements. They need to understand how regulations impact financial markets and their clients' investments. Compliance officers, for example, need to ensure that their organizations comply with all relevant regulations, while financial planners need to ensure that their clients' investments are compliant with applicable regulations.

Business acumen:
Finance professionals also require business acumen to stay relevant in their careers. They need to understand the broader business environment, including industry trends, competitive dynamics, and macroeconomic factors. Investment bankers, for example, need to understand the strategic goals of their

clients and how they fit into the broader business landscape. Portfolio managers also need to understand the broader economic environment to make informed investment decisions.

Ethical standards:
Ethical standards are also essential for finance professionals to stay relevant in their careers. They need to act with integrity and avoid conflicts of interest. Financial advisors, for example, need to act in the best interests of their clients and avoid recommending investments that may not be suitable for them. Investment bankers also need to act ethically and avoid conflicts of interest when advising clients on mergers and acquisitions.

Conclusion:

In conclusion, finance professionals need a range of key skills and knowledge areas to stay relevant in their careers. Analytical skills, communication skills, technology skills, regulatory knowledge, business acumen, and ethical standards are all critical for success in the finance industry. By staying up-to-date with the latest trends, technologies, and regulations and continuously developing these key skillsets, finance professionals can stay relevant in their careers and achieve personal growth.

Discussion of the various ways in which finance professionals can continue to learn and develop their skills throughout their careers, such as through advanced degrees, professional certifications, and on-the-job training

As we have previously discussed, lifelong learning is crucial for finance professionals to remain relevant and competitive in their careers. However, the question remains: what are the various ways in which finance professionals can continue to learn and develop their skills throughout their careers? In this section, we will explore some of the most common methods for continuing education, including advanced degrees, professional certifications, and on-the-job training.

Advanced Degrees
One of the most traditional and well-respected methods for continuing education in finance is pursuing an advanced degree, such as a Master's in Business Administration (MBA) or a Master's in Finance (MSF). These degrees provide students with a rigorous curriculum that covers a broad range of finance-related topics, including accounting, economics, investment analysis, risk management, and financial reporting.

While pursuing an advanced degree can be time-consuming and expensive, it can also provide a significant return on investment in terms of career advancement and earning potential. For example, according to a survey by the Graduate Management Admission Council, the median salary for MBA graduates in the United States in 2020 was $105,000, compared to $67,000 for those with only a bachelor's degree. Furthermore, an advanced degree can help finance professionals develop critical thinking, leadership, and communication skills that are essential for success in the industry.

Professional Certifications
Another popular method for continuing education in finance is earning professional certifications, such as the Certified Financial Planner (CFP), Chartered Financial Analyst (CFA), or Certified Public Accountant (CPA) designations. These certifications require passing rigorous exams and meeting strict educational and professional requirements, and are widely recognized as indicators of expertise and credibility in the industry.

Earning a professional certification can provide many benefits for finance professionals, including enhanced job opportunities, higher salaries, and increased credibility with clients and employers. For example, according to the CFA Institute, CFA charterholders in the United States earn a median salary of $180,000, compared to $70,000 for financial analysts without the designation. Additionally, earning a certification can help finance professionals develop specialized knowledge and skills in specific areas of finance, such as investment analysis or financial planning.

On-the-Job Training
While advanced degrees and professional certifications are certainly valuable for continuing education in finance, they can also be time-consuming and costly. For this reason, many finance professionals opt for on-the-job training as a way to learn and develop new skills in a more practical and cost-effective manner.

On-the-job training can take many forms, including attending conferences and workshops, participating in mentoring programs, or simply learning from colleagues or superiors. This type of training allows finance professionals to learn new skills and techniques in real-world settings, and can be particularly effective for developing soft skills such as communication, teamwork, and problem-solving.

In conclusion, finance professionals have a wide range of options for continuing education and developing their skills throughout their careers. Whether pursuing an advanced degree, earning a professional certification, or participating in on-the-job training, the key is to remain committed to lifelong learning and to seek out opportunities to expand one's knowledge and expertise. By doing so, finance professionals can enhance their careers, increase their earning potential, and contribute to the overall success of the industry.

Exploration of the benefits of lifelong learning for finance professionals, including enhanced career opportunities and increased earning potential

Exploration of the Benefits of Lifelong Learning for Finance Professionals, including Enhanced Career Opportunities and Increased Earning Potential

In today's rapidly evolving business world, finance professionals face constant challenges to keep up with new technologies, regulations, and market trends. Lifelong learning is a critical tool for finance professionals to stay relevant and competitive in their careers. In this section, we will explore the benefits of lifelong learning for finance professionals, including enhanced career opportunities and increased earning potential.

Enhanced Career Opportunities

One of the most significant benefits of lifelong learning for finance professionals is the ability to enhance their career opportunities. The finance industry is highly competitive, and professionals who stay up-to-date with the latest industry developments have a better chance of advancing their careers.

Advanced degrees, professional certifications, and on-the-job training are all effective ways for finance professionals to enhance their skills and knowledge, making them more attractive to potential employers. For example, an investment banker who earns an MBA in finance will have a better chance of securing a high-level management position than someone with only a bachelor's degree. Similarly, a financial planner who earns the Certified Financial Planner (CFP) designation will have a competitive advantage over someone who has not obtained this certification.

In addition to enhancing job prospects, lifelong learning can also lead to opportunities for professional growth and career change. Finance professionals who develop new skills and knowledge through lifelong learning may be able to move into different areas of finance or related industries. For example, a portfolio manager who develops expertise in sustainable investing may be able to transition to a role in environmental finance or impact investing.

Increased Earning Potential

Another significant benefit of lifelong learning for finance professionals is the potential for increased earning potential. Finance is a highly competitive industry, and employers are willing to pay a premium for professionals with advanced skills and knowledge. According to a study by the Financial Times, finance professionals who earn advanced degrees, such as an MBA, can expect to earn a higher salary than those with only a bachelor's degree.

Professional certifications are also associated with higher salaries in the finance industry. For example, a financial analyst with the Chartered Financial Analyst (CFA) designation can expect to earn a higher salary than someone without this certification. The CFA Institute reports that finance professionals with the CFA designation earn, on average, 23% more than those without the certification.

In addition to higher salaries, lifelong learning can also lead to promotions and other opportunities for career advancement. For example, a securities trader who earns the Financial Risk Manager (FRM) designation may be able to move into a risk management role, which could lead to a higher salary and greater responsibility.

Continuing Professional Development (CPD) Certificates

Many professional organizations and regulatory bodies require finance professionals to participate in Continuing Professional Development (CPD) programs to maintain their licenses and certifications. CPD programs are designed to ensure that professionals remain up-to-date with the latest industry developments and best practices.

CPD programs offer several benefits for finance professionals, including:

Increased knowledge and skills: CPD programs provide professionals with the opportunity to deepen their knowledge and acquire new skills.

Enhanced credibility: Participating in CPD programs demonstrates a commitment to professional development and enhances professionals' credibility with clients and employers.

Improved career prospects: CPD programs can lead to new career opportunities and promotions.

License/certification maintenance: Many professional organizations and regulatory bodies require finance professionals to participate in CPD programs to maintain their licenses and certifications.

Examples of CPD programs in the finance industry include online courses, seminars, workshops, and conferences. These programs cover a range of topics, including risk management, investment analysis, financial planning, and ethical considerations in finance.

Conclusion

Lifelong learning is critical for finance professionals who want to stay relevant and competitive in their careers. Advanced degrees, professional certifications, and on-the-job training are just a few ways in which finance professionals can continue to learn and develop their skills throughout their careers. By keeping up-to-date with the latest industry trends, technologies, and regulations, professionals can enhance their competence, advance their careers, and achieve personal growth.

The benefits of lifelong learning for finance professionals are numerous. One of the most significant benefits is the potential for enhanced career opportunities. Employers often seek out professionals who have demonstrated a commitment to continuing education, as it demonstrates a desire to stay current in their field and an ability to adapt to changing industry trends. Additionally, professionals who pursue advanced degrees or certifications may be eligible for higher-level positions, increased responsibilities, and higher salaries.

Another significant benefit of lifelong learning is increased earning potential. Professionals who pursue advanced degrees, such as a master's degree or doctorate, or who obtain professional certifications, such as a Chartered Financial Analyst (CFA) or Certified Financial Planner (CFP), may be able to command higher salaries than their peers who do not have these credentials. Additionally, professionals who invest in their ongoing education and professional development may be better positioned to negotiate higher salaries and bonuses, as they can demonstrate the value they bring to their organization.

Finally, lifelong learning can lead to personal growth and fulfillment. Finance professionals who are committed to ongoing education are often more engaged in their work, more innovative in their thinking, and more motivated to achieve their goals. They may also feel a greater sense of satisfaction in their work, as they are continually improving their skills and contributing to the success of their organization.

CPD certificates are also a key benefit of lifelong learning for finance professionals. Continuing Professional Development (CPD) is the process of tracking and documenting the skills, knowledge, and experience that professionals gain through formal and informal learning activities. CPD certificates demonstrate to employers, clients, and regulators that professionals are committed to ongoing learning and development, and have the necessary skills and knowledge to perform their job effectively.

In conclusion, lifelong learning is essential for finance professionals who want to stay competitive and advance their careers. By pursuing advanced degrees, obtaining professional certifications, and investing in on-the-job training, professionals can enhance their competence, increase their earning potential, and achieve personal growth. Additionally, CPD certificates provide a tangible demonstration of a professional's commitment to ongoing learning and development. By embracing lifelong learning, finance professionals can ensure that they remain relevant and valuable contributors to their organization for years to come.

THE
CPD
GROUP

ACCREDITED PROVIDER

#781205

Verify @ https://thecpdregister.com

www.ingramcontent.com/pod-product-compliance
Lightning Source LLC
Chambersburg PA
CBHW061322190326
41458CB00011B/3865